OCR
A LEVEL

LAW

Second Edition

Nicholas Price
Richard Wortley
Nigel Briggs
Series editor: Sue Teal

HODDER
EDUCATION
AN HACHETTE UK COMPANY

The teaching content of this resource is endorsed by OCR for use with the 2020 specifications AS Level Law (H018) and A Level Law (H418). In order to gain OCR endorsement, this resource has been reviewed against OCR's endorsement criteria.

This resource was designed using the most up to date information from the specification. Specifications are updated over time which means there may be contradictions between the resource and the specification, therefore please use the information on the latest specification and Sample Assessment Materials at all times when ensuring students are fully prepared for their assessments.

Any references to assessment and/or assessment preparation are the publisher's interpretation of the specification requirements and are not endorsed by OCR. OCR recommends that teachers consider using a range of teaching and learning resources in preparing learners for assessment, based on their own professional judgement for their students' needs. OCR has not paid for the production of this resource, nor does OCR receive any royalties from its sale. For more information about the endorsement process, please visit the OCR website, www.ocr.org.uk.

Text credits

p.35 The Times / News Licensing; **p.183** Byelaws for Skateboarding. https://www.rother.gov.uk/byelaws-and-legal-notices/byelaws-for-skateboarding/; **pp.184-85** Adapted from the Croydon Council website: www.croydon.gov.uk/community/safercroydon/law_enforcement/ drinkbans; **p.191** The Times / News Licensing; **p.326** Criminal and civil legal aid in England and Wales from 2005–2006 to 2018–2019, Commons Library Briefing Paper, September 2020. Derived from www.statista.com.

Every effort has been made to trace all copyright holders, but if any have been inadvertently overlooked, the Publishers will be pleased to make the necessary arrangements at the first opportunity.

Although every effort has been made to ensure that website addresses are correct at time of going to press, Hodder Education cannot be held responsible for the content of any website mentioned in this book. It is sometimes possible to find a relocated web page by typing in the address of the home page for a website in the URL window of your browser.

Hachette UK's policy is to use papers that are natural, renewable and recyclable products and made from wood grown in well-managed forests and other controlled sources. The logging and manufacturing processes are expected to conform to the environmental regulations of the country of origin.

Orders: please contact Hachette UK Distribution, Hely Hutchinson Centre, Milton Road, Didcot, Oxfordshire, OX11 7HH. Telephone: +44 (0)1235 827827. Email education@hachette.co.uk Lines are open from 9 a.m. to 5 p.m., Monday to Friday. You can also order through our website: www.hoddereducation.co.uk

ISBN: 978 1 3983 2647 7

© Richard Wortley, Nick Price and Nigel Briggs 2021

First published in 2021 by Hodder Education,
An Hachette UK Company
Carmelite House
50 Victoria Embankment
London EC4Y 0DZ

www.hoddereducation.co.uk

Impression number 10 9 8 7 6 5 4 3 2 1

Year 2025 2024 2023 2022 2021

Cover photo © Alexandre Rotenberg / Alamy Stock Photo

Illustrations by Aptara, Inc.

Typeset in India by Aptara, Inc.

Printed in Slovenia

A catalogue record for this title is available from the British Library.

Contents

Section 4 The law of tort

Section 5 The nature of law

Section 6 Human rights law

Section 7 The law of contract

Introduction

This textbook has been written and designed for the new OCR A Level Law specification (H418) introduced for first teaching in September 2020, with first assessment 2022. To view the full specifications, planning and teaching resources, delivery guides and examples of assessment material for OCR A Level Law, please visit OCR's website **https://www.ocr.org.uk/qualifications/as-and-a-level/law-h018-h418-from-2020/**

The law is as we believe it to be on 1 June 2020.

How to use this book

Each chapter has a range of features that have been designed to present the course content in a clear and accessible way, to give you confidence and to support you in your revision and assessment preparation.

Introduction

Each chapter starts with an overview of the content.

Link

Links to content in other chapters help you navigate through the material.

Key terms

Key terms, in bold in the text, are defined.

Case study

Description of a case and a comment on the point of law it illustrates.*

Tips

These are suggestions to help clarify what you should aim to learn.

Extension activity

These include challenging activities for students striving for higher grades.

Look online

These weblinks will help you with further research and reading on the internet.

Activities

Activities appear throughout the book and have been designed to help you apply your knowledge and develop your understanding of various topics.

Quick questions

Questions at the end of each chapter will help consolidate your knowledge.

Summary

These boxes contain summaries of what you have learned in each section.

* There will be cases in the OCR Teacher Guides that are not covered in this textbook, so do not expect to see every case in the textbook.

Table of cases

vii

Chapter 17

Chapter 18

No cases

Chapter 19

Chapter 20

No cases

Chapter 21

Chapter 35

Chapter 36

xix

Chapter 44

Table of legislation

Chapter 17

Acts

Chapter 18

Acts

Chapter 19

Acts

Chapter 20

Acts

Chapter 21

Chapter 22

Acts

Chapter 23

Acts

Other

Chapter 24

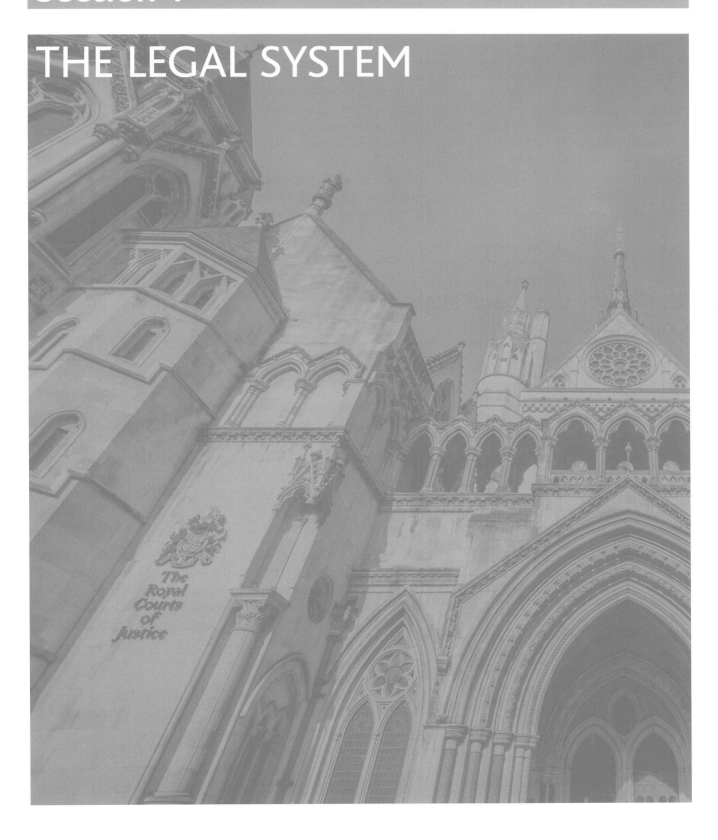

Section 1

THE LEGAL SYSTEM

Chapter 1 Civil courts and other forms of dispute resolution

Introduction

Civil courts exist to resolve disputes between individuals or businesses, if the dispute cannot be settled in any other way. Using the courts to resolve a dispute can be costly for the parties in terms of money and time. It can also be traumatic for the individuals involved and may not lead to the most satisfactory outcome. More and more people and businesses are seeking other ways of resolving their disputes without going to court.

Alternative methods are referred to generally as 'ADR', which stands for 'alternative dispute resolution', and include any method of resolving a dispute without using a civil court. There are different methods, ranging from informal negotiations between the parties to a comparatively formal employment tribunal dealing with specific claims arising from employment matters.

1.1 County Court and High Court

Since the Crime and Courts Act 2013 came into force, there has been one County Court in England and Wales, sitting in nearly 500 centres. There is one High Court, based in the Royal Courts of Justice in London, but also sitting in a number of centres around the country.

1.1.1 Jurisdiction

County Court

The County Court can try most civil claims of up to £100,000 in value. Typical cases heard in this court include:

- negligence claims where a person has suffered injury or loss as a result of the action or failure of another
- other tort-based claims such as nuisance or trespassing
- debt claims and consumer disputes which generally involve a breach of contract
- housing claims, including possession of residential and commercial properties, and other landlord and tenant matters, such as eviction
- bankruptcy and insolvency matters
- probate claims and other claims in relation to wills and trusts.

Claims will be heard in open court by a single judge – usually a Circuit Judge but some cases are heard by a Recorder. If the case is straightforward and of relatively low value, it can be heard by a District Judge. The judge will read the case papers before the hearing and can hear evidence and legal arguments in court. At the end of the hearing the judge will decide:

- liability – which side 'wins'
- the compensation payable, if any, or
- any other remedy requested, such as an eviction notice, and
- who should pay the costs of the case.

The Small Claims Track is part of the County Court and deals with claims of less than £10,000 (£1000 in personal injury claims) in an informal way. Cases are heard by a District Judge and lawyers are discouraged. As a result, there is less legal argument and costs will not be awarded.

Link

See Chapter 21 for claims in Negligence and Chapter 23 for tort-based claims relating to land. For the different types of judges, see Chapter 3. See Chapters 26 and 43 for the ways damages are calculated in tort and contract claims.

High Court

As with the County Court, claims will be heard in open court by a single judge of the High Court. Judges will be assigned to one of the three Divisions – Queen's Bench, Chancery and Family – and will only hear cases relating to that Division's work. As before, the judge will read the case papers before the hearing and can hear evidence and legal arguments in court.

As with the County Court, at the end of the hearing the judge will decide:

- liability – which side 'wins'
- the compensation payable, if any, or
- any other remedy requested, such as an eviction notice, and
- who should pay the costs of the case.

The Royal Courts of Justice

The Queen's Bench Division

This is the largest of the three divisions. It has the jurisdiction to hear a wide variety of cases including contract and tort claims over £100,000 in value and smaller claims where there is a complicated issue of law involved.

There are several specialist courts of the Queen's Bench Division, including:

- the Administrative Court which hears:
  - applications for judicial review and applications for *habeas corpus*
  - case stated appeals in criminal cases decided at the Magistrates' Court or Crown Court
- Circuit Commercial Courts.

Link

See Chapter 15 for judicial review and Chapter 33 for *habeas corpus*. See Chapter 2 for case stated appeals.

Extension activity

Research the work of the Circuit Commercial Courts.

The Chancery Division

This court has jurisdiction to deal with the following types of cases:

- disputes relating to business, property or land where over £100,000 is in issue
- disputes over trusts
- contentious probate claims
- disputes about partnership matters.

Specialist courts of the Chancery Division include the Insolvency and Companies List.

Family Division

Cases in this Division are generally heard in private as they are often dealing with sensitive matters. It has the jurisdiction to hear:

- cases where a child is to be made a ward of the court and cases relating to the welfare of children under the Children Act 1989
- appeals from lower courts such as Family Proceedings Courts, which are part of the Magistrates' Court, and complicated family cases transferred from the County Court
- cases with a foreign element such as international child abduction, forced marriage, female genital mutilation and where a divorce has taken place outside England but the parties are disputing property situated within England.

1.1.2 Pre-trial procedures

A court claim should only be considered as a last resort if a negotiated settlement cannot be reached or a form of Alternative Dispute Resolution has failed.

Pre-action protocols

The first step to take before issuing any court claim is to follow an appropriate pre-action protocol. They explain the conduct and set out the steps the court would normally expect parties to take before starting any court action.

The aim of a pre-action protocol is to ensure that as many problems as possible can be resolved without the need for a court hearing.

Which court to use?

If a settlement cannot be reached, issuing a court claim may be the only course of action. Which court is used will depend on the amount of compensation being claimed.

Amount of claim	Which court?
Less than £10,000 (or £1000 in a personal injury claim)	Can be started in the Small Claims Court
Less than £100,000 (or £50,000 in a personal injury claim)	Must be started in the County Court
More than £100,000 (or more than £50,000 in a personal injury claim)	Can be started in either the County Court or, more likely, in the High Court

Figure 1.1 Which court to use?

Issuing a claim

A claim form N1 has to be completed with the names and addresses of the parties, brief details of the reason for the claim and the amount of money being claimed. The form can be filed at:

● a County Court office
● the High Court if it is a high value claim
● online, for a debt claim.

A fee will be charged for issuing the claim, and the amount of the fee depends on the amount being claimed.

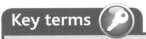

Activity

Miguel bought a set of golf clubs from Direct Sports costing £750. When he first used the clubs, he found several of them bent when he tried to hit the ball and one club broke completely. He complained to the retailer but they refused to refund his money or enter into negotiations with him.

1 Download a Form N1 from **https://assets.publishing.service.gov.uk/government/uploads/system/uploads/attachment_data/file/688390/n1-eng.pdf**

2 Complete the N1 claim form for Miguel.

Key terms

Claimant – the person injured or suffering loss who intends to claim money from the defendant.

Defendant – the person or business causing the loss or damage or owing money to the claimant.

Defending a claim

The court will generally send, or serve, the claim on the defendant who then has a choice of actions:

1 Admit the claim and pay the full amount to the claimant or the court. If this option is chosen, the case will end.

2 Admit the claim and pay in instalments. If this option is accepted by the claimant, the case will end when the full amount has been paid.

3 Dispute the claim and file a defence setting out why the claim should not be paid, either in full or part.

4 File an Acknowledgement of Service confirming receipt of the claim form but asking for time to file a defence.

If the defendant fails to respond when receiving the claim, the claimant can apply for judgment in default. This means that the claim is 'won' and an attempt can be made to force the defendant to pay the sum claimed.

1.1.3 The three tracks

If the claim is defended, a judge must allocate it to an appropriate case management track for it to be dealt with in the most just and cost-effective way. There are three tracks that a case can be allocated to, as shown in Figure 1.2.

Type of track	Value of claim	Explanation
Small claims track	Less than £10,000 (or £1000 in personal injury cases)	● The claim will be heard by a District Judge and lawyers are not encouraged. ● The time allocated to a hearing will be a maximum of 2–3 hours and each party will be allowed a limited number of witnesses.
Fast track	£10,000–£25,000	● A case allocated to this track will have a strict timetable set at a maximum of 30 weeks. If the parties do not follow the timetable, the claim can be thrown out or judgment in default can be awarded. ● The hearing will be a maximum of one day in open court, with a limited number of witnesses called and usually heard by a Circuit Judge. ● Each of the parties can be represented by a lawyer.
Multi track	£25,000–£50,000	● Usually allocated to the County Court. ● The hearing will take place before a Circuit Judge. ● The case will be strictly case-managed by the Circuit Judge, who sets a strict timetable, the disclosure of relevant documents, the number of witnesses and how long the case will last. ● If the case involves complicated points of law or evidence, or it involves more than £50,000 in value, it can be passed up to the High Court.

Figure 1.2 Explaining the three tracks

1.2 Appeals and appellate courts

If one of the parties is dissatisfied with the decision of the trial judge about liability and/or the amount of compensation awarded, they can appeal. What does this mean?

- An appeal hearing usually consists of legal arguments as to why the original decision should be altered.
- An appeal is usually made to the next highest court in the hierarchy, and heard by a panel of three judges.
- It is rare for new evidence to be heard. There must be legal grounds for an appeal – more than 'the judge got the decision wrong'.
- An appeal usually has to be made within 21 days of the original hearing.
- If an appeal is made, costs will increase as lawyers will probably be required to argue the reasons for appeal.
- The appeal court can agree with the original decision or reverse it. It can agree the original amount of compensation awarded or alter the amount.

1.2.1 Appeals from the County Court

1 If the original decision was made by a District Judge, for example, in the Small Claims Court, an appeal will be heard by a single Circuit Judge of the same court.
2 If the original decision was made by a Circuit Judge, an appeal can be made to a High Court Judge of the Division that is relevant to the case. For example, if the claim is for personal injury, an appeal will be made to a judge of the Queen's Bench Division.
3 An appeal can be made directly to the Court of Appeal if the case raises an important point of principle or practice, and the Court of Appeal agrees to hear it.

1.2.2 Appeals from the High Court

An appeal from a decision of a High Court Judge will generally be heard by the Court of Appeal (Civil Division).

If one of the parties wishes to appeal further, it can be taken to the Supreme Court, but only if permission

is granted by the Court of Appeal. The Supreme Court is the highest court for hearing civil appeals, and permission will only be given if there is a point of law of general public importance involved.

In rare cases, a 'leapfrog' appeal may be made directly from the High Court to the Supreme Court if there is an issue of national importance involved, or the case raises issues of sufficient importance to justify the leapfrog.

Tip

- Make sure you understand the courts that can hear civil cases and the three-track allocation system. These are the basis of the whole court system.
- Be clear about the grounds on which an appeal can be made in civil cases and the courts that can hear appeals.

1.3 Employment tribunals and Alternative Dispute Resolution

Tribunals exist alongside the court system. Some matters have to be heard by a tribunal and cannot be dealt with in court. Employment tribunals deal solely with employment issues, but there are other tribunals which deal with specific issues such as landlord and tenant claims. In addition, there are forms of Alternative Dispute Resolution (ADR) which exist to resolve disputes without having to go through the court or tribunal process.

1.3.1 Employment tribunals

Employment tribunals deal with issues such as a claim of unfair dismissal, discrimination in the workplace or redundancy. An employment tribunal sits in a separate building and has a set process, but this is less formal than a court – no wigs or gowns are worn.

Preliminary matters

A claim on an employment issue has to be brought within three months, less one day, from the event – for example, a dismissal.

In most cases, ACAS (the Advisory, Conciliation and Arbitration Service) must be contacted within this time for early conciliation to see if there can be a resolution. Only if the matter cannot be resolved can a claim be issued.

Most claimants obtain advice on the strength of the case before issuing a claim, though it is possible for a claimant to take their own case. Advice can be obtained from a specialist lawyer or a trade union.

The claim must set out detailed reasons for the action and must be filed with the tribunal within the time limit. Unlike a court claim, there is no fee involved. The claim will be passed to the employer who will have the opportunity to make comment on it.

Link

For more information on ACAS, see section 1.3.4, Conciliation.

The hearing

Hearings are held in individual tribunal rooms. There will be a tribunal panel made up of:
- a judge specialising in employment law who will run the proceedings
- one person representing the employer's organisation
- one person representing the employee's organisation.

If a preliminary hearing is needed, it takes place before a judge sitting without panel members.

In the full hearing, evidence is taken on oath and there are rules about the procedure and the evidence that can be accepted. Either side can represent themselves or be represented by a lawyer or, for example, a union official.

Most hearings are open to the public, though they are rarely publicised.

Hearings are generally quite short as most of the issues will have been identified beforehand and the panel will have read the papers. At the end of the hearing, the panel might decide on the day or give it later in writing.

A collective decision of the panel will subsequently be issued in writing:
- If the tribunal finds in favour of the employee, they may encourage a settlement which could include, for example, writing a favourable reference and some compensation.
- If a settlement cannot be reached, the tribunal can award compensation.
- If the claim is lost, the employee will not have to pay the employer's costs, though they will be responsible for the costs of any lawyer they use.
- If either side is dissatisfied with the panel's decision they can ask, within 14 days, for the tribunal to review its decision.

Appeals

Either side may then appeal within 42 days of the tribunal decision to an Employment Appeal Tribunal, but only on a point of law.

Further appeals can be made to the Court of Appeal (Civil Division) and the Supreme Court, but, again, only on a point of law and with permission from the Employment Appeal Tribunal.

Look online

Use the search term 'Employment tribunal hearing' to find a video on YouTube on how an employment tribunal hearing takes place.

1.3.2 Negotiation and ADR

Anyone in dispute with another person or business can negotiate to settle the dispute in the easiest and least confrontational way possible.

Negotiation can be carried out by:
- face-to-face talking
- writing
- phone or e-mail
- any other suitable method.

It is an attempt to come to an agreement or settlement. The agreement can be verbal or more formally set down in writing.

Negotiation can be conducted by the parties themselves, their representatives, their lawyers or any combination of these. If the negotiation is carried out by the parties, it should not cost them anything, but the involvement of lawyers will inevitably involve cost.

Even if original negotiations are unsuccessful and court proceedings are issued, it can take place right up to a court hearing.

1.3.3 Mediation

This is where a neutral person helps the parties to reach a compromise. The parties will usually be in separate rooms or locations, and the mediator acts as a facilitator, shuttling between the parties to put forward points and opinions.

The parties have control over the process, so they can stay as long as they wish and can withdraw at any time. The mediator will not offer an opinion to either party unless asked to do so.

A successful mediation depends on both parties embracing the concept and actively participating. Eventually it is hoped that the parties themselves will reach a compromise and agreement acceptable to both.

Mediation is often used in family disputes over children and financial issues. The parties have to show that they have attempted the process before starting court proceedings. A charity such as Relate will provide the mediation service in this case. Another charity offering mediation services is the Centre for Effective Dispute Resolution (CEDR), which promotes the service as an effective form of alternative dispute resolution and provides training for mediators.

Key term

Mediator – a trained person who acts as a go-between in an attempt to help people in a dispute come to an agreement.

Look online

1 Look at the services provided by West Kent Mediation at **http://wkm.org.uk/** and the Centre for Effective Dispute Resolution at **www.cedr.com/**
2 List the areas in which they each can help.

A more formal method of mediation is a 'mini-trial':
- Each side presents its case to a panel, composed of a neutral party plus a decision-making executive from each party in the dispute.
- Once all the submissions have been made, the executives, with the help of the neutral adviser, will evaluate the two sides' positions and try to come to an agreement.
- If the executives cannot agree, the neutral adviser will act as a mediator between them.

Even if the whole matter is not resolved, this type of procedure may be able to narrow down the issues so that if the case does go to court, it will not take so long.

1.3.4 Conciliation

This is similar to mediation, but the conciliator plays a more active role, discussing the issues with both parties and suggesting grounds for compromise or settlement. The parties still have control over the process and may withdraw at any time.

As with mediation, both parties must agree to a final compromise and the process may not lead to a resolution, especially if one or both parties are fixed in their position.

ACAS is an example of a conciliation service:
- It tries to encourage the parties in an employment dispute to reach a settlement before a claim can be issued in an employment tribunal.
- It also gets involved in industrial disputes – for example, if a trade union calls a strike action, ACAS will attempt to conciliate between the parties to reach a compromise.

1.3.5 Arbitration

Arbitration is where both parties voluntarily agree to let their dispute be left to the judgment of a neutral arbitrator or a panel of arbitrators. The arbitrator will normally have experience in the field of the dispute.

The agreement providing for arbitration will usually be in writing, and will be contained in the initial contract between the parties which will be made before any dispute arises. This arbitration clause is called a *Scott v Avery* clause: see Figure 1.3.

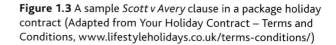

D Complaints

3. Disputes arising out of, or in connection with, this contract which cannot be amicably settled may (if you so wish) be referred to arbitration under a special scheme devised by arrangement with the Association of British Travel Agents (ABTA) but administered independently by the Chartered Institute of Arbitrators. The scheme provides for a simple and inexpensive method of Arbitration on documents alone, with restricted liability on you in respect of costs. The scheme does not apply to claims greater than £1,500 per person or £7,500 per booking form or to claims which are solely or mainly in respect of physical injury or illness or the consequences of such injury or illness. If you elect to use the scheme, written notice requesting arbitration must be made within 9 months after the scheduled date of return from holiday.

Figure 1.3 A sample *Scott v Avery* clause in a package holiday contract (Adapted from Your Holiday Contract – Terms and Conditions, www.lifestyleholidays.co.uk/terms-conditions/)

- Such agreements are governed by the Arbitration Act 1996, which provides that a court will normally refuse to deal with a dispute when there is a *Scott v Avery* clause.
- The initial agreement will either name an arbitrator or provide a method for choosing one. If there is no selection procedure, a court may appoint an arbitrator.
- It is common to find a *Scott v Avery* clause in building contracts, package holiday contracts and mobile phone contracts.

The parties will agree the procedure for dealing with the dispute which can range from a 'paper' arbitration – where all the points are set out in writing and the arbitrator makes a decision based on this – to a formal court-like hearing. The date, time and place of any hearings are decided by the parties in conjunction with the arbitrator. Any formal hearing will be held in private.

Legal representation is not always necessary. This saves the parties the expense of employing lawyers, and is likely to be less confrontational.

The arbitrator's decision is called an 'award', and is final and binding on the parties. If necessary, it can be enforced in court. An award can only be challenged if there is a serious irregularity in the proceedings or on a point of law.

Activities ❓

1. Find an arbitration clause in a consumer contract; for example, in the insurance contract for your mobile phone.
   - Who will the arbitrator be?
   - How will any hearing be conducted?
2. Make a table explaining the different types of ADR. Include:
   - who deals with the dispute
   - the type of cases dealt with
   - how the dispute is dealt with
   - the possible outcomes
   - whether an appeal is possible.

1.4 Advantages and disadvantages of using the civil courts and ADR to resolve disputes

1.4.1 The civil courts – evaluation

Advantages	Disadvantages
● The case will be presided over by a qualified judge, whether in the County Court or the High Court. Judges are experienced, qualified lawyers who can deal with complex legal matters. They will apply established rules of evidence and procedure to ensure the case is dealt with fairly and without favouring one side or the other. When giving their decision on liability, judges will provide reasoned opinions so that the parties can see how a decision is reached.	● The rule in civil cases is that the loser pays the winner's costs as well as their own. As a result, the costs of taking a case to court can be more than the sum claimed. This can especially be the case with a claim in the High Court. There is a need for lawyers to be used in more complicated cases, whose time has to be paid for.
● Reasoned judgments can be studied for accuracy of the law used by the judge to reach a decision. If there are inaccuracies, there is a clear, structured appeal route. Appeals can also be made against the amount of compensation awarded.	● Even with the three-track system, there can be considerable delay in completing the preliminary stages of a claim. Once these stages are completed, there is often a further delay in arranging a hearing date. Some complicated cases may take several years to be resolved.
● A judge will allocate a defended case at an early stage to the most suitable track and court. It will be case managed through the process to a court hearing to minimise delays. Both parties will know, in advance, the number of witnesses allowed and the length of a hearing.	● A claimant can only apply to their lawyer for a no-win, no-fee arrangement in personal injury claims. A lawyer will only agree such an arrangement if a claim stands a high chance of succeeding. If the lawyer decides there is a low chance of success, a claimant must fund the claim from their own resources. Claimants in other cases will have to accept responsibility for their lawyer's fees, and hope that they win the case and can recover their costs from the loser, in addition to any compensation.
● A legally binding and enforceable decision will be made by the judge. The parties are guaranteed a resolution at the end of the hearing and an enforceable remedy is guaranteed.	**Cont.**

Advantages	Disadvantages
● The court system provides open justice as the public and press are able to sit in and report most cases. This can stop individuals and businesses hiding disputes and outcomes that the public should be aware of. ● By considering precedent, lawyers can give informed advice to their clients, at an early stage, of the likely outcome of the case. The client can then assess the strength of the case and whether it is worth pursuing. Precedent can be quoted in court in support of the arguments. ● In some types of claim, a form of funding may be available for the payment of lawyers' fees; for example, in personal injury claims it may be possible to use a no-win, no-fee arrangement	● Except in small claims, it is very difficult for a claimant to take a case without the assistance of a lawyer. This is due to the requirements of pre-action protocols, the Civil Procedure Rules and the formal nature of hearings. Failure to observe these rules may result in the claim being dismissed. More complicated rules apply if an appeal is required. ● Despite the system of precedent, there will be uncertainty of the outcome, and no guarantee of winning a case until a judge (or an appeal court) makes a final ruling. ● Using lawyers tends to lead to greater confrontation between the parties. This can produce further delay and costs.

Figure 1.4 Evaluating civil courts

Link

See Chapter 17 for an explanation of precedent. See Chapter 1 for an explanation of the Civil Procedure Rules.

1.4.2 Alternative Dispute Resolution – evaluation

Advantages	Disadvantages

● Using a method of ADR is less formal than using the courts:
  ○ Negotiation can involve just the parties themselves.
  ○ In mediation and conciliation, the parties are encouraged to reach a settlement themselves.
  ○ In arbitration, the parties can set the form of the process.
 	
● Lawyers are not encouraged as:
  ○ the processes are flexible and less formal
  ○ there is no rule that the loser pays the winner's costs. This is likely to mean lower costs for the parties and less confrontation throughout the process: there will not be a winner/loser situation, and the parties can continue a personal or business relationship.
 	
● It is quicker and easier to arrange a resolution than going through the courts. If there is a hearing, it is likely to be in private and there will be little or no publicity to embarrass the parties.
 	
● Especially in negotiation, mediation and conciliation, the decision does not have to be strictly legal, and is more likely to be based on commercial common sense and compromise. Again, this is likely to preserve the future relationship between the parties.
	● In all forms of ADR, except for tribunals, the parties cannot be forced to engage in the process, and one of them may decide not to. The process will have to be abandoned and court action may be required to resolve the dispute, which will result in further delay and cost.
	
	● If a claim is settled using one of the methods of ADR, the claimant is likely to receive lower compensation than may be awarded by the courts.
	
	● No funding is available for claimants using ADR. This may put an unrepresented claimant at a disadvantage in arbitration and employment tribunals, where a business or employer is likely to be legally represented.
	
	● If an unexpected legal issue appears in either arbitration or an employment tribunal:
	  ○ an unrepresented claimant (one who does not engage a lawyer) might be at a disadvantage
	  ○ a non-legally qualified arbitrator might not be able to resolve it.
	
	● Proceedings and hearings in employment tribunals have a certain formality, which may be intimidating for unrepresented claimants.
	
	● There are limited rights of appeal for most forms of ADR:
	  ○ In arbitration, an appeal can only be made on the grounds of serious irregularity.
	  ○ With employment tribunals, an appeal can only be made if there is a point of law involved.
	Any appeal is likely to require a lawyer and involve more costs for a claimant.

Figure 1.5 Advantages and disadvantages of Alternative Dispute Resolution

Advantages	Disadvantages
● Claims will be heard by a specialist panel. ● ACAS will encourage the parties to settle the claim before a hearing. ● The hearing will often be heard without public or press present. This will ensure confidentiality for both parties. ● The hearings will generally be informal and short – less than a day in length. ● The employee can be represented by a non-lawyer including a trade union representative. It will then be cheaper. ● The panel will give a written judgment after the hearing. ● Each party will pay their own costs. ● There are limited appeal rights.	● A claim has to be issued quickly after the issue arises. ● Funding is not available. An employee may be at a disadvantage against an employer who can pay for legal representation. ● It is a more formal process than other forms of ADR – if settlement is not possible. ● Appeals are limited to issues of law. ● There may be delays in setting hearing dates.

Figure 1.6 Advantages and disadvantages of employment tribunals

Advantages	Disadvantages
● It can be by straightforward contact between the parties. ● Low or no cost – no need for lawyers. ● The parties themselves are in control. ● Relationships between the parties are preserved. ● Continued business relationship.	● One of the parties may not be prepared to negotiate with the other. ● One of the parties may be hostile towards the other. ● Either party may believe they are 'right' and not prepared to settle. ● Court proceedings may be the only way to resolve the dispute.

Figure 1.7 Advantages and disadvantages of negotiation

Advantages	Disadvantages
● Cheaper than taking a court case. ● The parties have some control choosing the conciliator and the process. ● Future business relationship can be preserved.	● The conciliator may force a resolution on one or both of the parties. ● The process may not bring about a resolution. ● The result may not be binding on one or both parties.

Figure 1.8 Advantages and disadvantages of conciliation

Advantages	Disadvantages
● Cheaper than a court case. ● The parties are in control over the process. ● Future business and personal relationships can be maintained.	● One of the parties may be unwilling to take part in the process. ● The parties may be unwilling or unable to reach a settlement. ● The result may not be binding on one or both the parties.

Figure 1.9 Advantages and disadvantages of mediation

Advantages	Disadvantages
● Cheaper than a court case. ● The arbitrator will be qualified and experienced. ● The arbitrator's decision is final and binding. ● The arbitrator's decision can be enforced in court.	● The process can be formal and complicated. ● It is likely to be more expensive than other forms of ADR. ● It is not a suitable process if there is a complicated point of law involved.

Figure 1.10 Advantages and disadvantages of arbitration

Quick questions

1   Name the civil trial and appeal courts.
2   Describe how a civil claim for compensation can be taken in court.
3   Describe how a claim for unfair dismissal can be taken.
4   Describe the process of mediation.
5   Describe the process of arbitration.
6   Assess the advantages and disadvantages for an individual claimant taking a civil court action to recover a debt.

Summary

Civil courts

- Civil cases are tried in the County Court or High Court, depending on their value.
- Claims are started by filing a Form N1, setting out what is being claimed and why.
- If a claim is defended, it is allocated to one of three tracks, again based on its value: small claims track, fast track, or multi-track.
- An appeal can be made from the trial court to the Court of Appeal on the grounds of liability and/or the amount of compensation.
- A further appeal lies to the Supreme Court based on an issue of law of public importance.
- Advantages of using the civil courts include: fair process, judge is a legal expert, easier to enforce decisions, appeal system.
- Disadvantages of using the civil courts include: the cost of taking an action, delays, complicated process, uncertain outcome until a final decision is made.

Employment tribunals

- The employment tribunal deals only with employment issues which have to be heard there.
- Cases are heard in the first-tier tribunal by a tribunal judge sitting with two lay members.
- There may be a right of appeal to an upper tribunal and ultimately to the appeal courts.

- Compared to going to court, employment tribunals are cheaper, quicker, more informal, and cases are heard by experts in employment issues.
- Disadvantages of using employment tribunals are: no funding for applicants, more formal than other forms of ADR, delay in complex cases.

Other forms of ADR

- Negotiation is where the parties or their representatives make direct contact to see if an agreement can be made.
- Mediation is where an independent trained mediator helps the parties themselves to reach a compromise.
- Conciliation is where an independent trained conciliator plays a more active role in helping the parties to reach a compromise.
- Arbitration is where an independent qualified arbitrator decides the case after hearing evidence from both parties.
- ADR is cheaper than using the courts, is more flexible, there are fewer delays and less confrontation and it allows the parties to remain on good terms with each other.
- Disadvantages of using forms of ADR are that one of the parties may be unwilling to use a form of ADR and not be prepared to be bound by it.

Chapter 2 Criminal courts and lay people

Introduction

Criminal cases are heard in the Magistrates' Court or the Crown Court, depending on the seriousness of the offence. An adversarial trial will take place when the defendant pleads not guilty. The role of the magistrates or jury is to decide if a defendant is guilty or not guilty. The magistrates can then impose a sentence, but in the Crown Court, this is for the judge to decide. There is a range of sentences that can be imposed, from imprisonment to community penalties, fines or discharges. The court will take into account the aims of sentencing and any aggravating and mitigating factors. There is a long-established tradition of using lay people (people who are not legally qualified) in the decision-making process in criminal cases, as 'trial by your peers' is seen as the fairest form of justice.

2.1 Criminal process

The two courts that hear trials of criminal cases are the Magistrates' Court and the Crown Court. Which court is used for the trial is decided by the category of crime involved (see section 2.1.3).

If a defendant pleads guilty to the charge against them, they will receive a sentence. Where the accused pleads not guilty, there will be a trial to decide if the accused is guilty or not guilty. The burden of proof is on the prosecution who must prove the case beyond reasonable doubt.

The form of the trial is adversarial, with prosecution and defence presenting their cases and cross-examining each other's witnesses. The role of the judge or magistrates is that of a referee, overseeing the trial and making sure that legal rules are followed correctly. The judge or magistrates cannot investigate the case, nor ask to see additional witnesses.

Guilt will be decided by:
- a District Judge or lay magistrates in the Magistrates' Court
- a jury in the Crown Court.

If a guilty verdict is reached, a sentence will be imposed.

2.1.1 Jurisdiction of Magistrates' Courts

There are about 160 Magistrates' Courts in England and Wales. They were established as local courts and deal with cases that have a connection with their geographical area.

Cases are heard by magistrates, who may either be legally qualified District Judges or non-legally qualified lay magistrates (also called justices).

Leeds Magistrates' Court

Magistrates' Courts have the following jurisdiction:
1 To try all summary cases.
2 To try any triable either way cases that can be dealt with in the Magistrates' Court.
3 To deal with the first hearing of all indictable offences. These cases are then immediately sent to the Crown Court.
4 To deal with all preliminary matters connected to criminal cases, such as issuing warrants for arrest and deciding bail applications.
5 To try cases in the Youth Court where defendants are aged 10–17 inclusive.

(The first two categories account for about 97 per cent of all criminal cases.)

2.1.2 Jurisdiction of the Crown Court

The Crown Court sits in about 84 different locations throughout England and Wales. The Crown Court deals with all indictable, or serious, offences. It also deals with any triable either way offences that are sent for trial from the Magistrates' Court.

A judge sits alone to hear pre-trial matters in cases at the Crown Court, and where a defendant pleads guilty. However, when a defendant pleads not guilty, a jury is used to decide the verdict. The judge will:
- control the court
- rule on relevant issues of law
- direct the jury on the law and evidence
- impose a sentence if the defendant is found guilty.

Party	Description
Prosecution	• It is the Crown Prosecution Service (CPS) which initially advises the police on what offence to charge. • Lawyers work for the CPS. They may direct the police on what evidence is required and needs to be obtained. • Once the case comes to court, lawyers present the case and try to prove the defendant guilty beyond reasonable doubt.
Defendant	• This is the person charged with a criminal offence. • They (and their lawyer) do not have to disprove the prosecution case but to cast sufficient doubt on it.

Figure 2.1 Key facts: the prosecution and the defendant

2.1.3 Classification of criminal offences

Summary offences

These are the least serious criminal offences and have to be tried in the Magistrates' Courts. They are subdivided into offences of different 'levels', which carry maximum fines:
- Level 1: maximum £200
- Level 2: £500
- Level 3: £1000
- Level 4: £2500
- Level 5: unlimited.

Examples of summary offences include driving while disqualified, common assault, being drunk and disorderly in a public place and theft from a shop where the value of the goods stolen is less than £200.

Triable either way offences

These offences can be tried in either the Magistrates' Court or the Crown Court.

If it is decided that the case will be dealt with in the Magistrates' Court, then the procedure is the same as for trial of a summary offence. The only difference is that, if the defendant pleads guilty or is found guilty, the magistrates have the power to send the defendant to the Crown Court for sentencing. The magistrates can only do this if they think that they cannot impose an adequate sentence.

If the case is tried in the Crown Court, the trial will proceed in the same way as an indictable offence. If the defendant pleads (or is found) guilty, the judge can impose any sentence up to the maximum for that offence.

Triable either way offences include assault causing actual bodily harm and theft of property over £200.

Indictable offences

These are the most serious offences and can only be tried in the Crown Court.

The first preliminary hearing to establish the defendant's identity will take place in the Magistrates' Court.
- If the defendant pleads not guilty, a jury will decide if the defendant is guilty or not guilty after hearing all the evidence.
- If the defendant pleads guilty, the judge will impose a sentence.

When sentencing, the judge can impose any sentence up to the maximum that is set by the Act that imposes the offence. Examples of indictable offences include murder, manslaughter and robbery.

Type of offence	Description
Summary offences	The least serious offences: have to be tried in the Magistrates' Court
Triable either way offences	More serious offences: can be tried in either the Magistrates' Court or in the Crown Court
Indictable offences	The most serious offences: have to be tried in the Crown Court

Figure 2.2 Key facts: types of offence and their description

2.1.4 Pre-trial procedures

Summary offences

There is a case management system which aims to complete the case at the earliest opportunity. At the first hearing, the clerk of the court will check the defendant's name and address and take the plea – guilty or not guilty. Over 90 per cent of defendants in the Magistrates' Court plead guilty.

- Whether or not the defendant has legal representation, the magistrates will proceed to consider a sentence if the defendant has pleaded guilty. A sentencing hearing will hear the brief facts of the offence from the prosecution and any statements the defendant wishes to make. The magistrates will then decide on and announce their sentence.
- In some minor driving offences, the defendant can plead guilty by post, so that attendance at court is unnecessary.
- If the defendant pleads not guilty, the magistrates will try to discover the issues involved and then set a date for trial.

Triable either way offences

The procedure is set out in the Magistrates' Courts Act 1980.

Plea before venue

The defendant will be asked to plead.

- If the plea is guilty, the matter is automatically heard by the Magistrates' Court and a sentencing hearing will take place in the same way as with summary offences.
- If the defendant pleads not guilty, the magistrates must decide where the case will be tried and a Mode of trial procedure will take place.

The defendant has no right to request a hearing at the Crown Court but the case can be sent there by the magistrates if they consider they have insufficient sentencing powers.

Mode of trial

This procedure is to decide the most appropriate court for the case to be dealt with. The magistrates decide if the case is suitable for a Magistrates' Court trial and whether they are prepared to accept jurisdiction. They must consider the nature and seriousness of the offence, their powers of punishment and any representation of the prosecution and defence.

- If the case involves complex questions of law, breach of trust or offences committed by organised gangs, it should be sent to the Crown Court.
- If the case is referred to the Crown Court, or the defendant chooses trial there, all pre-trial matters will be dealt with by the Crown Court.

Indictable offences

First hearing

The first hearing will be in the Magistrates' Court shortly after the defendant is charged. The magistrates will deal with:

- establishing the defendant's identity
- whether bail or custody should be ordered
- whether the defendant should receive legal aid for representation.

All further pre-trial matters will then be dealt with in the Crown Court, by a Crown Court judge sitting alone.

Plea and Trial Preparation Hearing (PTPH)

This takes place at the Crown Court as soon as possible after the case has been sent there from the Magistrates' Court. An effective PTPH will:

- 'arraign' the defendant (take the defendant's plea) unless there is good reason not to
- set a trial date
- identify the issues for trial, so far as they are known at that stage
- provide a timetable for pre-trial preparation and give appropriate directions for an effective trial
- make provision for any Further Case Management Hearing (FCMH) that may be required to take place when it can have maximum effectiveness.

The indictment

This document will be prepared before trial and formally sets out the charges against the defendant.

Although the defendant will have been sent for trial charged with specific crimes, the indictment can be drawn up for any further offence that the evidence reveals. In more complicated cases the indictment may have several counts (charges), each relating to a different offence.

Disclosure by prosecution and defence

Both prosecution and defence have to make certain points known to the other before trial. The prosecution must set out all the evidence they propose to use at the trial. They must also disclose previously undisclosed material 'which in the prosecutor's opinion might reasonably be considered capable of undermining the case for the prosecution against the accused'.

The defence must give a written statement to the prosecution that includes:

- the nature of the accused's defence, including any legal defences intended to be relied on
- any matters of fact on which issue is taken with the prosecution
- any point of law to be argued, and the case authority in support
- any alibi and the witnesses to support that alibi – this information allows the prosecution to run police checks on the alibi witnesses.

2.2 Appeals and appellate courts

2.2.1 Appeals from the Magistrates' Court to the Crown Court

This appeal is only available to the defence.

- If the defendant pleaded guilty at the Magistrates' Court, then an appeal can only be made against sentence. The Crown Court can confirm the sentence, or they can increase or decrease it. However, any increase can only be up to the magistrates' maximum powers for the case.
- If the defendant pleaded not guilty and was convicted, an appeal can be made against

conviction and/or sentence. The Crown Court, consisting of a judge sitting with two lay magistrates, will hold a complete rehearing of the case including any evidence that was not available in the Magistrates' Court. They can confirm or vary the conviction and/or sentence or find the defendant guilty of a lesser offence.

2.2.2 Case-stated appeals

These are appeals on a point of law that go to the Queen's Bench Divisional Court, either directly from the Magistrates' Court or following an appeal to the Crown Court. Both the prosecution and the defence can use this appeal route.

The magistrates (or the Crown Court) are asked to state the case by setting out their findings of fact and their decision. The appeal is argued on the basis of what the law is on those facts; no witnesses are called. The appeal is usually heard by a panel of two or three judges.

The approach will be that the magistrates came to a wrong decision because they made a mistake about the law. The Divisional Court may confirm, vary or reverse the decision, or send the case back for the magistrates to implement the decision on the law.

There are usually fewer than one hundred case-stated appeals made each year. There is a possibility of a further appeal to the Supreme Court such as in *C v DPP* (1994).

> ### Case study
>
> **C v DPP (1994)**
>
> A boy of 13 was convicted in the Magistrates' Court of interfering with a motorcycle with intent to commit theft or to take and drive it away without consent. The appeal concerned the presumption of criminal responsibility of children between the ages of 10 and 14. Until this case, it had been accepted that such a child could only be convicted if the prosecution proved that the child knew he was doing wrong. The Divisional Court held that times had changed, children were more mature and the rule was not needed.
>
> The case was further appealed to the House of Lords who overruled the Divisional Court, holding that the law was still that a child of this age was presumed not to know they were doing wrong, and therefore not to have the necessary intention for any criminal offence. The original conviction was confirmed.

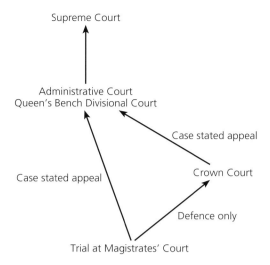

Figure 2.3 Appeal routes from the Magistrates' Court

2.2.3 Appeals from the Crown Court

Figure 2.4 Routes of appeal from a Crown Court trial

Appeals by the defendant

If a defendant has been found guilty following a Crown Court trial, they should be advised by their lawyers on the possibility of an appeal. An appeal can be made against conviction and/or sentence to the Court of Appeal (Criminal Division).

Leave to appeal

The Criminal Appeal Act 1995 requires that the defendant must obtain leave (or permission) to appeal, decided by a single judge of the Court of Appeal. The aim is to filter out cases without merit and save the court's time.

The Criminal Appeal Act 1995

The Criminal Appeal Act 1995 simplified the grounds under which the court can allow an appeal. The Act states that the Court of Appeal:

> shall allow an appeal against conviction if they think that the conviction is unsafe; and shall dismiss such an appeal in any other case.

Since the European Convention on Human Rights was incorporated into law by the Human Rights Act 1998, the Court of Appeal has taken a broad approach to the meaning of 'unsafe'. In particular, a conviction has been held to be 'unsafe' where the defendant has been denied a fair trial.

Link

See Chapter 34 for more on Article 6 of the European Convention on Human Rights.

New evidence

The defendant can apply to introduce new evidence but:

- it must appear to be capable of belief and afford a ground for an appeal
- it has to be considered whether it would have been admissible at the trial, and why it was not produced at that trial.

The Court of Appeal's powers

The Court of Appeal can:

- allow a defendant's appeal and quash a conviction, or
- vary the conviction to that of a lesser offence of which the defendant could have been convicted, and/or
- decrease, but not increase, any sentence imposed, or
- dismiss the appeal, or
- order that there should be a retrial of the case in front of a new jury.

Appeals by the prosecution against an acquittal

The prosecution has limited rights to appeal against an acquittal as follows:

1 Where the acquittal was the result of the jury being 'nobbled'. This is where one or more jurors was bribed or threatened by associates of the defendant.
2 Where there is new and compelling evidence of the acquitted person's guilt, and it is in the public interest for the defendant to be retried. This power is given by the Criminal Justice Act 2003 and it is only available for some thirty serious offences, including murder, manslaughter, rape and terrorism

offences. It is known as double jeopardy, since the defendant is being tried twice for the same offence. The Director of Public Prosecutions has to consent to the reopening of investigations in the case.

> ### Key term 🔑
> Acquittal – the defendant is found not guilty.

Case studies

Stephen Lawrence

In 2011, two defendants who had been previously acquitted of the murder of black teenager Stephen Lawrence were retried and convicted using the double jeopardy rules, some 19 years after the murder. Part of the new evidence was a DNA match with Stephen's blood found on the clothing of one of them. This evidence became available due to improved DNA testing techniques.

Michael Weir

Michael Weir was jailed for life for the murders of two pensioners. He was convicted twenty years after the killings in a unique double jeopardy case. His original murder conviction was dismissed on appeal on a technicality when prosecutors were late filing legal papers, despite DNA evidence from a glove found at the scene linking him to one of the attacks. By 2018, new DNA evidence linking him to both murders was discovered. Weir was the first defendant to be found guilty of the same murder twice.

Referring a point of law after an acquittal

Following an acquittal, under s 36 of the Criminal Justice Act 1972, the Attorney-General can refer a point of law to the Court of Appeal in order to get a ruling on the law.

The decision by the Court of Appeal on that point of law does not affect the acquittal but it creates a precedent for any future case involving the same point of law.

> ### Link
> See Chapter 17 for more information on judicial precedent.

Against sentence after conviction

Also, under s 36 of the Criminal Justice Act 1988, the Attorney-General can apply for leave to refer an unduly lenient sentence to the Court of Appeal.

Cases are brought to the Attorney-General's attention by the Crown Prosecution Service. It is also possible for a member of the public to contact the Attorney-General's office if they feel that the original sentence was too lenient.

Further appeals

Both the prosecution and the defence may appeal from the Court of Appeal to the Supreme Court, but they need to have the case certified as involving a point of law of general public importance, and to get leave to appeal from either the Supreme Court or the Court of Appeal.

An appeal can only be made against conviction or acquittal. The appeal will consist of legal arguments only, and fewer than twenty criminal appeals are usually heard by the Supreme Court each year.

2.3 Sentencing and court powers for adults

Whenever a defendant is found guilty of a criminal offence, the court must impose a sentence as punishment for the wrongful behaviour. In the Magistrates' Courts, the magistrates will decide the sentence. In the Crown Court, the judge will decide the sentence.

There are guidelines on what type and level of sentence are appropriate for each offence. Both judges and magistrates will have to take account of the guidelines and the general aims of sentencing in their decision making.

2.3.1 Aims of sentencing

When judges or magistrates are passing sentence, they look at the sentences available but also have to decide what they are trying to achieve by the punishment. Section 142 of the Criminal Justice Act 2003 sets out the purposes of sentencing for those aged 18 and over:

- punishment of offenders
- reduction of crime (including its reduction by deterrence)
- reform and rehabilitation of offenders
- protection of the public
- offenders making reparations to their victims.

Punishment of offenders

The idea of punishment is that the offender deserves punishment for carrying out a criminal act or acts. It does not seek to reduce crime or alter the offender's future behaviour.

This idea was expressed in the nineteenth century by Kant in *The Metaphysical Elements of Justice* when he wrote:

> **"** Judicial punishment can never be used merely as a means to promote some other good for the criminal himself or for civil society, but instead it must in all cases be imposed on him only on the ground that he has committed a crime. **"**

Punishment is concerned only with:
- the offence that was committed
- making sure that the punishment fits the crime.

Punishment contains an element of revenge: society and the victim are being avenged for the wrong done. This is how long prison sentences for serious offences are justified.

The crudest form of punishment can be seen in the old saying, 'an eye for an eye and a tooth for a tooth and a life for a life'. This was one of the factors used to justify the death penalty for the offence of murder.
- One US judge has put this theory into practice in sentencing other offences, by giving victims of burglary the right to go, with a law officer, to the home of the burglar and take items up to the approximate value of those stolen from them!
- In other crimes it is not so easy to see how this principle can operate, to produce an exact match between crime and punishment.

Punishment and tariff sentences

Sentencing is based on the idea that punishment for each offence should have a set minimum term. The Sentencing Council produces guidelines on sentencing for the most common crimes. These include a starting point and a range for the sentence. They also set out factors that make an offence more serious or less serious.

When producing guidelines, the Council also has to identify whether they will probably increase the numbers being sent to prison or using the probation service. This allows the government to forecast the requirements of the prison and probation services.

This system upholds the aim of punishing offenders and leads to consistency in sentencing. However, it can be difficult for courts to impose sentences aimed at reforming offenders, and the guidelines leave very little discretion in sentencing with the judges.

Activity ❓

Research the Sentencing Council's guidelines for the guideline sentences for:
- involuntary manslaughter
- assault occasioning actual bodily harm
- robbery.

Reduction of crime including deterrence

There are two main kinds of deterrence:
- **Individual deterrence** aims to ensure that the offender does not reoffend, through fear of future punishment.
- **General deterrence** aims at preventing other potential offenders from committing crimes.

Both are aimed at reducing future levels of crime.

Individual deterrence

By imposing a severe penalty, the theory is that the offender will think twice in the future, for fear of punishments such as a prison sentence, a suspended sentence or a heavy fine. However, prison does not appear to deter, as about 45 per cent of adult prisoners reoffend within one year of release.

Critics of the theory of deterrence point out:
- It assumes that an offender will stop to consider what the consequences of their action will be. In fact, most crimes are committed on the spur of the moment, often under the influence of drugs or alcohol. These offenders are unlikely to stop and consider the possible consequences of their actions.
- Fear of being caught is more of a deterrent, and because crime detection rates are low, the threat of an unpleasant penalty seems too remote. Use of CCTV in town centres, business and residential properties may act as a deterrent for some potential offenders.

General deterrence

The value of this aim is more doubtful, as potential offenders are rarely deterred by severe sentences passed on other people. However, judges do occasionally make an example of one offender in order to warn other potential offenders of the type of punishment they might face.
- General deterrence relies on publicity, so that potential offenders are aware of the level of punishment they can expect.

- Deterrent sentences are less effective in cases of drug or people smuggling by foreign nationals, as the rewards are considered attractive.
- A number of terrorist offences have been created by Parliament with severe maximum sentences. However, the beliefs of potential offenders seem to outweigh the deterrent effect of these offences and of punishment.

General deterrence is in direct conflict with the principle of retribution, since it involves sentencing an offender to a longer term than is deserved for the specific offence. It is probably the least effective and least fair principle of sentencing.

Reform and rehabilitation

The main point of this aim to reduce crime is to reform the offender and rehabilitate them into society. It is a forward-looking aim: to alter the offender's behaviour so that they don't reoffend.

This principle of sentencing grew in the second half of the twentieth century with the development of community sentences.

- Judges or magistrates will be given information about the defendant's background and, if relevant, they will consider school reports, job prospects or medical issues.
- Community orders, especially drug testing and treatment orders and drug abstention orders, aim to rehabilitate drug abusers.

Persistent offenders are usually thought less likely to respond to a sentence with rehabilitation as a principal aim.

The Sentencing Council guidance asks courts to consider previous attempts at rehabilitation when passing sentence.

Individualised sentences

Where the court considers rehabilitation as a main aim, the sentence used is an individualised one aimed at the needs of the offender. This is in direct contrast to the concept of tariff sentences for retribution.

Criticisms of this approach:
- It leads to inconsistency in sentencing. Offenders who have committed exactly the same type of offence may be given different sentences because the emphasis is on the individual offender.
- It tends to discriminate against offenders from poor home backgrounds – they are less likely to be seen as possible candidates for rehabilitation.

Protection of the public

The Legal Aid Sentencing and Punishment of Offenders Act 2012 (LASPO) introduced new sentences where the main aim is to protect the public from violent or prolific offenders.

Custodial sentences are the main way of protecting the public. If the offender presents a significant risk to members of society, they must be sent to prison where they cannot commit further crimes.

- Long-term custodial sentences appear to be more effective at preventing reoffending than short-term custodial sentences. In 2017, the number of people who reoffended within one year of release was approximately:
  - 44 per cent of adults who served over 12 months' imprisonment
  - 60 per cent of those serving less than 12 months' imprisonment.
- The Extended Determinate Sentence, introduced by LASPO, protects the public from offenders who have committed serious sexual or violent offences. The offender has to serve a custodial sentence and an extended period on licence. The minimum custodial period is 12 months.
- Also, LASPO introduced a new mandatory life sentence for offenders convicted of a *second* very serious sexual or violent crime. They will be removed from circulation to protect society. But this raises questions:
  - How long should the public be protected for?
  - Should the offender serve all of the sentence imposed, or should they be released early, on licence?
- Those who commit murder or other serious crimes are given life sentences. When they are considered no longer to be a danger to the public, the parole board might consider releasing them on licence.

Community sentences can also protect the public:
- A curfew removes the offender from a certain area or place at certain times of the day, making those places safe for the public.
- Wearing an electronic tag allows the probation service and the police to monitor an offender's location and compliance with their curfew order. LASPO increased:
  - the curfew requirement from 6 to 12 months
  - the maximum period for the curfew from 12 to 16 hours per day.

- Community Orders offer treatment and education to offenders who are dependent on drugs and alcohol.
- The public are protected when people convicted of driving offences are taken off the road, either in prison or banned. LASPO introduced a maximum of five years' imprisonment for causing serious injury by dangerous driving.
- Section 142 LASPO introduced the offence of threatening with an offensive weapon or article containing a blade or point in public or on school premises.

Making reparations to the victim

This is aimed at compensating the victim of the crime, usually by ordering the offender to pay a sum of money to the victim or to make reparation, for example, by returning stolen property to its rightful owner.

The idea that criminals should pay compensation to the victims of their crimes is long established. Judges and magistrates are required to consider ordering compensation to the victim of a crime, as well as any other appropriate penalty. Under s 130 of the Powers of Criminal Courts (Sentencing) Act 2000, courts are under a duty to give reasons if they do not make a compensation order.

Restorative justice

Offenders and victims are brought together so that the offenders may see the effect of their crimes and make direct reparation, perhaps by doing decorating or gardening at the victim's home.

The offender might also make reparation to society by doing unpaid work on a community project, supervised by the probation service.

2.3.2 Factors in sentencing

Before sentencing an adult offender, the judge or magistrates will weigh up any relevant aggravating and mitigating factors.
- Aggravating factors will increase a sentence.
- Mitigating factors will reduce a sentence.

In order to do this, the court must know details of the offence, so where the offender pleads guilty the prosecution will outline the facts of the case and the defendant can make a statement.

Where the offender has pleaded not guilty and been convicted after a trial, the judge or magistrates will have heard full information about the case during the trial. However, they may still require a pre-sentence report to be prepared.

The main factors in sentencing include:
- pre-sentence reports
- medical reports
- sentencing guidelines
- reduction in sentence for a guilty plea
- the offender's background.

Pre-sentence reports

These are prepared by the probation service for consideration by the court before sentencing. This report might not be relevant for very serious offences, but is important when the court is considering a community sentence.

The report will give information about the offender's background and suitability for a community-based sentence. It might show why the offender committed the crime, and indicate the likely response to a community-based penalty.

Medical reports

Where the offender has medical or psychiatric problems, the court will usually ask for a report to be prepared by an appropriate doctor. Medical conditions may be important factors in deciding the appropriate way of dealing with the offender; the courts have special powers where the offender is suffering from mental illness.

Sentencing guidelines

The Sentencing Council was established in 2010 to bring greater consistency and transparency to sentencing practice. It has responsibility for:
- developing sentencing guidelines and monitoring their use
- assessing the impact of guidelines on sentencing practice
- promoting awareness among the public about the realities of sentencing
- publishing information about sentencing practice in Magistrates' and Crown Courts.

Judges and magistrates are now under a duty to impose a sentence that follows the guidelines. They should only depart from the guidelines when this would bring better justice. This should help produce more consistent sentencing.

There are guidelines on sentencing for specific offences, including aggravating and mitigating factors. The most important point to establish is how serious the offence was, of its type. This is now set out in s 143(1) of the Criminal Justice Act 2003:

> In considering the seriousness of the offence, the court must consider the offender's culpability in committing the offence and any harm which the offence caused, or was intended to cause or might reasonably foreseeably have caused.

Aggravating factors

The Act lists these aggravating factors that make an offence more serious:
- previous convictions for offences of a similar nature or relevant to the present offence
- if the offender was on bail when the offence was committed
- any racial or religious hostility in the offence
- any hostility to disability or sexual orientation being involved in the offence
- if the offender pleaded not guilty.

The sentencing judge or magistrates will also want to know:
- in a case of theft – how much was stolen and whether the offender was in a position of trust
- in a case of assault – what injuries were inflicted, whether the assault was premeditated and whether the victim was particularly vulnerable (young or elderly)
- whether the offender was in a position of trust and abused that trust – the offence will be considered as being more serious and merit a longer than usual sentence
- where several offenders are convicted of committing a crime jointly – whether any of them played a greater part than the others, and who was involved in planning it.

Mitigating factors

Before sentencing, mitigating factors will also be considered. Examples of mitigating factors include:
- no previous convictions
- showing genuine remorse
- taking a minor part in the offence
- mental illness or disability
- pleading guilty.

Look online

Go to **www.sentencingcouncil.org.uk/offences/crown-court/item/domestic-burglary/** for the sentencing guidelines for domestic burglary. What is the range of sentences for the following?
1 A first-time offender who reaches into an open window of an empty house and takes a bottle of beer.
2 A couple of friends who enter an empty house at night as they know the owners are on holiday, disable the alarm and steal a quantity of valuable jewellery.
3 A group of four knife-carrying burglars who break into a house by smashing patio doors and trash the house, looking for a safe which they think contains a quantity of cash. The house-owner is threatened and tied up.

Reduction in sentence for a guilty plea

A guilty plea at the first reasonable opportunity should reduce the sentence by up to one-third, but where the prosecution case is overwhelming, only 20 per cent. A plea of guilty after the trial has started would only be given a 10 per cent reduction.

The amount of reduction is on a sliding scale. The reason for this as set out by the Sentencing Council is:

> A reduction in sentence is appropriate because a guilty plea avoids the need for a trial, shortens the gap between charge and sentence, saves considerable cost, and, in the case of an early plea, saves victims and witnesses from the concern about having to give evidence.

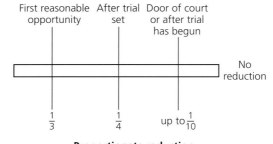

Stage in the proceedings

First reasonable opportunity | After trial set | Door of court or after trial has begun | No reduction

$\frac{1}{3}$ | $\frac{1}{4}$ | up to $\frac{1}{10}$

Proportionate reduction

Figure 2.5 Maximum reduction in sentence for guilty plea

The offender's background

1 Previous convictions: these are treated as an aggravating factor, and so include:
   - failure to respond to previous sentences
   - the past record of the offender
   - whether the offender was on bail when the offence was committed.
2 If there are no previous convictions and the offence was not committed while on bail, this will be treated as a mitigating factor.
3 The financial situation of the offender, where the judge or magistrates consider that a fine is a suitable penalty.

As from 1 October 2020, the Sentencing Council set new guidelines for those suffering mental disorders such as:
- schizophrenia, depression or PTSD
- developmental disorders such as autism
- neurological impairments such as acquired brain injury or dementia.

The court should take any of these conditions into account, but it will not necessarily have an impact on sentencing. The guidelines ask courts to take an individualistic approach and focus on the issues in the case.

2.3.3 Types of sentences

The main types of sentence that can be imposed on adult offenders are: custodial, community, fines and discharges.

Custodial sentences

A custodial sentence is the most serious punishment that a court can impose. Custodial sentences for adults range from a short period in custody to life imprisonment. The different custodial sentences are:
- mandatory life sentences
- discretionary life sentences
- fixed-term sentences
- suspended sentences.

Custodial sentences are meant to be used only for serious offences. This is confirmed by s 152 of the Criminal Justice Act 2003 which states:

> The court must not pass a custodial sentence unless it is of the opinion that the offence, or the combination of the offence and one or more offences associated with it, was so serious that neither a fine alone nor a community sentence can be justified for the offence.

Mandatory life sentences

The only sentence a judge can impose for a murder conviction is a life sentence.

However, after imposing the mandatory life sentence, the judge must set the minimum number of years' imprisonment that the offender must serve before being eligible for release on licence. This could be a minimum of 12 years to a maximum whole life order.

Aggravating factors that can increase the minimum term ordered by the judge include whether the victim was particularly vulnerable because of age or disability, or any mental or physical suffering inflicted on the victim before death.

Mitigating factors include that the offender had an intention to cause grievous bodily harm rather than an intention to kill, a lack of premeditation or that the offender acted to some extent in self-defence (though not sufficient to give them a defence).

A further type of mandatory life sentence was introduced by s 122 LASPO 2012. If an offender aged 18 or over commits a second serious offence then the court must impose a life sentence on the offender. Serious offences include manslaughter, ss 18 and 20 Offences Against the Person Act 1861 and robbery.

Whole life order

This is imposed for an offence of murder where the sentencing judge decides that the offender is so dangerous, they should never be released from prison. There are approximately 75 prisoners currently serving whole life sentences in England and Wales and include some of Britain's most notorious criminals.

Look online

Research a list of prisoners serving whole life sentences. Choose one of those offenders.

Why was a whole life sentence imposed on that offender?

Release on licence

When sentencing an offender, the judge will impose a minimum term of imprisonment that has to be served – this is called the 'tariff' period. At the end of this time, the Parole Board will decide whether the offender is fit for release back into the community. They will take into account:

- whether the offender admits the crime
- whether they are considered to still be a danger
- their behaviour during the tariff period.

If the offender is considered fit for release, this will be subject to conditions such as where they will live, what job they can take, wearing a tag and who they can associate with.

For offenders sentenced to a whole life term, these licence conditions will remain for the rest of their life. If the offender breaches any of the terms of the licence, they can be brought back to prison to serve a further term of imprisonment.

Discretionary life sentences

For the first commission of a serious offence, such as manslaughter, rape and robbery, the maximum sentence set by statute is life imprisonment, but the judge does not have to impose this. The judge has discretion in sentencing and can choose to give any sentence less than the maximum.

Fixed term sentences

For other less serious crimes, the maximum length of the sentence will again be set by statute – for a fixed term. For example, the maximum sentence for theft, imposed by the Theft Act 1968, is seven years.

The sentence imposed by a judge or magistrates will depend on several factors, including:

- the seriousness of the crime
- the defendant's previous record.

The length of a sentence can be increased if it is racially or religiously aggravated.

Only offenders aged 21 and over can be given a sentence of imprisonment.

Prisoners do not serve the whole of the sentence passed by the court:

- Anyone sent to prison is released on licence after they have served half of the sentence.

- For terrorism offences, offenders are released on licence after serving two-thirds of the sentence.

Release on licence has to be approved by the Parole Board and may be subject to conditions such as residence and the need to report to the police station or probation service.

Suspended prison sentences

A suspended sentence of imprisonment is one where the offender will only serve the custodial period if there is a breach of one of the terms of the suspension.

- The prison sentence can only be between fourteen days and two years.
- The period of suspension can be between six months and two years.

The idea is that the threat of prison during this period of suspension will deter the offender from committing further offences. If the offender complies with the requirements of the suspended sentence, they will not serve the term of imprisonment, but the sentence will be 'activated' if they do not comply.

The suspended sentence can be combined with any of the requirements used in a community order (see below).

A suspended sentence should only be given where the offence is so serious that an immediate custodial sentence would have been appropriate but there are exceptional circumstances in the case that justify suspending the sentence.

Non-custodial sentences

Community orders

These orders can be imposed when the judge or magistrates do not think that the offence is serious enough to warrant imprisonment.

The Criminal Justice Act 2003 created one community order under which the court can combine any requirements they think are necessary. The judge or magistrate can 'mix and match' requirements, allowing them to fit the restrictions and rehabilitation to the offender's needs.

The sentence is available for offenders aged 18 and over. The full list of requirements available to the courts is set out in s 177 of the Criminal Justice Act 2003. This states:

Activity

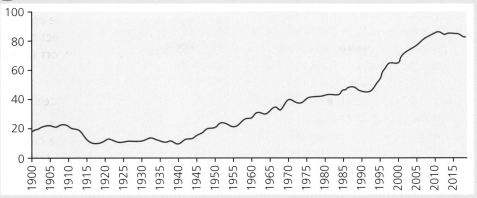

Figure 2.6 The prison population of England and Wales from 1900 to 2019

Source: **https://commonslibrary.parliament.uk/research-briefings/sn04334/**

There has been an explosion in the prison population between 1900 and 2019, quadrupling in size (half of this increase has taken place since 1990). If we calculate the number of prisoners per 100,000 people in the general population, by 2019 there were:

- 173 prisoners per 100,000 of the population in England and Wales
- 162 per 100,000 in Scotland
- 96 per 100,000 in Northern Ireland.

In 2019, England and Wales had the eighth highest rate of imprisonment among EU countries and the highest among western European jurisdictions.

1 Why do you think that England and Wales have the highest prison population in western European countries?
2 Consider ways in which the prison population could be reduced.

Source: Information adapted from report in House of Commons Library, 3 July 2020.

> 177(1) Where a person aged 18 or over is convicted of an offence, the court by or before which he is convicted may make an order imposing on him any one or more of the following requirements:
>
> (a) an unpaid work requirement
>
> (aa) a rehabilitation activity requirement
>
> (c) a programme requirement
>
> (d) a prohibited activity requirement
>
> (e) a curfew requirement
>
> (f) an exclusion requirement
>
> (g) a residence requirement – to live at a certain address
>
> (ga) a foreign travel prohibition requirement
>
> (h) a mental health treatment requirement
>
> (i) a drug rehabilitation requirement
>
> (j) an alcohol treatment requirement
>
> (ja) an alcohol abstinence and monitoring requirement
>
> (l) in the case where the offender is aged under 25, an attendance centre requirement
>
> (m) an electronic monitoring requirement.

Each of these orders is defined in the Criminal Justice Act 2003. Most are self-explanatory from their name but some specific orders need explanation:

- Drug rehabilitation or alcohol treatment requirement – much crime is linked to drug and/or alcohol abuse, and the idea is to tackle the causes of crime and prevent future offences.
- Programme requirement – this requires the offender to undertake an educational or practical course, for example, a course in building relationships for a person found guilty of a domestic violence offence.
- The time and length of the restrictions will be set together with conditions such as not contacting a victim or witnesses.
- Mental health treatment is also aimed at the cause of the offender's behaviour.

- Unpaid work requirements for a set number of hours. The type of work involved will vary, depending on what schemes the local probation service is running. Examples include painting school buildings, helping build a play centre or working on conservation projects. When Eric Cantona, the French footballer, was found guilty of assaulting a football fan in 1995, the court ordered him to help at coaching sessions for young footballers.
- Prohibited activity requirement – a wide variety of activities are banned, to prevent the offender from committing another similar crime, for example:
  - Often, the offender is forbidden to go into certain areas such as a town centre, or banned from wearing a 'hoodie'.
  - In one case, an offender who was found guilty of criminal damage was banned from carrying paint, dye, ink or marker pens.
- Exclusion requirement – offenders are ordered not to go to certain places where they are most likely to commit crime.

Fine

This is the most common sentence imposed in the Magistrates' Court – about 70 per cent of offenders are fined – whereas very few offenders receive a fine in the Crown Court. The maximum fines for summary offences are shown in 2.1.3 above.

When deciding the amount of a fine, the courts must take into account the income and assets of the offender.

Discharge

This may be either a conditional discharge or an absolute discharge.
- A conditional discharge means that the court discharges an offender on the condition that they commit no further offence during a set period of up to three years. If an offender reoffends within the time limit, the court can impose another sentence in place of the conditional discharge, as well as imposing a penalty for the new offence. Conditional discharges are widely used by Magistrates' Courts for first-time minor offenders.
- An absolute discharge means that, effectively, no penalty is imposed. This sentence is often used where an offender is technically guilty but morally blameless. This could be imposed, for example, where a person is found in possession of a small

quantity of cannabis for personal use, but there is a medical reason for the taking of the drug.

Type of sentence	Comment
Custodial sentence	<ul><li>Mandatory life sentence for murder</li><li>Discretionary life sentence for other serious offences</li><li>Fixed-term sentence</li><li>Suspended sentence – can be combined with conditions</li></ul>
Non-custodial sentences:	
Community order	<ul><li>Sentence served in the community</li><li>Court can impose suitable requirements, e.g. unpaid work, exclusion, drug rehabilitation, curfew</li></ul>
Fine	<ul><li>Used in 70% of cases in the Magistrates' Courts</li><li>Offender's income and assets must be taken into account</li></ul>
Discharge	<ul><li>Conditional: for a set length of time offender must not reoffend</li><li>Absolute: effectively no penalty imposed</li></ul>

Figure 2.7 Key facts: sentencing powers of the courts for adult offenders

Update

The Sentencing Act 2020 came into force on 1 December 2020. The Act contains a 'Sentencing Code' to provide a single reference point for the law on sentencing for adults and young offenders, rather than to have the law and procedure on sentencing contained in parts of several different Acts. The Sentencing Code is concerned with sentencing procedure and does not introduce any new law or change any sentences. It will apply to all offenders convicted of an offence after 1 October 2020. For further information about the Act, go to **www.lawgazette.co.uk/legal-updates/an-analysis-of-the-sentencing-code/5104692.article**

2.4 Lay magistrates and juries

There is a long-established tradition of using lay people (people who are not legally qualified) in the decision-making process in the English legal system. This applies particularly in criminal cases to the Magistrates' Courts where lay magistrates are used and the Crown Court where there is a jury to try cases.

2.4.1 Lay magistrates

Qualifications

Lay magistrates do not have to have any legal qualifications, but there are some general qualifications as follows:

- Lay magistrates must be aged between 18 and 65 on appointment, and have to retire at 70.
- Lay magistrates are expected to live or work within or near to the local justice area to which they are allocated.
- Lay magistrates must be prepared to commit themselves to sitting at least 26 half days each year, together with a number of training sessions.

There are, however, some requirements as to their character, in that they must be suitable in character, integrity and understanding for the work they have to perform. In 1998, the Lord Chancellor set out six key qualities that candidates should have. These are:

1 Good character
2 Understanding and communication
3 Social awareness
4 Maturity and sound temperament
5 Sound judgement
6 Commitment and reliability

They must have certain 'judicial' qualities — it is particularly important that they are able to absorb factual information and make a reasoned decision upon it. They must also be able to take account of the reasoning of others and work as a team.

Some people are not eligible to be appointed as lay magistrates, such as:

- those with serious criminal convictions, though a conviction for a minor motoring offence will not automatically disqualify a candidate
- those who are undischarged bankrupts
- members of the forces
- police officers and traffic wardens
- relatives of those working in the local criminal justice system — it would not appear 'just' if, for example, the wife of a local police officer were to decide cases
- those whose hearing is impaired or who by reason of infirmity cannot carry out all the duties of a Justice of the Peace
- close relatives to other magistrates on the same Bench.

Activities

1 Put the list of six key qualities into order, with the one that you think is most important first and the least important last.
2 Compare your list with a partner.
3 Can you think of any other qualities a magistrate would need?

Selection of lay magistrates

About 1200 new lay magistrates are appointed each year. The appointments are made by the Senior Presiding Judge. In order to decide who to appoint, the Senior Presiding Judge relies on recommendations made by the Local Advisory Committees.

Local Advisory Committees

The committee should have a maximum of twelve members and these should include a mixture of magistrates and non-magistrates. The committees try to encourage as wide a range of potential candidates as possible to put themselves forward. Advertisements may be placed in local papers, or on community noticeboards, radio adverts or using social media. The intention is to create a panel that is representative of all aspects of society.

The selection process

When applying, the candidate must fill in an application form and give the names of two referees. There is then a two-stage interview process:

- At the first interview, the panel tries to find out more about the candidate's personal attributes, in particular looking to see if they have the six key qualities required. The interview panel will also explore the candidate's attitudes on various criminal justice issues such as youth crime or drink driving.
- A second interview is aimed at testing candidates' potential judicial aptitude, and this is done by a discussion of at least two case studies that are typical of those heard regularly in Magistrates' Courts. The discussion might, for example, focus on the type of sentence that should be imposed on specific case facts.

Appointment of lay magistrates

The local advisory committees will interview candidates and then submit names of those they think are suitable to the Senior Presiding Judge, who will then appoint new magistrates from this list.

Role of lay magistrates in criminal cases

Magistrates have a very wide workload that is mainly connected to criminal cases, although they also deal with some civil matters.

Lay magistrates will normally sit as a panel of three, but a District Judge (Magistrates' Court) will sit alone. Magistrates try 97 per cent of all criminal cases. In addition to their trial role, they can grant search and arrest warrants to the police and consider, in serious cases, requests for an extension in police custody up to a maximum of 96 hours.

Summary offences

Magistrates deal with the case from start to finish. They will hear evidence from the prosecution and defendant and any legal arguments and decide if the defendant is guilty or not guilty.

If the defendant is found guilty, they will decide on a sentence. Their sentencing powers are limited to a maximum of six months' imprisonment for one offence. For a serious Level 5 offence, they can impose an unlimited fine.

Triable either way offences

Magistrates deal with plea before venue hearings (see section on Triable either way offences above).

Indictable offences

Magistrates will hold an Early Administrative Hearing before transferring the case to the Crown Court (see section on Indictable offences).

Youth Court

Specially nominated and trained magistrates form a Youth Court panel to hear criminal charges against young offenders aged 10 to 17. These panels must usually include at least one man and one woman. Hearings are informal and private.

Appeals

Lay magistrates can also sit in a Crown Court to hear appeals from a Magistrates' Court against conviction and/or sentence. In these cases, two lay magistrates form a panel with a qualified judge.

2.4.2 Jurors

Qualifications

The Juries Act 1974 (as amended) sets out the qualifications for jurors. To qualify for jury service, a person must be:

- aged 18 and over, and under 76
- registered as a parliamentary or local government elector
- ordinarily resident in the United Kingdom, the Channel Islands or the Isle of Man for at least five years since their 13th birthday.

In addition, the person must not be:

- a person detained or resident in a hospital under a Mental Health Order, or
- disqualified from jury service.

Disqualification

Some criminal convictions will disqualify a person from jury service. Disqualified permanently from jury service are those who at any time have been sentenced to:

- imprisonment, detention or custody for life
- detention during Her Majesty's Pleasure or during the Pleasure of the Secretary of State
- imprisonment for public protection or detention for public protection
- an extended sentence
- a term of imprisonment of five years or more or a term of detention of five years or more.

People are disqualified for ten years if at any time in the last ten years they have:

- served a sentence of imprisonment
- had a suspended sentence passed on them
- had a community order or other community sentence passed on them.

In addition, anyone who is currently on bail in criminal proceedings is disqualified from sitting as a juror. If a disqualified person fails to disclose that fact and turns up for jury service, they may be fined up to £5000.

Lack of capacity

A judge may discharge a person from being a juror for lack of capacity to cope with the trial. This could be because the person does not understand English adequately or because of some disability that makes them unsuitable as a juror. This includes blind people, as they would be unable to see plans and photographs produced in evidence.

Deaf jurors

In June 1995, a deaf man was prevented from sitting on a jury at the Old Bailey despite wishing to serve and bringing with him a sign-language interpreter. The judge pointed out that that would mean an extra person in the jury room and this was not allowed by law.

Discretionary excusals

Anyone who has problems that make it very difficult for them to do their jury service may ask to be excused or for their period of service to be put back to a later date. The court has discretion to grant such an excusal but will only do so if there is a sufficiently good reason.

Such reasons include being too ill to attend court, suffering from a disability that makes it impossible for the person to sit as a juror, or being a parent with a small baby. Persons aged over 70 can apply to be excused. Other reasons could include doing essential work, for example, doctors or other medical staff.

There are sometimes temporary events that would make it difficult for a person to do jury service, such as business appointments that could not be undertaken by anyone else, being due to sit examinations or having a holiday booked. In these situations, the court is most likely to defer jury service to a more convenient date rather than excuse the person completely.

If a person is not excused from jury service, they must attend on the date set or they may be fined up to £1000 for non-attendance.

Members of the forces

There is a special rule for full-time serving members of the forces. They may be excused from jury service if their commanding officer certifies that their absence from duty (because of jury service) would be prejudicial to the efficiency of the service.

Lawyers and police on juries

Lawyers and police are eligible to serve on juries despite the feeling that this could lead to bias or to a legally well-qualified juror influencing the rest of the jury. The test to be applied in such cases is:

> whether the fair-minded and informed observer, having considered the facts, would conclude that there was a real possibility that the tribunal was biased.

Case study

Hanif v United Kingdom (2012)

The European Court of Human Rights ruled that having a police officer on the jury was a breach of Article 6(1) of the European Convention on Human Rights – the right to a fair trial. In this case, the police officer juror had immediately alerted the court to the fact that he knew one of the prosecution police witnesses. It was particularly important as the evidence of this witness was crucial to the case against the defendant. However, the trial judge had ruled that this did not matter.

The case continued with the police officer juror being the foreman of the jury and the defendant was convicted. The Court of Appeal, somewhat surprisingly, upheld the conviction.

Judges on jury service

In June 2004 (just two months after the rules on jury service changed), a judge from the Court of Appeal, Lord Justice Dyson, was summoned to attend as a juror. This prompted the Lord Chief Justice, Lord Woolf, to issue observations to judges who are called for jury service. These point out that:

- A judge serves on a jury as part of his duty as a private citizen.
- Excusal from jury service will only be granted in extreme circumstances.
- A judge should defer jury service to a later date if they have judicial commitments at that time.
- At court, if a judge knows the presiding judge or other person in the case, they should raise this with the jury bailiff or a member of the court staff if they consider it could interfere with their responsibilities as a juror.
- It is a matter of discretion for an individual judge sitting as a juror as to whether they disclose the fact of their judicial office to the other members of the jury.
- Judges must follow the directions given to the jury by the trial judge on the law and should avoid the temptation to correct guidance that they believe to be inaccurate as this is outside their role as a juror.

Discuss whether you think the following people should sit on a jury:
- a woman who was fined for shoplifting a month ago
- a man who was fined and disqualified from driving for taking cars without the consent of the owner
- a doctor who works in general practice
- an 18-year-old student who has exams in three weeks
- a Circuit Judge who frequently tries cases in the Crown Court.

Selection of jurors

At each Crown Court there is an official who is responsible for summoning enough jurors to try the cases that will be heard in each two-week period.

This official will arrange for names to be selected at random from the electoral registers for the area the court covers. This is done through computer selection at a central office.

It is necessary to summon more than twelve jurors as most courts have more than one courtroom, and it will not be known how many of those summoned are disqualified or will be excused.

Those summoned must notify the court if there is any reason why they should not or cannot attend.

All others are expected to attend for two weeks' jury service, though, of course, if the case they are trying goes on for more than two weeks, they will have to stay until the trial is completed. Where it is known that a trial may be exceptionally long, such as a complicated fraud trial, potential jurors are asked if they will be able to serve for such a long period.

Vetting

Once the list of potential jurors is known, both the prosecution and the defence have the right to see that list. In some cases, it may be decided that this pool of potential jurors should be 'vetted'; that is, checked for suitability. There are two types of vetting:
- Disclosure and Barring Service (DBS)
- authorised jury checks.

DBS checks

Checks can be made on prospective jurors to eliminate those who are disqualified.

Authorised jury checks

This is where a wider check is authorised into a juror's background and political affiliations. This practice was brought to light by the 'ABC' trial in 1978 where two journalists and a soldier were charged with collecting secret information. It was discovered that the jury had been vetted for their loyalty. The trial was stopped and a new trial ordered before a fresh jury. Following these cases, the Attorney-General published guidelines in 1980 (revised in 1988) on when political vetting of jurors should take place. They state that:
- Vetting should only be used in exceptional cases involving national security, where part of the evidence is likely to be given in camera (in secret) such as in terrorism cases.
- Vetting can only be carried out with the Attorney-General's express permission.

Challenging

The jurors are usually divided into groups of fifteen and allocated to a court. At the start of a trial the court clerk will select twelve out of these fifteen at random. Once the court clerk has selected the panel of twelve jurors, these jurors come into the jury box to be sworn in as jurors. At this point, before the jury is sworn in, both the prosecution and defence have certain rights to challenge one or more of the jurors.

There are three challenges that can be made:
- to the array
- for cause
- the prosecution right to stand by.

To the array

This is a challenge to the whole jury on the basis that it has been chosen in an unrepresentative or biased way.

This challenge was used successfully against the 'Romford' jury at the Old Bailey in 1993 when, out of a panel of twelve jurors, nine came from Romford, with two of them living within twenty doors of each other in the same street.

In *R v Fraser* (1987), this method of challenging a jury was also used, as the defendant was of a black or minority ethnic (BAME) background but all the jurors were white. The judge in that case agreed to empanel another jury.

However, in *R v Ford* (1989), it was held that if the jury was chosen in a random manner then it could not be challenged simply because it was not multiracial.

For cause

This involves challenging the right of an individual juror to sit on the jury. To be successful, the challenge must point out a valid reason why that juror should not serve on the jury, such as being disqualified or knowing/being related to a witness or defendant.

If such people are not removed from the jury, there is a risk that any subsequent conviction could be quashed.

Appointment of jurors

When a jury has been chosen, they will individually be required to swear an oath that they will faithfully try the defendant according to the evidence.

Once this has been done, the jury has been empanelled and will start to hear the speeches and evidence. A jury will be empanelled to hear just one case.

Role of jurors in criminal cases

Juries are used in the Crown Court where they decide whether the defendant is guilty or not guilty.

Jury trials account for less than 1 per cent of all criminal trials – about 20,000 cases per year. This is because 97 per cent of cases are dealt with in the Magistrates' Court, and about two-thirds of defendants plead guilty at Crown Court.

A jury in the Crown Court has twelve members.

Split function

A trial is presided over by a judge and the functions are split between the judge and jury:
- The judge decides points of law.
- The jury decides the facts.

At the end of the prosecution case, the judge has the power to direct the jury to acquit the defendant if it is decided that, in law, the prosecution's evidence has not made out a case against the defendant. This is called a directed acquittal.

The defence will then put their case and call any witnesses. At the end of the evidence, the judge will sum up the case and direct the jury on any law involved.

The jury will retire to a private room and make a secret decision on the guilt or not of the accused. Initially the jury must try to come to a unanimous verdict – that is, one on which they are all agreed. The judge must accept the jury's verdict, even if they do not agree with it. This long-established principle goes back to Bushell's Case (1670). The jury does not give any reasons for their decision.

Majority verdicts

If, after at least two hours (longer where the case involves several defendants), the jury have not reached a verdict, the judge can call them back into the courtroom and direct that a majority verdict can be accepted. Where there is a full jury of twelve, the majority verdict can be 10–2 or 11–1. If the jury has fallen below twelve, then only one can disagree with the verdict; that is, if there are 11 jurors, the verdict can be 10–1; if there are 10 jurors, it can be 9–1. If there are only 9 jurors, the verdict must be unanimous as a jury cannot go below 9 members.

Majority verdicts were introduced because of the fear of jury 'nobbling'; that is, jurors being bribed or intimidated by associates of the defendant into voting for a not-guilty verdict. When a jury had to be unanimous, only one member needed be bribed to cause a 'stalemate' in which the jury was unable to reach a decision. Acquittal rates in jury trials were also too high, and it was thought that majority decisions would result in more convictions.

Where the jury convicts a defendant on a majority verdict, the foreman of the jury must announce the numbers both agreeing and disagreeing with the verdict in open court. This provision is contained in s 17(3) of the Juries Act 1974 and is aimed at making sure the jury have come to a legal majority, and not one, for example, of 8–4 that is not allowed.

Aspects	Magistrates	Juries
Qualifications	<ul><li>Aged 18–65 on appointment</li><li>No specific qualifications but should have the six key qualities</li><li>Live or work in local justice area</li><li>Commit to sitting at least 26 half-days each year</li></ul>	<ul><li>Aged 18 and over, and under 75</li><li>Registered to vote</li><li>Resident in UK for at least 5 years since age 13</li></ul>
Disqualified	<ul><li>If convicted of serious criminal offence</li><li>Undischarged bankrupts</li><li>Members of armed forces</li><li>Police and traffic wardens and others whose work is incompatible</li></ul>	<ul><li>Sentenced to 5 years' or more imprisonment = disqualified for life</li><li>Served a prison sentence OR suspended sentence OR a community order = disqualified for 10 years</li><li>On bail = disqualified while on bail</li></ul>
Excusals	N/A	<ul><li>Members of the armed forces</li><li>Discretionary: ill, business commitments or other 'good reason'</li></ul>
Selection	<ul><li>Adverts placed looking for volunteers</li><li>Selected by local advisory committee following interviews</li><li>Committee try to achieve balance on the bench</li></ul>	<ul><li>A central office selects names from the lists of electors</li><li>Summons sent to these people</li><li>Must attend unless disqualified or excused</li></ul>
Vetting	<ul><li>Likely to be checked for criminal record</li></ul>	<ul><li>May be checked for criminal record (R v Mason (1980))</li><li>In cases of national security may be subject to a wider check on background subject to Attorney-General's guidelines</li></ul>
Challenges	N/A	<ul><li>Individual juror may be challenged for cause, e.g. knows defendant</li><li>Whole panel may be challenged for biased selection – but no right to a multiracial jury (R v Ford (1989))</li><li>Prosecution may 'stand by' any juror</li></ul>
Function	<ul><li>Decide verdict in summary offences, some either-way offences and in Youth Court</li><li>Decide on sentences where defendant pleads guilty or is found guilty by them</li><li>Deal with preliminary matters before passing indictable offences to the Crown Court</li></ul>	<ul><li>Decide verdict: guilty or not guilty</li><li>Sole arbiters of fact but judge directs them on law</li></ul>Verdict:<ul><li>Must try for a unanimous verdict</li></ul>BUT<ul><li>If cannot reach a unanimous verdict, then a majority verdict can be accepted of 10–2 or 11–1</li></ul>

Figure 2.8 Key facts: the selection and use of lay magistrates and jurors in criminal cases

2.5 Advantages and disadvantages of using juries in criminal cases

2.5.1 Advantages of using juries

Public confidence

The jury is considered one of the fundamentals of a democratic society. The right to be tried by one's peers is a bastion of liberty against the state and has been supported by eminent judges. For example:

- Lord Devlin said juries are 'the lamp that shows that freedom lives'.
- Michael Mansfield QC, in an article in response to the Runciman Commission on criminal justice in the 1990s, claimed that the jury 'is the most democratic element of our judicial system'. He also thought that it 'poses the biggest threat to the authorities'.

The tradition of trial by jury is very old and people seem to have confidence in the impartiality and fairness of a jury trial.

Jury equity

Since juries are not legal experts, they are not bound to follow the praecedent of past cases or even Acts of

Parliament, and do not have to give reasons for their verdict, they can decide cases on their own ideas of 'fairness'.

Several cases have shown the importance of this. A particular example was *Ponting's* case (1985) in which a civil servant was charged under the s 2 of the Official Secrets Act 1911. He had leaked information on the sinking of a ship, the *General Belgrano*, in the Falklands war to a Member of Parliament. At his trial he pleaded not guilty, claiming that his actions had been in the public interest. The jury refused to convict him even though the judge ruled he had no defence.

These examples show that, in some cases, the jury may use its ideas of fairness and justice to ignore the actual law or the judge's directions.

Case studies

R v Kronlid (1996)

Three protestors were charged with causing criminal damage of £1.5 million to a Hawk jet plane that had been bought by the Indonesian government and was due to be sent there. The defendants admitted that they had done the damage but claimed that they had a lawful excuse for their actions. They claimed that the jet was going to be used against the civilian population in the East Timor region of Indonesia as part of an alleged genocidal campaign against the people of East Timor. The jury obviously sympathised with the defendant's views and found them not guilty.

R v Randle and Pottle (1991)

The defendants were charged with helping the spy, George Blake, escape from prison. Their prosecution did not take place until 25 years after the escape, when they wrote about what they had done. They were acquitted as the jury possibly decided it was unfair to convict with such a time lapse between the offence and the prosecution.

Open system of justice

The use of a jury is viewed as making the legal system more open:
- Justice is seen to be done as members of the public are involved in a key role and the trial takes place in public.
- It keeps the law clearer as points have to be explained to the jury, enabling the defendant to understand the case more easily.

Secrecy of decisions

The jury discussion on the verdict takes place in secret. The Criminal Justice and Courts Act 2015 makes it a criminal offence intentionally to disclose or solicit or obtain any particulars of statements made, opinions expressed, arguments advanced or votes cast by members of a jury in the course of their deliberations in any legal proceedings. As a result of this secrecy, the jury is free from pressure in their discussion. This allows jurors the freedom to ignore the strict interpretation of the law or the judge's directions as shown above.

It has been suggested that people would be less willing to serve on a jury if they knew that their discussions could be made public. However, disclosure is allowed where it is in the interests of justice, such as reporting juror misconduct.

Impartiality

A jury should be impartial as they are not connected to anyone in the case. The process of random selection should result in a cross-section of society and this should also lead to an impartial jury as they will cancel out each other's biases. A jury is not case-hardened since they sit for only two weeks and are unlikely to try more than three or four cases in that time.

Representative nature

Juries are much more representative of all sections of society than professional judges or lay magistrates. The age limits for jury service are wide (18–75), so there is likely to be a wide range of ages on a jury. Members of a jury will usually have a wide range of social backgrounds, in contrast to the Judiciary.

2.5.2 Disadvantages of using juries

Selection of juries

The method of selecting jurors from the electoral register is open to criticism as it does not always give a representative sample of the population.
- This method excludes some groups who are not eligible to vote, such as the homeless, and those who choose not to register.
- It is debatable whether those on lower incomes or unemployed are sufficiently represented.

Perverse decisions

This is when juries refuse to convict as in the cases of *Ponting*, *Kronlid* and *Randle and Potter* referred to earlier. Such decisions can be seen as perverse (wrong) and there can be a loss of public confidence in the fairness of the jury system.

Secrecy of decision making

The secrecy of the jury room can be a disadvantage:
- No reasons have to be given for a verdict, so there is no way of knowing if the jury did understand the case and have come to the decision for the right reasons.
- There can be no investigation of any possible malpractice within the jury room.

Events outside the jury room

The appeal courts have always been prepared to investigate events outside the jury room that might have affected the way a jury came to their decision. The best-known example of this is the case of *R v Young (Stephen)* (1995).

Case study

R v Young (Stephen) (1995)

The defendant was charged with the murder of two people. The jury had to stay in a hotel overnight as they had not reached a verdict by the end of a day of deliberations. At the hotel, four of the jurors held a séance using a Ouija board to try and contact the dead victims and ask them who had killed them. The next day the jury returned a guilty verdict.

When the use of the Ouija board became known, the Court of Appeal quashed the conviction and ordered a retrial.

Extraneous material

The appeal court will also inquire into events where extraneous material has been introduced into the jury room. Examples have included telephone calls in and out of the jury room, papers mistakenly included in the set of papers given by the court to the jury and information from the internet. This last happened in *R v Karakaya* (2005).

Case study

R v Karakaya (2005)

The defendant was accused of rape. A juror carried out an internet search at home and brought into the jury room the printed-out results of the search. The jury convicted Karakaya but this conviction was quashed because of the outside information that the jury had access to during their deliberations. A retrial was ordered and Karakaya was acquitted by the jury in the second trial.

Bias

One or more jurors on a panel may have a prejudice that can affect the deliberations and therefore the verdict. It may be a bias against the police or racial prejudice. However, if this is only shown in the jury room there can be no appeal or investigation made.

Media influence

Media coverage of the case they are sitting on may influence jurors. This is especially true in high-profile cases where there has been a lot of publicity about police investigations.

Case studies

R v West (1996)

Rosemary West was convicted for the murders of ten young girls and women, including her own daughter. From the time the bodies were first discovered, the media coverage was intense. In addition, some newspapers had paid large sums of money to some of the witnesses in order to secure their story after the trial was completed.

One of the grounds on which Rosemary West appealed against her conviction was that the media coverage had made it impossible for her to receive a fair trial. The Court of Appeal rejected the appeal, pointing out that otherwise it would mean that if 'allegations of murder were sufficiently horrendous so as to inevitably shock the nation, the accused could not be tried'. They also said that the trial judge had given adequate warning to the jury to consider only the evidence they heard in court.

R v Taylor and Taylor (1993)

Two sisters were charged with murder. Some newspapers published a still from a video sequence that gave a false impression of what was happening. After the jury convicted the two defendants, an appeal was made on the grounds of the possible influence this picture could have had on the jury's verdict; the Court of Appeal quashed the convictions.

Use of the internet

There have been several cases, such as in *R v Karakaya* (2005), where it was found that at least one member of the jury had researched aspects of the case on the internet. Judges usually direct jurors not to look at the internet for information, but it seems that the use of internet research by jurors is becoming more common.

The risk of using the internet is that the information may be prejudicial to the defendant; for example, doing a search on a defendant's name may find newspaper reports of previous convictions, which the jury should not know about. Also, defendants have been known to upload highly personal information regarding their own behaviour, including crimes, on to social networking sites.

Because of the increasing use of the internet, the Criminal Justice and Courts Act 2015 makes it a criminal offence with a maximum penalty of two years intentionally to research the internet for information relevant to the case. The Act also makes it a criminal offence to disclose such information to another member of the jury.

Fraud trials

When complex financial accounts are being given in evidence, special problems can be created for some jurors. Even jurors who can easily cope with other evidence may have difficulty understanding a fraud case. These cases are also often very long, so that the jurors have to be able to be away from their own work for months. A long fraud trial can place a great strain on jurors.

As long ago as 1986, the Roskill Committee suggested that juries should not be used for complex fraud cases but this proposal has never become law. However, in the Domestic Violence, Crime and Victims Act 2004 there is a special provision for cases where there is a large number of counts on the indictment. This allows a trial of sample counts with a jury and then, if the defendant was convicted on those, the remainder could be tried by a judge alone.

This provision balances the defendant's right to jury trial against the difficulty of a jury having to deal with large numbers of charges.

Jury tampering

In a very few cases, people connected to the defendant may try to bribe jury members or make threats against them so that they are too afraid to find the defendant guilty. In such cases police may be used to try to protect the jurors, but this may not be effective, and is also expensive, and removes the police from their other work.

To combat this, s 44 of the Criminal Justice Act 2003 provides that where there has already been an effort to tamper with a jury in the case, the prosecution can apply for the trial to be heard by judge alone. This was the case in *R v Twomey and others* (2009).

Activity

Juries are up to the job — whether complex fraud or simple theft

[A former] Lord Chief Justice has suggested that we ought to reconsider introducing jury-less trials for serious fraud cases and lesser criminal offences in response to financial cuts to our criminal justice system. I believe his suggestion is quite mistaken.

There is nothing special about fraud trials. Every large criminal case nowadays involves huge volumes of evidence and disclosure – an unavoidable fact of our electronic lives.

In the many fraud trials I have conducted, I have seen how quickly the jury cuts to the heart of the case and typically returns verdicts showing they are on top of the issues – just as efficiently as a professional judge.

Fraud usually boils down to some pretty basic form of dishonesty. Juries are simply the best at spotting that or attempts to conceal it.

The collective view of the jury is also important when assessing a witness; it is easy for a single person to form a strong, even distorted, view about a crucial piece of testimony when that conclusion would not be shared by a majority of 12.

While our judges are all unquestionably fair, some might be fairer than others. There have been instances in the past of senior judges giving somewhat slanted summings-up to the jury based on their own views of the defendant. Would we really feel comfortable letting those judges decide the facts too?

In less serious criminal cases where the defendant can choose between judge-only and trial by jury, I believe most elect for Crown Court trial.

Removing the distinction between the judge of law and the judges of fact becomes problematic. The judge must put out of mind any extraneous material they may have read and disregard any evidence they have ruled inadmissible. And, of course, the judge has no one to discuss the evidence with.

The power to order judge-only fraud trials where the case is thought too long or complex for a jury has been on the statute books for over ten years but has never been brought into force because of lack of political support.

Source: Adapted from an article by Alex Bailin QC from *The Times* 13/03/2014; accessed 20/10/20

Using the article, assess the arguments for and against the continuation of jury trials in serious fraud cases.

R v Twomey and others (2009)

The defendants were charged with committing a large robbery from a warehouse at Heathrow. Three previous trials had collapsed and there had been a 'serious attempt at jury tampering' in the last of these. The trial proceeded to a conclusion before a single judge.

High acquittal rates

Juries can be criticised that they acquit too many defendants: about 60 per cent of those who plead not guilty at the Crown Court are acquitted.

However, this figure does not give a true picture of the workings of juries, as it includes cases where the judge rules there is insufficient evidence. When these decisions are excluded from the statistics, it is found that juries actually acquit in about 30 per cent of cases. This seems acceptable.

Jury service

- The compulsory nature of jury service is unpopular, so that some jurors may be against the whole system, while others may rush their verdict in order to finish as quickly as possible.
- Jury service can be a strain, especially where jurors have to listen to horrific evidence. Jurors in the *Rosemary West* case were offered counselling after the trial to help them cope with the evidence they had had to see and hear.
- The use of juries makes trials slow and expensive, because each point has to be explained carefully to the jury and the whole procedure of the case takes longer. On the other hand, as observed above, this can be of benefit to a defendant who is able to understand the charges.

Advantages of use of juries	Criticisms of use of juries

Public confidence
 • Long-established system
 • Jury is considered as a fundamental requirement of a democratic society
 • Lord Devlin: 'the lamp that shows that freedom lives'
 • Michael Mansfield: 'the jury is the most democratic element of our judicial system'
 	
 Jury equity
 • Decisions based on fairness; no reasons given
   ○ *R v Ponting* 1985 – jury refused to convict when his defence was that he acted in public interest
   ○ *R v Kronlid* 1996 – jury refused to convict when defence was lawful excuse
   ○ *R v Randle and Potter* – jury refused to convict for helping spy escape from prison due to time lapse
 	
 Open justice
 • Trial in public
 • Explaining issues to jury will help defendant understand law and process
 	
 Impartiality
 • Jury free of pressure in making decisions
 • Members of jury not connected to the case
 • Members of jury will not be case-hardened
 	
 Representative nature
 • Due to random selection, there will be a wide range of ages and backgrounds – this means the jury will be representative
	Lack of public confidence
	 • Public confidence can be lost by juries making perverse decisions or acquitting a percentage of defendants
	 • Service is compulsory, so may be unpopular
	 • Juries may be subject to tampering or influence
	
	 Perverse decisions
	 • Decisions such as *Ponting*, *Kronlid* and *Randle & Potter* can be considered perverse (wrong)
	 • How juries reach verdicts cannot be investigated
	
	 BUT
	 • *R v Young* 1995 – some members used a Ouija board outside jury room
	 • *R v Karakaya* 2005 – member shared internet search results about case with other members
	 • Secret discussions may result in jury members influencing others, just to reach a verdict
	
	 Unrepresentative and unfitness
	 • Selection based on electoral register may mean jury is unrepresentative
	 • No intelligence tests used – long, complicated trials may not be understood by some jurors
	 • Lack of reasoning for decisions could suggest jury did not understand the case, especially in fraud trials
	 • Jury may be influenced by reporting of case – *R v Taylor and Taylor*

Figure 2.9 Key facts: advantages and disadvantages of juries

Look online

The case of *R v Young* (1995) is an interesting example of how a jury reached its verdict. Make an internet search for this case and read about what happened in more detail.

Quick questions

1 Describe the work of lay magistrates in the criminal justice process.
2 Describe the selection process for members of a jury.
3 Outline the aims of sentencing.
4 Describe how magistrates or judges decide a sentence for an offender in the criminal courts.
5 Assess the value of lay persons (lay magistrates and juries) in the criminal justice process.

Summary

- There are three categories of criminal offence:
  - summary offences which can only be tried in the Magistrates' Court
  - either-way offences which can be tried in either the Magistrates' Court or the Crown Court, and
  - indictable offences which can only be tried in the Crown Court before a judge and jury.
- The defendant can appeal against conviction and/ or sentence. The prosecution has only limited appeal rights when the defendant is acquitted.
- When an offender is convicted the court must impose a sentence. The sentences for adult offenders are
  - imprisonment
  - community orders
  - fines, or
  - discharges.
- The aims of sentencing are the:
  - punishment of offenders
  - reduction of crime
  - reform and rehabilitation of offenders
  - protection of the public
  - making of reparation by offenders to persons affected by their offences.

- The court takes into account relevant aggravating and mitigating factors when deciding on a sentence.
- Lay magistrates are not legally qualified but are selected for their judicial qualities.
- They decide conviction and sentences of summary and either-way offences.
- Juries are used at the Crown Court to hear indictable and either-way cases.
- Juries are selected at random from the electoral register and there are certain qualifications such as age and being registered on the electoral register. A juror must not be disqualified and can be excused from service for specific reasons.
- Jurors decide if a defendant is guilty or not guilty following the hearing of evidence and legal arguments. They have a secret discussion on their verdict. The judge will decide the sentence following a guilty verdict.

Chapter 3 Legal personnel

3.1 Barristers, solicitors and legal executives

3.1.1 Role of barristers

There are about 16,500 barristers in practice in England and Wales, including about 3000 barristers employed by organisations such as the CPS, independent businesses, local government and the Civil Service.

Collectively, practising barristers are referred to as 'the Bar'. All practising barristers must also be a member of one of the four Inns of Court: Lincoln's Inn, Inner Temple, Middle Temple and Gray's Inn. These are all situated close to the Royal Courts of Justice in London.

Barristers practising at the Bar are self-employed, and usually work from a set of chambers where they can share administrative expenses with other barristers. Chambers can vary in size from small with 10–20 barristers, to larger sets with 50 or more. The Chambers will employ a clerk as a practice administrator – to book in cases and negotiate fees – and they will have other support staff.

A barrister owes a duty of confidentiality to a client, but also owes a duty to the court. This means that a barrister:

- must not mislead a court or a judge or waste a court's time
- may need to make sure the court has all the relevant information it needs, even if it weakens his client's case.

But it does not require them to breach their duty of confidentiality to their client. This means that if a client confesses his guilt to the barrister, they cannot continue to represent the client in a not guilty defence.

As we will see below, a lot of barrister work is providing opinions on the action that should be taken in a case, including whether or not a case should go to court.

Barristers have full rights of audience. This means they can present a case in any court in England and Wales. The majority of barristers in private practice will concentrate on advocacy which is the presentation of cases in court.

Key term

Rights of audience – the right to present a case in court, as an advocate.

Advocacy in criminal cases

Barristers generally specialise in either prosecution or defence work.

Prosecution

When prosecuting, the barrister will be instructed by the CPS. Then the barrister will advise on the likely success of the charges that have been brought, and work with the CPS and the police to ensure that there is sufficient evidence available to prove those charges.

Defence

When acting for a defendant, a barrister will be instructed by a solicitor who has seen a defendant from the outset. The barrister will advise on the strength of the prosecution evidence and any weaknesses in the defence. Ultimately, it is for the defendant to decide whether to plead guilty or not guilty.

After a conviction and sentence, the barrister can advise on the possibility of an appeal against conviction and/or sentence. The barrister can then present an appeal to an appeal court. An appeal is likely to consist of legal arguments. Witnesses are unlikely to be required for further evidence.

Advocacy in civil cases

Barristers tend to specialise in certain fields such as personal injury or commercial work. They can be instructed by a solicitor or directly by a client in all matters except publicly funded (legally aided) criminal and family cases.

In a civil case, much of the evidence and the legal arguments will be presented in writing before any court hearing and will usually be drafted by a barrister. A barrister may attend meetings to negotiate a settlement.

In the court hearing, the advocacy will concentrate on important pieces of evidence and legal issues. When liability is decided by the judge, a barrister for the successful party will argue for an award, usually the amount of damages, and for the award of costs.

After the hearing, the barrister for either party will advise on the possibility of an appeal against liability and/or the amount of damages and, if necessary, will draft the appeal papers. As with criminal cases, an appeal is likely to consist of legal arguments with no further evidence.

Direct access (also known as public access)

Professionals, such as accountants and surveyors, can brief a barrister directly without using a solicitor. Members of the public can also use this service; it is accessed through the Bar Council Direct Access Portal.

To carry out direct access work, a barrister must have completed additional training.

Limited advocacy work

Some barristers specialise in areas such as tax or company law, and rarely appear in court.

Cab rank rule

Normally, barristers operate what is known as the 'cab rank rule': they cannot turn down a case if it is in the area of law they deal with and they are free to take the case.

However, in direct access, the cab rank rule does not apply. Barristers can turn down a case that requires investigation or support services that they cannot provide.

Employed barristers

Barristers can be employed by government organisations, the Civil Service, local government or businesses. In particular, the CPS employs a large number of barristers to prosecute criminal cases. Employed barristers have the same rights of audience (right to present cases in court) as self-employed barristers.

Queen's Counsel

After at least ten years' practising as a barrister, it is possible to apply to become a Queen's Counsel (QC). About 10 per cent of the barristers practising at the Bar are Queen's Counsel.

Becoming a Queen's Counsel is known as 'taking silk'. A QC:
- usually takes on more complicated and high-profile cases than junior barristers (all barristers who are not Queen's Counsel are known as 'juniors')
- can command higher fees for their recognised expertise
- often has a junior barrister to assist with the case.

There is an application process to become a QC. An application fee has to be paid and, if successful, an appointment fee. Applicants must:
- provide references from other lawyers including judges before whom they have appeared
- be interviewed by an independent selection panel which recommends those who should be appointed to the Lord Chancellor.

3.1.2 Role of solicitors

There are over 149,000 solicitors practising in England and Wales, and they are controlled by their own professional body, the Law Society. About 75 per cent work in private practice and the remainder are in employed work, such as for local government, the Civil Service, the CPS or private businesses.

The majority of those qualifying as a solicitor will work in private practice in a solicitors' firm. However, as with barristers, there are other careers available including working in the CPS, for a local authority or government departments or as legal advisers in commercial businesses or in industry.

A solicitor in private practice will generally work in a partnership, ranging from a 'high street' practice to a big city firm. The number of partners is not limited, and some of the biggest firms have over a hundred partners, as well as employing assistant solicitors and legal executives. The type of work done by a solicitor will largely depend on the firm. A high street firm will probably be a general practice advising individual clients on a whole range of topics including:

- conveyancing (the legal side of buying and selling flats, houses, office buildings and land)
- the making of wills, and probate (dealing with the affairs of deceased persons)
- consumer problems
- business matters
- personal injury claims
- family matters.

This work is likely to involve interviewing clients, negotiating on their behalf, writing letters and emails, drafting contracts, leases or other formal documents.

Some solicitors act for clients in civil or criminal cases. This is known as litigation. Solicitors with an advocacy qualification, and who litigate in the higher courts, are able to apply to become a Queen's Counsel (QC) in the same way as barristers.

Civil cases

Generally, a solicitor will be the first source of legal advice. The solicitor's role is to:

- collect evidence, both documentary and oral
- prepare and issue court papers if the case is straightforward
- carry out advocacy, usually in the County Court
- instruct a barrister to advise on the case if it is more complex, to draft the court papers and to carry out the advocacy
- support the barrister throughout the case, including obtaining any further evidence.

Criminal cases

A solicitor might initially meet a client who has been arrested, in the police station, though it is more likely now that a solicitor will have a telephone consultation rather than a face-to-face meeting. In serious cases they may sit in on police interviews.

In less serious cases a client may have been issued with a summons by post and the initial meeting will take place in the solicitor's office or at the first court appearance.

- If the police press charges, the solicitor will obtain details of the prosecution case (known as disclosure) and advise the client on the strength of the evidence.
- If the case is a summary or either-way case heard in the Magistrates' Court, the solicitor can carry out the advocacy.
- If the case is more a serious either-way or indictable offence, the solicitor is likely to brief a barrister or a solicitor-advocate to advise and to carry out the advocacy. Again, the solicitor will support the barrister throughout the court hearings.

Although some solicitors may handle a variety of work, it is more usual for a solicitor to specialise in one particular field. The firm itself may handle only certain types of cases (perhaps only civil actions) and not take any criminal cases, or a firm may specialise in family matters. In large city firms there will be an even greater degree of specialisation, with departments dealing with just one area of law or a limited number of clients.

Advocacy

All solicitors have rights of audience in the lower courts – the Magistrates' and County Courts.

Solicitors who wish to exercise rights of audience in the higher courts must satisfactorily complete the appropriate higher courts' advocacy qualification.

Solicitors with an advocacy qualification are eligible to be appointed as Queen's Counsel and also to be appointed as judges.

3.1.3 Role of legal executives

Most legal executives work for a firm of solicitors in private practice. Their work is charged at an hourly rate in the same way as solicitors' work is charged but it is likely to be charged at a lower rate. In this way a legal executive makes a direct contribution to the income of a firm. Legal executives can also work for local authorities, the CPS and in company legal departments.

A qualified Legal Executive will need to be a fellow of the Chartered Institute of Legal Executives (CILEX), to have obtained the CILEX Professional Qualification and to have completed three years' supervised legal experience. There are over 20,000 legal executives currently practising.

Legal executives are likely to specialise in a particular area of law, and their work is similar to that of a solicitor although they tend to deal with more straightforward matters. For example, they can:
- handle parts of a property transfer
- assist in the formation of a company
- draft wills
- advise people with matrimonial problems
- advise clients accused of a crime, advise a client detained in a police station and interview witnesses.

There are three different advocacy certificates a legal executive can obtain:
1 A Civil Proceedings Certificate: this allows appearances in the County Court.
2 A Criminal Proceedings Certificate: this allows legal executives to make applications for bail or deal with cases in the Youth Court.
3 A Family Proceedings Certificate: this allows appearances in the Family Court of the Magistrates' Court.

3.1.4 The regulation of the legal professions

Regulation of barristers

Bar Standards Board

This body sets training and entry standards but also regulates the barrister's profession. It sets out a Code of Conduct that barristers have to comply with.

The Board investigates any alleged breach of the Code of Conduct. It can discipline any barrister who is in breach of the Code. If the matter is serious, it will be referred to a Disciplinary Tribunal arranged by an independent Bar Tribunals and Adjudication service. A tribunal has several sanctions it can impose, including:
- reprimanding the barrister (formally warning them about their behaviour)
- making the barrister complete further professional development training
- ordering the barrister to pay a fine
- suspending the barrister for up to three years
- in extreme cases, disbarring barrister (striking off) the barrister.

If a complainant is unhappy with the decision of the Bar Standards Board, a complaint can be made to the Legal Ombudsman.

Liability

A barrister enters a contract with a client on the Direct Access scheme and such client can sue for breach of contract. A barrister can be liable in negligence for a poor quality of advocacy (but this must be more than just losing a civil claim or being convicted in a criminal case).

Regulation of solicitors

Solicitors Regulation Authority

Although every solicitor must belong to the Law Society, it is the SRA who deals with complaints about professional misconduct of solicitors.
- It will initially investigate the complaint. If there is evidence of serious professional misconduct, it can bring the case to the Solicitors' Disciplinary Tribunal.
- If the Tribunal upholds the complaint, it can fine or reprimand the solicitor or, in more serious cases, it can suspend a solicitor from the Roll, so that they cannot practise for a certain time.
- In very serious cases, the Tribunal can strike off a solicitor from the Roll so that they are prevented from practising again as a solicitor.

Liability in contract and negligence

As a solicitor deals directly with a client, a contract is entered into. This means that:
- If the client does not pay, the solicitor has the right to sue for outstanding fees.
- The client can sue the solicitor for breach of contract if the solicitor fails to do the agreed work.
- The client can also sue the solicitor in negligence if they suffer loss due to poor quality of work. It was decided in *Hall v Simons* (2000) that loss suffered as a result of negligent advocacy can also be claimed.
- Solicitors can be liable in negligence to persons who are not their clients but who are affected by their negligent work. This is shown in *White v Jones* (1995).

Hall v Simons (2000)

Three firms of solicitors were sued by their clients for negligent advocacy. The lower courts were bound by the decision of *Rondel v Worsley* (1969) which decided that lawyers could not be liable for negligent advocacy.

Using the Practice Direction 1966, the House of Lords reversed *Rondel v Worsley* and ruled that the protection given to advocates was no longer appropriate, because of changes in the law of negligence, the working of the legal professions, the administration of justice and public perceptions. As a result, barristers and solicitors carrying out negligent advocacy could be sued by a client.

White v Jones (1995)

A father wanted to make a will leaving each of his daughters £9000. He wrote to his solicitors instructing them to draw up a will to include this. The solicitors received this letter on 17 July 1986 but had done nothing about it by the time the father died on 14 September 1986. As a result, the daughters did not inherit any money. They successfully sued the solicitor for the £9000 they had each lost.

Regulation of Legal Executives

Chartered Institute of Legal Executives

All legal executives are members of the Chartered Institute of Legal Executives (CILEx). This organisation provides education, training and development of skills for legal executives. It also protects the status and interests of legal executives. Another aim is to:

> " promote and secure professional standards of conduct amongst members and those who are registered with the Institute. "

CILEx publishes a code of conduct and guides to good practice but regulation of members is done by the CILEx Regulation Board, which investigates complaints about legal executives.

When an investigation is complete, a summary of the issues is prepared and the matter is put to the Professional Conduct Panel for consideration. The Panel will decide if there has been misconduct. If there has been misconduct it may reprimand or warn a member. It will refer serious matters to the Disciplinary Tribunal. The Disciplinary Tribunal has the power to:

- exclude a person from membership of the Institute
- reprimand or warn the member
- order the legal executive to pay a fine and costs.

Regulation of all the legal professions

In addition to the separate regulatory bodies there is an Office for Legal Complaints set up by the Legal Services Act 2007. This Office provide a free service to investigate how the individual regulatory body investigated a complaint and refers the case to the Legal Ombudsman

3.2 The Judiciary

3.2.1 Types of judges

Collectively, judges are referred to as 'the Judiciary'. There are different levels of judges:

- Superior judges are High Court Judges and above.
- Inferior judges are Circuit Judges and below.

Which level they are affects the selection process, the training, the work and the terms on which they hold office. The head of the Judiciary is the Lord Chief Justice.

Justices of the Supreme Court

Justices of the Supreme Court are appointed from those who hold high judicial office; for example, as a judge in the Court of Appeal, or from those who have been qualified to appear in the senior courts for at least 15 years.

As the Supreme Court is the final appellate court for Scotland and Northern Ireland as well, judges can also be appointed from those who have qualified to appear in courts in Scotland or Northern Ireland for at least 15 years.

The Constitutional Reform Act 2005 provides that there should be a maximum of 12 Justices and they are the most senior judges in the country. They sit in the Supreme Court to hear final appeals from all courts in the UK.

Lords Justices of Appeal

Lords Justices of Appeal must have been qualified as a barrister or solicitor and have gained experience in law for at least seven years or be an existing High Court Judge. Lords Justices of Appeal are officially appointed by the Queen.

A Lord Justice of Appeal will sit in either:

- the Civil Division of the Court of Appeal where they will hear appeals from cases in the County Court or High Court, or
- the Criminal Division of the Court of Appeal where they will hear appeals from trials in the Crown Court.

High Court Judges

In order to be eligible to be appointed as a High Court Judge, it is necessary either to have been qualified as a barrister or solicitor, and have gained experience in law for at least seven years, or to have been a Circuit Judge for at least two years.

The vast majority of High Court Judges are appointed to serve full time from barristers who have been in practice for twenty or thirty years. Deputy High Court Judges, who sit part-time, are also appointed and this is a way of testing the suitability of a person to become a High Court Judge. Candidates are usually expected to have previous judicial experience at a lower level. High Court Judges are officially appointed by the Queen.

High Court Judges are assigned to one of the Divisions of the High Court and will hear the cases assigned to that Division:

1 Judges of the Queen's Bench Division will hear high value civil claims of contract and tort. In addition, judges of this Division will hear serious criminal cases such as murder in the Crown Court.
2 Judges of the Chancery Division will hear high value commercial claims and cases of liquidation of companies and partnership disputes.
3 Judges of the Family Division will hear claims relating disputes of property and financial matters of married and unmarried partners and relating to children of relationships.

In addition, judges of the High Court can sit as judges of the Court of Appeal alongside Lords Justices to hear appeals relating to work of the respective Divisions.

Circuit Judges

In order to become a Circuit Judge, it is necessary to be a solicitor or barrister who has held a 'right of audience' for at least ten years. They should generally also have served either part-time as a Recorder in criminal cases or full-time as District Judges in civil cases before they can be appointed.

They will hear both civil and criminal cases:

1 In the County Court they will hear a wide range of tort and contract claims, claims relating to possession of land and property disputes and some family work.
2 In the Crown Court they will take charge of criminal trials, hearing more serious cases as they gain seniority, and sentence offenders who have pleaded guilty.

This is a part-time post for qualified barristers or solicitors who have gained at least seven years' experience. An applicant is appointed as a Recorder in training first and then appointed as a Recorder. They will hear less serious civil cases in the County Court and less serious criminal cases in the Crown Court.

District Judges

A District Judge is a full-time post and an applicant must have been qualified as a barrister or solicitor and have gained experience in law for at least five years or have been a Deputy District Judge. The vast majority of District Judges in the County Court are former solicitors. It is usual to have sat part-time as a Deputy District Judge before being considered for the position of District Judge.

Under the Tribunals, Courts and Enforcement Act 2007, CILEx Fellows are now eligible to be appointed as a Deputy District Judge.

District Judges will hear civil and criminal cases:

- In the County Court and particularly the Small Claims Court, they will hear low value civil claims of tort and contract.
- In the Magistrates' Court, they will sit alone to hear summary and either-way criminal trials and impose sentences on offenders of those crimes.

3.2.2 The role of judges in civil courts

The general role of a judge is to resolve disputes in a fair, unbiased way, applying the law to each case before them.

In civil courts of first instance – the County Court and High Court – a judge will sit on their own to deal with all aspects of the case. The judge will be responsible for pre-trial matters such as case management and setting timetables to make sure

43

that the parties in the case are ready for trial at a set date.

At trial, the judge will:

- hear evidence from all the witnesses
- listen to legal arguments
- look at any relevant case papers
- decide the facts, how the law applies to those facts, and make the decision as to who has won the case (also known as who is liable)
- in a contract and tort case, decide the amount of damages payable, or other remedy requested such as specific performance of a contract
- decide who should bear the legal costs of the case.

Appeal court judges in the Court of Appeal (Civil Division) and Supreme Court have a different role. They do not hear evidence from witnesses. Instead, they hear arguments on legal points in the case and decide if the decision made at the trial should stand or whether the appeal should be allowed.

- In the Court of Appeal (Civil Division), an appeal may be heard against the finding of liability or about the remedy awarded; for example, the amount of money awarded as damages. The court can either allow or dismiss the appeal or vary the amount of damages.
- A case can only be appealed to the Supreme Court if there is an important point of law involved or an issue of general public importance. Five Justices will normally sit to hear the appeal. Often appeals involve complicated and technical areas of law and how legislation should be interpreted. Any decision the Supreme Court makes on a point of law will become a precedent for all lower courts to follow.

3.2.3 The role of judges in criminal courts

The general role of a judge in a criminal case is to oversee the case and ensure that correct procedures are followed, to rule on points of law that arise, to direct the jury on the law and evidence and, if the defendant is found guilty, to impose a sentence.

In the Magistrates' Court, a District Judge (Magistrates' Courts) can sit on their own to decide:

- whether the defendant is guilty or not guilty
- the sentence when a defendant pleads guilty or is found guilty.

They generally have the same sentencing powers as lay magistrates.

In the Crown Court, a judge will:

- sit with a jury when a defendant pleads not guilty to an either-way offence or an indictable offence
- decide any legal issues in the case and direct the jury on the relevant law
- decide on the sentence where a defendant pleads guilty, or is found guilty by a jury
- take into account any legal submissions on behalf of the defendant and consider any reports.

A convicted defendant can appeal to the Court of Appeal (Criminal Division) against sentence and/ or conviction. Three judges will hear legal arguments from the defence and prosecution and can either confirm the original decision and/or sentence, vary the sentence or find the defendant not guilty. If this is their decision, they can order a retrial.

A further appeal against the decision of the Court of Appeal can be taken to the Supreme Court but only if leave is granted because there is an issue of general public importance to be decided. Five Justices will hear legal arguments from the defence and prosecution – no evidence will be heard. The Court can agree or overrule the decision of the Court of Appeal. They will not make a decision on the sentence.

Activity ?

Find a law report on a site such as **www.bailii.org**, or from an authorised series of law reports. The case can be about any topic, civil or criminal.

Write a short report of the case containing the names of the parties, the court hearing the case, the name(s) and status of the judge(s) and, briefly, what the case is about.

3.3 The separation of powers and the independence of the Judiciary

3.3.1 The separation of powers

The theory of separation of powers was first put forward by Montesquieu, a French political theorist, in the eighteenth century. The theory states that there are three primary functions of the State and that the only way to safeguard the liberty of citizens is by keeping these three functions separate. As the power of each is exercised by independent and separate bodies, each can keep a check on the others and thus limit the amount of power wielded by any one group.

Ideally this theory requires individuals not to be members of more than one 'arm of the state'. Some countries, for example, the USA, have a written constitution that clearly embodies this theory. In the United Kingdom there is no written constitution, but even so, the three organs of state are roughly separated. There is some overlap as the Lord Chancellor is involved in all three functions of the state.

Key term

> The Lord Chancellor – due to the Constitutional Reform Act 2005, the role of the Lord Chancellor was changed. Rather than being the head of the Judiciary, the role is now managing the Judiciary system and the courts. The Lord Chancellor is an MP, so a member of the Legislature, and a member of the Cabinet, so part of the Executive.

The three arms of the state identified by Montesquieu are as follows:

1 The Legislature. This is the law-making arm of the state and, in the English system, this is Parliament.
2 The Executive or the body administering the law. In the British political system, this is the government of the day.
3 The Judiciary – the judges, who apply the law.

There is an overlap between the Executive and the Legislature: ministers forming the government also sit in Parliament and are active in the law-making process.

With the exception of the Lord Chancellor, there is very little overlap between the Judiciary and the other two arms of the state. This is important because it allows the Judiciary to act as a check and ensure that the Executive does not overstep its constitutional powers. This is in accordance with Montesquieu's theory. However, it is open to debate whether the Judiciary is truly independent from the other organs of government.

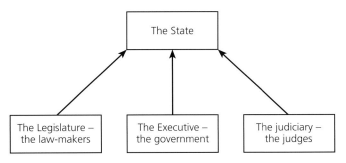

Figure 3.1 The separation of powers according to Dicey

3.3.2 Independence of the Judiciary

Security of tenure

Superior level judges cannot be dismissed by the government. They can only be dismissed by the monarch following a petition presented by both Houses of Parliament. Inferior level judges do not have the same level of security of tenure. The Lord Chancellor, with the consent of the Lord Chief Justice, has the power to dismiss inferior level judges for incapacity or misbehaviour.

Judicial independence is guaranteed under s 3 of the Constitutional Reform Act 2005. This states:

- The Lord Chancellor, other ministers in the government and anyone with responsibility for matters relating to the Judiciary or the administration of justice, must uphold the continued independence of the Judiciary.
- The Lord Chancellor and government ministers must not seek to influence particular judicial decisions.

Immunity from suit

This allows a judge to perform judicial duties without fear of repercussions. Judges of all levels are given immunity from criminal prosecution for any acts they carry out in performance of their judicial duties. They also have immunity from being sued in any civil case while they are performing their judicial duties. This includes a defamation claim for anything said about the parties or witnesses in a case they are hearing.

Case study

Sirros v Moore (1975)

In a case heard in the Crown Court, the judge wrongly ordered a person's detention. The person then launched a claim for false imprisonment against the judge. The Court of Appeal decided that, although the order of detention was unlawful, no action lay against the judge as he had acted in good faith, believing he had the power to imprison.

Independence of judges from other arms of the state

The Legislature

Judges are generally not involved in the law-making functions of Parliament. Full-time judges are not allowed to be members of the House of Commons. The rule is not as strict for part-time judges so that Recorders and Assistant Recorders can be Members of Parliament.

There used to be judges in the House of Lords when the Appellate Committee of the House of Lords was the final court of appeal. The main reason for the creation of the Supreme Court in 2009 was to separate the Judiciary from the Legislature. Judges of the Supreme Court are not allowed to be members of the House of Lords.

Judges are given a certain degree of financial independence. Their salaries are paid out of the Consolidated Fund, which doesn't need Parliament's authorisation. However, they are not completely protected from parliamentary interference in the terms on which they hold office: Parliament can change judicial retirement ages and qualifying periods of service for pensions.

Independence of judges from the Executive

Superior level judges cannot be dismissed by the government. They can make decisions that may displease the government, without the threat of dismissal. The extent to which judges are prepared to challenge or support the government is considered below.

Judicial independence is guaranteed under s 3 of the Constitutional Reform Act 2005. This states:

- The Lord Chancellor, other ministers in the government and anyone with responsibility for matters relating to the Judiciary or the administration of justice must uphold the continued independence of the Judiciary.
- The Lord Chancellor and government ministers must not seek to influence particular judicial decisions.

Independence from the case

Judges must not hear or try any case in which they have an interest in the issues involved. This was confirmed by the *Pinochet* case.

Case study

Re Pinochet (1999)

A claim was made to extradite the former dictator, Augusto Pinochet, back to Chile to face charges of carrying out torture and murder. The House of Lords initially ordered that he could be extradited. It was then found that one of the judges, Lord Hoffman, was an unpaid director of Amnesty International, one of the parties to the case. Pinochet's lawyers asked for the original decision to be set aside and for a new hearing to take place before a different panel. The Law Lords decided that their original decision could not stand as all the panel had to be seen as completely unbiased and unconnected to the case. The case was retried by the Lords with a different panel.

Judicial review

One way that judges can show their independence from the Executive is the process of Judicial Review. An initial hearing will take place in the Divisional Court of the Queen's Bench Division when decisions of government ministers or public authorities can be challenged by a person who has 'standing' – in other words is affected by the decision. Judges are prepared to find against ministers if they have acted unlawfully, as shown in the cases below.

Case studies

R v Home Secretary, ex parte Fire Brigades Union (1995)

It was held that the changes to the Criminal Injuries Compensation Scheme made by the Home Secretary were unlawful.

R v Secretary of State for Foreign Affairs, ex parte World Development Movement (1995)

It was decided that the Foreign Secretary, Douglas Hurd, had acted unlawfully over the development of the Pergau Dam.

R (on the application of Q) v Secretary of State for the Home Department (2003)

Collins J in the High Court declared that the Home Secretary's power to refuse to provide assistance to asylum seekers who had not immediately, on their entry to this country, declared their intention to claim asylum was unlawful. The Court of Appeal upheld this decision, although they did suggest how the relevant Act could be made compatible with human rights.

Human rights

Judges are also able to hear cases involving human rights, and again are prepared to find against the government. The Human Rights Act 1998 incorporates the European Convention on Human Rights (ECHR) into UK law and judges have the power to declare that an Act is incompatible with the Convention: this happened for the first time in *H v Mental Health Review Tribunal* (2001). Decisions of this nature put pressure on the government to change the law to comply with the ECHR. Some examples of these decisions are shown below.

Case study

A and another v Secretary of State for the Home Department (2004)

The House of Lords declared that the Anti-Terrorism, Crime and Security Act 2001 was incompatible with the ECHR. The Act allowed foreign nationals to be detained indefinitely without trial where there was suspicion that they were involved in terrorist activity. The Lords held that this breached both Article 5 (the right to liberty) and Article 14 (no discrimination on basis of nationality). This decision forced the government to change the law.

3.4 Evaluation of the Judiciary, including the advantages of judicial independence

One of the main criticisms in the past of the Judiciary has been that it is dominated by elderly, white, upper-class males and, as such, they are out of touch with current issues and the concerns of those appearing in front of them.

3.4.1 Age

On 1 April 2020, 76 per cent of all court judges were over the age of 50, and 40 per cent over the age of 60. It is unusual for any judge to be appointed under the age of 40, with superior judges usually being well above this age.

3.4.2 Women in the Judiciary

On 1 April 2020, 32 per cent of all court judges were women and 26 per cent of superior level judges were women.

The increasing number of women judges is partly due to the open and competitive method of selection. But it is also partly due to the fact that there is an increasing number of women barristers and solicitors, and so more possible applicants for judicial posts.

3.4.3 BAME representation

There has also been an increase over the past twenty years in the number of judges from a BAME (black, Asian and minority ethnic) background. On 1 April 2020, 8 per cent of all court judges were from a BAME background.

Judges from a BAME background are still very much in the minority

Look online

Look at the up-to-date statistics for judicial diversity at **www.judiciary.uk/**

Find out how many women judges and BAME judges are in post in the:
- Supreme Court
- Court of Appeal
- High Court
- inferior courts.

The system of selection by the Judicial Appointments Commission has led to improved diversity in the Judiciary. This can be seen by comparing the percentage of women and ethnic minority judges now with those in the past.

3.4.4 Should there be a career judiciary?

In many other European countries, becoming a judge is a career choice made by students once they have their basic legal qualifications. They will usually not practise as a lawyer first, but instead are trained as judges. Once they have qualified as a judge, they will sit in junior posts and then hope to be promoted up the judicial ladder.

This has two distinct advantages over the system in use in this country:

- The average age of judges is much lower, especially in the lower ranks where judges will be in their twenties. In England and Wales, an Assistant Recorder will normally be in their late thirties or early forties when appointed, and the average age for appointment to the High Court Bench tends to be late forties/early fifties.
- Judges have had far more training in the specific skills they need as judges.

A disadvantage of this system is that judges may be seen as too closely linked to the state and government as they are civil servants.

3.4.5 The advantages of judicial independence

An independent judiciary is seen as important in protecting the liberty of the individual from abuse of power by the Executive. If a government could make judges decide the way it wanted, this could lead to opponents of the government being imprisoned without reasonable cause. A government needs to value and abide by the rule of law in order to command the respect and confidence of the electorate. An independent judiciary is vital in a democracy.

It is an advantage of judicial independence that a government cannot force a judge to resign if that judge makes a decision with which the government of the day disagrees. In judicial review cases, judges often

Case study

Judges and the Executive

Following the 2016 referendum on withdrawing membership of the European Union, the government announced, without obtaining the approval of Parliament, that it would start the process for leaving. There was then a legal challenge, by judicial review, as to whether the Executive was acting lawfully by attempting to take this action without consulting, or obtaining the approval, of Parliament. In *R (Miller) v Secretary of State for Exiting the European Union* (2017), the Supreme Court confirmed the decision of the High Court that the government could not start the process for leaving without consulting Parliament. The decision confirmed that the Royal Prerogative, exercised by the Prime Minister and government, cannot be used to invalidate rights that Parliament has granted through an Act of Parliament. This decision was attacked by some who felt that the Judiciary should not interfere. However, the then Prime Minister, Theresa May, publicly upheld the right of the Judiciary to be independent and to decide cases against the government if it considered that the government had acted unlawfully.

A further challenge was made in 2019 against the government's decision to prorogue, or suspend, Parliament for an extended period. This case, *R (Miller) v The Prime Minister* (2019) again concerned the use of the Royal Prerogative. The Queen, advised by the Privy Council, gave her consent to prorogation for a six-week period in September and October 2019. The argument against this action was that it would prevent Parliament debating and confirming the UK exit from the European Union which was originally scheduled for 31 October.

The Supreme Court relied on the principles of parliamentary sovereignty and the accountability of Parliament to the electorate. It considered that if the power of prorogation of Parliament was unchecked, then the Executive could indefinitely prorogue Parliament, undermining its sovereignty and obligation to make and scrutinise laws.

Lord Bingham's statement that the government's conduct being accountable to Parliament 'lies at the heart of Westminster democracy' was approved. The court ruled that any prorogation would be unlawful 'if it has the effect of frustrating or preventing, without reasonable justification, the ability of Parliament to carry out its constitutional functions as a legislature and as the body responsible for the supervision of the Executive'. In this case the court found that the House of Commons, in particular, had the right to scrutinise any Brexit plans from the government. Further, that suspending Parliament for five of the eight weeks leading up to 31 October prevented it from exercising its constitutional functions. This was particularly the case as the government had not provided a justification for such a lengthy suspension. As a result, the Supreme Court found that the government's action was unlawful and could not be allowed.

Both of these decisions show that judges are capable of acting independently and are not afraid of finding that the government of the day acted unlawfully. This will also mean that any government should ensure that it acts lawfully, in any and every decision it makes and actions it takes.

have to decide if an act or decision by a government department is reasonable. It is important that the judges can carry out this function without fear of repercussions.

It is an advantage of judicial independence that judges are, and are seen to be, impartial in their decisions. It is vital that each judge is able to decide cases solely on the evidence presented in court by the parties and in accordance with the law. Judges must be free to exercise their judicial powers without interference from litigants, the state, the media or powerful individuals or entities, such as large companies.

Quick questions

1 Describe what is meant by 'direct access' to a barrister and the areas of law in which it is allowed.
2 Describe the role of a judge in a civil case of tort or contract law.
3 Define the theory of separation of powers.
4 Compare the advocacy role of barristers, solicitors and legal executives in both civil and criminal cases.
5 Discuss the following statement: 'In the twenty-first century, there is a definite need for lawyers'.

Summary

Barristers

- They are usually self-employed, providing advocacy services in civil and criminal cases and expert opinions on questions of law.
- They are usually accessed through a solicitor but can also be instructed by direct access.
- Senior barristers can apply to be appointed as QC to provide specialist services in very important cases.

Solicitors

- They will often work in private practice in partnerships.
- They are often the first port of call for individuals or companies requiring legal services.
- They can carry out contentious work which can involve advocacy in courts or tribunals.
- They will often carry out non-contentious work, drafting documents and the legal processes of property sale and purchase work.

Legal executives

- Legal executives are fee earning and usually work for solicitors.

Regulation

- Barristers are subject to regulation by the Bar Standards Board. They can be sued for negligent advocacy by their clients. They can sue and be sued in contract when they have a direct access arrangement with their client.
- Solicitors are regulated and disciplined by the Solicitors Regulation Authority. They can sue and

be sued in contract by their clients. They can be sued for carrying out negligent work.

- Legal Executives are regulated by CILEx Regulation Board.
- There is a separate Office for Legal Complaints which deals with complaints that the professional bodies have not adequately dealt with.

Judges

- Justices of the Supreme Court hear appeals on matters of law of general public importance in both civil and criminal cases.
- Lord Justices of Appeal hear appeals in the Court of Appeal. In civil cases, appeals can be against liability and amounts of compensation. In criminal cases, appeals can be against conviction and sentence.
- High Court judges deal with trials of cases of high value and in criminal cases sit with a jury to try serious criminal cases.
- Superior level judges sit in the High Court, the Court of Appeal and the Supreme Court.
- Inferior level judges try civil and criminal cases, and include Circuit Judges, part-time Recorders and District Judges. They can try both lower-level civil and criminal cases. In civil cases, they decide liability and the amount of compensation. In the Crown Court, they sit with a jury and can sentence guilty offenders. District Judges can sit on their own in the Magistrates' Court.

Judicial independence

- Judicial independence is achieved by:
  - Security of tenure – superior level judges can only be removed from office following a petition passed by Parliament to the monarch. Inferior level judges can be removed by the Lord Chancellor with agreement of the Lord Chief Justice.
  - Independence from the Legislature and the Executive.
  - Immunity from suit, and that they have no interest in the cases they hear.

- Judicial independence is an advantage because:
  - Those involved in a case see that the judge is not subject to any influence – their decisions are made only on the facts and law.
  - Ordinary citizens are protected against unlawful acts of government who must act lawfully at all times.
  - The public have confidence in the judicial system.

Chapter 4 Access to justice

Introduction

A client using a lawyer will have to pay for their services, which are usually charged at an hourly rate. Legal aid, paid for by the state, only provides limited funding in civil cases, more in criminal cases as the client's liberty may be at risk. A main source of civil funding is where a lawyer enters a Conditional Fee Agreement with their client, but only where the case stands a high chance of success. There are other sources of advice in civil cases, but with limited exceptions, they will not be able to represent the clients if the case comes to court.

4.1 Government funding for civil and criminal cases

4.1.1 The Legal Aid Agency

This government agency is responsible for the administration of civil and criminal legal aid in England and Wales. Their role is to:
- make sure that legal aid services provided by solicitors, barristers and the not-for-profit sector are available to the general public
- fund the Civil Legal Advice service
- run the Public Defender Service to give a range of services within the criminal defence market.

4.1.2 Civil cases

The Civil Legal Advice (CLA) service

This organisation provides free and specialist initial legal advice to people across England and Wales who qualify for legal aid. It advises on matters such as debt, education, discrimination, housing and family issues.

Civil legal aid

Civil legal aid provides funding for claimants in certain civil disputes when legal advice, mediation or representation in court are required.

The claimant will have to pass a means and merits test. The means test looks at both the claimant's income and capital. It will also look at their partner's finances unless they have a contrary interest. The figures alter each year.

Look online

Look at www.gov.uk/guidance/civil-legal-aid-means-testing under the heading 'Eligibility limits' for civil legal aid. What are the current maximum figures for:
- gross monthly income
- disposable income
- disposable capital?

The merits test looks at the reason for taking the action, and the chance of success.

Only certain limited types of claims are able to be funded by civil legal aid. These include repossession of a property, homelessness, asylum and immigration cases or protection from violence or harassment.

If civil legal aid is granted, this will pay for advice, assistance and legal representation by a lawyer. If a claimant does not qualify for legal aid, or the case they are taking is not within the qualifying types of case, they will have to pay their own legal costs unless they can obtain a Conditional Fee Agreement (see below).

4.1.3 Criminal cases

Criminal legal aid services are under the jurisdiction of the Legal Aid Agency. The Agency enters into contracts with legal firms to provide legal services to people charged with criminal offences.

Advice and assistance for individuals held in custody

Under s 13 Legal Aid, Sentencing and Punishment of Offenders Act 2012, legal aid for advice and assistance

51

is provided for a suspect detained in police custody and who has requested legal advice.

- The scheme is not means tested.
- Advice is provided by duty solicitors, usually over the telephone at first.
- The duty solicitor decides whether a suspect qualifies for the scheme and for either telephone or face-to-face advice.
- Solicitors can only claim for attending at the police station if they can show that attendance was expected to 'materially progress the case'.

Advice and assistance for criminal proceedings following charge

A defendant needs to pass a means and merits test in order to receive legal aid for advice and assistance from a solicitor or barrister.

Means test

The defendant's income and capital and those of their partner will be considered together, unless the partner has a contrary interest – in other words, they are the victim. Their income is means tested for cases in both the Magistrates' Court and Crown Court.

If the defendant receives state benefits, they will automatically pass this test.

> **Look online**
>
> Look at www.gov.uk/guidance/work-out-who-qualifies-for-criminal-legal-aid under heading 'Means' and sub-heading 'Crown Court trial'. What are the current minimum and maximum limits for income, and the maximum for capital, if a defendant faces a trial in the Crown Court?

Merits test: 'the interests of justice'

This test considers the merits of the case and whether legal aid should be granted – for example, if there are any previous convictions, the nature of the offence and the risk of custody if found guilty. The more serious the charge or possible consequences, the more likely it is that their case will qualify for legal aid.

This test also takes into account the 'Widgery criteria' which apply to the case.

> **Look online**
>
> Look at www.gov.uk/guidance/work-out-who-qualifies-for-criminal-legal-aid under the heading 'Merits: interests of justice' and list the 'Widgery criteria'.

4.2 Private funding, conditional fees, other advice agencies

4.2.1 Private funding

Anyone who can afford it can pay for legal advice from a solicitor and/or a barrister. Solicitors have offices in most towns. However, many solicitors specialise in certain areas of work, so if a person has an unusual problem, they may need to do some research to find a solicitor's firm that can help them.

Solicitors charge an hourly fee, and it can be expensive to obtain legal advice. A solicitor will probably not be able to give a fixed fee for taking a case, as it will depend on how many hours will be spent on it, how easy the evidence is to obtain, whether a settlement could be reached or the case has to go to trial, and whether a specialist barrister will be required.

In some areas of civil law, it may be possible to instruct a barrister under the Direct Access scheme.

4.2.2 Conditional fees

A solicitor can enter into a written Conditional Fee Agreement (CFA) with their client in many types of civil cases. These are particularly used in personal injury claims, but cannot be used in family or criminal cases.

- A CFA ensures that the client only pays the solicitor if they win the case for the client.
- It will place a cap – or maximum – on the amount the solicitor can charge.
- If the case is lost, the solicitor cannot claim any costs. Therefore, a solicitor will usually only agree a CFA if it is considered that the claim has a good chance of success – usually more than a 75 per cent chance.
- The agreement will usually contain a 'success fee' clause. This is the added fee that a solicitor becomes entitled to under a CFA if their client's case is successful. The amount of the success fee is usually determined by the complexity and risk of the claim and is a percentage of the amount of compensation recovered. If the client wins the case, they cannot claim the success fee from the loser in addition to their costs.
- Due to the rule in civil cases that the loser pays the winner's legal costs, it will be a term of the CFA that the client takes out an 'after the event' insurance policy (see section on insurance below) to cover the costs of the other party in the case, if the case is lost.

4.2.3 Other advice agencies

Citizens Advice

This is a charitable organisation and there are bureaux in many towns and cities across the country. They are staffed by both full-time employees and trained volunteers who give general advice across a wide range of issues by face-to-face contact, telephone consultations and by email and webchat. The main areas of advice are for debt, consumer issues, claiming welfare benefits, housing problems and employment matters.

Many Citizens Advice offices have arrangements with local solicitors who offer clinics to give advice on purely legal issues. The solicitors are likely to offer a cheap, or free, first advice session.

Law Centres

Law Centres offer free, non-means tested advice to people living in their area, and advice and representation in areas where there are no or few solicitors. At the time of writing there were only 41 law centres across the country. They are funded by central or local government but have found it increasingly difficult to gain enough funding, despite covering a need.

Most law centres will have a qualified solicitor working full-time, supported by volunteers.

Citizens Advice can be a first stop for legal advice

Look online

Use this link to find your local law centre www.lawcentres.org.uk/about-law-centres/law-centres-on-google-maps/geographically

What legal services does your local law centre provide? What is suggested if you do not have a law centre in your area?

Pro Bono unit (now known as Advocate)

Volunteer barristers staff a Bar Pro Bono unit, based in London, which gives free legal advice on a range of legal issues to members of the public who cannot afford legal fees and who do not qualify for CLA. The unit may also represent a member of the public in any civil legal proceedings.

Free Representation Unit (FRU)

This body, based in London and Nottingham, provides advice and legal representation in social security and employment tribunals. They help members of the public who are not eligible for legal aid and cannot afford lawyers.

Their work is carried out by volunteers, who are often law students and legal professionals in the early stages of their career. All FRU's representatives are trained and supervised by legal officers. In addition, many universities around the country encourage their law students to offer free legal advice to members of the public in their area.

Trades unions

They will usually offer their members free legal advice on a range of employment-related matters and other matters such as a personal injury in an accident outside work.

Members of a union generally pay a subscription which will cover the giving of advice and, if necessary, representation throughout a case. A union often employs full-time specialist advisers to deal with work-related issues and who will negotiate with an employer on behalf of their members.

In personal injury claims, a union will usually refer a member to a specialist lawyer and then cover the lawyer's costs.

Insurance companies

Many insurance policies include cover for help with legal fees for advice and, if necessary, taking a case to court. For example:
- Vehicle insurance covers the insured for advice on claims arising from road accidents.
- A house insurance policy will cover advice and assistance if a visitor is injured on the premises.

There are also special insurance policies that can be bought to cover legal costs:
- 'Before the event' policies are taken out where there is no known claim at the time of purchase.

- 'After the event' policies are required when a conditional fee agreement is entered into. This policy covers the lawyer's fees and the winner's legal costs if the claim is lost.

Charities

Many charities offer some form of free specialist advice in their area of work. They will employ either trained advisers or volunteers to provide initial advice and assistance to those who contact them.

Some charities have telephone helplines offering legal advice. For example:

- Gingerbread offers advice on any issues which may impact on a single or shared parent. This can include matters of child maintenance, contact with children after a family breakdown, employment issues, education, welfare benefits, housing, and debt.
- Shelter offers local teams who provide face-to-face advice, a telephone helpline and online chats for free advice on a range of housing issues, including homelessness, eviction, tenancy agreements, repairs and housing benefits.

4.3 Evaluation of access to justice

4.3.1 Civil cases

On the one hand, it is positive that:

1 There are many ways in which a claimant in a civil case can obtain legal advice and assistance from a variety of sources.
2 Claimants don't have to rely solely on lawyers for such advice and assistance.
3 Many sources of free or cheap advice and assistance are specialists in their fields, and have much greater knowledge and skills than high street lawyers in matters of employment law, housing and entitlement to welfare benefits.
4 It is possible to obtain legal advice and representation in a number of fields, if it is necessary to take a case further than just obtaining advice.
5 For those unable to pay privately there is, in certain specific cases, state-funded legal aid.
6 CFAs with lawyers are the main source of funding for those claiming compensation for personal injuries suffered in an accident. They allow a claim to be made if the claimant is unable to afford to fund a case privately.
7 Using private funding for legal advice and representation allows the choice of the best or most experienced lawyer for the case.

On the other hand, there are a number of problems with obtaining access to justice:

1 Legal fees: lawyers are generally unable to give an estimate of their fees at the start of a case, as discussed in section 4.2.1. In addition, the client might have to pay two amounts of fees, due to the rule that the loser of a civil case has to pay the winner's costs. Private funding of claims will be expensive and out of the reach of many.
2 Problems with the system of CFAs:
- A lawyer has to be convinced at the outset that there is a high chance of the claim succeeding before an agreement can be entered into.
- A potential claimant has to take out an 'after the event' insurance policy which is likely to cost several hundred pounds – the premium will be based on the chances of the claim succeeding.
- The amount of compensation paid to the claimant will be reduced by the deduction from the lawyer's success fee which cannot be recovered from the defendant.
3 Civil legal aid funding has been cut. From a peak of just over £1 billion in 2010–11, the allocation fell to £600 million in 2015–16, though it rose again to £739 million in 2018–19. At the same time, the number of civil court claims has increased as more people are prepared to take action to enforce their rights.
4 As a result of the lack of funding in civil cases, there has been a rise in the number of litigants in person, which in turn has led to more delays in court.
5 With the cuts to funding and the expense of using lawyers, more pressure is being put on other advice agencies at a time when their budgets are stretched. This means there are likely to be greater delays in accessing legal advice

4.3.2 Criminal cases

On the one hand, it is positive that:

1 A suspect in police detention is able to obtain legal advice and assistance, as it will prevent the police from breaking the rules in the Police and Criminal Evidence Act 1984.

2 When a suspect is detained, all their possessions are taken from them and they cannot access any of their documents or salary details, so the availability of free advice without being means tested is vital.

3 A person facing criminal charges that could seriously affect their future should be able to instruct a lawyer to investigate those charges, obtain evidence and, if appropriate, put forward a defence on their behalf. In this way, justice can be seen to be done.

On the other hand, there are a number of problems:

1 The government has cut the budget for criminal legal aid: in 2018–19 the criminal legal aid budget for England and Wales was £879 million, down from £891 million in 2017–18. The criminal legal aid budget peaked in 2007–08 at just over £1.2 billion, and between 2010–11 and 2015–16 it was cut by £314 million. This has the following consequences:

2 There has not been a corresponding drop in the number of crimes being committed, or coming to court, so the amount of money available to fund the scheme has been steadily reducing.

3 Fewer firms are providing criminal legal aid services as it does not pay them to do so. In 2010, there were 1861 firms undertaking criminal legal aid work. At the time of writing this number stands at 1147.

4 This has caused a rise in the number of defendants both in the Magistrates' and Crown Courts who are not represented by lawyers. This means that:
   ○ cases are taking longer as points and procedures have to be explained in simple terms to defendants
   ○ there is a greater chance of defendants being found guilty and denied justice.

5 The longer-term future for solicitors' firms practising in the area is not promising:
   ○ Solicitors do not want to practise in criminal law as it is not as well remunerated as other areas of law.
   ○ Unsociable work hours: they can be called out during the night to attend a police station and then go to court the following morning.

6 The only alternative to the present system is for the government to set up a public defender service, to represent all defendants charged with criminal offences. This is likely to cost far more than is presently being spent.

7 As a result of the strict means test, especially in the Magistrates' Court, about three-quarters of adults appearing do not qualify for legal aid. In Crown Courts, there are less severe financial limits, but cases dealt with there are more serious and it is more expensive to defend a case – therefore, there is less money available for each case and a greater risk of injustice.

8 The 'interests of justice' test is strictly applied and it has to be shown there is a real prospect of imprisonment to satisfy this test. One result of this is that a defendant with a greater number of past convictions is more likely to be imprisoned and, therefore, they are more likely to receive legal aid. A defendant who is charged with a serious offence but less likely to go to prison is less likely to receive legal aid.

Look online

- Read some stories of the clients helped by the Bar's pro bono unit at https://weareadvocate.org.uk/applicant-stories.html.
- Look online to see what legal services and advice a trade union such as Unison can provide for its members.

Activity

Where might it be possible for the following clients to obtain legal advice and, if necessary, legal aid?

- Aiden is arrested on suspicion of robbery and taken to a police station.
- Bob has been charged with manslaughter and is shortly due to appear for the first time in a Magistrates' Court.
  Clara has been dismissed by her employer who refuses to give reasons for the dismissal.
  David is in dispute with his landlord who has threatened him with eviction.
  Eden is injured in a road accident which was due to the fault of a motorcyclist who was driving too fast.
- Faisal has bought a computer from an online store. After two weeks, the computer will not turn on and the store refuses to answer Faisal's complaints.

1 What are the two tests that have to be passed in order to claim civil legal aid?
2 What are the two tests that have to be passed to claim criminal legal aid?
3 If granted, what does legal aid pay for?
4 Is legal aid free for a claimant?
5 List three sources of legal advice apart from lawyers.
6 Assess the value of Conditional Fee Agreements (CFA).

Summary

- The Legal Aid Agency oversees the operation of both civil and criminal legal aid.
- Civil legal aid provides funding in a limited number of civil cases. Claimants have to pass both a means test and a merits test to qualify.
- Legal aid is more likely to be granted in criminal cases as the liberty of an individual may be at stake. Claimants have to pass a means test and an 'interests of justice' test.
- A client can pay their lawyer privately in both civil and criminal cases.

- Conditional Fee Agreements can be used in many civil cases. The client only pays their lawyer if the case is won. If the case is lost, the lawyer does not get paid. A case will be taken only if there is a high chance of success.
- Other sources of advice in mostly civil cases include the Citizens Advice service, law centres, Pro Bono Unit (Advocate), Free Representation Units, trade unions if the client is a member, insurance companies for their policyholders and charities.

Section 2

CRIMINAL LAW

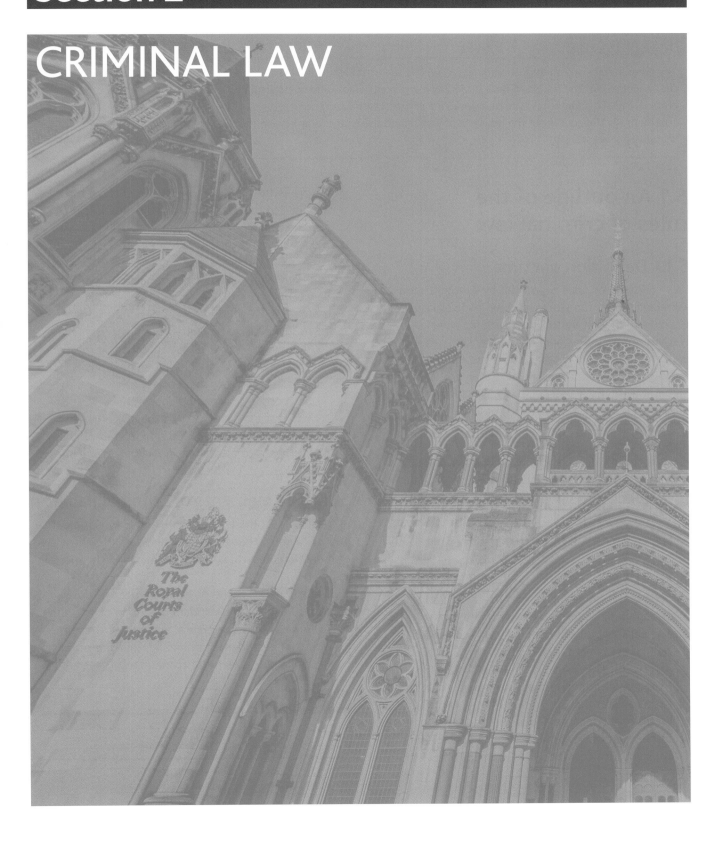

Chapter 5 Rules and theory

5.1 An outline of the rules of criminal law

5.1.1 Definition of crime

Law is a body of rules supported by sanctions and administered by the state. A crime involves conduct which is forbidden by the state and for which there is a punishment. This area of the law sets out what is deemed to be acceptable (and unacceptable) conduct in the UK. There are also offences which can be committed by a British citizen abroad, but then prosecuted under English law in the UK.

Key term

Crime – conduct which is forbidden by the state and for which there is a punishment.

5.1.2 Sources of criminal law

Criminal law ensures every citizen understands what is acceptable conduct. The state sets out and describes criminal behaviour, either through Acts of Parliament or through judicial interpretation of the law.

1 The vast majority of criminal law is contained in Acts of Parliament, such as the Theft Act 1968, and the Offences Against the Person Act 1861. However, murder and manslaughter are mostly not based on statute.
2 Occasionally a criminal offence is created by judges rather than the state. An example is the offence of conspiracy to corrupt public morals. This offence has never been enacted by Parliament, but the judges recognised that it existed in *Shaw v DPP* (1962).
3 Judges interpret the law set out in Acts of Parliament and occasionally change their view as to the meaning of an Act or the definition of what constitutes a particular crime. For example:
   ○ In *R v R* (1991), the courts decided that a husband could be guilty of raping his wife, as she was no longer assumed, by being married, to consent to sexual intercourse with him. This reflected the fact that society's views on the position of women had changed.
   ○ The test for dishonesty in the law of theft under s 2 Theft Act 1968 and related offences has changed as set out in *R v Barton and Booth* (2020).

5.1.3 The elements of criminal liability

In most crimes, there are two elements which must be proved to show that the defendant is guilty. These two elements are known as the *actus reus* and the *mens rea*:

● The *actus reus* is the physical element of the crime – what the defendant has done or not done.
● The *mens rea* is the mental element of the crime – what the defendant is intending, thinking or failing to think about when the crime is committed.

Key terms

Actus reus – the physical element of the crime.
Mens rea – the mental element of the crime.

Each crime has its own *actus reus* and *mens rea*. Many crimes require a *mens rea* of intention or recklessness as to the *actus reus*. Some crimes have specific *mens rea*. For example, in theft:

- the defendant must appropriate property belonging to another for the *actus reus*, and
- do this dishonestly and intend to permanently deprive the other of it for the *mens rea*.

Some criminal offences can be committed by proof of *actus reus* alone – the defendant need not be proved to have any *mens rea* relating to the offence. These are known as crimes of strict liability. For example:

- a driving offence such as exceeding the speed limit – for a person to be convicted, all that must be proved is that the driver exceeded the prescribed speed limit.

Key term

Crime of strict liability – a crime that can be committed by proof of *actus reus* alone.

5.1.4 People involved in a criminal case – prosecution and defence

Criminal proceedings are usually initiated by the police, and the Crown Prosecution Service (CPS) prepares the case to be brought to a Magistrates' Court or the Crown Court.

- Almost all criminal cases start in the Magistrates' Court, but depending on the nature and seriousness of the offence, the case might be passed to the Crown Court, to be tried before a judge and jury.
- The accused has the chance to defend the case brought against him by supplying evidence to the court to challenge evidence put forward by the prosecution.
- If the defendant is found guilty, a punishment (sentence) will be imposed by the Court. In deciding on sentence, the court considers the aims of sentencing as well as aggravating and mitigating factors.

Link

See Chapter 2 for more information on sentencing.

Private prosecutions are also sometimes pursued by bodies such as the Royal Mail, and very occasionally, an individual.

5.1.5 The burden of proof, the standard of proof and reverse onus

An accused person is presumed to be innocent until proven guilty.

The burden (sometimes referred to as the onus) of proof is on the prosecution to prove the defendant is guilty. This means that the prosecution must prove both the required *actus reus* and *mens rea* for the offence for which the defendant is charged.

Key terms

Burden of proof – the prosecution must prove that the defendant is guilty.
Standard of proof – the extent to which the burden of proof must be made.
Reverse onus – shifting the burden of proof to the defendant.

For a successful prosecution of any crime, there must be proof of the elements of the offence.

Traditionally, this is known as 'beyond reasonable doubt', but current guidance to judges is to use the word 'sure' – this is the standard of proof in criminal cases. The judge will usually explain to the jury that it should only convict if it is satisfied, on the evidence, that it is *sure* of the defendant's guilt.

The idea of beyond reasonable doubt as the standard of proof to be found by the jury from the evidence is unofficially described as the '99 per cent' test.

If the defendant raises a defence (a reason why they should not be found guilty of the crime), then it is for the prosecution to disprove that defence.

- For all common law defences, except insanity, there must be some evidence of the key points of the defence given at the trial. This can be from evidence given by the defence or by the prosecution.
- If evidence of a defence is given at the trial then, even where the defendant has not specifically raised the defence, the prosecution must disprove at least one element of that defence. The trial judge must direct the jury to acquit unless it is satisfied that the defence has been disproved by the prosecution.

However, for some defences, for example, insanity, the burden of proof is on the defendant – they must prove to the court that this defence can be used. This shifting of the burden of proof to the defendant is known as the reverse onus. Where the burden of proof is on the defendant to prove a defence, the standard is the civil one of 'on the balance of probabilities'. This is the standard of proof in civil law that is unofficially described as the '51 per cent' test.

5.2 An overview of the theory of criminal law

A person who breaks the criminal law and commits an offence is seen as committing a wrong against society as a whole. They might face criminal prosecution by the state and, if convicted, will receive an adequate punishment.

The question of why an act should or should not be considered a criminal act is a matter for moral philosophy.

> **Link**
>
> The relationship between law and morality is examined in Chapter 29. The relationship of law and justice is explored in detail in Chapter 30.

5.2.1 The aims and purpose of criminal law

Criminal law is often seen as retributive justice. This is a theory of justice that considers proportionate punishment a morally acceptable response to crime.

Today, criminal law is not purely about punishment; it is also concerned with:
- deterrence and corrective justice to encourage citizens not to commit crimes, or
- educating an offender to change their behaviour and avoid reoffending.

For example, minor offences are sometimes dealt with in ways that avoid a criminal prosecution, such as attending a speed awareness course after breaking the speed limit; and courts might decide to impose non-custodial sentences.

The criminal law also provides a form of social control over society. This may reflect the general morality of the time and changing social attitudes. For example, the general public's attitude to the offences of drink- (or drug-) driving or holding a mobile phone while driving has become less tolerant.

> **Link**
>
> See Chapter 31 for the relationship between law and society.

The purpose of the criminal justice system, stated by the Ministry of Justice, is to deliver justice for all, by convicting and punishing the guilty and helping them to stop offending, while protecting the innocent.

It aims to do so by detecting crime and bringing offenders to justice and carrying out the orders of court, such as collecting fines, and supervising community and custodial sentences.

Activity

Here is a list of the aims and purposes and theories of criminal law.

For each bullet write a short sentence, preferably with an example, that explains the point.

The aims and purposes of criminal law
● Protect individuals from harm
● Protect people's property from harm/theft
● Preserve order in society
● Enforce prevailing moral standards
● To balance conflicting interests
● Punish those at fault
● Educate society about appropriate behaviour
● To achieve justice
● Provide a deterrent

Theories of criminal law
● Legal paternalism
● Individualism and collectivism
● Legal necessity
● Legal moralism
● The harm principle
● Distributive justice
● Socio-economic and public policy factors
● Symbolic criminalisation

Follow a criminal case, perhaps at a visit to your local Magistrates' Court.

Identify:

- how the case is presented to court
- the offence with which the defendant is charged
- the *actus reus* and *mens rea* for that offence.

At the end of the case, consider:

- Was the result just?
- Will the sentence be seen as a deterrent by the defendant and others in the locality?

Write down reasons for your views.

The Magistrates' Court in Colchester

5.2.2 The principles of criminal law

Fault, in a legal sense, is some form of wrongdoing. This is described as **an offence** in criminal law or being **negligent** in the civil law of tort.

Fault is the term used to convey the idea of blameworthiness. The person at fault usually has legal responsibility. Sometimes a person can be at fault even if the offence or action carried out is termed 'no fault'.

In criminal law, there is a general presumption that liability is based upon fault. A person should not be held liable for a criminal offence unless they are, to some extent, blameworthy or at fault.

This underpins the concept of *mens rea* in a criminal offence – it is what is in a person's mind

that distinguishes between an accident and a criminal offence. For example:

- A minor car accident when parking a car will not normally be considered criminal. It is an error by the driver and might, in civil law, give rise to a claim in negligence. The event only becomes criminal when the accident contains an element of mens rea, showing an intention or recklessness to cause damage to the other car.

The principle of innocent until proven guilty means that a defendant is presumed to be not guilty until the court makes a verdict of guilty. Guilt can only be established by the prosecution providing evidence that all the elements of the crime with which the defendant are charged are present. This must be done to the standard of beyond reasonable doubt in the minds of the jury or magistrates.

The evidence collected by the prosecution is subject to the defendant having the right to remain silent. The defendant does not have to incriminate himself while being questioned by the police who must obtain evidence in accordance with the Police and Criminal Evidence Act 1984. The purpose of this Act is to set out police powers under one Act and to balance carefully the rights of the individual against the powers of the police.

The defendant has the right to raise any defence that the law may make available to him. These may be general defences applicable to all crimes or specific defences to particular crimes. The purpose of defences is to make sure that fault is attached correctly as guilt leads to a sanction and a sense of moral wrongness in the eyes of society.

Quick questions

1. State the main sources of English criminal law.
2. Explain the difference between *actus reus* and *mens rea*.
3. What are the aims of criminal law?
4. Explain the principle of fault in criminal law.
5. What is meant by the right to remain silent?

Summary

- A crime can be defined as conduct which is forbidden by the state and for which there is a punishment.
- Criminal law is mainly set down by the state, though some conduct is criminalised by judges.
- The two elements of a crime are the *actus reus* and the *mens rea*.
- The standard of proof is beyond reasonable doubt.
- The burden of proving guilt is on the prosecution: the defendant is presumed innocent until proven guilty.

- Ideas of what conduct is criminal can change over time.
- Criminal law involves the concept of justice.
- Criminal law has a close relationship with morality and the requirements of society.
- In criminal law, there is a general presumption that liability is based upon fault.

Chapter 6 General elements of criminal liability

Introduction

This chapter deals with the central concepts of *actus reus* and *mens rea* in criminal law.

6.1 *Actus reus*

As already stated in Chapter 5, the *actus reus* is the physical element of a crime. In most cases, the *actus reus* will be something the defendant *does*, but there are situations in which a *failure to act* is sufficient for the *actus reus*.

6.1.1 Conduct and consequence crimes

Crimes can be categorised as either a conduct crime or a consequence (result) crime.

1 A conduct crime is where the accused's conduct forms the offence, and there is no required consequence from that conduct. For example:
   ○ The offence of drink-driving is a criminal offence; merely driving with excess alcohol in your bloodstream is the offence. No consequence (such as causing an accident) is required.
2 For a consequence crime, the consequence element must happen for the offence to be committed. For example:
   ○ In the offence of assault occasioning actual bodily harm (s 47 of the Offences Against the Person Act 1861), there must be an assault but there must also be a consequence of actual bodily harm.

      A consequence crime requires proof that the defendant's *actus reus* (the assault) caused the prohibited consequence (the actual bodily harm).

Link

The offence of assault is explained in Chapter 8.

6.1.2 Voluntary acts (including state of affairs) and omissions

Voluntary acts

The act or omission must be voluntary on the part of the defendant. If the defendant has no control over his or her actions, then he or she has not committed the *actus reus*. This was explained in *Hill v Baxter* (1958).

Case study

R v Hill v Baxter (1958)

The defendant ignored a road sign that said 'halt' and carried on, causing his van to crash. He claimed to have remembered nothing for some time before the crash and said he was an automaton (behaving like a mechanical machine).

He was convicted as there was no real evidence of him being an automaton, but the court gave examples where a driver of a vehicle could not be said to be doing the act of driving voluntarily such as losing control of the vehicle while being stung by a swarm of bees, being struck on the head by a stone or having a heart attack while driving.

State of affairs

There are some rare instances in which the defendant has been convicted even though the act was not desired by the defendant, but occurred through actions against his will. These situations involve what are known as state of affairs cases, such as *R v Larsonneur* (1933).

Case study

R v Larsonneur (1933)

The defendant, a French woman, had been ordered to leave the United Kingdom. She decided to go to Ireland, but the Irish police deported her and took her back to the UK. She did not wish to go back and was certainly not doing this voluntarily. She made every effort to avoid deportation but was taken to England against her will.

When she landed in the UK she was immediately arrested and charged with 'being an alien to whom leave to land in the UK had been refused, was found in the UK', in other words, an illegal immigrant. She was convicted of the offence. It did not matter that she had been brought back by the Irish police against her will.

Omissions

The normal principle is that the *actus reus* must be a positive act. Therefore, an omission, a failure to act, cannot make a person guilty of an offence. There is no requirement on a person to go to the aid of another in danger. However, there are situations where an omission can give rise to liability in criminal law. These are where:

- an Act of Parliament creates an offence involving an omission
- a contractual duty to act exists
- a duty exists because of a relationship between the victim and the accused
- a duty toward the victim has been taken on voluntarily by the accused
- a duty to act arises as a consequence of the accused's official position
- a duty to act arises because the defendant has set in motion a chain of events.

An Act of Parliament creates an offence involving an omission

Many of these statutory offences are regulatory and concern matters such as prevention of pollution and public safety; for example, building standards or failing to take a breath test as a driver. These offences often require proof of only an *actus reus* to establish guilt. These offences are known as offences of **strict liability**.

A contractual duty to act exists

An example of this can be seen in the case of *Pittwood* (1902).

Case study

R v Pittwood (1902)

A railway-crossing keeper omitted to shut the gates so that a person crossing the line was struck and killed by a train. The keeper was guilty of manslaughter, by virtue of a contractual duty, because of his failure to close the gate.

A more modern example would be of a lifeguard at a beach who leaves their post unattended, contrary to their contractual duty. Failure to do their duty could make them guilty of an offence if a swimmer was injured.

A duty exists because of a relationship between the victim and the accused

A duty because of a relationship could be, for example, that between a parent and a child. This was shown in *Gibbins and Proctor* (1918).

Case study

R v Gibbins and Proctor (1918)

The child's father and his mistress failed to feed the child so that it died of starvation. They had a duty to feed the child as a result of the relationship of parent to child, so had a duty to act. Their omission to act formed the *actus reus* of the offence, and they were guilty of murder.

A duty toward the victim has been taken on voluntarily by the accused

A duty which has been taken on voluntarily can give rise to *actus reus* where the duty is not carried out. This can be seen in the cases of *Stone and Dobinson* (1977) and *Evans* (2009).

Case study

R v Stone and Dobinson (1977)

Stone's elderly sister came to live with the defendants. She became ill and unable to care for herself. She died, and the two defendants were convicted of manslaughter.

As the deceased was Stone's sister, he owed a duty of care to her. Dobinson had undertaken some care of her and so also owed her a duty of care. The duty was either to help her themselves or to summon help from other sources. Their failure to do either of these meant that they were in breach of their duty. This formed the *actus reus* of the crime.

R v Evans (2009)

The victim was a 16-year-old heroin addict who lived with her mother and her older half-sister. The half-sister bought some heroin and gave it to the victim who injected the drug herself. It became obvious that she had overdosed, but neither the mother nor the half-sister tried to get medical help. They put her to bed and hoped she would recover, but she died.

The mother owed a duty of care to her daughter. The half-sister had created a situation which she knew or ought reasonably to have known was life-threatening, and therefore owed her a duty.

A duty toward the victim arises from an official position

The official position can give rise to a duty to act, and failure to act can then become the *actus reus* of a crime. This is unlike in some countries whose law requires every person to act in situations where another is in danger or distress. An example can be seen in *Dytham* (1979).

Case study

R v Dytham (1979)

Dytham, a police officer, witnessed a violent attack on the victim but took no steps to intervene or summon help; instead he drove away from the scene. The officer was guilty of wilfully and without reasonable excuse neglecting to perform his duty.

A duty toward the victim arises because the defendant has set in motion a chain of events

This concept of owing a duty and being liable through omission was created in the case of *Miller* (1983).

Case study

R v Miller (1983)

The defendant, a squatter, fell asleep in an empty house. His lit cigarette fell onto his mattress, and a fire started. When he realised this he left the room and went to sleep in another room. He did not attempt to put out the fire or summon help. He was guilty of arson under the Criminal Damage Act 1971, s 1.

This can also be seen in the case of *Evans* (2009) discussed above.

Source	Examples
Statutory duty	Failing to provide a specimen of breath (s 6 of the Road Traffic Act 1988)
Under a contract, especially of employment	Pittwood (1902)
Because of a relationship such as parent and child	*Gibbins and Proctor* (1918)
A duty voluntarily undertaken, e.g. care of an elderly relative	*Stone and Dobinson* (1977); *Evans* (2009)
Because of a public office, e.g. police officer	*Dytham* (1979)
As a result of a dangerous situation created by the defendant	*Miller* (1983); *Evans* (2009)

Figure 6.1 Key cases and legislation: when an omission can form the *actus reus* of a crime

Involuntary acts

The concept of an involuntary act can be seen where someone suffers an epileptic fit. Whether this excuses criminal liability is discussed in Chapters 9 and 10 on defences and in particular the defence of automatism.

6.1.3 Causation

Where a consequence must be proved, then the prosecution has to show that:

- the defendant's conduct was the factual cause of that consequence (legal causation), and

- the defendant's conduct was in law the cause of that consequence (legal causation), and
- there was no intervening act which broke the chain of causation.

Factual cause

The defendant can only be guilty if the consequence would not have happened 'but for' the defendant's conduct: see *Pagett* (1983). The opposite situation was seen in *White* (1910).

R v Pagett (1983)

The defendant used his pregnant girlfriend as a shield while he shot at an armed policeman. The police fired back and the girlfriend was killed. Pagett was convicted of her manslaughter. She would not have died 'but for' him using her as a shield in the shoot-out.

R v White (1910)

The defendant put cyanide in his mother's drink, intending to kill her. She died of a heart attack before she could drink it. The defendant was not the factual cause of her death; he was not guilty of murder, though he was guilty of attempted murder.

Legal causation

There are a number of things to consider here:
- the 'thin skull rule', and
- the chain of causation.

The 'thin skull rule'

The defendant must take the victim as he or she finds them. This is known as the 'thin skull rule'. If the victim has something unusual about their physical or mental state which makes an injury more serious, then the defendant is liable for the more serious injury. For example, if the victim has an unusually thin skull which means that a blow to the head gives them a serious injury, then the defendant is liable for that serious injury. This is so, even though that blow would have only caused bruising in a 'normal' person. An example is the case of *Blaue* (1975).

Case study

R v Blaue (1975)

A young woman was stabbed by the defendant. She was told she needed a blood transfusion to save her life but she refused to have one as her religion forbade blood transfusions. She died and the defendant was convicted of her murder.

Despite the fact that her religious belief made the wound fatal, the defendant was still guilty because he had to take his victim as he found her.

The chain of causation

Once it is established that there is factual causation, the prosecution must also prove that there is legal causation so that there is little chance of an innocent person being convicted. The link between the act and the consequence is known as the chain of causation – this must remain unbroken if there is to be criminal liability. Imagine the following scenario:

- You have invited a friend to your house. On the way to your house your friend is attacked and seriously injured. We could say that 'but for' your invitation, your friend would not have been attacked. However, you clearly did not inflict the injuries as your invitation was not the operating and substantial cause of the injuries, the key test for legal causation. The injuries caused by the attack were the operating and substantial cause of the injuries.

Figure 6.2 Breaking the chain of causation

The chain of causation can be broken by:
- an act of a third party
- the victim's own act
- a natural but unpredictable event.

In order to break the chain of causation so that the defendant is not responsible for the consequence, the intervening act must be both sufficiently independent of the defendant's conduct and sufficiently serious enough.

An act of a third party: medical treatment

There are a number of cases where it was asked whether poor medical treatment was the operating or substantial cause of the injuries. Medical treatment is unlikely to break the chain of causation unless it is so independent of the defendant's acts and 'in itself so potent in causing death' that the defendant's acts are insignificant. The following three cases show this.

Case study

R v Smith (1959)

Two soldiers had a fight and one was stabbed in the lung by the other. The victim was carried to a medical centre by other soldiers, but was dropped on the way. At the medical centre the staff gave him artificial respiration by pressing on his chest. This made the injury worse and he died. If he had been given the proper treatment, his chance of recovering would have been as high as 75 per cent. Despite this, the original attacker was still guilty of his murder. This was because the stab wound was the overwhelming cause of the death – it was the operative and substantial cause of death. This means that the significant cause, the stabbing, was more than a minimal contribution to the death (the de minimis rule).

R v Cheshire (1991)

The defendant shot the victim in the thigh and the stomach. The victim had problems breathing and was given a tracheotomy (a tube was inserted in his throat to help him breathe). The victim died from rare complications of the tracheotomy, which were not spotted by the doctors. By the time he died, the original wounds were no longer life-threatening. The defendant was still held to be liable for his death.

R v Jordan (1956)

The victim had been stabbed in the stomach. He was treated in hospital and the wounds were healing well. He was given an antibiotic but suffered an allergic reaction to it. One doctor stopped the use of the antibiotic but the next day another doctor ordered that a large dose of it be given. The victim died from the allergic reaction to the drug. In this case, the actions of the doctor were held to be an intervening act which caused the death. The defendant was not guilty of murder. The stab wound was not the significant cause and was therefore de minimis.

However, switching off a life-support machine when a patient is brain-dead does not break the chain of causation. If discontinuance of medical treatment is in the best interests of the patient, this is not an omission which can form the actus reus. This was decided in Airedale NHS Trust v Bland (1993) in which the NHS Trust was given permission to stop artificial feeding of a man who had been in a persistent vegetative state for over three years.

Link

See Chapter 28, section 28.2.1 for case details for Airedale.

Victim's own act

If the defendant causes the victim to react in a foreseeable way, then any injury to the victim will have been caused by the defendant. This occurred in Roberts (1971).

Case study

R v Roberts (1971)

A girl jumped from a car in order to escape from sexual advances. The car was travelling at between 20 and 40 mph and the girl was injured through jumping from the car. The defendant was held to be liable for her injuries.

However, if the victim's reaction is unreasonable, then this may break the chain of causation, as in Williams (1992).

Case study

R v Williams (1992)

A hitch-hiker jumped from Williams' car and died from head injuries caused by his head hitting the road. The car was travelling at about 30 mph. The prosecution alleged that the driver had attempted to steal the victim's wallet and that was the reason for his jumping from the car. The court stated that the victim's act had to be foreseeable and also had to be in proportion to the threat. Here it was not in proportion to the threat, and so the injury to the victim was not caused by the defendant.

Case	Principle
Pagett (1983)	She would not have died 'but for' him using her as a shield in the shoot-out.
White (1910)	The defendant was not the factual cause of her death.
Blaue (1975)	The defendant was guilty because he had to take his victim as he found her.
Smith (1959)	The original attacker was still guilty because the stab wound was the overwhelming cause of the death, it was the significant and operative cause and not *de minimis*.
Cheshire (1991)	Even though the original wounds were no longer life-threatening, the defendant was still held to be liable for his death.
Jordan (1956)	The actions of the doctor were held to be an intervening act which caused the death. The defendant was not guilty of murder.
Roberts (1971)	The defendant was held to be liable for her injuries as the victim's reactions to his attack were reasonably foreseeable in relation to the threat.
Williams (1992)	Here it was not in proportion to the threat and so the injury to the victim was not caused by the defendant.

Figure 6.3 Key cases: causation

A natural but unpredictable event

This would be where the injury or loss was caused by something such as an earthquake or flood.

Activity

Apply the rules of causation for each person in the death of Charlie in the following circumstances:

Anne was driving down the motorway late at night when her drunken passengers, Bill and Charlie, started having a violent argument. She stopped the car on the hard shoulder and Bill, who had been sitting behind her, got out, leaving the door open into the nearside lane of the motorway. Charlie undid his seatbelt and leaned over and shut the door after a passing lorry driver blew his horn and moved towards the middle lane. Dave, who was very tired and driving at over 100 miles per hour, saw the lorry move but in trying to move past it, lost control of his car and hit Anne's parked car. Charlie was killed in the crash.

(Note that it is illegal to stop on a motorway except in an emergency.)

6.2 Mens rea

Mens rea is the mental element of an offence. Each offence has its own *mens rea* or mental element, except offences of strict liability.

6.2.1 Fault

The concept of fault has been discussed in Chapter 5. In deciding whether a defendant is to be blamed for their conduct, the criminal law generally presumes that a defendant is responsible for their actions and the consequences of those actions.

The courts recognise four main instances when the defendant is not to blame, or not fully to blame for the consequences of his actions.

1. Some people are exempt from criminal prosecution, such as:
   - Children under the age of criminal responsibility (in England and Wales this is the age of ten, the lowest age of criminal responsibility in Europe).
   - People who are insane. However, if it is decided that they committed an unlawful act while insane, they can be detained in a hospital under the Mental Health Act 1983.
2. A person may not be liable for some involuntary acts. An example of this is the case of *R v Mitchell* (1983), discussed in section 6.2.6: the defendant punched a man who fell onto a woman. She died; the man who was punched was not charged with any criminal offence as his falling was an involuntary act caused by the punch.
3. A person is in control of their actions but does not have the required mental state (*mens rea*) for the particular offence. For example, if a man accidentally takes someone else's coat from the coat rack at a restaurant, he is not liable for theft as he does not have the intention necessary for theft.
4. There are some defences where, even though the defendant had the necessary mental state for the offence, they are not to be blamed. These defences include:
   - self-defence or defence of another
   - duress where the defendant had been threatened with death or serious injury if they did not commit the crime.

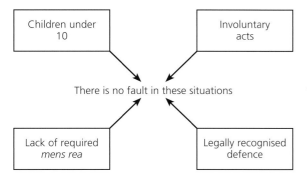

Figure 6.4 Situations where there is no fault

Where the defendant has been at fault and committed an offence, the court will impose a punishment that reflects the level of fault. The most severe punishment will be imposed on those who commit the most serious offences. This can be seen in the hierarchy of non-fatal offences in Chapter 8.

6.2.2 Intention

In the case of *Mohan* (1975), the court defined intention as:

> a decision to bring about, in so far as it lies within the accused's power [the prohibited consequence], no matter whether the accused desired that consequence of his act or not. "

This makes it clear that the defendant's motive or reason for doing the act is not relevant. The important point is that the defendant decided to bring about the prohibited consequence for there to be direct intention. Other types of *mens rea* are different.

Case study

R v Mohan (1975)

The defendant refused to stop when a policeman signalled for him to do so. Instead, he drove towards the officer. This shows a direct intention to scare or injure the policeman.

In most cases, the defendant's intention is clear. For example, where someone deliberately punches another person, he or she has an intention to use unlawful force on the victim. This is also known as direct intent.

The main problem with proving intention is when the defendant's main aim was not the prohibited consequence, but, in achieving the aim, they realised or foresaw that they would cause those consequences. This is referred to as 'foresight of consequences' and forms the basis of 'oblique' or 'indirect' intent.

Oblique intention

The first rule about foresight of consequences is that it is not the same as intention but can be evidence of intention. A jury may use this evidence to find that the defendant had intention, but only where harm caused as a result of their actions was a virtual certainty and the defendant realised this. This was explained in *Woollin* (1998).

Case study

R v Woollin (1998)

The defendant lost his temper and threw his three-month-old son towards his pram which was against a wall just over a metre away. The baby suffered head injuries when he hit the wall and died.

The court ruled that the consequence must be a virtual certainty and the defendant must realise this. If the jury were satisfied on both these two points, then the jury could find intention on this evidence.

Intention is a concept which affects many offences, but most of the cases we will consider involve murder. Section 8 of the Criminal Justice Act 1967 tried to make the law clear on this point. It states:

> A court or jury in determining whether a person has committed an offence—
>
> (a) shall not be bound in law to infer that he intended or foresaw a result of his actions by reason only of its being a natural and probable consequence of those actions; but
>
> (b) shall decide whether he did intend or foresee that result by reference to all the evidence, drawing such inferences from the evidence as appear proper in the circumstances. "

The main problems in the law are on foresight of consequences. Courts have tried on many occasions to explain it:
- In *R v Moloney* (1985) it ruled that foresight of consequences was not intention; it was only evidence from which intention could be inferred in accordance with s 8 above.
- The later decision in *R v Woollin* (1998) made the law uncertain, when the House of Lords spoke about intention being found from foresight of consequences.

R v Matthews and Alleyne (2003)

The two defendants had pushed the victim from a bridge over a deep wide river so that he fell 25 feet into the river and drowned. The defendants knew that the victim could not swim. They were convicted for murder.

The court thought that if the jury were sure that the defendants had appreciated the virtual certainty of the victim's death when they threw him into the river, it was 'impossible' to see how the jury could not have drawn the inference that the defendants intended the victim's death.

6.2.3 Subjective recklessness

This is a lower level of *mens rea* than intention. Recklessness is the taking of an unjustifiable risk. It has to be proved that the defendant realised the risk, but decided to take it. This is a subjective test. This can be seen in the case of *Cunningham* (1957).

This is the most common form of *mens rea*. If an offence requires a *mens rea* of intention or recklessness, the prosecution only need to prove recklessness which is much easier to prove than intention.

Key term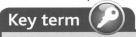

Recklessness – where the defendant realised the risk, but decided to take it.

Case study

R v Cunningham (1957)

The defendant tore a pre-payment gas meter from the wall of an empty house in order to steal the money in it. This caused gas to seep into the house next door, where a woman was affected by it. Cunningham was charged with an offence of maliciously administering a noxious thing, which has a *mens rea* of recklessness or intention to do so.

It was held that he was not guilty since he did not realise the risk of gas escaping into the adjacent house. He had not intended to cause the harm, nor had he taken a risk he knew about – he was not reckless.

6.2.4 Negligence

The concept of negligence is not widely used in the criminal law. However, in Chapter 7 you will be studying the offence of gross negligence manslaughter.

For gross negligence manslaughter:

- all the elements of negligence (duty, breach and damage) must be proved
- the jury must find the conduct of the defendant was so bad as to amount to a criminal act or omission.

Recklessness is about defendants who realise that they are exposing others to certain unjustified risks, whereas negligence is about not realising the risk, and this being unreasonable.

6.2.5 Strict liability

The concept of strict liability

For all criminal offences, there is a presumption that *mens rea* is required. The courts will always start with this presumption, but if they decide that the offence does not require *mens rea* for part of the *actus reus*, then the offence is one of strict liability – there is no requirement for *mens rea* for all of the *actus reus*.

This idea of not requiring *mens rea* for part of the offence can be seen in the case of *Pharmaceutical Society of Great Britain v Storkwain Ltd* (1986).

Case study

Pharmaceutical Society of Great Britain v Storkwain Ltd (1986)

The defendant, a pharmacist, had supplied drugs on prescriptions, but the prescriptions were later found to be forged. He had not acted dishonestly, improperly or even negligently. The forgery was sufficiently good to deceive the pharmacist. Despite this, he was convicted of supplying drugs without a genuine prescription.

No fault

Even though the defendant was totally blameless in respect of the consequence, he or she can be convicted as in *Callow v Tillstone* (1900).

Case study

Callow v Tillstone (1900)

A butcher asked a vet to examine a carcass to see if it was fit for human consumption. The vet assured him that it was, so the butcher offered it for sale. In fact, it was unfit and the butcher was convicted of the offence of exposing unsound meat for sale.

This shows there is no automatic due diligence defence.

Key term

Due diligence – where the defendant has done all that was within his power not to commit an offence.

Even where the defendants took all reasonable steps to prevent the offence, they are still guilty, as in *Harrow LBC v Shah and Shah* (1999).

Case study

Harrow LBC v Shah and Shah (1999)

The defendants owned a newsagents business where lottery tickets were sold. They had told their staff and reminded them frequently not to sell tickets to anyone under 16 years old.

One of their staff sold a lottery ticket to a 13-year-old boy, without asking for proof of age. The salesperson mistakenly believed the boy was over 16 years old. The defendant owners were convicted of selling a lottery ticket to a person under 16, despite their best efforts.

Similarly, there is no defence of mistake. This can be seen in *Cundy v Le Cocq* (1884).

Case study

Cundy v Le Cocq (1884)

The defendant was charged with selling intoxicating liquor to a drunken person. The individual had not displayed any signs of being drunk but the offence was complete on proof that a sale had taken place and that the person served was drunk, so the defendant was convicted.

In summary, where an offence is held to be one of strict liability, the following points apply:
- The defendant must be proved to have done the *actus reus*.
- This must be a voluntary act on his part.
- There is no need to prove *mens rea* for at least part of the *actus reus*.
- No 'due diligence' defence will be available.
- The defence of mistake is not available.

Is it a strict liability offence?

There are several thousand strict liability offences. Most involve matters such as regulating the sale of food, alcohol and lottery tickets, the prevention of pollution and the safe use of vehicles. Strict liability offences created by an Act of Parliament will not contain any words requiring *mens rea* in their definition. However, the courts will still look at a number of factors before deciding that a statutory offence is one of strict liability.

The starting point for deciding which offences are ones of strict liability is the presumption of *mens rea*. Nearly all strict liability offences have been created by statute, so this presumption will have been in the mind of parliamentary law-makers.

If the Act doesn't make it clear that *mens rea* is not required, judges will look for words in an Act of Parliament that indicate *mens rea* (such as 'knowingly', 'intentionally', 'maliciously' or 'permitting'). If there are no such words, judges will still presume that all criminal offences require *mens rea*. This was made clear in the case of *Sweet v Parsley* (1969).

Case study

Sweet v Parsley (1969)

The defendant let a farmhouse to students. The police found cannabis at the farmhouse and the defendant was charged with 'being concerned in the management of premises used for the purpose of smoking cannabis resin'. She did not know that cannabis was being smoked there. It was decided that she was not guilty as the court presumed that the offence required *mens rea*. Lord Reid said:

 There has for centuries been a presumption that Parliament did not intend to make criminals of persons who were in no way blameworthy in what they did.

In *Gammon (Hong Kong) Ltd v Attorney-General of Hong Kong* (1984) the court needed to decide whether:
- it had to be proved that the defendants knew that their deviation from planned building works was material, or

- the offence was one of strict liability so their knowledge was irrelevant.

Starting with the presumption that *mens rea* is required for a criminal offence, four other factors were set out for consideration:

1 The presumption can only be displaced (ruled out) if this is clearly or by necessary implication the effect of the words of the statute.
2 The presumption is particularly strong where the offence is 'truly criminal' in character.
3 The presumption can only be displaced if the statute is concerned with an issue of social concern such as public safety.
4 Strict liability should only apply if it would help enforce the law by encouraging greater vigilance to prevent the prohibited act.

This allows strict liability to be justified in a wide range of offences, as issues of social concern can be seen to cover any activity which is a potential danger to public health, safety or morals. Thus, strict liabilities are found in regulations covering health and safety matters in relation to food, drink, pollution, building and road use, as well as possession of an offensive weapon such as an unlicensed gun.

Extension activity

Search for details of cases involving strict liability.
1 What type of activity is the subject matter of each offence?
2 Why are these offences of strict liability?
Some examples to get you started:
- *R v Blake* (1997)
- *Alphacell v Woodward* (1972)

6.2.6 Transferred malice

This is the principle that the defendant can be guilty if he or she intended to commit a similar crime but against a different victim.

An example is aiming a blow at one person with the necessary *mens rea* for an assault occasioning actual bodily harm, but actually hitting another person. This occurred in the cases of *Latimer* (1886) and *Mitchell* (1983).

Case	Facts	Law/Comment
Pharmaceutical Society of Great Britain v Storkwain Ltd (1986)	Pharmacist did not realise that a prescription was a forgery.	Supplying the drugs without a genuine prescription made them guilty of the offence, even though the forgery was very difficult to spot. An example of strict liability.
Callow v Tillstone (1900)	A butcher sold meat that had been passed fit to sell by a vet. The meat was found to be unfit.	The butcher was guilty even though he was not at fault in any way. No defence of no fault is available.
Harrow LBC v Shah and Shah (1999)	A lottery ticket was sold to an under-age boy although defendants had asked staff to check proof of age. Defendants were guilty.	The offence was one of strict liability. Defendants were guilty even though they had done their best to prevent such an offence happening.
Cundy v Le Cocq (1884)	The defendant was charged with selling intoxicating liquor to a drunken person. The individual had not displayed any signs of being drunk.	The defendant was guilty as it was a strict liability offence.
Sweet v Parsley (1969)	Tenants in a farmhouse owned by the defendant smoked cannabis there. The landlord did not know.	Defendant was not guilty as there was a presumption that *mens rea* was required.

Figure 6.5 Key cases: strict liability offences

R v Latimer (1886)

The defendant aimed a blow with a belt at a man in a pub after that man had attacked him. The belt bounced off the man and struck a woman in the face. Latimer was guilty of malicious wounding against the woman, although he had not meant to hit her. There was, however transferred malice so he could be found guilty of hitting the woman.

R v Mitchell (1983)

The defendant tried to jump the queue at a Post Office. An elderly man questioned his behaviour and challenged him. The defendant hit the old man and pushed him. The man fell back onto others in the queue, including an elderly lady who fell and broke her leg. She later died. Here, the *mens rea* directed towards the old man was transferred to the offence against the old woman.

However, where the *mens rea* is for a completely different type of offence, the defendant might not be guilty. This was the situation in *Pembliton* (1874).

Case study

R v Pembliton (1874)

The defendant had been fighting and threw a stone, intending it to hit people with whom he had been fighting. The stone hit and broke a window, which was criminal damage. The intention to hit people could not be transferred to breaking the window as there was a different *mens rea* for the two offences.

6.2.7 Coincidence of *actus reus* and *mens rea*

In order for an offence to take place, both the *actus reus* and the *mens rea* must be present at the same time. This is also known as the 'contemporaneity' rule.

For example:

- Suppose you decide you do not like your next door neighbour's fence and set off to knock it down. Before you get to their house you change your mind, and decide the fence is not so bad. You do not actually damage the fence. You cannot be guilty of criminal damage even though you had the *mens rea* for that offence as there is no *actus reus*.
- A week later, you are driving your car out of your driveway and knock down the fence accidently.

You have now done what could be the *actus reus* for criminal damage. However, you are not guilty of any criminal offence since at the moment you damaged the fence, you did not have the necessary *mens rea*. The *mens rea* and the *actus reus* were not present at the same time.

Link

Although there is no crime, there may be liability in the tort of negligence; see Chapter 21.

However, there are some circumstances where the courts will view the events as a continuing act. When the *mens rea* and *actus reus* do coincide, the defendant will be guilty. This can be seen in the case of *Fagan v Metropolitan Police Commissioner* (1968).

In *Church* (1965) the court had to decide whether the *actus reus* and *mens rea* were present together. Unlike *Fagan*, where the *actus reus* started before the *mens rea* occurred, the *mens rea* started before the *actus reus* occurred.

Case studies

Fagan v Metropolitan Police Commissioner (1968)

Fagan was told by a police officer to park by the pavement. Fagan drove onto the policeman's foot without realising he had done so. The policeman pointed out what had happened and asked Fagan several times to move the car off his foot. Initially he refused to move his car and swore at the policeman, telling him he could wait. Eventually Fagan did move the car.

The court stated that once Fagan knew the car was on the police officer's foot, he had the required *mens rea* for the offence. As the *actus reus* (the car putting force on the foot) was still continuing, the two elements were then present together so coincided.

R v Church (1965)

The victim mocked the defendant's ability to satisfy her sexually and slapped his face. A fight developed during which he knocked her unconscious. He tried but failed to wake her for 30 mins. He then believed she was dead and threw her body into a river.

Medical evidence revealed that the cause of death was drowning and the victim therefore had been alive when the defendant threw her into the river. This was a series of events and he was convicted of manslaughter.

Extension in these areas can be developed by considering the effect of the following cases/materials.

- A duty based on a special (often familial) relationship – *R v Hood* (2004)
- A duty to avert a danger created (supervening fault) – *DPP v Santa-Bermudez* (2004)
- Victim's self-neglect or suicide (not a *novus actus interveniens* (NAI)) – *R v Wallace* (2018)
- Drugs case: voluntary act of self-injection by victim is an NAI – *R v Kennedy (No 2)* (2007)
- Motive is irrelevant – *R v Steane* (1947)
- D foresees a risk of the relevant element of the *actus reus* and unreasonably takes that risk – *R v G and Another* (2003)
- The presumption against strict liability applies to statutory offences, and can be displaced only by clear wording in the statute or by necessary implication based on the effect of the statute – *R v Lane and Letts* (2018)
- The presumption in favour of *mens rea* stands unless strict liability would encourage observance of the law – *Lim Chin Aik v The Queen* (1963)

Case	Facts	Law/Comment
Latimer (1886)	The defendant aimed a blow with a belt at a man in a pub but struck a woman in the face. He was guilty of a malicious wounding against the woman.	Latimer had not meant to hit her but was found guilty. There was transferred malice.
Mitchell (1983)	The defendant pushed an old man. The man fell back onto an elderly lady who fell and broke her leg.	The *mens rea* directed towards the old man was transferred to the offence against the old woman.
Pembliton (1874)	During a fight, the defendant threw a stone and broke a window, but he had intended it to hit other people.	The intention to hit people could not be transferred to breaking the window as there was a different *mens rea* for the two offences.
Fagan v Metropolitan Police Commissioner (1968)	The defendant drove on to the policeman's foot without realising he had done so. When told about it, he initially refused to move his car.	Once he knew the car was on the police officer's foot, he had the required *mens rea* for the offence. The two elements were then present together.
Church (1965)	The defendant had a fight with a woman and knocked her unconscious; he then threw her body into a river, believing she was dead.	As the *actus reus* and *mens rea* must coincide at some point, the defendant was guilty.

Figure 6.6 Key cases: transferred malice and coincidence of *actus reus* and *mens rea*

Quick questions

1 What is the difference between a conduct crime and a consequence crime?
2 State three situations where an omission can give rise to liability in criminal law; explain each by reference to a decided case.
3 Explain by reference to decided cases the difference between direct and oblique (indirect) intention.
4 Explain the meaning of 'an offence of strict liability'.
5 Explain the 'contemporaneity' rule.

Summary

- Different crimes require different levels of *mens rea*.
- Intention is the highest form of *mens rea*. This can be:
  - direct intent where the defendant's aim, purpose or desire is to bring about the consequence; or
  - oblique where the defendant does not desire the consequence but foresees it as virtually certain.
- Foresight of consequences is not the same as intention, but it is evidence from which a jury may 'find' intention.

- Subjective recklessness requires proof that the defendant knew the risk and still took it.
- Negligence is where the defendant fails to meet the standards of the reasonable man. Gross negligence is so bad that a jury considers it to be a criminal act or omission.
- Strict liability offences require no *mens rea*.
- Transferred malice is where the defendant intends to commit a crime against one person, but inadvertently commits it against another person.
- There must be coincidence of *actus reus* and *mens rea*: this can be through a continuing act.

Chapter 7 Fatal offences against the person

Introduction

Homicide is the unlawful killing of a human being. There are different offences, depending on the *mens rea* of the defendant and whether there is a special defence available to the defendant. These offences and the relationship between them can be seen in Figure 7.1 and will be discussed in this chapter.

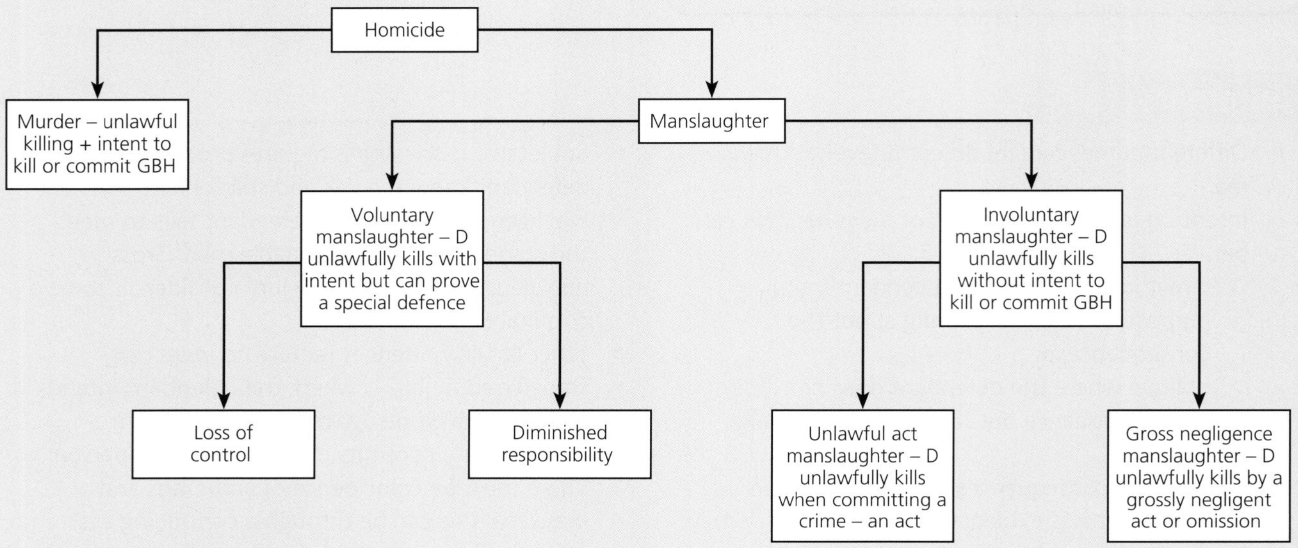

Figure 7.1 Overview of fatal offences against the person

7.1 Murder

7.1.1 Definition of 'murder'

Murder is the most serious of the fatal offences. This is reflected in the sentence for a conviction for murder being mandatory life imprisonment.

Murder is a common law offence – it is not defined by any Act of Parliament. It has been defined by the decisions of judges in different cases, and the accepted definition is based on one given by a seventeenth-century judge, Lord Coke:

> Murder is the unlawful killing of a reasonable person in being and under the King's (or Queen's) Peace with malice aforethought, express or implied.

7.1.2 *Actus reus* of murder

The following have to be proved for the *actus reus* of murder:

- the defendant killed
- a reasonable creature in being
- under the Queen's Peace, and
- the killing was unlawful.

'Killed'

The *actus reus* of killing can be by an act or omission, but it must cause the death of the victim. Usually the *actus reus* is an act, but an omission (a failure to act) can make a person liable for an offence. This was seen in the case of *R v Gibbins and Proctor* (1918), where failure to feed a seven-year-old girl was enough for the *actus reus* of murder.

Link

See Chapter 6, section 6.1.2 for full details of this case.

The defendant cannot be guilty of murder unless their act or omission caused the death. In most cases there is no problem with this. For example, the defendant shoots the victim in the head and the victim is killed instantly.

However, there might be other causes contributing to the death, such as poor medical treatment. This type of situation raises questions of causation, which have been discussed in Chapter 6.1.3, and the cases of *R v Smith* (1959) and *R v Jordan* (1956) relate to the offence of murder.

'Reasonable creature in being'

This phrase means 'a human being'. So, for murder, a person must be killed. Normally, this part of the definition does not cause any difficulties. In *Attorney-General's Reference (No 3 of 1994)* (1997), it was stated by the House of Lords that where the foetus is injured and the child is born alive but dies afterwards as a result of the injuries, this can be the *actus reus* for murder or manslaughter.

A person who is 'brain-dead'

It is not certain whether such a person would be considered as a 'reasonable creature in being' or not. However, doctors are allowed to switch off life-support machines without being liable for murder or manslaughter.

The Law Reform (Year and a Day Rule) Act 1996 sets no time limit on when the death may occur after the unlawful act, although where it is more than three years after the attack, the Attorney-General's consent is needed for the prosecution.

'Queen's Peace'

'Under the Queen's Peace' means that killing an enemy in the course of war is not murder. However, killing a prisoner of war would be sufficient for the *actus reus* of murder.

'Unlawful'

The killing must be unlawful. For example, the killing is *not* unlawful if it is:
- in self-defence
- in defence of another
- in the prevention of crime and the defendant used reasonable force in the circumstances.

7.1.3 *Mens rea* of murder

The *mens rea* for murder is stated as being 'malice aforethought, express or implied'. This means that there are two different intentions, either of which can be used to prove the defendant guilty of murder:
- express malice aforethought – the intention to kill, or
- implied malice aforethought – the intention to cause grievous bodily harm.

A defendant has the *mens rea* for murder if he or she has either of these intentions. This means that a person can be guilty of murder even though they did not intend to kill. This was decided in *R v Vickers* (1957).

Case study

R v Vickers (1957)

Vickers broke into the cellar of a sweet shop. He knew that the old lady who ran the shop was deaf. However, the old lady came into the cellar and saw Vickers. He then hit her several times with his fists and kicked her once in the head. She died as a result of her injuries.

The Court of Appeal upheld Vickers' conviction for murder. It pointed out that where a defendant intends to inflict grievous bodily harm and the victim dies, that has always been sufficient in English law to imply malice aforethought.

The same point was considered by the House of Lords in *R v Cunningham* (1981) when it confirmed that an intention to cause grievous bodily harm was sufficient for the *mens rea* of murder.

The other issue is what is meant by 'grievous bodily harm'. In *DPP v Smith* (1961), the House of Lords decided that 'grievous bodily harm' has the natural meaning of 'really serious harm'. However, even if the judge directed the jury, leaving out the word 'really' and just saying 'serious harm', this was not a misdirection.

Link

Grievous bodily harm is dealt with in more detail in Chapter 8.

The general rules on intention, as discussed in Chapter 6, section 6.2.2, apply to murder.

	Law	Source/Case
Definition	'The unlawful killing of a reasonable person in being and under the King's (or Queen's) Peace, with malice aforethought, express or implied.'	Lord Coke (17th century)
Actus reus	● Must unlawfully kill a person under the Queen's Peace. ● Can be an act or an omission. ● A foetus is not considered a person for the purposes of murder.	*R v Gibbins and Proctor* (1918) *Attorney-General's Reference (No. 3 of 1994)* (1997)
Mens rea	● Intention to kill (express malice aforethought) or intention to cause grievous bodily harm (implied malice aforethought). ● Foresight of consequences is evidence of intention. ● Jury can find intention if death or serious injury was a virtual certainty as a result of the defendant's actions and the defendant appreciated this.	*Vickers* (1957) *Cunningham* (1981) *Moloney* (1985) *Woollin* (1998)

Figure 7.2 Key facts: murder

Activity

In each of the following situations, explain whether the defendant has the required elements to be charged with murder:

1   Jim knows he has a contagious disease that can prove fatal. He goes to visit his ex-wife Lola whom he dislikes intently. He pretends to be trying to reconcile them, and gives her a hug. A few days later, Lola dies from the same contagious disease that Jim suffered from.

2   Raj is annoyed by vandals damaging goods in his yard. He fixes a trip wire just inside the fence, so any intruder will get an electric shock. Wayne breaks into the yard and dies from electrocution when he gets tangled up in the wire.

3   Peta's business has been losing a great deal of money. She decides to arrange for one of her lorries to crash and be destroyed, along with the cargo, by rolling off an unguarded cliff-edge road, so that she can claim insurance on it. Unfortunately, the lorry lands on people walking under the cliff who die.

Extension activity ✓

You can explore these further issues, cases and principles for murder:

● When does life end? – *Re: A (a child)* (2015)
● With malice aforethought (intention to kill or cause GBH) – *R v Cunningham* (1982)
● 'Malice' does not mean ill-will or malevolence – *R v Inglis* (2011)
● Intention to cause GBH – *DPP v Smith* (1961)

7.2 Voluntary manslaughter

Voluntary manslaughter arises where the defendant appears to satisfy the *actus reus* and *mens rea* of murder. However, there are two special defences to a charge of murder which reduce murder to manslaughter. These are where the killing occurs when the defendant suffers from:

● Loss of control – set out in s 54 of the Coroners and Justice Act 2009.
● Diminished responsibility – set out in s 2 of the Homicide Act 1957 as amended by s 52 of the Coroners and Justice Act 2009.

These defences are available only to murder.

They are also only partial defences. This means that the defendant is not completely acquitted. Instead, when one of these defences is successful, the offence of murder is reduced to manslaughter. This type of manslaughter is known as voluntary manslaughter because the defendant had the necessary *mens rea* for murder.

This verdict of manslaughter instead of murder is important because it means that the judge has discretion in passing sentence. When a person is found guilty of murder, there is a mandatory life sentence. However, for manslaughter the judge can give a lesser sentence where suitable.

Key term

Voluntary manslaughter – the verdict when the defendant has a partial defence to murder, where the killing was carried out when the defendant was suffering from loss of control or diminished responsibility.

7.2.1 Defence of loss of control

The law on loss of control is set out in s 54 of the Coroners and Justice Act 2009. Section 54(1) states:

> Where the defendant kills or is a party to the killing of another, the defendant is not to be convicted of murder if:
>
> (a) the defendant's acts and omissions in doing or being a party to the killing resulted from the defendant's loss of self-control,
>
> (b) the loss of self-control had a qualifying trigger, and
>
> (c) a person of the defendant's sex and age, with a normal degree of tolerance and self-restraint and in the circumstances of the defendant, might have reacted in the same or in a similar way to the defendant.

So, the following points must be proved for the defence to be successful:

1 The defendant must have lost self-control.
2 There must be a qualifying trigger.
3 A person of the same sex and age would have reacted in the same way as the defendant in the same circumstances.

Key term

Loss of control – a partial defence to a charge of murder which reduces the offence to one of manslaughter under s 54(1) of the Coroners and Justice Act 2009.

Defendant must have lost self-control

Section 54(2) of the 2009 Act sets out that the defendant's loss of self-control does not have to be sudden.

Whether the defendant lost self-control will be a matter for the jury to decide and will have to be a total loss of self-control – a partial loss will not be sufficient. The jury is entitled to draw upon their life experiences when considering the evidence to decide if this requirement is satisfied.

Temper, anger or a reaction out of character, or even acting spectacularly out of character, are not sufficient. The defendant must have really 'lost it', or 'snapped'. In *R v Jewell* (2014), the fact that the defendant was unwell, sleeping badly, tired, depressed and unable to think straight was not enough to prove that there was loss of control.

Where the defendant has the normal capacity of self-restraint and tolerance then, unless the circumstances were extremely grave, any normal irritation or even serious anger will not come within 'loss of control' for the Act's purposes.

Case study

R v Jewell (2014)

The defendant shot the victim at point blank range with a shotgun and fled in his car. When he was arrested, his car was found to contain a survival kit including a tent, clothes, passport etc., as well as weapons and ammunition. He stated that when he got out of his car at the victim's house:

'I did it because I lost control. I could not control my actions. I could not think straight. My head was fucked up. It was like an injection in the head, an explosion in my head.'

There was insufficient evidence of the defendant having lost his self-control.

If this first component is not met, there is no need to consider the other components.

Qualifying trigger

Section 55 sets out the qualifying triggers for loss of control:

- The defendant's fear of serious violence from the victim against the defendant or another identified person (s 55(3)), or
- A thing or things done or said (or both) which
  (a) constituted circumstances of an extremely grave character, and
  (b) caused the defendant to have a justifiable sense of being seriously wronged (s 55(4)).

Alternatively, the qualifying trigger can be a combination of these two matters (s 55(5)).

Fear of violence

The defendant does not have to fear violence by the victim. Fear of violence on another person, who must be identified, can amount to a qualifying trigger. This was illustrated in *R v Ward* (2012).

Case study

R v Ward (2012)

The defendant successfully pleaded loss of control after killing the victim, who had physically attacked the defendant's brother at a house party. The defendant and his brother went outside to wait for a taxi, but it was delayed and it was very cold so they tried to get back in. They were refused re-entry and the defendant's brother was head butted by the victim. The defendant then hit the victim with a pick axe handle, the injuries from which caused his death.

It cannot be a general fear of violence; however, under s 55(6)(a) where the defendant has incited the violence, he or she cannot rely on the qualifying trigger of fear of violence. This was emphasised in *R v Dawes* (2013).

Case study

R v Dawes (2013)

The defendant had returned home to find his wife and the victim asleep on the sofa with their legs entwined. There was an altercation and he stabbed and killed the victim.

He could not rely on fear of violence where he had induced that violence.

Things said or done

This is the anger trigger. It is an objective test. Therefore the jury decides whether a reasonable person would lose control.

The question of whether the circumstances are *extremely grave* and whether the defendant had a justifiable sense of being *seriously wronged* should be judged objectively, and not as a matter of opinion, as in the cases of *R v Zebedee* (2012) and *R v Bowyer* (2013).

Case studies

R v Zebedee (2012)

The defendant lost control when his 94-year-old father, who suffered from Alzheimer's and was doubly incontinent, repeatedly soiled himself. He killed his father. He put forward the defence of loss of control.

The appeal court ruled that neither condition was present in this case. He was convicted of murder.

R v Bowyer (2013)

The defendant and the victim were both having a relationship with the same prostitute. The victim was also her pimp. The defendant was not aware she was a prostitute. The defendant and the victim knew about the other's relationship with the woman. The defendant went to the victim's house to burgle him, but the victim disturbed him and a fight developed.

The victim told the defendant that the woman was a prostitute and taunted him by saying that she was his best earner.

The defendant lost his control, beat the victim and tied him up. He was left alive but was found dead the following afternoon.

The defendant had no justifiable sense of being wronged as he was committing a burglary. The court concluded that the victim was entitled to say and do anything reasonable, including using force, to eject a burglar from his home and that this did not give the defendant any justifiable sense of being wronged, let alone seriously wronged.

Excluded matters

The 2009 Act specifically states that sexual infidelity can never be a qualifying trigger for the defence of loss of control.

The Court of Appeal made this point in *R v Clinton* (2012) and in *R v Dawes* (2013). However, sexual infidelity could be considered if it was integral to and formed an essential part of the context where there were other factors which could be qualifying triggers.

Case study

R v Clinton (2012)

Both the defendant and his wife suffered from depression and required medication. He lost control due to a number of factors and killed his wife as previously she had told him she was having sexual relations with many men, taunted him about suicide websites that he had recently visited and told him she no longer wanted their children. Here, the defence of loss of control should be decided by the jury.

The defence also cannot be allowed if the defendant acted in a 'considered desire for revenge'.

Normal standards of self-control

The defendant is expected to show a normal degree of tolerance and self-control. Being hot-tempered cannot be taken into account when looking at the level of self-control expected.

Although the Act refers to the accused's circumstances, s 54(3) emphasises that general circumstances which might affect the defendant's tolerance or self-restraint are not to be considered. There is an objective test for this part of the defence and, apart from sex and age, the jury cannot consider any circumstance of the defendant which might have made him have less self-control.

Circumstances of the defendant

Although only age and sex can be considered in deciding the level of self-control expected from the defendant, other circumstances may be taken into consideration such as mental illness and a history of sexual abuse.

In *R v Rejmanski* (2017), the court confirmed that a mental disorder may be a relevant circumstance of the defendant but cannot be relevant to the question of the normal degree of tolerance and self-restraint exercised.

Case study

R v Rejmanski (2017)

The defendant's defence was that he suffered from PTSD as a result of his army service in Afghanistan, and that the deceased had provoked him with negative comments about his role in the army.

The court stated that, while in principle a disorder such as PTSD may be a relevant circumstance, there was insufficient evidence of that being the case here. Additionally, it was specifically excluded from being a part of the description of a hypothetical 'normal person', but the judge was correct to direct the jury to consider the defendant's army experiences when looking at the qualifying trigger.

Voluntary intoxication and the defendant's circumstances

In *R v Asmelash* (2013), the court refused to allow voluntary intoxication to be considered for either loss of control or diminished responsibility.

However, if a sober person in the defendant's circumstances, with normal levels of tolerance and self-restraint, might have behaved in the same way when confronted by the relevant qualifying trigger, then the defendant might still be able to use the defence of loss of control, even though they were intoxicated.

If a defendant with a severe problem with alcohol or drugs was mercilessly taunted about this problem so that it was a qualifying trigger, the alcohol or drug problem would then form part of the circumstances for consideration.

The jury then has to consider whether the 'normal person' in the circumstances of the defendant would have reacted as the defendant did. The defence will fail if the jury considers that a normal person might have lost control but would not have reacted in the same way.

Sufficient evidence

The Coroners and Justice Act 2009 has given the trial judge the task of deciding if there is sufficient evidence of each of the three components to leave the defence of loss of control to the jury.

Section 54(5) and (6) of the Coroners and Justice Act 2009 states that if sufficient evidence is adduced to raise an issue with respect to the defence of loss of control, the jury must assume that the defence is satisfied unless the prosecution proves beyond reasonable doubt that it is not.

This was considered in *R v Christian* (2018).

Case study

R v Christian (2018)

The defendant fatally stabbed the two victims during an altercation in their shared living accommodation about the temperature of the water in the communal shower. The judge ruled that loss of control should not be left to the jury in this case as, although there was evidence of both a loss of control and a qualifying trigger, the defendant's reaction was so extreme and so protracted that no jury could conclude that the notional reasonable person might have reacted or behaved in the same or a similar way.

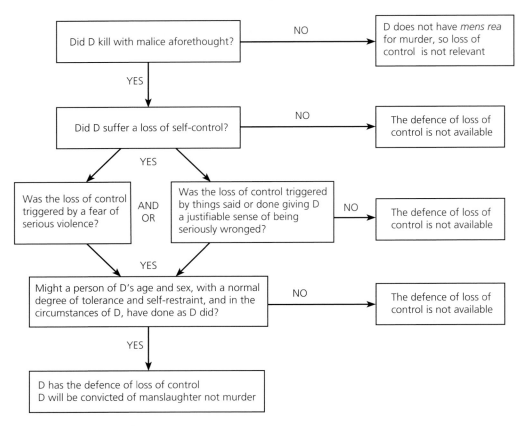

Figure 7.3 Loss of control

	Law
Main points of defence	D must have lost self-control. There must be a qualifying trigger. A person of the same sex and age would have reacted in the same way as D in the same circumstances.
Loss of control	This need not be sudden.
Qualifying triggers	Either or both of the following: ● fear of serious violence ● a thing or things done or said which constituted circumstances of an extremely grave character and caused D to have a justifiable sense of being seriously wronged.
Standard of self-control	That of a person of D's sex and age, with a normal degree of tolerance and self-restraint.
Circumstances of D	Circumstances of D (which do not have a bearing on capacity for self-control) can be taken into consideration in deciding whether a normal person might have reacted in the same way.
Effect of defence	Reduces charge of murder to manslaughter.

Figure 7.4 Key facts on loss of control

7.2.2 Defence of diminished responsibility

The diminished responsibility defence was introduced by the Homicide Act 1957.

The defence is set out in s 2(1) of the Homicide Act as amended by s 52 of the Coroners and Justice Act 2009. The effect of this section is that:

A person who kills or is a party to the killing of another is not to be convicted of murder if he or she was suffering from an abnormality of mental functioning which:

(a) arose from a recognised medical condition,

(b) substantially impaired the defendant's ability to:
- understand the nature of his conduct; or
- form a rational judgment; or
- exercise self-control and

(c) provides an explanation for the defendant's acts and omissions in doing or being a party to the killing.

The burden of proving the defence is on the defendant, but the defendant need only prove it on the balance of probabilities.

Key term

Diminished responsibility – a partial defence to a charge of murder which reduces the offence to one of voluntary manslaughter.

There is, therefore, a four-stage test, of which all four elements must be proved:

1. Whether the defendant was suffering from an abnormality of mental functioning.
2. If so, whether it had arisen from a recognised medical condition.
3. If so, whether it had substantially impaired their ability either to understand the nature of their conduct or to form a rational judgement or to exercise self-control (or any combination).
4. If so, whether it provided an explanation for their conduct.

Abnormality of mental functioning

What is meant by 'abnormality of mental functioning'? In *R v Byrne* (1960), the Court of Appeal described this as 'a state of mind so different from that of ordinary human beings that the reasonable man would term it abnormal'.

Case study

R v Byrne (1960)

The defendant was a sexual psychopath who strangled a young woman and then mutilated her body. The medical evidence was that, because of his condition, he was unable to control his perverted desires. He was convicted of murder but the Court of Appeal quashed the conviction and substituted a conviction for manslaughter.

Although this case was on the old definition of 'abnormality of mind', amended by s 52 of the Coroners and Justice Act 2009, the courts still use the same standard of abnormality. Examples of medical conditions in cases before the 2009 Act include: *R v Gittens* (1984) (depressions), *R v Ahluwalia* (1992) (Battered Spouse Syndrome), *R v Campbell* (1987) (epilepsy). These conditions will still be regarded as recognised medical conditions under the 2009 Act.

Recognised medical condition

The phrase 'recognised medical condition' as a cause of the abnormality of mental functioning was introduced into s 2 of the 1957 Homicide Act by the 2009 Act.

- In *R v Conroy* (2017), all four psychiatrists and the Court of Appeal agreed that Autism Spectrum Disorder is a 'recognised medical condition'.
- In *R v Squelch* (2017), all three psychiatrists and the Court of Appeal agreed that paranoid personality disorder was a 'recognised medical condition' for the purposes of s 2.

Thus 'recognised medical condition' is wide enough to cover:
- psychological and physical conditions
- any recognised mental disorder

- any physical condition which affects mental functioning such as epilepsy, sleep disorders or diabetes.

The defence must produce medical evidence of a recognised medical condition in the trial.

Substantially impaired

The abnormality of mental functioning must substantially impair the defendant's mental responsibility for his acts or omissions in doing or being a party to the killing.

- In *R v Byrne* (1960), the appeal court said that the question of whether the impairment was substantial was one of degree and that it was for the jury to decide.
- In *R v Lloyd* (1967), it was held that substantial does not mean total, nor does it mean trivial or minimal. It is something in between and it is for the jury to decide if the defendant's mental responsibility is impaired and, if so, whether it is substantially impaired. However, as it is a question of fact, the judge can withdraw the point from the jury if there is not sufficient evidence.

These two cases were decided on the law before it was amended in 2009. In *R v Golds* (2016), the Supreme Court pointed out that there is no indication in the 2009 Act that Parliament wished the words to carry a different meaning; the old law is still relevant.

Case study

R v Golds (2016)

The defendant killed his partner. He admitted the killing. The medical evidence was that he had an abnormality of mental functioning arising from a medical condition. The only issue was whether he was in a psychotic state at the time of the killing.

It was decided that the judge must direct that, while an impairment must be more than merely trivial to be substantial, it is not the case that any impairment that is more than trivial will suffice.

What must be substantially impaired?

Section 2(1A) of the Homicide Act 1957 sets out that the defendant's ability to do one of three things must be substantially impaired:

- to understand the nature of his conduct

- to form a rational judgement
- to exercise self-control.

The amendments made by the Coroners and Justice Act 2009 have effectively put the decision in *Byrne* into statutory form:

- **Ability to understand the nature of his conduct**: this covers situations such as where the defendant is in an automatic state, does not know what he or she is doing or suffers from delusions. It also covers people with severe learning difficulties.
- **Ability to form a rational judgement**: the concept of rational judgement was introduced by the 2009 Act but is not defined there. Those suffering from paranoia, schizophrenia or Battered Spouse Syndrome may well not be able to form a rational judgement. The jury may consider all relevant circumstances before or after the killing.
- **Ability to exercise self-control**: this was the situation in *R v Byrne* (1960). Byrne was a sexual psychopath, and this condition meant he was unable to control his perverted desires. The defence of diminished responsibility was therefore available to him.

Provides an explanation for the defendant's conduct

The defendant has to prove that the abnormality of mental functioning provides an explanation for his acts and omissions in doing or being a party to the killing.

This is a new principle of diminished responsibility, introduced by the amendments made by the Coroners and Justice Act 2009. There must now be some causal connection between the defendant's abnormality of mental functioning and the killing.

The abnormality of mental functioning does not have to be the only factor which caused the defendant to do or be involved in the killing. However, it must be a significant factor. This is particularly important where the defendant is intoxicated at the time of the killing.

7.2.3 Diminished responsibility and intoxication

1 There is a clear rule that intoxication alone cannot support a defence of diminished responsibility, as shown by the case of *R v Dowds* (2012).

Case study

R v Dowds (2012)

The defendant and his girlfriend, the victim, were heavy binge-drinkers. In a drunken state, he stabbed her sixty times, killing her. He was convicted of murder. He appealed on the ground that his state of 'acute intoxication' should have been left to the jury as providing a possible defence of diminished responsibility.

His appeal was rejected and his conviction for murder upheld on the basis that voluntary acute intoxication is not capable of founding the defence of diminished responsibility.

2   There are difficulties in cases where the defendant has some pre-existing abnormality of mental functioning but, in addition, is intoxicated at the time he does the killing. This occurred in *R v Dietschmann* (2003).

Case study

R v Dietschmann (2003)

The defendant felt that the victim was disrespecting the memory of the defendant's aunt who had just died. He killed the victim by repeatedly kicking him and stamping on him. The defendant had drunk about a third of a bottle of whisky, and two and a half pints of cider before the killing.

Psychiatrists called by the prosecution and the defence agreed that the defendant was suffering from an adjustment disorder in the form of depressed grief reaction to the death of his aunt. However, they disagreed on whether this had substantially impaired his mental responsibility for the killing. He was convicted and appealed.

It was decided that if the defendant satisfied the jury that his abnormality of mind substantially impaired his mental responsibility for his acts in doing the killing, then even though he was intoxicated, the jury should not find him guilty of murder but, instead, guilty of manslaughter.

This can also be seen in the case of *R v Kay* (2017).

Case study

R v Kay (2017)

The defendant had a long history of alcohol and drug abuse, and was a diagnosed paranoid schizophrenic. During a three-day bender and in the grip of a psychotic episode where he believed he was Satan, he stabbed the victim, a complete stranger, to death in a frenzied and brutal attack. He relied on diminished responsibility as, at the time of the stabbing, he had been suffering from an abnormality of mental functioning which arose from a recognised medical condition – schizophrenia. The partial defence was only possible if the condition was so severe that it would have impaired responsibility without intoxication.

The court stated:

> In our view, it (the defence of diminished responsibility) rightly does not necessarily provide even a partial defence to everyone diagnosed with schizophrenia, who, well aware of the possible consequences, chooses to abuse drink and or drugs to excess and then kills.

3   There is a recognised medical condition called alcohol dependency syndrome (ADS). This means that the person cannot control their drinking. Under the old law, in *R v Tandy* (1989), where the defendant is unable to resist drinking so that it is involuntary, this could amount to diminished responsibility.

Case study

R v Tandy (1989)

Mrs Tandy had been an alcoholic for a number of years, usually drinking wine. One day, she drank nearly a whole bottle of vodka. That evening she told her mother that her (Tandy's) second husband had sexually abused her 11-year-old daughter. She then strangled her daughter.

The trial judge told the jury to decide whether Tandy was suffering from an abnormality of mind as a direct result of her alcoholism or whether she was just drunk. She was convicted. The court dismissed her appeal because she had not shown that her brain had been injured (a test under the old law) or that her drinking was involuntary.

The decision in this case was criticised as it only looked at whether the defendant was unable to prevent themselves from drinking. It did not consider whether alcoholism is a disease.

4   The point was considered again in *R v Wood* (2008) when the court pointed out that the 'sharp effect of the distinction drawn in *Tandy* between cases where brain damage has occurred as a result of ADS and those where it has not, is no longer appropriate'.

Case study

R v Wood (2008)

The defendant, after drinking heavily, had gone to the victim's flat and fell asleep. He was woken by the victim trying to perform oral sex on him. The defendant repeatedly hit the victim with a meat cleaver, killing him. At the trial, medical experts agreed that the defendant was suffering from ADS, but disagreed as to whether this had damaged his brain.

The judge directed the jury that the defendant could only use the defence of diminished responsibility if his drinking was involuntary. The defendant was convicted but successfully appealed as the judge's direction of the jury was wrong.

5   The issue was considered again in *R v Stewart* (2009) when the Court of Appeal set out a three-stage test for juries in such cases to consider:

   a) Was the defendant suffering from an 'abnormality of mind' (now mental functioning)? They pointed out that the mere fact that the defendant has ADS would not automatically amount to an abnormality. The nature and the extent of the ADS had to be considered.

   b) If so, was the defendant's abnormality caused by the ADS?

   c) If so, was the defendant's mental responsibility substantially impaired? To decide this, all the evidence, including the medical evidence, should be considered. This would involve such matters as the extent and seriousness of his dependency and the extent to which he could control his drinking.

Look online

Look at the case of *R v Stewart* (2009) and summarise the facts and arguments made in the judgment which can be found at https://www.bailii.org/ew/cases/EWCA/Crim/2009/593.html

Although these cases were decided before the change in the definition of diminished responsibility, it is likely that the same approach will be taken. In addition, under the new law, the jury must also decide whether the abnormality caused, or was a significant factor in causing, the defendant to kill the victim.

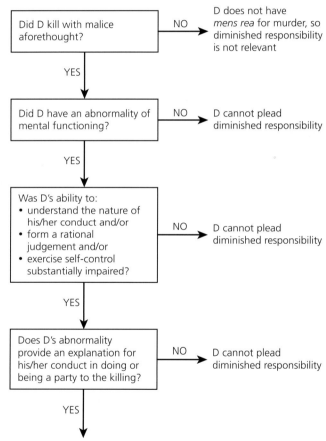

Figure 7.5 Diminished responsibility

	Law	Act/Case

Definition	Suffering from an abnormality of mental functioning which:
	● arose from a recognised medical condition
	● substantially impaired D's ability to do one or more of the following:
	  ○ understand the nature of the conduct
	  ○ form a rational judgement
	  ○ exercise self-control, and
	● provide an explanation for D's conduct.
		s 2(1) of the Homicide Act 1957 (as amended by the Coroners and Justice Act 2009)

Abnormality of mental functioning	A state of mind so different from that of ordinary human beings that the reasonable man would term it abnormal.	Byrne (1960)
Substantially impaired	A question of degree for the jury to decide. 'Substantial' does not mean 'total' nor 'trivial' or 'minimal' but something in between.	Byrne (1960) Golds (2016)
Provides an explanation for D's conduct	The abnormality of mental functioning provides an explanation for D's conduct if it causes, or is a significant contributory factor in causing, D to carry out that conduct.	s 2(1B) of the Homicide Act 1957
Effect of intoxication	● Transient effect of drink or drugs on brain cannot found the defence of diminished responsibility. ● Where the defendant has a pre-existing mental disorder, intoxication does not prevent him using the defence; the abnormality of mental functioning does not have to be the sole cause of the defendant doing the killing. ● Alcohol Dependency Syndrome can be an abnormality of mental functioning.	Dowds (2012) Dietschmann (2003) Wood (2008)
Burden of proof	It is for the defence to prove on the balance of probabilities.	s 2(2) of the Homicide Act 1957
Effect of defence	The charge of murder is reduced to manslaughter.	s 2(3) of the Homicide Act 1957

Figure 7.6 Key facts chart on diminished responsibility

Extension activity

You can explore further issues, cases and principles for diminished responsibility:

● Cases of examples of mental functioning for diminished responsibility – *R v Jama* (2004); *R v Wilcocks* (2016); *R v Gittens* (1984); *R v Seers* (1984); *R v Ahluawalia* (1993); *R v Wood* (2008); *R v Stewart* (2009); *R v Simcox* (1964); *R v Campbell* (1997); *R v Smith* (1982); *R v Reynolds* (1988); *R v Moyle* (2008); *R v Erskine* (2009); *R v Bunch* (2013); *R v Brennan* (2014).

7.3 Involuntary manslaughter

Involuntary manslaughter is an unlawful killing where the defendant does not have the intention, either direct or oblique, to kill or to cause grievous bodily harm.

7.3.1 Unlawful act manslaughter

Here the defendant has done a dangerous unlawful act (a crime) which caused the death. This makes the defendant liable even though they did not realise that death or injury might occur.

The elements of unlawful act manslaughter are:

- The defendant must do an unlawful act (the *actus reus*).
- That act must be dangerous on an objective test.
- The act must cause the death.
- The defendant must have the required *mens rea* for the unlawful act.

Unlawful act

The death must be caused by an unlawful act, which must be a *criminal* offence. A *civil* wrong (tort) is not enough. There must be a criminal unlawful act as in *R v Lamb* (1967).

Case study

R v Lamb (1967)

Lamb and his friend were fooling around with a revolver. They both knew that it was loaded with two bullets in a five-chamber cylinder but thought that it would not fire unless one of the bullets was opposite the barrel. They knew that there was no bullet in this position, but did not realise that the cylinder turned so that a bullet from the next chamber along would be fired. Lamb pointed the gun at his friend and pulled the trigger, killing him.

It was held that the defendant had not done an unlawful act. The pointing of the gun at the friend was not an assault as the friend did not fear any violence from Lamb.

There must be an act. An omission cannot create liability for unlawful act manslaughter. This was shown by the case of *R v Lowe* (1973).

Case study

R v Lowe (1973)

The defendant was convicted of wilfully neglecting his baby son and of his manslaughter. The trial judge had directed the jury that if they found the defendant guilty of wilful neglect he was also guilty of manslaughter.

The Court of Appeal quashed the conviction for manslaughter because a finding of wilful neglect involved a failure to act, and this could not support a conviction for unlawful act manslaughter.

In many cases the unlawful act will be some kind of non-fatal offence, but any criminal offence can form the unlawful act if it involves a dangerous act likely to cause injury. Examples of the offences which have led to a finding of unlawful act manslaughter include:

- arson – *R v Goodfellow* (1986)
- criminal damage – *DPP v Newbury and Jones* (1976)
- burglary – *R v Watson* (1989).

Dangerous act

The unlawful act must be dangerous on an objective test. In *R v Church* (1965), it was held that it must be:

> such as all sober and reasonable people would inevitably recognise must subject the other person to, at least, the risk of some harm resulting therefrom, albeit not serious harm.

The risk need only be of 'some harm'. The harm need not be serious. If a sober and reasonable person realises that the unlawful act might cause some injury, then this part of the test for unlawful act manslaughter is satisfied. It does not matter that the defendant did not realise there was any risk of harm to another person.

The case of *R v Larkin* (1943) illustrates both these requirements.

Case study

R v Larkin (1943)

The defendant threatened another man with an open cut-throat razor, in order to frighten him. The mistress of the other man tried to intervene and, because she was drunk, accidentally fell onto the open blade which cut her throat and killed her. On appeal, his conviction for manslaughter was upheld because:

- The act of threatening the other man with the razor was a technical assault.
- It was also an act which was dangerous because it was likely to injure someone.

Link

This is also shown by the case of *R v Mitchell* (1983), discussed in section 6.2.6.

The act need not be aimed at the victim. This was the situation in *Larkin* where the assault was against the man but the woman died.

Some harm

It is enough that the sober and reasonable person would foresee some harm, not the actual harm that was done. This was stated in *R v JM and SM* (2012).

Case study

R v JM and SM (2012)

JM lit a cigarette inside a nightclub and was asked to leave. After some pushing, both JM and his brother SM left. Later they both returned and kicked a fire door. This led to a fight between the brothers and doormen. During the fight, the victim, one of the doormen, collapsed and died shortly afterwards of loss of blood: his renal artery had ruptured.

The court stated that it has never been a requirement that the defendant should foresee any specific harm, or that the reasonable bystander should recognise the precise form which occurred. The test is whether reasonable and sober people would recognise that the unlawful activities of the defendant subjected the deceased to the risk of some physical harm.

Act against property

The unlawful act need not be aimed at a person; it can be aimed at property. This was illustrated by *R v Goodfellow* (1986).

Case study

R v Goodfellow (1986)

The defendant set fire to his council flat so that the council would have to rehouse him. The fire got out of control and his wife, son and another woman died in the fire. He was convicted of manslaughter and appealed. His conviction was upheld because all the elements of unlawful act manslaughter were present.

The facts of *Goodfellow* show the elements of unlawful act manslaughter. These were:
- The defendant does an unlawful act – arson is an offence under the Criminal Damage Act 1971.
- Arson is dangerous – a reasonable person would recognise that it might cause some harm to another person, there was an obvious risk that someone in the flat might be hurt.
- The unlawful act caused the death.

- The act was committed intentionally – Goodfellow intended to set the flat on fire.

Physical harm

The 'risk of harm' refers to physical harm. Something which causes fear and apprehension is not sufficient.
- In *R v Dawson* (1985), convictions for manslaughter were quashed although a petrol station attendant died from a heart attack during an attempted robbery.
- However, where a reasonable person would be aware of the victim's frailty and the risk of physical harm to him, then the defendant will be liable. This was stated in *R v Watson* (1989), when an elderly man died of a heart attack ninety minutes after being physically abused in an attempted burglary of his home.
- Burglary can become a 'dangerous' act if the victim's condition was apparent to the reasonable person, or the circumstances of the act make it dangerous. This happened in *R v Bristow, Dunn and Delay* (2013), where the owner of a car repair business in remote farm buildings tried to stop the defendants and was run over and killed by them as they were escaping after a burglary.

Causing the death

The unlawful act must cause the death. The rules on causation are the same as for murder that has been considered in Chapter 6.

An important point is that if there is an intervening act which breaks the chain of causation, then the defendant cannot be liable for manslaughter.

Cases where 'death results from the unlawful supply of drugs'

If a person supplies drugs or materials to administer a drug to someone else, who then administers the drug to himself and dies, this is not an unlawful act. This is the case even where a person performs preparatory acts, such as applying a tourniquet or preparing a syringe for injection.

This is because the criminal law assumes a person's free will. Subject to certain exceptions, informed adults of sound mind are treated as able to make their own decisions on how to act. This can be seen in *R v Kennedy* (2007).

R v Kennedy (2007)

The defendant and victim were living together in a hostel. The victim asked the defendant for 'a bit to make him sleep'. The defendant prepared a dose of heroin for the victim, then passed him the syringe so that he could inject himself. The victim did so, and died several hours later as a result of choking on his own vomit while under the influence of the drug.

As the victim was a fully informed and consenting adult, who had freely and voluntarily self-administered the drug without any pressure from the defendant, this was an intervening act and the defendant was not liable for manslaughter.

It is possible that in situations where the defendant has supplied the victim with drugs, the defendant could be liable for gross negligence manslaughter set out below.

Mens rea

It must be proved that the defendant had the *mens rea* for the unlawful act. It is not necessary for the defendant to realise that the act is unlawful or dangerous, as in the case of *DPP v Newbury and Jones* (1976).

DPP v Newbury and Jones (1976)

Two teenage boys pushed a paving stone from a bridge onto a railway line as a train was approaching. The stone hit the train and killed the guard. They were convicted of manslaughter.

The House of Lords confirmed it was not necessary to prove that the defendant foresaw any harm from his act. So, a defendant can be convicted provided that:

- the unlawful act was dangerous
- the defendant had the necessary *mens rea* for that act.

Case	Facts	Law
Lamb (1967)	Defendant fired gun at a friend. Both thought it was safe because there was no bullet in the firing chamber.	There must be an unlawful act. In this case there was no assault as the friend did not fear violence.
Lowe (1973)	Failed to care properly for baby.	There has to be an act – unlawful act manslaughter cannot be committed by an omission.
Larkin (1943)	Threatened a man with a razor – a woman fell on blade and died.	The unlawful act need not be aimed at the victim but it must be objectively dangerous in the sense that it is likely to cause harm.
Goodfellow (1986)	Set fire to flat, causing three deaths.	The unlawful act can be aimed at property. The test is whether it is objectively dangerous in the sense that it is likely to cause harm.
Dawson (1985)	Petrol station attendant died of a heart attack when his petrol station was robbed.	Causing fear is not enough. The unlawful act must put the victim at risk of physical harm.
Newbury and Jones (1976)	Pushed a paving stone onto a passing train, killing the guard.	Defendant need only have the intention to do the unlawful act, and does not have to foresee that it might cause some harm.

Figure 7.7 Key cases: unlawful act manslaughter

7.3.2 Gross negligence manslaughter

In a successful claim for negligence, in civil law, the person who caused the injury or damage is only liable if:

- they owe the claimant a duty of care, and
- they breached this duty, and
- the breach caused reasonably foreseeable injury or damage.

Whether a duty of care is owed in negligence comes from the three-stage test of *Caparo v Dickman* (1990), as clarified by *Robinson v Chief Constable of West Yorkshire* (2018) and *Poole BC v GN* (2019). (This is dealt with in Chapter 21.)

Gross negligence manslaughter is committed where the defendant owes the victim a duty of care but breaches that duty in a way that is so criminal it is negligent, causing the death of the victim.

- It can be committed by an act or an omission, neither of which has to be unlawful.
- This offence might be considered in many circumstances, but typically involves death following medical treatment or care, death in the workplace or death in custody.

The leading case on gross negligence manslaughter is *R v Adomako* (1994).

Case study

R v Adomako (1994)

The defendant was an anaesthetist. During an operation, one of the tubes supplying oxygen to the patient became disconnected. The defendant failed to notice this until some minutes later when the patient suffered a heart attack caused by the lack of oxygen. The patient suffered brain damage and died six months later as a result.

Doctors giving evidence in the trial said that a competent anaesthetist would have noticed the disconnection of the tube within 15 seconds and that the defendant's failure to react was 'abysmal'. The trial judge directed the jury on gross negligence manslaughter and they convicted. The conviction was upheld by the House of Lords.

Key term

Gross negligence manslaughter – a form of involuntary manslaughter where the defendant is grossly negligent in breach of a duty of care towards the victim, and this results in the victim's death.

From *Adomako* (1994) it can be seen that the elements of gross negligence manslaughter are:

- the existence of a duty of care by the defendant towards the victim
- a breach of that duty of care which causes death
- gross negligence which the jury considers to be so bad as to be criminal.

The tests were restated in the case of *R v Broughton* (2020):

> … six elements have been identified that the prosecution must prove before a defendant can be convicted of gross negligence manslaughter:
>
> i) The defendant owed an existing duty of care to the victim.
>
> ii) The defendant negligently breached that duty of care.
>
> iii) At the time of the breach there was a serious and obvious risk of death. Serious, in this context, qualifies the nature of the risk of death as something much more than minimal or remote. Risk of injury or illness, even serious injury or illness, is not enough. An obvious risk is one that is present, clear, and unambiguous. It is immediately apparent, striking and glaring rather than something that might become apparent on further investigation.
>
> iv) It was reasonably foreseeable at the time of the breach of the duty that the breach gave rise to a serious and obvious risk of death.
>
> v) The breach of the duty caused or made a significant (i.e. more than minimal) contribution to the death of the victim.
>
> vi) In the view of the jury, the circumstances of the breach were truly exceptionally bad and so reprehensible as to justify the conclusion that it amounted to gross negligence and required criminal sanction.

Case study

R v Broughton (2020)

At a music festival, the defendant supplied the drugs which his girlfriend had a bad reaction to. He remained with her as her condition deteriorated to the point where her life was obviously in danger. He was charged with being grossly negligent in failing to obtain medical assistance, which was a substantial cause of her death.

His conviction was quashed as the evidence could not prove causation – that she would have lived if he had called for help. This is the criminal standard of proof.

Drugs were supplied at a music festival, in *Broughton*

Case studies

R v Singh (1999)

The defendant was the landlord of property in which a faulty gas fire caused the deaths of tenants. It was recognised that there was a duty on the defendant to manage and maintain property properly.

R v Litchfield (1997)

The defendant was the owner and master of a sailing ship. He sailed, knowing that the engines might fail because of contamination to the fuel. The ship was blown onto rocks and three crew members died. It was held that the defendant owed a duty to the crew.

In these cases there was a contractual duty of care. However, there does not need to be a contractual duty. Other situations can lead to a duty of care, as shown by the case of *R v Khan and Khan* (1998), where the defendants had supplied heroin to the victim and then left her alone. She died. The defendants' conviction for unlawful act manslaughter was quashed but the Court

of Appeal stated, *obiter*, that duty situations could be extended to this type of area. A similar situation occurred in *R v Dias* (2002).

An actual extension of the type of duty recognised by the courts occurred in *R v Wacker* (2002).

Case study

R v Wacker (2002)

The defendant brought 60 illegal immigrants into England. They were put in the back of his lorry for a cross-Channel ferry crossing. The only air into the lorry was through a small vent and it was agreed that it should be closed at certain times to prevent the immigrants from being discovered. The defendant closed the vent before boarding the ferry. The crossing took an hour longer than usual and at Dover the Customs officers found that 58 of the immigrants were dead. The defendant's conviction for manslaughter was upheld by the Court of Appeal, who stated that the defendant knew that the safety of the immigrants depended on his own actions in relation to the vent, and he clearly assumed the duty of care.

In *Wacker* the victims were parties to an illegal act. In the civil law of negligence this would have meant that the victims (or their dependants) could not have made a claim against the defendant. However, for the criminal law, it was irrelevant that the victims were parties to an illegal act. This can be seen again in *R v Broughton* (2020).

Whether a duty is owed depends on the facts of each case:

- In *R v Kuddus* (2019), a restaurant owner could only owe a duty about allergies (in this case peanut allergy) of the customer that he actually knew about. Kuddus did not know of it so was acquitted.
- In *R v Zaman* (2017), the restaurant owner *did* know about it and was convicted.

The defendant has created a dangerous situation

A duty of care can exist where the defendant has created a state of affairs, which he or she knows or ought reasonably to know, has become life-threatening. This was seen in the case of *R v Evans* (2009): see Chapter 6, section 6.1.2 for case details.

Breach of duty causing death

Once a duty of care has been shown to exist, it must be proved that the defendant was in breach of that duty of care and that this breach caused the death of the victim.

Whether there is a breach of duty is a factual matter for the jury to decide. Did the defendant negligently do or fail to do something? Causation is important, as it must be proved that the breach of duty caused the death. The general rules on causation apply.

Gross negligence

The fact that a defendant has been negligent is not enough to convict them of gross negligence manslaughter. The negligence has to be 'gross'.

At the time of the breach, the jury must conclude that a reasonably prudent person would have foreseen a serious and obvious risk of death, and not merely a risk of injury.

- The meaning of 'serious' was considered by the Court of Appeal in *R v Rudling* (2016) where a GP, following a telephone call from a 12-year-old's mother on Friday night, suggested a visit to the surgery after the weekend. Unfortunately, the child died from the same condition the next day. The court stated that a serious risk of death is not the same as the inability to eliminate a possibility. This is because there may be many remote possibilities of very rare conditions, which cannot be eliminated but which do not present a serious risk of death.

- The meaning of 'obvious' was considered by the Court of Appeal in *R v Rose* (2017). Rose, a registered optometrist, had examined a boy who, five months later died suddenly of hydrocephalus. It was said that she should have identified this. Her appeal against conviction succeeded and the court stated:

  'A mere possibility that an assessment might reveal something life-threatening is not the same as an obvious risk of death. An obvious risk is a present risk which is clear and unambiguous, not one which might become apparent on further investigation.'

Elements	Comment	Cases
Duty of care	Defendant must owe the victim a duty of care. The civil concept of negligence applies. Covers wide range of situations, e.g. maintaining a gas fire. The fact that the victim was party to an illegal act is not relevant.	*Adomako* (1994) *Adomako* (1994) *Singh* (1999) *Wacker* (2003)
Breach of duty	This can be by an act or an omission.	
Gross negligence	Beyond a matter of mere compensation and showed such disregard for the life and safety of others as to amount to a crime. Conduct so bad in all the circumstances as to amount to a criminal act or omission.	*Adomako* (1994)
Risk of death	There must be a risk of death from the defendant's conduct.	*Adomako* (1994) *Rose* (2017)

Figure 7.9 Key facts: gross negligence manslaughter

Extension activity

You can explore further issues, cases and principles for gross negligence manslaughter:

- The role of the judge and jury – *R v Willoughby* (2004).
- Gross is a matter for the jury (and judge's guidance) – *R v Sellu* (2016).
- No breach of human rights – *R v Misra* (2004).

1 State the definition of murder.
2 What is meant by the expression 'malice aforethought'?
3 Explain the difference between voluntary and involuntary manslaughter.
4 State the qualifying triggers for loss of control.
5 On whom is the burden of proof with respect to the defence of diminished responsibility?
6 Explain the four stage test for diminished responsibility.
7 What is the *mens rea* for unlawful act manslaughter?
8 State the elements of the offence of gross negligence manslaughter.
9 State three examples of situations that could permit a charge of gross negligence manslaughter.
10 What is the meaning of 'gross' in gross negligence manslaughter?

Summary

- The offence of gross negligence manslaughter requires breach of an existing duty of care which it is reasonably foreseeable gives rise to a serious and obvious risk of death and does, in fact, cause death in circumstances where, having regard to the risk of death, the conduct of the defendant was so bad in all the circumstances as to go beyond the requirement of compensation but to amount to a criminal act or omission.
- There are six elements which the prosecution must prove in order for a person to be guilty of an offence of manslaughter by gross negligence:
  i)   The defendant owed an existing duty of care to the victim.
  ii) The defendant negligently breached that duty of care.
  iii) At the time of the breach there was a serious and obvious risk of death.
  iv) It was reasonably foreseeable at the time of the breach of the duty that the breach gave rise to a serious and obvious risk of death.
  v)   The breach of the duty caused or made a significant contribution to the death of the victim.
  vi) In the view of the jury, the circumstances of the breach were truly exceptionally bad and so reprehensible as to justify the conclusion that it amounted to gross negligence and required criminal sanction.

  The question of whether there is a serious and obvious risk of death must exist at, and is to be assessed with respect to, knowledge at the time of the breach of duty.
- A recognisable risk of something serious is not the same as a recognisable risk of death.
- A mere possibility that an assessment might reveal something life-threatening is not the same as an obvious risk of death: an obvious risk is a present risk which is clear and unambiguous, not one which might become apparent on further investigation.

Chapter 8 Non-fatal offences against the person

Introduction

There are five offences to be explored in this chapter:
- assault
- battery
- assault occasioning actual bodily harm under s 47 Offences Against the Person Act (OAPA) 1861
- malicious wounding or inflicting grievous bodily harm under s 20 OAPA 1861
- malicious wounding or inflicting grievous bodily harm with intent to do some grievous bodily harm under s 18 OAPA 1861.

Assault and battery are common law offences – there is no statutory definition. These offences are collectively known as common assault. Although assault and battery are common law offences, they are charged under s 39 of the Criminal Justice Act 1988. This sets out that the maximum punishment for them is six months' imprisonment or a fine of £5000, or both. They are both basic intent offences.

The actus reus involved is different for assault and battery.
- For assault, there is no touching, only the fear of immediate, unlawful force.
- For battery, there must be actual force.

There are often situations in which both occur, such as when a defendant approaches the victim shouting that he or she is going to 'get them', then punches the victim in the face:
- The approaching, shouting and raising his arm prior to the punch constitute an assault.
- The punch is the battery.

A defendant is charged with either assault or assault by beating where a battery is involved.

The consequences of the *actus reus* are central to each offence: a punch could have a minimal physical consequence on the victim, or could cause serious harm.

> **Link**
>
> You will need to evaluate these offences. See Chapter 13.

8.1 Assault

Assault is defined as an act which causes the victim to apprehend the infliction of immediate, unlawful force. The defendant either intends to cause another to fear immediate unlawful personal violence or is reckless as to whether such fear is caused.

8.1.1 *Actus reus* of assault

There must be:
- an act
- which causes the victim to apprehend the infliction of immediate, unlawful force.

An act

An assault requires some positive act (not an omission) including words. Words can be verbal or written, as in *R v Constanza* (1997).

Case study

R v Constanza (1997)

The defendant had written over 800 letters and made a number of phone calls to the victim. The victim interpreted the last two letters as clear threats. There was an assault as there was a 'fear of violence at some time, not excluding the immediate future'.

In *R v Misalati* (2017) there was no actual violence. Spitting is an assault, whether it makes contact with the victim or causes fear of immediate unlawful physical contact.

Case study

R v Misalati (2017)

The defendant verbally and racially abused staff at a Job Centre and spat at a third member of staff. There was evidence that the members of staff feared violence and he was convicted of assault.

In *R v Ireland* (1997) it was held that even silent telephone calls can be an assault.

Apprehend immediate unlawful force

The important point is that the act or words must cause the victim to apprehend that immediate force is going to be used against him.

There is no assault if the situation is such that it is obvious that the defendant cannot actually use force. For example:

- Where the defendant shouts threats from a passing train, there is no possibility that they can carry out the threats in the immediate future.

It was decided in *R v Lamb* (1967) (see 7.3.1 above) that pointing an unloaded gun at someone who knows that it is unloaded cannot be an assault. This is because the other person does not fear immediate force. However, if the other person thought the gun was loaded, this could be an assault.

Fear of any unwanted touching is sufficient, as the force or unlawful personal violence which is feared need not be serious.

The force which is threatened must be:

- unlawful – if it is lawful, there is no offence of assault
- immediate – this does not mean instantaneous, but 'imminent', as in *Smith v Chief Superintendent of Woking Police Station* (1983).

Case study

Smith v Chief Superintendent of Woking Police Station (1983)

The defendant went into a garden and looked through the female victim's bedroom window on the ground floor at about 11 p.m. one evening. She was terrified and thought that the defendant was about to enter the room, even though he was outside the house and no attack could be made at that immediate moment. Fear of what he might do next was sufficient.

Words indicating that there will be no violence might prevent an act from being an assault. This is a principle which comes from the old case of *Tuberville v Savage* (1669): the defendant placed one hand on his sword and said, 'If it were not assize time, I would not take such language from you'. This was held not to be an assault, because what he said showed he was not going to do anything.

8.1.2 *Mens rea* of assault

The *mens rea* for an assault is either:

- an intention to cause another to fear immediate unlawful personal violence, or
- subjective recklessness as to whether such fear is caused.

Assault is classed as an offence of basic intent. This is important when dealing with the defence of intoxication, considered in Chapter 10.

Extension activity

You can explore further issues, cases and principles for assault:

- Definition – *R v Nelson* (2013).
- Some 'act' or 'words' required – *Lodgon v DPP* (1976).
- Can be caused indirectly – *R v Dume* (1986).
- *Mens rea* – *R v Venna* (1976); *R v Spratt* (1990).

8.2 Battery

Battery, or assault by beating, is the second part of common assault. It is defined as the application of unlawful force to another person, intending either to apply unlawful physical force to another or being reckless as to whether unlawful force is applied.

8.2.1 *Actus reus* of battery

The *actus reus* of battery is the application of unlawful force to another person. Force is a misleading word, as it can include the slightest touching, as shown by the case of *Collins v Wilcock* (1984). In this case, the court pointed out that touching a person to get his attention was acceptable, provided that no greater degree of physical contact was used than was necessary. However, physical restraint was not acceptable.

Case study

Collins v Wilcock (1984)

The defendant appealed against her conviction for assaulting a police constable in the execution of his duty. His intention was to caution her with respect to activity as a prostitute. The law did not give him power to detain her, but he took hold of her. She resisted, and injured him.

As there was no arrest, and no power implied or otherwise to arrest her, the attempted restraint was a battery and she was entitled to free herself.

An element of the offence of battery is that the prosecution must establish that the offence was committed unlawfully. However, this does not rely solely on direct evidence from the victim, and can be suggested by other evidence. It could be a technical assault for a police officer physically to detain a person without violence and without any intention to arrest the person. This can be seen in the case of *Pegram v DPP* (2019).

Case study

Pegram v DPP (2019)

A police officer took hold of Pegram's arm with what he judged to be just enough force to get his attention, to warn him that he may be about to commit a public order offence.

The court stated that the police officer was acting in the execution of his duty. It is lawful for a police officer or any other person to make moderate and generally acceptable physical contact with another person to attract their attention. The appeal was dismissed.

Each case turns on its facts as, for example, in *Wood v DPP* (2008), where a police officer took hold of Wood's arm to check his identity. In that case, the police officer had no power of arrest so could not detain him without committing a technical battery.

Even touching the victim's clothing can be sufficient to form a battery. In *R v Thomas* (1985), the defendant touched the bottom of a girl's skirt and rubbed it. The Court of Appeal stated that if you touch a person's clothes while they are wearing them, that is equivalent to touching the person even if they do not notice it.

Continuing act

A battery may be committed through a continuing act, as in *Fagan v Metropolitan Police Commissioner* (1968) discussed in Chapter 6. In this case, it became an offence of battery the moment the defendant intended to leave the wheel on the officer's foot.

Indirect act

A battery can also be committed through an indirect act. In this situation, the defendant causes force to be applied, even though they do not personally touch the victim, as in *DPP v K* (1990).

Case study

DPP v K (1990)

A 15-year-old school boy took some acid from a science lesson to the toilets. When he heard someone else coming, he hid it into a hot air hand drier, intending to come back for it later. Before he returned, another pupil came into the toilet and used the hand drier. The nozzle was pointing upwards and acid was squirted into his face causing permanent scars. The court stated that a common assault could be committed by an indirect act.

Another example of indirect force occurred in *Haystead v Chief Constable of Derbyshire* (2000) where the defendant caused a small child to fall to the floor by punching the woman holding the child. The defendant was found guilty because he was reckless as to whether or not his acts would injure the child. In this case, there could also be transferred malice.

Omissions

As the *actus reus* of battery is the application of unlawful force, omitting to perform an act is rarely battery. However, it can be seen in the case of *DPP v Santa-Bermudez* (2003).

Case	Facts	Law
Constanza (1997)	Defendant wrote 800 letters and made phone calls to victim.	Written words can be an assault if they cause victim to fear immediate violence.
Smith v Chief Superintendent (Woking) (1983)	Defendant looked through victim's bedroom window late at night.	Fear of what defendant would do next was sufficient for the *actus reus* of assault.
Tuberville v Savage (1669)	Defendant put hand on sword and said, 'Were it not assize time, I would not take such language from you'.	Words can prevent an act from being an assault, but it depends on the circumstances.
Collins v Wilcock (1984)	A police officer held a woman's arm to prevent her walking away.	Any touching may be a battery, and always is if there was physical restraint.
Wood (Fraser) v DPP (2008)	An officer took hold of W's arm to check his identity.	This was a battery by the police and W was entitled to struggle to release himself.
Fagan v MPC (1968)	Defendant, unknowingly, stopped his car with a wheel on a policeman's foot and refused to move when requested.	The *actus reus* of battery can be an ongoing act so that the complete offence is committed when defendant forms the *mens rea*.
DPP v K (1990)	Defendant put acid in a hand drier – the next person to use it was sprayed with acid.	An indirect act can be the *actus reus* of battery.
DPP v Santa-Bermudez (2003)	Defendant failed to tell a policewoman that he had a needle in his pocket – she was injured when she searched him.	An omission is sufficient for the *actus reus* of battery.

Figure 8.1 Key cases: assault and battery

Case study

DPP v Santa-Bermudez (2003)

A policewoman, before searching the defendant's pockets, asked him if he had any needles or other sharp objects on him. He said 'no', but when the police officer put her hand in his pocket, she was injured by a needle which caused bleeding. The defendant's failure to tell her about the needle could amount to the *actus reus* of the offence.

Unlawful force

For a battery to be committed, the force must be unlawful. This means that the defences of consent or self-defence are particularly appropriate.

Link

These defences are explained in Chapter 11.

Battery without an assault

It is possible for there to be a battery even though there is no assault. This can occur where the victim is unaware that unlawful force is about to be used on them, such as where the attacker comes up unseen or while the victim is asleep.

8.2.2 *Mens rea* of battery

The *mens rea* for battery is either:

- an intention to apply unlawful physical force to another, or
- subjective recklessness as to whether unlawful force is applied.

Extension activity

You can explore further issues, cases and principles for battery:

- Definition – *R v Rolfe* (1952).
- A requirement of hostility – *Faulkner v Talbot* (1981); *R v Brown* (1994).
- *Mens rea* – *R v Venna* (1976); *R v Spratt* (1990).

8.3 Assault occasioning actual bodily harm under s 47 OAPA 1861

The lowest level of injury is actual bodily harm under s 47 OAPA 1861. The section states:

> Whosoever shall be convicted of any assault occasioning actual bodily harm shall be liable to imprisonment for five years.

This is a triable either way offence. The elements of the section need to be considered to establish the requirements for conviction.

8.3.1 *Actus reus* of s 47

The *actus reus* has three elements that must be proved:
- assault
- occasioning
- actual bodily harm.

Unlawful force and consent

As with battery, the force must be unlawful. This means that the defences of consent or self-defence are particularly appropriate. However, in *Brown* (1994) it was stated that in the absence of good reason, the victim's consent is no defence to a charge under OAPA 1861 (this includes ss 47, 20 and 18).
- Surgery involves intentional violence resulting in actual or sometimes serious bodily harm, but surgery is a lawful activity.
- Tattooing, ear-piercing and violent sports including boxing are lawful although they involve actual bodily harm activities.
- Other activities are not lawful and cannot be consented to, such as female genital mutilation.

- Some activities, as in *Brown* (1993), are considered unacceptable as a matter of public policy, which may also be considered in the relationship of law and morality.

Case study

Brown (1994)

The defendants were convicted of ss 47 and 20, after having performed consensual acts of sado-masochism on each other and inflicted non-permanent physical injuries to each other. They had pleaded guilty after a ruling that the prosecution had not needed to prove the absence of consent.

The court stated it was not in the public interest that injuries should be allowed to be inflicted on others without good reason. Sado-masochism was not a good reason. Articles 7 and 8 of the ECHR do not apply in these circumstances.

The principle in *Brown* (1994) was continued in *R v BM* (2018) (a s 18 case), which confirmed that it would not be in the public interest to allow members of the public to wound each other without 'good reason' and remains good law.

Element	Explanation
Assault	Assault means common assault so it could be an assault or a battery as set out above. All the elements of the *actus reus* and *mens rea* of the assault or battery must be proved.
Occasioning	Occasioning means causing. It is necessary to prove that there was an assault or battery and that this *caused* actual bodily harm. The normal principles of causation are applied.
Actual bodily harm	The injury caused is what differentiates actual bodily harm from other non-fatal offences: 1 *R v Miller* (1954): actual bodily harm is 'any hurt or injury calculated to interfere with the health or comfort of the victim'. 2 *R v Chan Fook* (1994): • 'Actual' means not so trivial as to be wholly insignificant. • 'Harm' is injury which goes beyond interference with the health and comfort of the victim. • 'Bodily' is not limited to harm to skin, flesh and bones but includes injury to the nervous system and brain such as recognised and identifiable psychiatric harm. 3 *R(T) v DPP* (2003): loss of consciousness, even momentarily, was held to be actual bodily harm. The defendant and a group of other youths chased the victim who fell to the ground and saw the defendant coming towards him. He covered his head with his arms and was kicked. He momentarily lost consciousness, which was sufficient for actual bodily harm. 4 *DPP v Smith* (2006): physical pain is not necessary; cutting a substantial amount of the victim's hair could amount to actual bodily harm.

Figure 8.2 Elements required for *actus reus* of battery, s 47

R v BM (2018)

The defendant, BM, was a registered tattooist and body piercer who also provided body modification. He had no formal medical qualifications.

His conviction for three counts of causing actual bodily harm was based on the following procedures that BM had performed, all without anaesthetic:

- removal of a customer's ear
- removal of a customer's nipple
- splitting a customer's tongue to resemble a reptile's tongue.

All customers had consented to these serious, irreversible injuries.

8.3.2 *Mens rea* of s 47

The section in the Act makes no reference to *mens rea* but, as the essential element is assault or battery, the courts have held that the *mens rea* for the underlying assault or battery is sufficient for the *mens rea* of a s 47 offence.

This means that if the underlying offence is battery, the defendant must intend or be subjectively reckless as to whether the victim fears or is subjected to unlawful force. There is no need for the defendant to intend or be reckless as to whether actual bodily harm is caused.

Extension activity

You can explore further issues, cases and principles for this area of the law:

- *Actus reus – R v Roberts* (1972).
- Psychiatric injury – *R v Ireland* (1997).

8.4 Malicious wounding or inflicting grievous bodily harm under s 20 OAPA 1861

Section 20 OAPA 1861 states:

> Whosoever shall unlawfully and maliciously wound or inflict any grievous bodily harm upon any other person, either with or without a weapon or instrument, shall be guilty of an offence and shall be liable ... to imprisonment for not more than five years.

There are two offences: malicious wounding and inflicting grievous bodily harm.

Section 20 is a triable either way offence.

8.4.1 Elements of the offences

Three parts of the definition need explanation:

- unlawful
- wound
- grievous bodily harm.

Unlawful

As with s 47, the act must be unlawful. The main issues revolve around consent and specific exceptions such as surgery. For example:

- In *R v Melin* (2019), consent to injection with Botox resulting in serious harm was no defence when the consent was given on the understanding that the defendant was medically qualified, which he was not.

Link

Consent and the evaluation of that defence are considered in more detail in Chapters 11 and 13.

Wound

A wound is a cut or a break in the continuity of the whole skin. A cut of internal skin, such as in the cheek, is sufficient but internal bleeding, where there is no cut of the skin, is not sufficient. This can be seen in *JJC v Eisenhower* (1983).

Case study

JJC v Eisenhower (1983)

The victim was hit in the eye by a shotgun pellet. This did not penetrate the eye but did cause severe bleeding under the surface. As there was no cut, it was held that this was not a wound. The cut must be of the whole skin – both layers.

Evidence of a wound is usually visible bleeding. A rupture of the inner skin of the cheek or of the urethra (connected to the bladder) can be considered a wound if the bleeding becomes visible.

Grievous bodily harm

Grievous bodily harm means really serious harm, which may be physical, psychiatric or by deliberate infection with a serious disease. This offence has developed over recent years to ensure that convictions can be achieved:

- *DPP v Smith* (1961): grievous bodily harm means 'really serious harm'.
- *Saunders* (1985): the harm does not have to be life-threatening. A jury can be directed that there need be 'serious harm', not including the word 'really'.
- *R v Bollom* (2004): the severity of the injuries should be assessed according to the victim's age and health. Bruising would be less serious on an adult in full health than on a very young child.

Case study

R v Bollom (2004)

A 17-month-old child had bruising to her abdomen, both arms and left leg. While the defendant was convicted of assault occasioning actual bodily harm, the Court of Appeal stated that bruising could amount to grievous bodily harm.

- *R v Burstow* (1997): serious psychiatric injury can be grievous bodily harm – the victim of a stalker suffered a severe depressive illness as a result of the stalker's conduct. The conduct included some silent telephone calls and some abusive calls to her. He distributed offensive cards in the street where she lived. He was often at her home and place of work for no reason. He took photographs of the victim and her family. He sent her a note which was menacing.
- *R v Dica* (2004): the first ever conviction for causing grievous bodily harm through infecting victims with the HIV virus.

Case study

R v Dica (2004)

The defendant had had unprotected but consensual sex with two women without telling them he was HIV-positive. Both women became infected as a result. This could amount to grievous bodily harm, as consent to sex did not involve consent to the risks of a known but undisclosed infection.

- *R v Golding* (2014): raised the issue of whether genital herpes could be described as 'really serious bodily harm' within s 20 of the Act.

Case study

R v Golding (2014)

The defendant did not disclose his diagnosis of genital herpes to the victim which he passed on to her. He understood that he had the infection and how it is transmitted. By not preventing transmission, or disclosing his condition and allowing the victim to make an informed consent to the risk, he was guilty of recklessly inflicting grievous bodily harm under s 20.

Inflicting grievous bodily harm

Section 20 uses the word 'inflict'. Originally, this was taken as meaning that there had to be a technical assault or battery, although the section was interpreted quite widely.

- *R v Lewis* (1974): the defendant shouted threats at his wife through a closed door in a second-floor flat and tried to break his way through the door. The wife was so frightened that she jumped from the window and broke both her legs. He was convicted of an s 20 offence.
- *R v Burstow* (1997): it was decided that 'inflict' does not require a technical assault or a battery. It need only be shown that the defendant's actions have led to the consequence of the victim suffering grievous bodily harm. This means that there is now little, if any, difference in the *actus reus* of the offences under s 20 and s 18, which uses the word 'cause'.

8.4.2 *Mens rea* of s 20

The word used in the section is 'maliciously'. In *Cunningham* (1957), it was held that 'maliciously' did not require any ill will towards the person injured. It simply meant either:

- intention to do the particular kind of harm that was in fact done, or
- recklessness as to whether such harm should occur or not.

In *R v Parmenter* (1991), the House of Lords confirmed that the *Cunningham* meaning of recklessness applies to *all* offences in which the statutory definition uses the word 'maliciously'. So, for the *mens rea* of s 20, the prosecution has to prove that the defendant:

- intended to cause another person some harm, or that

- was subjectively reckless as to whether another person suffered some harm.

Although the *actus reus* of s 20 requires a wound or grievous bodily harm, there is no need for the defendant to foresee this level of serious injury.

Extension activity

You can explore further issues, cases and principles for this area of the law:
- Wounding – *Moriarty v Brooks* (1834); *Wood* (1830).
- Inflicting – *R v Wilson* (1984).
- Inflicting a disease – *R v Konzani* (2005).
- *Mens rea* – *R v Mowatt* (1968).

8.5 Malicious wounding or inflicting grievous bodily harm with intent to do some grievous bodily harm under s 18 OAPA 1861

Section 18 is considered a much more serious offence than s 20, as can be seen from the difference in the maximum punishments:
- Section 20 = five years' imprisonment.
- Section 18 = life imprisonment.

The definition in OAPA 1861 states:

> Whosoever shall unlawfully and maliciously by any means whatsoever wound or cause any grievous bodily harm to any person, with intent to do some grievous bodily harm to any person, or with intent to resist or prevent the lawful apprehension or detainer of any person, shall be guilty of ... an offence.

It can be viewed as an offence where there would have been a charge of murder if the victim had died. As with s 20, the act must be unlawful.

8.5.1 *Actus reus* of s 18

This can be committed in two ways:
- wounding, or
- causing grievous bodily harm.

The meanings of 'wound' and 'grievous bodily harm' are the same as for s 20.

The word 'cause' is very wide so that it is only necessary to prove that the defendant's act was a substantial cause of the wound or grievous bodily harm.

8.5.2 *Mens rea* of s 18

This is a specific intent offence – recklessness is not enough for the *mens rea* of s 18.

It must be proved that the defendant intended to:
- do some grievous bodily harm, or
- resist or prevent the lawful apprehension or detainer of any person.

The word 'maliciously' appears in s 18, but this adds nothing to the *mens rea* of this section.

Activity

Since May 2020, there has been an increase on reports that key workers are being spat on and coughed at by members of the public during the global Covid-19 pandemic. One example is rail worker, Belly Mujinga, who was allegedly spat and coughed on in London Victoria's station by a man claiming to have contracted coronavirus. She sadly died two weeks later from Covid-19.

The CPS warned that anyone who deliberately coughs or spits at an emergency worker will face serious criminal charges. Police forces, such as Cumbria Police, stated they will arrest anyone who demonstrates this type of behaviour for common assault.

- Outline the arguments for and against prosecuting those who cough and/or spit at another while claiming to have contracted coronavirus for each of the non-fatal offences discussed above.
- Could it be argued that a defendant in such a case might also be guilty of murder or manslaughter?

Extension activity

You can explore further issues, cases and principles for this area of the law:

- *Mens rea* and wounding: an intention to wound is insufficient *mens rea* for s 18 if it does not amount to GBH – *R v Taylor* (2009).
- With resisting/preventing arrest, the offence requires proof of a specific intent to resist/prevent but need only be reckless as to causing a wound or injury – *R v Morrison* (1989).

Offence	Actus reus	Consequence (injury) required	Mens rea
Assault	Causing victim to fear immediate unlawful violence Requires an act but can be by silent telephone calls: *Ireland* (1997), or letters: *Constanza* (1997)	None needed	Intention of, or subjective reckless as to, causing victim to fear immediate unlawful violence
Battery	Application of unlawful violence, even the slightest touching: *Collins v Wilcock* (1984)	None needed	Intention of, or subjective reckless as to, applying unlawful force
Assault occasioning actual bodily harm s 47 OAPA 1861	Assault, i.e. an assault or battery	Actual bodily harm (e.g. bruising) This includes: ● momentary loss of consciousness: *R(T) v DPP* (2003) ● psychiatric harm: *Chan Fook* (1994)	Intention or subjective recklessness as to causing fear of unlawful violence or of applying unlawful force, i.e. the *mens rea* for an assault or battery
Maliciously wounding or inflicting grievous bodily harm: s 20 OAPA 1861	A direct or indirect act or omission: *Martin* (1881) No need to prove an assault: *Burstow* (1998)	Either a wound – a cutting of the whole skin: *JJC v Eisenhower* (1984) OR Grievous bodily harm (really serious harm) which includes psychiatric harm: *Burstow* (1998)	Intention or subjective recklessness as to causing some injury (though not serious): *Parmenter* (1991)
Wounding or causing grievous bodily harm with intent: s 18 OAPA 1861	A direct or indirect act or omission which causes victim's injury	A wound or grievous bodily harm (as above)	Specific intention to cause grievous bodily harm

Figure 8.3 Key facts: non-fatal offences

Quick questions

1 Distinguish between the offences of assault and battery.
2 Explain the meaning of 'assault occasioning actual bodily harm'.
3 Distinguish between s 47 and s 20 Offences Against the Person Act 1861.
4 In what circumstances can a person consent to a non-fatal offence?
5 Give an example of when there can be a battery without an assault.

- The law on non-fatal offences against the person, apart from assault and battery, is set out in the Offences Against the Person Act (OAPA) 1861.
- Common assault can be either an assault or battery. Both are common law offences.
- An assault is an act which intentionally or recklessly causes another to fear immediate and unlawful violence.
- Battery is the application, intentionally or recklessly, of unlawful force to another person.
- Assault occasioning actual bodily harm (s 47 OAPA 1861) is assault or battery which causes actual bodily harm. 'Actual bodily harm' is 'any hurt or injury calculated to interfere with the health or comfort' of the victim. It includes psychiatric injury.

- For unlawfully and maliciously wounding or inflicting grievous bodily harm upon another person (s 20 OAPA 1861), the defendant must intend to cause another person some harm or be subjectively reckless as to whether they suffer some harm. There is no need for the defendant to foresee serious injury.
- Wounding or causing grievous bodily harm with intent to do so (s 18 OAPA 1861) is a specific intent offence. D must be proved to have intended to do some grievous bodily harm.
- For both ss 20 and 18, grievous bodily harm means 'really serious harm' but this does not have to be life-threatening.
- 'Wound' means a cut or a break in the continuity of the whole skin.

Chapter 9 Offences against property

Introduction

There are three property offences to consider in this chapter, all of which are found in the Theft Act 1968. There are some concepts, such as dishonesty, which are essential components of each of these offences.

9.1 Theft under s 1 Theft Act 1968

When the Theft Act 1968 was passed, the definition of 'theft' was meant to be in simple, everyday language that ordinary people could understand. However, there have been some case decisions on the elements of theft which show that is not always the case.

Theft is defined in s 1 of the Theft Act 1968:

> A person is guilty of theft if he dishonestly appropriates property belonging to another with the intention of permanently depriving the other of it.

Sections 2–6 of the Act help with the meaning of the words or phrases in the definition. This is done in the order that the words or phrases appear in the definition, making it easy to remember the section numbers. They are:

- s 2 – dishonestly (part of the *mens rea*)
- s 3 – appropriates (part of the *actus reus*)
- s 4 – property (part of the *actus reus*)
- s 5 – belonging to another (part of the *actus reus*)
- s 6 – with the intention of permanently depriving the other of it (part of the *mens rea*).

Remember that a person charged with theft is always charged with stealing 'contrary to s 1 of the Theft Act 1968'. Sections 2–6 are definition sections explaining s 1. They do not themselves create any offence.

All the elements of the *actus reus* and *mens rea* must be proved for there to be theft.

9.1.1 *Actus reus* of theft

Sections 3, 4 and 5 make up the *actus reus* of theft.

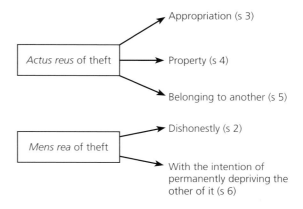

Figure 9.1 The elements of theft

Section 3 – Appropriation

Section 3(1) states:

> Any assumption by a person of the rights of an owner amounts to an appropriation, and this includes, where he has come by the property (innocently or not) without stealing it, any later assumption of a right to it by keeping or dealing with it as owner.

Appropriation is the act of a taking.
- The more obvious situations involve a physical taking, for example, taking a wallet from someone's pocket.
- But a wide variety of acts can be considered as appropriation. They include the physical picking up of an item, destroying property, throwing items away, selling property, switching price labels on items, giving worthless cheques in payment for goods, receiving a gift and deciding to keep an item.
- Taking goods from a shelf in a supermarket and placing them in your pocket or your own shopping bag is an example of an appropriation. This is clearly assuming the rights of an owner. But it has been decided that even the action of taking the goods

from a shelf in a supermarket is an appropriation. The important words are 'any assumption by a person of the rights of an owner amounts to appropriation'.

Tip

Remember that appropriation alone does not constitute theft. It is only one of the five elements that must be proved for there to be theft.

The rights of the owner include selling the property or destroying it, as well as possessing it, consuming it, using it, lending it or hiring it out. So, for there to be appropriation, the thief must do something which assumes (takes over) at least one of the owner's rights. This can be seen clearly in the case of *R v Vinall* (2011). (This case is in fact a robbery case, but as we will see in the next chapter, the offence of robbery requires a theft to have taken place.)

Case study

R v Vinall (2011)

The defendants encountered two cyclists, subjected them to verbal abuse, punched one from his bike, made other threats and chased them for a short distance. The defendants then walked away, one of them having picked up the bike. The bike was left by a bus shelter some 45 metres further on and the police stopped them about half a mile away. The appeal against conviction raised issues of appropriation, intention permanently to deprive, and the time at which, and the purpose for which, force was used in determining whether robbery had been committed.

The Court of Appeal stated either of two actions could be regarded as appropriation, sufficiently assuming of the rights of owner:

- the initial taking of the bike
- the subsequent act of abandoning the bike.

The rights of an owner also include the right to sell property. An appropriation by assuming the right to sell is demonstrated by the case of *R v Pitham and Hehl* (1977).

Case study

R v Pitham and Hehl (1977)

The defendants 'sold' furniture belonging to another person and in that person's house. This was held to be an appropriation. It did not matter whether or not the furniture was removed from the house and the owner was never deprived of the property.

The right to destroy property is also an owner's right. This means that:

- if the defendant destroys property belonging to another person, he or she can be charged with theft. If the property is not destroyed but merely thrown away, there is an infringement of the owner's rights.

The wording in s 3(1) is 'any assumption by a person of the rights of an owner'. Does the assumption have to be of *all* of the rights or can it just be of *any* of the rights? This was considered in *R v Morris* (1983), which decided that there does not have to be an assumption of all of the rights of an owner.

Case study

R v Morris (1983)

Morris had switched the price labels of two items on the shelf in a supermarket. He had then put one of the items, which now had a lower price on it, into a basket provided by the store and taken the item to the checkout, but had not gone through the checkout when he was arrested.

His conviction for theft was upheld as he had switched the price labels of two items on the shelf in a supermarket. He had assumed an owner's right.

Case	Facts	Law
R v Vinall (2011)	Defendants took a bike and abandoned it a short distance away.	Appropriation occurred in the initial taking of the bike and/or the abandoning of the bike.
R v Pitham and Hehl (1977)	Defendants 'sold' furniture belonging to another person and in that person's house.	Appropriation occurred by assuming the right to sell another's goods.
R v Morris (1983)	Defendant switched the price labels of two items in a supermarket.	Appropriation was of the owner's right to put labels on the goods. Appropriation does not have to be all the rights of an owner.

Figure 9.2 Key cases: elements of appropriation – s 3 Theft Act 1968

Consent to the appropriation

What is the position where the owner has allowed the defendant to take something because the owner thought that the defendant was taking what was owed to them? This point was considered in *Lawrence v Commissioner for Metropolitan Police* (1972).

Case study

Lawrence v Commissioner for Metropolitan Police (1972)

An Italian student, who spoke very little English, arrived at Victoria Station and showed an address to Lawrence, a taxi driver. The journey should have cost 50p, but Lawrence told him it was expensive. The student got out a £1 note and offered it to the driver. Lawrence said it was not enough and so the student opened his wallet and allowed Lawrence to help himself to another £6.

Lawrence put forward the argument that he had not appropriated the money as the student had consented to him taking it. The court stated that there was appropriation in this situation.

In *R v Morris*, the whole system of supermarket shopping is shown to rely on the customer taking goods from shelves and the idea of the 'honest shopper'. This means that there is an implied consent from shops operating a self-service style of shopping to customers removing items from shelves or petrol from a pump as they intend to purchase the goods at the price stated. Switching labels involves an interference with the goods that is not consented to.

The point was considered again in the case of *R v Gomez* (1993), from which it can be seen that any removal of goods from a shelf in a shop is an appropriation.

Case study

R v Gomez (1993)

The defendant worked as a shop assistant. He had persuaded the manager to accept, in payment for goods, two cheques which he knew to be stolen and had no value. The court stated that an act expressly or impliedly authorised by the owner of goods or consented to by him or her could amount to an appropriation of the goods within the meaning of the Theft Act 1968.

So, to have committed an appropriation, the defendant need not do anything contrary to the owner's apparent wishes. The issue of theft will still depend on, for example, dishonesty, and usually what the defendant is doing is not consistent with the victim's actual wishes (because the victim does not usually know the facts behind the defendant's actions).

Consent without deception – the problem of gifts

Does the decision in *Gomez* (1993) extend to situations where a person has given property to another without any deception? This was the problem raised in the case of *R v Hinks* (2000).

Case study

R v Hinks (2000)

The defendant, aged 38, was friendly with John Dolphin, aged 53 and of limited intelligence. Dolphin understood the concept of ownership of property and making a valid gift. The defendant described herself as his main carer. In the period April to November 1996, Dolphin withdrew sums totalling around £60,000 from his building society account and deposited them in Hinks's account. He also gave her a television set. During the summer of that year he made withdrawals of the maximum permissible sum of £300 every day so that he lost most of his savings and moneys inherited from his father.

The House of Lords decided that even though there was a valid gift, there was an appropriation. The question remained as to whether the jury would see the act as dishonest for there to be theft.

Case	Facts	Law
Lawrence v Commissioner for Metropolitan Police (1972)	Taxi driver took too much money from proffered wallet of his passenger who did not speak the same language.	The consent to appropriation of the money was only to the correct amount, not the excess, because of the deception.
R v Gomez (1993)	Goods were handed over in exchange for worthless cheques.	The consent to appropriation of the goods was not genuine because of the deception about the value of the cheques.
R v Hinks (2000)	Victim was of limited intelligence, but understood the concept of ownership of property and making a valid gift.	Even though there was a valid gift, there was appropriation.

Figure 9.3 Key cases: consent to appropriation

When does appropriation take place?

Another effect of the decision in *Gomez* is that the appropriation is viewed as occurring at one specific point in time. We have already seen that in the case of *R v Vinall* (2011). The reason that this is important is that criminal law has a basic principle of coincidence of *actus reus* and *mens rea*. The later act, in a case such as *Vinall*, might be the relevant one if, for example, it was impossible to prove an intention permanently to deprive at the time of the initial taking of the bike.

This is further illustrated by the case of *R v Atakpu and Abrahams* (1994), where it can be seen that appropriation occurs the first time a person assumes the rights of the owner.

Case study

R v Atakpu and Abrahams (1994)

The defendants hired cars in Germany and Belgium using false driving licences and passports. They were arrested at Dover and charged with theft. The Court of Appeal quashed their convictions because the moment of appropriation under the law in *Gomez* was when they obtained the cars. So the thefts had occurred outside the jurisdiction of the English courts and as the defendants had already stolen the cars in Germany and Belgium, keeping and driving them in England was not a new appropriation – a later assumption of the right of an owner or a continuing act.

A later assumption of a right

Section 3(1) makes it clear that there can also be an appropriation where the defendant acquires property without stealing it, but then later decides to keep or deal with the property as owner. The appropriation in this type of situation takes place at the point of 'keeping' or 'dealing'.

Section 4 – Property

For there to be theft, the defendant must have appropriated 'property'. Section 4 gives a very comprehensive definition of property, which means that almost anything can be stolen. The definition is in s 4(1) of the Theft Act 1968:

> 'Property' includes money and all other property, real or personal, including things in action and other intangible property.

Section 4 lists five types of items which are included in the definition of 'property', and are discussed below.

Money

In this list, 'money' means coins and banknotes of any currency.

Real property

Real property is the legal term for land and buildings. Under s 4(1), land can be stolen, but s 4(2) states that this can only be done in three particular circumstances:

1. The person dealing with the land does so in a special capacity, such as a trustee or under a power of attorney, and appropriates the land or anything forming part of it by dealing with it in breach of the confidence reposed in him.
2. Someone not in possession of the land severs anything forming part of the land from the land.
3. Being in possession of the land under a tenancy, the tenant appropriates the whole or part of any fixture or structure let to be used with the land. An example of this might be removing and selling a kitchen cupboard fixed to the wall of a rented flat.

Personal property

Personal property covers all moveable items such as books, jewellery, clothes and cars, as well as trivial items such as a sheet of paper or a ball point pen.

- *R v Kelly and Lindsay* (1998): dead bodies and body parts can be personal property for the purposes of theft.
- Regenerative body materials, such as hair (*R v Herbert* (1961)), blood (*R v Rothery* (1976)) and urine (*R v Welsh* (1974)), can be the subject of property rights and are capable of being stolen in certain circumstances.

Case study

R v Kelly and Lindsay (1998)

Kelly was a sculptor who asked Lindsay to take body parts from the Royal College of Surgeons where he worked as a laboratory assistant. Kelly made casts of the parts. They were convicted of theft and appealed on the point of law that body parts were not property. The Court of Appeal held that, though a dead body was not normally property within the definition of the Theft Act 1968, the body parts were property as they had acquired 'different attributes by virtue of the application of skill, such as dissection or preservation techniques, for exhibition or teaching purposes'.

Things in action

A thing in action is a right which can be enforced against another person by taking legal action. The right itself is property under the definition in s 4. For example:

- A cheque itself is a thing in action, but it is also a piece of paper. This is property which can be stolen, and it is a 'valuable security' that can also be stolen under the definition of property.

Other intangible property

This refers to other rights which have no physical presence but can be stolen under the Theft Act 1968 such as data in a computer game.

However, confidential information cannot be stolen, as seen in *Oxford v Moss* (1979), where knowledge of the questions on an examination paper was held not to be property.

Case study

Oxford v Moss (1979)

A civil engineering undergraduate dishonestly obtained a copy of his forthcoming exam paper, read its contents, and returned the paper to where he had found it. He was charged with theft of confidential information but was not convicted because information is not property within the Theft Act 1968 s 4. The court noted there were many options for the University in the civil courts.

Things which cannot be stolen

There are some things which *cannot* be stolen except in specific circumstances. These are set out in ss 4(3) and 4(4) of the Theft Act 1968.

- Section 4(3): Plants growing wild cannot be stolen, but it is possible to steal cultivated plants. Taking apples from trees in a farmer's orchard would be theft, but picking wild blackberries or mushrooms would not be theft unless it was done for sale or reward or other commercial purpose.
- Section 4(4): Wild animals cannot be stolen unless held in captivity, such as in a zoo. Once the animal or its carcass has been taken into possession by someone, it can then be stolen. This would happen where game is shot and then collected by the hunter. There are other criminal offences with respect to capturing or killing certain types of animal.

Type of property	Example
Money	Coins and banknotes of any currency
Real property	Land and buildings on the land
Personal property	All moveable items such as jewellery or cars
Things in action	A right which can be enforced against another person by an action in law such as a bank account
Other intangible property	Things which have no physical presence such as a computer game

Figure 9.4 Examples of property – s 4 Theft Act 1968

Section 5 – Belonging to another

In order for there to be a theft of the property, that property must 'belong to another'. However, s 5(1) of the Theft Act 1968 gives a very wide definition of what is meant by this – possession or control of the property or any proprietary interest in it is sufficient. One reason for making it so wide-ranging is so that the prosecution does not have to prove who the legal owner is.

Possession or control

Obviously, the owner of property normally has possession and control of it, but there are many other situations in which a person can have either possession or control of property:

- Someone who hires a car has both possession and control during the period of hire.
- If the car is stolen during this time, the thief can be charged with stealing it from the hirer.
- As the car-hire firm still owns the car (a proprietary right), the thief could be charged with stealing it from them.

The possession or control of the item does not have to be lawful. Where B has stolen jewellery from A and then C steals it from B, B is in possession or control of that jewellery and C can be charged with stealing it from B. This is useful where it is not known who the original owner is, as C can still be guilty of theft.

- This wide definition of 'belonging to' has led to the situation in which an owner was convicted of stealing his own car, in *R v Turner (No. 2)* (1971).

Case study

R v Turner (No. 2) (1971)

The defendant left his car at a garage for repairs. It was agreed that he would pay for the repairs when he collected the car after the repairs had been completed. When the repairs were almost finished, the garage left the car parked on the roadway outside its premises. The defendant used a spare key to take the car during the night without paying for the repairs.

The garage was in possession or control of the car because, as repairers, it has a right to retain possession of the item being repaired until payment is made (a repairer's lien). The defendant was convicted of theft.

- It is possible for someone to be in possession or control of property even though he or she does not know it is there. This happened in *R v Woodman* (1974).

Case study

R v Woodman (1974)

A company had sold all the scrap metal on its site to another company which arranged for it to be removed. However, a small amount of the scrap had been left on the site. The company was in control of the site itself as it had put a fence round it and had notices warning trespassers to keep out. The defendant took the remaining scrap metal. He was convicted of theft even though the company was unaware there was any scrap left.

- Where goods are left for someone, the goods belong to the original owner until the new owner takes possession of them. This occurred in *R (on the application of Ricketts) v Basildon Magistrates' Court* (2010).

Case study

R (on the application of Ricketts) v Basildon Magistrates' Court (2010)

In the first offence, Ricketts took bags containing items of property from outside a charity shop. He argued that the original owner had abandoned the property and, therefore, it did not belong to another. The court ruled that the goods had not been abandoned – the giver had attempted to deliver them to the charity and delivery would only be complete when the charity took possession. Until then, they were the property of the giver.

In the second offence, Ricketts had taken bags of goods from a bin at the rear of another charity shop. These goods were still in the possession of the charity at the time they were appropriated by Ricketts.

Proprietary interest

Where the defendant owns property and is in possession and control of property, they can still be guilty of stealing it if another person has a proprietary interest in it. This point was the key issue in the case of *R v Webster* (2006).

Case study

R v Webster (2006)

The defendant was an army sergeant who had served in Iraq. He had been awarded a medal for his service there. By mistake the Ministry of Defence sent him a second copy of the medal. He sold this second medal on eBay. He was convicted of theft of the medal.

On appeal his conviction was upheld on the basis that the Ministry of Defence had retained an equitable (proprietary) interest in the medal.

Section 5 makes it clear that in certain situations a defendant can be guilty of theft even though the property may not 'belong to another'. These are situations in which the defendant is acting dishonestly and has caused a loss to another or has made a gain. These are:

- trust property
- property received under an obligation
- property received by another's mistake.

Section 5(2): Trust property

This is simply where property is held by a trustee on behalf of another who can be liable for theft of trust property.

Section 5(3): Property received under an obligation

There are many situations in which property (usually money) is handed over to the defendant on the basis that they will keep it for the owner or will deal with it in a particular way. The Theft Act 1968 tries to make sure that such property is still considered to 'belong to the other' for the purposes of the law of theft.

Case	Facts	Law
R v Turner (No. 2) (1971)	Defendant took his car from repairer without paying using spare key.	Repairer had right to retain car until payment. That right over the car was stolen.
R v Woodman (1974)	All scrap on a site had been sold and buyer removed it but left some behind subsequently taken by defendant.	The scrap left behind was capable of being stolen.
R (on the application of Ricketts) v Basildon Magistrates' Court (2010)	Goods left outside charity shop as a donation to the charity.	These goods could be stolen as they either belonged to the donor of the goods or the charity shop.

Figure 9.5 Key cases: property belonging to another – s 5

Under this section there must be an obligation to retain and deal with the property in a particular way. This means:

- Where money is paid as a deposit to a business, the prosecution must prove that there was an obligation to retain and deal with those deposits in a particular way.
- If the person paying the deposit only expects it to be paid into the bank account of the business and that is what happens, there cannot be theft – even if all the money from the account is used for other business expenses and the client does not receive the goods or service for which they paid the deposit.
- The key aspect is then the question of dishonesty, if an offence is to be established. An example can be seen in *R v Hall* (1972).

Case study

R v Hall (1972)

The defendant was a travel agent who received deposits from clients for air trips to America. He paid these deposits into the firm's general account but never organised any tickets and was unable to return the money. He was convicted of theft.

On appeal his conviction was quashed, because when he received the deposits he was not under an obligation to deal with them in a particular way. The Court of Appeal stressed that each case depended on its facts.

- In *R v Klineberg and Marsden* (1999), there was a clear obligation to deal with deposits in a particular way.

Case study

R v Klineberg and Marsden (1999)

The two defendants operated a company which sold timeshare apartments in Lanzarote to customers in England. Each purchaser paid the purchase price on the understanding that the money would be held by an independent trust company until the apartment was ready for the purchaser to occupy. Over £500,000 was paid to the defendants' company but only £233 was actually paid into the trust company's account.

The defendants were guilty of theft. They were under a clear obligation to the purchasers 'to retain and deal with that property or its proceeds in a particular way' and that they had not done this.

- There can be an obligation in less formal situations, such as paying a shared bill. This was shown in the case of *Davidge v Bunnett* (1984).

Case study

Davidge v Bunnett (1984)

The defendant was given money by her flatmates to pay the gas bill but instead she used it to buy Christmas presents. There was a legal obligation to deal with the money in a particular way and, as she had not fulfilled that obligation, she was guilty of theft.

Section 5(4): Property received by another's mistake

Section 5 also provides for situations where property has been handed over to the defendant by another's mistake and so has become the defendant's property.

If there were no special provision in the Act, this could not be 'property belonging to another' for the purposes of the law of theft. This section was considered in *Attorney-General's Reference (No. 1 of 1983)* (1985).

Case study

Attorney-General's Reference (No. 1 of 1983) (1985)

The defendant, a police officer, had received an overpayment of wages when her pay went into her bank account. She recognised it was an overpayment. She did not withdraw any part of the money, but did not return it. She was convicted of theft of the property (a thing in action) as she was under an obligation to return it.

- There must be a legal obligation to restore the property. In some situations there is no legal obligation to restore money. This is shown by *R v Gilks* (1972).

Case study

R v Gilks (1972)

The defendant, Gilks, had placed a bet on a horse race. The bookmaker made a mistake about which horse the defendant had backed (two horses had similar names) and overpaid him. Gilks realised the error and decided not to return the money. The ownership of the money had passed to him, so the only way he could be guilty of theft was if s 5(4) applied. It was held that as betting transactions were not at that time enforceable at law, s 5(4) did not apply and Gilks was not guilty.

Case	Facts	Law
R v Webster (2006)	An army sergeant sold a duplicate medal sent to him by mistake.	Guilty: The Ministry of Defence retained an equitable interest in the medal so defendant was guilty.
R v Hall (1972)	A travel agent received travel deposits from customers but did not arrange tickets for the customers.	Not guilty: defendant was not under an obligation to deal with the deposits in a particular way under s 5(3).
R v Klineberg and Marsden (1999)	The defendants took deposits for the purchase of timeshare apartments but didn't place them in the agreed separate account.	Guilty: there was a clear obligation to deal with deposits in a particular way; they appropriated the victim's proprietary interest.
Davidge v Bunnett (1984)	The defendant bought Christmas presents with money collected from her flatmates to pay the gas bill.	Guilty: there was a legal obligation to deal with the money in a particular way and she had not fulfilled that obligation.
Attorney-General's Reference (No. 1 of 1983) (1985)	Defendant received an overpayment of wages into her bank account. She neither withdrew nor returned it.	Guilty: she was under an obligation to return the thing in action – the overpayment in her bank accounts.
R v Gilks (1972)	A bookmaker paid out a bet in error over the name of the horse. The bettor kept the money.	Not guilty: no rights were appropriated as betting transactions could not be enforced by law.

Figure 9.6 Key cases: proprietary interest

Activity

In each of the following situations, explain whether the *actus reus* of theft is present.

1   Roland works in a small factory where there are only 20 employees. One day he finds a small purse in the washroom. He opens it. It contains a £10 note and some coins. There is no name or other identification in it. Roland decides to keep the money as he does not think he can find the owner.

2   Natalie is given a Christmas cash bonus by her employer in a sealed envelope. She has been told by her boss that the bonus would be £50. When she gets home and opens the envelope she finds there is £60 in it. She thinks her employer decided to be more generous and so keeps the money. Would your answer be different if:
   • Natalie realised there had been a mistake but did not return the money?
   • The amount in the envelope was £200?

3   Errol is given permission by his employer to borrow some decorative lights for use at a party. Errol also takes some candles without asking permission. When putting up the lights, Errol smashes one of them. He lights two of the candles so that by the end of the evening they are partly burnt down. One of the guests admires the remaining lights and asks if he can have them to use at a disco at the weekend. Errol agrees to let him take the lights.

4   Ilsa and Jools are in the habit of borrowing each others records when DJing together. At the end of one night, Jools took home a number of records that in fact belong to Ilsa. Jools' flatmate, Kamala, noticed that one record was particularly valuable. She substituted her much less valuable record and sold Ilsa's valuable version.

9.1.2 *Mens rea* of theft

There are two elements to the *mens rea* of theft:
- s 2 – dishonestly
- s 6 – with the intention of permanently depriving the other of it.

Section 2 – Dishonestly

Proof of dishonesty is now the main distinguishing point between theft and an honest appropriation. There is no definition of what is meant by dishonesty in the Act. Section 1(2) states that:

> it is immaterial whether the appropriation is made with a view to gain, or is made for the thief's own benefit.

In other words, if all the elements of theft are present, the motive of the defendant is not relevant. This means that a modern-day Robin Hood stealing to give to the poor would be guilty of theft. The defendant does not have to gain anything from the theft.

The Act does set out behaviour which is not dishonest, despite the difficulty of proving something through a negative.

Behaviour which is not dishonest

Section 2(1) provides that a person's appropriation of property belonging to another is *not* to be regarded as dishonest if he or she appropriates the property in the belief that:

1 he or she has in law the right to deprive the other of it, on behalf of themselves or of a third person (s 2(1)(a))
2 he or she would have the other's consent if the other knew of the appropriation and the circumstances of it (s 2(1)(b)), or
3 the person to whom the property belongs cannot be discovered by taking reasonable steps (s 2(1)(c)).

All these three situations depend on the defendant's belief. It does not matter whether it is a correct belief or even whether it is a reasonable belief. If the defendant has a genuine belief in one of these three, then he or she is not guilty of theft.

The legal right to deprive the other of it

This exception requires an honest, but not necessarily reasonable, belief by the defendant of their right to take the item. This is a subjective test, so the sole concern is for the defendant to convince a jury that they held that belief.

An example of this is where an employee is instructed to collect goods from a third party: they will not be dishonest in taking the goods if they honestly believe they have the legal right to do so.

A person will not be considered dishonest where they believe they have in law the right to deprive the other of the property. *R v Holden* (1991) and *R v Robinson* (1977) illustrate this 'claim of right' defence.

Case studies

R v Holden (1991)

The defendant was charged with the theft of scrap tyres from the tyre supply and fitting company where he worked. He claimed that other people had taken tyres with the permission of the supervisor. However, taking tyres was a dismissible offence under his contract of employment. His conviction was quashed as the defendant subjectively believed he had the right to take them.

R v Robinson (1977)

The defendant was owed £7 by the victim's wife. When he went to collect the money, a fight developed between him and her husband, during which a £5 note dropped out of the husband's pocket. The defendant kept the £5 note. There was no theft because he had an honest belief that he was entitled to the money.

Consent if the other knew of the appropriation

Examples of this rule are:
- borrowing your friend's ruler without asking, using it and then returning it
- continuing a habitual practice of borrowing tools and machinery between neighbours.

The owner of the property cannot be discovered

An example would be finding a one pound coin in the street. Here, there is usually an honest belief that the owner could not reasonably be found, but that would not be so if the defendant had just seen someone pull the coin out of their pocket along with a handkerchief and dropped the coin. Clearly, the more valuable the item, the less likely the owner cannot reasonably be found. This can also be seen in the case of *R v Small* (1987).

Case study

R v Small (1987)

The defendant noticed an old car parked in the road for some time with the key in the ignition. Parts were missing, and there was no petrol in it. The defendant thought the car had been dumped and therefore decided to get it going and drive it. His defence to stealing the car was that he believed it had been abandoned by its owner and therefore he had a legal right to take it.

As there is no requirement that the defendant's belief is reasonable, it does not matter that a reasonable person would have known to contact the Vehicle Licensing Agency to discover the owner. Therefore, he was not guilty of theft.

The situation where a person is willing to pay for something

In some situations, the defendant may say that they are willing to pay for the property or may, on taking property, leave money to pay for it.

This does not prevent the defendant's conduct from being dishonest, as s 2(2) states that:

> a person's appropriation of property belonging to another may be dishonest notwithstanding that he is willing to pay for the property.

The test for dishonesty

Where these exceptions do not apply, the courts have developed a test for what amounts to dishonesty. There is usually little argument about whether an act is dishonest – for example, shoplifting is obviously dishonest and a jury would have little difficulty with that.

However, sometimes defendants would claim that they had not been dishonest and there was no standard test to apply. Examples include borrowing from the petty cash at work without permission and contrary to the company rules but intending to replace the money the next day, or borrowing from the till and leaving an IOU.

The case of *R v Ghosh* (1982) used to be the leading case on what is meant by 'dishonestly'. However the case of *Ivey v Genting Casinos Ltd t/a Crockfords* (2017) was accepted as the correct test even though it is a civil case and so strictly speaking did not overrule the

Case study

Ivey v Genting Casinos Ltd t/a Crockfords (2017)

The case involved the defendant using a card technique called 'edge-sorting' while gambling – giving himself an advantage in order to win, despite being subject to a gaming contract, which implied a term that he would not cheat. He won £7.7 million. However, he was refused payment after the casino pored over video footage of all his games and finally figured out how he had gamed the casino. The court reviewed the test for dishonesty and stated that the court will now decide what it is the defendant believed and then will determine whether the defendant's actions are dishonest by the standards of ordinary, reasonable and honest members of society (the jury).

The case of *Barton and Booth* (2020) clarifies the matter. The criminal test for dishonesty is as set out in *Ivey v Genting Casinos* (2017) and not that in *R v Ghosh* (1982). The test is:

1 What was the defendant's actual state of knowledge or belief as to the facts?
2 Was his conduct dishonest by the standards of ordinary decent people?

Case study

Barton and Booth (2020)

Barton was the owner of a luxury nursing home; Booth was the general manager. For many years Barton used his position to groom, defraud and steal from elderly and dependent residents who were wealthy, vulnerable and childless. He obtained over £4,000,000 from his criminal activities. Booth was accused of facilitating this fraud.

The Court of Appeal confirmed that the test for dishonesty in criminal cases was that set out in *Ivey v Genting* (2017).

Tip

The test for dishonesty is used for many offences, so it is essential you know the test accurately.

Case	Facts	Law
R v Small (1987)	The defendant believed that an old car had been abandoned, so fixed it up and took it.	The defendant honestly believed he had the legal right to take the car, so was not dishonest.
R v Holden (1991)	The defendant was charged with the theft of scrap tyres from his workplace.	As the test is subjective, a person was not dishonest if he genuinely believed that he had a legal right to the property.
R v Robinson (1977)	The defendant went to collect money he was owed, and kept a £5 note which dropped out of the debtor's husband's pocket.	There was no theft because he had an honest belief that he was entitled to the money.
Ivey v Genting Casinos Ltd t/a Crockfords (2017)	The defendant used unfair techniques while playing cards in a casino.	Deciding whether or not a defendant's conduct should be considered dishonest should reflect what ordinary, decent people would consider it to be. The defendant does not have to be aware of this.
R v Barton and Booth	The defendants ran a nursing home and preyed on elderly and vulnerable residents.	The test for dishonesty in the criminal law is that set out in the case of *Ivey v Genting*.

Figure 9.7 Key cases: dishonesty – s 2

Section 6 – Intention of permanently depriving

The final element that has to be proved for theft is that the defendant had the intention permanently to deprive the other of the property.

- In many situations there is no doubt that the defendant had such an intention, for example, where an item is taken and sold to another person or where cash is taken and spent by the defendant. This is true even if the defendant intends to replace the money later, as was shown in *R v Velumyl* (1989).

Case study

R v Velumyl (1989)

The defendant, a company manager, took £1050 from the office safe. He said that he was owed money by a friend and he was going to replace the money when that friend repaid him. The Court of Appeal upheld his conviction for theft as he had the intention of permanently depriving the company of the banknotes which he had taken from the safe, even if he intended replacing them with other banknotes to the same value later.

- There is a clear intention to permanently deprive where the defendant destroys property belonging to another.

There are, however, situations where it is not so clear and, to help in these, s 6 of the Theft Act 1968 explains and expands the meaning of the phrase. It provides that,

even though a person appropriating property belonging to another does not mean the other permanently to lose the thing itself, they can be regarded as having the intention to permanently deprive the other of it if their intention is to treat the thing as their own to dispose of, regardless of the other's rights. In *DPP v Lavender* (1994), the court ruled that the dictionary definition of 'dispose of' was too narrow, as a disposal could include 'dealing with' property.

Case study

DPP v Lavender (1994)

The defendant took doors from a council property which was being repaired and used them to replace damaged doors in his girlfriend's council flat. The doors were still in the possession of the council but had been transferred without permission from one council property to another. Here he was dealing with the doors as his own by moving them from one property to another without permission.

Borrowing or lending

Normally borrowing would not be an intention to permanently deprive, such as where a student takes a textbook from a fellow student's bag in order to read one small section and then replaces the book.

Section 6 states that borrowing is not theft unless it is for a period and in circumstances making it equivalent to an outright taking or disposal. In *R v Lloyd* (1985), it was held that this meant borrowing the property and keeping it until 'the goodness, the virtue, the practical value . . . has gone out of the article'.

Case study

R v Lloyd (1985)

The projectionist at a local cinema gave the defendant a film that was showing at the cinema so that the defendant could make an illegal copy. He returned the film in time for the next screening at the cinema. His conviction for theft was quashed because, by returning the film in its original state, it was not possible to prove an intention to permanently deprive.

Conditional intent

Another difficulty is where the defendant examines property to see if there is anything worth stealing. What if they decide it is not worth stealing and return it? This is what happened in *R v Easom* (1971).

Case study

R v Easom (1971)

The defendant picked up a handbag in a cinema, rummaged through the contents and then replaced the handbag without having taken anything.

His conviction for theft of the handbag and its contents was quashed. There was no evidence that the defendant had intended to permanently deprive the owner of the bag or items in it so he could not be guilty of theft.

Intent permanently to deprive and throwing things away

Vinall can be compared with *Easom*, in which the handbag was replaced approximately in the position from which it had been removed.

Subsequent 'disposal' of the property may be evidence either of an intention at the time of the taking or evidence of an intention at the time of the disposal.

- When the allegation is theft, a later appropriation will be sufficient.
- When the allegation is robbery, it almost certainly will not.

How the property was disposed of is evidence supporting the inference of section 6(1) intention. This was shown *DPP v Lavender* (1994), *R v Marshall* (1998) and *R v Raphael* (2008).

Case study

The Chief Constable of Avon and Somerset Constabulary v Smith (1984)

The defendant broke into a parked car and removed two cases. Having searched them they concealed the cases, one in a nearby hedge and the other in a public lavatory cubicle. The court stated that when the cases were taken from the car, there was plain evidence capable of establishing intent:

- permanently to deprive the owner of them, and
- to treat the cases as the respondent's own, to dispose of regardless of the true owner's rights.

The cases were in fact so disposed of – they were not taken back to the car.

Case	Facts	Law
R v Velumyl (1989)	Defendant took cash from the office safe. He was going to replace the money later.	He had the intention of permanently depriving the company of the banknotes, even if he intended to replace them.
DPP v Lavender (1994)	Defendant used doors from a council property to replace damaged doors in his girlfriend's council flat.	Defendant was dealing with the doors as his own by moving them from one property to another without permission.
R v Lloyd (1985)	The projectionist at a local cinema gave the defendant a film to make an illegal copy.	By returning the film in its original state, it was not possible to prove an intention to permanently deprive.
R v Easom (1971)	Defendant rummaged through a handbag in a cinema, and replaced it without taking anything.	The defendant had not intended to permanently deprive the owner of the bag or items in it so he could not be guilty of theft.
Chief Constable of Avon and Somerset Constabulary v Smith (1984)	The defendant broke into a parked car and removed two cases. They inspected the contents and hid the cases away from the car.	The defendant had intended to permanently deprive the owner of the bag or items in it so he was guilty of theft.

Figure 9.8 Key cases: intention to permanently deprive – s 6

Activity

1 Has there been an appropriation in this situation?

The owner of a shop asks Parvati, who is a lorry driver, to pick up a load of computer equipment and take it to a warehouse. Parvati agrees to do this but, after collecting the equipment, she decides not to take it to the warehouse and instead sell it for cash.

2 Would the item in this situation be property for the purposes of theft?

Della discovers the examination papers she is to sit next week in the next-door office. She writes out the questions from the first paper on her own notepad. The second paper is very long, so she uses the office photocopier to take a copy, using paper already in the machine.

Extension activity

You can explore further issues, cases and principles for theft:

- No need to touch/handle property to appropriate – *R v McPherson* (1973).
- Appropriation without *mens rea* – *Eddy v Niman* (1981).
- Things in action – *Darroux v R* (2018); *R v Kohn* (1979).
- Other intangible property – *AG of Hong Kong v Chan Nai-Keung* (1987).
- Bodies and body parts (unless held or controlled) – *Yearworth v North Bristol NHS Trust* (2009).
- Possession or control – *R v Rostron* (2003); *R v Dyke and Munro* (2002); *Powell v McRae* (1977).
- Proprietary interest – *R v Marshall* (1998).
- Property got by mistake – *R v Gresham* (2003).
- Ownerless, lost and abandoned property – *Hibbert v McKiernan* (1948); *Williams v Phillips* (1957).
- To dispose of or treat as your own – *R v Marshall* (1998).
- An intention to sell or ransom property back to the victim – *R v Raphael* (2008).
- An intention to abandon the property – *R v Mitchell* (2008).
- Where defendant intends to part with victim's property but cannot be sure of its return – *R v Fernandes* (1996).
- Would have the other's consent if the other knew of the appropriation and the circumstances of it – *Boggeln v Williams* (1978).

9.2 Robbery

Robbery is an offence under s 8 of the Theft Act 1968. It is a theft which is aggravated by the use or threat of force.

Section 8 states:

> A person is guilty of robbery if he steals, and immediately before or at the time of doing so, and in order to do so, he uses force on any person or puts or seeks to put any person in fear of being then and there subjected to force.

The three men arrested in connection with the Great Train Robbery leaving Linslade Court

9.2.1 *Actus reus* of robbery

The elements of the *actus reus* which must be proved for robbery are:

- theft
- force or putting or seeking to put any person in fear of force.

There are two conditions on the force:

1 It must be immediately before or at the time of the theft.
2 It must be in order to steal.

There must be a completed theft

We have already considered what amounts to theft. This means that all the elements of theft have to be present. If any one of them is missing then there is no robbery, just as there would be no theft. For example:

- There is no theft where the defendant takes a car, drives it a few metres and abandons it, if it can be shown there is no intention permanently to deprive.

- There is no robbery where the defendant uses force to take that car as there was no theft. There is no offence of theft, so using force cannot make it into robbery, as in *R v Waters* (2015).

Case study

R v Waters (2015)

There was some hostility between a group of young people in a park. The defendant snatched the victim's phone from her and told her that she could have it back if one of her friends would speak to him. The police were immediately called to the scene, and he was charged and convicted of robbery.

The Court of Appeal quashed the conviction because the evidence did not establish an intention to permanently deprive the victim of her phone. The defendant's condition for returning the phone could have been 'fulfilled in the near future'. This meant that there was no theft and, therefore, no robbery.

Where force is used in order to steal, then the moment the theft is complete there is a robbery. This is demonstrated by the case of *Corcoran v Anderton* (1980).

Case study

Corcoran v Anderton (1980)

One of the defendants hit a woman in the back and tugged at her bag. She let go of the bag and it fell to the ground. The defendants ran off without the bag (because the woman was screaming and attracting attention). It was held that the theft was complete so the defendants were guilty of robbery.

However, if the theft is not completed, for instance if the woman in the case of *Corcoran v Anderton* had not let go of the bag, then there is an attempted theft and the defendant could be charged with attempted robbery.

There must be force or threat of force

As well as theft, the prosecution must prove force or the threat of force. The amount of force can be small. This is clearly shown by the case of *R v Dawson and James* (1976), and confirmed in *R v Clouden* (1987).

Case studies

R v Dawson and James (1976)

One of the defendants pushed the victim, causing him to lose his balance which enabled the other defendant to take his wallet. They were convicted of robbery. The Court of Appeal held that 'force' was an ordinary word and it was for the jury to decide if there had been force.

R v Clouden (1987)

The Court of Appeal held that the defendant was guilty of robbery: he approached a woman who was carrying a shopping basket in her left hand from behind, wrenched it down and out of her grasp with both hands and ran off with it. It was also stated that the question of whether the defendant had used force on a person was a question to be answered by the jury.

It can be argued that using force on the bag was effectively using force on the victim as the bag was wrenched from her hand. However, if a thief pulls a shoulder bag so that it slides off the victim's shoulder, would this be considered force? It would certainly not be force if a thief snatched a bag which was resting (not being held) on the lap of someone sitting on a park bench. This can be seen in *P v DPP* (2012).

Case study

P v DPP (2012)

The defendant snatched a cigarette from the victim's hand without touching the victim in any way. The Court stated:

> The unexpected removal of a cigarette from between the fingers of a person is no more the use of force on that person than would be the removal of an item from her pocket. This offence is properly categorised as simple theft.

The situation in *P v DPP* is similar to pickpocketing, where the victim is unaware of any contact. However, where the pickpocket (or accomplice) jostles the victim to distract the victim, as in *R v Dawson and James* (1976), while the theft is taking place, there is force which could support a charge of robbery rather than theft.

The definition of robbery makes clear that robbery is committed if the defendant puts or seeks to put a person in fear of force. It is not necessary that the force be applied. Putting the victim 'in fear of being there and then subjected to force' is sufficient for robbery. This covers:

- threatening words, such as, 'I have a knife and I'll use it unless you give me your wallet'
- threatening gestures, such as holding a knife in front of the victim.

Robbery is also committed even if the victim is not actually frightened by the defendant's actions or words. If the defendant seeks to put the victim in fear of being then and there subjected to force, this element of robbery is present. So if the victim is a plain-clothes policeman put there to trap the defendant and is not frightened, the fact that the defendant sought to put the victim in fear is enough. *B and R v DPP* (2007) illustrates this point, and the fact that the amount of force does not have to be great.

Case study

B and R v DPP (2007)

The victim, a schoolboy aged 16, was stopped by five other school boys. They asked for his mobile phone and money. As this was happening, another five or six boys joined the first five and surrounded the victim. No serious violence was used against him, but he was pushed and his arms were held while he was searched.

The Court upheld the convictions for robbery on these grounds:

- There was no need to show that the victim felt threatened; the defendant only has to seek to put any person in fear of being then and there subjected to force.
- There could be an implied threat of force; in this case, surrounding the victim by so many created an implied threat.
- In any event, there was some limited force used by holding the victim's arms and pushing him.

On any person

This means that the person threatened does not have to be the person from whom the theft occurs. An obvious example is an armed robber who enters a bank, seizes a customer and threatens to shoot that customer unless a bank official gets money out of the safe. This is putting a person in fear of being then and there subjected to force. The fact that it is not the customer's property which is being stolen does not matter.

Force immediately before or at the time of the theft

This requires deciding when a theft is completed, so that the force is 'at the time of stealing'. This was considered in *R v Hale* (1979), and the decision there was followed in *R v Lockley* (1995).

Case studies

R v Hale (1979)

The defendants forced their way into the victim's house. One put his hand over the victim's mouth to stop her screaming while the other went upstairs and took a jewellery box. Before they left the house they tied up the victim. Here there was force immediately before the theft when one of the defendants put his hand over the victim's mouth. Tying up the victim could also be force in order to steal, as the theft was still continuing.

R v Lockley (1995)

The defendant was caught shoplifting cans of beer. He used force on the shopkeeper who tried to stop him from escaping. The court stated that for the purposes of robbery, appropriation is a continuing act and it is for the jury to decide whether the theft is complete before the use of force.

As shown in the cases of *Hale* (1979) and *Lockley* (1995), the courts have been prepared to view appropriation as a continuing act. In *Lockley*, the defendant used force to escape after he had stolen. Although the appropriation for the theft occurred before the force, the defendant was guilty of robbery. This conflicts with the courts' approach in theft cases, particularly *R v Atakpu and Abrahams* (1994).

There must be a point when the theft is complete and so any force used after this point does not make it robbery. When the defendant is running down the street and uses force this is no longer robbery but theft plus common assault.

The force must be used in order to steal. If the force was not used for this purpose, then any later theft will not make it into robbery.

Imagine the defendant has an argument with the victim and punches them, knocking them out. The defendant then sees that some money has fallen out of the victim's pocket and decides to take it. The force was not used for the purpose of that theft and the defendant is not guilty of robbery, but guilty of two separate offences: an offence of actual bodily harm and theft.

Activity

Are the elements of robbery present in these examples?

- A bank official is attacked at their home by a gang in order to steal keys and security codes. The gang then drives to the bank and steals money. The theft has taken place an hour after the use of force. Is this 'immediately before'?
- The attack on the manager takes place on Saturday evening but the theft of the money not until 24 hours later. Does this come within 'immediately before'?

9.2.2 *Mens rea* of robbery

There are two elements to the *mens rea* of robbery. The defendant must have:

- had the *mens rea* for theft
- intended to use force to steal.

If a defendant were to punch a victim and knock them out, and then decided to steal the victim's watch, this would be theft but not robbery. If the victim was punched so that his watch could easily be stolen, this would be robbery.

Element	Law	Case
Theft	There must be a completed theft; if any element is missing, there is no theft and therefore no robbery.	*R v Waters* (2015)
	The moment the theft is completed (with the relevant force), there is robbery.	*Corcoran v Anderton* (1980)
Force or threat of force	The jury decides whether the acts amounted to force, using the ordinary meaning of the word.	*R v Dawson and James* (1976)
	It includes wrenching a bag from the victim's hand.	*R v Clouden* (1987)
On any person	The force can be against any person.	
	It does not have to be against the victim of the theft.	
Immediately before or at the time of the theft	For robbery, theft has been held to be a continuing act. Using force to escape can still be at the time of the theft.	*R v Hale* (1979) *R v Lockley* (1995)
In order to steal	The force must be in order to steal.	
	Force used for another purpose does not become robbery if the defendant later decides to steal.	
Mens rea	*Mens rea* for theft plus an intention to use force to steal.	

Figure 9.9 Key facts: robbery

Activity

Explain whether or not a robbery has occurred in each of the following situations:

1. Blake is angry with Conroy. Blake lies in wait and attacks Conroy, knocking him unconscious. When Conroy is unconscious, Blake notices that Conroy is wearing a very expensive watch and decides to steal the watch.
2. Albert holds a knife to the throat of a three-year-old girl and orders the child's mother to hand over her purse or he will 'slit the child's throat'. The mother hands over her purse.
3. Brendan threatens staff in a post office with an imitation gun. He demands that they hand over the money in the till. One of the staff presses a security button and a grille comes down in front of the counter so that the staff are safe and Brendan cannot reach the till. He leaves without taking anything.
4. Carla snatches at Delia's handbag. Delia is so surprised that she lets go of the bag and Carla runs off with it.
5. Ellie breaks into a car in a car park and takes a briefcase out of it. As she is walking away from the car, the owner arrives, realises what has happened and starts to chase after Ellie. The owner catches hold of Ellie, but she pushes him over and makes her escape.
6. Freya tells Hamid to hand over his Rolex watch and that, if he does not, Freya will send her friend, Grant, round to beat Hamid up. Hamid knows that Grant is a very violent man. Hamid takes his watch off and gives it to Freya.

Extension activity

You can explore further issues, cases and principles for this area of the law:

- There must be a complete theft – *R v Robinson* (1977); *R v Zerei* (2012).
- Force need not be on the owner of the property – *Smith v Desmond* (1965).
- The *mens rea* of robbery is the *mens rea* of theft. The defendant must also intend to use force to steal. If he or she accidentally uses force while stealing there would be no robbery – *R v Forrester* (1992).

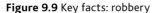

9.3 Burglary

There are two separate offences under the Theft Act 1968 s 9:
- Section 9(1)(a) – entering a building or part of a building as a trespasser with intent to commit theft, grievous bodily harm or criminal damage.
- Section 9(1)(b) – having entered as a trespasser, stealing or inflicting or attempting to inflict grievous bodily harm.

9.3.1 The common elements of ss 9(1)(a) and 9(1)(b)

Although ss 9(1)(a) and 9(1)(b) create different ways of committing burglary, they do have common elements of entering a building or part of a building as a trespasser.

'Entry'

'Entry' is not defined in the Theft Act 1968, but there have been several cases on the meaning of the word.
- *R v Brown* (1985): entry was said to mean an effective entry.
- *R v Ryan* (1996): a partial entry is enough to amount to entry. If a defendant puts any part of his body within the building, this can amount to burglary.

Case studies

R v Brown (1985)

The defendant was standing on the ground outside but leaning in through a shop window, rummaging through goods. His conviction for burglary was upheld as clearly in this situation his entry was effective.

R v Ryan (1996)

The defendant became trapped when trying to get through a window into a house in the early hours of the morning. His head and right arm were inside the house but the rest of his body was outside. The fire brigade had to be called to release him. He was convicted of burglary as there was sufficient evidence on which the jury could find that the defendant had entered.

'Building or part of a building' (s 9(4))

The Theft Act 1968 s 9(4) gives an extended meaning to the word 'building' so that it includes inhabited places such as houseboats or caravans. However, it does not give any basic definition for 'building'.

Usually there is no problem. Clearly houses, blocks of flats, offices, factories and so on are buildings. The word also includes outbuildings and sheds.

There are two cases on whether a large storage container is a building: *B and S v Leathley* (1979) and *Norfolk Constabulary v Seekings and Gould* (1986). The courts came to different decisions after looking at the facts.

Case studies

B and S v Leathley (1979)

A 25-foot-long freezer container had been kept as a storage unit in a farmyard for over two years. It rested on sleepers, had doors with locks and was connected to the electricity supply. This was held to be a building.

Norfolk Constabulary v Seekings and Gould (1986)

A lorry trailer with wheels had been used for over a year for storage. It had steps up to it and was connected to the electricity supply, but was held not to be a building: because it still had wheels, it remained a vehicle.

The phrase 'part of building' is used to cover situations in which the defendant may have permission to be in one part of the building (and therefore is not a trespasser in that part) but does not have permission to be in another part. This can be seen in *R v Walkington* (1979).

Case study

R v Walkington (1979)

The defendant went into the counter area in a shop and opened a till. This area was clearly marked by a three-sided counter. The defendant's conviction for burglary under s 9(1)(a) was upheld as he had entered part of a building (the counter area) as a trespasser with the intention of stealing.

The critical point in *Walkington* was that the counter area was not an area where customers were permitted to go. It was an area for the use of staff, so he was a trespasser.

Other examples include:
- storerooms in shops where shoppers would not have permission to enter
- a student residence where one student would be a trespasser if he or she entered another student's room without permission.

The courts view domestic burglary more seriously and therefore give a broad interpretation of what amounts to a dwelling. This was specifically considered by the Court of Appeal in the case of *R v Rodmell* (1994).

Case study

R v Rodmell (1994)

This defendant was convicted of burglary of a garden shed, and the theft of power tools in it. The shed stood in the large grounds of a house, and was about 50 metres from the house. The Court made the following sentencing remarks:

> A garden shed is part of a person's home. Burglars should be under no illusion that burglary of outbuildings is just as much burglary of domestic premises as breaking into the front door, although it can be said to be not quite as serious as breaking into the place where people live.

'As a trespasser'

In order for the defendant to commit burglary, he or she must enter as a trespasser. If a person has permission to enter, they are not a trespasser. The prosecution must prove that the defendant knew they were trespassing or was subjectively reckless as to whether they were trespassing.

Where a defendant is given permission to enter but then goes beyond that permission, they may be considered a trespasser. This was decided in *R v Jones and Smith* (1976).

Case study

R v Jones and Smith (1976)

Smith and his friend, Jones, went to Smith's father's house in the middle of the night and took two television sets without the father's knowledge or permission. The father stated that his son would not be a trespasser in the house; he had a general permission to enter. The Court of Appeal upheld their convictions for burglary, stating:

> a person is a trespasser for the purpose of s 9(1)(b) of the Theft Act 1968 if he enters premises of another knowing that he is entering in excess of the permission that has been given to him to enter, or being reckless whether he is entering in excess of that permission.

There are many situations where a person has permission to enter for a limited purpose:

- A person buys a ticket to attend a concert in a concert hall, or to look round an historic building or an art collection. The ticket is a licence (or permission) to be in the building for a very specific reason and/or time. If someone buys a ticket intending to steal one of the paintings from the art collection, these cases mean that they are probably guilty of burglary.
- Shoppers have permission to enter a shop. It is obvious that if a person has been banned from entering a shop, they will be entering as a trespasser if they go into that shop. Such a person would be guilty of burglary if:
  - they intended to steal goods (s 9(1)(a)), or
  - after entering, they then stole goods (s 9(1)(b)).

The case of *R v Jones and Smith* (1976) takes matters further than this, as it means that any person who enters a shop intending to steal is going beyond the permission to enter the shop in order to buy goods. They will be guilty of burglary under s 9(1)(a). However, it is rare for anyone to be charged with this as, unless the defendant admits they intended to steal when they entered, it is difficult for the prosecution to prove the intent.

The law is also clear where the defendant gains entry through fraud, such as claiming to be an electricity meter reader but not in fact being that person. There is no genuine permission to enter and the defendant is a trespasser.

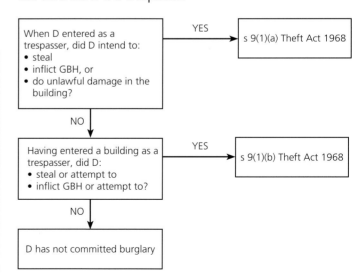

Figure 9.10 Different ways of committing burglary

9.3.2 *Mens rea* for burglary

There are two parts to the *mens rea* in burglary. These are in respect of entering as a trespasser, and the ulterior offence.

1 For both s 9(1)(a) and s 9(1)(b), the defendant must know, or be subjectively reckless, as to whether they are trespassing.
2 There is a difference between the subsections:
   ○ For s 9(1)(a), the defendant must have the intention to commit one of the three offences of theft, grievous bodily harm or criminal damage

at the time of entering the building. Where the defendant enters intending to steal anything they can find which is worth taking, then this is called a conditional intent. This is sufficient for them to be guilty under s 9(1)(a), even if there is nothing worth taking and they do not actually steal anything.
   ○ For s 9(1)(b), the defendant must also have the *mens rea* for theft or grievous bodily harm when committing (or attempting to commit) the *actus reus* of one of these offences.

See Figure 9.11.

Offence	Common elements	Underlying offences	Key differences
S 9(1)(a)	There must be: ● entry ● of a building or part of a building ● as a trespasser.	Intent to commit: ● theft ● grievous bodily harm ● criminal damage.	Defendant enters the building with an *intention* to commit the listed crimes. None of these crimes needs to be committed.
S 9(1)(b)	There must be: ● entry ● of a building or part of a building ● as a trespasser.	Commits or attempts to commit theft. *OR* Commits or attempts to commit grievous bodily harm.	Defendant enters the building and then commits the listed crimes. The intention to commit the offences occurs *after* his entry to the building. Criminal damage is not a listed offence.

Figure 9.11 Common elements of burglary

Elements	Comment	Case/Section
Entry	This has changed from: ● 'effective and substantial' entry to ● 'effective' entry to ● evidence for the jury to find D had entered.	*Collins* (1972) *Brown* (1985) *Ryan* (1996)
Building or part of a building	Must have some permanence. Includes inhabited vehicle or vessel. Can be entry of part of a building.	*B and S v Leathley* (1979) *Norfolk Constabulary v Seekings and Gould* (1986) s 9(4) of the Theft Act 1968/*Walkington* (1979)
As a trespasser	If D has permission s/he is not a trespasser. If D goes beyond permission then s/he can be a trespasser.	*Collins* (1972)/*R v Jones and Smith* (1976)
Mens rea	D must know or be subjectively reckless as to whether s/he is a trespasser PLUS EITHER Intention at point of entry to commit: ● theft, or ● grievous bodily harm, or ● criminal damage OR *Mens rea* for theft or grievous bodily harm at point of committing or attempting to commit these offences in a building.	s 9(1)(a) of the Theft Act 1968 s 9(1)(b) of the Theft Act 1968

Figure 9.12 Summary chart for burglary

You can explore further issues, cases and principles for this area of the law:

- Conditional intent is sufficient for *mens rea* – *AG's Ref (Nos 1 & 2 of 1979) (1979)*.

Quick questions

1 Explain the meaning of 'appropriation' in the law of theft.
2 Explain the meaning of 'property' in the law of theft.
3 Explain the meaning of 'belonging to another' in the law of theft.
4 What is meant by 'intention to permanently deprive' in the law of theft?
5 State the test for dishonesty in the law of theft and the name of the case that is authority for the definition in criminal law.

6 Explain the connection between force and theft in robbery.
7 What is the *mens rea* of the offence of robbery?
8 Explain the meaning of the terms 'entry' in the law of burglary
9 Explain the meaning of the term 'building or part thereof' in the law of burglary.
10 Outline the *mens rea* of burglary.

Summary

Theft

- Theft is defined by s 1 of the Theft Act 1968.
- In order to prove theft, there must be:
  - appropriation
  - of property
  - belonging to another
  - with the intention of permanently depriving that other of it and
  - dishonesty.
- Appropriation occurs where there is an assumption of the rights of an owner.
- Property includes money and all other property, real or personal. Things which cannot be stolen are set out in the Act.
- Property belongs to another if they have possession of control of it or any proprietary interest in it or it has been received under an obligation or by mistake.
- Dishonesty is not defined in the Theft Act 1968. The test is set out in R v Barton and Booth (2020).
- The defendant is regarded as having the intention to permanently deprive if it is his intention to treat the thing as his own to dispose of.

Robbery

- Robbery is defined by s 8 of the Theft Act 1968.
- It is a theft which is aggravated by the defendant's use or threat of force.
  - There must a completed theft.
  - The defendant must use force or put or seek to put any person in fear of force.
  - The force must be immediately before or at the time of the theft.
  - The amount of force can be small.
  - The defendant must intend to steal and intend to use force to steal.

Burglary

- Burglary is defined by s 9 of the Theft Act 1968.
- There are two ways of committing burglary:
  - Section 9(1)(a) – entering a building or part of a building as a trespasser intending to steal, inflict GBH or do unlawful damage.
  - Section 9(1)(b) – having entered a building or part of a building as a trespasser, steals or attempts to steal or inflicts or attempts to inflict GBH.
- Being a trespasser includes where the defendant goes beyond the permission to enter.
- Building includes inhabited vehicles and boats.

Chapter 10 Mental capacity defences

Introduction

Every person is presumed to be sane, and to possess a sufficient degree of mental capacity to be responsible for his crimes. There are three defences that allow a defendant to establish that he or she did not have the mental capacity for the offences with which he or she is charged. The defences are insanity, automatism and intoxication.

10.1 Insanity

The burden of proving insanity is on the defence, and it must be proved on the balance of probabilities. If the defendant proves this, then there is a special verdict of 'not guilty by reason of insanity'.

10.1.1 The *M'Naghten* Rules

The rules on insanity are based on the *M'Naghten* Rules, set as a result of the decision in the case of 1843.

Case study

M'Naghten (1843)

The defendant suffered from extreme paranoia. He thought he was being persecuted by the 'Tories' (the then government). He tried to kill a member of the government, Sir Robert Peel, but instead killed his secretary. Because of his mental state he was found not guilty of murder.

In fact, he was committed to a mental hospital because of his mental state, but this was not as a result of the verdict. The fact that he could be found not guilty and need not have been sent to a mental hospital caused a public outcry, leading the judges to answer a series of questions in order to clarify the law in respect of insanity. The answers to those questions have created the rules on insanity which are used in legal cases today.

Three elements need to be proved. These are that the defendant was suffering from:
- a defect of reason
- which must be the result of a disease of the mind
- which caused the defendant not to know the nature and quality of their act, or not to know they were doing wrong.

Insanity does not mean an absence of *mens rea*. A person who lashes out in a fight and causes injury is probably reckless as to an assault. But they may be insane if they do so while deluded as to the nature and quality, or wrongness, or what they are doing.

Insanity can be a defence to a strict liability offence, if the person does it because of a delusion as the nature and quality of the act. This can be seen in *Loake v DPP* (2017).

Link

See Chapter 6 for an explanation of strict liability offences.

Defendant is suffering from defect of reason	+	Defect is due to disease of the mind	+	Defendant does not know nature and quality of his action, or if he or she does know it, does not know it is wrong

Figure 10.1 The *M'Naghten* rules

Defect of reason

This means that the defendant's powers of reasoning must be impaired. If the defendant is capable of reasoning but has failed to use those powers, then this is not a defect of reason. This was decided in *R v Clarke* (1972), where it was held that the defect of reason must be more than absent-mindedness or confusion.

Case study

R v Clarke (1972)

The defendant went into a supermarket, picked up three items, put them into her own bag and then left the store without paying. She was charged with theft but claimed in her defence that she lacked the *mens rea* for theft as she had no recollection of putting the items into her bag. Indeed, she did not even want one of the items as neither she nor her husband ate it. She said she was suffering from absent-mindedness caused by diabetes and depression. The trial judge ruled that this amounted to a plea of insanity, so she pleaded guilty to the theft but later appealed.

The court quashed the conviction and held that the phrase 'defect of reason' in the *M'Naghten* Rules applied only to 'persons who by reason of a "disease of the mind" are deprived of the power of reasoning'. The Court also said that the rules of insanity do not apply to people who simply have moments of confusion or absent-mindedness.

Disease of the mind

The defect of reason must be due to a disease of the mind. This is a legal term, not a medical one. The disease can be a mental disease or a physical disease which affects the mind. An example of this is seen in *R v Kemp* (1956).

Case study

R v Kemp (1956)

The defendant was suffering from hardening of the arteries. This interfered with the supply of blood to his brain and caused him to have moments of temporary loss of consciousness. During one of these moments, he attacked his wife with a hammer, causing her serious injury. The question arose as to whether this condition came within the rules on insanity.

He admitted that he was suffering from a 'defect of reason' but said that this was not due to a 'disease of the mind' as it was a physical illness causing the problem and not a mental illness. As the law was not concerned with the brain but with the mind, his ordinary mental faculties of reason, memory and understanding had been affected and so his condition came within the rules on insanity.

In *R v Sullivan* (1984), the House of Lords was asked to decide whether epilepsy came within the rules of insanity.

Case study

R v Sullivan (1984)

The defendant had suffered from epilepsy since childhood. He was known to have fits and had shown aggression to those trying to help him during a fit. He injured an 80-year-old man during a visit to a neighbour's flat. The trial judge ruled that he would be directing the jury to return a verdict of 'not guilty by reason of insanity'. Because of the insanity direction, he pleaded guilty to assault occasioning actual bodily harm but then appealed.

The court ruled that the source of the disease was irrelevant. It could be 'organic, as in epilepsy, or functional', and it did not matter whether the impairment was 'permanent or transient and intermittent', provided that it existed at the time at which the defendant did the act.

- Organic insanity is when the brain has been damaged by a physical cause such as epilepsy or a degenerative disease like Alzheimer's.
- Functional insanity is when there is no organic reason for the damage to the brain.

This ruling means that, for the purpose of the *M'Naghten* Rules, the disease can be of any part of the body provided it has an effect on the mind. In *R v Hennessy* (1989), high blood sugar levels because of diabetes was classed as insanity because the sugar levels affected his mind.

Case study

R v Hennessy (1989)

The defendant was a diabetic who had not taken his insulin for three days. He drove a stolen car, and was charged with taking a motor vehicle without consent and driving while disqualified. He had no recollection of taking or driving the car. The judge ruled that he was putting forward a defence of insanity (and not non-insane automatism which the defendant wanted to use as a defence – see section 10.2). He then pleaded guilty and appealed on the grounds that he should have been allowed to put forward the defence of non-insane automatism.

The court held that the correct defence was insanity as the diabetes was affecting his mind. This brought diabetes within the definition of insanity.

Another case in which a condition amounted to insanity was *R v Burgess* (1991). In this case, it was decided that, in some instances, sleep-walking was within the legal definition of insanity.

Case study

R v Burgess (1991)

The defendant and his girlfriend had been watching videos. They both fell asleep and, in his sleep, he attacked her. There was no evidence of any external cause for this sleep-walking and evidence was given that, in this case, it was due to an internal cause – a sleep disorder. The judge ruled that this was evidence of insanity and the defendant was found 'not guilty by reason of insanity'. The Court of Appeal agreed with this finding rather than the defence of automatism.

Where the defendant is in a state where they do not know what they are doing due to an external cause, it does not amount to a disease of the mind and the defence of insanity does not apply. The defence of automatism may be available (see section 10.2).

Similarly, where the defendant voluntarily takes an intoxicating substance and this causes a temporary psychotic episode, the defendant cannot use the defence of insanity. This is because the intoxicating substance is an external factor (see section 10.3).

Not knowing the nature and quality of the act

Nature and quality refer to the physical character of the act. There are two ways in which the defendant may not know the nature and quality of the act. These are when:

1 they are unconscious or have impaired consciousness, or
2 they are conscious but due to their mental condition, they do not understand or know what they are doing.

If the defendant can show that either of these states applied to them at the time of the act, then they satisfy this part of the *M'Naghten* rules. A case of a defendant not knowing the nature and quality of his act was *R v Oye* (2013).

Case study

R v Oye (2013)

The police were called to a café where the defendant was behaving oddly. He threw crockery at the police and was arrested and taken to a police station. At the police station he continued to behave oddly including drinking water out of a lavatory cistern. When the police moved him to the custody suite, he became aggressive and punched a police officer, breaking her jaw. He was charged with assault occasioning actual bodily harm and two charges of affray.

His defence was that he believed the police had demonic faces and were agents of evil spirits. Medical evidence at the trial was that he had had a psychotic episode and that he had not known what he was doing and/or that he was doing wrong. The verdict was of not guilty by reason of insanity.

Where the defendant knows the nature and quality of the act, they still can use the defence of insanity if they do not know that what they did was wrong.

- *Wrong*, in this sense, means legally wrong, not morally wrong. If the defendant knows the nature and quality of the act and that it is legally wrong, they cannot use the defence of insanity. This is so even if the defendant is suffering from a mental illness, as shown by *R v Windle* (1952).

Case study

R v Windle (1952)

The defendant's wife constantly spoke of committing suicide. One day the defendant killed her by giving her 100 aspirins. He gave himself up to the police and said, 'I suppose they will hang me for this.' He was suffering from mental illness, but these words showed that he knew what he had done was legally wrong. As a result he could not use the defence of insanity and was found guilty of murder.

The decision in *Windle* was followed in *R v Johnson* (2007).

Case study

R v Johnson (2007)

The defendant forced his way into a neighbour's flat and stabbed him. He was charged with wounding with intent. At his trial, two psychiatrists gave evidence that he was suffering from paranoid schizophrenia and suffering from hallucinations. However, they both agreed that, despite this, he knew the nature and quality of his acts and that they were legally wrong. This meant that the defence of insanity was not available.

The special verdict

When a defendant successfully proves insanity, then the jury must return a verdict of 'not guilty by reason of insanity'. The judge can then impose:
- a hospital order (with or without restrictions as to when the defendant may be released), or
- a supervision order, or
- an absolute discharge.

Extension activity

You can explore further issues, cases and principles for insanity:
- Voluntary intoxication is considered an external factor (see section 10.2) – *R v Coley* (2013).

10.2 Automatism

There are two types of automatism:
- Insane automatism: the cause of the automatism is a disease of the mind within the *M'Naghten* Rules. The defence is insanity and the verdict is 'not guilty by reason of insanity'.
- Non-insane automatism: the cause of the lack of control is external. Where such a defence succeeds, it is a complete defence and the defendant is not guilty.

	Law	Case(s)
Definition	Defendant must be labouring under a defect of reason from disease of the mind *AND* must either not know the nature and quality of the act he or she is doing *OR* not know he or she is doing wrong	*M'Naghten* (1843)
Defect of reason	Defendant's powers of reasoning must be impaired Absent-mindedness is not enough	*R v Clarke* (1972)
Disease of the mind	This is a legal term NOT a medical one There must be an internal cause It need not be permanent: it can be 'transient and intermittent' An external cause is not sufficient	*R v Kemp* (1956) *R v Sullivan* (1984)
Not know nature and quality of act *OR* Not know he or she is doing wrong	This can be because the defendant is in a state of unconsciousness or impaired consciousness *OR* they are conscious but do not understand or know what they are doing Defendant must not know it is legally wrong: if they do, they cannot rely on the defence of insanity	*R v Oye* (2013) *R v Windle* (1952) *R v Johnson* (2007)
Special verdict	Not guilty by reason of insanity	

Figure 10.2 Key facts: insanity

Case	Facts	Law
M'Naghten (1843)	Suffering from paranoia, defendant shot Sir Robert Peel's secretary	House of Lords clarified the law on insanity Defendant must be labouring under a defect of reason, from disease of the mind *AND* must either not know the nature and quality of the act they are doing *OR* not know they were doing wrong.
Loake v DPP (2017)	The defendant was charged with harassment	Insanity is a general defence and not limited to crimes requiring *mens rea*.
R v Clarke (1972)	Absent-mindedly, defendant took items from a supermarket	Mere absent-mindedness or confusion is not insanity.
R v Kemp (1956)	Defendant suffering from hardening of the arteries which caused blackouts	Within the rules of insanity – his condition affected his mental reasoning, memory and understanding.
R v Sullivan (1984)	Injured friend during epileptic fit	Insanity includes any organic or functional disease, even where it is temporary.
R v Hennessy (1989)	Diabetic took a car after failing to take his insulin	If the disease affects the mind then it is within the definition of insanity.
R v Burgess (1991)	Injured girlfriend while sleepwalking	If the cause of sleepwalking is internal, it is a disease within the definition of insanity.
R v Oye (2013)	Defendant had very odd behaviour	Insanity could be applied here – he had a psychotic episode, didn't know what he was doing and/or that it was wrong.
R v Windle (1952)	Defendant suffered from a mental disorder and killed his wife	Defendants knew what they had done was legally wrong, so they were not insane by the *M'Naghten* Rules.
R v Johnson (2007)	Defendant stabbed his neighbour while suffering from paranoid schizophrenia and hallucinations	He knew the nature and quality of his acts and that they were legally wrong. Therefore, he was not insane by the *M'Naghten* Rules.

Figure 10.3 Key cases: insanity

Key term

Automatism – a defence to a criminal offence: an act done by the muscles without any control by the mind or by a person who is not conscious of what they are doing.

There is an overlap between insanity and automatism. It will have to be decided whether the defendant's condition is due to a mental illness or due to external factors. The courts have decided that those suffering from any mental or physical illness which affects their mind amounts to insanity. This means that the defence of non-insane automatism has been removed from such people as epileptics and diabetics.

This can be shown in *R v Quick* (1973), where the defence of automatism applied.

Case study

R v Quick (1973)

The defendant was a diabetic who had taken his insulin but had not eaten enough food. This caused him to have low blood sugar levels which affected his brain. He was a nurse at a mental hospital and assaulted a patient.

The Court ruled that his condition did not come within the definition of insanity. It was caused by an external factor, the insulin, which meant that the correct defence was automatism

This has consequences:
- Those successfully using the defence of automatism are entitled to a complete acquittal.
- On a finding of 'not guilty by reason of insanity', the judge is likely to impose some form of order on the defendant.

In *Bratty v Attorney-General for Northern Ireland* (1963), automatism was defined as:

> An act done by the muscles without any control by the mind, such as a spasm, a reflex action or a convulsion; or an act done by a person who is not conscious of what he is doing such as an act done whilst suffering from concussion or whilst sleep-walking.

10.2.1 Non-insane automatism

This is a complete defence:
- The *actus reus* of a crime committed by the defendant is not a voluntary action.
- There is an external cause such as in *R v Quick* (1973).
- Because of the automatism, the defendant does not have the required *mens rea*.

As a result, the defendant is not at fault for their uncontrolled actions.

The cause of the automatism must be generally external to the defendant, for example:
- a blow to the head
- the effect of post-traumatic stress disorder (PTSD)
- the effect of taking a drug, which might raise issues of self-induced automatism (see section 10.2.2).

This concept of no fault when the defendant was in an automatic state through an external cause was approved in *Hill v Baxter* (1958).

Case study

Hill v Baxter (1958)

The defendant drove through a halt sign without stopping, and collided with another car. He was charged with dangerous driving but there was little evidence to support a defence of automatism. However, it was stated a person should not be made liable where, through no fault of his own, he becomes unconscious when driving, for example, a person who has been struck by a stone or overcome by a sudden illness.

There has to be a *total* loss of voluntary control, as set out in *Attorney-General's Reference (No. 2 of 1992)* (1993). A reduced or partial control of one's actions is not sufficient to amount to automatism.

Case study

Attorney-General's Reference (No. 2 of 1992) (1993)

The defendant was a lorry driver, who after driving for several hours, drove along the hard shoulder of a motorway for about half a mile. He hit a stationary broken-down car, killing two people. He said that he was suffering from a condition of 'driving without awareness' which puts a driver into a trance-like state. This could be brought on by driving for long distances on featureless motorways.

However, because this condition only causes partial loss of control, it does not amount to automatism. Even in this state, a driver has still enough awareness to drive a vehicle.

This principle also applies to PTSD as in *R v T* (1990).

Case study

R v T (1990)

The defendant stabbed her victim and leaned into her victim's car to take her bag. The medical evidence was that she was suffering from post-traumatic stress disorder after having been raped three days earlier. This was viewed as arising from external sources so was sufficient for the defence of automatism.

10.2.2 Self-induced automatism

This is where the defendant knows that their conduct is likely to bring on an automatic state. Examples include:
- a diabetic, who knows the risk of failing to eat after taking insulin such as *R v Quick* (1973)
- a person who drinks alcohol after taking medication when they have been told by their doctor not to do so.

How the defence (and the defence of intoxication) works depends on whether the offence committed is one of *specific* intent or *basic* intent.

Link

See Chapter 8 for an explanation of specific and basic intent offences.

When the state of automatism comes about from the defendant's own voluntary conduct, the intoxication rules apply. This is illustrated by *R v Coley* (2013).

Case study

R v Coley (2013)

The defendant had been taking cannabis which led him to attack his neighbours. As well as arguing the defence of insanity, the defendant argued automatism.

The Court dismissed this argument as (a) he was not acting wholly involuntarily (he was able to dress himself in certain clothes and use keys to enter the neighbour's house) and (b) he had induced his condition by voluntary intoxication.

The same approach was taken in the case of *R v McGhee* (2013).

Case study

R v McGhee (2013)

The defendant, suffering from tinnitus, took temazepam (a sedative and muscle relaxant) and drank alcohol. He was charged with s 47 and s 18 offences but claimed he had no recollection of the assaults. The court ruled that even if he had been in a state of automatism, the defence would have failed on the grounds that he induced it through his voluntary fault. He had voluntarily drunk himself into a state of intoxication which was worsened by the combination of temazepam with alcohol, and he was well aware of the dangers of taking them together.

- If automatism results from some perfectly *appropriate action* but with unanticipated consequences, it will be a defence to offences of both specific and basic intent. This could occur, for example, from a wholly unexpected adverse reaction to taking a legitimate prescription drug.

- If the automotive state results from some kind of *improper action* or failure by the defendant – for example, if a diabetic took an excessive dose of insulin or failed to eat sufficient food having taken insulin – automatism:
  - *will* be a defence to specific intent offences, because they cannot be in a worse position than they would be in if their state resulted from intoxication (*R v Hardie* (1984))
  - *will not* be a defence to a basic intent offence if they knew the risk that if they did become an automaton, they might engage in dangerous or aggressive conduct (*R v Bailey* (1983)).

This is similar to the position with the defence of voluntary intoxication.

Case study

R v Bailey (1983)

The defendant was a diabetic who had failed to eat enough after taking his insulin to control his diabetes. He went to sort out matters between himself and his ex-lover's new boyfriend. After asking for some sugar and water, he failed to eat anything, became aggressive and hit the victim over the head with an iron bar. He was charged with s 18 OAPA 1861. While the defence of automatism was available to him, the result was not affected because there was no significant evidence of automatism.

Case study

R v Hardie (1984)

The defendant was depressed and took some Valium tablets which he had not been prescribed. His girlfriend encouraged him to take the tablets, saying that they would calm him down. He then set fire to a wardrobe in the flat. His defence was automatism as he did not know what he was doing because of the Valium, and it had the opposite effect on him of what he expected. Therefore, the defendant had not been reckless and the defence of automatism should have been left to the jury to consider.

The main problem when automatism is raised is whether it should be treated as insane automatism or non-insane automatism. This is very important as the effect of these two types of automatism as a defence is so different, as seen in section 10.2.1.

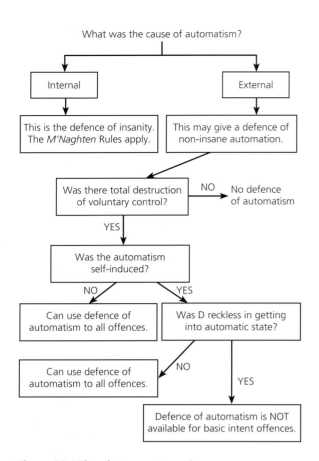

What was the cause of automatism?

Internal → This is the defence of insanity. The *M'Naghten* Rules apply.

External → This may give a defence of non-insane automation.

Was there total destruction of voluntary control? → NO → No defence of automatism

YES ↓

Was the automatism self-induced?

NO → Can use defence of automatism to all offences.

YES → Was D reckless in getting into automatic state?

NO → Can use defence of automatism to all offences.

YES → Defence of automatism is NOT available for basic intent offences.

Figure 10.4 Flowchart on automatism

Extension activity ✓

You can explore further issues, cases and principles for automatism:

● Defendant is hyperglycaemic (has high blood sugar) because they failed to take insulin (an internal factor) – *R v Bingham* (1991).

10.3 Intoxication

This covers intoxication by alcohol, drugs or taking other substances such as sniffing glue. To consider this defence, it has to be shown that the defendant was so intoxicated by the drink, drug or other substance that they were incapable of forming the *mens rea* of the offence. This will usually require evidence that the defendant had more than just a drink or two or a small amount of a drug.

The defendant being found guilty or not depends on whether:

● the intoxication was voluntary or involuntary, and
● the offence charged is one of specific or basic intent.

Case	Facts	Legal principle
R v Quick (1973)	Diabetic who failed to eat after taking his insulin assaulted patient.	This was an external cause (the effect of the drug) and not insanity.
Hill v Baxter (1958)	Defendant was charged with dangerous driving but there was little evidence to support a defence of automatism.	Examples of what might be automatism given.
Attorney-General's Reference (No. 2 of 1992) (1993)	A lorry driver crashed on a motorway killing two people, while suffering from a condition of 'driving without awareness'.	Automatism not available as there has to be a total loss of voluntary control.
R v Coley (2013)	The defendant took cannabis and attacked his neighbours.	Defence failed, because not acting wholly involuntarily and he had induced his condition by voluntary intoxication.
R v McGhee (2013)	The defendant, suffering from tinnitus, took temazepam and drank alcohol.	Even if he had been in a state of automatism, the defence would have failed as he induced it through his voluntary fault.
R v Bailey (1983)	A diabetic failed to eat enough after taking insulin and was charged with s 18 OAPA 1861 (a specific intent offence).	The jury should be able to consider automatism as a defence to specific intent offence.
R v Hardie (1984)	Defendant took some Valium tablets because he was depressed and set fire to a wardrobe (a basic intent offence).	Defendant had not been reckless and the jury should consider his defence of automatism.

Figure 10.5 Key cases: automatism

Specific intent offences	Basic intent offences
• these have intent only as the *mens rea*, e.g. murder, s 18 OAPA 1861	• these have recklessness as part of the *mens rea*, e.g. manslaughter, ss 20 and 47 OAPA 1861, assault, battery, criminal damage

Figure 10.6 Specific and basic intent offences

10.3.1 Voluntary intoxication

Voluntary intoxication is where the defendant:
- has chosen to take an intoxicating substance
- knows that the effect of taking a prescribed drug will be to make them intoxicated.

Voluntary intoxication occurs if a person chooses to consume a dangerous drug known to cause unpredictability or aggressiveness. Taking a 'non-dangerous drug' might also count as voluntary intoxication, depending on whether the defendant knows about the likely effects of the drug in the quantity and circumstances in which it was consumed.

The case considered under automatism of *R v Coley* (2013) illustrates this.

Case study

R v Coley (2013)

The defendant was a regular user of cannabis and one evening watched a violent video game. Later that night he entered a neighbour's house and attacked her and her partner with a knife. When arrested he was calling for his mother and threatening suicide. He said he had blacked out and had no recollection of what had happened. The psychiatric evidence was that he could have suffered a brief psychotic episode induced by taking cannabis, and that he might have been acting out the role of a character in the video game he had been playing.

He was convicted of attempted murder as his state of mind was caused by voluntary intoxication and therefore it was not a case of insanity.

Voluntary intoxication and specific intent offences

If the defendant is voluntarily intoxicated, this could mean they did not form the *mens rea* of the offence due to the intoxication. Originally, the test set by Lord Birkenhead in *DPP v Beard* (1920) was:

> If he [the defendant] was so drunk that he was incapable of forming the intent required, he could not be convicted of a crime which was committed only if the intent was proved.

Later authority, such as *R v Sheehan and Moore* (1975), says that the true test is whether, because of intoxication, the defendant did not form the intent, irrespective of whether they were incapable of doing so.

Case study

R v Sheehan and Moore (1975)

The defendants, in a drunken state, poured petrol over a homeless man and set light to the petrol, causing his death. It was decided that the relevant question was not whether the defendants were capable of forming the *mens rea*; it was whether they *had* in fact formed the *mens rea* – a drunken intent is still an intent.

It is for the prosecution to prove that the defendant had the intent. In this case, they were unable to do so and the defendants were convicted of unlawful act manslaughter.

So, where there is an alternative basic intent offence, the defendant may be charged with both a specific intent offence and a basic intent offence, and it can be left to the jury to decide whether the defendant had the *mens rea* for the specific intent offence. For example, a defendant could be charged with both murder (specific intent) and manslaughter (basic intent). In this case, the prosecution will know that they will at least get a conviction for the lesser offence if the jury finds that the defendant did not form the *mens rea* of murder. This was seen in *R v Lipman* (1970).

Case study

R v Lipman (1970)

The defendant and his girlfriend took LSD. While they were tripping, the defendant stuffed a sheet down her throat as he thought he was fighting a snake and going to the centre of the earth. He was charged with his girlfriend's murder and with unlawful act manslaughter.

He was acquitted of murder, as he was unable to form the *mens rea* of the offence. However, he was convicted of manslaughter as that is a basic intent offence to which voluntary intoxication is no defence.

Where the defendant has the necessary *mens rea* despite their intoxicated state, then they are still guilty of an offence, as a drunken intent is still intent. This can be shown by *Attorney-General for Northern Ireland v Gallagher* (1963).

Attorney-General for Northern Ireland v Gallagher (1963)

The defendant decided to kill his wife. He bought a knife to do the killing and also a bottle of whisky. He drank a large amount of the whisky to give himself 'Dutch courage' before killing his wife. His conviction for murder was upheld as he had formed the intent to kill before he became intoxicated. This case shows the defendant's prior fault being punished – in other words, he made up his mind to kill before, allegedly, becoming so drunk that he killed while having no *mens rea*.

Voluntary intoxication and basic intent offences

Where the offence charged is one of basic intent, then voluntary intoxication is not a defence. This is because becoming intoxicated voluntarily is considered a reckless course of conduct, and recklessness is enough to constitute the necessary *mens rea*. This can be seen in *DPP v Majewski* (1977).

DPP v Majewski (1977)

The defendant consumed large quantities of alcohol and drugs and then attacked the landlord of the pub where he was drinking. He also attacked the police officers who tried to arrest him and damaged the pub and the police station where he was taken. All the offences he was charged with were basic intent offences.

The defendant claimed that he had no memory of what he had done due to the drink and drugs he had consumed. The court held that becoming intoxicated by drink and/or drugs was a reckless course of conduct, and as recklessness was enough for the necessary *mens rea* in the offences with which he was charged, he could not use the defence of intoxication.

If the defendant does not realise the strength of the intoxicant, for example, where street drugs have been cut with other substances, there could still be a defence.

R v Allen (1988)

The defendant drank some home-made wine which had a much greater effect on him than he expected. While under the influence of this wine, he committed sexual assaults. He claimed he was so drunk he did not know what he was doing and that he had not voluntarily put himself in that condition as the wine was much stronger than he realised.

It was decided that his intoxication was still voluntary, even though he had not realised the strength of it. Sexual assault is a crime of basic intent and therefore the defendant could not rely on his intoxicated state to negate the *mens rea*.

10.3.2 Involuntary intoxication

Involuntary intoxication covers situations where the defendant did not know they were taking an intoxicating substance. This may be where, for example, a soft drink has been 'laced' or 'spiked' with alcohol or drugs. It also covers situations where a prescribed drug has the unexpected effect of making the defendant intoxicated and the defendant does not realise its effect.

If the defendant was intoxicated through no fault of their own, they are allowed to argue that they did not form the *mens rea*, whether the offence is of specific or basic intent. If the prosecution can prove that they *did* form the *mens rea*, they will be guilty of the offence, even if they would not have committed it without being involuntarily intoxicated. This was decided in *R v Kingston* (1994).

Case study

R v Kingston (1994)

The defendant was invited to a house where his drink was drugged by a man who wanted to blackmail him. He was then shown a 15-year-old boy who was drugged and unconscious in the room, and he was invited to abuse him. The defendant, who had paedophile tendencies, did so and was photographed by the blackmailer. He was convicted of indecent assault: if a defendant had formed the *mens rea* for an offence before becoming intoxicated, then involuntary intoxication could not be a defence.

10.3.3 Intoxicated mistake

If the defendant is mistaken about a key fact because they are intoxicated, it depends on what the mistake was about as to whether or not there is a defence:

- There is a defence to a specific intent offence where the mistake is about something which means that the defendant did not have the necessary *mens rea* for the offence.
- Where the offence is one of basic intent, the defendant has no defence.

If the mistake is about another aspect, for example the amount of force needed in self-defence, the defendant will not have a defence. This applies to crimes of both basic intent and specific intent offences. This was stated in *R v O'Grady* (1987) and confirmed in *R v Hatton* (2005).

Case studies

R v O'Grady (1987)

After the defendant and the victim, who were friends, had been drinking heavily, they fell asleep. The defendant claimed that he awoke to find the victim hitting him, so he picked up a glass ashtray and hit the victim with it, and then went back to sleep. When he woke the next morning, he found that his friend was dead. On a charge of manslaughter, the court said a defendant is not entitled to rely, so far as self-defence is concerned, upon a mistake of fact which has been induced by voluntary intoxication.

R v Hatton (2005)

The defendant had drunk over twenty pints of beer. He and the victim went back to the defendant's flat. In the morning he claimed he found the victim dead from injuries caused by a sledgehammer. He said he could not really remember what had happened but thought the victim had hit him with a five-foot-long stick and he had defended himself. He was convicted of murder.

The court held that the decision in *O'Grady* (1987) was not limited to basic intent offences, but also applied to specific intent offences. A drunken mistake about the amount of force required in self-defence was not a defence.

Tip

When considering the appropriateness of various defences, look for potential indicators in the facts, such as alcohol (intoxication), drugs (intoxication or perhaps automatism) or some form of condition (insanity). This should help you to decide which defences are relevant.

10.3.4 Criminal Justice and Immigration Act 2008

Section 76 of the Criminal Justice and Immigration Act 2008 states that reasonable force may be used for the purposes of self-defence, defence of another or prevention of crime. However, s 76(5) says that this:

> does not enable the defendant to rely on any mistaken belief attributable to intoxication that was voluntarily induced.

The words 'attributable to intoxication' in s 76(5) are broad enough to encompass a mistaken state of mind:

- as a result of being drunk or intoxicated at the time
- immediately or after earlier drinking or drug-taking, so that, even though the defendant was not drunk or intoxicated at the time, the short-term effects could have triggered subsequent episodes or, for example, paranoia. This was seen in *Taj* (2018).

Taj (2018)

Taj began abusing drugs and alcohol as a child, which eventually brought on a psychosis that made him hear voices and become aggressive and paranoid. This psychosis would linger for a while even after the intoxication wore off.

Taj drank heavily and later, while in the grip of post-intoxication psychosis, he became convinced that a Muslim man he saw was a terrorist trying to detonate a bomb. He attacked and nearly killed him, but pleaded self-defence to the charge of attempted murder, arguing that he was entitled to the benefit of his honest, albeit unreasonable, beliefs about the circumstances that existed at the time of the attack.

The phrase 'attributable to intoxication' was not confined to cases in which alcohol or drugs were still present in a defendant's system. That was consistent with common law principles but this did not extend to long-term mental illness caused, perhaps over a considerable period, by alcohol or drug misuses.

Tip

In relation to the defence of intoxication, in examination scenarios, you may find references to the defendant's consumption of alcohol, for example: 'they drank five pints of beer' or 'half a bottle of whisky' or even 'they had a lot to drink'. These do not show, in themselves, that the defendant was intoxicated. You still have to make the point that the defendant could not form the *mens rea* of the offence for the defence of intoxication.

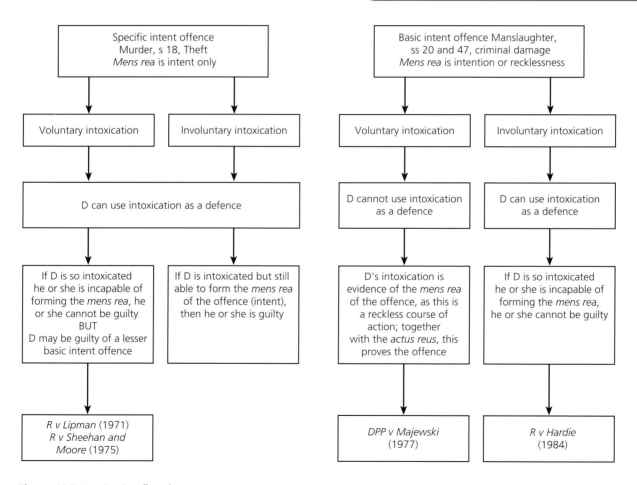

Figure 10.7 Intoxication flowchart

Case	Facts	Legal principle
R v Lipman (1970)	The defendant and his girlfriend took an LSD trip and he stuffed a sheet down her throat.	Could not form the *mens rea* of the offence, so he was not guilty of murder (a specific intent crime) but was convicted of manslaughter (it is a basic intent offence to which intoxication is no defence).
Attorney-General for Northern Ireland v Gallagher (1963)	The defendant decided to kill his wife and drank whisky to give himself 'Dutch courage'.	He was convicted of murder as he had formed the intent to kill before he became intoxicated.
DPP v Majewski (1977)	The defendant consumed large quantities of alcohol and drugs and then assaulted the landlord of the pub and the police and damaged property (all basic intent offences).	His reckless behaviour formed the necessary *mens rea* in these offences, so he could not use the defence of intoxication.
R v Kingston (1994)	The defendant had paedophile tendencies, and was drugged and filmed abusing a boy.	Guilty of indecent assault as he had formed the *mens rea* for an offence before becoming intoxicated, and involuntary intoxication could not be a defence.
R v O'Grady (1987)	A man killed his friend after a drinking session, claiming he did so in mistaken self-defence.	The defendant cannot rely on self-defence for a mistake of fact which has been induced by voluntary intoxication.
R v Hatton (2005)	The defendant had drunk a lot of beer and found the victim dead. He thought he had acted in self-defence but could not remember the events.	The decision in *O'Grady* applied to both specific and basic intent offences. A drunken mistake about the amount of force required in self-defence was not a defence.
R v Taj (2018)	Defendant drank heavily and later, while in the grip of post-intoxication psychosis, became convinced that a man was a terrorist.	The phrase 'attributable to intoxication' was not confined to cases in which alcohol or drugs were still present in a defendant's system. The appeal failed.

Figure 10.8 Key cases: intoxication as a defence

Activity

Consider whether there would be a defence available in the following situations.

1 Jameela suffered from paranoid schizophrenia, which caused her to believe that people were intending to harm her. When she found herself in a large crowd in town, she began to panic and lash out at anyone nearby. In doing so, she knocked down Ken, an elderly man. In his fall, Ken broke his hip. What defence(s) might be available to her if she is charged with offences under ss 18 and 20 OAPA 1861?

2 Michael was driving to work when he realised that he had forgotten to bring an important document that he needed. Without thinking, he suddenly tried to swing his car round to go back in the opposite direction. However, he lost control of the car, struck a kerb and injured Nick, a passing cyclist. Michael himself suffered a head injury in the collision and he staggered away from the car with little idea of what was happening. When Tina tried to help him, he punched her, cutting her lip. What defence(s) might be available to him if he is charged with offences under ss 20 and 47 OAPA 1861?

Quick questions

1 State the three elements that must be proved for the defence of insanity.
2 Explain the difference to the defendant between a successful plea of insanity and one of automatism.
3 Explain the legal principles with respect to self-induced automatism.
4 Distinguish between voluntary and involuntary intoxication.
5 Explain the legal principles with respect to an intoxicated mistake.

Summary

Insanity

- The definition of insanity is based on the *M'Naghten* Rules.
- The defendant must prove that they were 'labour-ing under such a defect of reason, from disease of the mind, as not to know the nature and quality of the act they were doing, or if they did know it, that they did not know they were doing what was wrong'.
- Disease of the mind includes physical diseases which affect the mind: it does not include the effect of an external factor.
- If the defendant knows the act is legally wrong, then they cannot use the defence of insanity.
- If the defence is successful, the verdict is not guilty by reason of insanity.
- A judge now has a discretion to impose whatever sentence is considered appropriate.

Automatism

- This is an act done by the muscles without any control by the mind.
- Automatism can be categorised as insane (covered by the defence of insanity) or non-insane.
- If the defendant's automatism is caused by an external factor then there is a defence and the defendant is not guilty.

- The external factor has to cause a total loss of voluntary control.
- If the automatism is self-induced, the defendant will be able to use the defence for a specific intent offence.
- If the automatism is self-induced because of the defendant's recklessness, they will have no defence for a basic intent offence.

Intoxication

- Voluntary intoxication can only be a defence to a specific intent offence where the defendant is so intoxicated that they do not have the necessary *mens rea* for the offence.
- Voluntary intoxication is not a defence to a basic intent offence, as becoming intoxicated is a reckless course of conduct.
- Involuntary intoxication is a defence to a specific intent offence where the defendant did not have the necessary *mens rea* for the offence.
- Involuntary intoxication can be a defence to a basic intent offence, as the defendant has not been reckless in becoming intoxicated.
- Where the defendant makes a mistake because they are intoxicated, then if the mistake means that the defendant did not have the necessary *mens rea* for the offence, they can use intoxication as a defence.

Chapter 11 General defences

Introduction

In this chapter we will discuss the defences of self-defence, duress by threats, duress of circumstances and necessity where the situation has affected the defendant to the extent that he or she takes criminal action, and the defence of consent where the defendant's actions have been permitted by the victim.

11.1 Self-defence

This is a complete defence in criminal law and, if successful, the defendant will be found not guilty. It covers not only actions needed to defend oneself from an attack, but also actions taken to defend another person, or one's property. The defence is now set out in both common law and statute.

- The common law defence of self-defence (including defence of another) and defence of property are as amended by the Criminal Justice and Immigration Act 2008.
- The statutory defence is in s 3(1) of the Criminal Law Act 1967 of self-defence in the prevention of crime or effecting or assisting in a lawful arrest.

Both permit the use of such force as is reasonable in the circumstances. They are governed by much the same rules. Section 76 of the Criminal Justice and Immigration Act 2008 confirms the rules to be applied when 'the question arises whether the degree of force used by the defendant against a person was reasonable in the circumstances' (s 76(1)(b)).

There are two questions to be asked in answering the question on whether the force used was reasonable in the circumstances in self-defence:

- Was it necessary to use any degree of force?
- If so, was the degree of force actually used proportionate or reasonable (to the harm threatened or the risk to be averted)?

Thus, if the use of some force was unnecessary, then the second question of proportion never arises and the use of force cannot be reasonable.

If the use of some force was necessary, the first hurdle is overcome but the second hurdle of proportionate force must then also be overcome. If it is not, the force used will not have been reasonable in the circumstances.

The defence applies to all fatal and non-fatal offences and, if accepted by the jury, is a complete defence.

Was it necessary to use force? Subjective test	+	Was the force used reasonable? Objective test

Figure 11.1 Requirements of self-defence

11.1.1 Was it necessary to use some force?

The defendant will be judged according to the facts as he or she genuinely believed them to be (a subjective test).

In the following cases in this section, the defendants had genuinely mistaken views of the facts, so the courts had to decide how they should be judged.

Case study

R v Williams (Gladstone) (1983)

The defendant was on a bus when he thought he saw a man assaulting a youth in the street. In fact, the man was trying to arrest the youth for mugging an old lady. The defendant got off the bus and asked what was happening. The man said that he was a police officer arresting the youth, but could not show his police ID card. There was then a struggle in which the man was injured.

The court quashed the defendant's conviction because the jury should have been told that if they thought the mistake was genuine, they should judge the defendant according to his genuine, mistaken view of the facts, regardless of whether this mistake was reasonable or unreasonable.

Section 76 of the Criminal Justice and Immigration Act 2008 puts the decision in *R v Williams (Gladstone)* onto a statutory footing. It states in s 76(3) the question whether the degree of force used by the defendant was reasonable in the circumstances is to be decided by reference to the circumstances as the defendant believed them to be.

This means, in each situation, the important point is to establish the facts as the defendant genuinely believed them to be.

In s 76(4) it states:

> If the defendant claims to have held a particular belief as regards the existence of any circumstances –
>
> (a) the reasonableness or otherwise of that belief is relevant to the question whether the defendant genuinely held it; but
>
> (b) if it is determined that the defendant did genuinely hold it, the defendant is entitled to rely on it for the purposes of subsection (3), whether or not –
>
> (i) it was mistaken, or
>
> (ii) (if it was mistaken) the mistake was a reasonable one to have made.

This means that if the defendant genuinely made a mistake, they should be judged on the facts as he or she believed them to be. This is so, even if the mistake was unreasonable.

Section 76(5) states that if a defendant made the mistake because he or she had voluntarily got drunk or taken drugs, and made a mistake because of their intoxicated state, then he or she cannot rely on their mistaken belief.

An example would be where a defendant had taken drugs which caused hallucinations, causing them to believe that he or she was being attacked by snakes. If he or she then assaults someone believing that that person is a snake, then he or she cannot use the defence of self-defence. He or she might genuinely believe they are being attacked by a snake, but this mistake has been caused by voluntary intoxication.

11.1.2 The effect of mental conditions on self-defence

The defendant's genuine belief can include delusions resulting from a psychiatric condition or another condition such as PTSD. This had to be considered in *R v Oye* (2013) who was not guilty by reason of insanity (see Chapter 10).

In *R v Press and Thompson* (2013), the Court of Appeal applied the same principles to PTSD suffered by the defendants who were both serving soldiers. It was alleged they had launched an unprovoked and vicious assault on an innocent victim in a fast-food shop. While the PTSD might cause them to misunderstand whether defensive action is necessary, the reasonableness in the degree of force used is objective.

Parliament, when enacting s 76 of the Criminal Justice and Immigration Act 2008, had sought to set an already existing principle in law. It did not intend to change the objective criteria for reasonable force.

11.1.3 Is a pre-emptive strike allowable?

In other words, does a person have to wait until they are attacked before they can use force? This can be illustrated by *R v Bird* (1986).

Case study

R v Bird (1986)

The defendant's ex-boyfriend turned up at her birthday party with his new girlfriend. There was an argument and he was asked to leave. He did but returned and there was another argument and he was injured. The defendant argued she acted in self-defence.

The court ruled that while withdrawing or showing an unwillingness to fight is good evidence that the defendant is acting reasonably and in good faith, there is no requirement to show an unwillingness to fight or a willingness to retreat, but it is a factor to be taken into account. Her conviction was quashed.

This principle is now set out in s 76(6A) of the Criminal Justice and Immigration Act 2008.

This makes it clear that a person is not under a duty to retreat when acting for a legitimate purpose. But the possibility that the person could have retreated should be considered as a relevant factor in deciding whether the degree of force was necessary.

11.1.4 What if the defendant is the aggressor?

Even if the defendant is the initial aggressor, they may use force if the victim's response is wholly disproportionate and seriously threatens the defendant. But this will only be a defence if it was not the defendant's aim all along to give themselves an excuse to use much more serious violence. This was the issue in *R v Rashford* (2005).

R v Rashford (2005)

The defendant sought out the victim, intending to attack him in revenge for an earlier dispute, but the victim and his friends responded out of proportion to the defendant's aggression. The defence was successful.

The court held that a defendant will only lose the defence by being the aggressor throughout the situation. Whether a defendant can rely on self-defence depends on whether they feared that they were in immediate danger and if the violence used was no more than was necessary to protect themselves from serious injury or death.

Generally, a person who starts a fight, the aggressor, cannot rely upon self-defence to make actions lawful, as such actions are not lawful – they are unlawful acts of violence.

11.1.5 Was the force used proportionate?

The reasonableness of the force used is considered on the facts as they were or, if the defendant made a mistake, on the facts as the defendant genuinely believed them to be.

The basic rule is set out in s 76(6) of the Criminal Justice and Immigration Act 2008 which states that, except in a 'householder case', force which is disproportionate will not be reasonable. This gives additional protection to a householder who, for example, tackles a burglar.

The test is objective as referred to in *R v Oye* (2013) and *R v Press and Thompson* (2013) above. It balances the risk of harm to the defendant with the risk of harm to the victim, but takes into account that:

- a person with a legitimate purpose might not be able to work out the exact measure of any necessary action (s 76(7)(a)), and
- evidence of them only doing what they honestly and instinctively thought was necessary for a legitimate purpose shows that they took reasonable action (s 76(7)(b)).

The following points may be taken into account:

- There is no simple reckoning of equality. It will not be the case that, for example, a 'fight of fists has to be with fists'. It may be proportionate for a weapon to be used in extreme cases, where the defendant is attacked without the use of a weapon.
- Initially proportionate force may develop into disproportionate force, for example, if the defendant does not stop after the danger has been removed or passed.
- The defence is lost entirely when the force used is disproportionate (excessive).

These points can be illustrated by considering two cases where the defendants were both charged with murder but both pleaded the defence of self-defence; *R v Clegg* (1995) and *R v Martin* (2002).

R v Clegg (1995)

The defendant was a soldier on duty at a checkpoint in Northern Ireland during the Troubles and had orders to stop joyriders. A car came towards the checkpoint at speed with its headlights full on. One of the soldiers shouted for it to stop but it did not. The defendant fired three shots at the windscreen of the car and one as it had passed. This final shot hit a passenger in the back and killed her. As the evidence showed that the fatal shot had been fired as the car had gone past, the defendant could not use the defence of self-defence. The danger had passed when the fatal shot was fired and excessive force had been used.

R v Martin (2002)

Two burglars broke into the defendant's isolated farmhouse. He fired several shots at them; one of the intruders died and the other suffered serious injuries. The defendant claimed he had shot in self-defence but the evidence showed that they were leaving when he shot them, so the defence was not effective.

Tony Martin, defendant in *R v Martin* (2002)

Householder cases

Section 76(5A) of the Criminal Justice and Immigration Act 2008 states that, in a 'householder case', force which is grossly disproportionate will not be seen as reasonable. This means that a householder can use reasonable force, and now disproportionate force, to protect themselves and others in the house, but not grossly disproportionate force.

To be a householder case:
- the force must be used by the defendant while in or partly in a building that is a dwelling
- the defendant must not be a trespasser
- the defendant must have believed that the victim was a trespasser.

In a householder case, and assuming that the defendant genuinely believed that it was necessary to use force to defend themselves, the tests to be considered are:

1 Was the degree of force the defendant used grossly disproportionate in the circumstances as they believed them to be? If the answer is 'yes', they cannot use the defence of self-defence. If 'no', then:

2 Was the degree of force the defendant used nevertheless reasonable in the circumstances they believed them to be? If it was reasonable, they have a defence. If it was unreasonable, they do not.

A case considering these rules is *R v Ray* (2017).

Case study

R v Ray (2017)

The defendant and the victim's former partner were in a relationship and spending time in the former shared home. In the course of a fight, and fearing that the victim would use a knife against him, the defendant fatally stabbed the victim. The defence failed, but the Court of Appeal confirmed the interpretation of the defence in *R (Denby Collins) v Secretary of State for Justice* (2016).

This confirms that in householder cases, the law is as follows:

1 Whether the degree of force used is reasonable depends on the circumstances as the defendant believed them to be (this is contained in the common law and s 76(3)).

2 A householder is not regarded as having acted reasonably in the circumstances if the degree of force used was grossly disproportionate (s 76(5A)).

3 A degree of force that went completely over the top would, on the face of it, be grossly disproportionate.

4 However, a householder may or may not be regarded as having acted reasonably in the circumstances if the degree of force used was disproportionate. This will be a matter for the jury to decide.

The jury might have to consider matters such as:
- the shock of coming across an intruder in the house
- the time of day
- the presence and vulnerability of others in the house, especially any children
- if any weapon or object was being used or picked up
- the conduct (or previous conduct, if known) of the intruder.

Basic rule	In householder cases
The defendant can use reasonable force to protect themselves, others or property.	The defendant can use reasonable force to protect themselves or others in the home *BUT* they can use disproportionate force if it is honestly and instinctively thought to be required.
The defendant cannot use disproportionate (excessive) force.	The defendant cannot use grossly disproportionate force.

Figure 11.2 The amount of force that can be used in self-defence

11.1.6 The statutory defence – also known as the public defence

Section 3(1) of the Criminal Law Act 1967 states that:

> A person may use such force as is reasonable in the circumstances in the prevention of crime, or in effecting or assisting in the lawful arrest of offenders or suspected offenders or of persons unlawfully at large.

So, reasonable force can be used by an individual in the prevention of any crime or in making an arrest to:

- allow a person to defend himself from any form of attack, so long as the attack is criminal
- prevent an attack on another person, or
- defend their property – this can include possessions such as a watch, bag or wallet demanded by a mugger, where there might also be physical danger to the owner.

The tests that apply to both the private defence and the public defence are very similar:

- Whether the defendant believed that force was necessary to prevent crime or assist a lawful arrest is a *subjective* test.
- Whether the force used was reasonable is an *objective* test.

A clarification arose in the case of *R v Williams* (2020). Neither the common law defence of self-defence nor that of crime prevention under s 3 Criminal Law Act 1967 allows force to be used in trying to recover stolen property. The s 3 defence was only available in relation to preventing crimes in progress, not in relation to reacting to crimes already committed.

Case study

R v Williams (2020)

The victim stabbed the defendant and took a necklace from him at a party. The victim ran away and was chased by a group from the party led by the defendant. They caught up with the victim some distance away and fatally stabbed him. Self-defence was not available here.

Case	Facts	Legal principle
R v Williams (Gladstone) (1983)	The defendant thought he witnessed a fight. He intervened and injured a man.	The defendant should be judged according to their genuine, mistaken, view of the facts, regardless of whether the mistake was reasonable or unreasonable.
R v Oye (2013)	The defendant attacked police in the cafe, claiming he was being threatened and 'rushed' by evil spirits.	Where the defendant has delusions, their mental illness is not to be taken into account in the objective test, unless the reference is to s 76(7).
R v Bird (1986)	The defendant hit her ex-boyfriend but argued she acted in self-defence as she hit him before he hit her.	Withdrawing or showing an unwillingness to fight is evidence that the defendant is acting reasonably and in good faith. There is no requirement to show an unwillingness to retreat.
R v Rashford (2005)	The defendant switched from aggression to defence when the victim and his friends responded out of proportion to the defendant's aggression.	The defendant loses the defence if they are the aggressor throughout the situation. The defendant can use the defence if they feared they were in immediate danger and used only necessary violence to protect themselves from death or serious injury.
R v Ray (2017)	The defendant stabbed the victim during a fight in the victim's former home.	In householder cases, the defendant: • can use reasonable force to protect themselves or others in the home • can use disproportionate force if it is honestly thought to be required • cannot use grossly disproportionate force.

Figure 11.3 Key cases: the defence of self-defence

Extension activity

You can explore further issues, cases and principles for self-defence:

- Private defence at common law is the right to use reasonable force to defend yourself, another, your property or the property of another – *R v Duffy* (1967).
- The defence applies to the offence of obstructing a police officer – *Oraki v DPP* (2018).
- Only such force may be used as is reasonable in the circumstances. This is a question for the jury – *R v Scarlett* (1993); *R v Owino* (1995).

11.2 Duress by threats

The starting point of the common law in criminal law is that an adult of sound mind is responsible for any crime they commit. There is a limited exception to this if the defendant has been forced to commit a crime against their will because of threats that have been made to them. It is a common law defence and, if successful, it is a full defence so that the defendant will be found not guilty. However it is not a defence for:

- murder (*R v Howe* (1987))
- attempted murder (*Gotts* (1992)).

Key term

Duress by threats – a defence in criminal law: the defendant has been effectively forced to commit the crime by threats made to him.

Case studies

R v Howe (1987)

With others, the defendant took part in torturing and abusing two men who were then strangled by one of the others. He claimed that he took part in the killings because of threats that had been made against him.

Lord Hailsham said:

> I do not at all accept in relation to the defence of murder it is either good morals, good policy or good law to suggest … that the ordinary man of reasonable fortitude is not to be supposed to be capable of heroism if he is asked to take an innocent life rather than sacrifice his own.

R v Gotts (1992)

Gotts, a sixteen-year-old boy, tried to kill his mother by stabbing as he claimed that his father had threatened to shoot him unless he did so. Gotts caused serious injuries but, fortunately, his mother survived. He was charged with attempted murder and was not permitted to use the defence of duress for such an offence.

11.2.1 The tests for the defence

In *R v Hasan* (2005), the court set out the following tests which must be satisfied for the defence to succeed:

1. There must be a threat to cause death or serious injury.
2. The threat must be directed against the defendant or their immediate family or someone close to them.
3. Whether the defendant acted reasonably in the light of the threats will be judged objectively.
4. The threats relate directly to the crime committed by the defendant.
5. There was no evasive action the defendant could have taken.
6. The defendant cannot use the defence if they have voluntarily laid themselves open to the threats.

Case study

R v Hasan (2005)

The defendant worked for a woman who ran an escort agency involving prostitution. He would drive women to clients and act as a minder. The woman had a new boyfriend, a dangerous and violent drug dealer who boasted about committing three murders to the defendant, and took over much of the defendant's work. He and another man known only as 'Lunatic Yardie' ambushed the defendant outside his home. The defendant was told to commit a burglary on a house owned by one of the woman's clients. The boyfriend told him that 'Lunatic Yardie' would accompany him to ensure that the burglary was carried out and threatened that if he did not do so, he and his family would be harmed. The defendant complied and was convicted of aggravated burglary, but his defence of duress was rejected because he failed the sixth part of the test.

The threat

The threat has to be of death or serious injury. Serious injury will be given its normal meaning, so the victim will have to be subject to injury equivalent to grievous bodily harm. A lesser threat, such as a threat to disclose a previous conviction, is not sufficient.

However, provided there are serious threats, the cumulative effect of the threats can be considered, as in *R v Valderrama-Vega* (1985).

Case study

R v Valderrama-Vega (1985)

The defendant illegally imported cocaine. He claimed he had done this because of death threats made by a mafia-type organisation involved in drug-smuggling, because of threats to disclose his homosexuality and also because of financial pressures.

The jury was entitled to look at the cumulative effects of all the threats made against him. If there had not been a threat of death, then the other threats in this case would not be enough on which to base a defence of duress. But as there had been a threat of death, the jury was entitled to consider all the threats.

In *R v Hammond* (2013), the defence of duress was not available because the evidence was insufficient to show that the threat was imminent or immediately likely to have serious consequences.

Case study

R v Hammond (2013)

The defendant walked out of an open prison because he believed that he would be unable to stop himself causing serious injury to a fellow inmate who was threatening to sexually assault him.

The threat must be effective at the moment the crime is committed but this does not mean that the threats need to be able to be carried out immediately, as in *R v Hudson and Taylor* (1971).

Case study

R v Hudson and Taylor (1971)

Two teenage girls committed perjury by failing to identify the defendant in a case. They pleaded duress, on the basis that they had been warned by a group, including a man with a reputation for violence, that if they identified the defendant in court, the group would get the girls and cut them up. They decided to tell lies, and did so when they arrived at court and saw the man that had made the threat in the public gallery.

The Court said that the threat had to be a 'present' threat but that this was in the sense that it was effective to neutralise the will of the defendant at the time of committing the offence: the defence should be put to the jury.

Against whom must the threat be made?

The threat must be directed against:
- the defendant, or
- their immediate family, or
- someone close to them, or
- a person for whose safety they would reasonably regard themselves responsible.

Did the defendant act reasonably?

R v Graham (1982) set out that if the defence should succeed, the jury must consider a two-stage test:

1 Was the defendant compelled to act as they did because they reasonably believed they had good cause to fear serious injury or death?

   The defendant must genuinely believe in the effectiveness of the threat. They must also reasonably believe in it – an objective test. If this test is satisfied, the second stage can apply. This is a subjective test with an objective element.

2 Would a sober person of reasonable firmness, sharing the characteristics of the accused, have responded in the same way? This is an objective test.

Case study

R v Graham (1982)

The defendant was a homosexual who lived with his wife and another homosexual man, K. K was violent and bullied both the defendant and his wife. The defendant was taking drugs for anxiety, which made him more susceptible to bullying. After drinking heavily, K put a flex around the wife's neck and told the defendant to pull the other end of the flex. He did so, killing his wife. He claimed his fear of K caused him to act as he did and amounted to duress. The court stated that if a defendant's will to resist a threat has been eroded by voluntarily consuming drink or drugs, or both, the defence of duress will not be available.

The jury is allowed to take some of the defendant's characteristics into account, as the reasonable person is regarded as sharing the relevant characteristics of the defendant. This can be seen in *R v Bowen* (1996).

Case study

R v Bowen (1996)

The defendant had a low IQ of 68. He obtained goods by deception for two men who had told him they would petrol-bomb him and his family unless he carried out this offence. It was held that his low IQ was irrelevant in deciding whether the defendant found it more difficult to resist any threats, so the defence failed. The relevant characteristics must go to the ability to resist pressure and threats.

In *Bowen*, it was accepted that the following could be relevant:
- Age: very young people and the very old could be more susceptible to threats.
- Pregnancy: there is the additional fear for the safety of the unborn child.
- Serious physical disability: this could make it harder for the defendant to protect themselves.
- Recognised mental illness or psychiatric disorder: this could include post-traumatic stress disorder or any other disorder which meant that a person might be more susceptible to threats.
- Gender: even though many women might have as much moral courage as men.

Did the threats relate directly to the crime committed by the defendant?

The defendant can only use the defence if the threats are made in order to make him commit a specific offence. The offence must be one stated by the person making the threat, for example, 'I will maim your son if you do not steal this car for me'. This is known as the threat/offence nexus. If there was none, the defence will not be available as can be seen in the case of *R v Cole* (1994).

Case study

R v Cole (1994)

The defendant claimed that he, his girlfriend and child had been threatened in order to make him repay money he owed to a loan shark. He then robbed

building societies to get sufficient money to repay the debt. He said he only did this because of the threats of violence to him and his family.

The threats to him were directed at getting repayment and not directed at making him commit a robbery. This meant there was not a sufficient connection between the threats and the crimes he committed, so the defence of duress was not available.

Could the defendant have taken any evasive action?

Duress can only be used as a defence if the defendant is put in a situation where they have no safe avenue of escape.

Case study

R v Gill (1963)

In *R v Gill* (1963), the defendant claimed that he and his wife had been threatened unless he stole a lorry. However, there was a period of time during which he was left alone and so could have raised the alarm. As he had the possibility of a 'safe avenue of escape', he could not rely on the defence of duress.

If police protection is possible, the defendant cannot rely on duress. It should be made clear to a jury that if the threat is not likely to be carried out almost immediately, the defendant could probably have taken evasive action, either by going to the police or in some other way, to avoid committing the crime. However, in *R v Hudson and Taylor* (1971), the court accepted that police protection could not be completely foolproof. Even where a defendant had the opportunity to go to the police and tell them of the duress, they might be so afraid of the consequences that they would not go to the police.

Did the defendant lay himself open to the threats?

The defendant cannot use the defence if he or she has voluntarily laid themselves open to the threats. The court in *R v Sharp* (1987), a case involving a gang of robbers, stated:

> Where a person has voluntarily, and with knowledge of its nature, joined a criminal organisation or gang which he knew might bring pressure on him to commit an offence and was an active member when he was put under such pressure, he cannot avail himself of the defence of duress.

We have already seen that in *R v Hasan* (2005) above. A typical example is the case of *R v Shepherd* (1987).

Case study

R v Shepherd (1987)

The defendant joined a shoplifting gang, but was threatened with violence when he tried to leave. He did not know this was likely when he decided to leave so future shoplifting could now have the defence available, but not offences committed before he was aware of the threat of violence.

Case	Facts	Legal principle
R v Howe (1987)	The defendant took part in two killings, one as principal, the other as secondary party.	Duress is not available as a defence to murder or attempted murder (*R v Gotts* (1992)).
R v Valderrama-Vega (1985)	The defendant illegally imported cocaine because of death threats, threats to disclose his homosexuality and financial pressures.	The cumulative effects of all the threats should be considered by the jury.
R v Bowen (1996)	The defendant had a low IQ and obtained goods by deception for two men who had told him they would petrol-bomb him and his family unless he carried out the offence.	Low IQ was irrelevant in deciding whether the defendant found it difficult to resist any threats.
R v Graham (1982)	The defendant took drugs and claimed his fear of K caused him to kill his own wife.	The defence will not be available when a defendant's will to resist a threat has been eroded by the voluntary consumption of drink or drugs, or both.
R v Cole (1994)	The defendant and his family had been threatened if he did not repay the debt, so he carried out two robberies to get money.	There was insufficient connection between the threats and the crimes committed, so the defence was not available.
R v Hasan (2005)	The defendant was charged with aggravated burglary. He claimed he was forced to commit the offence because of threats made to him.	The six tests for the defence to succeed: • There must be a threat to cause death or serious injury. • The threat must be directed against the defendant or their immediate family, or someone close to them. • Whether the defendant acted reasonably in the light of the threats will be judged objectively. • The threats relate directly to the crime committed by the defendant. • There was no evasive action the defendant could have taken. • The defence is not available if the defendant voluntarily lays themselves open to the threats.
R v Shepherd (1987)	The defendant joined a shoplifting gang, but was threatened with violence when he tried to leave.	The defence could only be raised with respect to offences committed after he had been threatened.

Figure 11.4 Key cases: duress

11.3 Duress of circumstances and necessity

11.3.1 Duress of circumstances

Duress of circumstances differs from duress by threats in that the circumstances dictate the crime rather than a person.

- This defence was used in *R v Willer* (1986) and *R v Martin* (1989).
- In *R v Conway* (1988), the threats were to a passenger, rather than the driver.

Case studies

R v Willer (1986)

The defendant and a passenger were driving down a narrow alley when their car was surrounded by a gang of youths who threatened them. He realised that the only way to get away from the gang was by driving on the pavement. The court allowed his appeal for reckless driving because the jury should have been allowed to consider whether the defendant drove 'under that form of compulsion, that is, under duress'.

R v Conway (1988)

A passenger in the defendant's car had been shot at by two men a few weeks earlier. The passenger saw two men running towards the stationary car. He thought they were the two men who were after him (in fact they were plain-clothes policemen). He yelled at the defendant to drive off who did so very fast. He was charged with reckless driving.

The trial judge refused to leave duress for the jury to consider and the defendant was convicted. The court ruled that a defence of duress of circumstances was available if, on an objective standpoint, the defendant was acting in order to avoid a threat of death or serious injury.

R v Martin (1989)

The defendant's wife became hysterical and threatened suicide unless he drove her son (who was late and at risk of losing his job) to work. The defendant had been disqualified from driving but he eventually agreed to drive the boy to work. He was convicted of driving while disqualified.

On appeal it was ruled that duress of circumstances could be available. The same two-stage test as for duress by threats applied.

The decision in *R v Pommell* (1995) confirmed that duress of circumstances could be a defence to all crimes except murder or attempted murder, the same as duress by threats.

Case study

R v Pommell (1995)

The defendant was found by police at 8 a.m. lying in bed with a loaded sub-machine gun. He told police that earlier, at about 1 a.m., he had taken it from another man who was going to use it 'to do some people some damage'. He said he had intended getting his brother to hand the gun in to the police that morning, but was denied the opportunity to put the defence to the jury.

The Court of Appeal confirmed that the defence of duress of circumstances was available for all offences except murder and attempted murder. His conviction was quashed and the case was sent for retrial.

In *R v Cairns* (1999) and *R v Abdul-Hussain* (1999), the court had to consider whether the defence was available where the defendant reasonably perceived a threat of serious physical injury or death, even though there was no actual threat.

Case study

R v Cairns (1999)

The victim threw himself across the bonnet and windscreen of the defendant's car. Several of the victim's friends were nearby shouting and the defendant felt threatened. He drove off with the victim on his bonnet and some of the victim's friends following. These friends were in fact trying to help rather than be threatening. The victim fell under the car and was seriously injured.

The defendant's conviction was quashed as he reasonably perceived a threat of serious physical injury or death.

Case study

R v Abdul-Hussain (1999)

The defendants, who were Shi'ite Muslims, fled to Sudan from Iraq because of their religion and the risk of punishment and execution. They feared that, when they landed, they would be sent back to Iraq. They hijacked the plane which eventually landed in the UK. The defendants were charged with hijacking and pleaded duress of circumstances.

The trial judge decided that the danger they were in was not sufficiently 'close and immediate' as to give rise to a 'virtually spontaneous reaction' and he ruled that the defence could not be considered by the jury. The defendants were convicted and appealed.

The Court of Appeal quashed their convictions, holding that the threat need not be immediate, but it had to be imminent in the sense that it was hanging over them.

The Court of Appeal in *Abdul-Hussain* ruled that:
- There must be immediate peril of death or serious injury to the defendant, or to those for whom he or she has responsibility.
- The peril must operate on the defendant's mind at the time of committing the otherwise criminal act, so as to overbear their will; this is a matter for the jury.
- Execution of the threat need not be immediately in prospect.
- There is no avenue of escape.

In duress of circumstances, the defence may be used for any offence which is an appropriate response to the danger posed by the circumstances. As seen in *Abdul-Hussain*, the danger was of torture and execution, and the offence committed was hijacking which enabled them to get to a safe venue.

	Law	Case
Availability	All offences EXCEPT: ■ murder ■ attempted murder.	*R v Howe* (1987) *R v Gotts* (1992)
Seriousness of threat	Must be of death or serious injury BUT can consider cumulative effect of other threats with threat of injury.	*R v Valderrama-Vega* (1985)
Subjective and objective tests	There are two tests: ■ Was the defendant compelled to act because they feared serious injury or death (subjective)? ■ Would a sober person of reasonable firmness have responded in the same way (objective)? Some of the defendant's characteristics can be taken into account, especially: ■ age ■ pregnancy ■ serious physical disability ■ recognised mental illness.	*R v Graham* (1982) *R v Bowen* (1996)
Avenue of escape	Duress is NOT available as a defence if there is a safe avenue of escape.	*R v Gill* (1963)
Imminence of threat	The threat need not be immediate but it must be imminent.	*R v Hudson and Taylor* (1971) *R v Abdul-Hussain* (1999)
Self-induced duress	Duress is NOT available where: ■ the defendant joins a criminal gang which they know is violent ■ the defendant puts themselves in a position where they foresaw (or should have foreseen) the risk of being subjected to compulsion.	*R v Sharp* (1987) *R v Hasan* (2005)

Figure 11.5 Key facts: duress

11.3.2 Defence of necessity

The defence of necessity first arose in the case of *R v Dudley and Stephens* (1884): the defence was put forward by shipwrecked sailors who ate the cabin boy to survive and had been charged with murder. The principle set out was that there must be circumstances which force a person to act in order to prevent a worse evil from occurring. The defence, therefore, has similarities with the defence of duress of circumstances, yet the courts have been reluctant to recognise necessity as a defence in its own right.

- The defence has been recognised by courts when making an order in some civil cases, such as *Re F* (1990), a case about sterilisation of a patient with learning difficulties for whom pregnancy would be exceedingly problematic.
- In *Re A (Conjoined Twins)* (2000), doctors sought a declaration that it would be lawful for them to operate to separate conjoined twins, although this would cause one of them to die. In this case, the defence of necessity was considered and held to be available as a defence, even to a potential charge of murder.
- Necessity was also considered in the case of *R v Shayler* (2001). The Court of Appeal held that the tests for duress of circumstances and/or necessity were as follows:
  - The act must be done only to prevent an act of greater evil.
  - The evil must be directed towards the defendant or a person or persons for whom they were responsible.
  - The act must be reasonable and proportionate to the evil avoided.

11.4 Consent

Consent may be a defence to some non-fatal offences against the person. However, it is never a defence to murder or to offences where serious injury is caused.

Consent is strictly speaking not a defence, as where the other person consents, there is no offence. For example, where the other person consents to being touched, there is no battery as there is no unlawful force. This is illustrated by *R v Donovan* (1934).

Case study

R v Donovan (1934)

The defendant caned a 17-year-old girl for the purpose of sexual gratification. This caused bruising and he was convicted of indecent assault and a common assault. The defendant appealed on the basis that the victim had consented to the act. His conviction was quashed.

A more extreme case illustrating the same point is *R v Slingsby* (1995) where the defendant was charged with manslaughter.

Case study

R v Slingsby (1995)

The defendant was charged with involuntary manslaughter by an unlawful act. He and the victim had taken part in sexual activity which was described as 'vigorous' but which had taken place with the victim's consent. During this, a signet ring which he was wearing caused small cuts to the victim and this led to blood poisoning from which she died. The victim's consent meant that there was no battery or other form of assault and so he was held to be not guilty of manslaughter as there was no unlawful act.

In *R v Brown* (1993) and *R v BM* (2018), it was stated it would not be in the public interest to allow members of the public to wound each other without 'good reason'.

11.4.1 Real consent

There must be real consent. Consent can be affected by the identity of the defendant and non-disclosure of disease

The effect of identity on consent

Medical qualifications were in question in *R v Tabassum* (2000).

Case study

R v Tabassum (2000)

The defendant had pretended to be medically qualified so as to obtain the opportunity to examine women's breasts. He appealed against his conviction for indecent assault, saying that the complainants had consented to the examinations. However, the consent was given only because the victim was misled into believing that the defendant was medically qualified, so his fraud vitiated (destroyed) the consent.

In *R v Richardson* (1998), a dentist carried out work on patients after being suspended from practice by the dentists' governing body. The patients would not have consented to the treatment had they known she had been suspended. However the court decided that the patients had consented to the treatment. There was no fraud as to the identity of the person performing the treatment. The fraud related to the defendant's right to practise dentistry.

In *R v Melin* (2019) the issue of real consent and identity arose again.

Case study

R v Melin (2019)

The defendant twice injected what was said to be Botox into two complainants. Following the second injection, they both suffered really serious harm. The prosecution case was that, in both cases, they only consented to the treatment because the defendant had said that he was medically qualified, which he was not. Here, there was a deception as to identity, which was capable of vitiating (invalidating) consent. This included a deception as to qualifications or attributes. If having the injection administered by a medically qualified practitioner was a condition of each complainant giving her consent, this would go to the question of the defendant's identity and the legal validity of the consent.

The effect of consent on transmission of disease

With respect to consent and transmission of disease, in *R v Dica* (2004), the Court had to consider the position where the victim had consented to sex but did not know that the defendant was HIV-positive. Here, even though the victim had consented to sex, there was no consent to being infected with HIV and so the defendant could be guilty of an offence under s 20 OAPA 1861.

Similarly, in *R v Golding* (2014), the herpes virus was added to the list of communicable diseases that cause really serious harm, where the defendant was reckless as to causing the infection.

Activity

Could a person who breaks social distancing rules during the coronavirus pandemic be charged with a non-fatal offence?

- Write down the arguments for and against this suggestion.
- Would there be a defence of consent in such cases?

11.4.2 Implied consent

There are situations in which the courts imply consent to minor touchings, which would otherwise be a battery. These are the everyday situations where there is a crowd of people and it is impossible not to have some contact. In *Wilson v Pringle* (1987), it was held that the ordinary 'jostlings' of everyday life were not battery. Nobody can complain of the jostling which is inevitable from their presence in, for example, a supermarket, an underground station or a busy street; nor can a person who attends a party complain if their hand is seized in friendship, or even if their back is (within reason) slapped.

This also applies to contact sports. When people take part in organised sport such as football, rugby or judo, they are agreeing to the contact which is part of that sport. However, if the contact goes beyond what is allowed within the rules, then it is possible for an offence to be committed. For example, a rugby player consents to a tackle within the rules of the game, but they do not consent to an opposition player stamping on their head.

The breach of the rules of the sport must be a serious one. In *R v Barnes* (2004), it was decided that where an injury is caused during a match, there should only be a criminal prosecution when the conduct was sufficiently grave to be properly categorised as criminal.

Case study

R v Barnes (2004)

The defendant had inflicted a serious leg injury upon the victim while attempting to make a sliding tackle during an amateur football match. He accepted that the tackle had been hard, but fair, and that the injury caused had been purely accidental. The court stated that contact sports are exceptions, on public policy grounds, to the general rule that consent is no defence to bodily harm; implied consent exists where the situation is within what can reasonably be expected, as it was here.

11.4.3 Consent to minor injuries

There have been arguments as to whether consent could be a defence to an offence under s 47 OAPA 1861.

It used to be thought that consent could be a defence where the injuries were not serious. However, in *Attorney-General's Reference (No. 6 of 1980)* (1981), where two young men agreed to fight in the street to settle their differences following a quarrel, it was held that consent could not be a defence to such an action as it was not in the public interest.

Generally, it is acceptable and in the public interest to allow regulated sports and games, and also the other cases that provide some sort of exemption at common law, including horseplay, consensual casual fighting, voluntary participation in dangerous exhibitions or displays, religious mortification, and tattooing and similar treatment.

11.4.4 Consent to medical procedures

Consent to medical procedures is usually sought and given by the patient. This is presumed in life-saving circumstances but consent can be refused as in *R v Blaue* (1975) – discussed in Chapter 6.

11.4.5 Mistaken belief in consent

Where the defendant genuinely but mistakenly believes that the victim is consenting, then there may be a defence to a charge of a non-fatal offence against the person. These cases usually involve horseplay such as giving someone 'the bumps' in *Jones* (1986) and *R v Aitken* (1992), a case where a practical joke that had previously caused no harm resulted in serious injury.

Where the victim submits to the defendant's conduct through fear, the consent is not real. This was shown in *R v Olugboja* (1982), where the defendant intimidated his victim into having sex so there was no consent.

If consent is obtained by fraud, as in *Tabassum*, duress or influence or because of the victim's age (as in *Burrrell v Harmer* (1967) involving tattooing of a 12 year old who had 'consented') or lack of mental capacity, that will not amount to true consent.

Offence	Can consent be a defence?	Comment/Case
Murder s 18 OAPA 1861	Never a defence to these crimes	Not in the public interest.
s 20 OAPA 1861 s 47 OAPA 1861	Generally not a defence	Not in public interest, e.g. fighting (*Attorney-General's Reference (No. 6 of 1980)* (1981)) *OR* sado-masochistic acts (*Brown* (1993))
	BUT there are exceptions where consent is a defence	Properly conducted sports, surgery, dangerous exhibitions (*Jones* (1986)) *Chapter 17* personal adornment such as tattoos
Battery	Always allowed as a defence	Consent can also be implied to the 'jostlings' of everyday life (*Wilson v Pringle* (1986)).

Figure 11.6 Key facts: consent

Quick questions

1. State three matters the jury might have to consider to decide whether a householder may or may not be regarded as having acted reasonably in the circumstances if the degree of force used was disproportionate for self-defence.
2. Explain the statutory defence (also known as the public defence) under s 3(1) of the Criminal Law Act 1967.
3. In *R v Hasan* (2005), the court set out the tests which must be satisfied for the defence of duress to succeed; state them.
4. Why was the defence of duress unsuccessful in the case of *R v Cole* (1994)?
5. Explain, using case examples, implied consent in the defence of consent.

Summary

Self-defence

This includes the need to defend oneself and action taken to defend another.

Section 76 of the Criminal Justice and Immigration Act 2008 sets out rules:

- Degree of force must be reasonable and not disproportionate.
- In householder cases, the degree of force must not be 'grossly disproportionate'.
- Where the defendant is acting under a mistake, he or she is judged on the facts as they genuinely believed them to be.
- Where the defendant is acting under a drunken mistake, he or she cannot use the defence.

Duress

This is where the defendant is effectively forced by threats to commit an offence.

- Not available for murder or attempted murder.
- Threat must be of death or serious injury – but cumulative effect of threats can be considered.
- Threat must be to the defendant or his family.
- There are two tests:
  - (a) subjective – was the defendant compelled to act as they did because he or she reasonably believed that they had good cause to fear death or serious injury?
  - (b) objective – if (a) is satisfied, would a sober person of reasonable fitness, sharing the same characteristics as the defendant, have responded in the same way?
- Relevant characteristics include age, pregnancy, gender, serious physical disability, recognised mental illness or psychiatric disorder (low IQ is not included).

Duress of circumstances

This is where the defendant is forced to act because of circumstances.

- The defence is not available for murder or attempted murder.
- The circumstances must mean that there is a threat of death or serious injury.

Necessity

This is where circumstance forces a person to act to prevent a worse evil.

- Criminal courts have been reluctant to recognise the defence.
- Civil courts have recognised the defence.
- In the criminal case of *R v Shayler* (2001), it was concluded that necessity and duress of circumstances were the same defence.

Consent

Consent can be a defence to some offences against the person.

- It cannot be a defence to murder nor where serious injury is caused.
- The consent must be real.
- The victim must have knowledge of relevant facts, such as the defendant being HIV positive.
- There is implied consent to ordinary 'jostlings' of everyday life.
- In sport there is consent to contact which is within the rules of that sport.
- For minor injuries it has been held that it is not in the public interest that people should try to cause each other bodily harm for no good reason.
- The exceptions to this rule include properly conducted games and sports, lawful chastisement, reasonable surgical interference, dangerous exhibitions.
- A genuine mistaken belief that the victim is consenting can be a defence.

Chapter 12 Preliminary offences: Attempts

Introduction

An attempt occurs when someone tries to commit a crime but fails. It seems unfair to punish or convict someone for a failure to commit a crime, but prosecution aims to prevent reoffending by punishing them for the attempt to offend. Attempt is an inchoate offence, one where a substantive offence may not have been completed but nevertheless an offence of a different kind has been committed because of the actions or agreements in preparation for the substantive offence.

Key term

Inchoate offence – an offence relating to a criminal act which has not, or not yet, been committed.

12.1 What is meant by 'an attempt'?

An attempt is where a person tries to commit an offence, has the *mens rea* to do so, but, for some reason, fails to complete it. For example:

- The defendant fires a gun at the victim, intending to kill the victim.
- Just as the defendant pulls the trigger, the victim stoops to tie her shoelace. The bullet misses the victim and goes over her head.
- The defendant intended to kill the victim but has not succeeded, so the defendant cannot be charged with murder as the victim is still alive.
- In this type of situation, the defendant can be charged with attempted murder.

We have already seen a case of an attempt to commit murder in *R v White* (1910).

Link

See Chapter 6 for case details of *R v White* (1910).

12.1.1 Definition of 'attempt'

'Attempt' is defined by s 1(1) of the Criminal Attempts Act 1981, which states:

> If, with intent to commit an offence to which this section applies, a person does an act which is more than merely preparatory to the commission of the offence, he is guilty of attempting to commit the offence.

A charge of attempting to commit an offence can only be brought if the full offence is one which is triable on indictment; this includes an either-way offence charged via an indictment. In general, offences which are triable summarily only cannot be charged as an attempt of that crime.

The Act specifically requires an act. This clearly implies that there cannot be an attempt at a crime that can only be committed by an omission.

As with all offences, the prosecution must prove the *actus reus* and the *mens rea* of attempt. The definition above sets these out. They are:

- *Actus reus* – a person does an act which is more than just preparing to commit the offence.
- *Mens rea* – with intent to commit that offence.

12.2 *Actus reus* of attempt

The act that the defendant commits has to be more than preparation for the main crime. Some acts are obviously mere preparation, but other acts are more difficult to categorise.

Activity

Take the example where the defendant decides to rob a bank. Consider each point and decide what your view is. Discuss this in groups.

1 Clyde buys himself a shotgun and converts it into a sawn-off shotgun. Are both the buying of the gun and converting it 'merely preparatory'?

2 Clyde drives around the area, checking escape routes. Is it 'merely preparatory'?

3 On the day of the robbery, Clyde steals a car and drives to the bank. 'Merely preparatory'?

4 Clyde stands on the pavement outside the bank, carrying the sawn-off shotgun in a bag. Is this still only 'merely preparatory'?

5 Clyde walks into the bank. Has he now gone beyond mere preparation, and can he be charged with attempted robbery?

6 Clyde spots several police and a bank guard so pretends to check his balance on a machine and walks out. Can he still be charged with attempted robbery?

12.2.1 Cases showing mere preparation

There have been many cases on the meaning of 'merely preparatory'. It is difficult to draw any general principle from them.

In *R v Gullefer* (1987), it was said that 'more than merely preparatory' means that the defendant must have gone beyond purely preparatory acts and be 'embarked on the crime proper'.

Case study

R v Gullefer (1987)

The defendant jumped onto a greyhound race track in order to have the race declared void and so enable him to reclaim money he had bet on the race. His conviction for attempting to steal was quashed because his action was merely preparatory to committing the offence.

So, although the defendant in *R v Gullefer* (1987) had tried to interfere with the race, he had several other acts to do before the theft (the point at which he would get his betting money back):

- He had to go to one of the betting points and ask for his money back. Even just going towards the betting point would not be sufficient. However, asking for the money would change his actions into 'more than merely preparatory'. He would be guilty of attempted theft. It is when the money was handed to him that he would be guilty of theft.

In *Attorney-General's Reference (No. 1 of 1992)* (1993), it was decided that the defendant need not have performed the last act before the crime proper, nor need they have reached the 'point of no return'.

Case study

Attorney-General's Reference (No. 1 of 1992) (1993)

The defendant dragged a girl up some steps to a shed. He lowered his trousers and sexually assaulted her. His penis remained flaccid. He argued that he could not therefore attempt to commit rape. His conviction for attempted rape was upheld.

Looking at the whole of the defendant's acts, this seems a sensible decision. However, if he had been stopped immediately after he had dragged the girl to the shed, and before he lowered his trousers or interfered with her, then it is unlikely that he could have been convicted. His act of dragging her into the shed was probably 'merely preparatory'.

An attempt begins when the merely preparatory acts have come to an end and the defendant embarks upon the crime proper. When this moment occurs will depend on the facts in any particular case. The case of *R v Geddes* (1996) also illustrates acts which were only preparatory.

Case study

R v Geddes (1996)

The defendant was found in the boys' toilet block of a school, in possession of a large kitchen knife, some rope and masking tape. He had no right to be in the school. He had not contacted any of the pupils. This appears to be a situation of attempted false imprisonment but his conviction was quashed on appeal.

The Court of Appeal stated that attempts should be considered by asking two questions:

1 Had the accused moved from planning or preparation to execution or implementation?

2 Had the accused done an act showing that he was actually trying to commit the full offence, or had he got only as far as getting ready, or putting himself in a position, or equipping himself, to do so?

Using these two questions, it can be seen that Geddes had not quite moved from planning or preparation to execution. Also, it can be argued that he had got only as far as getting ready, or putting himself in a position, to commit the full offence.

A difficult case is *R v Campbell* (1991).

Case study

R v Campbell (1991)

The defendant, who had an imitation gun, sunglasses and a threatening note in his pocket, had been seen loitering outside a post office. He went away but returned a few minutes later with a slightly changed appearance. When he was in the street one metre from the post office, he was arrested and admitted he was going to rob the post office. His conviction for attempted robbery was quashed as this was still merely preparatory.

The next step in this case would have been for the defendant to enter the post office. Again, if the law of attempt is to be effective in protecting people from the main offence, surely he should have been guilty of an attempt at the point of arrest? Is it sensible to wait until he enters the post office? If the gun had been real then customers and staff in the post office would have been put at risk.

Activity

Now review your decisions in the first activity in this chapter.

12.2.2 Cases in which there was an attempt

The following three cases show situations where the defendant had gone beyond mere preparation. In each case, the defendants were held to be guilty of an attempt to commit the full offence.

Case studies

R v Boyle and Boyle (1987)

The defendants were found standing by a door which had a broken lock and hinge. Their conviction for attempted burglary was upheld. The test to use was whether the defendant was embarking on the crime proper. In this case, once the defendants had entered they would be committing burglary, so trying to gain entry was an attempt.

R v Tosti and White (1997)

The defendant intended to burgle premises. He took metal cutting equipment with him and hid it behind a hedge near to the premises. He then examined the padlock on the door. He did not damage the padlock. He was found guilty of attempted burglary.

The difference from *Campbell* for both these cases is:
- Burglary is committed at the moment the defendant enters as a trespasser with intent to steal (or do certain other offences).
- Robbery is not committed until the defendant actually steals and uses force. Walking into a building still leaves another step before the crime proper is committed.

In the next case, *R v Jones* (1990), the defendant had done almost everything he could before committing the full offence.

Case study

R v Jones (1990)

The defendant's partner told him that she wanted their relationship to end and that she was seeing another man, the victim. The defendant bought a shotgun and shortened the barrel. He then found the victim, who was in his car. The defendant, who was wearing a crash helmet with the visor down, got into the car and pointed the gun at the victim, who grabbed the gun and managed to throw it out of the car window. The defendant's conviction for attempted murder was upheld.

The defendant had tried to argue that, as the safety catch was still on, he had not done the last act before the crime proper. The Court of Appeal said that buying the gun, shortening it, loading it and disguising himself with the visor were all preparatory acts. But once the defendant got into the victim's car and pointed the gun, then there was sufficient evidence to leave to the jury the question of whether there was an attempt.

Activity

Consider these points about the case of *Campbell* (1991) above:

1 If he entered the post office and showed the gun and the note to the person behind the counter and thus obtained money, there is clearly robbery.
2 If, having shown the gun and note, he did not obtain any money or changed his mind at that point, then there is no theft, so no robbery, but the acts are more than preparatory – attempted robbery.
3 If he went into the post office with his note and gun hidden, this is more problematic, although it would almost certainly be burglary. With respect to attempted robbery, this may still be merely preparatory.
4 If he does not enter the post office, there should be no offence of robbery or burglary as:
    - carrying the note and gun are merely preparatory to a robbery
    - he has not entered the building for there to be a possible burglary.

To what extent do you agree with them, and why?

Extension activity

You can explore further issues, cases and principles for this area of the law:

- Cases where the defendant had not gone beyond mere preparation – *Mason v DPP* (2009).

12.3 *Mens rea* of attempt

For an attempt, the defendant must normally have the same intention as would be required for the full offence. If the prosecution cannot prove that the defendant had that intention then they are not guilty of the attempt. This was shown by the case of *R v Easom* (1971): there was no evidence that the defendant had intended permanently to deprive the owner of the bag or items in it, so he could not be guilty of attempted theft.

Link

See Chapter 9 for case details of *R v Easom* (1971).

A similar decision was made in the case of *R v Husseyn* (1977).

Case study

R v Husseyn (1977)

The defendant and another man were seen loitering near the back of a van. When the police approached, they ran off. The defendant was convicted of attempting to steal some sub-aqua equipment that was in the van. The Court of Appeal quashed his conviction as he had been charged specifically with attempting to steal the diving equipment when, in fact, his true intention was to steal anything.

This issue was resolved in *Attorney-General's Reference (Nos 1 and 2 of 1979)* (1979) where the Court of Appeal decided that if the defendant had a **conditional intent** (the defendant intended stealing if there was anything worth stealing), he could be charged with an attempt to steal some or all of the contents.

- Easom would now be charged with attempting to steal some or all of the contents of the bag, rather than the bag itself and specific items in it.
- Husseyn would be charged with attempting to steal some or all of the contents of the van.

In this way they could be found guilty of attempted theft.

12.3.1 *Mens rea* of attempted murder

The *mens rea* for attempted murder involves proving a higher level of intention than for the full offence of murder.

- The full offence requires that the prosecution proves the defendant had the intention either to kill or to cause grievous bodily harm (GBH).
- However, for attempted murder, the prosecution must prove an intention to kill. An intention to cause serious harm is not enough.

This can be seen in the case of *R v Whybrow* (1951).

Case study

R v Whybrow (1951)

The defendant wired up his wife's bath and caused her an electric shock. He was convicted of attempted murder. When he appealed, the court stressed that only an intention to kill was sufficient for the *mens rea* of attempted murder. As he only intended to cause GBH, he could not be guilty of attempted murder even though he would have been guilty of murder if she had died.

The justification for this rule is on grounds of public policy: a defendant should not escape a conviction for murder if the evidence shows that death occurred as a direct result of their assault intended to result only in GBH.

However, if no death occurs and there is evidence that the defendant intended really serious harm, then this is a s 18 offence rather than attempted murder. The maximum sentence is the same.

12.3.2 Is recklessness enough for the *mens rea* of attempt?

What if it can be proved that the defendant was reckless? Is this sufficient for them to be guilty of an attempt? In *R v Millard and Vernon* (1987), it was decided that it was not sufficient.

Case study

R v Millard and Vernon (1987)

The defendants repeatedly pushed against a wooden fence on a stand at a football ground. The prosecution claimed that they were trying to break it and they were convicted of attempted criminal damage, but, on appeal, their convictions were quashed. This was because recklessness is not normally sufficient *mens rea* for an attempt, even if it would suffice for the completed offence.

However, there is an exception where recklessness as to one part of the offence can be sufficient where there is intention for another part. This can be seen in *Attorney-General's Reference (No. 3 of 1992)* (1994).

Case study

Attorney-General's Reference (No. 3 of 1992) (1994)

The defendant threw a petrol bomb towards a car containing four men. The bomb missed the car. The defendant was charged with attempting to commit arson with intent to endanger life. He was convicted: it had to be proved that the defendant intended to damage property, but it was only necessary to prove that he was reckless as to whether life would be endangered.

There are some offences where recklessness is sufficient *mens rea* for the full offence. For an attempt of such offences, the prosecution must prove that the defendant had the intent to commit the offence.

12.4 Impossibility

In some situations, a person may intend to commit an offence and may do everything they possibly can to commit it, but in fact the offence is impossible to commit.

An example of this would be where the defendant goes to the victim's room and stabs the victim as they lie in bed. In fact, the victim died two hours before the defendant stabbed them. The defendant has merely stabbed a dead body so it cannot be murder, but can the defendant be guilty of attempting to murder the victim?

The Criminal Attempts Act 1981 s 1(2) states:

> A person may be guilty of attempting to commit an offence ... even though the facts are such that the commission of the offence is impossible.

After the Act was passed, the courts had to consider this section and the problem of attempting the impossible in the case of *Anderton v Ryan* (1985).

Case study

Anderton v Ryan (1985)

Mrs Ryan bought a video recorder very cheaply. She thought it was stolen. Later she admitted this to police who were investigating a burglary at her home. Her conviction was quashed because the video recorder was not in fact stolen; it was cheap because it was defective.

The House of Lords held that even though Mrs Ryan had gone beyond merely preparatory acts, in fact all her acts were innocent. The video recorder was not stolen. On this basis, they thought that s 1(2) did not make her guilty.

However, less than a year later, the House of Lords overruled this decision in *R v Shivpuri* (1986).

Case study

R v Shivpuri (1986)

The defendant agreed to receive a suitcase which he thought contained illegal drugs. The suitcase was delivered to him, but it contained nothing illegal and mostly harmless vegetable matter. The defendant was convicted of attempting to be knowingly concerned in dealing with prohibited drugs.

This time, the House of Lords said that both ss 1(2) and 1(3) were relevant. Subsection 1(3) states:

" In any case where—

(a) apart from this subsection a person's intention would not be regarded as having amounted to an intent to commit an offence; but

(b) if the facts of the case had been as he believed them to be, his intention would be so regarded, then, for the purpose of subsection (1) he shall be regarded as having an intent to commit that offence. "

The combined effect of ss 1(2) and 1(3) of the Criminal Attempts Act 1981 meant that a person could be guilty of an attempt even if committing the full offence was impossible. In *R v Shivpuri* the facts as he believed them to be were that the suitcase contained prohibited drugs. He intended dealing in drugs so his intention, under s 1(3), was regarded as being an intention to commit that offence. The House of Lords accepted that its decision in *Anderton v Ryan* (1985) had been wrong, and they used the 1966 Practice Statement to overrule that decision.

Activity

In these scenarios, explain whether there is an attempt to commit an offence.

1 Amir knows his girlfriend has been going out with Blake. Amir plans to disfigure Blake. He buys some acid, which he intends to throw in Blake's face, and he drives to Blake's house. As he is about to get out of the car, he sees a police car nearby. Amir immediately drives off.

2 Connor puts some poison in Donna's drink, intending to kill her. The amount he puts in the drink is insufficient to kill and Donna survives.

3 Faye sees a handbag in the ladies' cloakroom. She hopes there will be some money in it, so she opens it. In fact, the bag contains only make-up and tissues. Faye closes the bag and replaces it.

4 Greg and Hans are found in the garden of a house with masks, a torch and screwdrivers in their pockets. They admit they intended to burgle the house.

5 Ian fires a shot at Jani but misses her. He admits he intended to kill her.

Case	Facts	Offence attempted	Law
Cases where there was sufficient evidence for an attempt			
Attorney-General's Reference (No. 1 of 1992) (1993)	The defendant tried to rape a girl but could not get an erection	Rape	Need not have performed the last act
R v Boyle and Boyle (1987)	Standing by door with broken lock	Burglary	Had done part of a series of acts
R v Jones (1990)	Gun safety catch was left on	Murder	Sufficient evidence to leave the question of whether there was an attempt to the jury
Cases which were merely preparatory			
R v Gullefer (1987)	Disrupted race intending to reclaim bet	Theft	Has the defendant 'embarked upon the crime proper'?
R v Geddes (1996)	In school with knife, rope and tape	False imprisonment	Has the defendant 'actually tried to commit the offence in question'?
R v Campbell (1990)	Outside post office with imitation gun and threatening note	Robbery	Merely preparatory

Figure 12.1 Key cases: 'merely preparatory' in attempts

	Attempt	Case or statute
Definition of 'attempt'	With intent to commit an offence, a person does an act which is more than merely preparatory to the commission of the offence.	s 1(1) of the Criminal Attempts Act 1981
'More than merely preparatory'	The defendant must have embarked on the crime proper OR the defendant must be trying to commit the full offence.	R v Gullefer (1987) R v Geddes (1996)
Mens rea of attempt	The defendant must have intention for the full offence. A conditional intention is sufficient. Recklessness is not normally sufficient BUT recklessness as to part of the offence may be sufficient.	R v Easom (1971) Attorney-General's Reference (Nos 1 and 2 of 1979) (1979) R v Millard and Vernon (1987) Attorney-General's Reference (No. 3 of 1992) (1994)
Attempting the impossible	Sections 1(2) and 1(3) of the Criminal Attempts Act 1981 mean that the defendant is guilty even if the full offence is legally or physically impossible.	R v Shivpuri (1986)

Figure 12.2 Key facts: attempts

Offence	Indictable or either-way charged as indictable offence	Can there be a charge of the attempted offence?
Murder	Yes	Yes
Involuntary manslaughter	Yes	Yes*
Unlawful and malicious wounding or infliction of GBH (s 18 OAPA 1861)	Yes	Yes
Unlawful and malicious wounding or causing of GBH (s 20 OAPA 1861)	No	No
Assault (as assault or battery) occasioning actual bodily harm (s 47 OAPA 1861)	Yes	Yes
Assault	No	No
Battery	No	No
Robbery	Yes	Yes
Burglary	Yes	Yes
Theft	Yes	Yes
* For involuntary manslaughter, the *actus reus* requires proof that the defendant caused the victim's death, so the intention required for the attempt must be an intention to cause this death. This is the *mens rea* for murder, but there is no case on a charge of attempted involuntary manslaughter.		

Figure 12.3 Offences included on the OCR specification and the law on attempts

Quick questions

1 State one offence that cannot be an attempted offence. Why can't it be an attempted offence?
2 What is meant by 'more than merely preparatory'?
3 State the *actus reus* and *mens rea* of attempted theft.
4 Explain what is meant by conditional intent.
5 Distinguish between the *mens rea* of murder and the *mens rea* of attempted murder.

Summary

- Attempt is defined by s 1(1) of the Criminal Attempts Act 1981.
- The *actus reus* of attempt is doing an act which is more than merely preparatory to the commission of the offence.
- The *mens rea* of attempt is that the defendant must have the *mens rea* required for the full offence.
- For murder there must be an intention to kill.
- There can be a conditional intent – where the defendant intends to steal if there is something worth stealing.

- Recklessness is not normally sufficient for the *mens rea* of attempt.
- In *R v Shivpuri*, the courts overruled their previous decision and held that a person could be guilty of an attempt even though the commission of the full offence was impossible.
- An attempt cannot be committed by an omission.

Chapter 13 Evaluation

Introduction

This chapter investigates specific areas of law that are to be evaluated under the OCR specification. Ideas for reform are incorporated in each area of law.

13.1 Critical evaluation of non-fatal offences against the person

In the 1980s and 1990s, many reports on this area of law were published. All of these emphasised the need for reform. Police-recorded crime showed a 3 per cent increase in violence against the person offences, from 1,697,718 offences in the year ending June 2019 to 1,750,750 offences in the year ending June 2020.

The most recent report 'Reform of Offences Against the Person', Law Commission (2015), stated:

> In 1998 a draft bill was written, but no progress was made with that and there seems little political will to implement any proposals. Such Parliamentary debates as there have been have tended to refer to the 1861 Act and specific sections, usually referring to the law on abortion and criticisms of the UK law in this respect.

The areas of concern raise questions of justice and the balance between different criminal offences and potential punishment, while relying on judges' decisions to correct the imbalances.

The main areas of concern in the report are:
- There are too many narrowly defined offences about the same subject. The reality is that all non-fatal offences have a different level of seriousness depending on the outcome – a graze, a scratch, a cut, a deep cut etc. could be charged under several sections of the Act.
- Some sections appear to create multiple different offences. This can be seen in s 20 and s 18.
- The order and grading of the offences by seriousness is unclear. It is not clear whether grievous bodily harm and wounding are at the same or different levels of seriousness.
- When it is clear which offences are meant to be more serious, this is not reflected in sentencing. An example of this is the offences under s 47 and s 20.
- Vocabulary:
  - The Act uses vocabulary that is not in common usage today, such as 'grievous'.
  - It uses words without a clear meaning. For example, 'maliciously' has been explained by the courts.
  - It uses words that have different meanings in different contexts, such as 'assault'.

These areas of concern show the need for reform:
- The Offences Against the Person Act 1861 is out of date.
- The different offences show inconsistencies between them.
- There is no conformity with the correspondence principle.
- Much of the language used is archaic.

13.1.1 Out of date

The 1861 Act is over 150 years old. This has caused a number of problems.
1 When it was created, people did not have the understanding of mental health problems that we have today. The Act only referred to 'bodily' harm in the offences and did not mention any mental harm. As a result, for some time it was not sure that the offences could include those where the victim had suffered mental harm.

The courts in *Chan Fook* (1994) and *Burstow* (1997) decided that the meaning of 'bodily harm' did include injury to mental health. Since then, defendants causing such injury can be convicted of offences under the 1861 Act.

2   Another area which has created problems is whether inflicting bodily harm could cover the situation of infecting another person with a disease. In 1861 there was only limited understanding of how some diseases were transmitted from person to person. The idea that a criminal offence could be committed by infecting someone with a disease was certainly not thought of then.

   The courts filled this gap, as can be seen in the cases of *Dica* (2004) and *R v Golding* (2014), that infecting someone with HIV or genital herpes could come within the wording of inflicting grievous bodily harm.

3   Cosmetic surgery and body adornments have also had to be considered by the courts in, for example, *R v Melin* (2019) and *R v BM* (2018).

13.1.2 Inconsistency between offences

There are inconsistencies in the Act, especially with regard to the *mens rea* required for each offence. In particular:

1   Section 47 has the same *mens rea* as for an assault or battery. It does not require the defendant to intend or even realise that there is a risk of any injury. This appears unjust as s 47 carries a maximum sentence of five years' imprisonment, while assault and battery only carries a maximum of six months' imprisonment. As the outcome of the attack dictates the offence, there is no need for separate offences.

2   It is also unjust that a person who causes a small cut can be charged with the more serious offence of s 20 instead of the offence of 'occasioning actual bodily harm' under s 47. This is because s 20 refers to 'wound or grievous bodily harm'. Yet clearly there are different levels of wound, and many of them do not equate with serious harm. Currently, we have to rely on the prosecution to choose an appropriate offence and then rely on the court to decide an appropriate sentence within the range permissible for the offence.

3   The maximum sentence for both s 47 and s 20 offences is the same, yet the s 20 offence is meant to be more serious than s 47 as it requires more serious injury. Section 20 requires the defendant to intend or be reckless as to causing the victim some

harm, whereas for s 47 it is not necessary to prove that the defendant had any higher level of *mens rea* than that for assault or battery. It seems unjust that these two offences carry the same maximum penalty when the levels of blameworthiness are so different. There is no clear hierarchy of offences.

13.1.3 Correspondence principle

The 2015 Report also points out that the offences in the Act do not conform to the 'correspondence principle'. Under this principle the results which the defendant must intend or foresee should match the results which actually occur. A defendant should not be convicted for a kind and level of harm unless they meant to do it or at least knowingly ran the risk of it.

●   Under the 1861 Act, a defendant can be guilty of an s 20 offence without intending or being reckless as to causing serious harm.

●   Equally a defendant can be guilty of an s 47 offence without intending or being reckless as to causing any harm.

Both these are clear breaches of the correspondence principle.

13.1.4 Need for modern, simplified language

1   Section 20 uses the word 'maliciously'. In modern language today, the word 'maliciously' suggests acting deliberately and with ill-will to the victim. Yet the meaning of the word in the 1861 Act has been held to be that the defendant either intended to do the type of harm that was done or was reckless as to whether that type of harm occurred. The Law Commission has recommended that the word 'reckless' should be used. This would make sense, given that if you intend something, then you must have been more than reckless.

2   The Act is not consistent: for s 20, the word 'inflict' is used, yet for s 18, the word 'cause' is used. This led to considerable debate as to whether the word 'inflict' in s 20 meant that a technical assault had to take place. This was finally resolved by the case of *Burstow* (1997), in which it was ruled that it did not, so essentially meaning the same thing.

3   The word 'assault' is used in different ways, and can refer to:
   ○   the common law offence of assault, or to
   ○   assault and battery as in 'common assault', or to
   ○   either of the underlying offences of assault or battery in the context of s 47.

13.1.5 Ideas for reform

In 1998 the Home Office issued a Consultation Document, 'Violence: Reforming the Offences Against the Person Act 1861'. This included a draft Bill which set out four main offences. These were intended to replace ss 18, 20, 47 and assault and battery. Figure 13.1 shows how the proposals would work:

Any new statute should respect the following principles:

- It should provide a clear hierarchy of offences from the most serious to the least. The place of each offence in the hierarchy should reflect:
  - ○ the harm caused
  - ○ the culpability of the defendant
  - ○ the maximum penalty in proportion to the offence.
- Each offence should provide a clear and accurate label for the conduct in question and should be defined in language that is easy to understand.
- Each ingredient of an offence, whether an external element or a mental element, should be set out explicitly.

As can be seen from the table, the proposed Act seems to cover these points.

The recommendations would provide a more coherent set of offences than exists at present:

- There would be no overlap or inconsistency between the offences.

- The *actus reus* and the *mens rea* for each proposed new offence are clearly set out.
- The offences conform to the 'correspondence principle' – defendants would only be held liable for a given kind and level of harm where they either meant to do it or knowingly ran the risk of it.
- The law would be strengthened if the recommendation for a higher maximum penalty of seven years' imprisonment, the equivalent of s 20, is implemented. The proposed new offence of aggravated assault would carry a higher maximum penalty than common assault. This would give victims greater protection.

However, any reform of the law would inevitably be subject to criticism and cases will arise that challenge the meaning of words and phrases within the new legislation. Given the manner in which the legal system operates, the complete analysis of new legislation will be very lengthy. It requires a case to be brought and then work through the appeal system. There may be a delay while waiting for cases that have any particular point in them. Even then, an appeal has to be funded in an era of declining legal aid. Many defendants would rather the case was over and done with, particularly if the sentence is non-custodial.

Many argue that law reform should be for Parliament and not the Judiciary, yet we have already seen that there are many decisions interpreting the current legislation.

Current offences	Maximum sentence	Proposed offences	Maximum sentence
Wounding or causing grievous bodily harm, with intent to do grievous bodily harm, s 18	Life imprisonment	Intentionally causing serious injury	Life imprisonment
Malicious wounding or causing grievous bodily harm – the defendant must intend or foresee a risk of some harm, not necessarily serious	5 years	Recklessly causing serious injury – the defendant must foresee a risk of serious injury	7 years
Assault occasioning actual bodily harm – no need to intend or foresee any harm at all	5 years	Either intentionally or recklessly causing injury, not necessarily by assault – the defendant must foresee a risk of some injury OR Aggravated assault, that is assault causing injury – no need to foresee risk of injury	5 years 12 months
Assault and battery	6 months	Physical assault OR threatened assault	6 months

Figure 13.1 Proposed replacements for non-fatal offences

13.2 Critical evaluation of defences

In this section we will consider the defences of intoxication, self-defence and consent.

13.2.1 Intoxication

Historically, intoxication was not a defence as an intoxicated defendant should know the dangers of becoming intoxicated and then carrying out criminal acts. In *R v Gamlen* (1858), the court stated: 'Drunkenness is no excuse for crime'.

Since then, the law developed piecemeal to deal with different aspects of intoxication and its relationship with different offences.

The Law Commission 2009 report 'Intoxication and Criminal Liability' set out the following issues in the law as it stands:

- Whether the defendant's intoxication should be classified as 'voluntary' or 'involuntary'.
- Whether voluntary intoxication should be relevant to the fault element in the definition of an offence.
- Whether voluntary intoxication should be relevant to other defences where the defendant's state of mind may be relevant.
- The test to be applied in cases where voluntary intoxication is not relevant to the defendant's criminal liability.

Voluntary and involuntary intoxication

The report recommended that the distinction between voluntary and involuntary intoxication should be kept even though the distinction between voluntary and involuntary can be unclear. At present, all intoxicating substances are treated similarly, whether legal or illegal.

No account is taken of the effect of an intoxicating substance on an individual where their inhibitions are broken down by being made involuntarily intoxicated.

- The decision in *Kingston* (1994) makes such a defendant guilty if they formed the necessary *mens rea*. This ignores the fact that the defendant was not to blame for the intoxication.
- But an intoxicated defendant would be not guilty of a basic intent offence where the prosecution relied on recklessness (as in *Hardie* (1984)). This appears to be unfair to defendants in Kingston's situation.

If pleaded successfully, intoxication provides a complete defence. This includes the situation when prescribed medication is taken as directed but has an unpredictable effect. It is a defence where the defendant does not know they are taking an intoxicating substance, as in laced drinks, but there is no defence if the defendant has some awareness of intoxication.

The distinction between specific and basic intent

If the defendant intended to cause only minor harm to the victim, or damage to something other than a person, but the victim dies as a consequence, the defendant is not guilty of murder because they did not have the specific intent required. They could be liable for less serious offences (fallback offences), including manslaughter which carries a maximum sentence of life imprisonment. This allows the courts to deal appropriately with the consequences of the defendant's behaviour and provide justice, even if the victim and their relatives may not agree.

Murder has an alternative (fallback) offence of manslaughter. Section 18 OAPA has an alternative (fallback) offence of s 20 OAPA. One difficulty is that not every offence has a 'fallback' option. If, for example, a defendant is charged with theft and successfully claims that they did not form the *mens rea* because they were too intoxicated, there is no fallback option, the defendant will be not guilty of any offence and therefore there can be no conviction.

It can also be argued that the difference between specific and basic intent cases is almost arbitrary despite the different effect of the defence on the outcome of a trial for an offence of similar gravity:

- Crimes of specific intent include murder and s 18 wounding/GBH with intent, burglary and theft.
- Crimes of basic intent include manslaughter, rape and s 20 and s 47 OAPA offences.

In other words, there is no differentiation by seriousness of the offence, merely by the definition of the crime.

The level of intoxication

If a person is very intoxicated, it may prevent that person from forming the necessary *mens rea* of the crime. However, there is no fixed level of intoxication.

- In cases where the defence has been successful, the evidence is usually overwhelming. In *R v Lipman* (1970), the defendant hallucinated as a result of voluntarily taking LSD, attacking and killing the victim while imagining he had been attacked by snakes. He was convicted of manslaughter and not murder, as he was able to satisfy the court that he did not have the ability to form the *mens rea* of murder.
- In *R v Majewski* (1971), the defendant had taken drugs and then drank a great deal of alcohol. Taking such a quantity of drugs and alcohol was reckless, so he could not rely on the defence of intoxication where a *mens rea* including recklessness was sufficient for a conviction.

Given the problems of obtaining evidence that this raises, it seems that the defence of intoxication is only satisfactory for offences charged under a fallback position. Would Majewski or Lipman be convicted of theft if either had also stolen a mug from the premises where the incidents took place?

Competing interests in the defence of intoxication

There are competing interests of personal autonomy and social paternalism.
- Personal autonomy: an adult can make a choice to spend as much of their own money on buying intoxicating substances as they wish. With legal drugs such as alcohol, this can be done in public.
- Social paternalism: there is the view that excessive consumption of alcohol, and the consumption of illegal drugs, cause damaging consequences for society and for the individual and should be discouraged. This can be done through the criminal justice system. However, it sometimes allows a defence, whether the drugs are legal, illegal or prescribed.

The criminal justice system attempts to balance the rights of the defendant and the victims of crime. If intoxication was always allowed to be a defence, then victims' rights would not be protected, but if it was never allowed, then the defendant would not be protected, for example, when there is involuntary intoxication. It can also be argued that the distinction between legal and illegal drugs could be reflected in more severe sentencing being available for intoxication caused by illegal drugs as they have not been subject to taxation which funds the legal system and help

through social and medical services for the victims of crime.

Statutory intervention usually follows this paternalistic approach. An example is s 76(5) of the Criminal Justice and Immigration Act 2008. We have seen that this section, in relation to the defence of self-defence, means a person cannot rely on 'any mistaken belief attributable to intoxication that was voluntarily induced' when claiming this defence.

Intoxication and the coincidence of *actus reus* and *mens rea*

Some areas of the law on intoxication appear to be contrary to the normal rules on *mens rea* and *actus reus*. For example:
- In *DPP v Majewski* (1977), the defendant was guilty of a basic intent offence because getting drunk is a 'reckless course of conduct'. This ignores the principle that *mens rea* and *actus reus* must coincide. Majewski had taken drugs and had some drink before he went to the pub.
- In *O'Grady* (1987), the defendant had fallen asleep and only committed the act of hitting his friend some hours afterwards.

The recklessness in becoming intoxicated means that the defendant takes a general risk of doing something 'stupid' when drunk. At the time of becoming intoxicated, the defendant has no idea that they will actually commit an offence. Normally, for offences where recklessness is sufficient for the *mens rea* of an offence, it has to be proved that the defendant knew there was a risk of the specific offence being committed.

The Law Commission said in their 1993 report that the *Majewski* rule was arbitrary and unfair. It later changed its opinion on this point, suggesting that the effectiveness of the law remains uncertain in achieving justice and balancing conflicting interests.

Policy considerations

The law on intoxication as a defence is largely policy-based. There are two main reasons:
- Many offences are committed when the defendant is intoxicated. Statistics suggest that half of all violent crimes are committed by a defendant who is intoxicated through drink and/or drugs.
- There is a need to balance the rights of the defendant and the victim; if intoxication were always to be a defence, then victims' rights would not be protected.

As a result, there is conflict between public policy and legal principles. Public policy is based on public protection and the encouragement of good behaviour. Legal principles impose liability where there is fault. The fault must be voluntarily assumed or there must be the deliberate taking of a risk.

The law on intoxication has tried to balance these opposing points of view, but over the past thirty or so years it can be argued that public policy has become the main theme.

Proposals for reform

After previous proposals to reform the law on intoxication were rejected or abandoned, the Law Commission looked again at the defence in its 2009 report, 'Intoxication and Criminal Liability'. This report recommended:

1 While the distinction between voluntary and involuntary intoxication should be kept, the use of the terms 'specific intent' and 'basic intent' should be abolished. These terms would be replaced by categorising offences as those where:
   ○ *mens rea* is an integral fault element, where there has to be intention as to a consequence
   ○ *mens rea* is not an integral fault element, because the offence merely requires proof of recklessness.

2 Where the defendant was voluntarily intoxicated, the Law Commission proposed a general rule that where the charge is of an offence for which *mens rea* is *not* an integral fault element (the second bullet above), a defendant should be treated as being aware of anything they would have been aware of if they had been sober.

   This rule would not apply to offences where the required *mens rea* involved intention as to a consequence, knowledge, fraud or dishonesty.

3 The Law Commission proposed that there should be a list of situations which would count as involuntary intoxication, such as spiked drinks and situations where a drug is taken for a proper medical purpose. Where there is involuntarily intoxication, this should be taken into account in deciding whether the defendant has the required *mens rea*. This effectively confirms the law as set out in *Kingston* (1995).

No action has been taken on any of these proposals.

13.2.2 Self-defence

Problems with this defence are caused by the requirements for its success as a defence.

Is force necessary?

This is a question for the jury and, as with all questions for the jury, may be difficult for them to make a decision; in particular, whether a victim has to retreat before using force as in *R v Bird* (1985).

Section 76(6A) CJIA 2008 (an amendment added by s 148 of the Legal Aid, Sentencing and Punishment of Offenders Act 2012) now makes it clear that a person is *not* under a duty to retreat when acting for a legitimate purpose. But the possibility that the defendant could have retreated is to be considered when deciding whether the degree of force was necessary.

Section 76 CJIA 2008 makes it clear that, provided the mistake was not made due to intoxication, then the defendant can rely on their mistake.

Householder cases

A householder is morally justified in using force to defend themselves, others in the house and their property against an intruder. But questions remain:

● Is a householder morally justified in using any amount of force?
● Is a householder acting wrongfully in defending themselves or their property, whatever the force used?

Section 76(5A) now states that in a householder case, the degree of force will not be regarded as reasonable only where it was 'grossly disproportionate'. The law now appears to support the view that a householder has a moral right to defend themselves or their property using force, but only to a certain level (and a higher level than before the 2008 Act was introduced).

The terms 'reasonable', 'disproportionate' and 'grossly disproportionate' have not been defined in statute, so will require judicial interpretation when cases come to court.

This is intended to cover situations where a burglar, or other intruder, enters the defendant's house. It also applies where a building has a dual purpose as a place of residence and work, and there is an internal means of access between the two parts. For example:

● if a shopkeeper is confronted by an intruder in the shop area, there could be a risk to their family in the adjoining residential part.

But this extended defence does not apply to customers who happen to be in the shop and use force against an intruder. The normal rules of self-defence apply to them.

The defence is available even where the mistake the defendant made is unreasonable. Is it too generous to judge defendants on the basis of facts they unreasonably believe to be true?

- If the defence is not allowed where the defendant honestly believed (however unreasonably) they were about to be attacked, then the defendant is at risk of being convicted when they really were not at fault.
- Against this, there is the need to protect the innocent victim whom the defendant has assaulted due to a mistaken belief.

Do defendants have to wait until they are attacked before they can use force?

The law appears to be clear that they can act to prevent force. It is not necessary for an attack to have started. This appears to be a sensible rule, since it would be ridiculous if people had to wait until they were stabbed or shot before being allowed to defend themselves. In *Attorney-General's Reference (No. 2 of 1983)* (1984), it was held that someone who fears an attack can make preparations to defend himself. This is so even if the preparations involve breaches of the law.

The morality issue

It is morally right that a person should be able to use force to defend themselves and their property. This should apply whether the person who uses force is a householder or acting outside a house.

But limits have to be set on what force can be used to prevent people from taking the law into their own hands. If the limits are exceeded, then self-defence cannot be used and the person who uses force will be at fault. However, the level of fault can be taken into account by the judge when passing sentence.

This can be particularly unfair for a person who kills another while claiming to act in self-defence. If convicted, they must be given a life sentence. However, the level of their fault can be reflected in the tariff period.

An all or nothing defence

Although the level of the defendant's fault can be reflected in sentencing, critics say that self-defence is an 'all or nothing' defence. That is, the defendant either:

- succeeds completely with the defence and is found not guilty, or
- fails and is found guilty.

It can be argued that there should be a partial defence where the use of force in self-defence was justified, but the defendant used excessive force in the circumstances.

The relevance of the defendant's characteristics

Should the defendant's characteristics be taken into account in deciding if they thought that they needed to defend themselves?

- In *R v Martin (Anthony)* (2002), the psychiatric evidence that he had a condition where he perceived much greater danger than the average person was not relevant to the question of whether he had used reasonable force. One of the reasons for this decision was that self-defence is usually raised in cases of minor assault and it would be 'wholly disproportionate to encourage medical disputes in cases of that sort'.
- *R v Cairns* (2005) followed the decision in *Martin* (2002). In deciding whether the defendant had used reasonable force in self-defence, it was not appropriate to take into account whether he was suffering from a psychiatric condition (such as paranoid schizophrenia) which may have caused him to have delusions that he was about to be attacked.
- In *R v Oye* (2013), the law in *Martin* and *Cairns* still applied.

Statutory confusion

The Criminal Justice and Immigration Act 2008 was passed to clarify the common law on self-defence. Section 76(6) of the Act requires that the amount of force used in the circumstances as the defendant believed them to be should be reasonable. However, the Crime and Courts Act 2013 now gives a wider defence to householders where an intruder enters their property. They can use the defence of self-defence provided that the degree of force was not 'grossly disproportionate'. For other cases, the degree of force used in self-defence must not be 'disproportionate'.

The case of *Ray* (2017) tried to assist judges summing up to a jury who have to consider the application of evidence and words that have small differences in meaning. It is vital, when summing up in cases where the householder's defence is raised, that the judge explains to the jury that the law gives a little more protection to a householder in his own home. However, it must be made clear to the jury that the use of force that was 'grossly disproportionate' could never be reasonable.

This raises questions:
- Should the judge use everyday language to help the jury decide whether, on the evidence, the prosecution have proved that the degree of force used was unreasonable?
- Would it be helpful to spell out the kind of circumstances that might show the degree of force used by a householder was reasonable?
- Should every case use a common formula of words?

Reasonable force and property protection

In *R v Williams* (2020), the defence did not apply.

Case study

R v Williams (2020)

The victim had stabbed the defendant in the arm and taken a necklace from him at a party, run away and was chased by a group from the party led by the defendant who, 120 metres from the flat in which the party had taken place, fatally stabbed him.

Neither the common law defence of self-defence nor that of crime prevention under the Criminal Law Act 1967 s 3 allows the use of force to recover stolen property. The s 3 defence was only available in relation to preventing crimes in progress, not in relation to a reaction to crimes already committed. The defences were not available here.

If a shopkeeper chased a robber out of his shop and caught him just down the street, the court is unlikely to think the robbery was completed in the shop, and disallow the defence of reasonable force by the shop-keeper to recover the stolen goods. In *Williams* the argument may have been less successful as the defendants were 16-year-old gang members.

13.2.3 Consent

The limits to what a person can consent to reflect the relationship of law to society and to morality.

This is an area where the law tends to lag behind the views of society and often reacts to a particular situation in a way that is unpredictable. This makes the criminal law seem unjust, in that an individual who regulates their life in accordance with the law may suddenly find themselves guilty of a criminal act.

Policy matters and inconsistency

In *R v Brown* (1993), the House of Lords held that consent was not a defence to sado-masochistic acts done in private by homosexuals, even though all the participants were adult and the injuries inflicted did not require medical attention. The court clearly made this decision as a matter of public policy. Lord Templeman said:

> The question whether the defence of consent should be extended to the consequences of sado-masochistic encounters can only be decided by consideration of policy and public interest ... Society is entitled and bound to protect itself against a cult of violence.

In deciding what was in the public interest, the courts have come to decisions, some of which are difficult to reconcile. However, in *R v Wilson* (1996), it was decided that where a defendant branded his initials on his wife's buttocks with a hot knife at her request, this was not an unlawful act, even though she had to seek medical attention for the burns caused. It held it was not in the public interest that such consensual behaviour should be criminalised. This was a situation of 'personal adornment' like having a tattoo. The so-called 'rough sex' defence is currently a matter where policy is involved.

Section 74 Sexual Offences Act 2003 makes it clear that a person consents to any sexual penetration only if there is agreement by choice to that penetration and the person has the freedom and capacity to make that choice.
- Consent to sexual activity may be given to one sort of sexual activity but not another and be subject to conditions, such as wearing a condom.
- Consent can be withdrawn at any time during sexual activity and each time activity occurs.

To establish whether there is consent, the prosecution and defence look at evidence of consent or lack of consent. This involves whether the victim was targeted, the vulnerability of the victim and the context of the alleged offence. This puts a great burden on juries and is liable to end up with inconsistent decisions. It may also go some way to explain the reduction in successful prosecutions for sexual assaults.

Look online

Research the background and progress of the Domestic Abuse Bill 2019–21 such as **https://publications.parliament.uk/pa/cm5801/cmpublic/DomesticAbuse/memo/DAB20.htm**

The need for a defence of consent

There must be a defence of consent in some situations. For example, if there was no defence of consent, then contact sports would all be illegal. This is why the Court of Appeal in *Attorney-General's Reference (No. 6 of 1980)* (1981) stated that, although consent was not a defence to street fights, there were exceptions where consent was a defence.

The list of exceptions given in that case was:

> **"** properly conducted games and sports, lawful chastisement or correction, reasonable surgical interference, dangerous exhibitions, etc. **"**

These exceptions are based on public policy.

Sport

If there was no defence of consent in 'properly conducted games and sports', then team games such as football, rugby and hockey could never be played, neither could individual sports such as judo, karate and boxing.

The important phrase in the judgment is 'properly conducted games and sports'. There has to be a distinction between playing within the rules and behaviour which is outside the rules. A deliberate 'off-the-ball' tackle aiming at another player's legs with the intention of causing serious injury must surely be considered as criminal behaviour. A player who is injured in this way has not consented to such behaviour.

The case of *R v Barnes* (2004) set out matters which were to be considered in deciding whether an assault in the course of a match was criminal. The court said that in deciding whether conduct in the course of a sport is criminal or not, the following factors should be considered:

- Intentional infliction of injury will always be criminal.
- For reckless infliction of injury, did the injury occur during actual play, or in a moment of temper or over-excitement when play had ceased?
- 'Off-the-ball' injuries are more likely to be criminal.
- The fact that the play is within the rules and practice of the game and does not go beyond them will be a firm indication that what has happened is not criminal.

By applying these factors, a good balance should be achieved between allowing contact sports to be played without unnecessary restrictions on their rules and upholding the criminal law on assault. Only those who

Without the defence of consent, rugby could not be played

deliberately inflict injury or who go beyond the rules of the game should be liable under the criminal law.

Medical procedures

Another exception where consent is allowed as a defence is 'reasonable surgical interference'. Clearly where the surgery is needed to save the patient's life or to improve a patient's health in some way, then consent to the operation is a defence to any charge of an offence against the person.

Mentally capable adults can consent to reasonable medical treatment or they can refuse it. If they refuse consent, then if surgery or other treatment was performed it would be a criminal act. For example, if a person refuses a blood transfusion because of his religious beliefs, then such treatment cannot be given.

If a patient is unconscious so that their consent cannot be asked, medical staff will try to obtain consent from relatives. If this is not possible then, where treatment is necessary and must be performed quickly, such an operation can be performed without actual consent.

What actually amounts to reasonable medical procedures leads to difficulties with respect to cosmetic procedures and body adornments. This has been seen in cases such as *R v BM* (2018) and *R v Melin* (2019).

Consent and euthanasia

No one can consent to another person assisting in bringing about their own death. This means that if a terminally ill patient wishes to die, they must take their own life. If anyone helps bring about the death, they will face a charge of murder or assisting suicide. This was decided in *R (on the application of Pretty) v DPP* (2001). This decision leads to the situation where the law recognises the personal autonomy of a person being entitled to take their own life and not committing any crime by trying to do so.

But in cases where people who wish to commit suicide are physically incapable of doing so, then they are denied their wishes as anyone who helps them will be guilty of an offence. There have been several attempts to challenge this rule, including Tony Nicklinson in 2014. In this and other cases, the courts have said that this is an issue for Parliament to consider. However, at the time of writing, Parliament has been unwilling to legislate, despite there being broad public support for their doing so.

Extension activity

You can explore further issues, cases and principles for this area of the law. With respect to consent, the following is an exhaustive list of aspects of the defence in the context of non-fatal offences.

Intentional injury

Boxing (and similar aggressive contact sports)

Due to their alleged entertainment value, public matches conducted with protective equipment, a referee and within the rules are lawful but street fighting and 'bare-knuckle' fighting are not lawful since the higher risk to the combatants outweighs any alleged entertainment value: *R v Coney* (1882).

Reasonable surgical and medical treatment

Most surgery is expressly consented to and has a high utility factor in its benefit to the patient. This is clearly lawful. There can be issues around 'informed consent' but this is usually a civil matter: *Corbett v Corbett* (1971).

Ritual circumcision

Male circumcision for religious purposes is lawful where both parents agree to it but so-called female circumcision is prohibited under the Female Genital Mutilation Act 2003: *Re: J (Circumcision)* (2000).

Tattooing, ear and body piercing and branding

In most circumstances the victim will give express consent to a piercing or tattoo which is considered to have some social utility as a personal adornment. There are issues around the age of consent to such procedures. But, note the limits set in the recent decision re: 'tongue splitting' in: *R v BM* (2018); *R v Wilson* (1997); *Burrell v Harmer* (1967).

Sado-masochism

The law has not generally accepted the idea of consent being a defence to injuries inflicted for sexual gratification in sado-masochistic sexual activity – certainly not where they are serious: *R v Brown & others* (1993); *R v Emmett* (1999); *R v Donovan* (1934).

Risk of accidental injury

Properly conducted sports

Deliberate and unnecessary infliction of injury cannot be consented to even in a rough sport like boxing or rugby: *R v Johnson* (1986).

As a general rule, any incident which takes place outside the rules of the game will not be considered to have been consented to. See *Barnes* for guidance: *R v Lloyd* (1989); *R v Billinghurst* (1978); *R v Barnes* (2005).

Rough and undisciplined horseplay

Consent to rough and undisciplined play could provide a defence as long as there was no intention to cause injury and a victim can give effective consent to the risk of accidental injury in the course of rough undisciplined play: *R v Jones* (1986); *R v Aitken* (1992).

Reasonable and lawful chastisement of children

Reasonable and lawful chastisement (corporal punishment) of children is lawful if 'reasonable and proportionate in the circumstances, involving no cruelty': *A v UK* (1998); s 58 Children Act 2004.

Sexual activity

The risk of injury involved in consensual sexual activity short of 'vigorous' or 'sado-masochistic' activity will be a viable defence: *R v Boyea* (1992); *Brown*; *Donovan*.

Risk of STD/HIV transmission

The victim can validly consent to the risk of infection in a sexual encounter provided they were fully informed of the risk. Obviously, this does not include situations where either party intends the infection to be spread: *R v Dica* (2004); *R v Konzani* (2005).

Express consent

These are situations where we are explicitly asked verbally or in writing before a procedure that would otherwise be an assault such as ear-piercing, surgery or dental treatment.

Implied consent

It is possible to 'impliedly' consent to minor batteries through situations where, for example, people inevitably come into contact with one another such as at football matches, on the underground or a pop concert: *Wilson v Pringle* (1987).

Real consent

Just because the victim appears to consent, this does not mean the consent is valid in law: *R v Tabassum* (2000).

Submission is not the same thing as consent

Consent is not the same as reluctant submission: *R v Olugboja* (1981).

Consent gained by fraud

Not all frauds will vitiate consent: *R v Linekar* (1995).

Fraud as to the identity of the defendant can vitiate: *R v Elbekkay* (1995); *R v Dica* (2004).

Fraud as to the nature and quality of the act consented to can also vitiate: *R v Williams* (1923).

Children and consent

Children under 16 with sufficient intelligence to understand fully the implications of the proposed treatment can give effective consent (a 'Gillick-competent' child): *Gillick v West Norfolk & Wisbech HA* (1985).

Mentally incapacitated and consent

If medical staff are acting in the patient's best interests, the absence of consent would not be unlawful: *F v West Berkshire HA* (1989).

Evaluation

Striking a balance between law and morality; privacy and public policy; should judges determine social, moral and public policy issues?

Quick questions

1. What is meant by the correspondence principle?
2. Outline the proposals for replacement of the offences in the Offences Against the Person Act 1861 set out in the draft bill of 1998.
3. There are competing interests of personal autonomy and social paternalism in the defence of intoxication. Explain these competing ideas.
4. Discuss the moral issues in the defence of self-defence.
5. Discuss the moral issues in the defence of intoxication.

Summary

Non-fatal offences against the person

- The Offences Against the Person Act 1861 is out of date.
- There are too many overlapping offences.
- The different offences show inconsistencies between them.
- There is no conformity with the correspondence principle.
- Much of the language used is archaic.

The defence of intoxication

- The distinction between specific and basic intent.
- The level of intoxication.
- Competing interests in the defence of intoxication.
- Should there be a distinction between legal and illegal drugs?
- Intoxication and the coincidence of *actus reus* and *mens rea*.
- Policy considerations.

The defence of self-defence

- Whether force is necessary if retreat is possible.
- Distinction between householder and others.
- Can there be a pre-emptive strike?
- The defence and morality.
- An all-or-nothing defence.
- The relevance of the defendant's characteristics.
- Statutory terminology not defined.
- Can force be used to protect property?

The defence of consent

- Inconsistent application of policy aspects.
- The need for the defence.
- Medical procedures.
- What can a person consent to?
- How genuine is consent?

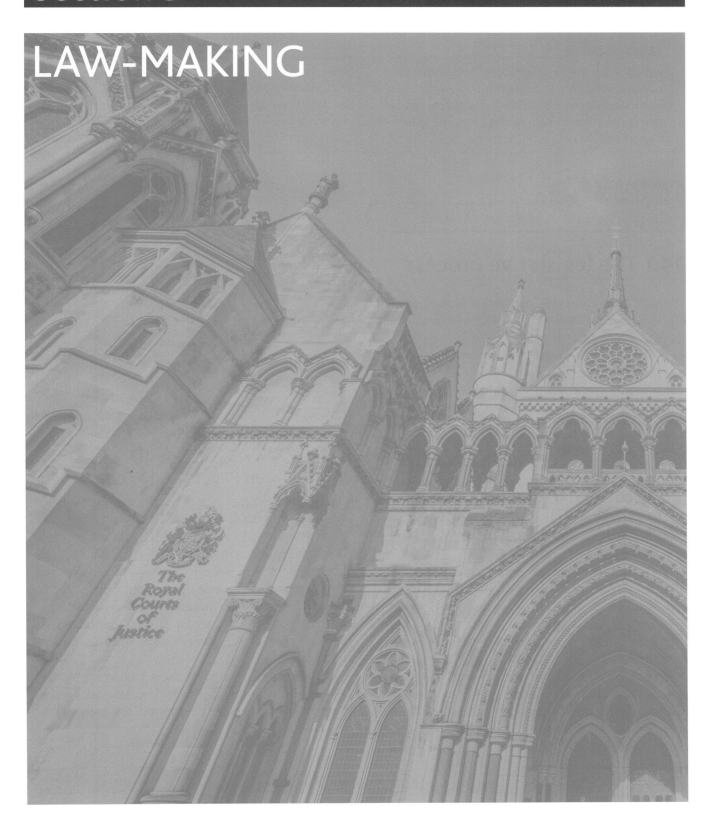

Section 3

LAW-MAKING

Chapter 14 Parliamentary law-making

Introduction

The main legislative (i.e. law-making) body in the UK is Parliament, which meets in the Palace of Westminster. In a democracy, the view is that laws should only be made by the elected representatives of society and, as such, MPs are elected to the House of Commons.

Laws passed by Parliament are known as Acts of Parliament, and this source of law is usually referred to as statute law. About sixty to seventy Acts are passed each year and are called primary legislation. These Acts provide the framework of law.

Key term

Primary legislation – laws passed by Parliament.

14.1 The legislative process

The United Kingdom Westminster Parliament consists of the House of Commons, the House of Lords and the Queen all acting together:

- Members of the House of Commons are elected.
- Members of the House of Lords are either hereditary peers or are appointed life peers.
- The Queen has to give her assent before a law can become an Act of Parliament.

Members of Parliament (MPs) sit in the House of Commons and represent a political party. They are elected by the public, with the country being divided into constituencies and each of these returning one MP.

The government of the day is formed by the political party that has a majority of MPs in the House of Commons.

Parliament considers proposed legislation for the whole of the United Kingdom and that which applies only to England. It has to be passed by both the House of Commons and the House of Lords and then assented to by the Queen – which is a mere formality.

As a result of devolution some powers have been given away by the Westminster Parliament. Scotland and Wales have their own elected Parliaments to make laws that relate only these countries. Northern Ireland has its own elected Assembly to make laws for that province.

The United Kingdom Houses of Parliament at Westminster

14.1.1 Green Papers and White Papers

If a government is unsure about the details of a law it wishes to introduce, it issues a Green Paper. This is a document for consultation, issued by the government department with responsibility for the issue. The government's view is put forward with their proposals for the new law. Interested parties are then invited to send comments to the government department, so that a full consideration of all views can be made and any necessary changes made to the government's proposals.

Following this, the government publishes a White Paper with its firm proposals for new law, taking into account the views received from the Green Paper consultation.

Alternatively, if the government has firm views on a topic, it can just issue a White Paper without consultation.

Consultation before any new law is framed is valuable as it allows time for mature consideration. From time to time governments are criticised for responding in a 'knee-jerk' fashion to incidents or a situation and, as a result, rushing through law that has subsequently proved to be unworkable. This occurred with the Dangerous Dogs Act 1991.

Look online

- Find an example of a recent Green Paper and a recent White Paper issued by the UK government.
- Have either of your findings resulted in legislation being passed?

14.1.2 Different types of Bill

A Bill is the name given to a proposed law introduced into Parliament. It will be drafted by lawyers in the civil service known as Parliamentary Counsel to the Treasury. They are given instructions on what is to be included and the effect the proposed law is intended to have by the proposer, usually the responsible government department.

The Bill has to be drafted so that it represents the proposer's wishes, while at the same time using correct legal wording so that there will not be any difficulties applying it in the future. It must be unambiguous, precise and comprehensive. Achieving all of these is not easy, and there may be unforeseen problems with the language used, as discussed in Chapter 16 on statutory interpretation.

A Bill will only become an Act of Parliament if it successfully completes all the necessary stages in Parliament. The government will set out a timetable when they introduce the Bill into Parliament and their Bills take priority over all other business.

Public Bills

These are the most frequent form of Bill. They usually involve matters of public policy that will affect either the whole country or a large section of it. Most government Bills are in this category; for example:

- the Constitutional Reform Act 2005
- the Legal Services Act 2007

- the Equality Act 2010
- the Legal Aid, Sentencing and Punishment of Offenders Act 2012
- the Criminal Justice and Courts Act 2015.

Not all Bills are aimed at changing the law for the entire country. Some may affect just one, or more, of the devolved countries – Scotland, Wales and Northern Ireland – as well as England.

It is also possible for a Private Members' Bill (see below) to be a Public Bill if it affects the whole population. The Abortion Act 1967 is such an example.

Private Bills

Some Bills are designed to pass a law that will affect only individual people or corporations, not the whole country. These are called Private Bills. An example of a Private Bill is:

- the University College London Act 1996, which was passed in order to combine the Royal Free Hospital School of Medicine, the Institute of Neurology and the Institute of Child Health into University College Hospital.

Private Members' Bills

Private Members' Bills are introduced and sponsored by individual MPs. Under the parliamentary process, there can be a ballot in each parliamentary session in which twenty private members are selected who can take their turn in presenting a Bill to Parliament. The time for debate of Private Members' Bills is limited, so only the first six or seven members in the ballot have a realistic chance of introducing a Bill on their chosen topic.

Relatively few Private Members' Bills become law, but there have been some important laws passed as the result of such Bills. Examples are:

- the Abortion Act 1967, which legalised abortion in Great Britain
- the Marriage Act 1994, which allowed people to marry in any registered place, not only in register offices or religious buildings
- the Household Waste Recycling Act 2003, which places local authorities under a duty to recycle waste.

A rarer form of Private Members' Bills can be introduced by a member of the House of Lords.

Using www.legislation.gov.uk, search for a recent example of a Private Members' Bill which has become law.

Type of Bill	Description
Government Bills	These are introduced by the government. They are likely to become law as government business takes priority in Parliament.
Private Members' Bills	They are introduced by individual members of either the House of Commons or the Lords. They will seldom become law.
Public Bills	These affect everyone and every business in the country.
Private Bills	These only affect individual persons or companies.

Figure 14.1 Key facts: types of Bills

14.1.3 Legislative stages in the House of Commons and the House of Lords, and the role of the Crown

In order to become an Act of Parliament, a Bill usually has to be passed by both Houses of Parliament.

A Bill will normally start in the House of Commons, and Finance Bills must start here. Occasionally a Bill will be introduced in the House of Lords. Whichever House a Bill is introduced in, it must go through all the stages explained below.

House of Commons

First Reading

This is a formal procedure where the name and main aims of the Bill are read out. Usually no discussion takes place, and usually there will be no vote.

Second Reading

This is the main debate on the whole Bill in which MPs debate the principles behind the Bill. The debate usually focuses on the main principles rather than smaller details. Those MPs wishing to speak in the debate must catch the Speaker's eye, since the Speaker controls all debates and no one may speak without being called on by the Speaker. At the end of the debate there will be a vote. There must be a majority in favour of the Bill for it to progress.

Committee Stage

If the Bill passes the Second Reading, the Committee Stage will thoroughly examine every clause of the Bill.

A committee of between 16 and 50 MPs form a Standing Committee, chosen specifically for that Bill. The MPs on the Committee will usually be those with a special interest in, or knowledge of, the subject of the Bill that is being considered. For Finance Bills the whole House sits in Committee.

Members of the Committee can propose amendments or additions, and these will be voted on by the Committee.

Report Stage

The Committee reports back to the House on amendments or additions accepted by them. If there were no amendments, there will not be a Report Stage – instead the Bill will continue to the Third Reading.

Amendments will be debated in the House and accepted or rejected. Further amendments can be added.

Third Reading

This is the final vote on the Bill. It is almost a formality since a Bill that has passed through all the previous stages is unlikely to fail at this late stage. A Bill will then be passed to the House of Lords for further debate and consideration. If it passes the stages in the House of Lords, it will be put forward for Royal Assent.

1 Go to www.parliament.uk/bills/ This page lists the Bills currently before Parliament.
2 Click on any Bill and you will see what stage of the Parliamentary process it has reached. It will also usually give the next part of the process with a date, if one has been fixed. Write brief notes on when the Bill was introduced and the dates of the stages it has passed. Keep checking the progress of the Bill during your course until you see that it has become an Act.

The House of Lords

If a Bill is introduced in the House of Lords, it will follow the following process:

1 First Reading – this is a formality when the short title of the Bill is read out and an order is made for the Bill to be printed.

2 Second Reading – the main debate on the Bill takes place. The Government Minister in the Lords explains the Bill and answers questions. This gives members of the Lords the opportunity to debate the main principles and purpose of the Bill. After this, a majority vote will be required for the Bill to proceed.

3 Committee Stage – there is a detailed scrutiny of every clause of the Bill at this stage. Unlike the House of Commons, all Bills are considered by the whole House in the Lords chamber and any peer can participate. The Bill may be amended, agreed to and voted on. All amendments are considered and members can discuss an issue for as long as they want. The government cannot restrict the subjects under discussion or impose a time limit.

4 Report Stage – all members of the Lords have another opportunity to examine the proposals and make amendments. Any member of the Lords can take part. Votes on any amendments take place.

5 Third Reading – amendments can still be made at this stage as long as the point was not considered and voted on at the Committee or Report stages.

6 The Bill will now be passed to the House of Commons for their consideration.

The Parliament Acts 1911 and 1949

The power of the House of Lords to reject a Bill is limited by the Parliament Acts 1911 and 1949. These allow a Bill to become law even if the House of Lords rejects it, provided that the Bill is reintroduced into the House of Commons in the next session of Parliament and passes all the stages again there.

The role of the Crown

The final stage is where the monarch formally gives approval to the Bill and it then becomes an Act of Parliament and part of the law.

This is now a formality and, under the Royal Assent Act 1967, the monarch will not even have the text of the Bills to which she is assenting; she will only have the short title. The last time that a monarch refused assent was in 1707, when Queen Anne refused to assent to the Scottish Militia Bill.

A Bill has to pass all three parliamentary stages before it can become an Act.
Most Bills are introduced into the House of Commons where they will be debated and receive detailed scrutiny.
The House of Lords will further debate and scrutinise the Bill after it has passed through the House of Commons.
They can suggest amendments which can either be accepted or rejected by the Commons.
The will of the House of Commons will eventually prevail as they have elected representatives.
The Queen's Royal Assent is necessary, but a mere formality, for a Bill to become an Act and part of the law of the land.

Figure 14.3 Key facts: the Parliamentary law-making journey

14.2 Advantages and disadvantages of the legislative process

14.2.1 Advantages of the legislative process

- Law is being made by elected representatives. This means it is democratic. As there has to be a general election at least once every five years, the electorate can vote out any government if it has not performed as the public expected and introduced promised law reforms.
- Before a Bill is presented to Parliament, there will often have been consultation on the proposed changes to the law such as in Green Papers. This allows the government to take into consideration objections and further suggestions on their original proposals.
- As all Bills have to go through the lengthy discussion process in both Houses of Parliament, especially in committee stages, any new law will have been thoroughly discussed and scrutinised before being brought into force.
- Parliament can act on reports and draft Bills prepared by the Law Commission, who will have consulted widely and investigated the state of existing law and the need for reform. This research is more likely to result in less contentious and better drafted legislation. There is a greater possibility of codification of existing law and practice, such as that introduced by the Sentencing Act 2020.

Wild Animals in Circuses Act 2019

2019 CHAPTER 24

An Act to make provision to prohibit the use of wild animals in travelling circuses.

[24th July 2019]

BE IT ENACTED by the Queen's most Excellent Majesty, by and with the advice and consent of the Lords Spiritual and Temporal, and Commons, in this present Parliament assembled, and by the authority of the same, as follows:—

1   Prohibition on use of wild animals in travelling circuses in England

(1)   A circus operator may not use a wild animal in a travelling circus in England.

(2)   For the purposes of this section, a circus operator uses a wild animal in a travelling circus if the animal performs or is exhibited as part of the circus.

(3)   A circus operator who contravenes subsection (1) is guilty of an offence and liable on summary conviction to a fine.

(4)   Where an offence under this section is committed by a body corporate and is proved—

(a)   to have been committed with the consent or connivance of an officer of the body corporate, or

(b)   to be attributable to any neglect on the part of an officer of the body corporate,

the officer (as well as the body corporate) is guilty of the offence and liable to be proceeded against and punished accordingly.

(5)   In this Act—

"animal" has the meaning given by section 1(1) of the Animal Welfare Act 2006;

"circus operator", in relation to a circus, means—

(a)   the owner of the circus,

(b)   any other person with overall responsibility for the operation of the circus, and

(c)   if neither the owner of the circus nor any person with overall responsibility for its operation is present in the United Kingdom, the person in the United Kingdom who is ultimately responsible for the operation of the circus;

"officer", in relation to a body corporate, means—

(a)   a director, manager, secretary or other similar officer of the body corporate, and

(b)   any person purporting to act in any such capacity;

"wild animal" means an animal of a kind which is not commonly domesticated in Great Britain.

Figure 14.2 Excerpt from the Wild Animals in Circuses Act 2019 (Source: www.legislation.gov.uk/ukpga/2019/24/introduction)

1   What is the purpose of this Act?

2   What is a wild animal?

3   To which part of the UK does the Act apply?

4   When does the Act come into force?

- Under the principle of Parliamentary Sovereignty, law passed by Parliament is the highest form of law. It cannot be questioned and must be applied by judges in their decisions in court. There is a clear separation of powers between the legislature who make laws and the judiciary who apply those laws.
- A Government minister introducing law into Parliament will have the full knowledge, support and expertise of their department in the proposal and they will have been consulted in the drafting of the law.
- In times of emergency, law can be introduced, debated and enacted quickly. A clear example of this approach was seen with the introduction of the Coronavirus Act 2020 which gave the government emergency powers to handle the pandemic. It passed all the parliamentary stages and received Royal Assent within a week of its introduction.

14.2.2 Disadvantages of the legislative process

- It is argued that the legislative process is undemocratic because:
  - the House of Lords is unelected
  - the approval of the Crown is undemocratic
  - although MPs are democratically elected, they are often obliged to 'take the whip' and vote on party lines rather than voting with their conscience or in the interests of their constituents.
- Government and Parliament do not always have the time or inclination to deal with all the reforms that are proposed. This is particularly true of reform of 'lawyers' law' such as areas of criminal law or the law of contract.

  An example of law that is still awaiting reform is the law on assaults and other non-fatal offences against the person. This is discussed in more detail in Chapter 8.
- Even where government introduces a Bill into Parliament, the process of it becoming an Act, with all the different readings, committee and report stages, and the possible 'ping-pong' between the Commons and the Lords, can take several months. For example, the Consumer Rights Act 2015 took fourteen months from first reading to Royal Assent.

  On the other hand, where there is a need for emergency laws, such as with the COVID-19 pandemic in 2020, laws to deal with an emergency can be passed very quickly.

- The government is in control of the parliamentary timetable, which often allows very little time for considering Private Members' Bills. Even when a private member does manage to introduce a Bill, it can easily be voted out by the government as they have the majority of seats in the House of Commons. Often a Private Members' Bill will involve a moral issue such as the right to die. The result is that very few Private Members' Bills become law.
- Because of the principle of Parliamentary Sovereignty it is difficult to remove or amend a badly drawn or outdated piece of legislation such as the Dangerous Dogs Act 1991. It means that another Act will be required to amend or remove the original legislation.
- The principle of Parliamentary Sovereignty is undermined when Parliament has not passed a law in an area of law. If this is discovered when a case comes to court, judges are allowed to create precedent which contradicts Parliamentary Sovereignty.
- An Act can come into force immediately it completes the parliamentary stages. However, in many cases, an Act will not come into force until a later date or dates. It may be necessary to consult several documents to find exactly when the relevant part of an Act came into force.
- MPs are not specialists in all areas of legislation, which may mean that some pieces of legislation will not receive detailed scrutiny in the House of Commons. It is more likely that there will be specialists in the House of Lords who can provide appropriate scrutiny. However, as the will of the Commons will prevail, there is limited likelihood of success of amendments suggested by the House of Lords.

Quick questions

1. Identify the parliamentary stages of an Act of Parliament.
2. Explain Private Members' Bills and identify one example.
3. Explain the nature and purpose of Green Papers and White Papers.
4. Explain why the will of the House of Commons always prevails over that of the House of Lords.
5. Assess the effectiveness of Parliament as a law-maker.

Summary

- The Westminster Parliament makes laws for the whole of the UK. Each of the devolved nations can make laws for themselves on certain issues.
- Green Papers are issued if Government wish to consult on a new law. White Papers set out their formal ideas before issuing a Bill in Parliament.
- A Public Bill will affect the whole country and will usually be issued by the Government. Private Members can promote a Bill through Parliament. Private Bills are required for large projects and affect only the company promoting them.
- A Bill will usually be introduced in the House of Commons where it has to pass through various stages of debate and approval. On passing all stages, it will proceed to the House of Lords for further debate and approval.
- In case of dispute between the two Houses, the will of the Commons has to prevail as it is the elected House.

Chapter 15 Delegated legislation

Introduction

As well as Parliament directly making laws through Acts of Parliament, other people or bodies can be given the power by Parliament to create laws. This can include the Privy Council, government ministers, local authorities and certain companies. Law created in this way is known as delegated legislation.

As the power to make law is given to unelected people or bodies, there are various checks and controls made on the making and operation of delegated legislation.

15.1 Types of delegated legislation

Delegated legislation is law made by some person or body other than Parliament, but with the authority of Parliament. That authority is usually laid down in a 'parent' Act of Parliament, known as an enabling Act. This creates the framework of the law and then delegates power to others to make more detailed law in the area.

An example of an enabling Act is the Police and Criminal Evidence Act 1984, which gives powers to make Codes of Practice for the use of police powers.

Key terms

Delegated legislation – laws or rules written outside Parliament when a person or body has been given the authority, by Parliament, to make those laws or rules.

Enabling Act – a law passed by Parliament which gives a person or body the authority to make laws.

15.1.1 Orders in Council

The Queen and the Privy Council have the authority to make Orders in Council. Its membership mainly comprises senior politicians who are current or former members of either the House of Commons or the House of Lords.

This type of delegated legislation effectively allows the government to make legislation without it having to be debated or voted on in Parliament. Orders in Council can be made on a wide range of matters, especially:

- Transferring responsibility between government departments; for example, when the Ministry of Justice was created, the powers of the previous Department of Constitutional Affairs and some of the powers of the Home Office were transferred to this new ministry. Another example of a similar type of order is the Northern Ireland (Restoration of Devolved Powers) Order 2000, made under the Northern Ireland Act 2000.
- Bringing Acts (or parts of Acts) of Parliament into force.
- To make law in emergencies under the Civil Contingencies Act 2004.

Orders in Council can also be used to make other types of law. For example:

- In 2003, an Order in Council was used to alter the Misuse of Drugs Act 1971 to downgrade cannabis to a Class C drug. Five years later the government decided that it had been a mistake and another Order in Council was issued, upgrading cannabis back to a Class B drug.

An Order in Council was used to upgrade cannabis to a Class B drug

There must be an enabling Act allowing the Privy Council to make an Order in Council. The enabling Act for the change of category of cannabis was the Misuse of Drugs Act 1971.

Look online

Look up recent Orders in Council on the Privy Council website at **https://privycouncil.independent.gov.uk/**
- On the home page, click on Privy Council, then click on Privy Council Meetings. You should now see a series of dates on which meetings took place.
- Click on any of these dates and you should see a list of Orders in Council made at that meeting.
- Can you see which enabling Acts have allowed the Orders to be made? The enabling Act is usually given on the left-hand side of the list of Orders.

15.1.2 Statutory Instruments

The term 'Statutory Instrument' refers to rules and regulations made by government ministers. Ministers in government departments can be given authority to make regulations.

Each department deals with a different area of policy and the minister in charge can make rules and regulations in respect of matters it deals with. For example:
- The Minister for Work and Pensions can make regulations on work-related matters, such as health and safety at work.
- The Minister for Transport can deal with road traffic regulations.

Statutory Instruments can be very short, covering one point, such as making the annual change to the minimum wage. However, other Statutory Instruments may be very long, with detailed regulations that were too complex to include in an Act of Parliament. Examples of Statutory Instruments that include a lot of detail are the following:
- Chemicals (Hazard Information and Packaging for Supply) Regulations 2009. This Statutory Instrument was made by the Minister for Work and Pensions under powers given in the European Communities Act 1972 and the Health and Safety at Work etc. Act 1974.
- Police codes of practice in relation to such powers as stop and search, arrest and detention: these were made by the Lord Chancellor and Secretary of State for Justice under powers given by the Police and Criminal Evidence Act 1984.

The use of Statutory Instruments is a major method of law-making. In 2014, 3481 Statutory Instruments were made but in 2019 the number was 1410.

Key term

Statutory Instrument – a piece of delegated legislation created by a government minister under the authority of an enabling Act. It will often be used to complete the detail of the enabling Act.

STATUTORY INSTRUMENTS

2020 No. 105

CIVIL AVIATION

The Air Navigation (Restriction of Flying) (Streatham) (Emergency) Regulations 2020

| Made | - - - - | at 2.40 p.m. on 2nd February 2020 |
| Coming into force - - | | with immediate effect |

The Secretary of State for a reason affecting the public interest deems it necessary to restrict flying in the area specified in the Schedule by reason of an emergency having arisen in that area.

The Secretary of State makes the following Regulations in exercise of the powers conferred by article 239 of the Air Navigation Order 2016(a).

Citation and commencement

1. These Regulations may be cited as the Air Navigation (Restriction of Flying) (Streatham) (Emergency) Regulations 2020 and come into force with immediate effect.

Restricted airspace

2. No aircraft is to fly below 2,500 feet above mean sea level over the area specified in Column 1 of the Schedule, being an area bounded by a circle of the radius specified in Column 2 and centred on the position specified in Column 3.

3. These Regulations do not apply to any aircraft flying in accordance with directions given by the Metropolitan Police Service.

Signed by authority of the Secretary of State for Transport

Carole Lovstrom
Grade 6
At 2.40 p.m. on 2nd February 2020
Department for Transport

SCHEDULE
Regulation 2

Table 1

Column 1	Column 2	Column 3
Specified area	Radius of circle	Position of centre of circle (latitude and longitude)

(a) S.I. 2016/765, to which there are amendments not relevant to these Regulations.

Figure 15.1 The Air Navigation (Restriction of Flying) (Streatham) (Emergency) Regulations 2020

Source: www.legislation.gov.uk/uksi/2020/105/pdfs/uksi_20200105_en.pdf

Look online

Look up the most recent Statutory Instrument for changing the National Minimum Wage. At the time of writing, the responsibility for setting the wage was with the Department of Business, Energy and Industrial Strategy.

- Who has signed the most recent change?
- What is the name of the enabling Act?
- What are the old and new amounts of the minimum wage?

Similarly, the Gaming Act (Variation of Monetary Limits) Order 1999 was made under the authority of the Gaming Act 1968.

- Who signed this Order?
- What is the name of the enabling Act?
- What are the amounts of the permitted prizes at gaming clubs?

15.1.3 By-laws

These can be made by local authorities to cover matters within their own area: a county council can pass by-laws affecting a whole county, while a district or town council can only make by-laws for its district or town. Usually, these by-laws will be made under the Local Government (Miscellaneous Provisions) Act 1982.

- Many local by-laws involve traffic control, such as parking restrictions.
- Other by-laws may be made for regulating behaviour such as banning drinking in public places or banning people from riding bicycles in a local park.
- By-laws can also be made by public corporations and certain companies for matters within their jurisdiction that involve the public. This means that bodies such as the British Airports Authority and railway companies can enforce rules about public behaviour on or about their premises. An example is the South West Trains Limited Railway Bylaws (made under s 129 of the Railways Act 1993).

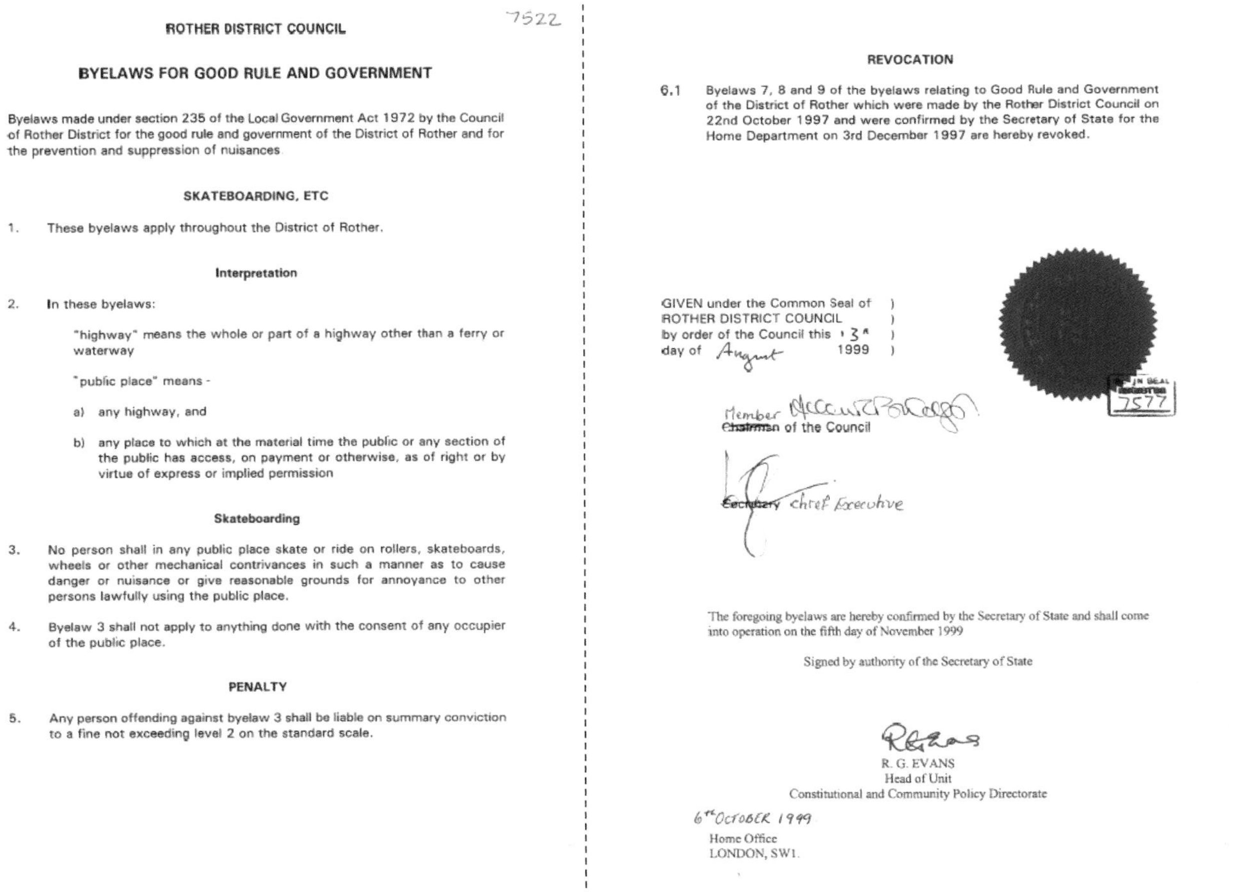

7522

ROTHER DISTRICT COUNCIL

BYELAWS FOR GOOD RULE AND GOVERNMENT

Byelaws made under section 235 of the Local Government Act 1972 by the Council of Rother District for the good rule and government of the District of Rother and for the prevention and suppression of nuisances.

SKATEBOARDING, ETC

1. These byelaws apply throughout the District of Rother.

Interpretation

2. In these byelaws:

"highway" means the whole or part of a highway other than a ferry or waterway

"public place" means -

a) any highway, and

b) any place to which at the material time the public or any section of the public has access, on payment or otherwise, as of right or by virtue of express or implied permission

Skateboarding

3. No person shall in any public place skate or ride on rollers, skateboards, wheels or other mechanical contrivances in such a manner as to cause danger or nuisance or give reasonable grounds for annoyance to other persons lawfully using the public place.

4. Byelaw 3 shall not apply to anything done with the consent of any occupier of the public place.

PENALTY

5. Any person offending against byelaw 3 shall be liable on summary conviction to a fine not exceeding level 2 on the standard scale.

REVOCATION

6.1 Byelaws 7, 8 and 9 of the byelaws relating to Good Rule and Government of the District of Rother which were made by the Rother District Council on 22nd October 1997 and were confirmed by the Secretary of State for the Home Department on 3rd December 1997 are hereby revoked.

GIVEN under the Common Seal of)
ROTHER DISTRICT COUNCIL)
by order of the Council this 3rd)
day of August 1999)

7577

Member ~~Chairman~~ of the Council

~~Secretary~~ Chief Executive

The foregoing byelaws are hereby confirmed by the Secretary of State and shall come into operation on the fifth day of November 1999

Signed by authority of the Secretary of State

R. G. EVANS
Head of Unit
Constitutional and Community Policy Directorate

6th OCTOBER 1999

Home Office
LONDON, SW1.

Figure 15.2 Example of a by-law (Source: Rother District Council)

Activity

Look at the following two sources and answer the questions on the next page.

Source A

STATUTORY INSTRUMENTS

2020 No. 447

PUBLIC HEALTH, ENGLAND

The Health Protection (Coronavirus, Restrictions) (England) (Amendment) Regulations 2020

Approved by both Houses of Parliament

Made	*21st April 2020*
Laid before Parliament	*at 12.30 p.m. on 22nd April 2020*
Coming into force	*at 11.00 a.m. on 22nd April 2020*

The Secretary of State makes the following Regulations in exercise of the powers conferred by sections 45C(1), (3)(c), (4)(d), 45F(2) and 45P of the Public Health (Control of Disease) Act 1984(**1**).

These Regulations are made in response to the serious and imminent threat to public health which is posed by the incidence and spread of severe acute respiratory syndrome coronavirus 2 (SARS-CoV-2) in England.

The Secretary of State considers that the restrictions and requirements imposed by these Regulations are proportionate to what they seek to achieve, which is a public health response to that threat.

In accordance with section 45R of that Act the Secretary of State is of the opinion that, by reason of urgency, it is necessary to make this instrument without a draft having been laid before, and approved by a resolution of, each House of Parliament.

Citation and commencement

1. These Regulations may be cited as the Health Protection (Coronavirus, Restrictions) (England) (Amendment) Regulations 2020 and come into force at 11.00 a.m. on 22nd April 2020.

Amendment of the Health Protection (Coronavirus, Restrictions) (England) Regulations 2020

2.—(1) The Health Protection (Coronavirus, Restrictions) (England) Regulations 2020(**2**) are amended as follows.

(2) In regulation 3, after paragraph (4), insert—

Figure 15.3 SI for Coronavirus restrictions, 2020

Source: www.legislation.gov.uk/uksi/2020/447/introduction/made

Source B

Drinking ban zones

The Safer Croydon Partnership has implemented four drinking ban zones. The correct term for a drinking ban zone is a Designated Public Place Order. These were introduced as part of the Criminal Justice and Police Act 2001. Prior to implementing a drinking ban zone, consultation must take place with the police and local residents, businesses and all of the licensed premises within the proposed area. Within the designated area, alcohol consumption is restricted in any open space, other than licensed premises.

It is important to note that this is a discretionary power, so where alcohol is being consumed without causing a problem (e.g. a family picnic in the park) the police would be unlikely to take action.

People are required to hand over alcohol in their possession when requested to do so by a police officer. The police officer will generally dispose of the alcohol by pouring it away. Failure to surrender alcohol on request may result in an arrest.

Although the vast majority of people drink and behave responsibly, a small minority of individuals engage in alcohol-related crime and disorder, causing distress to others and generally creating a negative impact on local communities. The legislation gives extra power to the police to help them deal with alcohol related problems.

1 What type of delegated legislation is Source A?
2 Which Act is the enabling Act which allowed this delegated legislation to be made?
3 Which government minister was responsible for making this legislation?
4 Which type of delegated legislation is Source B referring to?
5 Which body made the order referred to in Source B?
6 Who will enforce the Order?
7 Will the Order be enforced on everyone drinking alcohol in the designated public areas?

15.2 Controls on delegated legislation and their effectiveness

15.2.1 Control by Parliament
Approval of the parent Act

Parliament has initial control over what powers are delegated, as the enabling Act sets out the limits within which any delegated legislation must be made. For example, the enabling Act will state:
- which government minister can make the regulations
- the type of laws to be made and whether they can be made for the whole country or only for certain places
- whether the government department must consult other people before making the regulations.

Parliament also retains control over the delegated legislation as it can repeal (withdraw) the powers in the enabling Act at any time. If it does this, then the right to make legislation will cease.

Negative resolution procedure

Most Statutory Instruments will be subject to a negative resolution. This means that the relevant Statutory Instrument will become law unless rejected by Parliament within forty days of publication.

The main problem with this procedure is that very few of the Statutory Instruments will be looked at, as so many are made each year.

Affirmative resolution procedure

A small number of Statutory Instruments will be subject to this procedure. It means that the Statutory Instrument will not become law unless specifically approved by Parliament.

The need for an affirmative resolution will be included in the enabling Act. For example:
- an affirmative resolution is required before new or revised police Codes of Practice under the Police and Criminal Evidence Act 1984 can come into force.

One of the disadvantages of this procedure is that Parliament cannot amend the Statutory Instrument; it can only be approved, annulled or withdrawn.

Scrutiny by Committees

These bodies are an effective check on Statutory Instruments:
- the Joint Committee on Statutory Instruments (usually called the Scrutiny Committee)
- the Secondary Legislation Scrutiny Committee in the House of Lords.

As stated above, these committees can only check the legislation once it has been made and has come into force. They can review all Statutory Instruments and, where necessary, draw the attention of Parliament to points that need further consideration. However, the review is a technical one and not based on policy. The main grounds for referring a Statutory Instrument back to Parliament are that:
- it imposes a tax or charge – this is because only an elected body (Parliament) has such a right

- it appears to have retrospective effect which was not provided for by the enabling Act
- it appears to have gone beyond the powers given under the enabling legislation
- it makes some unusual or unexpected use of those powers
- it is unclear or defective in some way.

Effectiveness of Parliamentary controls

Scrutiny of statutory instruments by the Secondary Legislation Scrutiny Committee can be said to be effective as the committee are able to, at least, check a number of statutory instruments. However, due to the number of statutory instruments made each year, the Committee are unable to thoroughly check all of them.

As has been stated, the Delegated Powers and Regulatory Reform Committee is a committee of the House of Lords and any inappropriate provisions can be brought to the attention of the House before the Committee stage. This is considered to be an effective control because, if enabling provisions are made appropriately, it is more likely that legislation made under the authority of them will also be appropriate.

The various Scrutiny Committees can only report back their findings to either House; they have no power to alter any Statutory Instrument.

The main problem with this form of scrutiny is that the review is only a technical one, limited to reporting back. Even if a Committee discovers a breach, they cannot alter the regulations or stop them from becoming law. They can only draw the attention of Parliament to the matter.

When the Affirmative Resolution procedure is required there will, at least, be some debate in Parliament and it will usually be used for very important and potentially controversial matters. However, it is a time-consuming procedure and it relies on time being allocated to debate. If there is a dispute, then the Government will generally win a vote due to its majority in the House of Commons. Parliament cannot amend the statutory instrument; it can only be approved, annulled or withdrawn.

The majority of Statutory Instruments are subject to the negative resolution procedure but, as there are so many to be considered, it is likely that only a few will be looked at in detail. This procedure is considered to have limited effect as there is no strict requirement to look at Statutory Instruments made under this procedure. Most legislation made this way is not challenged and automatically becomes law after

40 days. On the other hand, a member of either House can raise an objection which may provide opportunity for debate and more detailed consideration.

The Delegated Powers and Regulatory Reform Committee

This role of this Committee is to report whether the provisions of any Bill inappropriately delegate legislative power, or whether the exercise of legislative power is subjected to an inappropriate degree of parliamentary scrutiny.

The Committee considers Bills when they are introduced into the Lords (at present there is no equivalent committee in the Commons). A memorandum is provided for each Bill, identifying each of the delegations, its purpose, the justification for leaving the matter to delegated legislation, and explaining why the proposed level of Parliamentary control is thought appropriate.

The Committee examines whether the delegations in each Bill are appropriate. The Committee restricts its consideration to the delegation in question, and not the merits of the overall policy.

The Committee's recommendations are made in reports to the House of Lords, usually before the start of the Committee Stage of the Bill.

Activity

Look at the Health Protection (Coronavirus, Restrictions) (England) (Amendment) Regulations 2020 above. Is this Regulation subject to the negative or affirmative resolution procedure? What is the reason for the procedure you have identified?

15.2.2 Control by the courts

Judicial review

A piece of delegated legislation can be challenged in court by the procedure of judicial review. It will be heard in the Queen's Bench Division Divisional Court, usually by two judges. The person making the challenge must have sufficient standing or interest in the case and is therefore directly affected by the legislation. The challenge will be made on the ground that the legislation is *ultra vires* – that it goes beyond the powers granted by the enabling Act.

Procedural *ultra vires*

It is *ultra vires* because the correct procedure set out by the enabling Act has not been followed. For example, in the *Aylesbury Mushrooms* case (1972), the Minister of

Labour had to consult 'any organisation ... appearing to him to be representative of substantial numbers of employers engaging in the activity concerned'. His failure to consult the Mushroom Growers' Association, which represented about 85 per cent of all mushroom growers, meant that an order setting up a training board was invalid as it was against the interests of mushroom growers generally.

Another example is *R v Secretary of State for Education and Employment, ex parte National Union of Teachers* (2000) in which it was ruled that a Statutory Instrument setting conditions for appraisal and access to higher rates of pay for teachers was beyond the powers given to the Education Secretary by the Education Act 1996. In addition, the procedure used was unfair as only four days had been allowed for consultation.

Substantive *ultra vires*

This is when a rule-making body has no substantive power under the empowering Act to make the rules in question. This would include, for example, acting beyond what is authorised. Any such rule will be *ultra vires* and void. An example is *R v Home Secretary, ex parte Fire Brigades Union* (1995) where changes made by the Home Secretary to the Criminal Injuries Compensation scheme were decided to have gone beyond the delegated powers given in the Criminal Justice Act 1988.

Activity

Another case example of substantive *ultra vires* is *R v Secretary of State for Social Security ex parte Joint Council for the Welfare of Immigrants* (1996). What were the facts in this case and what decision was ruled *ultra vires*?

'*Wednesbury* unreasonableness'

This is when a decision is so unreasonable (or irrational) that no reasonable body or authority would ever consider imposing it. If this test is met, the decision will be *ultra vires* and void. It was set in the case of *Associated Picture Houses v Wednesbury Corporation* (1948). An example *is R (Rogers) v Swindon NHS Trust* (2006) when a woman with breast cancer was prescribed the non-approved drug Herceptin. Her NHS Trust refused to provide her with the drug as it said her case was not exceptional, though it did provide the drug for some patients in its area. This decision was decided to be unreasonable and therefore *ultra vires*.

Effectiveness of judicial controls

It is positive that an individual person or body has the ability to challenge a piece of delegated legislation or a decision made by a public body. However, there are a number of limitations on judicial controls.

This type of action is dependent upon a case being brought before a court.

In a judicial review action, the person making the challenge will have to have 'standing' or an interest in the action or be directly affected by the legislation or decision. It is likely that a challenge will be made against a government department or public body, which are likely to have greater resources and funding to defend the legislation or decision. Finally, an action will have to be launched within three months of the decision having been made, and there will be no state funding or legal aid available for the challenge. The persons or body available to afford to take such action will be limited and there will be minimal time to appeal for crowdfunding.

A court does not have the power to strike down a piece of legislation due to the principle of Parliamentary Supremacy. It can only check that a piece of legislation has been made in accordance with the requirements of the parent Act.

15.3 Reasons for the use of delegated legislation

1 Parliament does not have time to consider and debate every small detail of complicated regulations.
2 Parliament may not have the necessary technical expertise or knowledge required; for example, health and safety regulations in different industries need expert knowledge. Modern society has become very complicated and technical, so that it is impossible for MPs to have all the knowledge needed to draw up laws on controlling technology, ensuring environmental safety, dealing with a vast array of different industrial problems or operating complex taxation schemes. It is thought that it is better for Parliament to debate the main principles of a law thoroughly, but to leave the detail to be filled in by those who have expert knowledge of it.
3 Ministers can have the benefit of further consultation before detailed regulations are drawn up. Consultation is particularly important for rules on technical matters, where it is necessary to make sure that the regulations are technically accurate and workable.

Some Acts require consultation before regulations are created; for example, before any new or revised police Code of Practice under the Police and Criminal Evidence Act 1984 is issued, there must be consultation with a wide range of people including:

a) persons representing the interests of police authorities

b) the General Council of the Bar, and

c) the Law Society.

4 The process of passing an Act of Parliament can take a considerable time and, in an emergency, Parliament may not be able to pass law quickly enough. The Privy Council can meet at short notice and pass necessary emergency rules and Ministers can draft Statutory Instruments which can have immediate effect.

5 Local councils can deal with issues that are of concern to them and can use by-laws to regulate behaviour in certain areas such as parks and beaches.

6 Delegated legislation can be easily amended or revoked when necessary, so that the law can be kept up to date. Ministers can respond to new or unforeseen situations by amending or updating existing regulations. For example, government ministers have issued a number of Statutory Instruments to issue orders on the closing of shops and licensed premises, the wearing of face coverings and restrictions on travel during the COVID-19 pandemic.

15.4 Advantages and disadvantages of delegated legislation

15.4.1 Advantages of delegated legislation

- Time-saving: Delegated legislation is quicker to pass and amend than an Act of Parliament, which must be debated and passed by both Houses. Also, Parliament's business is controlled by the government; its procedure can be complicated and it does not sit all year. New laws to deal with changing situations, like the Covid-19 pandemic, have been introduced to deal with changing situations.

- Policy over detail: It is better for Parliament to focus on wider issues of policy rather than detail; for example, the Road Traffic Act (1988) made a general requirement for motorcycle helmets to be worn but detailed specifications of the nature of approved helmets were set out in separate regulations.

- Speed: Delegated legislation allows for a quick response in an emergency as Parliament might not be sitting at weekends or during Parliamentary holidays. One old example is the Food Protection Order (1986), which was laid before Parliament within two hours of notification of the nuclear disaster at Chernobyl to protect the movement of sheep which might have been contaminated by the fallout. Other current examples relate to the restrictions on international travel due to the Covid-19 pandemic and the locking down of specific areas where infections have arisen.

- Expertise: It is better to initially involve and use technical expertise, or local knowledge, when making detailed laws for specific industries or local areas. The law-making system would lose public support if laws were introduced and then found to be unworkable for failure to consult or lack of knowledge.

- Flexibility: Delegated legislation can be easily amended or revoked without having to go back to Parliament. An example is the annual updating of the amount of the minimum wage each year.

- Acts of Parliament can be brought into force by commencement orders as and when preparations to implement the rules have been put into place.

- Controls: Both forms of control – parliamentary and judicial – help to avoid any abuse of power by ministers or others exercising delegated law-making powers.

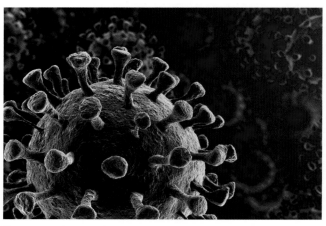

The coronavirus up close

15.4.2 Disadvantages of delegated legislation

- It takes law-making away from the democratically elected House of Commons and allows non-elected people to make law. This is acceptable provided there is sufficient control but, as already seen, Parliament's control is fairly limited. This criticism cannot be made of by-laws made by local authorities since these are elected by local citizens.
- Sub-delegation – this means that law-making authority is handed down another level. Government ministers do not have the time or expertise to make delegated legislation themselves. They rely on civil servants working in their departments. This brings comment that much law is made by unelected civil servants and merely 'rubber-stamped' by the minister of that department.
- The large volume of delegated legislation also gives rise to criticism since it makes it difficult to discover what the present law is. This problem is aggravated by a lack of publicity, as much delegated legislation is made in private, in contrast to public debates in Parliament. This was particularly seen when dealing with the COVID-19 pandemic, as several Statutory Instruments were passed with little if any debate, at short notice, imposing new rules in addition to existing rules. This left the public confused as to the state of the law as it affected them.
- Delegated legislation shares with Acts of Parliament the same problem of obscure wording that can lead to difficulty in understanding the law and requiring judges to interpret the meaning.

Quick questions

1. Identify the body that makes Orders in Council. Who sits on this body?
2. Who can make Statutory Instruments? Where do they get the power to make these regulations?
3. Describe two ways judges can control delegated legislation.
4. Describe two ways Parliament can control delegated legislation
5. Assess the reasons for the use of delegated legislation.

Summary

- Delegated legislation is law made by a person or body outside Parliament, but with the authority of Parliament in an enabling Act.
- Orders in Council are made by the Privy Council.
- Statutory Instruments are made by government ministers.
- By-laws are made by local authorities and public companies.
- Delegated legislation is controlled by Parliament by:
  - Approval of the Enabling Act.
  - The negative resolution procedure – the Statutory Instrument becomes law unless it is rejected within forty days of publication.
  - The affirmative resolution procedure – Parliament's approval has to be given before the Statutory Instrument comes into force.
  - Scrutiny committees check the delegated legislation after it comes into force.
- Delegated legislation is also controlled by the courts by judicial review and a declaration of *ultra vires* on the grounds of:
  - procedural *ultra vires*
  - substantive *ultra vires*, or
  - unreasonableness.
- Reasons for the use of delegated legislation include:
  - Parliament does not have time to consider every small detail of law.
  - Parliament does not have technical expertise.
  - Further consultation may be required before detailed rules are introduced.
  - There may be a need to introduce laws quickly.
  - By-laws deal with local issues.
  - Delegated legislation can be amended or revoked more easily than primary legislation.

Chapter 16 Statutory interpretation

Introduction

Many acts or statutes are passed by Parliament each year. The meaning of the law in these statutes should be clear, but this is not always achieved. In order to help understand the meaning of a statute, Parliament will include definition clauses which give the meaning of certain words used in that statute; such clauses are called 'interpretation sections'.

For example, in the Theft Act 1968, the definition of 'theft' is given in section 1, and then sections 2–6 define key words in that offence. However, not all words in all Acts are given definitions, and it will then be for judges in cases in court to give meanings to words used by Parliament. When acting in this way, judges use certain rules.

16.1 Rules of statutory interpretation

Statutory interpretation is where judges give a meaning to the words of an Act of Parliament when they are delivering their judgment in court. When acting in this way, judges use certain rules:

1 the literal rule
2 the golden rule
3 the mischief rule.

The three rules take different approaches and a judge may prefer the use of one rule over another. This means that the interpretation of words in a statute may differ from one judge to another. However, once an interpretation has been set, particularly in the appeal courts, it might then form a precedent for future cases.

Link

See Chapter 17 for an explanation of judicial precedent.

16.1.1 The literal rule

This rule developed in the early nineteenth century and has been the main rule applied ever since then. Using this rule, a judge will give words their plain, ordinary or literal (dictionary) meaning, even if the result is not very sensible.

This idea was expressed by Lord Esher in *R v Judge of the City of London Court* (1892) when he said:

> " If the words of an Act are clear then you must follow them even though they lead to a manifest absurdity. The court has nothing to do with the question whether the Legislature has committed an absurdity. "

The use of this rule was illustrated in *Whiteley v Chappell* (1868), where the defendant was charged under an Act that made it an offence to impersonate 'any person entitled to vote'. The defendant had pretended to be a person whose name was on the voters' list, but who had died. The court held that the defendant was not guilty since a dead person is not, in the literal meaning of the words, 'entitled to vote'.

The use of the rule has been criticised because it can lead to what are considered harsh decisions.

Case studies

London & North Eastern Railway Co. v Berriman (1946)

A railway worker was killed while doing maintenance work, oiling points on a railway line. His widow tried to claim compensation because there had not been a look-out man provided by the railway company in accordance with a regulation under the Fatal Accidents Act. This stated that a look-out should be provided for men working on or near the railway line 'for the purposes of relaying or repairing' it.

The court took the words 'relaying' and 'repairing' in their literal meaning. They said that oiling points was maintaining the line and not relaying or repairing, so that Mrs Berriman's claim failed.

Fisher v Bell (1961)

A shopkeeper had a flick-knife displayed in his shop window with a price tag on it. The Restriction of Offensive Weapons Act 1959 made it an offence to 'offer' such flick-knives for sale. In ordinary contract law, goods on display in shops are not 'offers' in the technical sense but an 'invitation to treat', preparatory to a customer making an offer.

Lord Justice Parker applied the literal rule of statutory interpretation to the offence and found that the shopkeeper had committed no offence.

Link

This case relates to contract law – what amounts to an invitation to treat and an offer.

Key term

The literal rule – words in an Act are given their ordinary, natural, dictionary meaning.

Activity

Read the following law report and answer the questions below.

Lurking policeman not 'passengers'

Cheeseman v Director of Public Prosecutions (1990)

Section 81 of the Public Health Acts Amendment Act 1907 gave the word 'street' the meaning of 'any place of public resort under the control of a local authority'. The defendant, Cheeseman, was charged with wilfully and indecently exposing his person in a street to the annoyance of passengers contrary to s 28 Town Police Clauses Act 1847. He was seen by police officers who were stationed in a public toilet following complaints. The issue was whether the stationary officers were 'passengers'.

Lord Justice Bingham said that the *Oxford English Dictionary* showed that in 1847, when the Act was passed, 'passenger' had a meaning of 'a passer-by or through; a traveller (usually on foot); a wayfarer'. Before the meaning of 'street' was enlarged in 1907, that dictionary definition of passenger was not hard to apply: it clearly covered anyone using the street for ordinary purposes of passage or travel. The dictionary definition could not be applied to a place of public resort such as a public lavatory, but on a commonsense reading, 'passenger' had to mean anyone resorting in the ordinary way to a place for one of the purposes for which people would normally resort to it. If that was the correct approach, the two police officers were not 'passengers'. They were stationed in the public lavatory in order to apprehend persons committing acts which had given rise to earlier complaints. They were not resorting to that place of public resort in the ordinary way but for a special purpose and thus were not passengers.

Source: Adapted from *The Times*, 2 November 1990

1 The meaning of the word 'passenger' was also important. How did the court discover what this word meant in 1847?

2 The court decided that 'passenger' meant 'a passer-by or through; a traveller (usually on foot); a wayfarer'. Why did that definition not apply to the police officers who arrested the defendant?

3 The defendant was found not guilty because of the way the court interpreted 'passenger'. Do you think this was a correct decision? Give reasons for your answer.

16.1.2 The golden rule

This rule is a modification of the literal rule as it starts by looking at the literal meaning of words but the judge is then allowed to avoid an interpretation that would lead to an absurd result.

There are two views on how far the golden rule should be used.

1 A very narrow view, as shown by Lord Reid's comments in *Jones v DPP* (1962), when he said:

> It is a cardinal principle applicable to all kinds of statutes that you may not for any reason attach to a statutory provision a meaning which the words of that provision cannot reasonably bear. If they are capable of more than one meaning, then you can choose between those meanings, but beyond this you cannot go.

Under this narrow application of the golden rule, the court may only choose between the possible meanings of a word or phrase. If there is only one meaning then that must be taken. This narrow view of the golden rule can be seen in practice in *Adler v George* (1964).

Case study

Adler v George (1964)

The Official Secrets Act 1920 made it an offence to obstruct Her Majesty's Forces 'in the vicinity' of a prohibited place. The defendant had obstructed HM Forces actually in their base, the prohibited place. The defendants argued they were not guilty as the literal wording of the Act did not apply to anyone *in* the prohibited place – it only applied to those 'in the vicinity', i.e., outside but close to it.

The Divisional Court found the defendant guilty. The words 'in the vicinity of' were interpreted in a narrow way as meaning 'being in or in the vicinity of' the prohibited place.

2 The words have only one clear meaning, but if that meaning was used, it would lead to a repugnant situation – a result which should not be allowed. In such a case a judge will modify the words of a statute to avoid that problem. Here are two examples:

Case studies

Re Sigsworth (1935)

A son had murdered his mother. The mother had not made a will, so normally her estate would have been inherited by her next of kin according to the rules set out in the Administration of Estates Act 1925. This meant that the murderer son would have inherited as her 'issue'.

There was no ambiguity in the words of the Act, but the court was not prepared to let a murderer benefit from his crime, so it was held that the literal rule should not apply, and a wider use of the golden rule would be used to prevent the repugnant situation of the son inheriting. Effectively the court was writing into the Act that the 'issue' would not be entitled to inherit where they had killed the deceased.

R v Allen (1872)

The defendant attempted to marry the niece of his first wife, to whom he was still married. This could not have been a valid marriage because of the close relationship of the two women. He was charged under s 57 Offences Against the Person Act 1861 which makes it an offence for 'whosoever being married shall marry again without the previous marriage being ended'. The defendant argued that he could not be guilty as his second 'marriage' was void.

The court, using the narrow application of the golden rule decided that 'shall marry' be interpreted as going through a ceremony of marriage so the defendant was guilty. If any other meaning was given to these words, the offence was incapable of being committed.

Key terms

The golden rule – a judge can choose the best interpretation of ambiguous words *OR* avoid an absurd or repugnant result.

A narrow approach of the rule – the court chooses a possible meaning of words but if there is only one meaning, that must be given. Examples are *Adler v George* (1964) and *R v Allen* (1872).

A broad approach of the rule – if a clear meaning of the words would lead to a repugnant result, the judge will modify the meaning of the words. An example is *Sigsworth* (1935).

16.1.3 The mischief rule

This rule gives a judge more discretion when interpreting legislation than the previous two rules. The definition of the rule comes from *Heydon*'s case (1584), where it was said that there were four points the court should consider. These, in the original language of that old case, were:

1 What was the common law before the making of the Act?
2 What was the mischief and defect for which the common law did not provide?
3 What was the remedy the Parliament hath resolved and appointed to cure the disease of the commonwealth?
4 The true reason of the remedy.

> Then the office of all the judges is always to make such construction as shall suppress the mischief and advance the remedy.

Under this rule, therefore, the court should look to see what the law was before the Act was passed in order to discover what gap (or 'mischief') the Act was intended to cover. The court should then interpret the Act in such a way that the gap is covered. This is quite a different approach from the literal rule.

A good example of the way the mischief rule operates is seen in *Smith v Hughes* (1960). There was disagreement over using the mischief rule or the literal rule in *Royal College of Nursing v DHSS* (1981).

- The mischief rule is similar to the purposive approach (see section 16.2), except that it does require the identification of a problem or 'mischief' before it can be used.
- It may often rely on the use by judges of extrinsic aids (see section 16.3), to help detect the intention of Parliament and/or the mischief that preceded the passing of the Act.

Case studies

Smith v Hughes (1960)

The judges had to interpret s 1(1) of the Street Offences Act 1959, which said 'it shall be an offence for a common prostitute to loiter or solicit in a street or public place for the purpose of prostitution'.

The court considered appeals against conviction under this section by six different women. In each case the women had not been 'in a street'; one had been on a balcony and the others had been at the windows of ground-floor rooms, with the window either half open or closed. In each case the women were attracting the attention of men by calling to them or tapping on the window. They argued that they were not guilty under this section since they were not literally 'in a street or public place'. The court decided that they were guilty, with Lord Parker, the Lord Chief Justice saying:

> For my part I approach the matter by considering what is the mischief aimed at by this Act. Everybody knows that this was an Act to clean up the streets, to enable people to walk along the streets without being molested or solicited by common prostitutes. Viewed in this way it can matter little whether the prostitute is soliciting while in the street or is standing in the doorway or on a balcony, or at a window, or whether the window is shut or open or half open.

It can be seen from this that the judge was putting his own interpretation on Parliament's words.

Royal College of Nursing v DHSS (1981)

The Abortion Act 1967 provided that a pregnancy should be 'terminated by a registered medical practitioner' – a doctor. Medical improvements led to the normal method of terminating a pregnancy using drugs. Part of the procedure was carried out by a doctor, and part was performed by nurses without a doctor present. It had to be decided if this procedure was lawful.

The majority of judges in the House of Lords decided it was lawful. They pointed out that the mischief Parliament was trying to remedy was the unsatisfactory state of the law before 1967 and the number of illegal abortions. They also said that the policy of the Act was to broaden the grounds for abortion and ensure that they were carried out with proper skill in hospital.

The judges in the minority took the literal view, and said that the words of the Act were clear and that terminations could only be carried out by a registered medical practitioner. They said that the other judges were not interpreting the Act but 'redrafting it with a vengeance'.

Key term

The mischief rule – the judge looks at the gap in the law before the Act was passed and interprets the words to cover the gap and deal with the mischief.

16.2 The purposive approach

This is a complete contrast to the literal rule and goes beyond the mischief rule:

- The court is not just looking at the meaning of individual words or to see what the gap was in the old law; the judges are deciding what they believe Parliament meant to achieve and giving effect to that purpose.

The champion of this approach in English law was Lord Denning. His attitude towards statutory interpretation was shown when he said in the case of *Magor and St Mellons v Newport Corporation* (1950):

> We sit here to find out the intention of Parliament and carry it out, and we do this better by filling in the gaps and making sense of the enactment than by opening it up to destructive analysis.

However, his attitude was criticised by judges in the House of Lords when they heard the appeal in the case. Lord Simonds called Lord Denning's approach: 'a naked usurpation of the legislative function under the thin disguise of interpretation' and pointed out that 'if a gap is disclosed the remedy lies in an amending Act'.

Another judge, Lord Scarman, said:

> If Parliament says one thing but means another, it is not, under the historic principles of the common law, for the courts to correct it. The general principle must surely be acceptable in our society. We are to be governed not by Parliament's intentions but by Parliament's enactments.

This speech shows the problem with the purposive approach. Should the judges refuse to follow the clear words of Parliament? How do they know what Parliament's intentions were? It has to be remembered that, due to the principle of Parliamentary Supremacy, judges should be interpreting and giving effect to the words of an Act, they should not be making law themselves. There is a problem in that it may be very difficult to discover Parliament's intentions; only the words of the statute can show what Parliament wanted.

This approach to interpretation is the style used in many other European countries and, while the UK was a member of the EU, it was recognised by the Judiciary that, when interpreting legislation which had been passed to comply with EU law, the correct view to take was to use the purposive approach.

Case study

R (Quintavalle) v Secretary of State for Health (2003)

The House of Lords decided that organisms created by cell nuclear replacement (CNR) came within the definition of 'embryo' in the Human Embryology and Fertilisation Act 1990. Section 1(1)(a) of this Act states that 'embryo means a live human embryo where fertilisation is complete'. CNR was not possible in 1990 when the Act was passed and the problem is that fertilisation is not used in CNR. Lord Bingham said:

> The court's task, within permissible bounds of interpretation, is to give effect to Parliament's purpose … Parliament could not have intended to distinguish between embryos produced by, or without, fertilisation since it was unaware of the latter possibility.

It can be seen how this approach goes beyond the mischief rule. At the time of the Act, Parliament was considering the mischief (or gap in the law) of the risk of wrong use of embryos created through fertilisation. The Act was aimed at that. Parliament did not know of any gap in relation to CNR embryos: they hadn't been invented. As a result:

- the purposive approach is used at the judge's discretion to make sure the purpose of the Act is given effect, whereas
- the mischief rule looks at the gap in the law before the Act was passed and the judge interprets the words to deal with the mischief.

R v Registrar-General, ex parte Smith (1990)

Section 51(1) of the Adoption Act 1976 stated:

> the Registrar-General shall, on an application ... by an adopted person, ... supply to that person ... such information as is necessary to enable that person to obtain a certified copy of the record of his birth.

Mr Smith wanted information to enable him to obtain his birth certificate. He had been convicted of two murders and was detained in Broadmoor.

Taking a literal interpretation, the Registrar-General had to supply him with the information as the Act used the phrase 'shall . . . supply'.

A psychiatrist thought that it was possible he might be hostile towards his natural mother. The court had to decide – should they use the literal rule or use an alternative approach? The Court of Appeal decided to use the purposive approach, saying that, despite the plain language of the Act, Parliament could not have intended to promote serious crime. In view of the possible risk to Mr Smith's natural mother if he discovered her identity, the Registrar-General did not have to supply any information.

Jones v Tower Boot Co. (1997)

A young black worker was physically and verbally abused at work by fellow workers. He sued his employers, arguing that they were responsible for the actions of their workers. It had to be decided whether the workers were acting in the 'course of their employment' under s 32 of the Race Relations Act 1976. The employers argued that the abuse was not part of a job and fell outside the 'course of their employment'.

The Court of Appeal ruled, using the purposive approach, that Parliament's intention when passing the Act was to eliminate discrimination in the workplace and this would not be achieved by giving a narrow interpretation to the words 'course of employment'. As a result, the employers were liable.

16.3 Intrinsic and extrinsic aids to interpretation

16.3.1 Intrinsic aids

Judges can use certain items within the statute to help make the meaning of some words clearer.

- A judge can consider the **long title**, the **short title** and the **preamble** (if any) of the Act.
- Older statutes usually have a preamble that sets out Parliament's purpose in enacting that statute.
- Modern statutes either do not have a preamble or contain a very brief one; for example, the Theft Act 1968 states that it is an Act to modernise the law of theft.
- The **long title** may also explain briefly Parliament's intentions.
- Other useful internal aids are any **headings** before a group of sections, and any **schedules** attached to the Act.
- There are often also **marginal notes** explaining different sections, but these are not generally regarded as giving Parliament's intention as they will have been inserted after the Parliamentary debates and are only helpful comments put in by the printer.
- An unusual approach was taken in the Arbitration Act 1996, where a statement of the principles of the Act is set out in an **interpretative section**, s 2. This is a new development in statutory drafting and one that could both encourage and help the use of the purposive approach.

Look up any recent Act of Parliament on **www.parliament.uk**

Try to find all or any of the internal aids. Remember that modern Acts do not necessarily have all these aids written in them.

16.3.2 Extrinsic aids

These are items outside an Act which may help a judge to find the meaning of words in an Act. They include:

- any relevant pre-legislative documents such as *travaux préparatoires*, Green Papers, White Papers, Law Commission reports or reports of law reform bodies

- previous Acts of Parliament on the same topic
- dictionaries of the time the Act was passed such as used in *Cheeseman v DPP* (1990) (above)
- academic books and publications.

In addition, the following can be, and will be, considered by judges:
- Hansard
- explanatory notes published in, or with, the Act
- international treaties or Conventions
- the Interpretation Act 1978.

Hansard

This is the official report of what was said in Parliament when the Act was debated.

In *Pepper v Hart* (1993), the House of Lords relaxed the previous rule that courts could not look at what was said in Parliamentary debates and accepted that Hansard could be used in a limited way. This case was unusual in that seven judges heard the appeal, rather than the normal panel of five. These seven judges included the Lord Chancellor, who was the only judge to disagree with the use of Hansard. The majority ruled that Hansard could be consulted.

Case study

Pepper (Inspector of Taxes) v Hart (1993)

Teachers at an independent school were having their children educated at a reduced rate, which was a taxable benefit based on the 'cash equivalent' of the reduction. By s 63 Finance Act 1976, 'cash equivalent' could be interpreted to mean either
- the additional cost of providing the reduction to the teachers, or
- the average cost of providing the schooling to the public and the teachers.

In their decision, the House of Lords referred to statements made by the Financial Secretary to the Treasury in Parliament, which showed that the intention was to tax employees on the basis of the additional cost to the employer of providing the reduction.

The result of the decision is that Hansard may be considered but only where the words of the Act are ambiguous or obscure or lead to an absurdity. Even then, it should only be used if there was a clear statement by the

minister introducing the legislation, which would resolve the ambiguity or absurdity. The Lord Chancellor in *Pepper v Hart* opposed the use of Hansard on practical grounds, pointing out the time and cost it would take to research Hansard in every case.

Hansard – the official report of what is said in Parliament

Reports of law reform bodies and the Law Commission

As with the use of Hansard, reports by law reform agencies, including the Law Commission, used not to be considered by judges.

However, this rule was relaxed in the *Black Clawson* case in 1975, when it was accepted that such a report should be looked at to discover the mischief or gap in the law that the legislation based on the report was designed to deal with. After all, a piece of legislation drafted following a detailed investigation and report is likely to follow closely the recommendations of the reform body and their reasoning.

International treaties and conventions

In *Fothergill v Monarch Airlines Ltd* (1980), the House of Lords decided that an international convention should be considered, as it was possible that in translating and adapting the convention to the legislative process, the true meaning of the original might have been lost.

The House of Lords in that same case also held that an English court could consider any preparatory materials or explanatory notes published with an international convention. The reasoning behind this was that other countries allowed the use of such material (known as *travaux préparatoires*), and the UK judiciary should also be allowed to do so, for consistent international interpretation.

Laroche v Spirit of Adventure (UK) Ltd (2009)

Several extrinsic aids were considered in this case. The claimant had been injured as the result of the sudden landing of a hot-air balloon in which he was travelling. The meaning of the word 'aircraft' was important. Was a hot-air balloon within the definition of 'aircraft'? If so, then the claim would fail as it had not been made within two years of the accident.

In deciding the case, the Court of Appeal looked at:

- The definition of 'aircraft' in the *Pocket Oxford Dictionary*. This defined 'aircraft' as 'aeroplane(s), airship(s) and balloon(s)'.
- The Air Navigation Order 2000 (a Statutory Instrument). This supported the view that a hot-air balloon should be regarded as an 'aircraft'.
- The fact that English law had to be interpreted in a similar way to international carriage by air, which is ruled by an international convention: the Warsaw Convention.

As a result of considering these three extrinsic aids, the court ruled that a hot-air balloon was regarded as an 'aircraft'. This meant that the claim failed as it had not been brought within the two-year time limit.

The Interpretation Act 1978

This Act provides a definition of certain words that are frequently used in legislation. For example:

- 'Land' includes building and other structures, land covered with water, and any estate, interest, easement, servitude or right in or over land.
- 'Month' means calendar month.

The Act also provides that, unless the contrary intention appears:

1 words importing the masculine gender include the feminine
2 words importing the feminine gender include the masculine
3 words in the singular include the plural and words in the plural include the singular.

Look up Schedule 1 of the Interpretation Act 1978 at **www.legislation.gov.uk/ukpga/1978/30/schedule/1**

Find out the meanings of the following words:

- 'Person'
- 'Writing'
- 'England'

When explaining any of the rules, approaches or aids to interpretation, illustrate your description with a case and/or the exact words used in a statute to show the words that required interpretation.

16.4 Impact of the European Union law and the Human Rights Act 1998 on statutory interpretation

16.4.1 Impact of EU law

Most European countries prefer the purposive approach when interpreting their own legislation. The Court of Justice of the European Union has also adopted this approach when interpreting European Union law. This preference for the purposive approach has affected English judges in two ways:

1 They accepted that the purposive approach is the correct one to use when dealing with European Union law.
2 Using the purposive approach for European Union law made judges more accustomed to it, and therefore more likely to apply it to cases involving purely English law. Even though the UK has left the European Union, judges in England are likely to continue using the purposive approach as it has become so well used and accepted in English law.
3 Using the purposive approach allowed the Judiciary in England to confirm the supremacy of EU law over UK law. An example of this was the well-known case of *Factortame* (1990). The House of Lords, using the purposive approach, decided to 'disapply' the Merchant Shipping Act 1988 which, as originally enacted, affected the rights of Spanish fishermen to trawl in UK waters – a right recognised under EU law. The court considered it was acting by the European Communities Act 1972, s 2 (4) of which provided that EU law is to prevail over inconsistent Acts of Parliament 'passed or to be passed'. This decision could be said to be in conflict with the principle of Parliamentary Supremacy.
4 The European Communities Act 1972 was repealed by the European Union (Withdrawal) Act 2018, which allowed the UK to leave the EU. This meant that from the time of leaving, EU law was no longer

supreme to that of UK law. Due to the principle of Parliamentary Sovereignty, a decision such as Factortame would not be made by UK judges.

16.4.2 Impact of Human Rights Act 1998 (HRA)

Section 3 HRA says that, as far as possible to do so, legislation must be read and given effect in a way which is compatible with the European Convention on Human Rights (ECHR). This approach applies where one of the Convention rights is in issue, but it does not apply otherwise.

An example of the effect of HRA on statutory interpretation is the case of *Godin-Mendoza v Ghaidan* (2002).

Case study

Godin-Mendoza v Ghaidan (2002)

The Rent Act 1977 allowed an unmarried partner to succeed to a tenancy if 'a person who was living with the original tenant as his or her wife or husband shall be treated as the spouse of the original tenant'. The question for the Court of Appeal was whether this section covered same-sex partners.

A previous House of Lords decision ruled that same-sex partners did not have the right to take over a tenancy.

The Court of Appeal decided that the Rent Act had to be interpreted according to the ECHR which forbids discrimination on the grounds of gender. In order to make the Rent Act compliant with ECHR, it interpreted the words 'living with the original tenant as his or her wife or husband' to mean 'as if they were his or her wife or husband'. This allowed same-sex partners to have the same rights as unmarried heterosexual couples. The Court of Appeal observed that:

> in order to remedy this breach of ECHR, the Court must, if it can, read the Schedule [to the Rent Act] so that its provisions are rendered compatible with ECHR rights of the survivors of same-sex partnerships.

This decision was later confirmed by the House of Lords.

16.5 Advantages and disadvantages of the different approaches to statutory interpretation

Advantages of use of the literal rule	Disadvantages of use of the literal rule
• The rule follows the words that Parliament has used. Since Parliament is the democratic law-making body, it is right that judges should apply the law exactly as it is written. Using the literal rule to interpret Acts of Parliament prevents unelected judges from making law.	• The literal rule assumes every Act will be perfectly drafted. In the Dangerous Dogs Act 1991, Parliament used the word 'type' of dog, whereas they should have used the word 'breed' as there is no such thing as a type of dog.
• Using the literal rule should make the law more certain, as the law will be interpreted exactly as it is written by Parliament. This makes it easier for lawyers and the public to know what the law is and how judges will interpret it.	• When the law is drafted it is not always possible to cover every situation that Parliament intended: see *Whiteley v Chappell* (1868).
• The rule focuses the mind of Parliament, forcing them to be clear in their language when considering the wording of an Act.	• Words may have more than one meaning so that the Act is unclear.
• It respects Parliamentary Sovereignty over judicial discretion as use of the rule gives effect to the precise words in an Act.	• Following the words in an Act exactly can lead to unfair decisions: see *London & North Eastern Railway Company v Berriman* (1946). Professor Michael Zander has denounced the literal rule as being mechanical and divorced from the realities of the use of language.
• It respects the Separation of Powers doctrine as judges have minimal or no legislative function.	• Use of the rule can demand unrealistic perfection of wording by the draftsmen and foresight of how the Act will cover every future situation.

Figure 16.1 Advantages and disadvantages of the literal rule

Advantages of the golden rule	Disadvantages of the golden rule
• This rule respects the exact words of Parliament except in limited situations. The narrow approach allows the judge to choose the most sensible meaning: see *R v Allen* (1872). • The wider approach can provide sensible decisions in cases where the literal rule would lead to a repugnant situation: see *Re Sigsworth*.	• It is very limited in its use, so it is only used on rare occasions and it is not always possible to predict when courts will use the golden rule over the literal rule. • Michael Zander has described it as a 'feeble parachute'. In other words, it is an escape route but it cannot do very much.

Figure 16.2 Advantages and disadvantages of the golden rule

Advantages of the mischief rule	Disadvantages of the mischief rule
• The mischief rule promotes the purpose of the law as it allows judges to look back at the gap in the law that the Act was designed to cover. This is more likely to produce a 'just' result, as seen in *Smith v Hughes*. From the public's point of view, would it have been 'just' if the prostitutes had been found not guilty just because they were not actually on the street? • The Law Commission prefers the mischief rule and, as long ago as 1969, recommended that it should be the only rule used in statutory interpretation.	• There is the risk of judicial law-making when this rule is used: see Lord Parker's comments. • The split decision of the Law Lords in *Royal College of Nursing v DHSS* shows that even senior judges do not always agree on the use of the mischief rule. • Use of the mischief rule may lead to uncertainty in the law, making legal advice difficult. • The mischief rule is not as wide as the purposive approach as it is limited to looking back at the gap in the old law. It cannot be used for a more general consideration of the purpose of the law.

Figure 16.3 Advantages and disadvantages of the mischief rule

Activities

1 Referring to the case of *Fisher v Bell* – how do you think it would have been decided if the judge had used the mischief rule?

2 Referring to the case of *Smith v Hughes* – how do you think that it would have been decided using the literal rule?

Advantages of use of the purposive approach	Disadvantages of use of the purposive approach
• As can be seen from the case examples, justice (or the 'right' result) was achieved in each case. For example, it can be said to be 'just' that in the *Jones v Tower Boot* case, the employers were liable as they should have been keeping greater control over their workers as the victimisation occurred in the workplace. • Judges can take account of new technology introduced after the passing of the Act, as in *RCN v DHSS*. • Judges can fill in any gaps in the law left by Parliament or dealing with new situations.	• It is undemocratic as judges are interpreting laws in a way they consider Parliament meant, and judges are not accountable for the decisions they make in court. An alternative view is that Parliament should make clear the meaning when they pass an Act. • It may be time consuming to find what Parliament meant. Hansard and government statements have to be studied. • Litigation is notoriously uncertain and expensive. Legal advice is difficult as lawyers will not know until the final judgment whether the judges are prepared to use this approach.

Figure 16.4 Advantages and disadvantages of the purposive approach

Tip

When evaluating one of the rules or approaches to statutory interpretation, try to support and illustrate each point you make with a relevant case example.

Quick questions

1 Define the literal rule of interpretation.
2 Identify three cases in which the literal rule was used.
3 Define the golden rule of interpretation.
4 Identify, with examples, two external aids to interpretation used by judges.
5 Evaluate the advantages and disadvantages of judges using the mischief rule to interpret the words in a statute.

Summary

- Statutory interpretation is carried out by judges giving a meaning to words in an Act of Parliament. They can use a number of rules and aids to help them do so.
- The literal rule is when words are given their ordinary, natural, dictionary meaning.
- The golden rule has two approaches – the narrow approach is when words have more than one possible meaning – the judge will choose a meaning which is the least absurd. The wider approach is when the words have one meaning but if this is used it could lead to a repugnant situation. In this case, the judge will alter the meaning to avoid that problem.
- The mischief rule looks at what the law was before the Act was passed to discover the mischief or gap that the Act was intended to cover. The judge will give a meaning that deals with the mischief.

- The purposive approach is the widest approach and judges give a meaning that they think Parliament was trying to achieve when passing the Act. This is the approach used in most European countries.
- Judges can use intrinsic aids – within the Act – which may help to make the meaning of words clearer.
- They can also use extrinsic aids – outside the Act. The most obvious is Hansard – a record of what was said in Parliament. This can be used where the meaning of words is ambiguous or unclear and where there is a clear statement by the minister promoting the Bill which resolves the ambiguity or lack of clarity.
- Legislation must be read and given effect to in a way that is compatible with the European Convention on Human Rights.

Chapter 17 Judicial precedent

Introduction

Judicial precedent is a source of law where decisions of judges create law for future judges to follow. This is also known as case law. Judges' decisions were historically very important to the development of the common law, and remain a major source of law today. The level of the court making the decision is important when considering whether other judges have to follow it.

17.1 The doctrine of precedent

17.1.1 *Stare decisis*

Judicial precedent is based on the Latin maxim *stare decisis et non quieta movere* (usually shortened to *stare decisis*), which loosely translated means 'stand by what has been decided and do not unsettle the established'.

Judges are able to make decisions in court, either to interpret Parliamentary law, or to decide a rule where there is no Parliamentary law. These decisions, when reported, can be looked at by other judges in later cases. If the later case uses similar rules then a judge in the later case can follow the earlier decision. This supports the idea of fairness and provides certainty in the law.

17.1.2 *Ratio decidendi*

Precedent can only operate if the legal reasons for a past decision are known. Therefore, at the end of a case there will be a judgment (speech) in which the judge will:

- give a summary of the facts of the case
- review the arguments put by the advocates or the parties
- explain the principles of law being used to come to the decision.

These principles are the important part of the judgment and are known as the *ratio decidendi*, which means 'the reason for deciding'. This is what creates a precedent for judges to follow in future cases. Sir Rupert Cross defined the *ratio decidendi* as:

> any rule expressly or impliedly treated by the judge as a necessary step in reaching his conclusion.

If the *ratio* is given by a judge in a higher court, particularly an appeal court, it will carry great authority and must be followed by all lower level judges in later cases.

In appeal cases where there is a particularly important or complicated point of law, more than one judge may want to explain the legal reasoning that led to a decision. This can cause problems in later cases as each judge may have had a different reason for their decision, so there will be more than one *ratio decidendi*. It will be for lawyers and judges in later cases to choose which *ratio* they prefer and which to use in court.

17.1.3 *Obiter dicta*

The remainder of the judgment is called *obiter dicta*, meaning 'other things said' and judges in future cases are not bound to follow it.

Sometimes a judge will speculate on what the decision would have been if the facts of the case had been different. This hypothetical situation is part of the *obiter dicta* and the legal reasoning put forward may be considered in future cases, although, as with all *obiter* statements, it is not a binding precedent (see section 17.3.1).

A major problem when looking at a past judgment is to divide the *ratio decidendi* from the *obiter dicta*, as the judgment is usually in a continuous form, without any headings specifying what is meant to be part of the *ratio decidendi* and what is not. Lawyers and judges dealing with later similar cases have to make their own decisions as what the *ratio* of a decision is and what forms the *obiter*.

- An example of a *ratio decidendi* in a decision is in the case of *R v Howe* (1987). The House of Lords decided that the defence of duress was not available to a charge of murder. They also expressed the opinion that duress is not a defence to a charge of attempted murder. This opinion was *obiter dicta*, as Howe was not charged with attempted murder and it was directly relevant to the facts of the case.
- *Obiter* statements such as this can become persuasive in later cases. For example, in the case of *R v Gotts* (1992), the House of Lords followed the *obiter* statement in *R v Howe* and, in their *ratio decidendi*, ruled that duress cannot be a defence to a charge of attempted murder.

Link

See Chapter 11, section 11.2, for case details of *R v Howe* (1987) and *R v Gotts* (1992).

Activity

Refer to the leading negligence case of *Donoghue v Stevenson* (1932) in Chapter 21. What was the *ratio decidendi* of the House of Lords in that case?

17.2 The hierarchy of the courts

In England and Wales, the courts operate a very rigid doctrine of judicial precedent, which has the effect that:

- every court is bound to follow any decision made by a court above it in the hierarchy, following the principle of *stare decisis*, and
- in general, appellate courts (courts that hear appeals) are bound by their own past decisions.

17.2.2 The Supreme Court

Until October 2009, the senior court in the UK legal system was the House of Lords. This court was then abolished and replaced by the Supreme Court. The lower courts have to follow decisions of the Supreme Court, and also decisions by the House of Lords that have not been changed by the Supreme Court.

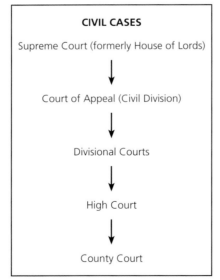

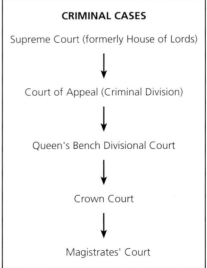

Figure 17.1 Cascade model of judicial precedent operating in the hierarchy of the courts

Court	Courts bound by it	Courts it must follow
Supreme Court	All courts below it	–
Court of Appeal	High Court, County Court, Crown Court, Magistrates' Court	Supreme Court
High Court	County Court, Magistrates' Court	Supreme Court, Court of Appeal
Crown Court	Possibly Magistrates' Court	Supreme Court, Court of Appeal
County Courts and Magistrates' Courts do not create precedent and are bound by all higher courts		

Figure 17.2 Key facts: court hierarchy and judicial precedent

Does the Supreme Court bind itself?

The main debate about the Supreme Court (and previously the House of Lords) is the extent to which it should follow its own past decisions. In *London Street Tramways v London County Council* (1898), the House of Lords decided that certainty in the law by following a past decision was more important than preventing individual hardship. It was completely bound by its own past decisions unless the decision had been made *per incuriam*, that is, 'in error'.

In the middle of the twentieth century this approach was not felt to be satisfactory, as the law could not alter to meet changing social conditions and opinions, nor could any possible 'wrong' decisions be changed except by legislation. It was felt that the highest court of appeal should have greater flexibility in its decision making.

The Practice Statement

In 1966, the Lord Chancellor issued a Practice Statement announcing a change to the rule in *London Street Tramways v London County Council* which allowed them to depart from a previous decision when it appears right to do so. This approach was confirmed by Practice Directions 3 and 4 issued by the Supreme Court in 2009.

Use of the Practice Statement

The Practice Statement allowed the House of Lords to change the law when it believed that an earlier case was wrongly decided. It had the flexibility to refuse to follow an earlier case when 'it appeared right to do so'. This phrase is vague and there was little guidance on when the House of Lords might overrule a previous decision.

- The first major use did not occur until 1972 in *British Railways Board v Herrington* (1972), which involved the law on the duty of care owed to a child trespasser. The earlier case of *Addie v Dumbreck* (1929) had decided that an occupier of land would only owe a duty of care for injuries to a child trespasser if those injuries had been caused deliberately or recklessly. In the *Herrington* case, the Lords held that social and physical conditions had changed since 1929, and the law should also change, allowing the injured child trespasser's claim.
- *Pepper v Hart* (1993) (see Chapter 16) is also an example of the use of the Practice Statement.

Look online

In the case of *British Railways Board v Herrington* (1972), the House of Lords completely changed the previous law about occupiers' liability to child trespassers.
- Do an internet search for this case.
- Why did the House of Lords decide that the previous law needed to be changed?

The Practice Statement in criminal law

The Practice Statement stressed that criminal law needs to be certain and the Supreme Court does not often use it in criminal cases. When it is used, there is a recognition that an error may have been made previously and the most important thing is to put the law right.

Where the Practice Statement is used to overrule a previous decision, that past case is then effectively ignored. The law is now that which is set out in the new case.

R v R and G (2003)

The House of Lords used the Practice Statement to overrule the earlier decision of *R v Caldwell* (1982) on the offence of criminal damage. In *Caldwell*, the House of Lords had ruled that recklessness included the situation where the defendant had not realised the risk of his actions causing damage, but an ordinary careful person would have realised there was a risk (an objective test).

In *R v R and G*, it was held that this was the wrong test to use. The Law Lords overruled *Caldwell* and held that a defendant is only reckless if he realises that there is a risk of damage and goes ahead and takes that risk (a subjective test). This case showed the House of Lords as being prepared to use the Practice Statement where they thought it 'right to do so'.

The Supreme Court's relationship to the Practice Statement

From October 2009, the Constitutional Reform Act 2005 transferred the House of Lords' powers to the Supreme Court. Initially, it was not clear if this included the use of the Practice Statement. In *Austin v London Borough of Southwark* (2010), which was about tenancy law, the Supreme Court confirmed that the power to use the Practice Statement had been transferred to it.

Read the following passage, which comes from an extra explanatory note that was given to the press when the Practice Statement was issued, and answer the questions below

> The statement is one of great importance, although it should not be supposed that there will frequently be cases in which the House thinks it right not to follow their own precedent. An example of a case in which the House might think it right to depart from a precedent is where they consider that the earlier decision was influenced by the existence of conditions which no longer prevail, and that in modern conditions the law ought to be different.
>
> One consequence of this change is of major importance. The relaxation of the rule of judicial precedent will enable the House of Lords to pay greater attention to judicial decisions reached in the superior courts of the Commonwealth, where they differ from earlier decisions of the House of Lords. That could be of great help in the development of our own law. The superior courts of many other countries are not rigidly bound by their own decisions and the change in the practice of the House of Lords will bring us more into line with them.

1. Why was the Practice Statement of great importance?
2. Does the note suggest that the Practice Statement was likely to be used often?
3. Do you agree that 'in modern conditions the law ought to be different'? Give reasons and examples to support your answer.
4. Why would the House of Lords have wanted to consider decisions from Commonwealth countries? What authority do such decisions have in the English legal system?

Research the case of *Knauer v Ministry of Justice* (2016). This was the first case after 2009 to consider the use of the Practice Statement. Read paragraphs 20–23 in the joint judgment of Lord Neuberger and Lady Hale.
1. What reasons did they give for certainty in the law?
2. Do you agree with their reasoning?

The Supreme Court and Europe

The European Court of Justice

The application of EU law in the UK has always been a matter for the UK courts, ultimately the Supreme Court, not for the Court of Justice of the European Union (CJEU). UK courts have always accepted their obligation to enforce EU law during the period of UK membership of the EU. A case can be referred to the CJEU for an opinion; there is no right of appeal to the CJEU from a UK court. The role of the CJEU within the UK is therefore an indirect one, based on the preliminary ruling procedure, controlled by the UK courts themselves.

Until the UK left the EU, the position was specified in s 3 of the European Communities Act 1972. UK courts, including the Supreme Court, were bound by rulings on EU law by the CJEU.

Following withdrawal, existing rulings of the CJEU on EU law (rulings given before withdrawal) could, in principle, be overridden by a contrary ruling of the Supreme Court. In respect of CJEU rulings given after withdrawal, it is suggested that UK courts 'need not [but may where appropriate] have regard to' any ruling of the CJEU on a point of EU law, apparently including rulings relating to the period of UK membership but delivered after that date.

The European Court of Human Rights

In giving effect to rights contained in the European Convention on Human Rights, the Supreme Court must take account of any decision of the European Court of Human Rights (ECtHR) but it is not bound to follow them.

In *Manchester City Council v Pinnock* (2010), Lord Neuberger said:

> This Court (the Supreme Court) is not bound to follow every decision of the ECtHR. Not only would it be impractical to do so: it would sometimes be inappropriate, as it would destroy the ability of the Court to engage in the constructive dialogue with the ECtHR. Of course, we should usually follow a clear and constant line of decisions by the ECtHR. But we are not actually bound to do so or (in theory, at least) to follow a decision of the Grand Chamber.

On occasions, the Supreme Court has effectively sent issues back to the ECtHR for reconsideration. For example, in 2009 the Court declined to follow a decision of the ECtHR in *R v Horncastle*. In December 2011, the ECtHR gave judgment in *Al-Khawaja* which raised the same issue as in *Horncastle*. It was noted that the ECtHR had taken into consideration the UK Supreme Court's judgment in *Horncastle*, demonstrating the 'dialogue' between the two courts.

The UK's exit from the EU does not change the jurisdiction of the ECtHR as this is separate from the EU.

17.2.3 The Court of Appeal

There are two divisions of this court: the Civil Division and the Criminal Division. The rules for departing from precedent are not quite the same in these two Divisions.

The first rule is that decisions by one Division of the Court of Appeal will not bind the other Division. However, within each Division, previous decisions are normally binding on later decisions, especially for the Civil Division.

Civil Division

Young's case

This rule comes from the case of *Young v Bristol Aeroplane Co. Ltd* (1944). The only exceptions allowing the Court of Appeal Civil Division to depart from a previous decision are where:

- there are conflicting decisions in past Court of Appeal cases – the court can choose which one to follow
- there is a decision of the Supreme Court that effectively overrules a Court of Appeal decision
- the decision was made *per incuriam*, that is, carelessly or by mistake.

Instances of *per incuriam*

- *Williams v Fawcett* (1986): the Court of Appeal refused to follow previous decisions of their own because these had been based on a misunderstanding of the County Court rules.
- *R v Cooper* (2011): the Court of Appeal appears to have extended the scope of the *per incuriam* exception, to be followed in the Crown Court when barring a convicted individual from working with children or vulnerable adults. A new system was being brought in under the Safeguarding Vulnerable Groups Act 2006 and it was not clear what procedure should be followed.

The Court of Appeal (Criminal Division)

The Criminal Division, as well as using the exceptions from *Young*'s case, can also refuse to follow a past decision of its own if the law has been 'misapplied or misunderstood'. This extra exception arises because in criminal cases, people's liberty is involved.

- This idea was recognised in *R v Taylor* (1950) and in *R v Gould* (1968). Also, in *R v Spencer* (1985), the judges said that there should not in general be any difference in the way that precedent was followed in the Criminal Division and in the Civil Division:

> save that we must remember that we may be dealing with the liberty of the subject and if a departure from authority is necessary in the interests of justice to an appellant, then this court should not shrink from so acting.

- In *R v Simpson* (2003), the Court of Appeal (Criminal Division), a five-judge panel, overruled an earlier decision made by a three-judge panel on the basis that the law had been misunderstood or misapplied.
- However, in *R v Magro* (2010), the Court of Appeal itself pointed out that Simpson had not given them the right to overrule a three-judge panel where that decision had been made after full argument and close analysis of the relevant legislative provisions.

17.3 Binding, persuasive and original precedent

17.3.1 Binding precedent

This is a precedent from an earlier case that must be followed if the decision was made by a court that is senior to (or in some cases the same level as) the court hearing the later case. For example, a precedent set by the Court of Appeal Civil Division must be followed by all lower courts in the hierarchy and will generally be followed by later cases heard by the Court of Appeal. This follows the principle of *stare decisis*.

17.3.2 Persuasive precedent

This is a precedent that is not binding on a court, but the judge may consider it, decide that it is a correct principle and be persuaded that it should be followed. Persuasive precedent can come from a number of sources such as:
- Courts lower in the hierarchy: an example can be seen in *R v R* (1991), where the House of Lords (now the Supreme Court) agreed with and followed the same reasoning as the Court of Appeal in deciding that a man could be guilty of raping his wife. In this case, the judgment of the Court of Appeal was persuasive and the House of Lords followed it.
- Decisions of the Judicial Committee of the Privy Council: this court is not part of the court hierarchy in England and Wales and so its decisions are not binding but, since many of its judges are also members of the Supreme Court, their judgments are treated with respect and may often be followed. An example of this can be seen in the law on remoteness of damages in the law of negligence

in tort and the decision made by the Privy Council in the case of *The Wagon Mound (No. 1)* (1961). In later cases, courts in England and Wales followed this decision. This means that law made as a result of a case from another country can have an effect on the law in England and Wales.
- Statements made *obiter dicta* as seen in section 17.1.3 in the cases of *R v Howe* (1987) and *R v Gotts* (1992).
- A dissenting judgment: where a case has been decided by a majority of judges (for example, two to one in the Court of Appeal), the judge who disagreed will also have explained the reasons for reaching that decision. If that case goes on appeal to the Supreme Court, or if there is a later case on the same point that goes to the Supreme Court, it is possible that the Supreme Court may prefer a dissenting judgment and decide the case in the same way. The dissenting judgment has persuaded the higher court to follow it. An example of this is Lord Denning's dissenting judgment in *Candler v Crane, Christmas & Co.* (1951) which was later upheld in *Hedley Byrne v Heller* (1963). These cases were to do with the tort of negligent misstatement.
- Decisions of courts in other countries: this is especially so where the other country uses the same ideas of common law as in the English system. This applies to Commonwealth countries such as Canada, Australia and New Zealand. An example of such a decision is *Bazley v Curry* (1999), a Canadian case which was considered in *Lister v Hesley Hall Ltd* (2001), seen in Chapter 24.

17.3.3 Original precedent

If the point of law arising in a case has never been decided before, then whatever the judge decides will form a new precedent for future cases to follow; that is, it is an original precedent.
- As there are no past cases for the judge to base the decision on, previous cases that are the closest in principle will be considered with similar rules used. This way of arriving at a judgment is called reasoning by analogy. The judge will try to say something specific about the case being dealt with based on the fact that it is 'like' another example in a certain way. This was done in *Hunter v Canary Wharf* (1997) (see Chapter 23, section 23.1.2) where a principle from *Aldred*'s case of 1610 was used by Lord Hoffman. In his

view, anyone may build whatever they like upon their land even if it interferes with the light, air or view of a neighbour.

- Some legal commentators used to have the view that the judge is only declaring what the law is (that is, the law has always been there, but it is the first time a judge has had to decide it). This supports the view that judges do not create law; they merely declare what it has always been.
- The opposite view is that judges *do* have a law-making role in these situations – when a new point has to be decided, the judge is creating new law.

Case study

Fearn and others v Board of Trustees of the Tate Gallery (2020)

Residents of flats adjacent to the Tate Modern Gallery alleged that the enjoyment of their premises was being interfered with as visitors to the museum looked into their homes. The Court of Appeal had to decide whether the alleged intrusion amounted to a nuisance in law. They set a new precedent by declaring that overlooking could never be considered a nuisance.

Look online

Another example case to be considered here could be *Re: S (Adult: Refusal of Medical Treatment)* (1992). Research the facts of this case online and note why it was an original precedent.

17.3.4 Methods of handling precedent

Following

When a judge considers a precedent is relevant to the case, and it is binding, then the precedent must be followed.

Overruling

This is where a court, in a later case, states that the precedent decided in an earlier (different) case is wrong. Overruling may occur when a higher court changes, or overrules, a decision made in an earlier case by a lower court, such as the Supreme Court overruling a decision of the Court of Appeal.

As seen above, it can also happen when the Supreme Court uses the Practice Direction, as restated by Practice Directions 3 and 4 2009, to overrule a past decision of its own.

Case study

Pepper v Hart (1993)

The House of Lords ruled that Hansard (the record of what is said in Parliament) could be consulted when trying to decide what certain words in an Act of Parliament meant. This decision overruled the earlier decision in *Davis v Johnson* (1979), when the House of Lords had held that it could not consult Hansard.

17.3.5 Reversing

This is where a court higher in the hierarchy, in an appeal, overturns the decision of a lower court on appeal in the same case. For example, the Court of Appeal may disagree with a ruling of the High Court and come to a different view of the law. In this situation it reverses the decision made by the High Court. The decision of the appeal court will then be substituted for that of the lower court. An example of reversing is the case of *Sweet v Parsley* (1970), when the House of Lords reversed the decision of the Divisional Court of the Queen's Bench Division (see Chapter 6, section 6.2).

17.3.6 Distinguishing

This is a method that can be used by a judge to avoid following a past decision, which would otherwise have to be followed. It means that the judge finds that the material facts of the present case are sufficiently different to allow a distinction to be drawn between the present case and the previous precedent, so that the precedent in the previous case is not binding.

Examples of distinguishing are the criminal cases of *R v Brown* (1993) and *R v Wilson* (1996).

- In *Brown*, the House of Lords decided, by a majority, that consent to suffer injuries in the course of homosexual sado-masochistic activities is no defence to charges of s 20 OAPA 1861 or to charges of actual bodily harm.

- In *Wilson*, the defendants were a married couple and the defence of consent was allowed by the Court of Appeal to charges of actual bodily harm.

  In *Balfour v Balfour* (1919) and *Merritt v Merritt* (1971), both cases involved a wife making a claim against her husband for breach of contract.

- In *Balfour*, it was decided that the claim could not succeed because there was no intention between them to create legal relations; there was merely a domestic arrangement between a husband and wife and so there was no legally binding contract.
- In *Merritt*, a different decision was reached and the Court of Appeal distinguished the otherwise binding decision of *Balfour*. Although the parties were husband and wife, the agreement was made, in writing, and after they had separated. This was different as it was meant as a legally enforceable contract.

Activity

- In the case of *R v Brown* (1993), identify the ratio and the *obiter*.
- How was the *obiter dicta* in *R v Brown* then used in the case of *R v Wilson* (1996)?

17.4 Advantages and disadvantages of precedent

Advantage	Explanation
Certainty	- Because judges follow past decisions, people know what the law is and how it is likely to be applied in their case. - This allows lawyers to advise clients on the likely outcome of cases. - It also allows people to operate their businesses knowing that financial and other arrangements they make are recognised by law. - The House of Lords Practice Statement of 1966 pointed out how important certainty is.
Consistency and fairness in the law	It is seen as just and fair that similar cases should be decided in a similar way. The law must be consistent in its application if it is to be credible.
Precision	As the principles of relevant law are set out in actual cases, the law becomes very precise. It is well illustrated, and a body of rules gradually builds up through the different variations of facts in the cases that come before the courts.
Flexibility	There is room for the law to change with society as the Supreme Court can use the Practice Statement to overrule past cases that may not reflect current trends. - In *BRB v Herrington*, the House of Lords considered that there had been considerable social change since the previous precedent was decided in 1929.
Time saving	- When a principle has been established, it can be seen through the whole system of law reporting. - Lawyers are able to save time and advise their clients that a case with similar facts or principles of law to a precedent is unlikely to be worth taking through the lengthy and costly process of litigation.
Filling gaps	Where there is no statute law on a topic, such as the law on occupiers' liability towards trespassers before 1984, judges are able to fill gaps to ensure that the law is not at a standstill.

Figure 17.3 Advantages of judicial precedent

Disadvantages	Explanation
Rigidity	The law can be too inflexible and previous bad decisions may be continued, because: ● lower courts have to follow decisions of higher courts ● the Court of Appeal has to follow its own past decisions. Also, as so few cases reach the Supreme Court, change in the law will only take place if parties have the courage, the persistence and the money to appeal their case to the highest court.
Complexity	● Since there are nearly half a million reported cases, it may not be easy to find all the relevant case law, even with computerised databases. ● Court judgments can be very long, with no clear distinction between comments and the reasons for the decision. This makes it difficult in some cases to extract the *ratio decidendi*; indeed, in *Dodd's* case (1973), the judges in the Court of Appeal said they were unable to find the *ratio* in a previous decision of the House of Lords.
Illogical distinctions	● The use of distinguishing to avoid past decisions can lead to 'hair-splitting' so that some areas of the law have become very complex. ● The differences between some cases may be very small and appear illogical.
Slowness of growth	● Judges are well aware that some areas of the law are unclear or in need of reform; however, they cannot make a decision unless a case comes before the courts to be decided. ● This is one of the criticisms of the need for the Court of Appeal to follow its own previous decisions, as only about fifty cases go to the Supreme Court each year. There may be a long wait for a suitable case to be appealed as far as the Supreme Court to bring about a change in the law.
Uncertainty	This can arise when a higher court reverses a decision of a lower court. ● This happened in *R v Kingston* (1994): the House of Lords reversed the decision of the Court of Appeal and dismissed the defendant's argument that his involuntary intoxication could be used as a defence.

Figure 17.4 Disadvantages of judicial precedent

Tip

When describing one of the rules of precedent, or when making an evaluative point, try to support your description or evaluation by reference to a decided case.

Quick questions

1 Identify the three main elements of judicial precedent.
2 Identify the court hierarchy in either the civil courts or the criminal courts.
3 Explain how and why the Supreme Court can depart from one of its own precedents.
4 Analyse the power of the Court of Appeal to depart from a binding precedent.
5 Evaluate the advantages and disadvantages of judicial precedent.

- Judicial precedent is based on *stare decisis* ('keep to the decision').
- *Ratio decidendi* is the reason for the decision which creates a precedent for future cases: the *ratio* is identified by judges in later cases.
- *Obiter dicta* ('other things said') is the remainder of the judgment which does not create a precedent.
- There are separate hierarchies of civil and criminal courts.
- Judgments of higher courts are generally published in law reports.
- Courts lower in the hierarchy must follow a precedent set by a higher court.
- A court higher in the hierarchy can overrule a precedent made in a lower court.
- An appeal court can reverse a decision made by a lower court in the same case.
- The Supreme Court is normally bound by its previous decisions, but the Practice Statement allows it to depart from a previous decision when it is right to do so.
- The Court of Appeal is bound by its previous decisions: the only exceptions are those set out in *Young*'s case.

- While the UK was a member of the EU, all UK courts had to follow decisions of the ECJ. Once the UK left the EU, the Supreme Court need not (but may where appropriate) have regard to any ruling of the ECJ on a point of EU law.
- The Supreme Court must take account of any decision of the European Court of Human Rights.
- Binding precedent from a court higher in the hierarchy must be followed.
- A judge does not have to follow an otherwise binding precedent if it can be distinguished from the present case.
- An original precedent can be made on a point of law that has not been decided before.
- Advantages of judicial precedent include certainty, consistency, fairness, precision, flexibility, filling gaps and time saving.
- Disadvantages of judicial precedent include rigidity, complexity, illogical distinctions and slowness of growth.

Chapter 18 Law reform

Introduction

There may be many reasons why laws are debated in Parliament and introduced. Political parties are likely to have ideas when they come into power on the type of society they wish to create and the laws that are needed to achieve that. The general public, groups within it and the media may press for certain changes which may or may not be agreed by the government. Formal recommendations on changes to 'pure', non-political law may be made after detailed investigations by the Law Commission. All of these sources may produce proposals for change in the law.

18.1 Influences on Parliament

A government will have ideas on what laws they intend to introduce during their term of office. However, there will be a number of organisations or reasons that might encourage government ministers to consider introducing other laws, or to alter their ideas on the laws they had proposed.

18.1.1 Political influences

When there is a general election, all the political parties publish a list of their policies and suggest reforms and new laws they would introduce if they were elected as the next government. This is called the party's manifesto, and it is one of the ways in which each party tries to persuade people to vote for them. The manifesto can include policies on issues such as finance, education, transport and law and order. For example:

- In the December 2019 general election, the main manifesto policy of the Conservative Party was to 'get Brexit done', to implement the result of the 2016 referendum to withdraw the UK from the European Union. To achieve this, a number of new laws would have to be introduced to leave the EU and establish new systems previously covered by European Union rules. Once the election was won, the government then focused on drafting and passing these laws in order to keep their election promise, although their plans were deflected to a large extent to allow them to focus on the Covid-19 pandemic.
- Another example was the promise in the Labour Party manifesto before the 1997 election to 'bring rights home'. This was achieved by the government when the Human Rights Act 1998 was passed by Parliament.

During parliamentary sessions, individual MPs may be able to introduce legislation by Private Members' Bills. They may adopt campaigns started by others or have strong beliefs themselves that they want to promote. Two examples of Private Members' Bills that became law are the Abortion Act 1967, introduced and promoted by David Steel, and the Computer Misuse Act 1991, promoted by Michael Colvin.

Link

See Chapter 14, section 14.1.2 for further details on Private Members' Bills.

Look online

Search online for the Conservative Party manifesto and the manifesto of one other political party for the 2019 General Election.
- What promises did they each make for law and order and another topic of your choice?
- Can you find whether any laws have been introduced in Parliament on those topics?

18.1.2 Media

The term 'media' means the ways in which information is supplied to the public. It includes television and radio, newspapers, magazines and internet sources.

The media can play a large role in bringing public opinion to the government's attention. Where an issue is given a high profile on television, in newspapers or through social media, it will be brought to the attention of the public and politicians and may add to the weight of public opinion.

This is an advantage of a free press. The media are able to criticise government policy or demand government action. This can be especially effective in a general election campaign, where every political party is keen to gain public support.

The media can both represent and influence public opinion:

- Members of the public can make their views known by contacting media sources or by posting material on social media.
- Government regularly monitors social media to judge public opinion.
- Government also uses focus groups to gauge opinion on an issue or their overall popularity.

On the other hand, media, including now social media, may be used by government to make their views known and to attempt to influence public opinion.

Some media campaigns have successfully brought about changes to the law. Examples include:

- The Snowdrop campaign successfully used the media to campaign for handguns to be banned (see section 18.1.5 for more details).
- When 'dangerous dogs' attacked a number of adults and children, this led to the passing of the Dangerous Dogs Act 1991. This Act was subsequently considered to be a poorly drafted piece of legislation as it was introduced as a 'knee-jerk reaction' to media publicity.
- The reform of the 'double jeopardy' rule, allowing a person to be tried more than once if new evidence comes to light following an acquittal in the first trial. This was introduced by the Criminal Justice Act 2003 and was due to media campaigns after the suspects accused of killing black teenager Stephen Lawrence in 1993 were acquitted in their first trial, despite strong evidence against them.

Look online

- Find a current example of a newspaper or social media campaign on an issue.
- In your view, how likely is the government to introduce legislation as a result of this campaign?

18.1.3 Pressure groups

These are groups of people who campaign as they have a special interest in a subject or cause. They can bring their interest or cause to the attention of the general public and government. This can be done by lobbying a government minister or department responsible for an issue. There are two main types of pressure group: sectional and cause.

1 Sectional pressure groups exist to represent the interests of a group of people and often represent workers' groups or professions. Examples include:
   - the Law Society, which represents solicitors' interests
   - the British Medical Association, which represents doctors
   - trades unions, which represent workers in different types of jobs.
2 Cause pressure groups exist to promote a particular cause. Examples include:
   - environmental groups such as Greenpeace
   - animal welfare groups
   - human rights groups, such as Amnesty.

Pressure groups may make the government reconsider certain areas of law. For example, the passing of the Hunting Act 2004, which banned hunting foxes with dogs, was due to the efforts of the League Against Cruel Sports.

Hunting foxes with dogs was banned by the Fox Hunting Act (2004) after pressure from the League Against Cruel Sports

Sometimes pressure groups will campaign against a proposed change to the law. This was seen when, in 1997, government attempts to restrict the right to trial by jury were opposed by the Law Society and Bar Council. JUSTICE, an independent all-party legal and human rights organisation, published a paper in 2007 opposing plans to abolish jury trial for fraud cases, which was being considered by Parliament.

In addition to pressure groups, there are special interest groups such as the Trades Union Congress and the Confederation of British Industry, which have contributed to changes in employment law such as the Equal Pay Act 1970.

18.1.4 Lobbying

Lobbying means trying to persuade government ministers or individual MPs to support a cause. It is often carried out by members of pressure groups on behalf of a campaign to convince a minister or MP to act in a certain manner.

'Lobbying' gets its name from the practice of members of the public meeting MPs in the lobbies (small hallways) in the entry to the House of Commons. Lobbying can take the form of:

- individual meetings
- writing messages
- producing surveys or petitions to show wide support.

If a pressure group is successful in lobbying, it may persuade an MP to ask a question of a government minister, either privately or in Parliament, or the setting up of an inquiry.

Often lobbying by pressure groups will take many months or years to bring about government response or action. However, on occasions, a specific event may lead to a change in the law. For example:

- In the aftermath of the Dunblane massacre in 1996, when a gunman entered a school in Scotland and killed 16 children and their teacher, local families set up a single-issue pressure group called 'Snowdrop' to campaign for the banning of handguns. Their campaign led eventually to a public inquiry which published the *Cullen Report*. This in turn led to the passing of the Firearms (Amendment) Act 1997, which banned the private ownership of most handguns. As Snowdrop had achieved their aim and they had no reason to campaign on other issues, the group then disbanded.

Extension activity

Choose a pressure group to research that deals with national issues.

- What issues is the group presently campaigning on?
- Who should they be lobbying to promote their issues?
- Have they been successful in bringing about change to the law in the past?

18.2 Law reform by the Law Commission

This full-time body was set up by the Law Commission Act 1965. It consists of:

- a chairperson
- a High Court Judge
- four other Law Commissioners who are experts in certain areas of law.

There are also researchers and draftsmen who prepare proposed Bills.

The role of the Commission is to consider areas of law that need reform. This role is set out in s 3 of the Law Commissions Act:

- To review areas of law
- Where possible, to codify or consolidate areas of law
- To repeal old unnecessary law, and
- Where possible to simplify and modernise law.

18.2.1 How the Law Commission works

Topics may be referred to it by government, or it may select itself areas of law in need of reform. The process is as follows:

1. The Commission researches the area of law needing reform.
2. It publishes a consultation paper, seeking views on possible reform from lawyers, academics and anyone with an interest in the area under investigation. The consultation paper will suggest options for reform.

3 Following responses to the consultation paper, the Commission will then draw up proposals for reform presented in a researched report. There will often be a draft Bill attached to the report which can be considered by Parliament.

> ### Look online
>
> - Look at the Law Commission's website: www.lawcom.gov.uk
> - Find the areas of law that it is currently researching.

18.2.2 Repeal of existing law

There remain in force many old, unnecessary and irrelevant statutes. In order to deal with these, the Law Commission investigates whether they are still required and will prepare a Repeals Bill for Parliament to consider for those that are unnecessary or irrelevant.

By 2015 there had been 19 Statute Law (Repeals) Acts, and the whole of 3000 old Acts had been repealed.

This 'tidying-up' of the statute book helps to make the law more accessible.

18.2.3 Consolidation

In some areas of law there are a number of statutes which set out a small part of the total law. The aim of consolidation is to draw all the existing provisions together in one Act to make the law more accessible.

The Law Commission produces about five Consolidation Bills each year. However, consolidation is not always successful. For example, for many years the law on sentencing practice and procedure was contained in:

- the Powers of Criminal Courts (Sentencing) Act 2000,
- the Criminal Justice and Courts Services Act 2000,
- the Criminal Justice Act 2003, and
- the Legal Aid, Sentencing and Punishment of Offenders Act 2012.

The Sentencing Act 2020 has replaced sentencing practice and procedure from these Acts, as set out below.

18.2.4 Codification

This involves bringing together all the law, both statutory and judicial precedent, on a topic into one single law. Again, the intention is to make the law more understandable, consistent and easier to find.

The Law Commission worked on producing a Sentencing Code so that all the law on sentencing adult and young offenders is in one document instead of all the Acts referred to above. This was achieved by the passing of the Sentencing Act 2020, which came into force on 1 December 2020. The Sentencing Code is concerned with sentencing procedure and does not introduce any new law or change any sentences. It will apply to all offenders convicted of an offence after 1 October 2020. For further information about the Act, go to www.lawgazette.co.uk/legal-updates/an-analysis-of-the-sentencing-code/5104692.article

18.2.5 Success of the Law Commission

Although the Law Commission has not achieved its original idea of codification of many areas of law, it has been successful in some areas. After it was established, about 85 per cent of its proposals were enacted by Parliament. These included the Unfair Contract Terms Act 1977, the Supply of Goods and Services Act 1982 and the Occupiers' Liability Act 1984.

Following this, however, only about 50 per cent of its suggestions have become law due to lack of parliamentary time and lack of interest by Parliament in technical law reform. The Law Commission Act 2009 tried to deal with the issue of non-acceptance of its reports by requiring the Lord Chancellor to tell Parliament every year why the government has decided not to implement any of the previous year's crop of Law Commission proposals. The Commission's Annual Report of 2017–18 showed that there were twelve reports awaiting response from government, who also rejected about one in six of the Law Commission's reports.

But some important reforms have been passed in recent years. These include the following:

- The Fraud Act 2006, which simplified the law on fraud.
- The Corporate Manslaughter and Corporate Homicide Act 2007, which made corporations and organisations criminally liable for deaths caused by their working practices.
- The Criminal Justice and Courts Act 2015, which included reform of contempt by jurors and the creation of new offences of juror misconduct in relation to using the internet.

18.3 Advantages and disadvantages of influences on law-making

Advantages	Disadvantages
• Each political party has its proposals for law reform ready and published in a manifesto during an election campaign so that, if they are elected as the government, the electorate knows what they wish to do in future parliamentary sessions to achieve their aims. • If the government has a majority of seats in the House of Commons, virtually every one of their policy proposals will be passed. This can be said to make the law-making process popular with the majority of the population. • By publishing manifestos, the public know before an election what the broad proposals of each political party are, and have a choice as to which set of proposals and law reforms they would wish to see put in place. • Proposed changes to laws will be debated in Parliament and improvements to initial proposals can be suggested and included. • Members of the House of Lords have expertise in a wide range of topics. Suggestions made by the Lords to alter government proposals carry considerable weight and authority, and are generally non-political.	• If a different party is elected in a general election from the previous governing party, they may decide to repeal or alter some of the laws that the previous government passed. This is because their policies are likely to be different from the previous government. Such changes of policy can be costly, open to criticism and lead to piecemeal reform of laws. • If the government has a large majority of seats in the House of Commons, they can force through their policy proposals, ignoring criticism from opposition. • If the government only has a small majority, it may be difficult or impossible to achieve changes to the law or their manifesto commitments. • Suggestions to alter or improve the proposals made by experts in the House of Lords do not have to be accepted by the Commons or the government. • If a crisis occurs, such as the Covid-19 pandemic, the government's focus will be to take measures to deal with that crisis, which may differ from their manifesto commitments.

Figure 18.1 Advantages and disadvantages of political influence

Advantages	Disadvantages
• The media can raise awareness of public concern of an issue with government – for example, damage to the environment. Government may have greater willingness to act on a media campaign if they see it is popular. • The public can use the media to raise concern about issues and individual incidents, such as the Dunblane massacre and, more recently, terrorist related attacks. Individuals are much more prepared to use social media to raise concerns and voice opinions. • The media can inform and raise public awareness, which is essential to encourage government to form policy, to act and legislate. Government is ultimately responsible to the electorate and, especially before an election, they will fear losing public support if they are not seen to be responding to an issue of public concern.	• While radio and television channels are required to remain politically neutral, this is not the case with newspapers, which may be willing to promote inaccurate individual views and campaigns, and may not have wide public support. Some newspapers give support to a specific political party and regularly promote their views. • Newspapers are commercial businesses and may be prepared to sensationalise an issue to expand their readership. This can be seen as parts of the media manipulating the news and creating public opinion. • There is no regulation on the expression of views on social media. Any views expressed may be inaccurate or have limited public support. • Even if an issue appears to have wide public support, there is no guarantee that government will act on it.

Figure 18.2 Advantages and disadvantages of media as an influence

Advantages	Disadvantages
● Pressure groups have experts in their membership, or can employ experts, to effectively argue their cause. ● There are many pressure groups with different aims and issues to promote. A wide range of issues can be drawn to the attention of government. ● Pressure groups often raise important issues. Environmental groups have made the government much more aware of the damage being done to the environment from greenhouse gases and other pollutants.	● Pressure groups may seek to impose their ideas on the public or on government, even where there is limited public support. For example, when trades unions call strike action involving a public service, this can cause disruption for the general public who are unlikely to support the cause. ● Sometimes two pressure groups may have conflicting interests and will campaign for opposing actions. For example, when the ban against fox hunting was being considered, the League Against Cruel Sports wanted it banned, but the Countryside Alliance wanted it to continue.

Figure 18.3 Advantages and disadvantages of pressure groups as an influence

Advantages	Disadvantages
● If successful, action may be taken by government, laws introduced or inquiries set up. ● Pressure groups may be more successful as they have greater expertise and influence.	● Government ministers may have many requests made of them and be unable or unwilling to deal with all requests. ● Even lobbying by pressure groups may be unsuccessful or have delayed response.

Figure 18.4 Advantages and disadvantages of lobbying

Advantages	Disadvantages
● The Law Commission uses legally qualified Commissioners to investigate, who are experts in their field. Their reports are thoroughly researched and recommendations for reform are fully justified. Draft Bills accompany their reports so there is no need for delay in consideration of the recommendations by Parliament. ● It is politically independent and has the aim of improving the law – it does not get involved in matters of public policy. It reports to Parliament, not the government, thereby maintaining its independence. ● If Parliament accepts a recommendation to codify an area of law, it becomes easier for lawyers and the public to understand and apply. ● Many old, unnecessary and irrelevant laws are removed from the statute book.	● Governments are reluctant to find parliamentary time to consider and debate 'pure' law issues. As a result, Parliament has to wait for government to accept a Law Commission report and act on it. ● Parliament tends to concentrate on debating matters of broad policy, such as health and education, rather than on 'purely' legal issues where there is limited popular support. ● Government is not bound to accept Law Commission reports or implement any recommendations, either fully or in part. For example, the Law Commission recommended in 1993 reforms to the non-fatal offences in criminal law and, in 1998, to the civil law of negligence but neither area of law has been changed. ● The government is not bound to consult the Law Commission before bringing any changes in the law to Parliament – e.g., the Commission was not consulted on changes to sentencing practice and procedure before any of the four Acts were introduced on this issue.

Figure 18.5 Advantages and disadvantages of the Law Commission as an influence

Summary

- Political parties will set out ideas for new laws and reform of existing laws in a manifesto before an election. They will be judged according to how successful they are in introducing manifesto promises.
- MPs who are not members of the government can introduce Private Members' Bills or promote a cause.
- The general public can express their views by voting in an election, opinion polls and using social media. These views may or may not be acted upon by the government or Parliament.
- The media can inform the public and express the public's view on an issue. They can criticise government policy and/or support public opinion.
- Pressure groups can be sectional or cause groups. Both types can campaign on issues.
- A pressure group is likely to be well informed and campaigns can bring about change in the law or government action.
- Lobbying is carried out by individuals and pressure groups who try to persuade government ministers or individual MPs to take certain action or support a cause.
- The Law Commission is a non-political body charged with reviewing areas of law and making recommendations for reform.
- They carry out detailed investigations, issue reports and draft Bills for consideration by Parliament.
- They consider how areas of law could be consolidated or codified and recommend the repeal of old and unnecessary statute law.

Chapter 19 European Union law

Introduction

The United Kingdom (UK) was a member of the European Union (EU) from 1973 until January 2020. In that time, it accepted many laws and decisions of the EU in areas such as consumer protection and employment. Upon joining, the supremacy of EU law over national law had to be accepted and this was set out in the European Communities Act 1972.

19.1 Institutions of the European Union

The European Economic Community was set up by the Treaty of Rome in 1957 and consisted of six member countries. It became the European Union (EU) in 1993. Over the years more countries joined, to a total of 28 members (now 27). The UK joined the EU on 1 January 1973 and, after a referendum in 2016, left on 31 January 2020. To date it has been the only country to leave the EU.

19.1.1 The membership, role and legal functions of the European Commission

Each Member State has one Commissioner who is supposed to act independently of their national origin and interests.

Commissioners are appointed for a five-year term and can only be removed during this term of office by a vote of censure by the European Parliament. Each Commissioner heads a department with special responsibility for one area of Union policy, such as economic affairs, agriculture or the environment.

The Commission as a whole has several functions:

- It puts forward proposals for new laws to be adopted by the Parliament and the Council.
- It is the 'guardian' of the treaties and ensures that treaty provisions and other measures adopted by the Union are properly implemented. If a Member State has failed to implement Union law within its own country, or has infringed a provision in some way, the Commission has a duty to intervene and, if necessary, refer the matter to the Court of Justice of the European Union (ECJ). The Commission has

performed this duty very effectively and, as a result, Court judgments have been given in favour of the Commission and against Member States.
- It is responsible for the administration of the EU and it has powers to implement the Union's budget and supervise how the money is spent.

19.1.2 The membership, role and legal functions of the European Parliament

Members of the European Parliament (MEPs) are directly elected by the electorate of the Member States in elections which take place once every five years. The number of MEPs from each country is determined by the size of its population.

MEPs do not operate in national groups, but form political groups with those of the same political allegiance. The European Parliament meets on average about once a month for sessions that can last up to a week. It has standing committees which discuss proposals made by the Commission and then report to the full Parliament for debate. Decisions are made by the Parliament and the Council (see section 19.1.3).

The Parliament used to have only a consultative role, but it can now co-legislate on an equal footing with the Council in most areas. It can approve or reject a legislative proposal made by the Commission, or propose amendments to it. There are some areas, such as competition laws, where the Parliament cannot make law but only has the right to be consulted and put forward its opinion.

The Parliament also:
- decides on international agreements
- decides whether to admit new Member States
- reviews the Commission's work programme and asks it to propose legislation.

19.1.3 The membership, role and legal functions of the Council of the EU

The Council is the principal law-making and decision-making body of the EU.

It negotiates, amends and adopts laws, together with the European Parliament, based on proposals from the Commission, as well as co-ordinating EU policies.

The government of each member state sends a representative to the Council. The Foreign Minister is usually a country's main representative, but a government is free to send any of its ministers to Council meetings.

This means that, usually, the minister responsible for the topic under consideration will attend a meeting, so that the precise membership will vary with the subject being discussed. For example, the Minister for Agriculture will attend when the issue to be discussed involves agriculture. Ministers attending the Council have the authority to commit their governments to the laws and actions agreed upon. Usually, twice a year, government heads meet in the European Council or 'Summit' to discuss broad matters of policy.

Member States take it in turns to provide the President of the Council for a six-month period. A committee of permanent representatives assists with the day-to-day work of the Council.

19.1.4 The membership, role and legal functions of the Court of Justice of the EU (CJEU, formerly European Court of Justice)

Under Article 253 of the Treaty of the Functioning of the European Union (TFEU), judges are appointed from those who are eligible for appointment to the highest judicial posts in Member States or who are leading academic lawyers.

Each judge is appointed for a term of six years, and can be reappointed for a further term of six years. The judges select one of themselves to be President of the Court. The court sits in Luxembourg and has one judge from each Member State.

The CJEU is assisted by eleven Advocates General, who also hold office for six years. Each case is initially assigned to an Advocate General whose task under Article 253 is to research all the legal points involved and to present publicly, with complete impartiality and independence, reasoned conclusions on cases submitted to the Court with a view to assisting the latter in the performance of its duties.

The Court's function is set out in Article 19 Treaty of European Union (TEU). This states that the Court must 'ensure that in the interpretation and application of the Treaty the law is observed' uniformly in all Member States. It does this by:

- Hearing cases to decide whether a Member State has failed to fulfil its obligations under EU treaties. Such actions are usually initiated by the European Commission, although they can also be started by another Member State.

  An early example of such a case was *Re Tachographs: The Commission v United Kingdom* (1979) in which the court held that the UK had to implement a Council Regulation on the use of mechanical recording equipment (tachographs) in road vehicles used for the carriage of goods (see section 19.2.2 for the effect of Regulations).

- Hearing references from national courts for preliminary rulings on points of EU law. For example, if a national court had to consider a matter of EU law that had not arisen before, it could refer the point to the CJEU, which would then refer the case back to the national court when their ruling had been given.

- This reference function is important, as rulings made by the CJEU are then binding on courts in all Member States. This ensures that the law is indeed uniform throughout the European Union.

The status of the CJEU as a court of reference for UK courts after leaving the EU has yet to be finalised.

A request for a preliminary ruling is made under Article 267 TFEU, which says:

> the Court of Justice shall have jurisdiction to give preliminary rulings concerning:
>
> (a) the interpretation of treaties;
>
> (b) the validity and interpretation of acts of the institutions of the Union;
>
> (c) the interpretation of the statutes of bodies established by an act of the Council, where those statutes so provide.

Judges in session in the Court of Justice of the European Union

Commission	• Commissioners whose duty it is to act in the Union's interest • Proposes legislation • Tries to ensure that the Treaties are implemented in each Member State
European Parliament	• Members elected by citizens in each Member State • Can co-legislate on an equal footing with the Council in most areas
The Council of the European Union	• Consists of ministers from each Member State • Responsible for broad policy decisions
Court of Justice of the European Union	• One judge from each Member State • Decides whether Member States have failed in obligations • Rules on points of European Union law when cases are referred to it under Article 267 TFEU

Figure 19.1 The institutions of the European Union

19.2 Sources of European Union law

There are primary and secondary sources of EU law:
• Primary sources are mainly the treaties.
• Secondary sources are legislation passed by EU institutions under Article 288 TFEU. This secondary legislation is made up of Regulations, Directives and Decisions.

19.2.1 Treaties

The treaties are:
• The Treaty of Rome 1957, which established the Common Market, which eventually became the European Union.
• Treaties of Accession, when a new member joins the EU. The Treaty of Accession was signed in 1972 when the UK, Denmark and Ireland joined on 1 January 1973.
• Any amending Treaty such as the Treaty on European Union 1992 (the Maastricht Treaty), which introduced provisions for a shared European citizenship, for the introduction of a single currency (the Euro), and for common foreign and security policies.
• The Treaty of Lisbon 2007, also known as the TEU, which amended both the Treaty of Rome and the Maastricht Treaty.

While the UK was a member of the European Union, any Treaty made by the EU automatically became part of UK law and could be relied on by individual citizens. The same applied in every Member State. Once a Treaty was signed, it instantly becomes law in every Member State.

For the UK, s2(1) European Communities Act 1972 stated that:

> All such rights, powers, liabilities, obligations and restrictions from time to time created or arising by or under the Treaties and all such remedies and procedures from time to time provided for by or under the Treaties, as in accordance with the Treaties are without further enactment to be given legal effect or used in the United Kingdom, shall be recognised and available in law and be enforced, allowed and followed accordingly.

At the time of writing this section is still in force.

This meant that law contained in the Treaties was directly applicable and did not need an Act of Parliament to make them into UK law. This not only made EU law part of UK law but also it allowed an individual to rely on it. This is called direct effect.

EU citizens in the 27 member countries can rely on rights set out in the Treaty of Rome, as amended (such as freedom of movement and goods). National courts can apply EU law directly in their own countries.

19.2.2 Regulations

Under Article 288 TFEU, the EU has the power to issue EU Regulations which are 'binding in every respect and directly applicable in each Member State'. These laws will be made by the Council.

Such Regulations do not have to be adopted in any way by the individual states, as Article 288 makes it clear that they automatically become law in each member country. This means that they are directly applicable in the same way as Treaties. This prevents Member States from picking and choosing which Regulations they implement. As a result, laws are uniform across all the Member States. An example of a Regulation is the Unfair Terms in Consumer Contracts Regulations 1994.

Key term

EU Regulations – laws issued by the Council of Ministers which are binding on Member States, automatically apply and have direct effect, allowing an individual to rely on that law.

Look online

One of the first cases involving Regulations and the UK was *Re Tachographs: Commission v United Kingdom* (1979).

Research the facts and decision in this case.

19.2.3 Directives

A Directive is a legislative act that sets out a goal that all EU countries must achieve within a certain time frame. It is up to each Member State to write, and bring into effect, its own laws to reach the set goal.

Directives are the main way in which harmonisation of laws within Member States is reached. An example of an EU Directive is the Consumer Rights Directive 2011/83:

- It strengthened consumer rights across the EU by eliminating hidden charges and costs for goods and services bought on the internet, and extending the period under which consumers can withdraw from a sales contract.

The usual method of implementing Directives in the UK was by Statutory Instrument. For example:

- The provisions of the Consumer Rights Directive were implemented by the Payment Surcharges Regulations 2012, which took effect in April

2013, and the Consumer Contracts Regulations (Information, Cancellation and Additional Charges) Regulations 2013, which came into force on 13 June 2014.

Directives could, however, be implemented by other methods such as an Act of Parliament. An example was:

- The EU Directive on Liability for Defective Products, which was issued in July 1985. The Directive had to be implemented by 30 July 1988. This was done in the UK by the passing of the Consumer Protection Act 1987, which came into force on 1 March 1988.

Directives were also implemented by an Order in Council made by the Privy Council.

Directives are not directly effective, so they cannot be relied on by an individual until they have been enacted by domestic laws. If a Member State fails to implement a Directive within the time limit, an individual can take the Member State to court for non-implementation.

Key term

EU Directives – laws issued by the Council of Ministers requiring Member States to bring in their own law so that harmony of law is achieved throughout the EU.

19.3 Impact of European Union law on the law of England and Wales

19.3.1 The extension of rights of EU law to individuals – Treaties and Regulations

A citizen of a Member State (including the UK while it was a Member State) can rely on directly applicable laws contained in Treaties and Regulations to enforce their rights as these automatically become part of the law of a Member State. Since the UK left the EU on 31 January 2020, this right will not apply to UK citizens for EU laws made after that date. Whether it applies to laws made before that date is not yet decided.

In the case of *Van Gend en Loos* (1963), the CJEU established that provisions of the Treaty of Rome were capable of creating legal rights which could be enforced by individuals and companies in a national court. This is called direct effect.

Costa v ENEL (1964) confirmed the primacy of EU law over the laws of each Member State.

In *Internationale Handelsgesellschaft* (1970), the ECJ held that the validity of EU laws cannot be challenged on grounds of conflict with national law rules or concepts, even if that amounts to a violation of fundamental human rights provisions in a Member State's constitution.

In the event of a question of interpretation of EU law arising in a case, it can be referred to the CJEU. However, in *Bulmer v Bollinger* (1973), the House of Lords decided that this should be done only if absolutely necessary, not just where desirable or convenient.

Key term

Direct effect – an EU law that an individual can rely on as authority for their case. This applies to laws in Treaties and Regulations.

19.3.2 Directives

Under EU law, Member States have to implement EU Directives into their own national legislation. Usually, a time limit is set for this to be done. If a Member State fails to do this correctly, or within the time limit, they are in breach of their obligation. Once a Directive has been written into national law, individuals can rely on their rights under the national law. However, if the Directive has not been implemented by the required date, or if it has been inaccurately implemented, individuals can rely on the terms of the Directive itself against the Member State, and against any organisation or body that is said to be an 'emanation of the state'.

The reason is that a state cannot use its own failure to comply with EU law to deny an individual their rights if the state had properly implemented the Directive.

A private individual or body who is defending a claim based on an EU Directive is allowed to rely on national law, even if that does not properly implement a Directive. This is because Directives do not have direct effect between private individuals or bodies. In this case, the claimant would lose their claim and would then have to sue the state in a *Francovich* claim for damages for failing to implement the Directive.

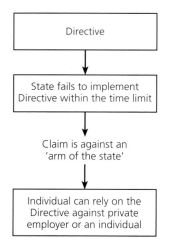

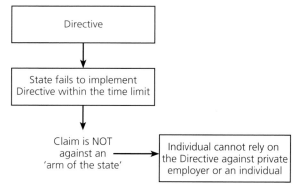

Figure 19.2 Vertical and horizontal direct effect

Case studies

Francovich v Italian Republic (1991)

The Italian government failed to implement a Directive aimed at protecting the wages of employees whose employer became insolvent. Francovich's employer became insolvent, owing him wages. He sued the State for his financial loss, and the ECJ ruled that he was entitled to compensation due to the State's failure.

R v Secretary of State for Employment, Ex p EOC (1995)

In *R v Secretary of State for Employment, Ex p EOC* (1995), the House of Lords decided that it was possible for a UK court to make a declaration that UK law was incompatible with a Directive – in this case the threshold conditions for redundancy pay was incompatible with the Equal Treatment Directive.

Vertical direct effect

Vertical direct effect is where the individual can claim against an emanation of the State (also known as an arm of the State) when a Directive has not been implemented or was implemented in a defective way.

This was the case in *Marshall v Southampton and South West Hampshire Area Health Authority* (1986). The Equal Treatment Directive had vertical effect, allowing an individual, such as Miss Marshall, to rely on it and take action against the UK.

Case study

Marshall v Southampton and South West Hampshire Area Health Authority (1986)

Miss Marshall was required to retire at age 62 while men doing the same work did not have to retire until 65. Under the Sex Discrimination Act 1975, this was not discriminatory in the UK; however, the Equal Treatment Directive had not been fully implemented in the UK and, if this had been in force, Miss Marshall would have succeeded.

The CJEU decided that the Directive was sufficiently clear and imposed obligations on Member States. Miss Marshall succeeded as her employers were 'an arm of the State'.

An 'arm of the State' covers a public service under the control of the State. This could cover hospitals in the health service (as above), the police or other emergency services.

Horizontal direct effect

On the other hand, if an EU law has horizontal direct effect, an individual can rely on it to claim against another individual or business. As explained above, Directives are usually incapable of being horizontally directly effective. For example, in *Duke v GEC Reliance Ltd* (1988), Mrs Duke was unable to rely on the Equal Treatment Directive as her employer was a private company.

However, under the *Kücükdeveci* (2010) principle, Directives which give rise to fundamental human rights, such as non-discrimination, can give rise to horizontal direct effect, allowing an individual to claim against another individual or business.

Indirect effect

Indirect effect is where a Member State has failed to implement a Directive — either correctly or at all. In *Von Colson and Kamann v Land Nordrhein-Westfalen*, the CJEU ruled that national courts should interpret national law in line with the Directive, 'in so far as it is given the discretion to do so under national law'. In *Marleasing v La Comercial Internacional de Alimentacion*, the CJEU extended indirect effect to situations where the Member State concerned had not implemented the Directive at all.

Statutory interpretation

As well as having to follow decisions of the CJEU, membership of the EU has affected UK court decisions in another way. This is because judges in the CJEU use a purposive approach to statutory interpretation. This approach has encouraged judges in English courts to greater use of the purposive approach in matters of statutory interpretation.

19.3.3 The concept of supremacy of EU law and sovereignty of UK Parliament

EU law takes precedence over the national law of every Member State.

- This was first established in *Van Gen den Loos* (1963), which involved a conflict between Dutch law and EU law on customs duties. The Dutch government argued that the CJEU had no jurisdiction to decide if EU law prevailed over Dutch law but the ECJ rejected this argument.
- In *Costa v ENEL* (1964), the CJEU decided that even if there was a later national law, it did not take precedence over EU law.
- This effect was seen in *R v Secretary of State for Transport, ex parte Factortame* (1990) (usually referred to as the *Factortame* case). The CJEU decided that the UK could not enforce the Merchant Shipping Act 1988. This Act had been passed to protect British fishermen by allowing vessels to register only if 75 per cent of directors and shareholders were British nationals. It was held that this contravened the Treaty of Rome. The Act could not be enforced against EU nationals.

From the cases given above it can be seen that Member States have definitely transferred sovereign rights to the EU. No Member State can rely on its own law if it is in conflict with EU law.

While the UK was a member of the EU it was true to say that the sovereignty of the UK Parliament had been affected and that, in the areas it operated in, EU law had supremacy over UK law. In fact, this supremacy was one of the main arguments for the

'Leave' campaigners. As the UK has now left the EU, it seems that the UK Parliament has regained its sovereignty and is free to pass any law it chooses, whether or not in conflict with EU law.

Whether any EU law passed while the UK was a Member remains in force will have to be seen. It will depend on whether the UK Parliament passes laws to alter, amend or accept EU law from the time that the UK was a Member State.

Case	Law
Van Duyn v Home Office (1974)	Individual entitled to rely on Treaty provision.
Re Tachographs: Commission v UnitedKingdom (1979)	Regulations are directly applicable in all Member States and can be relied on by individuals.
Marshall v Southampton and South West Hampshire Area Health Authority (1986)	<ul><li>Directives have vertical direct effect.</li><li>In an action against the State, or an emanation of the State, individuals can rely on a Directive which has not been implemented.</li></ul>
Francovich v Italian Republic (1991)	Individuals can claim compensation from the State for losses caused by the State's failure to implement a Directive.
Van Gend en Loos (1963)	EU law takes precedence over the national law of every Member State.
Costa v ENEL (1964)	Even if there is a later national law, it does not take precedence over EU law.
Factortame case (1990)	EU law takes precedence over national law even where the Member State has enacted its own law to the contrary.

Figure 19.3 Key cases: the effect of EU law

Activity (?)

Source A shows extracts from Articles 1 and 2 of the Equal Treatment Directive 76/207. Read these and then apply them, giving reasons for your decision, to the facts set out in Source B.

Source A: Council Directive 76/207

Article 1

1 The purpose of this Directive is to put into effect in the Member States the principle of equal treatment as regards access to employment, including promotion, and to vocational training and as regards working conditions . . . This principle is hereinafter referred to as the 'principle of equal treatment'.

Article 2

1 For the purposes of the following provisions, the principle of equal treatment shall mean that there shall be no discrimination whatsoever on the grounds of sex either directly or indirectly by reference in particular to marital or family status.

2 This Directive shall be without prejudice to the right of Member States to exclude from its field of application those occupational activities and, where appropriate, the training leading thereto, for which, by reason of their nature or the context in which they are carried out, the sex of the worker constitutes a determining factor.

3 This Directive shall be without prejudice to provisions concerning the protection of women, particularly as regards pregnancy and maternity.

4 This Directive shall be without prejudice to measures to promote equal opportunity for men and women, in particular by removing existing inequalities which affect women's opportunities in the areas referred to in Article 1(1).

Source B: Case facts

Amy Austin and Ben Bowen are employed by Green Gardens Ltd. There is a vacancy for a promotion to section manager, and both have applied for the post. Green Gardens have interviewed Amy and Ben and decided that both are equally qualified for the position. In this situation, if there are fewer women employed at the relevant level, Green Gardens have a policy of appointing the female applicant.

Ben complains that this is discriminatory and contrary to the Equal Treatment Directive.

Quick questions

1 Identify one source of primary EU law and briefly explain the principle of direct effect.
2 Explain the use of EU Directives and give one example.
3 Explain the role of the CJEU.
4 Explain what action an individual can take against a state that has not fully implemented a Directive into national law.
5 Discuss the concept of supremacy of EU law over national law.

Summary

- The European Union was established in 1957. The UK joined in 1973 but left in January 2020.
- The Council of Europe is the main law-making and decision-making body of the EU. It consists of ministers of all Member States.
- The Commission is a permanent body which proposes laws and policies to the Council.
- The European Parliament is directly elected and is consulted on Commission proposals.
- The Court of Justice interprets matters of EU law that have been referred to it by national courts.
- Treaties are a primary source of law and automatically become law in every Member State. They have direct effect, allowing individuals to rely on them.
- Regulations establish consistent laws across the EU. They also have direct effect and can be relied on by individuals.
- Directives introduce harmony in laws across the EU. They direct each Member State to introduce their own law to comply with the Directive within a time limit.
- Failure by a Member State to fully implement a Directive, or to do so within a time limit, allows an individual a claim against the State.
- An individual can rely on an unimplemented Directive if taking action against the State or an emanation of the State.
- An individual cannot rely on an unimplemented Directive if taking action against a private individual or company.
- EU law takes precedence over the national law of every Member State.
- Member States transferred sovereign rights to make laws to the EU. No Member State can rely on its own law if it is in conflict with EU law.

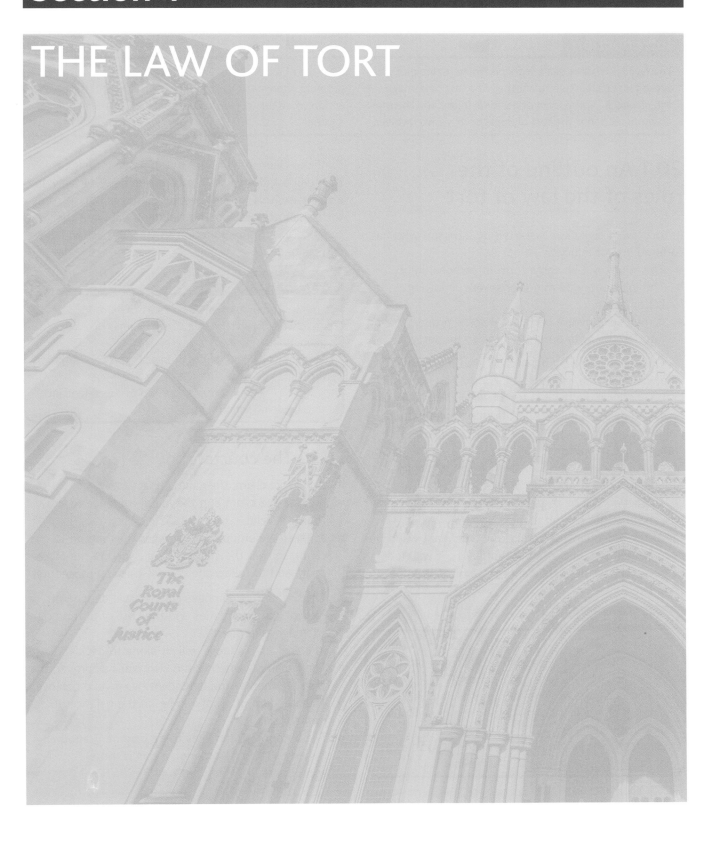

Section 4

THE LAW OF TORT

Chapter 20 Rules and theory of the law of tort

Introduction

The civil law of tort deals with cases where one party has caused loss or damage to another. The loss or damage will usually be some form of personal injury and the most common action is the tort of negligence, which involves a breach of a duty of care towards another. Tort law also protects interests in land. It allows a claimant to take action when one person accepts liability for the actions of another.

20.1 An outline of the rules of the law of tort

In tort law, a civil case is started by a person who has suffered loss or injury.
- The injury will be some form of personal injury.
- The injury may be minor or severe, involving lifelong care.
- It may also involve damage to some property or an interference with a right related to property.

The person suffering the loss is called the claimant who will usually be an individual. For the torts covered in this specification, the loss for an individual will usually be due to personal injury. Apart from personal harm, a claimant may have suffered damage to, or interference with, the use or enjoyment of their land, as in the tort of nuisance. A business can also claim in tort where it has suffered loss due to the fault of another.

The action will be taken against the individual or business that has caused the loss and they will be called the defendant. Generally, the defendant will have been at fault but, unlike criminal offences, it will not be necessary for the defendant's state of mind to be considered.

Key terms

Tort – a civil wrong. The word comes from the French for 'wrong'. The aim of the law of tort is to compensate an injured victim for the wrong done to them.

Claimant – an injured victim of a wrongdoing. The claimant brings an action to recover compensation for their loss or damage.

Defendant – the person or body responsible for the loss or damage and who, generally, has been at fault.

If the claimant is successful in proving their case, they will ask the court to award a remedy. Usually, in a tort case, this remedy will be damages but, in some torts such as nuisance, the claimant will want the court to award an injunction to stop the action being complained of.

Key terms

Remedy – an order made by a court to enforce or satisfy a tort claim. It is usually damages or an injunction.

Damages – the payment of money as compensation for the loss or damage suffered.

Injunction – a court order addressed to the defendant to stop doing something.

20.1.1 The courts

In a civil tort claim, the claimant has to:
- prepare the claim and the initial evidence to show that it is valid
- suggest the amount of damages they intend to claim, so that the claim can be issued in the correct court and to follow the correct tracking procedure.

The amount of damages claimed will depend on the severity of the injuries and the cost of putting right any damage to property.

In a civil trial, a judge will sit alone to decide:
- The liability – whether the claimant has proved the case or whether the defendant has a valid defence. The standard of proof will be on the balance of probabilities.
- The amount of damages to be paid or, if another remedy should be ordered, if this is more appropriate.

- If the winning party is entitled to the payment of their legal costs by the losing party. In civil cases the general rule is that the loser pays the winner's legal costs in addition to their own costs.

One of the parties can appeal against the decision of the judge, either:
- against liability – because the judge might have misdirected themselves on the relevant law, or
- against the amount of damages awarded – too much or too little.

20.1.2 The parties

- The claimant is generally an individual. If the claimant is under the age of 18, their parent or litigation friend will take the action on their behalf.
- The defendant can be either an individual person, or in some cases, a business which may exist in law as a company or a partnership.

It is likely that a defendant will only be worth suing for compensation if they are insured and the insurance company pays out for them. This will certainly be the case in road accidents.

However, if an individual defendant commits the tort while working, the principles of vicarious liability can make the employer liable as well as the individual worker. This will benefit the claimant as the employer might be able to pay the compensation or, more likely, they will have liability insurance to pay out if the worker commits the tort in the course of working.

20.1.3 Burden and standard of proof

In civil cases, the burden of proving that the defendant is liable (at fault) is on the claimant.

Link
Vicarious liability is explained in Chapter 24.

There are rules on the level to which the case has to be proved. This is referred to as the 'standard of proof'. The standard of proof in civil cases is 'the balance of probabilities' – the claimant's evidence is enough to suggest that the law is probably on their side.

This standard is lower than the standard of proof in criminal cases, because:
- In a criminal case the defendant is punished and could lose their freedom if found guilty.
- In a civil case the defendant is found responsible for the damage/injuries and only has to compensate the injured party.

20.1.4 Defences

There are fewer defences available to a defendant in civil law than in criminal law.

However, the defendant can dispute the claimant's case and, in some cases, suggest that the claimant wholly or partly caused their own injury.

20.2 An outline of the theory of the law of tort

Link
These defences are called consent and contributory negligence, and will be considered in Chapter 25.

20.2.1 The protected interests in tort

The main point of tort law is that a person has certain interests which others have the obligation or duty to respect. The existence of these interests, and the duty of others to respect them, does not depend upon promises or agreements, as in contract law. They are broader social obligations. The failure to respect the obligation is a 'tort', and tort law is the body of principles which defines these interests, duties, and the remedies available when the duties have not been met.

Tort law aims to protect individual interests from a harm that is actual or threatened. However, not all interests are protected and some benefit from better protection than others. They can change over time. The interests protected include:
- Personal harm, which can include physical, psychological and reputational harm and personal freedom. This interest will include the torts of assault, battery and false imprisonment. Reputational harm is covered by the tort of defamation which in turn can be by libel or slander.
- Harm to property, which can include direct and indirect interference with land and rights over land such as use and enjoyment of land. This interest will include the torts of trespass and private nuisance.
- Harm to financial interests.

Warning sign against possible trespassers

Tort law has more pronounced moral overtones than contract law. To breach a contractual obligation, especially in a purely commercial setting between parties of equal bargaining power, may be a matter of moral indifference to either party. However to breach a duty enforced by tort law is wrong and, for some torts (especially where there is a breach of trust), a very serious moral matter.

20.2.2 The aims of tort law

These include:

- To provide compensation in the form of damages to injured victims.
- To achieve or provide justice for an injured victim – this can be achieved by the payment of compensation but money can only partly achieve justice for a victim who has suffered serious physical injuries.
- It is morally fair that a person who has caused injury to another should be required to pay for the suffering caused, penalising a defendant for their fault; it may also act as a deterrent to others not to commit the same or similar actions.
- Loss distribution – there is a view that that greater liability should be imposed on businesses or companies whose activities cause physical injury and damage as they are in the best position to spread the cost of losses associated with their activities, either directly, by increasing the price of their products and services, or indirectly, by purchasing liability insurance.
- To achieve policy aims of improving standards – for example, of products sold or the quality of the environment, by making those who sell defective goods or pollute rivers pay for their shortcomings or actions.

20.2.3 The 'compensation culture'

This refers to an attitude to sue for even the most trivial reasons or where only minor injury or damage has been caused. This attitude developed in the United States and was promoted in this country by numerous claims management companies.

Critics of this culture suggest that people's approach to risk taking has changed to them being less risk averse because, if something goes wrong, a claim for compensation can be taken. It is argued that people should take greater personal responsibility and accept responsibility for accidents which are their own fault.

To counter this culture, the Compensation Act 2006 was passed to regulate claims management companies. It became an offence to run an unauthorised claims management company. This authorisation was intended to improve standards of service and to reduce instances of cold calling.

It may be that instances of cold calling of victims of accidents in hospital has reduced but claims management companies still persist in cold calling. There remains a general feeling in society that suffering personal injury should result in the payment of compensation and greater efforts should be made for individuals to take greater responsibility for their actions.

20.2.4 Remedies in tort

If the claimant successfully proves their tort claim, they will be entitled to a remedy. This is usually damages.

Link

The remedies available in tort are considered in Chapter 26.

20.2.5 Distinctions between tort law and contract law

Differences

The main difference between the two forms of law is the relationship between the parties.

- Contract law – there will be a relationship because of a previously entered contract, whether written or oral. It will contain agreed terms as to, for example, the nature and quantity of goods or services and the price. The parties will know at the outset the terms and what they each have to do to perform their respective terms.

- Tort law – the parties will not have a formal legal relationship before the incident, but a relationship commences when one of the parties is injured or suffers loss or damage. This relationship is used as the initial basis of a claim.

20.2.6 Distinctions between tort law and criminal law

As set out in detail in Chapter 28, there are many distinctions between tort and criminal law:

1 The purpose of the law:
   ○ Tort law – to provide a form of compensation for those injured by the wrongful, but not necessarily criminal, acts of others.
   ○ Criminal law – to maintain law and order in a civilised society and to punish wrong-doers.
2 Because of the effect of punishment, the standard for judging whether an action is criminal is high. If the action does not meet this high standard, then it may amount to a civil, tortious wrong.
3 Judiciary:
   ○ Tort law – a legally qualified judge decides whether a person is liable, using formal legal reasons.
   ○ Criminal law – a lay person, a magistrate or a jury decides whether a person is in breach of the law, unless there is a guilty plea.
4 Consequences of breaching the law:
   ○ Tort law – merely concerned with compensating the victim for the injuries suffered. Except in nuisance claims, it will not be concerned with the offender's future behaviour.
   ○ Criminal law – some form of punishment where the offender repays a debt to society. The ultimate aims of punishment are reparation, deterrence and reform so that the offender addresses their future behaviour.

Quick questions

1 Identify the aims of the law of tort.
2 Explain the role of a judge hearing a civil tort claim.
3 When would it be worth issuing a civil tort claim?
4 Identify the main remedies available in tort law.

Summary

- Tort law is a civil wrong. It protects interests which others have an obligation to observe.
- A claimant will be the person or business which has suffered loss or damage by the act or omission of another.
- The defendant will be the person or business who has caused the loss or damage to the claimant.
- A case will be heard in the civil courts and the main remedy that can be awarded is damages by way of compensation.
- Aims of tort law include obtaining compensation for loss suffered, justice for the victim, loss distribution and the raising of standards.
- There was a compensation culture but to some extent this has been reduced.
- There are some similarities with contract law in that they are both civil actions, involve a breach of obligation and the payment of compensation for damage or injury caused.
- However, contract law has to have evidence of a formal relationship from the outset.
- The purpose of criminal law is to maintain law and order in society, but the purpose of tort law is to provide a means of compensation for injuries suffered.

Chapter 21 Liability in negligence

Introduction

Negligence is a common law tort that has been created solely by judicial decisions. It can be alleged when harm is done to a protected interest of a claimant, causing personal injury or damage to their property by the carelessness of the wrong-doer – the defendant in any court action.

21.1 Liability in negligence for injury to people and damage to property

The tort of negligence can apply in a wide variety of situations where a person is injured or their property is damaged as a result of an accident. For example:

- A car crash in which vehicles are damaged and a driver and/or passenger(s) are injured. The injured person will want to claim compensation for their injuries and for damage to their vehicle.
- People being injured at work or through medical negligence.

Negligence needs proof of fault on the part of the person who caused the incident.

Negligence was defined in the case of *Blyth v Birmingham Waterworks Co.* (1856) by Baron Alderson as:

> failing to do something which the reasonable person would do or doing something which the reasonable person would not do.

According to this definition, negligence can arise from either an act or an omission.

Key term

Negligence – an act or a failure to act which causes injury to another person or damage to their property.

Look online

Find two examples online of incidents where negligence is alleged when someone was injured or property was damaged.

In a negligence claim, the claimant has to prove that the defendant was at fault and is to blame for the injuries or damage. As we saw in Chapter 20:

- The level of fault is on the balance of probabilities – it is more likely than not that the defendant's fault caused the injuries or damage.
- The burden of proving this fault and providing evidence is on the claimant.

In a successful claim for negligence, the person who caused the injury or damage is only liable if:

- they owe the claimant a duty of care, and
- they breached this duty, and
- the breach causes reasonably foreseeable injury or damage.

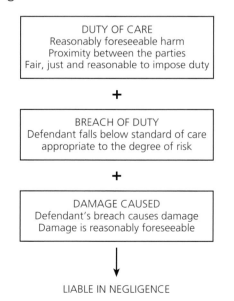

DUTY OF CARE
Reasonably foreseeable harm
Proximity between the parties
Fair, just and reasonable to impose duty

+

BREACH OF DUTY
Defendant falls below standard of care appropriate to the degree of risk

+

DAMAGE CAUSED
Defendant's breach causes damage
Damage is reasonably foreseeable

↓

LIABLE IN NEGLIGENCE

Figure 21.1 What must be proved for negligence

After these elements have been proved, the defendant may put forward a defence such as the contributory negligence of the claimant or that the claimant consented to run the risk of injury. These defences are explained in more detail in Chapter 25.

The aim of taking a negligence action is for the claimant to be awarded damages for the injury or damage. The basis for the award of damages is explained in more detail in Chapter 26.

21.2 The duty of care

The idea of a duty of care in the tort of negligence is to establish a legal relationship between the parties. It has developed through judicial precedent – judges making decisions in cases. The modern law of negligence began with the case of *Donoghue v Stevenson* (1932). In the judgments, the Law Lords used the principle from *Heaven v Pender* (1883) to set out when a duty of care is owed:

> a duty to take care did arise when the person or property of one was in such proximity to the person or property of another, that, if due care was not taken, damage might be done by one to another.

21.2.1 *Donoghue v Stevenson* (1932) and the neighbour principle

This famous case used the above statement to establish for the first time the broad principles of owing a legal duty of care and general liability in negligence, known as 'the neighbour principle'.

Case study

Donoghue v Stevenson (1932)

Mrs Donoghue went to a café with a friend who bought her a bottle of ginger beer and ice cream. The bottle had dark glass so that its contents could not be seen. After drinking some, Mrs Donoghue poured out the remainder of the ginger beer and saw that it contained a dead (and decomposing) snail. Because of the impurities in the drink, she suffered physical injuries and mental anguish from what she saw.

She wanted to claim compensation for these injuries but she could not use contract law as she had not bought the drink. Instead she sued the manufacturers of the drink in negligence, claiming that they owed her a duty of care and were at fault in the manufacturing process.

In the House of Lords, Lord Atkin set the test for when a person would be under a duty to another. He said:

> You must take reasonable care to avoid acts or omissions which you can reasonably foresee would be likely to injure your neighbour ... Who then is my neighbour? Persons who are so closely and directly affected by my act that I ought reasonably to have them in my contemplation as being affected when I am directing my mind to the acts or omissions in question.

Key term

The neighbour principle – the person who is owed a duty of care by the defendant. It is not the person living next door: it is anyone you ought to bear in mind, who could be injured by your act or omission.

21.2.2 Development of the duty of care

In subsequent years the highest courts were faced with the problem of deciding whether a duty of care should apply to new situations.

In *Dorset Yacht Co. v Home Office* (1970), Lord Reid said

> when a new point emerges one should ask not whether it is covered by authority but whether recognised principles apply to it. *Donoghue v Stevenson* may be regarded as a milestone, and the well-known passage in Lord Atkin's [judgment] should I think be regarded as a statement of principle ... it ought to apply unless there is some justification or valid explanation for its exclusion.

In other words, an incremental approach should apply when considering if a duty of care applied.

How to apply this incremental approach was dealt with in *Anns v Merton London Borough Council* (1978). A two-stage approach for deciding if a duty of care existed was developed by Lord Wilberforce where there was sufficient legal proximity between the parties unless there were policy reasons for not doing so.

Junior Books v Veitchi (1983) appeared to be a unique decision in negligence as it involved a purely contractual relationship between the parties. It was decided that the parties were sufficiently proximate to each other and there was a duty between them. It was found that this was not limited to a duty to avoid causing foreseeable harm to persons or property, but also created a duty to avoid pure economic loss, as a result of the work that had been defective.

Look online

Research the case of *Michael v Chief Constable of South Wales Police* (2015): **https://news.liverpool.ac.uk/2015/01/28/viewpoint-supreme-court-rejects-michael-familys-bid-sue-police/**

In *Michael's* case, and in *Hill v Chief Constable of West Yorkshire* (1989) below, there were said to be omissions by the police, whereas in the *Robinson* case below there was said to be a positive action. Identify the omissions and the positive action in each of the cases.

21.2.3 The *Caparo* test

Ultimately the case of *Caparo v Dickman* (1990) came before the House of Lords and they set a three-part test for deciding, in all cases, whether a duty of care existed:

1 Was damage or harm reasonably foreseeable?
And

2 Is there a sufficiently proximate (close) relationship between the claimant and the defendant?
And

3 Is it fair, just and reasonable to impose a duty?

Key term 🔑

Three-part test – an update of the neighbour principle to show who is owed a duty of care in negligence.

Figure 21.2 The *Caparo* three-part test

Case study

Caparo v Dickman (1990)

The claimant company wanted to take over another company – Fidelity Limited. They looked at the statutory accounts prepared by the defendant, which showed that the company made a profit. Based on these accounts, the claimants decided to take over Fidelity. After completing the purchase, they inspected the detailed accounts which showed a large loss. They sued the defendant in negligence for their loss.

The House of Lords, when deciding whether the defendant owed a duty of care, set the three-part test. They decided that the defendant did not owe a duty of care as the accounts were prepared for Fidelity and for statutory reasons, and not for prospective buyers.

Damage or reasonably foreseeable harm

Whether the injury or damage is reasonably foreseeable depends on the facts of the case. An example of this is the case of *Kent v Griffiths* (2000).

Case study

Kent v Griffiths (2000)

The claimant was suffering an asthma attack and an ambulance was called to take her to hospital. Despite repeated assurances by the control centre, and for no obvious reason, the ambulance failed to arrive within a reasonable time. As a result, the claimant suffered a respiratory arrest.

The court decided it was reasonably foreseeable that the claimant would suffer further illness if the ambulance did not arrive promptly. No good reason was given why it failed to do so. A duty of care came into existence when the control centre accepted the call and, as they failed in this duty, they were liable.

Proximity of relationship

Even if the harm is reasonably foreseeable, a duty of care will only exist if the relationship between the claimant and the defendant is sufficiently close or proximate. An example is the case of *Bourhill v Young* (1943).

Case study

Bourhill v Young (1943)

A pregnant woman heard an accident as she got off a tram. The accident was caused by a motorcyclist who died in the accident. She approached the scene of the accident and saw blood on the road. She suffered such shock from what she saw that she later gave birth to a still-born baby. She sued the relatives of the dead motorcyclist.

Under the neighbour test, she had to prove that she was proximate, or close, to the motorcyclist so that he owed her a duty of care. The House of Lords decided that he could not anticipate that, if he was involved in an accident, it would cause mental injury to a bystander. He was not proximate to her and did not owe her a duty of care.

One reason for the decision in this case could have been that Mrs Bourhill was not related to the victim and, if she could sue, it would open the floodgates to claims.

Fair, just and reasonable to impose a duty

The courts are often reluctant to find that it is 'fair, just and reasonable' to impose a duty of care on public authorities such as the police. In the case of *Hill v Chief Constable of West Yorkshire* (1990), it was pointed out that imposing a duty of care on police (and allowing them to be sued) could lead to policing being carried out in a defensive way, which might divert police resources and attention away from the prevention and detection of crime. This could lead to lower standards of policing, not higher ones.

Case studies

Hill v Chief Constable of West Yorkshire (1990)

The Yorkshire Ripper, a serial killer, had been attacking and murdering women in Yorkshire and across the North of England. The claimant's daughter was his last victim before he was caught. By the time of her death, the police had enough information to arrest him but failed to do so. The claimant alleged that the police owed her daughter a duty of care.

It was decided by the House of Lords that the relationship between the victim and the police was not sufficiently close (proximate) for the police to owe a duty of care to the victim, and that it was not fair, just and reasonable for the police to owe a duty of care to the general public. The police knew that the killer might strike again, but they had no way of knowing who the victim might be.

Mitchell v Glasgow City Council (2009)

A claim was brought by the family of a man who was killed by his neighbour who had threatened the deceased and others on the estate. The killing took place after a meeting called by the Council to discuss the behaviour. It was alleged that the Council owed a duty of care to the deceased to warn him about the meeting so that the deceased would have been more prepared.

It was decided that the Council did not owe a duty to the deceased as it was not fair, just and reasonable for the Council to warn the deceased of the steps they were taking to deal with the offending behaviour. Further, a duty to warn another person that he is at risk of loss, injury or damage as the result of the criminal act of a third party will arise only where the person who is said to be under that duty has, by his words or conduct, assumed responsibility for the safety of the person who is at risk.

21.2.4 Robinson v Chief Constable of West Yorkshire (2018)

The three-part test in *Caparo* was criticised because:
- It did not say when a duty of care should be imposed but after the decision, judges and lawyers applied the three-part test to every negligence claim.
- The police and other emergency services used the defence in *Hill* that, for policy reasons, it was not fair, just and reasonable for them to owe a duty of care to members of the general public with whom they had no previous dealing.

Robinson v Chief Constable of West Yorkshire (2018)

An elderly lady was walking along a street, and was injured when police officers tried to arrest a suspected drug dealer. There was a struggle, during which the suspect and the police fell to the ground, collided with the claimant and injured her.

The police defended the claim on the grounds of *Hill*, arguing that they did not owe the claimant a duty of care and, if they did, they were protected for policy reasons. The claimant argued that this was a novel case and that the police owed the claimant a duty of care.

In the Supreme Court it was said:

> It was not the House of Lord's intention [in *Caparo*] to create a rigid test for judges to use [in every case], as this would be impractical. The House of Lords, in *Caparo*, considered that when deciding to impose a duty, the courts had to take a more pragmatic approach.

And Lord Reed:

> The proposition that there is a *Caparo* test which applies to all claims in ... negligence, and that in consequence the court will only impose a duty of care where it considers it fair, just and reasonable to do so on the particular facts, is mistaken [paras 21–24]. It is normally only in novel cases, where established principles do not provide an answer, that the courts need to exercise judgment that involves consideration of what is 'fair, just and reasonable'. [para 27]

Following *Robinson*, the common law has developed bit by bit, using established authority.

The effect of the decision is:

- There is no single definitive test to assess whether a duty of care exists.
- If there is an existing, similar precedent (or some statutory authority) for deciding if a duty of care exists, then that should be followed. Alternatively, the law can be developed incrementally and by analogy with existing precedent.
- If there is a novel situation where it has not previously been decided if a duty of care exists, or when the court is being invited to depart from a decided precedent, then the *Caparo* three-stage test should be used.

As a result it was decided that there was no blanket protection for the police and that Mrs Robinson was owed a duty of care.

This approach was then applied in *Darnley v Croydon NHS Trust* (2018), when a patient left the hospital's A & E department after wrongly being told by a receptionist that there would be a wait of several hours when he felt really unwell. Unfortunately, he ultimately suffered permanent brain injuries. It was decided that the case fell within an established category of duty of care. A duty to take reasonable care not to cause physical injury is owed by those who provide and run a casualty department. In this case, as soon as the patient was 'booked in', he entered into a relationship with the hospital for them to take reasonable care not to provide misleading information which may foreseeably cause physical injury.

Another case where the Court of Appeal had to apply the *Robinson* principles was *Sumner v Colborne and others* (2018). A road accident took place at a junction where a motorist's view of the road was obscured by overgrown vegetation off the highway. The question for the court was whether the highway authority owed a duty of care to road users to cut the vegetation and improve the visibility at the junction. No precedent existed to say whether the owner of land adjoining a highway owed a duty of care to highway users in relation to overgrowing vegetation, so it was a novel situation. The court decided that it would not be fair, just and reasonable for a duty to be imposed. This was based on undue burdens being placed on landowners to keep the boundaries of their land free from obstruction and if a duty was imposed, it might lead to more claims by insured motorists against landowners.

Principle	Case	Judgment
Duty of care	*Donoghue v Stevenson* (1932)	You must take reasonable care not to injure your neighbour.
Three-stage test	*Caparo v Dickman* (1990)	<ul><li>Injury or damage has to be reasonably foreseeable.</li><li>There must be proximity of relationship.</li><li>It must be fair, just and reasonable to impose a duty of care.</li><li>Three-stage test only to be used in novel situations.</li></ul>
Current test for showing duty of care	*Robinson v Chief Constable of West Yorkshire* (2018)	No single definitive test of when a duty is imposed; existing precedent should be followed or there should be an incremental development of the law.
Reasonable foreseeability	*Kent v Griffiths* (2000)	It was reasonably foreseeable that if the ambulance took unreasonable time to reach the patient, greater injury would be caused.
Proximity of relationship	*Bourhill v Young* (1943)	Claimant not proximate to victim of road accident.
Fair, just and reasonable test	*Hill v Chief Constable of West Yorkshire Police* (1990)	It was not fair, just and reasonable for the police to owe a duty of care to a member of the public not known to them.
	Mitchell v Glasgow City Council (2009)	It was not fair, just and reasonable for the Council to owe a duty of care to victim of unlawful killing.

Figure 21.3 Key cases: duty of care

Activity

Read the blogs of the Supreme Court in the following cases, both of which consider the existence of a duty of care. The blogs contain links to the full judgments for detailed discussion of the issues.

James-Bowen v Commissioner of Police of the Metropolis (2018)

http://ukscblog.com/case-comment-james-bowen-ors-v-commissioner-of-police-of-the-metropolis-2018-uksc-40/

Poole BC v GN and another (2019)

http://ukscblog.com/new-judgment-poole-borough-council-v-gn-through-his-litigation-friend-the-official-solicitor-anor-2019-uksc-25/

Look online

What was the standard of care found by the court to apply in *Wells v Cooper* (1958)?

Key term

Reasonable person – the ordinary person on the street or someone doing the same task as the defendant.

21.3 Breach of duty

21.3.1 The objective standard of care and the 'reasonable man'

Once it has been shown that a duty of care is owed, the claimant has to prove that the duty of care has been broken. The standard is objective – that of the 'reasonable man' (or person), as set by Baron Alderson referred to above. This reasonable person is the ordinary person performing the task competently. It could be the reasonable driver, the reasonable doctor or the reasonable manufacturer.

The reasonable man/person

In *Vaughan v Menlove* (1837), the defendant's argument that he had used his best judgement was not relevant – his actions were judged objectively. There are a number of variations of the 'reasonable person' and the court may have to consider whether the defendant has a special characteristic. For example, are they a professional, an inexperienced learner or a child? If any of these apply, how should they be judged?

The reasonable learner

Learners are judged at the standard of the competent, more experienced person. This principle was set by the case of *Nettleship v Weston* (1971).

Nettleship v Weston (1971)

Mrs Weston arranged with her neighbour, Mr Nettleship, for him to give her driving lessons. She was driving on her third lesson with him when she failed to straighten the car after turning a corner. She hit a lamp post which fell onto the car, injuring Mr Nettleship. It was decided that Mrs Weston should be judged by the standard of the competent driver, not the inexperienced learner driver, so she was liable.

Although this decision seems unfair to learners, it is logical as far as motorists are concerned because she was covered by an insurance policy. It would be unjust on an injured claimant if the defence was put forward that 'I am only on my third lesson and you cannot expect me to be as good a driver as someone who has been driving for some time'.

The reasonable child

The standard is that of a reasonable person of the defendant's age at the time of the accident. This is shown by the case of *Mullin v Richards* (1998).

Case studies

Mullin v Richards (1998)

Two 15-year-old girls were play-fighting in class with plastic rulers. One of the rulers snapped and fragments entered Mullin's eye, resulting in her losing all useful sight in that eye. It was decided that Richards had to meet the standard of a 15-year-old schoolgirl (and not that of a reasonable adult). As she had reached the required standard, she had not breached her duty of care.

Orchard v Lee (2009)

The claimant was a dinner lady supervising in a school playground. She suffered injuries when a 13-year-old boy ran backwards into her while playing a game of tag. She sued the boy in negligence. The issue for the court was whether the boy had breached his duty of care, and the relevance of his age.

In *Mullin v Richards* the rule was set that a child should be judged as a reasonable child of his age rather than a reasonable adult. As a result, the level of careless behaviour of a child will be very high.

In this case the boy had not breached the duty of care and was not liable.

The reasonable professional

In *Wilsher v Essex Area Health Authority* (1988), a junior doctor's actions were judged at the standard of a qualified doctor. This is illustrated by the case of *Bolam v Friern Barnet Hospital Management Committee* (1957).

Case study

Bolam v Friern Barnet Hospital Management Committee (1957)

The claimant was suffering from a mental illness and the treatment at the time was to administer a type of electric shock (ECT). He signed a consent form but was not told of the risk of broken bones while receiving the shock and was not given relaxant drugs. While receiving the treatment, he suffered a broken pelvis.

There were two opinions within the medical profession for undertaking ECT. One opinion favoured the use of relaxant drugs in every case, while the other was that drugs should only be used if there was a reason to do so. There was no reason in *Bolam*'s case. It was decided that as the doctors had followed one of these courses of action, there had been no breach of the duty of care.

The principle from *Bolam*'s case, and which applies to all professionals, is to ask the following questions:
- Does the defendant's conduct fall below the standard of the ordinary, competent member of that profession?
- Is there a substantial body of opinion within the profession that would support the course of action taken by the defendant?

If the answer to the first question is 'No' and to the second 'Yes', then the defendant has not broken their duty of care.

In *Bolitho v City and Hackney Health Authority* (1997), the House of Lords suggested that a court should decide what standard of care applies in each case, rather than considering professional opinion as a whole.

The *Bolam* approach was altered by the Supreme Court decision in *Montgomery v Lanarkshire Health Board* (2015).

21.3.2 Risk factors

When the court decides whether there has been a breach of duty, it considers whether:
- the standard of care should be raised or lowered

Case study

Montgomery v Lanarkshire Health Board (2015)

The claimant gave birth to a son with cerebral palsy due to complications during delivery. She claimed damages against the hospital and the doctor responsible for her care during pregnancy and labour. Her appeal to the Supreme Court focused on the doctor's failure to disclose the risks and obtain her informed consent. The Court was invited to depart from precedent and reconsider the duty of a doctor towards a patient in relation to advice about treatment.

The Court decided that the doctor was under a duty to disclose the risk of a major obstetric emergency which involved considerable risk to the mother's health. The doctor would have been entitled to withhold information about the risk if it would have been harmful to the patient's health; however, this was not intended to enable doctors to prevent their patients taking informed decisions. The doctor should have explained, in this case, why a vaginal delivery was preferable to a caesarean, having taken care to ensure that the claimant understood the considerations for and against each option. As a result, patients should be treated, as far as possible, as adults who are capable of understanding that medical treatment is uncertain of success and may involve risk, accepting responsibility for taking risks affecting their own lives and living with the consequences of their choice.

- the reasonable person would have taken more or fewer risks in the same situation.

The following risk factors may be considered:
- Has the claimant any special characteristics?
- What was the size of the risk?
- Have all appropriate precautions been taken?
- Were the risks known about at the time of the accident?
- Is there a public benefit to taking the risk?

Special characteristics

This is shown in the case of *Paris v Stepney Borough Council* (1951).

The employers knew that the consequences of an injury to his good eye would be very serious. They should have taken greater care because of this and provided him with goggles, even though, at that time,

Case study

Paris v Stepney Borough Council (1951)

The claimant was known to be blind in one eye. He was given work to do by his employers which involved a small risk of injury to his eyes, but he was not given any protective goggles. While doing this work, his good eye was damaged by a small piece of metal and he was left totally blind. His employers were held to have broken their duty of care to him.

it was not thought necessary to provide goggles for other workers.

Also, the cost and effort of providing goggles was very small compared with the consequences of the risk.

The size of the risk

The principle that applies here is that the higher the risk of injury, the greater the precautions that need to be taken to prevent injury. Where a risk is small, the defendants will not be expected to take as great precautions. This is shown in *Bolton v Stone* (1951).

Case study

Bolton v Stone (1951)

A cricket ball hit the claimant in the street as she passed a cricket ground. Evidence showed that there was a 17-foot-high fence around the ground and the wicket was situated a long way from the fence. Also, balls had been hit out of the ground only six times in the previous thirty years.

It was decided that the cricket club had done everything it needed to do in view of the low risk, and it had not breached its duty to the claimant.

If there is a higher risk of injury, the standard of care is higher. This was shown by the case of *Haley v London Electricity Board* (1965).

Case study

Haley v London Electricity Board (1965)

Workers for the electricity board dug a trench for its cables and, following standard practice, put out warning signs but no barriers. The claimant, who was blind, fell into the trench and was injured. It was known that the road alongside the trench was used by a number of blind people. It was decided that greater precautions should have been taken and the Board had breached their duty of care.

Adequate precautions

The courts will consider the balance of the risk involved against the cost and effort of taking adequate precautions to eliminate the risk. A case to illustrate this is *Latimer v AEC Ltd* (1953).

Case study

Latimer v AEC Ltd (1953)

A factory was flooded and, as the floor was very slippery with a mixture of water and oil, the workers were evacuated. Sawdust was spread on the floor of the most used areas to minimise the risk of slipping. Workers were then required to go back. One worker slipped and was injured.

The court decided there was no breach of duty. The factory owners had taken all reasonable care and steps to reduce the risk of injury. There was no requirement on them to incur expense to eliminate every possible risk to their employees.

It is quite likely that if this situation occurred today, higher standards of health and safety would mean that the factory owners would have to do more than merely spread sawdust before allowing their workers back.

Also, if the risk had been much more serious, for example, if there was a risk of an explosion, then there would have been a higher standard of care on the owners. It would have been reasonable to expect them to close the factory until the problem had been dealt with.

Unknown risks

If the risk of harm is not known, there can be no breach. This is illustrated by the case of *Roe v Minister of Health* (1954).

Case study

Roe v Minister of Health (1954)

Anaesthetic was kept in glass tubes which were sterilised by a cleaning solution after each use. At the time, it was not know that invisible cracks could occur in the glass tubes which caused the anaesthetic to become contaminated by the cleaning solution. The claimant was paralysed when injected with some contaminated anaesthetic.

As the risk of contamination was not known at the time, there was no breach of duty.

Policy

If there is an emergency, greater risks can be taken and a lower standard of care can be accepted. This is consistent with the third part of establishing a duty of care (fair, just and reasonable).

Also, the courts take a realistic view of dealing with emergencies. They accept in hindsight the situation could have been dealt with differently but accept that speedy action was taken without the benefit of hindsight. This can be illustrated by the cases of *Watt v Hertfordshire County Council* (1954) and *Day v High Performance Sports* (2003).

Case studies

Watt v Hertfordshire County Council (1954)

The claimant was a firefighter. There had been a road accident a short distance from his fire station and the fire service was called to rescue a woman trapped underneath a lorry. A jack was needed to release the injured woman but the normal vehicle for carrying the jack was not available. A flatbed truck was found but there was no way to secure the jack on it. The claimant was injured when the jack slipped and fell on him as the lorry was on its way to the accident.

It was decided that the fire service had not breached its duty of care because greater risks could be taken in the emergency situation and the utility of saving a life outweighed the need to take precautions.

Day v High Performance Sports (2003)

The claimant was an experienced climber but fell from an indoor climbing wall and suffered serious injuries. She had to be rescued by the duty manager from a height of 9 metres when she became 'frozen' in her position. The way the manager rescued her was inappropriate, causing her fall.

It was decided that the manager and the centre had not breached their duty of care towards the claimant in view of the emergency and the need to rescue her.

Tip

When discussing breach of duty, start by explaining the reasonable person test and then deal with the relevant risk factors. Illustrate your answer by reference to relevant cases.

Person or risk factor	Case	Judgment
Professionals	*Bolam v Friern Barnet Hospital Management* (1957)	Judged according to the standards operating in the profession.
Medical treatment	*Montgomery v Lanarkshire Health Board* (2015)	Medical treatment involves risk. Patients should be treated as adults and be made aware of the risks. They should accept the consequences of their choice of treatment.
Learners	*Nettleship v Weston* (1971)	Judged according to the competent and experienced.
Children	*Mullin v Richards* (1998)	Judged according to a child of the same age.
Vulnerable victim	*Paris v Stepney Borough Council* (1951)	Are there any special characteristics of the victim to be taken into account?
Size of the risk	*Bolton v Stone* (1951) *Haley v LEB* (1965)	Greater care should be taken if there is a higher chance of injury.
Cost of taking precautions	*Latimer v AEC* (1954)	The risk involved should be balanced against the cost and effort of taking precautions.
Knowledge of the risk	*Roe v Minister of Health* (1954)	Was the risk known at the time?
Public benefit (utility)	*Watt v Hertfordshire C. C.* (1954) *Day v High Performance Sports* (2003)	Greater risks can be taken in emergencies.

Figure 21.4 Key cases: breach of duty

21.4 Damage

The third part of a negligence claim is for the claimant to prove that the damage suffered was caused by the breach of duty and that the loss or damage is not too remote. This is referred to as damage, and should be distinguished from damages, which is the payment of compensation.

Causation

- Factual causation is the idea that the breach of duty has caused the injury or damage being claimed.
- Legal causation is deciding whether the injury or damage suffered was reasonably foreseeable.

Both elements have to be proved for a negligence claim to succeed.

Key terms

Damage – the legal test that a claimant's loss was caused by a breach of a duty of care.
Causation – a link between the defendant's act or omission and the injury, loss or damage suffered by the claimant.

21.4.1 Factual causation

Factual causation is the starting point: if factual causation cannot be proved, there is no need to consider legal causation.

Factual causation is decided by the 'but for' test – but for the defendant's act or omission, the injury or damage would not have occurred. This is illustrated by the case of *Barnett v Chelsea and Kensington Hospital Management Committee* (1969).

Case study

Barnett v Chelsea and Kensington Hospital Management Committee (1969)

Three night-watchmen went to a hospital A & E department, complaining of sickness after drinking tea made by a fourth man. A nurse telephoned the duty doctor, who did not come to examine the men but, instead, recommended that they go home and see their own doctors. One of the men died a few hours later at home from poisoning by arsenic.

His widow sued the hospital, claiming that the doctor was negligent in not examining her husband and had caused his death. She was able to prove that the doctor owed her husband a duty of care and that he had breached the duty by not carrying out an examination. However, the evidence showed that by the time her husband had called at the hospital it was already too late to save his life, as there was so much arsenic in his system that he would have died, whatever treatment he received. This meant that his death was not caused by the doctor's breach of duty, and her claim failed.

21.4.2 Legal causation

Intervening events

In the same way as in criminal law, an intervening event can break the chain of causation. The principle to be applied is whether the injury or damage was a foreseeable consequence of the original negligent act or omission.

If there is a *novus actus interveniens*, there will be an intervening act to break the chain of causation. This intervening event can be:

- An act of the claimant: so in *McKew v Hollands* (1969), the claimant suffered a leg injury at work due to his employer's breach of duty. He tried to climb down a steep concrete staircase without a handrail, unaided. His leg gave way and he jumped ten steps to the bottom, breaking his leg, and was left with a permanent disability. The defendant accepted liability for the original injury but disputed liability for the further injuries. It was decided that climbing the stairs unaided was a *novus actus interveniens*. The defendant was not liable for the further injuries.
- An act of nature: so in *Carslogie Steamship Co. v Royal Norwegian Government* (1952), a ship (*H*) suffered damage in a collision with the *Carslogie*, which was solely to blame. Temporary repairs to *H* were carried out in England before it sailed to the USA for permanent repairs. During the crossing, the ship suffered further damage from a storm. As a result, it was out of action for longer, causing further financial loss. It was decided that the storm was a *novus actus interveniens* that broke the chain of causation and the owners of the *Carslogie* were not liable for the loss that arose from the storm damage.

- A third party, as in *Knightly v Johns* (1982): Johns drove negligently, resulting in a crash where his car overturned near the exit of a tunnel. Two police officers attended the scene but the senior officer forgot to close the tunnel. He ordered the other officer – the claimant – to ride his motorcycle down the one-way tunnel to do so but he was involved in a collision. It was held that the officer's order was a *novus actus interveniens* that would remove John's liability for the police officer's injuries. While it can be said that the police officers attending the tunnel for the crash was a foreseeable event, the negligent order to drive down a one-way tunnel into opposing traffic was not foreseeable. The test for causation is whether the damage is reasonably foreseeable and a 'natural and probable' cause of the defendant's action. In this scenario, the negligent order given by the officer could not be reasonably foreseen and it was a new intervening act that broke the chain of causation.

Remoteness of damage

The damage must not be too remote from the breach of duty by the defendant. The rule comes from an Australian case decided by the Privy Council: *Overseas Tankship (UK) v Morts Dock and Engineering Co. Ltd*, more commonly known as *The Wagon Mound* (1961).

Case study

The Wagon Mound (1961)

Fuel oil had been negligently spilled from the defendant's ship into Sydney harbour, which flowed towards the claimant's wharf, where welders were carrying out repairs to another ship. Two days later, the oil caught fire because of sparks from the welding. The fire spread to the wharf which burnt down.

It was decided that although damage done to the wharf by spilled oil was reasonably foreseeable, fire damage was not. This type of damage was too remote from the original negligent act of spilling the oil.

The test for remoteness of damage from this case is that the injury or damage must be reasonably foreseeable.

Key term

Reasonably foreseeable – loss, damage or injury which a reasonable person should predict or expect from his negligent act or omission.

A large tanker in dry dock

Type of injury to be foreseeable

The defendant will also be liable if the type of injury was reasonably foreseeable, even though the precise way in which it happened was not. This is illustrated by the case of *Bradford v Robinson Rentals* (1967).

Case study

Bradford v Robinson Rentals (1967)

The claimant was required by his employer to drive an old van from Exeter to Bedford, collect a new van and drive it back to Exeter. It was an extremely cold winter and neither van had a heater. He had to drive the whole return journey with the window open as the windscreen kept freezing over. The claimant suffered frostbite and was unable to work again.

It was decided that the employers were liable, even though the injuries suffered were very unusual. Some injury from the cold was reasonably foreseeable.

An example of when the type of injury was *not* reasonably foreseeable is the case of *Doughty v Turner Asbestos* (1964).

Case study

Doughty v Turner Asbestos (1964)

The claimant was injured when an asbestos lid was knocked into a vat of molten metal. Shortly afterwards a chemical reaction caused an explosion of the metal, which burnt the claimant. Scientific knowledge at the time could not have predicted the explosion and so the burn injuries were not reasonably foreseeable. It could be seen that knocking something into the molten metal might cause a splash, but the claimant's injuries were caused by something different.

Take your victim as you find him

This rule means that the defendant must take their victim as they find them. If the type of injury or damage is reasonably foreseeable, but it is much more serious because the claimant had a pre-existing condition, then the defendant is liable for all the subsequent consequences. In negligence this is known as 'the eggshell skull' rule.

Link

A similar rule operates in criminal law where it is known as the 'thin skull' rule. See Chapter 6, section 6.1.3 for an explanation.

The operation of this rule is illustrated in the case of *Smith v Leech Brain and Co.* (1962).

Case study

Smith v Leech Brain and Co. (1962)

Due to the defendant's negligence, a man working in a factory was burnt on the lip by molten metal. The man had an existing pre-cancerous condition. The burn eventually brought about the onset of full cancer, from which he died. His widow claimed against the defendants.

It was decided that as the burn was reasonably foreseeable, and because of the eggshell skull rule, the defendants were liable for the man's death.

Principle	Case	Judgment
Factual causation	*Barnett v Chelsea and Kensington Hospital Management Committee* (1969)	'But for' test – but for defendant's act or omission, the injury would not have happened.
Novus actus interveniens	*McKew v Hollands* (1969) *Carslogie Steamship Co. v Royal Norwegian Government* (1952) *Knightly v Johns* (1982)	An intervening event – of the claimant, a natural event or action of a third party will break the chain of causation.
Legal causation: Is the loss or damage too remote or reasonably foreseeable?		
Remoteness of damage	*The Wagon Mound* (1961)	Injury or damage can be claimed if reasonably foreseeable.
Foreseeability	*Hughes v Lord Advocate* (1963) *Bradford v Robinson Rentals* (1967) *Doughty v Turner Asbestos* (1964)	Consequence foreseeable even if exact cause of injury not foreseeable. Consequence foreseeable, even if more severe. Consequence not known so injury not foreseeable.
Eggshell skull/ take your victim as you find him	*Smith v Leech Brain and Co.* (1962)	Defendant liable for all consequences of negligence.

Figure 21.5 Key cases: causation and remoteness of damage

Activities

1   Because of his fault, Tariq's van and Rhona's car were involved in an accident which resulted in Rhona suffering injuries that have affected her mobility. She is no longer able to work as a cycle courier or play sport. Consider whether Tariq is liable for all of Rhona's injuries.

2   Polish Limited had developed a new floor polish that they were testing. Jade, a secretary of the company, did not know about the test and slipped and fell on the highly polished surface of the test area and fell down the stairs, breaking her leg. She was admitted to hospital where she developed a rare medical condition that was missed by Dr Hari, an inexperienced junior doctor. As a result, her leg had to be amputated. Consider whether Polish Limited would be liable for the injury caused to Jade.

3   William was sorting out some files which were on a high shelf next to the open window in his office. As he could not reach the files easily, he used a pole to push them to the end of the shelf and then tried to catch them as they fell. William failed to catch a heavy file, which fell out of the window onto Robyn who was sitting outside in her car. The car's sunroof shattered and Robyn suffered a broken collarbone. Because of the injury, she was unable to work as a freelance hairdresser and had to cancel a planned skiing holiday. Consider whether William would be liable for all the injuries and damage.

Tip

'Take your victim as you find them' applies in both negligence and in criminal law. When referring to this principle in tort law, you refer to it as the 'eggshell skull' rule.

Quick questions

1   Define the tort of negligence.
2   What is the purpose of finding the existence of a duty of care?
3   What test should a judge use to decide if there is a duty of care in a novel situation?
4   Who or what is a reasonable person in breach of duty?
5   Explain legal causation and factual causation.

Summary

- Negligence is where the defendant's act or omission causes loss or damage to the claimant.
- The defendant will have been at fault.
- The claimant will have to prove the negligence on the balance of probabilities.
- Negligence requires proof of a duty of care, breach of that duty and loss or damage caused by it.
- Duty of care shows a legal relationship between the parties.
- The *Caparo* three-stage test for a duty of care requires the harm to be reasonably foreseeable, proximity of relationship and it being fair, just and reasonable to impose a duty of care. This test is used for new categories of claim.
- Following *Robinson*, there is no single definitive test of when a duty is imposed; existing precedent should be followed or there should be an incremental development of the law. The *Caparo* three-stage test should be used for novel situations.
- Breach of duty is an objective test of what the reasonable person would have done or not done:
  - Professionals are judged at the standard of the reasonable professional.
  - Learners are judged at the standard of the competent and experienced.
  - Children are judged according to children of the same age.
- There are a number of risk factors to be taken into account such as:
  - The special situation of the claimant.
  - The size of the risk.
  - If adequate precautions have been taken.
  - Was the risk known at the time?
  - Are there policy reasons in place?
- Damage – it has to be shown that the loss or damage was caused by the breach of duty – both factual and legal causation have to be proved.
- Factual causation uses the 'but for' test to establish a chain of events leading to the loss or damage.
- A *novus actus interveniens* will break the chain of causation.
- Legal causation asks if the loss or damage is too remote.
- You must take your victim as you find them.

Chapter 22 Occupiers' liability

Introduction

The occupier of a property is responsible for the safety of visitors and can be legally responsible if a lawful visitor suffers injury. The basic common duty of care is owed to adult visitors but different duties are owed to children and workmen. If the visitor is a trespasser, a different duty of care is owed.

Occupiers' liability is a branch of negligence, created by statute. There are two separate statutes:

1 The Occupiers' Liability Act 1957: an occupier of premises owes a duty of care to lawful visitors, and if that duty is breached and the visitor is injured, the visitor is entitled to receive compensation.

2 The Occupiers' Liability Act 1984: a trespasser who is injured on the occupier's property is also owed a duty but to a lower standard.

The main remedy for a successful claim of occupiers' liability is damages for the injuries or property damage suffered.

22.1 Liability in respect of lawful visitors (Occupiers' Liability Act 1957)

22.1.1 Definition of a lawful visitor

Occupiers

Potential defendants are the same under either Act: occupiers of premises who may be, but do not have to be, the owner or tenant of the premises. There is in fact no statutory definition of 'occupier'. The test for deciding whether a person is the occupier is found in case law.

In practice, a decision of who is in control of premises may be influenced by whose insurance policy covers the premises and will meet a claim. However, sometimes the courts will find that no one is in control of the premises, leaving the injured visitor with no claim.

Case studies

Wheat v E Lacon & Co. Ltd (1966)

The manager of a pub was given the right to rent out rooms in his private area. He had no ownership rights in the premises. A paying guest fell on an unlit staircase and died. It was decided that both the manager and his employers could be liable, so there can be more than one occupier of premises.

Harris v Birkenhead Corporation (1976)

A local council had served a compulsory purchase notice on a house but had not taken possession or made it secure. A four-year-old boy was injured in the empty house. It was decided that the council were occupiers as they were effectively in control of the premises.

Bailey v Armes (1999)

The defendants lived in a flat above a supermarket. They allowed their son to play on the flat roof above the flat but forbade him to take anyone else there. The supermarket knew nothing of this use. The boy took a friend with him and he was injured when he fell from the roof. The Court of Appeal decided that neither the supermarket nor the defendants were liable as neither had sufficient control over the roof.

Premises

There is no full statutory definition of 'premises' except in s 1(3)(a) of the 1957 Act, where there is reference to a person having occupation or control of any 'fixed or moveable structure, including any vessel, vehicle and aircraft'. Besides the obvious such as houses, offices, buildings and land, 'premises' has also been held to include:

- a ship in dry dock
- a vehicle
- a lift
- a ladder.

A visitor

Lawful adult visitors include:

- Invitees – persons who have been invited to enter premises and who have express permission to be there.
- Licensees – persons who have express or implied permission to be on the premises for a particular period and purpose. In *Lowery v Walker* (1911), in a negligence case, a licence to be on the land was implied from repeated use by trespass which the defendant had not stopped.
- Those with contractual permission to be on the premises – for example, a person who has bought an entry ticket for an event.
- Those given a statutory right of entry, such as meter readers or a police constable exercising a warrant.

If a lawful visitor exceeds the permission they have for being on the premises, they may become a trespasser. For example, if a visitor is invited to use a staircase, they are not invited to slide down the bannister rail as quoted in *The Calgarth* (1927).

Children

Children are not defined in the Act, but the age of the child affects how the standard of care to be taken by the occupier will be assessed.

Workers

Again, these are not defined by the Act, but it will have to be decided whether the worker is injured by something that relates to the work, or by something else.

22.1.2 The duty owed to a lawful visitor and when that duty is breached

Adults

An adult visitor lawfully on premises is owed a common duty of care. According to s 2(2), this means that the occupier should:

> take such care as in all the circumstances . . . is reasonable to see that the visitor will be reasonably safe in using the premises for the purpose for which he is invited . . . to be there.

The occupier does not have to make the visitor completely safe in the premises – only to do what is reasonable.

Case study

Laverton v Kiapasha Takeaway Supreme (2002)

The defendants owned a small takeaway food shop. They had fitted slip-resistant floor tiles and used a mop and bucket to clean the floor when it had been raining. The claimant went into the crowded shop when it was raining. She slipped and broke her ankle. The Court of Appeal decided that the shop owners had taken reasonable care to ensure their customers were safe – they did not have to make the premises completely safe and were not liable.

Activity

Consider which of the following injured adults can be lawful visitors for the purposes of the Occupiers' Liability Act 1957, and why.

1 Trevor is a milkman delivering milk to Archie's front door when he trips on a protruding stone on the pathway.
2 Kurt is a relief milkman who cuts across the front garden of Archie's house to deliver to the neighbour's house. He trips and falls into a small pond.
3 Craig is making door-to-door deliveries of flyers for a pizza restaurant when he is hit by a falling roof tile.
4 Gordon has a ticket for a football match. He is injured when the turnstile traps him at the entrance.
5 Hannah is attacked and injured by a cow when crossing Farmer Giles' field using a well-worn public footpath.
6 Aaron, an electrician, is injured by a falling cupboard when he is fitting new wall lights at Jada's house.
7 Tariq, a police officer, is set upon by Brian's dog when he calls at the house to make routine enquiries about recent burglaries.

The Court commented in this case that the safety of visitors to premises was not guaranteed, and in this case that was not feasible as the shop had taken precautions and customers could be safe if they took reasonable care.

Case study

Dean and Chapter of Rochester Cathedral v Debell (2016)

The claimant was injured when he tripped and fell over a small piece of concrete protruding about two inches from the base of a traffic bollard in the precincts of a cathedral. The Court of Appeal decided that:

- Tripping, slipping and falling are everyday occurrences. The obligation on an occupier is to make premises reasonably safe for visitors, not to guarantee their safety.
- A visitor will be reasonably safe even if there may be visible minor defects which carry a foreseeable risk of causing an accident and injury.

The judgments in both these cases emphasise that the common duty of care imposes a duty on the occupier to keep the visitor reasonably safe, not necessarily to maintain completely safe premises.

If these cases had been decided in favour of the visitors, it could have opened the floodgates to a tide of claims against occupiers, and created a very high level of responsibility for the safety of visitors.

The common duty of care, however, does not extend to liability for pure accidents. A duty of care for a specific risk cannot last indefinitely, where there could be other causes of the damage.

Case study

Cole v Davies-Gilbert, The Royal British Legion and others (2007)

The claimant was injured when she trapped her foot in a hole on a village green where a maypole had been erected in the past. She claimed that the British Legion had failed to properly fill in the hole after the flagpole had been removed. The Court of Appeal held that as her injury had occurred nearly two years after the flagpole had been removed, the duty on the British Legion could not last that long. The incident was a pure accident and not claimable. As such, the claimant had not proved her case.

Look online

Look up other reported claims made by visitors injured on the land of another.

What is the general approach of the courts to such claims?

Children

The occupier will owe children coming onto the premises the common duty of care, but there is an additional special duty owed to child visitors. Under s 2(3)(a) of the Occupiers' Liability Act 1957, the occupier

> " must be prepared for children to be less careful than adults [and, as a result] the premises must be reasonably safe for a child of that age. "

So for children, the standard of care is measured subjectively, according to the age of the child. The younger the child, the greater the care that the occupier must take to make sure the child is not injured. The reasoning is logical: what may not pose a threat to an adult may be very dangerous to a child.

The occupier should guard against any kind of 'allurement' or attraction which places a child visitor at risk of harm.

Key term

Allurement – something on the premises that may be attractive to children and which may cause them injury.

Case study

Glasgow Corporation v Taylor (1922)

A seven-year-old child died from eating poisonous berries picked from a shrub in a public park. The shrub was not fenced off. The Council were liable as they were aware of the danger and the berries amounted to an allurement to young children.

Where very young children are injured, the courts are reluctant to find the occupier liable, as the child should be under the supervision of a parent or other adult.

Case study

Phipps v Rochester Corporation (1955)

A five-year-old child was playing on open ground owned by the Council with his seven-year-old sister. He fell down an open trench and was injured. The Council was not liable as the court decided the occupier is entitled to expect that parents will not allow their young children to go to places that are potentially unsafe.

A difficulty here is that there is no age limit set as to when this rule applies. It can be assumed that the rule applies to children up to primary school age, but probably does not apply to children of secondary school age.

If an allurement exists, there will be no liability on the occupier if the damage or injury suffered is not foreseeable.

Case study

Jolley v London Borough of Sutton (2000)

The Council failed to move an abandoned boat that had been on its land for two years. Children regularly played on and in the boat, which was a potential danger. When two 14-year-old boys jacked the boat up, it fell on one of them, causing serious injuries.

The House of Lords decided the Council were liable as it was foreseeable that children would play on an abandoned boat. It was not necessary for the Council to foresee exactly what children would do in their play. Children often find ways of putting themselves in danger, which needs to be taken into account by an occupier when considering how to keep them safe.

Workers

The occupier owes a common duty of care to workers coming on the premises to carry out repairs to the property or anything on it.

However, by s 2(3)(b) of the 1957 Act, an occupier can expect that a tradesperson 'in the exercise of their calling' (while they carry out their work) will:

> appreciate and guard against any special risks ordinarily incident to it so far as the occupier leaves him free to do so.

This means that an occupier will not be liable where workers do not guard against risks which they should know about, or be expected to know about.

Case study

Roles v Nathan (1963)

Two chimney sweeps died after inhaling carbon monoxide fumes while cleaning the chimney of a coke-fired boiler. They had been warned of the danger. The occupiers were not liable as they could expect the chimney sweeps to be aware of the potential danger and take necessary precautions.

This defence to an occupier only applies where the worker is injured by something related to their work. If the worker is injured by something different, the occupier will still owe the common duty of care.

In *Ogwo v Taylor* (1987), it was held that a duty could be owed to a rescuer (in this case a firefighter) if they are injured by something incidental to the rescue.

Section 2(5) provides that the common duty of care does not impose on an occupier any obligation to a visitor in respect of risks willingly accepted as his by the visitor.

Work of independent contractors

If a lawful visitor is injured by the negligent work of a workman engaged by the occupier, the occupier may have a defence and be able to pass the claim on to the workman. This is set out in s 2(4)(b) of the 1957 Act.

Three requirements apply, and all have to be satisfied.

1 It must be reasonable for the occupier to have given the work to the independent contractor. The more complicated and specialist the work, the more likely it will be for the occupier to have properly given the work to a specialist.

Case study

Hazeldine v Daw & Son Ltd (1941)

The claimant was injured when a lift plunged to the bottom of a shaft. The occupier was not liable for the negligent repair or maintenance of the lift as this is highly specialist work and it was reasonable to give this work to a specialist firm.

2   The contractor who is hired must be competent to carry out the task. The occupier should check the contractor's references and make sure that they carry insurance. Not being insured could indicate that the contractor is not competent.

Case study

Bottomley v Todmorden Cricket Club (2003)

The cricket club hired a stunt team to carry out a 'firework display'. The team chose to use ordinary gunpowder, petrol and propane gas rather than traditional fireworks. The claimant, an unpaid amateur with no experience of pyrotechnics, was used for the stunt. The claimant was burnt and broke an arm when the stunt went wrong. The stunt team had no insurance cover.

The cricket club was found liable as it had failed to exercise reasonable care in choosing safe and competent contractors.

3   The occupier must check the work has been properly done. The more complicated and technical the work, and the less expert the occupier, the more likely that the occupier will need to employ an expert such as an architect or surveyor.

Case study

Woodward v Mayor of Hastings (1945)

A child was injured on school steps that were left icy after snow had been cleared from them. The occupiers were liable as they had failed to take reasonable steps to ensure the work had been properly done, and the danger should have been obvious to them.

If all these conditions are satisfied:
- the occupier will have a defence to a claim
- the injured claimant will have to claim directly against the contractor.

In *Ferguson v Welsh* (1987), it was held by the House of Lords that an occupier would not be liable for the unsafe system of work of a sub-contractor, since he could not reasonably be expected to supervise it.

22.1.3 Defences for the occupier by claims from lawful visitors

Volenti (consent)

This complete defence is also set out in more detail in Chapter 25. It applies to occupiers' liability in the same way as for negligence.

If it is successfully argued, the defendant will not be liable to pay damages to the claimant, as the claimant has freely accepted to run the risk of injury while on the occupier's premises.

Contributory negligence

This partial defence has been set out in more detail in Chapter 25. It applies to occupiers' liability in the same way as claims based on negligence. It is set out in the Law Reform (Contributory Negligence) Act 1945.

The occupier will argue that the claimant is partly responsible for the injuries they have suffered while on the occupier's premises. If it is successfully argued, the amount of compensation will be reduced by an appropriate amount.

Exclusion clauses

By s 2(1) of the 1957 Act, an occupier is able:

> to restrict, modify or exclude his duty by agreement or otherwise.

This means that the occupier will, in an oral or written warning, be able to limit or exclude completely their liability for any injury caused to the visitor. This is the case for residential occupiers, though whether an exclusion clause would work against a child visitor may depend on the child's age and ability to understand the effect of the exclusion.

In addition, s 65 Consumer Rights Act 2015 provides that:

> a trader cannot by a consumer contract or a consumer notice exclude or restrict liability for death or personal injury resulting from negligence.

This means that if there are such clauses in a warning notice, in say a shop, they are ineffective and cannot operate as a defence to an occupier if a consumer is injured on the premises.

Warning notices

If there is a notice warning of a danger, this can be a complete defence for the occupier. A warning can be oral or written. By s 2(4)(a) of the 1957 Act, a warning is ineffective unless:

> in all the circumstances it was enough to enable the visitor to be reasonably safe.

What amounts to a sufficient warning will be a question of fact in each case, and will be decided by the judge on the evidence.

If the premises are extremely dangerous then according to *Rae v Mars (UK) Ltd* (1990), the visitor should be given specific notice of the danger. However, if the danger is obvious, and the visitor is able to appreciate it, no additional warning is necessary.

Case studies

Staples v West Dorset District Council (1995)

The claimant fractured his hip when he fell off a harbour wall that was covered in algae and slippery when wet. He argued there were no warning signs of the danger.

However, the court ruled that the dangers of slipping on wet algae on a sloping harbour wall were obvious and known to the claimant; therefore there was no duty to warn him.

Darby v National Trust (2001)

The claimant's husband drowned in a pond owned by the National Trust (NT). It was common for visitors to paddle and swim in the pond during summer months. Mr Darby had been paddling then swam to the middle, but got into difficulty and drowned. The claimant argued that because of NT's inactivity in preventing swimmers using the pond, she and her husband had assumed the pond was safe for swimming.

The Court of Appeal decided that the risk to swimmers was obvious and there was no duty on NT to warn of an obvious risk.

Activity

Look at the signs in Figure 22.1. Is either of these warning notices an effective defence for:

- an occupier of a private house
- a supermarket in their car park
- a department store by their escalator?

Figure 22.1 Warning notices

22.1.4 Remedies

If a claimant is successful, the court can award damages for personal injury and for damaged property (such as clothes). The standard principles for the award of damages as set out in Chapter 26 will apply.

22.2 Liability in respect of trespassers (Occupiers' Liability Act 1984)

22.2.1 Definition of a trespasser

By s 1(3) of the 1984 Act:

> An occupier of premises owes a duty to another (not being his visitor).

So, a trespasser is:

- a person who has no permission to be on the occupier's premises, or
- a lawful visitor who has gone beyond their permission to be on the premises – they have outstayed their welcome, they have been told to leave or have gone into an area where they are not supposed to be. For example, in *Tomlinson v Congleton Borough Council* (2003), when he paddled in the lake he was a lawful visitor, but when he dived in and started swimming he became a trespasser.

Case	Facts	Legal principle
Wheat v Lacon (1966)	Visitor fell down stairs and died	The occupier is the person with control of the premises. There can be more than one occupier with control.
Laverton v Kiapasha Takeaway Supreme (2002)	Customer fell and injured on wet floor in shop	The premises do not have to be completely safe. The occupier has to make the premises reasonably safe for visitors.
Glasgow Corporation v Taylor (1922)	Child poisoned by berries growing on bush in park	The occupier has to protect child visitors from allurements.
Phipps v Rochester Corporation (19550	Young child injured when falling into trench on building site	The occupier can expect very young children to be supervised by parents.
Jolley v London Borough of Sutton (2000)	Teenager injured playing on abandoned boat on Council's land	Occupier is liable for injuries suffered by children that are reasonably foreseeable.
Roles v Nathan (1963)	Chimney sweeps killed when working in industrial chimney	The occupier can expect workmen to appreciate and guard against risks that are incidental to their work.
Hazeldine v Daw & Son Ltd (1941)	Claimant injured when lift fell to foot of shaft due to faulty maintenance or repair	It was reasonable for the lift repair to be done by a specialist firm – occupier not liable.
Darby v National Trust (2001)	Claimant's husband drowned in pond	Occupier not liable for death or injury caused by obvious risk.

Figure 22.2 Key cases: occupiers' liability to lawful visitors

22.2.2 The duty owed to a trespasser and when that duty is breached

By s 1(1)(a) of the 1984 Act, a duty applies towards people other than lawful visitors (who are covered by the 1957 Act) for:

> injury on the premises by reason of any danger due to the state of the premises or things done or omitted to be done on them.

The 1984 Act provides compensation for personal injuries only. Damage to property is not covered, reflecting the view that trespassers deserve less protection than lawful visitors.

The occupier will only owe a duty under s 1(3) if:

1 They are aware of the danger or have reasonable grounds to believe it exists.
2 They know, or have reasonable grounds to believe, that the other person is in the vicinity of (near to) the danger concerned, or that they might come into the vicinity of the danger (in either case, whether or not the other has lawful authority for being in the vicinity of the danger). In *Swain v Natui Ram Puri* (1996), a nine-year-old boy was injured when he climbed onto the occupier's roof and was injured when he fell. It was held that the occupier did not have reasonable grounds to believe, or actual knowledge that the child could, or

might, enter the vicinity of the danger. 'Reasonable grounds to believe' does NOT mean 'ought to have been aware'. The child's claim failed.

And

3 They may be expected to protect the other person against the risk. In *Tomlinson v Congleton Borough Council* (2003), it was said that as the claimant had freely accepted the risk of injury while swimming, the Council were not expected to protect him. The duty owed under s 1(4) is to:

> take such care as is reasonable in the circumstances to see that he [the trespasser] is not injured by reason of the danger.

The 'danger' referred to in these sections is the thing which causes injury, or area of land or part of building on which the trespasser is injured. The Act is not concerned with risks due to anything other than the danger.

The standard of care is objective. What is required of the occupier depends on the circumstances of each case. The greater the degree of risk, the more precautions the occupier will have to take. Factors to be taken into account include the:

- nature of the premises
- degree of danger
- practicality of taking precautions
- age of the trespasser.

These two provisions appear to give trespassers a right to claim compensation when they have been injured while trespassing. However, a number of court decisions have restricted when an occupier owes a duty to trespassers and, if a duty is owed, whether the occupier is liable.

Cases involving adult trespassers

Under the 1984 Act, the courts have introduced the concept of obvious dangers, especially for adult trespassers. The occupier will not be liable if the trespasser is injured by an obvious danger.

Case study

Ratcliff v McConnell (1999)

A 19-year-old student climbed the fence of his college's open-air swimming pool at night. He dived into the pool, hit his head on the bottom and was seriously injured.

The Court of Appeal decided that an occupier was not required to warn adult trespassers of the risk of injury arising from obvious dangers. In this case, there was no hidden danger as it is well known that swimming pools vary in depth, and diving without checking the depth is dangerous.

The time of day and the time of year when the accident happened can be relevant for deciding whether the occupier owes a duty of care.

Case study

Donoghue v Folkestone Properties (2003)

The claimant was injured when he trespassed onto a slipway at a harbour. He dived into the sea and hit his head on a grid pile used for mooring boats, suffering serious injuries. The pile would have been visible at low tide. The incident took place in the middle of winter about midnight.

It was held that the occupier did not owe the claimant a duty of care under the 1984 Act as they could not expect a trespasser would be present, or jump into the harbour, at that time of day or year.

An occupier does not have to spend lots of money in making premises safe from obvious dangers.

Case study

Tomlinson v Congleton Borough Council (2003)

The council owned a park which included a lake. Warning signs were posted prohibiting swimming and diving but the Council knew these were generally ignored. They decided to make the lake inaccessible to the public but the work was delayed due to lack of funds. The claimant, aged 18, swam in the lake, struck his head on the sandy bottom and suffered paralysis as a result of a severe spinal injury. His claim for compensation failed in the House of Lords for three main reasons:

1. In order to succeed under the 1984 Act, there had to be a danger due to the state of the premises, or things done, or omitted to be done. In this case, the danger was due to the claimant swimming, not the state of the premises.
2. Trespassers had to take some responsibility for their actions.
3. It was not reasonable for the Council to spend a lot of money preventing visitors suffering injury by an obvious danger. In this case, the Council would not have breached their duty even if the claimant was a lawful visitor.

The occupier will not be liable if they had no reason to suspect the presence of a trespasser.

Case study

Higgs v Foster (2004)

A police officer investigating a crime entered the occupier's premises in order to carry out surveillance. He fell into an uncovered inspection pit, suffering such severe injuries that he had to retire from the force. He was judged to be a trespasser.

The occupiers were not liable as, although they knew the pit was a potential danger, they could not have anticipated the officer's presence on the premises, or in the vicinity of it.

The occupier will not be liable if they were not aware of the danger, or had no reason to suspect the danger existed.

Warning sign at a lake in Weston-super-Mare

Rhind v Astbury Water Park (2004)

The claimant ignored a notice stating, 'Private Property: Strictly no swimming' when he jumped into a lake and was injured by objects below the surface. The occupiers did not know of submerged fibreglass containers on the bottom of the lake.

There is no obligation on the occupier under s 1(3)(a) to check for hidden dangers if, as in this case, swimming is prohibited. This is different from a duty under the 1957 Act where the occupier should ensure that the visitor will be reasonably safe.

By s 1(8) the occupier will not be liable for any property damage, for example, clothes, suffered by the trespasser.

Warnings

Section 1(5) provides that the occupier can discharge his duty to the trespasser by giving a warning of the danger, or in some way discouraging the taking of the risk. In *Westwood v The Post Office* (1973), in an action under a different Act, an adult employee of the Post Office was injured when he entered an unlocked room which had a warning of danger on the outside. The Post Office was not liable as the notice was sufficient warning to an adult.

Whether a warning will be a sufficient defence against a child trespasser may depend on the child's age and understanding.

Warning sign on a construction site

Activity

Look at the warning sign in the photograph above. Do you think this will be an effective defence for an occupier against:

1   An adult trespasser?
2   A ten-year-old child trespasser?

Cases involving child trespassers

The same statutory rules and judges' approach apply to child visitors as for adult visitors.

Look online

Read a detailed report of *Keown v Coventry Health Care Trust* (2006) at www.birminghampost.co.uk/news/local-news/sex-beast-told-brain-damage-3986526

Case studies

Keown v Coventry Healthcare NHS Trust (2006)

An 11-year-old boy fell from a fire escape on the exterior of a hospital when he was showing off to his friends. The Court of Appeal held that as he appreciated the danger, it was not the state of the premises that was the problem, it was what the boy was doing on it. The hospital was not liable as there was no danger due to the state of the premises (the fire escape).

Baldaccino v West Wittering (2008)

On a summer's day, a 14-year-old boy climbed a navigational beacon sited off a beach as the tide was ebbing. He dived off the beacon, suffering neck injuries and tetraplegia. He was a lawful visitor to the beach, but a trespasser to the beacon. His claim failed as there was no duty on the occupiers to warn against obvious dangers, and the injuries did not result from the state of the premises.

22.2.3 Defences to claims by trespassers

Consent (also known as *volenti*)

This complete defence is set out in more detail in Chapter 25. It also applies to occupiers' liability to trespassers in the same way as claims made by lawful visitors.

If it is successfully argued, the defendant will not be liable to pay damages to the claimant as the claimant has freely accepted to run the risk of injury while on the occupier's premises. This defence is allowed by s 1(6) of the 1984 Act, if the trespasser appreciates the nature and degree of the risk, more than just its existence.

Contributory negligence

This partial defence is explained in more detail in Chapter 25. It applies to occupiers' liability to trespassers in the same way as claims made by lawful visitors.

The occupier will argue that the trespasser is partly responsible for the injuries they have suffered while on the occupier's premises. If it is successfully argued, the amount of compensation will be reduced by an appropriate amount.

Tip

You must be able to recognise whether the visitor is a lawful visitor or a trespasser and apply the correct rules to consider a possible claim.
Remember that a lawful visitor can become a trespasser if they exceed permission to be on the premises or enter a prohibited area.

Quick questions

1 Describe the statutory duty owed to lawful visitors.
2 Explain who is an 'occupier' of premises.
3 Describe how an occupier can avoid liability if they employ an independent contractor to do work on their premises.
4 Describe when a duty of care is owed to a trespasser.
5 Explain why a trespasser can make a claim for personal injury only.

Case	Facts	Legal principle
Ratcliff v McConnell (1999)	Trespasser seriously injured diving into swimming pool at night	Occupier does not have to warn adult trespassers of risk of injury against obvious dangers.
Donoghue v Folkestone Properties (2003)	Trespasser seriously injured by diving into harbour at night in winter	Occupier does not have to warn trespasser against obvious risks if the trespasser enters at unforeseeable time of day or year.
Tomlinson v Congleton Borough Council (2003)	Trespasser injured swimming in lake	Occupier does not have to spend lots of money making premises safe from obvious dangers.
Higgs v Foster (2004)	Police officer fell into inspection pit	Occupier does not owe a duty to trespasser he or she does not expect to enter premises.
Rhind v Astbury Water Park (2004)	Trespasser injured by submerged objects in lake	Occupier does not owe a duty if he or she is unaware of the danger.
Keown v Coventry Healthcare NHS Trust (2006)	Boy injured when falling off fire escape	Occupier not liable to child trespasser if there is no danger from the state of the premises.

Figure 22.3 Key cases: occupiers' liability to trespassers

Summary

1957 Occupiers' Liability Act

- The occupier of premises owes a lawful visitor the common duty of care.
- An occupier can be the owner or tenant of premises or someone with control over the premises.
- Premises include any land, buildings or some form of moveable structure.
- Lawful visitors are those with express or implied permission to be on the land. If a lawful visitor exceeds the permission to be on the land, they can become a trespasser.
- The common duty of care requires the occupier to do everything reasonable to ensure the visitor will be reasonably safe – the premises do not have to be made completely safe.
- Children are owed a higher duty – for the premises to be reasonably safe for a child of that age. Special care must be taken if there are allurements on the premises. The occupier can expect parents or another adult to take care of very young children. Any injury to a child visitor has to be reasonably foreseeable.
- A worker is owed the common duty of care but the occupier can expect the worker to guard against risks incidental to the work.
- If a visitor is injured by the work of an independent contractor, the liability can be passed on if it was reasonable to give the work to the contractor, it was checked that the contractor was competent and the work was inspected.
- The occupier can use defences such as the consent of the visitor to suffer the injury, contributory negligence of the visitor, an exclusion clause in any contract or any warning notice.
- A successful claimant can claim damages for personal injury and damage to property.

1984 Occupiers' Liability Act

- A trespasser is someone without permission, express or implied, to be on the premises.
- An occupier owes a trespasser a duty not to cause injury by reason of a danger.
- A duty is owed if the occupier is aware of a danger, the trespasser is known to be in the vicinity of the danger and where they may be expected to offer the trespasser some protection against the danger.
- It is an objective test, taking into account the premises, the danger, the cost of taking precautions and the age of the trespasser.
- The occupier will not be liable where the danger is not known, for obvious dangers, to make the premises completely safe, or to spend money making the premises safe from obvious dangers.
- The occupier will not be liable if a warning of the danger is given.
- Defences for the occupier are the consent of the trespassers and their contributory negligence.
- If successful, the trespasser can only claim damages for personal injury.

Chapter 23 Torts connected to land

Introduction

Although the owner of a property is, in theory, allowed to do what they want in their own property, there are limits. If a nuisance is caused to an adjoining owner, action can be taken to stop or limit the offending action. If non-naturally occurring material is stored on land which then escapes and causes damage to neighbouring land, then compensation can be claimed for repairing the damage.

23.1 Private nuisance

23.1.1 Basic elements of private nuisance

Private nuisance concerns neighbours and the competing claims of people to do as they wish on their own land.

It is not unreasonable to expect to be able to behave as you like on your own land. Problems only arise when this behaviour affects a neighbour's ability to enjoy their land, and when the use is termed 'unreasonable' and amounts to a nuisance. What is reasonable depends not so much on the defendant's actions, but whether the interference caused by that action is sufficient to give rise to a legal action.

Usually, but not always, unreasonable behaviour involves adjoining properties.

The usual definition of private nuisance is that it is:

> an unlawful interference with a person's use or enjoyment of land or some right over, or in connection with it.

In most cases the interference will be indirect, because any interference with use or enjoyment is likely to be caused by noise, smell or smoke. However, an action for nuisance by direct interference would be possible if, for example, the roots of trees encroached from one property into the neighbouring property, perhaps causing damage to foundations.

23.1.2 Who can claim?

Nuisance involves the competing rights of neighbours to use their land how they wish, so the basic rule is that anyone who has the use or enjoyment of land, and is affected by an interference, may claim.

The claimant must have an interest in the land. This will include being an owner or a tenant but not a member of the owner's family, such as a child or lodger, who has no legal interest in the property. This was confirmed in *Hunter v Canary Wharf* (1997).

Case study

Hunter v Canary Wharf Ltd (1997)

The claimants were a number of people living in the Docklands area of East London when the Canary Wharf office tower was being built. They claimed that the building affected their television reception.

The House of Lords decided that:

- This recreational facility was not sufficient to amount to a private nuisance – partly because other forms of reception, such as cable and satellite, were available.
- Only those claimants with an interest in land, and not members of families, were able to bring a claim.

23.1.3 What amounts to a nuisance?

The claimant will have to show:

> an unlawful interference with a person's use or enjoyment of land or some right over, or in connection with it.

In most cases the interference will be because of an indirect interference.

Mere interference on its own is not enough for a claim. The claimant must prove that the defendant's activity amounts to an 'unlawful' use of land. 'Unlawful' here does not mean illegal, but that the court accepts that the defendant's use of land is unreasonable in the way that it affects the claimant.

The proper question for the court is: in all of the circumstances, is it reasonable for the claimant to have to suffer the particular interference? There is a certain amount of fault involved by the defendant not having regard for their neighbour. However, fault, in the sense of how and why the interference occurred, does not have to be proved.

A variety of activities have been held to amount to private nuisance, including:
- fumes drifting over neighbouring land
- smell from farm animals or from a fish and chip shop, as in *Adams v Ursell* (1913)
- noise – from a children's playground, due to gunfire, and from a speedway and motor racing circuit, as in *Coventry v Lawrence* (2015)
- vibrations from industrial machinery
- hot air rising into other premises
- oily smuts from chimneys, as in *Halsey v Esso Petroleum* (1961)
- fire
- cricket balls being hit into a garden, as in *Miller v Jackson* (1977)
- known risk of flooding as in *Sedleigh-Denfield v O'Callaghan* (1940), below
- slippage of earth as in *Leakey v National Trust* (1980) and *Holbeck Hall Hotel v Scarborough B.C.* (2000).

Look online

Research the case of *Holbeck Hall Hotel v Scarborough Borough Council* (2000).
- Why were the defendant Council not liable on appeal?
- Was this decision fair to the hotel owners?

It can be seen that, with the exception of the last action, all the forms of interference have involved indirect interference.

Some forms of interference will not be protected. A claimant cannot take action to protect a right to:
- a view as claimed in *Fearn and others v Board of Trustees of the Tate Gallery* (2020) (see Chapter 17.3.3 above)
- light
- television reception, as shown in *Hunter v Canary Wharf Ltd* above.

However, the courts are sometimes prepared to protect offensive behaviour, affecting the character of the neighbourhood, or possibly behaviour which adversely affects property values. For example:

- *Thompson-Schwab v Costaki* (1956): the Court of Appeal decided that the running of a brothel in a respectable residential area of London amounted to a nuisance.
- *Laws v Florinplace Ltd* (1981): an injunction was awarded to prevent premises being converted into a sex shop in an area of shops, restaurants and some housing.

Look online

Read this news story: **www.bbc.co.uk/news/uk-englandsomerset-27067020**

Were fireworks the cause of the deaths of road users?

23.1.4 What amounts to an unreasonable interference?

Because the tort is all about balancing competing interests of the claimant and the defendant, the court will take into account various factors to decide whether or not the use of neighbouring land is reasonable.

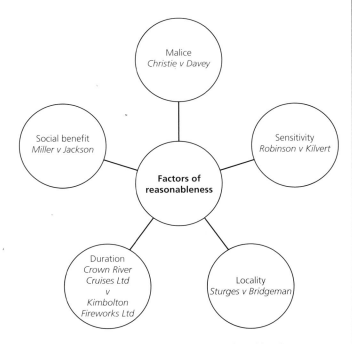

Figure 23.1 Factors of reasonableness considered by the court

The duration of the interference

To be actionable, the interference is likely to be continuous and at unreasonable hours of the day or night. In this way, regular, noisy, late-night parties might amount to a nuisance, but a noisy one-off party to celebrate a special occasion might not. *Crown River*

Cruises Ltd v Kimbolton Fireworks Ltd (1996) was an exception.

> ## Case study
>
> ### Crown River Cruises Ltd v Kimbolton Fireworks Ltd (1996)
>
> A river barge was set alight by flammable debris coming from a firework display lasting twenty minutes. It was held that the display amount to a private nuisance.

The fact that the interference is only temporary is not a sufficient reason to avoid a claim if it is an unreasonable interference with the claimant's use or enjoyment of land.

The sensitivity of the claimant

If it can be shown that the claimant is particularly sensitive, then the activity may not be a private nuisance.

> ## Case study
>
> ### Robinson v Kilvert (1889)
>
> The claimant stored brown paper on the ground floor of a building, while the defendant stored paper boxes in the basement. The defendant needed the conditions to be hot and dry. The heat from the basement caused the paper to dry out and the claimant sued for the loss in value. It was decided that the brown paper was particularly delicate and the heat from the basement would not have dried out normal paper, so there was no nuisance.

The law on nuisance is moving away now from the idea of 'abnormal sensitivity' to a general test of foreseeability, as shown in the following case.

> ## Case study
>
> ### Network Rail Infrastructure v Morris (2004)
>
> The claimant ran a recording studio near the main London to Brighton railway line. New track circuits were installed beside the railway which interfered with the amplification of electric guitars, causing the claimant to lose business.
>
> The Court of Appeal decided that the use of amplified guitars was abnormally sensitive equipment, and as the nuisance was not foreseeable, the defendants were not liable for private nuisance.

Locality

Nuisance is all about the use of land in the area where it is situated, so the character of the neighbourhood has to be considered. The court will consider whether the area:

- is purely residential
- is partly residential and partly commercial or industrial
- is situated in the town or country
- has changed in character over time.

As Thesiger LJ stated in *Sturges v Bridgman* (1879):

> " what would be a nuisance in Belgrave Square would not necessarily be so in Bermondsey. "

Malice

A deliberately harmful act will normally be unreasonable behaviour and considered a nuisance.

> ## Case study
>
> ### Christie v Davey (1893)
>
> The claimant was a music teacher who held musical parties and lessons in his house. The defendant became annoyed by the noise and responded by banging on the walls with his hands and with trays, blowing whistles and shouting. An injunction was granted against him due to his deliberate and malicious behaviour.
>
> ### Hollywood Silver Fox Farm v Emmett (1936)
>
> The claimant bred mink on his farm. The defendant had a disagreement with the claimant and told his son to shoot his guns near to the claimant's property to frighten the animals so they would not breed. This was held to be a deliberate and unreasonable act and a private nuisance.

Social benefit

If it is considered that the defendant is providing a benefit to the community, the court may consider the actions reasonable.

Case study

Miller v Jackson (1977)

The claimant's complained that their use of their garden was disrupted by cricket balls being hit into it from the adjoining recreation ground. The cricket club erected high fencing along the boundary and instructed batsmen to hit the ball on the ground. Despite the attempts to compromise, the claimants continued their action.

The court weighed up the public benefit of the use of the ground for recreational purposes against the private benefit of the claimant's use and enjoyment of their garden. It was decided the public benefit outweighed the private benefit and no private nuisance was being caused.

However, the opposite view was taken in *Adams v Ursell* (1913), when a well-used fish and chip shop was found to be causing a nuisance to local residents due to smells coming from it, and it was forced to close. Today, in a case like this, the court could make a positive order for the premises to fit extractors to remove excessive smells, rather than to order an outright ban.

Tip

Identify and explain the relevant factors of reasonableness from the scenario presented to you and support your explanation with relevant cases. You will not need to explain every factor of reasonableness.

23.1.5 Who may be sued?

- The person who causes the nuisance, or their successors in title, who have allowed the nuisance to occur. For example, in *Bybrook Barn Garden Centre v Kent County Council* (2001), the Council, as a highway authority, was responsible for the maintenance of a culvert which had overflowed, causing damage to the claimant's land. The culvert had originally been constructed by the Council's predecessor.
- The person who is causing, or allowing, the nuisance can be sued. For example, *in Tetley v Chitty* (1986), a local authority which allowed go-kart racing on its land was held liable for a nuisance.
- Where the occupier is not responsible for creating the nuisance, they might still be liable as a result of 'adopting' the nuisance – in other words, failing to deal with the problem, even if it was caused by a previous owner or a trespasser. This can be seen in the case of *Sedleigh Denfield v O'Callaghan* (1940).

- A defendant can also be liable where the nuisance is the result of natural causes which they are aware of but fail to deal with. In *Leakey v National Trust* (1980), the defendants owned land on which there was a large natural mound on a hillside. They were aware that the land could slip and, following a hot summer, it did slip, damaging the claimant's cottage. The defendants were liable as they had failed to prevent the slippage which they were aware of.

The defendant who is causing the nuisance does not have to have an interest in the land from which the nuisance is coming. This means that a short-term tenant, or a member of the neighbour's family, can be liable.

Case study

Sedleigh Denfield v O'Callaghan (1940)

The defendants were an order of monks who occupied land on which there was a ditch. Without the defendants' knowledge, the local authority laid a pipe to take water from the ditch. The grate was in the wrong place and became blocked, causing neighbouring land to flood. By this time the defendants knew about the pipe.

The House of Lords decided the defendants were liable in private nuisance, as an occupier who knows of a danger and allows it to continue is liable, even if they have not created the nuisance in the first place.

Activity

Consider whether there is a possible claim for private nuisance in the following situations:

1 Ray and Jas held a noisy party to celebrate their A-level results. The party lasted until 3 a.m., annoying their neighbours Ada and Florence.
2 Tara lives next door to Albert, an amateur radio enthusiast. When he is using his equipment, it causes interference with the sound and pictures on Tara's television.
3 Ricky, a music promotor, intends to hold a week-long open air pop concert on parkland at the head of a residential cul-de-sac.
4 Norris is annoyed because Rita's cat regularly comes into his garden and messes on his prize-winning flowers. Some of the flowers died just before he was going to exhibit them at a show.
5 Residents in a private care home object to the noise from football matches played on local authority playing fields opposite the home.

23.1.6 Defences

Prescription

This is a defence that is unique to nuisance. If the action has been carried on for at least twenty years, and there has been no complaint between the parties in that time, then the defendant has a prescriptive right to continue.

> ### Case study
>
> #### Sturges v Bridgeman (1879)
>
> The claimant, a doctor, had lived and worked next to the defendant's confectionary factory. The claimant built a consulting room on the boundary of his garden next to the factory. He then complained of feeling vibrations in the consulting room which came from the factory, and this amounted to a nuisance. The defendant argued he had a prescriptive right to continue as he had been using the factory for over twenty years without complaint.
>
> The court decided that the defence failed as the nuisance only began when the consulting room was built.

The operation of the defence was considered in *Coventry v Lawrence* (2014) below. The Supreme Court confirmed that the defence only applied to an activity that was an actionable nuisance for at least the last twenty years – not just that an activity had been carried on for that time without complaint.

Linked to this defence, the defence of *volenti non fit injuria* can apply. This means 'consent by the claimant to the nuisance': see Chapter 25.

Moving to the nuisance

The defendant may argue that the claimant is only suffering the nuisance as they have moved closer to the alleged problem (as in *Sturges v Bridgman*), or moved into the area (*Miller v Jackson*) and that there was no issue previously. This does not amount to a defence.

Statutory authority

As many of the activities that can amount to a nuisance are now regulated or licensed by environmental or other laws, statutory authority is one of the most effective defences.

> ### Case study
>
> #### Allen v Gulf Oil Refining (1981)
>
> The defendants operated an oil refinery. Local residents brought an action in nuisance. The defendants had been given statutory authority to acquire the site and build a refinery, but there was no express provision to operate it.
>
> The House of Lords said it must have been Parliament's intention when it gave permission for the building of the refinery for the owners to operate it. As the nuisance was the inevitable consequence of operating the authorised refinery, a defence of statutory authority applied.

If a statute provides the only possible remedy, an action in nuisance may not be possible as an alternative.

> ### Case study
>
> #### Marcic v Thames Water plc (2003)
>
> The claimant's home was flooded with sewage on many occasions due to failures of the defendants. The Water Industry Act 1991, which governed the workings of the defendants, provided procedures and remedies, and excluded an action in nuisance. As there were clear statutory procedures, the House of Lords decided that there could be no nuisance action; otherwise it would conflict with the intentions of Parliament.
>
> In addition to a claim in Private Nuisance, Marcic claimed there had been a breach of his human rights under Article 8 ECHR (see Chapter 34.3). In *Hatton v UK* (2003) the ECtHR makes it clear that the Convention does not give absolute protection to property. It requires a fair balance to be struck between those whose homes and property are affected and the interests of others, such as customers and the general public. In this case it was decided that Marcic had no right to claim as his minority interest of being subject to flooding conflicted with the interests of the water company's consumers who would have to pay for any remedial work.

Local authority planning permission can sometimes be lawful justification for a nuisance.

However, if the planning permission does not change the character of the neighbourhood, it will not operate as a defence.

Case studies

Wheeler v Saunders (1996)

A pig farmer was granted planning permission to expand by erecting two more pig houses, each containing 400 pigs. One of the new pig houses was only 11 metres from a neighbour's cottage, who took a nuisance action because of the strong smells he experienced.

The Court of Appeal decided that the grant of planning permission was only a defence if its effect was to change the character of the neighbourhood so that the nuisance was not unreasonable. This was not the case here, and the planning permission was not a defence.

Watson v Croft Promo-Sport (2009)

Planning permission was granted in 1963 to use a former aerodrome as a racing track. This use continued for 16 years but then ceased. In 1995, new owners reopened the track and it became very popular. The new owners applied for planning permission for the track to be used for 210 days a year and this was granted. The claimant, who lived about 300 metres from the track, brought a private nuisance action claiming noise disturbance, an injunction and damages.

The defendants argued the planning permission had changed the character of the area and the use of the circuit was reasonable. An injunction was granted by the Court of Appeal only allowing racing for 40 days a year, as they considered that as the area was essentially rural in nature and the character of the area had not changed, there was an actionable nuisance.

The Supreme Court has considered the law of nuisance more recently, in the case of *Coventry v Lawrence* (2014).

Case study

Coventry v Lawrence (2014)

The claimant bought a house in 2006, 864 metres from the defendant's motor sports stadium. Planning permission had been granted in 1975 for the stadium to be used for speedway and subsequently for stock cars, banger racing and motor-cross. The claimant brought an action in nuisance based on noise requiring an injunction to limit the use of the track. The Supreme Court confirmed that there was a noise nuisance which required an injunction to limit the use of the track. They decided that:

- The rule in *Sturges v Bridgeman* – about considering the character of the neighbourhood – still applies.
- If the claimant uses their property for the same purposes as their predecessor, the defendant cannot use the defence of moving to the nuisance.
- Where a claimant builds on their property or changes its use after the defendant has started the activity complained of, then the defence of coming to the nuisance may fail.
- Damages may be considered as a remedy more often in cases of nuisance, especially where planning permission has been granted, or where the public interest is involved such as employees losing their jobs if an injunction is awarded to completely stop an activity.

Volenti or consent

This may be a defence to a nuisance claim if there are active steps taken by the claimant encouraging the creation of the nuisance.

Link

For more detail on the defence of *volenti*, see Chapter 25.

Look online

Research online to find a report of a dispute between neighbours.
- What was the cause of the dispute?
- If it is ongoing, how do you think it could be resolved?
- If the dispute has ended, do you think it has been resolved to the satisfaction of both parties?

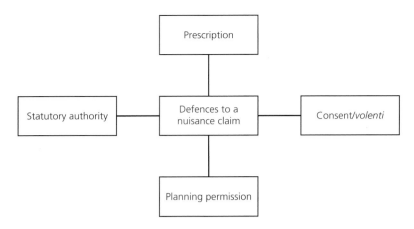

Figure 23.2 Defences to a nuisance claim

23.1.7 Remedies

Injunction

Until the case of *Coventry v Lawrence* (2014), the most common remedy for a nuisance claim, and the whole point of bringing an action, was an injunction. This would generally be prohibitory, ordering the defendant to stop causing the nuisance.

For example in *Kennaway v Thompson* (1981), an injunction was granted to limit the use of a lake, close to the claimant's house, for the racing of motor boats.

An injunction could also be positive in nature – for example, to order the defendant to install a filter to prevent the escape of smell or smuts. The injunction could be linked to the award of damages where a loss has occurred.

Abatement

A further remedy available to a claimant in nuisance is 'abatement'. For example, in *Lemmon v Webb* (1894), a claimant could chop down overhanging branches from his own land and return them to the neighbour's land.

Damages

The case of *Shelfer v City of London Electric Lighting Co.* (1895) set out that damages should only be awarded instead of an injunction when:

- the injury to the claimant's rights was small, and
- the claimant can be compensated by a small amount of money
- it would be unfair on the defendant to grant an injunction.

In *Coventry v Lawrence* (2014), the Supreme Court gave guidance as to the future use of injunctions and the award of damages in private nuisance:

- An injunction could be the default order in a nuisance claim.
- It is open to the defendant to argue that an award of damages would be a suitable alternative.
- The *Shelfer* test should not be applied rigidly.
- An injunction will not automatically be granted, even if the *Shelfer* test is satisfied.

One of the judges, Lord Sumption, suggested that damages would usually be an appropriate remedy in nuisance.

Following this guidance, the courts may award fewer injunctions in nuisance claims and be prepared to award damages instead.

Activity

Consider whether a defence to a nuisance claim exists in each of the following situations:

1 The noise from a busy railway line distresses homeowners living in houses next to the line.
2 Burglars break into Ravinder's home while he is away and leave his radio, TV and smart speaker all playing on maximum volume, which annoys his neighbours.
3 Ann lives in a flat below Roger's flat. She has to get up for work each morning at 6 a.m. but Roger arrives home from work at 1 a.m. and she is unable to sleep as she can hear his footsteps walking around for hours afterwards.
4 Residents of a small estate of houses suffer from the noise of children playing in an estate playground. It was a condition of the building of the estate that a playground is provided.
5 For more than 15 years Archie has kept pigs in his backyard. His neighbour, Reggie, eventually objects to the smell.

Case	Facts	Legal principle
Sedleigh Denfield v O'Callaghan (1940)	A pipe, laid by the local authority, but on the defendant's land, was blocked, flooding the neighbouring land.	An occupier who knows of a danger and allows it to continue is liable in nuisance, even if s/he has not created the danger him/herself.
Leakey v National Trust (1980)	There was a large natural mound on a hillside on the defendants' land. They were aware that it could slip and following a hot summer it did slip, damaging the claimant's cottage.	A landowner could be liable in nuisance if he/she knows a slippage might happen and fails to prevent it.
Hunter v Canary Wharf Ltd (1997)	Residents in Docklands complained of interference with TV reception when Canary Wharf was being built.	The loss of a recreational facility is not sufficient interference to give rise to an action in nuisance. Only those with an interest in the land, not members of families, have a right to bring an action in nuisance.
Crown River Cruises Ltd v Kimbolton Fireworks Ltd (1996)	A river barge was set alight by flammable debris, from a 20-minute firework display.	Even a short-term activity can amount to a nuisance.
Robinson v Kilvert (1889)	Paper boxes were stored in hot and dry conditions which caused paper stored above them to dry out.	If the claimant is unduly sensitive, a nuisance will not be found.
Christie v Davey (1893)	The defendant was annoyed by his neighbour's music and deliberately banged trays on the walls, blew whistles and shouted to disturb the neighbour.	The defendant's deliberate and malicious behaviour amounted to a nuisance.
Miller v Jackson (1977)	The claimants' use of their garden was disrupted by cricket balls being hit into it from the adjoining recreation ground.	The use of a sports ground and its benefit to the community was balanced against the claimants' use of their garden. The community use outweighed the private use.
Sturges v Bridgman (1879)	A doctor built consulting rooms in his garden on the boundary to a sweet factory. He complained of vibrations from machinery.	The defence of prescription failed as the nuisance began when the consulting room was built. The period before the building was erected did not count.
Allen v Gulf Oil Refining (1981)	Residents near an oil refinery brought a nuisance as the defendants did not have express permission to operate it.	The refinery had statutory authority to operate as this must have been Parliament's intention.
Coventry v Lawrence (2014)	Planning permission had been given for speedway and later for other motor sports. A claim of noise nuisance was made, limiting the use of the track.	The Supreme Court decided the rule in *Sturges v Bridgman* about the character of neighbourhood still applies.

Figure 23.3 Key cases: private nuisance

23.2 Rylands v Fletcher

23.2.1 Definition of the tort

This is a strict liability tort: the claimant does not have to prove that the defendant was at fault.

> **Case study**
>
> ### *Rylands v Fletcher* (1868)
>
> The defendant, Rylands, was a mill owner. He hired contractors to create a reservoir on his land to act as a water supply for the mill. The contractors negligently failed to block off disused mineshafts that were uncovered during the excavations. Unknown to the contractors, these shafts were connected to other mineworks on adjoining land, belonging to the claimant, Fletcher. When the reservoir was filled, water flooded the neighbouring mines.
>
> The defendant was liable.

There were four elements present in this case that now must be proved for a successful claim under the tort of *Rylands v Fletcher*:

1. A 'thing' is brought onto land and an accumulation (or storage) of it: the water.
2. The 'thing' is likely to cause mischief (or damage) if it escapes: again, the water.
3. The storage amounts to a non-natural use of the land: the storage of water was non-natural.
4. The 'thing' does escape and causes foreseeable damage: water escaped and flooded the mines.

A disused water mill wheel

Since the case of *Cambridge Water Co. v Eastern Counties Leather plc* (1994), the tort of *Rylands v Fletcher* has been considered to be a sub-tort of nuisance rather than a separate action of its own. It was suggested in that case that there are now statutory provisions, such as the Environmental Protection Act 1990, which are more suitable for dealing with this sort of problem.

23.2.2 Requirements to bring a claim

Potential claimants

A person who can take an action in this tort has to have an interest in the land affected, as shown in *Hunter v Canary Wharf* (1997). This means that they must own the land or rent it, or have some sort of property interest in it.

The House of Lords in *Transco plc v Stockport Metropolitan Borough Council* (2003) reviewed the past case law and approved the line taken in *Read v Lyons* below that the tort, being a sub-tort of nuisance, required a proprietary interest in land by the claimant.

Potential defendants

According to Viscount Simon's test in *Read v Lyons* (1947), a defendant to an action in *Rylands v Fletcher* will either be the owner or occupier of land who satisfies the four ingredients of the tort, and all of the elements must be present for liability. It is assumed that the defendant must have some control over the land on which the material is stored.

The bringing onto the land

If the 'thing' in question is already naturally present on the land, then there can be no liability. So, in *Giles v Walker* (1890) there was no liability when weeds spread onto neighbouring land as they were growing naturally.

There cannot be liability for a thing that naturally accumulates (is stored) on the land. So, in *Ellison v Ministry of Defence* (1997), rainwater that accumulated naturally on an airfield at Greenham Common did not lead to liability when it escaped and caused flooding on neighbouring land.

The 'thing' or substance is likely to do mischief if it escapes

This is a test of foreseeability. It is not the escape that must be foreseeable – only that damage is foreseeable, if the 'thing' or substance brought onto land does escape.

Examples of 'things' which courts have decided can do mischief are:

- gas and electricity
- poisonous fumes
- a flag pole
- tree branches
- an occupied chair from a chair-o-plane ride.

Case study

Hale v Jennings Bros (1938)

A 'chair-o-plane' car on a fairground ride became detached from the main assembly while in motion and injured a stallholder as it crashed to the ground. The owner of the ride was liable as the risk of injury was foreseeable if the car came loose.

A chair-o-plane ride

This case is one of the few in this tort where a claim for personal injury was successful. The House of Lords commented *obiter* in *Transco plc v Stockport Metropolitan Borough Council* (2003) that, as the tort is a sub-tort of nuisance, it is not possible to claim for personal injury.

The case of *Stannard* (t/a Wyvern Tyres) *v Gore* (2012) was an example of an action based on damage caused by fire. The claimant was successful at trial but the decision was reversed on appeal.

Case study

Stannard (T/A Wyvern Tyres) v Gore (2012)

A fire occurred in the defendant's tyre-fitting premises which spread to the claimant's adjoining premises. The claimant's action was dismissed in the Court of Appeal. In their view it was an essential requirement that an exceptionally dangerous 'thing' be brought and stored on the land and which had escaped. In this case, it was the fire that had escaped, not the tyres which were stored on the land, and tyres were not exceptionally dangerous.

In *Stannard,* Ward LJ concluded that in an appropriate case, damage caused by fire moving from an adjoining property might fall within a *Rylands v Fletcher* claim, but the appropriate case is likely to be very rare, because:

1 It is the 'thing' which had been brought onto the land which must escape, not the fire which was started or increased by the 'thing'.
2 As set out in *Transco v Stockport* (below), there must be an extraordinary or unusual use of the land.
3 While fire may be a dangerous thing, the occasions when fire is brought onto the land may be limited to cases where it has been deliberately or negligently started by the occupier.
4 In any event, starting a fire on the occupier's own land may well be an ordinary use of the land.

Stannard will have significant implications for damage by fire claims. In particular, it is clear from Ward LJ's comments that it will now be very difficult for a claimant to succeed in such cases without proof of negligence.

A non-natural use of land

Lord Cairns in the House of Lords in *Rylands v Fletcher* (1868) indicated the requirement of a non-natural use of land. He said:

> if the defendants, not stopping at the natural use of their close, had desired to use it for any purpose which I may term a non-natural use ... and in consequence of doing so ... the water came to escape ... then it appears to me that that which the defendants were doing they were doing at their own peril.

This concept of non-natural use was developed and explained by Lord Moulton in *Rickards v Lothian* (1913):

> it is not every use of land which brings into play this principle. It must be some special use bringing with it increased danger to others, and not merely by the ordinary use of land or such a use as is proper for the general benefit of the community.

Case study

Rickards v Lothian (1913)

An unknown person turned on water taps and blocked plugholes on the defendant's premises, causing damage to the flat below. The defendant was not liable in *Rylands v Fletcher* as the use of water in domestic pipes was a natural use of the land.

British Celanese v AH Hunt Ltd (1969)

The defendants stored strips of metal foil used in the manufacture of electrical components. Some strips blew off the defendant's land onto an electricity substation, causing a power failure. It was held that the use of land by the defendants was a natural use because of the benefit from the manufacture received by the local population.

The leading case of *Transco plc v Stockport Metropolitan Borough Council* (2004) ruled that 'non-natural' refers to some extraordinary or unusual use of land and a *Rylands v Fletcher* action can only take place where the defendant's use of land is extraordinary and unusual. In general, storage of things associated with the domestic use of land will not normally be classified as non-natural, even though they may be potentially hazardous. The following have been decided by courts as being a natural use of land:

- a fire in a grate which spread to the claimant's premises
- defective electric wiring that caused a fire which spread to the claimant's premises
- a domestic water supply.

Case study

Transco plc v Stockport Metropolitan Borough Council (2004)

The council were responsible for the maintenance of pipe work supplying water to a block of flats. A leak developed which was undetected for some time. The water collected at an embankment which housed the claimant's high-pressure gas main. The water caused the embankment to collapse and left the gas main exposed and unsupported. This was a serious and immediate risk and the claimant took action to avoid the potential danger. They then sought to recover the cost of the remedial works in a *Rylands v Fletcher* action.

The House of Lords decided that the Council were not liable as their use of the land was not a non-natural use. Lord Bingham said in relation to the use of land:

> I think it clear that ordinary user is a preferable test to natural user, making it clear that the rule in *Rylands v Fletcher* is engaged only where the defendant's use is shown to be extraordinary and unusual. This is not a test to be inflexibly applied: a use may be extraordinary and unusual at one time or in one place but not so at another time or in another place.

Further, Lord Hoffman said, in relation to personal injury claims in *Rylands v Fletcher*:

> I think that the point is now settled by two recent decisions of the House of Lords: Cambridge Water Co v Eastern Counties Leather plc 1994, which decided that *Rylands v Fletcher* is a special form of nuisance and *Hunter v Canary Wharf Ltd* 1997, which decided that nuisance is a tort against land. It must, I think, follow that damages for personal injuries are not recoverable under the rule.

Courts have been prepared to accept that certain activities may always lead to a potential level of danger, so that it amounts to a non-natural use of land, whatever the benefit to the public derived from the activity that has led to the danger.

However, in *Cambridge Water Co. v Eastern Counties Leather plc* (1994), the storage of chemicals in a factory was a classic example of a non-natural use of land. Just because the activity was an important source of local employment did not make the storage a natural use of land.

The thing stored must escape and cause foreseeable damage

The stored item must escape from one property onto another property. Note the comments in *Wyvern*, above, where the Court of Appeal observed that to come within the tort, it was not the fire that should escape but the stored tyres.

Case study

Read v J. Lyons & Co. Ltd (1947)

An inspector was checking the interior of a munitions factory and was injured, together with a number of workers, when a shell exploded. The House of Lords decided that *Rylands v Fletcher* did not apply as there was 'no escape at all of the relevant kind'. Viscount Simon explained that an escape for *Rylands v Fletcher* means:

> an escape from a place where the defendant has occupation or control over land to a place which is outside his occupation or control.

This rule is not always strictly applied: in *Hale v Jennings Bros* (1938), both stalls operated on the same piece of land and neither stallholder owned the land. Yet liability was imposed.

Case study

Cambridge Water Co. v Eastern Counties Leather (1994)

The defendants stored chemicals for their leather tanning business. There were frequent spillages and over the years, chemicals seeped into the concrete floors and into the soil below. An area where the claimants extracted water became polluted and involved the claimants spending over a million pounds to move its operation. They claimed this cost from the defendants but the House of Lords decided that the damage was not foreseeable and too remote from the site of the spillage.

Activity ?

Phil runs a microbrewery from a unit on a small industrial estate. One evening his apprentice leaves the boiler running, causing the brew to overheat and overflow. A considerable quantity of beer escapes into an adjoining bakery unit owned by Mac. As a result, several sacks of flour are damaged.

Advise Mac on:

- Whether he can take a claim in *Rylands v Fletcher* for the damage to the flour.
- The advantages and disadvantages of taking a claim in *Rylands v Fletcher* as opposed to a claim in negligence.

23.2.3 Defences

Despite the tort being described as strict liability, defences are possible in the event of a claim.

- Act of God – this defence may succeed where there are extreme weather conditions that 'no human foresight can provide against'. It is only likely to succeed if there are unforeseeable weather conditions.

Case study

Nichols v Marsland (1876)

The defendant made three artificial ornamental lakes by damming a natural stream. Freak thunderstorms accompanied by torrential rain broke the banks of the artificial lakes, and this water destroyed bridges on the claimant's land. The defendants were not liable as the extreme weather conditions amounted to an Act of God.

- Act of a stranger – if a stranger over whom the defendant has no control has been the cause of the escape causing the damage, then the defendant may not be liable.

Case study

Perry v Kendricks Transport (1956)

The defendants parked their bus on their parking space, having drained the tank of fuel. A stranger removed the fuel cap and a child was injured when another child threw a match into the tank, igniting fumes. A claim was made in the tort of *Rylands v Fletcher* but the defendants were not liable due to the act of a stranger.

- *Volenti non fit injuria* (consent) – there will be no liability where the claimant has consented to the thing that is accumulated by the defendant.

Case study

Peters v Prince of Wales Theatre (1943)

The claimant leased a shop next to a theatre from the defendant. The shop suffered flood damage when pipes from the theatre's sprinkler system burst due to icy weather conditions. The defendant was not liable in a *Rylands v Fletcher* action. It was decided that the sprinkler system was also for the benefit of the claimant who was ruled to have consented to it as it had been installed before the lease was signed.

(For more details of this defence, see Chapter 25.)

- Wrongful act of third party – this was shown in *LMS International Ltd v Styrene Packaging and Insulation Ltd* (2005).
- Statutory authority – if the terms of an Act of Parliament authorise the defendant's action, this may amount to a defence. This was argued unsuccessfully in *Charing Cross Electricity Co. v Hydraulic Power Co.* (1914)
- Contributory negligence – where the claimant is partly responsible for the escape of the 'thing', then the Law Reform (Contributory Negligence) Act 1945 applies and damages may be reduced according to the amount of the claimant's fault (see Chapter 25 for more details of this defence). This is shown in *Sayers v Harlow* (1958) – see Chapter 25, section 25.1.2 for case details.

23.2.4 Remedies

A claimant must show damage to, or destruction of, their property to succeed in a claim for damages. The level of damages will be the cost of repair or replacement of the property damaged or destroyed.

Case	Facts	Legal principle
Rylands v Fletcher (1868)	The defendant made a reservoir as a water supply for his mill. Mineshafts were not blocked off, causing flooding to a mine.	A claim could be made if material was brought onto land and stored, it was likely to cause mischief if it escapes, which amounted to a non-natural use of the land.
Transco plc v Stockport Metropolitan Borough Council (2004)	A water leak left a gas main exposed, requiring remedial work. The claimant sought to recover the cost of the work.	A claim in *Rylands v Fletcher* is a special form of nuisance when the use of land is extraordinary and unusual.
Rickards v Lothian (1913)	An unknown person turned on water taps and blocked plugholes, causing damage to the flat below.	There has to be a non-natural use of the land – not present in this case as domestic pipes were a natural use of land.
Read v Lyons (1947)	An explosion took place in a munitions factory, causing injury.	The material has to escape from one property onto adjoining property – no liability here as there was no escape.
Cambridge Water Co. v Eastern Counties Leather (1994)	Stored chemicals seeped through the concrete floor of a factory into the soil below, polluting an area where water was extracted.	Damage has to be reasonably foreseeable and not too remote from the escape.

Figure 23.4 Key cases: *Rylands v Fletcher*

Quick questions

1 Define the tort of private nuisance.
2 What damage must be caused by the interference?
3 Who can bring a claim in private nuisance?
4 Describe the factors that can make an activity unreasonable.
5 Describe the elements needed to be successful in a claim for *Rylands v Fletcher*.
6 What is the significance of the case of *Cambridge Water v Eastern Counties Leather* (1994)?

Tip

When explaining the requirements of the tort, make sure that you identify and explain, with cases to illustrate, all four of the elements of the tort.

Summary

- Private nuisance is the unlawful interference with the use or enjoyment of land coming from neighbouring land.
- The claimant is the person suffering the nuisance.
- The defendant will be the person who causes or allows the nuisance.
- The court will take factors into account such as the duration, the locality, whether there is any social benefit to the activity, any malice or the sensitivity of the claimant.
- Defences to an action include prescription, moving to the nuisance, statutory authority of the grant of planning permission.
- The court can order an injunction to stop or limit the nuisance or damages, the claimant can, if possible, try to abate the nuisance.
- *Rylands v Fletcher* is a strict liability tort. A claim can be made by a person who has an interest in the land affected.

- A defendant will be the owner or occupier of the land from where the material escaped and who has some control over that land.
- The elements to satisfy are:
  - There must be a storage of some non-naturally occurring material.
  - The material must escape from one property onto another.
  - The damage caused must be reasonably foreseeable.
- Defences to a claim include act of a stranger, act of God, statutory authority to the storage, consent to the storage and contributory negligence.
- The remedy will be damages for the damage caused to the claimant's property.

Chapter 24 Vicarious liability

24.1 Nature and purpose of vicarious liability

Vicarious liability is where one person (usually an employer) is responsible for the tort of another (usually the employee). This allows an injured claimant to sue the employee and the employer and discover which is better placed to pay the compensation. This may be because one of the parties (usually the employer) is more likely to be in a better financial position and/or insured. Without vicarious liability, an injured claimant will be left without compensation. The principle is usually justified because the employer employs, trains and supervises the employee, as well as benefitting from their work.

According to the 'Salmond test', employers are vicariously liable when:

- an employee commits an unintentional tort
- the person committing the tort is an employee, and
- the tort occurs in the course of the employment.

The parties in vicarious liability are:

- The tortfeasor – the person who commits the tort and causes the harm (usually the employee).
- The claimant – the victim who suffers harm.
- The defendant – the person liable for the tort (usually the employer).

The tortfeasor must have committed an unintentional tort which causes harm. In *Poland v Parr* (1927), this included the tortfeasor's action in protecting his employer's property, even outside the hours of employment.

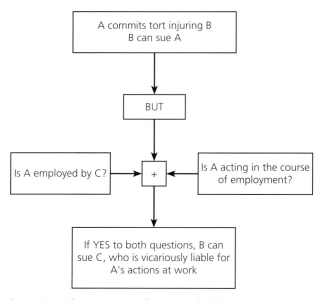

Figure 24.1 The operation of vicarious liability

24.2 Liability for employees

This section covers:

- traditional tests of employment status
- liability for torts committed in the course of employment.

24.2.1 Traditional tests of employment status

The old test of employment was whether a person was providing:

- a contract of service – they would be an employee, or
- a contract for services – they would be an independent contractor.

An employer can be vicariously liable for the actions of his employees, but not an independent contractor.

Key term

Independent contractor – also known as a self-employed person who is responsible for their own actions and can be sued by a victim of a tort committed by an independent contractor. No third party will be vicariously liable for the wrongdoings of an independent contractor.

Employee commits tort during course of employment	Independent contractor commits tort at work
↓	✖
Employer vicariously liable	Independent contractor remains liable for own tort

Figure 24.2 Employee and independent contractor liability

Working relationships have developed in recent times which may not fit into traditional definitions. Full-time and part-time work will often indicate employment, but what about casual, temporary or seasonal work or 'zero hours' contracts? And what about workers carrying out internships or volunteering or working from home? When should an employer be legally responsible for their acts or omissions?

Activity

Decide whether the following are employees or self-employed (independent contractors).

1 C is a caddie at a golf club. The club provides him with a uniform and a clothes locker. Caddying work is allocated according to a strict rotation and golfers pay the club a set rate, which is then passed on. Caddies can choose the hours they work but there is no guarantee of work.
2 Q is a dancer performing for guests at a private members' club. She pays the club a fee for each night that she performs. In return she decides for whom she dances, for how long and the fee that she collects.
3 M is a driver who owns his own car. He pays a mini-cab operator a weekly fee and in return has a radio installed and access to the company's computer system which allocates the work. He is required to wear a uniform and is prohibited from working for any other operator. He can choose the hours he works and keeps the fares he collects.

The courts have developed several methods of testing employee status:

- the control test
- the integration or organisation test
- the economic reality or multiple test.

The control test

Lord Thankerton, in *Short v J W Henderson Ltd* (1946), identified some key features which would show that the employer had control over the employee, including:

- the power to select the employee
- the right to control the method of working
- the right to suspend and dismiss
- the payment of wages.

Such a test is virtually impossible to apply accurately today. Nevertheless, there are circumstances in which a test of control is still useful, in the case of borrowed workers.

Case study

Mersey Docks & Harbour Board v Coggins and Griffiths (Liverpool Ltd) (1947)

A crane driver had been hired out by his employers, the Harbour Board, to stevedores who loaded and unloaded ships. Due to his negligence, the driver injured a person at work. In their contract, the Harbour Board continued to pay his wages and retained the power to sack him, but set out that he was the employee of the stevedores. The court decided that:

- the terms in any hire contract are not decisive, and
- the permanent employer is presumed liable, unless the contrary is proved.

If an employee is hired out without any equipment, there is an inference that the hirer becomes the employer. If the employee is hired out with equipment (as in this case with the crane), the inference is not as strong as the hirer may not have any control how the equipment can be used.

A more recent development of the control test concerns the activities of bouncers.

Case study

Hawley v Luminar Leisure (2006)

A bouncer was supplied to nightclubs by a specialist supplier. He assaulted a customer outside the defendant's club. The suppliers went into liquidation, so the injured customer claimed the club was vicariously liable. The court decided that as the club exercised so much control over the bouncer in how he should work, it employed him and was vicariously liable for his actions.

The integration or organisation test

Lord Denning in *Stevenson, Jordan and Harrison Ltd v McDonald and Evans* (1952) established this test. It provides that:

- A worker will be an employee if their work is fully integrated into the business.
- If a person's work is only accessory to the business, that person is not an employee.

According to this test:

- The master of a ship, a chauffeur or a newspaper staff reporter are all examples of employees.
- A pilot bringing a ship into port, a taxi driver and a freelance writer are not employees.

The economic reality or multiple test

In view of problems with these two tests, courts recognise that a single test of employment status is not satisfactory and may produce confusing results. This test considers various factors which may indicate employment or self-employment. It was established in *Ready Mixed Concrete (South East) Ltd v Minister of Pensions and National Insurance* (1968).

Case study

Ready Mixed Concrete (South East) Ltd v Minister of Pensions and National Insurance (1968)

Should the company be liable for the payment of national insurance contributions for drivers who drove company vehicles carrying the company logo?

Drivers bought vehicles from the company on hire-purchase, had to maintain them and only use them on company business. Working hours were flexible and pay was subject to an annual minimum rate according to the amount of concrete carried. Mackenna J established the test and set three conditions for an employment relationship:

1. The employee agrees to provide work or skill in return for a wage.
2. The employee expressly or impliedly accepts that the work will be subject to the control of the employer.
3. All other considerations in the contract are consistent with there being an employment contract, rather than any other relationship.

According to these tests, the drivers in this case were not employees.

The test has been updated so that all factors in the relationship should be considered and weighed according to their significance. They might include:

- The ownership of any tools, plant or equipment – an employee is less likely to own the plant and equipment used at work.
- The method of payment – a self-employed person is likely to take a payment for a whole job, where an employee will usually receive regular payments (salary) for the period of employment.
- Whether tax, national insurance and pension contributions are deducted from an employee's wages – a self-employed person will have to submit self-assessments and pay tax annually under schedule D.
- Any role description – a person may describe himself as an employee or as self-employed. This will usually, but not always, be an accurate description.
- Independence in doing a job – probably one of the most important tests of self-employed status is the amount of independence and flexibility in being able to take work from different sources, and when to do it.

All these factors are useful in identifying the status of the worker, but none is an absolute test or is definitive on its own, and cases can still bring conflicting decisions. For example:

- *Carmichael v National Power* (1999): tour guides employed on a casual basis were not employees as there was no formal contractual arrangement between the parties.
- *Ferguson v Dawson* (1976): there was a contract which stated that a building labourer was self-employed, but the court decided he was employed, and the employers were required to protect him under safety laws.
- *Viasystems (Tyneside) Ltd v Thermal Transfer (Northern) Ltd* (2005): the Court of Appeal decided that in some cases it was possible for two 'employers' to be dually (and equally) liable for an employee's negligent work. The question to be considered was:

  'Who was entitled and, in theory, obliged to control the employee's negligent acts in order to prevent it?'

24.2.2 Liability for torts committed in the course of employment

In order for the employer to be liable, the employee must commit the tort 'in the course of the employment'.

The court has to decide whether or not an action is in the course of employment. It will be a question of fact in each case. It is often difficult to see consistency in the judgments but there are two lines of cases:

1. There is vicarious liability because the employee is acting in the course of the employment.
2. There is no vicarious liability because there is a reason the employee is not acting in the course of employment.

In the following cases it was decided that the employee was acting in the course of employment.

Acting against orders

If the employee is doing their job but acts against orders in the way they do it, the employer can be liable for any tort committed by the employee.

Case studies

Limpus v London General (1862)

The employer instructed its bus drivers not to race other company's bus drivers when collecting passengers. One driver caused an accident when racing. The employer was liable to the injured claimant as the driver was doing what he was employed to do – even against orders.

Rose v Plenty (1976)

A dairy instructed its milkmen not to use child helpers on their milk rounds. One milkman did use a boy to help him, but the boy was injured on the round due to the milkman's negligent driving of the electric milk float. The dairy was vicariously liable for the milkman's negligent driving as it was suggested that the dairy benefitted from the work done by the boy.

An electric milk float from the 1960s

Employee committing a negligent act

If the employee does a job badly and causes injury to another, the employer can be liable for those actions. This was shown in *Century Insurance v Northern Ireland Road Transport Board* (1942).

275

Century Insurance v Northern Ireland Road Transport Board (1942)

A petrol tanker driver was delivering petrol to a garage when he lit a cigarette and threw a match on the ground. This caused an explosion, which destroyed several cars and damaged some nearby houses. The driver's employer was vicariously liable as the driver was doing his job, even though negligently.

In the following cases it was decided that the employee was not acting in the course of employment.

If the employee causes injury or damage to another while doing something outside the area or time of their work, the employer will not be liable. This is said to be acting on a 'frolic' of one's own.

Hilton v Thomas Burton (Rhodes) Ltd (1961)

Some employees were working on a site away from their workplace. They took an unauthorised break and drove their firm's van to a café for tea but had an accident on the way back to the site. One of the men was killed and his widow sued the employer.

It was decided the employers were not vicariously liable as the men were on an unauthorised 'frolic' of their own and not acting in the course of their employment.

If the employee gives an unauthorised lift, the employer will not be liable.

Twine v Bean's Express (1946)

The claimant's husband was killed through the negligence of a driver who had been forbidden to give lifts. This instruction was supported by notices on the side of the van stating who could be carried in it.

The employers were not vicariously liable, as the driver was doing an unauthorised act and the employers were gaining no benefit from it.

If the employee is acting against orders, and the act was not part of his job, then the employer will not be liable.

Beard v London General Omnibus Co. (1900)

A bus conductor, employed to collect fares, drove a bus without the authority of his employer, injuring the claimant. The employer was not liable as the conductor was doing something outside the course of his employment.

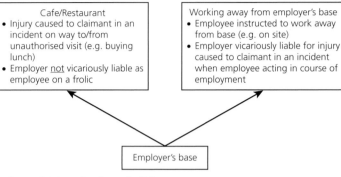

Figure 24.3 Acting 'on a frolic'

24.3 Recent approaches

The courts have in recent years developed an alternative approach to the conventional *Salmond* test for considering whether the employer is vicariously liable. This has come about as a number of cases involving non-traditional working relationships have come before the courts. This approach started in the case of *Lister v Hesley Hall*. The court asks:

- Was the relationship between the employer and employee 'akin to employment'?
  And
- Was the commission of the alleged tort 'closely connected' to the employment?

The court will decide these questions in each case. Judgments can be inconsistent, but recently they appear to be weighted in favour of claimants who have been injured by an employee.

If an employee commits a criminal act at work, the case of *Lister v Hesley Hall* (2001) introduced the concept of the employer being liable to the victim of the crime, if there is a 'close connection' between the crime and what the employee was employed to do.

Case study

Lister v Hesley Hall (2001)

The warden of a school for children with emotional difficulties was convicted of sexually assaulting some of the children. The House of Lords decided that there was a close connection between his job and what he did, as the assaults were carried out on school premises. As a result, the warden's employer was liable for his actions.

Since this decision, a number of cases have refined this principle:

- In *Catholic Child Welfare Society v Various Claimants (FC) and the Institute of the Brothers of the Christian Schools* (2012), a case involving sexual abuse by teachers on children in their care, the following principles were set out:
  - ○ Was the relationship between the Institute and its members akin to an employer and employee relationship?
  - ○ Was the sexual abuse connected to that relationship in such a way as to give rise to vicarious liability?
- In *Cox v Ministry of Justice* (2016), there was an assault by a prisoner on a catering manager employed at the prison. The government department responsible for the prison was sued.
  - ○ It was said that the organisation does not have to be carrying out a commercial activity or making a profit. It is enough for the organisation to carry on activities furthering its own interests. The department was liable for the prisoner's actions.
- In *Mohamud v Morrisons Supermarkets* (2016), an employee at a petrol station assaulted a customer, causing him serious injuries.
  - ○ The Supreme Court considered the job that the employee was doing, and whether there was a sufficient connection between that job and the assault on the customer. It decided that as the employee was acting within the field of his employment – the assault took place at the workplace and within working hours – there was a close connection between what he did and what he was required to do. As a result, the employers were vicariously liable for his actions.
- In *Armes v Nottingham County Council* (2017), a child was abused by foster carers with whom she was placed by the Council. It was decided that:
  - ○ foster carers were sufficiently integral to the local authority's 'business activity', and the local authority had sufficient control over them to make them vicariously liable.

Look online

You can read more detail about the *Cox v Ministry of Justice* and *Mohamud v Morrisons Supermarkets* cases at **www.pureemploymentlaw.co.uk/two-recent-supreme-court-cases-consider-vicarious-liability/**

24.3.1 Akin to employment

In the *Catholic Child Welfare Society* case above, Lord Phillips set out five criteria which can make it fair, just and reasonable to find a relationship akin to employment and impose vicarious liability on the employer. These criteria are:

(i) the employer is more likely to have the means to compensate the victim than the employee and can be expected to have insured against that liability;

(ii) the tort will have been committed as a result of activity being taken by the employee on behalf of the employer;

(iii) the employee's activity is likely to be part of the business activity of the employer;

(iv) the employer, by employing the employee to carry on the activity, will have created the risk of the tort committed by the employee; and

(v) the employee will, to a greater or lesser degree, have been under the control of the employer.

In *Barclays Bank v Various Claimants* (2020), a number of claimants who were prospective employees of the bank brought an action alleging sexual assaults during required medical examinations. The doctor who carried out the examinations was not an employee of the bank. In the Supreme Court, Lady Hale confirmed that, although the above five criteria might be helpful in establishing whether workers who are technically self-employed (or agency workers) are part of the employer's business, the court must instead look at the underlying details of the relationship. If a contractor is, 'carrying out his or her own independent business it is not necessary to consider the five incidents'. As a result, the Court found the doctor was an independent contractor and the bank was not liable for his actions.

24.3.2 Close or sufficient connection

- The first question for the court is what functions or 'field of activities' have been given by the employer to the employee, or, in everyday language, what was the nature of his job?
- Secondly, the court must decide whether there was sufficient connection between the position in which he was employed and his wrongful conduct to make it right for the employer to be held liable under the principle of social justice.

24.3.3 Independent contractors

As shown in the *Barclays Bank* case above, if the tortfeasor is an independent contractor, the business alleged to be their employer will not be vicariously liable for their actions. The victim will then have to rely on the financial worth of the contractor or their insurer in order to receive compensation.

The status of the tortfeasor was again considered in *Morrisons Supermarket v Various Claimants* (2020).

Morrisons Supermarket v Various Claimants (2020)

An unhappy employee uploaded personal details of colleagues to a file-sharing site and sent the data to three national newspapers. The employee was imprisoned, but the colleagues also sued the employee and employer for breach of statutory duty (under the Data Protection Act), misuse of personal information and breach of confidence.

The Supreme Court considered what 'close connection' meant and stated that employers would not be liable for a wrongful act, whether or not the act promotes the employer's business or is an effort to deliberately harm the employer as part of a vendetta. So, there was no vicarious liability as the employee's actions were outside the course of employment.

Case	Facts	Legal principle
Mersey Docks & Harbour Board v Coggins and Griffiths (Liverpool Ltd) (1947)	Hired crane driver negligently injured another worker	If worker and equipment are hired out, there is a presumption the original employer is liable. If only worker is hired out, the presumption is that hirer is liable.
Hawley v Luminar Leisure (2006)	Bouncer provided by specialist suppliers assaulted nightclub customer	Club employed bouncer so vicariously liable for his actions.
Ready Mixed Concrete (South East) Ltd v Minister of Pensions and National Insurance (1968)	Should the driver or the company be responsible for paying National Insurance contributions?	Three conditions required to show an employment relationship: 1 A relationship similar to employment. 2 Which was established by a close connection. 3 It was fair and just to impose liability on the employer.
Limpus v London General (1862)	Bus driver caused accident when racing, despite being instructed not to do so	Employer liable to victim – the driver was doing his job = even against orders.
Rose v Plenty (1976)	A dairy instructed its milkmen not to use child helpers. Boy injured while helping a milkman on his round	Dairy vicariously liable – it was benefitting from the boy's work.

Case	Facts	Legal principle
Hilton v Thomas Burton (Rhodes) Ltd (1961)	Employees took unauthorised break and had accident while driving firm's van, killing one of them	Employer's not liable as the workers were on a 'frolic' of their own.
Twine v Bean's Express (1946)	Claimant's husband killed by negligent driving of worker who had been forbidden to give lifts	Employers not liable – the driver was doing an unauthorised act and the firm was gaining no benefit.
Beard v London General Omnibus Co. (1900)	Bus conductor drove bus negligently injuring the victim	Employers not liable as conductor acted outside the course of his employment.
Lister v Hesley Hall (2001)	Warden sexually assaulted children with emotional difficulties at his school	Employers liable as there was a 'close connection' between his job and what he did.
Catholic Child Welfare Society v Various Claimants (FC) and the Institute of the Brothers of the Christian Schools (2012)	Teachers sexually abused pupils at the school in which they were employed	Employers liable as: ● Relationship between employers and teachers 'akin' to employer/employee relationship, and ● Abuse was connected to that relationship.
Cox v Ministry of Justice (2016)	Prison employee assaulted by prisoner	Not necessary for employer to be carrying out commercial activity. It is enough to be carrying on activities in furtherance of its own interests to be liable.
Mohamud v Morrisons Supermarkets (2016)	Employee assaulted customer at petrol station	Employee acted in the field of his employment, making employers liable.
Armes v Nottingham County Council (2017)	Child abused by foster carers	Foster carers integral to employer's 'business activity' to make them liable.
Barclays Bank v Various claimants (2020)	Doctor assaulted prospective employees while carrying out medical examinations on behalf of bank	Bank not liable for actions of independent contractor.

Figure 24.4 Key cases: vicarious liability

Quick questions

1 Define vicarious liability.
2 Describe the tests that are used to decide whether a person is an employee.
3 Explain who is liable for the torts of an independent contractor.
4 Explain the term 'frolic of its own'.
5 Assess the effect that *Lister v Hesley Hall Ltd* (2001) has had on the law relating to vicarious liability.

Summary

- Vicarious liability imposes liability onto someone who did not commit a tort. It is usually seen in an employee/employer relationship.
- The 'Salmond test' establishes this liability when the employee commits an unintentional tort, the person committing the tort is an employee and the tort is committed in the course of employment.
- The tortfeasor has to be an employee rather than an independent contractor who is solely liable for their torts.
- One way of judging is a person is an employee is the control test – how much control does the employer have over the worker?
- Another test is the integration test – how integrated is the worker into the business?
- The economic reality test looks at all factors in the relationship.
- It is a question of fact in each case if the tort is committed in the course of employment. It can include if the employee, doing his job, acted against orders or committed a negligent act but not if the employee acted on a 'frolic' of his own or when acting against orders and not doing his job.

- Recent cases have had to consider non-traditional working relationships and ask:
  - Was the working relationship akin to employment?

  And

  - Was there a close or sufficient connection between the tort and the employment?
- 'Akin' to employment has five criteria to satisfy:
  - the employer has the means or insurance cover;
  - the employee acted on behalf of the employer;
  - it was part of the business activity of the employer;
  - the employer created the risk of the tort; and
  - the employee was under the control of the employer.
- If there is a close or sufficient relationship, this requires the court to look at the nature of the job and then if there is a sufficient connection between the job and the conduct to make it right that the employer is vicariously liable.

Chapter 25 Defences

Introduction

There are limited defences that can be put forward in a tort claim. Contributory negligence is a part defence and can be argued where the claimant has, in some way, contributed to the accident and injuries. *Volenti* (also known as consent) can be argued where the claimant has agreed to run the risk of injury. There are, in addition, some defences specific to the actions of occupiers' liability and nuisance which are fully dealt with in the chapters relating to those torts.

25.1 Contributory negligence

25.1.1 A part defence

This is a part defence to claims of negligence and occupiers' liability. The defendant argues that the claimant *partly* caused the injuries suffered, and asks the court to reduce the blame and therefore the damages to be paid.

25.1.2 How it operates

The Law Reform (Contributory Negligence) Act 1945 provides that any damages awarded to the claimant can be reduced according to the extent or level to which they had contributed to their own harm.

- The judgment will firstly set the full amount of the damages as if there was no contributory negligence.
- The judge will then decide the percentage that the claimant is responsible for, and then reduce the amount of damages by this percentage. As it is a partial defence, it will only result in a reduction in the amount of damages.
- The defence does not require the defendant show that the claimant owed him a duty of care, just that the claimant failed to take the appropriate care in the situation.
- It will be necessary to prove causation – that the claimant's act or omission helped to cause the injuries suffered, despite the defendant's fault.

Case study

Sayers v Harlow Urban District Council (1958)

While waiting for a bus, the claimant went into the toilet at a bus station. She became trapped inside a cubicle as the door lock jammed. She tried to climb out of the cubicle by standing on the toilet roll holder, but fell and injured her leg.

The Council, who maintained the toilets, were liable but the damages were reduced by 25 per cent because of the careless way she tried to escape.

The defence is commonly used in claims for injuries or damage suffered in road traffic accidents. Damages were reduced in these cases:

- *O'Connell v Jackson* (1972): the motorcyclist failed to wear a crash helmet – damages were reduced by 15 per cent.
- *Froom v Butcher* (1976): the passenger in a vehicle was not wearing a seat belt – damages were reduced by 25 per cent.

It is possible for there to be a 100 per cent reduction in damages, as demonstrated in *Jayes v IMI (Kynoch) Ltd* (1985).

Case study

Jayes v IMI (Kynoch) Ltd (1985)

The claimant lost a finger while cleaning a machine at work, having removed the guard. The employers were liable for breach of statutory provision to maintain a guard on the machine, but the claimant was at fault for removing the guard and 100 per cent contributorily negligent.

Look online

Go to www.bbc.co.uk/news/uk-england-devon-22360093

Could this case open the floodgates to claims against highway authorities?

Is the outcome of this case fair to both parties?

25.2 Volenti non fit injuria

25.2.1 A complete defence

Consent, or *volenti*, is a *full* defence to a claim of negligence or occupiers' liability, when the defendant shows that the claimant voluntarily accepted a risk of harm or injury.

The phrase means that no injury is done to one who consents to the risk. If it successful, the claimant will receive no damages.

25.2.2 How it operates

To succeed, the defendant has to show that the claimant:

1 knew of the precise risk involved
2 exercised free choice, and
3 voluntarily accepted the risk.

One restriction on the use of the defence is s 149 of the Road Traffic Act 1988, which provides that the defence cannot be used for road traffic accidents. This is because of the existence of third-party insurance, which will compensate an injured victim.

- The test of *volenti* is subjective rather than objective.
- The defence will not apply merely because the claimant knows of the existence of the risk; they must fully understand the nature of the actual risk.
- The defence will not succeed where the claimant has no choice but to accept the risk: they must freely undertake the risk of harm.
- Where a person has a duty to act and is then injured because of the defendant's negligence, *volenti* will not be available as a defence. The duty means that the claimant had no choice but to act. This is particularly relevant in rescue cases.

Case studies

Smith v Baker & Sons (1891)

The claimant was employed to hold a drill in position while two other workers took it in turns to hit it with a hammer. Next to where he was working, another set of workers were engaged in taking out stones and putting them into a steam crane that swung over the area where the claimant was working. The claimant was injured when a stone fell out of the crane and struck him on the head. It was decided that the claimant may have been aware of the danger of the job, but had not consented to the lack of care. He was therefore entitled to recover damages.

Haynes v Harwood (1935)

The claimant policeman was injured trying to restrain a horse that had not been properly tied by the defendant. The defence failed as the claimant was acting under a duty to protect the public – he was not acting voluntarily.

It will not help the defendant to argue that the claimant ought to have been aware of the risk. The defence only applies where the claimant does actually know of the risk of injury.

A defendant could argue both contributory negligence and *volenti*. If *volenti* fails, the amount of damages could still be reduced.

See Chapter 21 for full case details of *Nettleship v Weston* (1971). Mrs Weston raised the defence of *volenti* by agreeing to get in the car; knowing she was a learner, Mr Nettleship had voluntarily accepted the risk. It was decided that *volenti* did not apply as he had checked the insurance cover which showed he did not waive any rights to compensation. However, damages were reduced by 50 per cent due to his contributory negligence as he was partly in control of the car.

Activity

Will a defence be available in the following situations?

- Mike was injured when a helicopter piloted by Noel crashed. Mike knew that Noel did not have a current flying licence.
- Jade breaks Remy's collarbone during a kick-boxing contest.
- Terry accepts a lift from John whose estate car is already full. Terry sits on the floor at the rear where there is no seat belt. Terry is injured when the car is involved in an accident due to John's bad driving.
- Heidi is badly injured when her horse pulls up at a fence during a show-jumping competition.
- Tom and Peter are fooling around. Tom aims a punch at Peter, not intending to hit him, but Peter is injured when he ducks to avoid the punch.

Tip

When answering a tort question, consider whether both defences of contributory negligence and *volenti* could apply.

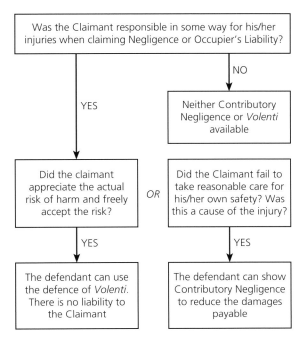

Figure 25.1 How to work out whether a claimant is responsible for their injuries

25.3 Specific defences

Figure 25.2 shows a summary of specific defences for tort.

Link

See Chapter 22 for detailed information on specific defences to occupiers' liability, and Chapter 23 for specific defences to private nuisance and *Rylands v Fletcher*.

Area of tort	Specific defences
Occupiers' liability	Lawful visitors: • Volenti • Contributory negligence • Exclusion clauses • Warning notice Trespassers: • Volenti • Contributory negligence • Warning notice
Private nuisance	• Statutory authority • Prescription
Rylands v Fletcher	• Act of God • Act of a stranger • Wrongful act of third party • Statutory authority

Figure 25.2 A summary of specific defences

Case	Facts	Legal principle
Sayers v Harlow Urban District Council (1958)	The claimant was trapped in a toilet and was injured trying to escape.	Reduced damages by 25% because of claimant's carelessness in escape attempt.
Jayes v IMI (Kynoch) Ltd (1985)	The claimant lost a finger at work, having removed the guard to a machine.	Claimant was 100% contributorily negligent; he was solely at fault by removing the guard.
Smith v Baker & Sons (1891)	The claimant was injured when a stone fell out of a crane.	Claimant did not consent to lack of care by crane operators.
Haynes v Harwood (1935)	The claimant policeman was injured trying to restrain a horse.	No defence of *volenti* as claimant was acting under a public duty – not voluntarily.

Figure 25.3 Key cases: defences

Activity

Explain which defence can be used in the following scenarios.

1 Virat was a passenger in a car which was involved in an accident. His injuries were made worse because he was not wearing a seatbelt.
2 When Charlotte entered a road race, she signed a disclaimer form stating that the organisers would not be liable for any personal injury or death that occurred during the race. She was badly injured when she fell down a pothole in the road.
3 Steven was riding his bike when he was involved in a collision with a car and was injured. He was wearing a helmet but had not fastened the strap.

Quick questions

1 Explain the meaning of '*volenti non fit injuria*' and the effect of this defence.
2 Identify the Act that applies in relation to contributory negligence.
3 Describe the effect of contributory negligence on a tort claim.
4 Consider whether the defence of contributory negligence is effective and fair.

Summary

- Contributory negligence is a part defence where it is shown that the claimant partly contributed to the injuries suffered.
- The court can reduce the damages by such percentage that the claimant bears responsibility.
- It is possible for the claimant to be 100 per cent contributory negligent.
- *Volenti* or consent is a full defence where it is shown that the claimant agrees to run the risk of injury and provided the extent of the risk is known.

Chapter 26 Remedies

Introduction

The main remedy awarded in tort claims will be damages to compensate the claimant for the loss or injury suffered. This addresses one of the main aims of tort law. However, there are other specific remedies such as an injunction to stop or limit the continuation of a nuisance or abatement (self-help) to deal with a nuisance problem.

26.1 Compensatory damages

In a tort claim, the court can award a successful claimant compensation for the injuries they have suffered and/or damage to their property. This award is known as damages.

The aim of the award of damages is to place the claimant in the same position as if the tort had not been committed, as far as money can do so. This is possible where the claim is for damage to property as, for example, a car damaged in an accident can be repaired. However, if the claimant has suffered a serious disabling personal injury, this is not possible as no amount of money can make good such injuries.

26.1.1 Pecuniary and non-pecuniary loss

Pecuniary loss is a loss that can be easily calculated in money terms, such as the cost of:
- hiring a car while the claimant's own car is being repaired
- damaged clothes or fares getting to and from hospital for treatment.

Non-pecuniary loss is loss that is not wholly money-based and not strictly quantifiable. This can include, for example:
- pain and suffering as a result of the accident
- loss of amenity or a change in lifestyle, such as not being able to play a sport.

26.1.2 Special and general damages

Special damages

These are amounts which can be calculated specifically up to the date of the trial or settlement. In other words, they are the pecuniary loss.

- This could include, as set out above, vehicle repairs and the hire of a replacement or replacing damaged clothes.
- Any loss of earnings while recovering from the accident can also be claimed as special damages.
- The cost of any necessary medical treatment such as physiotherapy if this is not otherwise available.

General damages

These are non-pecuniary losses and are looking forward from the trial or settlement date. They can include:
- an amount for pain and suffering
- loss of amenity
- future loss of earnings
- future medical expenses, including adapting a house or car to be suitable for a severely injured person and paying for specialist care.

These amounts are speculative, and evidence will have to be obtained to support the claim. This will include medical evidence of the effect of the accident on the victim and how long the suffering or injuries will take to heal, if at all.

For future loss of earnings and future medical expenses, there has to be an annual calculation of the loss, multiplied by the number of years of the loss. For example, five years' loss of earnings at £25,000 each year will lead to a total loss of earnings of £125,000.

26.1.3 Lump sums and structured settlements

When the court makes an award for pain and suffering and loss of amenity, they can only award a lump sum. This also has to be a once-only award. The claimant cannot come back to court to say that they have exhausted the damages received.

This can be unfair to a claimant whose condition in the future might become worse than originally diagnosed. Also, where a large award is made for future medical expenses, there is the problem of inflation.

On the other hand, an award of a lump sum might be unfair to the defendant if the claimant's condition improves considerably and there is no longer a need to pay for care.

To deal with these situations, the Damages Act 1996 allows for structured settlements to be made.

- This allows parties who settle a claim to agree that all or part of the damages can be paid as periodical payments: an amount per month or a year. This is arranged by the defendant (or probably the defendant's insurer) who will purchase an annuity through a financial company.
- Parties can agree that the payments may be made for life or for a specific period – for example, ten years – and the amount can be reassessed at intervals to ensure that its value in real terms is maintained. This type of settlement protects the claimant whose condition may become worse, and the defendant, if the claimant's condition improves.

This arrangement will have to be agreed by the parties, as the courts have no power to order such arrangements.

26.2 Mitigation of loss

The claimant is entitled to be fully compensated for their loss but the amount of damages should be reasonable. This is called mitigation of loss.

For example:

- While the claimant's Ford car is being repaired, the cost of hiring a Bentley cannot be claimed as a replacement.
- The cost of private health treatment cannot be claimed if the treatment is available on the NHS.

Claiming for hiring a Bentley while your Ford is repaired is not realistic!

The same principle applies if the claimant is claiming for damage to property. The cost of repairing like-for-like can be claimed, but not a more expensive or extensive repair.

When calculating general damages for loss of earnings, the claimant will be expected to mitigate the loss:

- If they can work part-time or at a lower wage, they will be expected to do so.
- The amount of this wage will be deducted from the award.

An example of the court penalising the claimant for failing to mitigate his loss is *Marcroft v Scruttons* (1954), when the claimant was injured due to the defendant's negligence. He then refused to attend hospital and his injuries worsened. The claimant was unable to claim his losses after his refusal to attend hospital due to his refusal to mitigate his loss.

Look online

Go to www.dailymail.co.uk/news/article-7632445/Boy-receives-30million-court-payout-hospital-blunders-left-brain-damaged.html

1. Consider why the award of damages was so high.
2. Will the payment be made in one amount or over a period of time?

Activity

Go to www.fieldfisher.com/en/injury-claims/insights/great-ormond-street-hospital-settle-claim-for-maisha-najeeb-after-she-was-injected-with-glue

1. How were Maisha's damages calculated?
2. Will the award of such a large amount of compensation put her back in the position she was in before the incident?
3. Will the payment be made in one amount or over a period of time?

26.3 Injunctions

Apart from damages, the other main remedy in tort is an injunction. This was explained in the tort of nuisance in Chapter 23.

An injunction is a discretionary order for the defendant to stop doing something (continuing the nuisance) or to limit the hours of an activity, as seen in *Coventry v Lawrence*. In the judgment, it was commented that if the loss or inconvenience suffered by the claimant is slight, then damages could be considered as a more suitable alternative.

If the person on whom the injunction is placed fails to follow the terms of the injunction, they will be in contempt of court and can be punished with a fine or imprisonment for a maximum of two years.

Key term

Contempt of court – failure to comply with an order of a civil court. The court can order punishment in the form of a fine or even imprisonment for failure to comply with an injunction.

Link

See Chapter 23 for the remedy of abatement, or self-help, to remove the nuisance from the claimant's land.

Quick questions

1 Explain the main aim of the award of damages in tort.
2 Explain the award of special damages.
3 Explain the award of general damages.
4 Explain 'mitigation of loss'.
5 Consider the following statement: 'Awards of damages in tort do not provide just remedies to all claimants in all circumstances.' To what extent do you agree with the statement?

Summary

- The main aim of the award of damages in tort is to put the claimant back in the position they were in before the accident, as far as money can do so.
- Pecuniary losses are those that can be easily calculated in money terms.
- Non-pecuniary losses cannot be easily quantified and are speculative.
- Specific damages are specific payments incurred by the claimant between the date of the accident and the court case.
- General damages are calculated looking forward from the date of the court case. They include awards for pain and suffering, loss of amenity, future loss of earnings and future medical expenses.
- A claimant can either be paid in one lump sum or when large amounts are due to be paid in instalments known as structured settlements.
- The claimant is expected to mitigate or reduce his loss as far as possible.
- An alternative to payment of damages is the award of an injunction to stop an action or limit the hours. It is generally awarded in nuisance claims.
- Abatement, or self-help, can be used in nuisance claims to remove the cause of the nuisance.

Chapter 27 Evaluation

27.1 Critical evaluation of liability in negligence

27.1.1 Duty of care

The purpose of the duty of care is to allow the possibility of legal liability being imposed. It establishes the range of persons, relationships and interests that should be legally protected from negligently inflicted harm. Deciding whether a duty exists is an effective way of filtering negligence claims before issues of breach, causation and the amount of damages are considered, and this may help to reduce the number of claims brought to court.

The law does not impose a duty for a person to act to prevent foreseeable harm – for example, to save a person drowning in a river, sea or lake. It only imposes a duty where a person has assumed certain responsibility and created or adopted a risk of harm to others. Causing physical injury and damage to property are normally within the scope of a duty of care. Financial or other losses not directly related to physical harm may not be within its scope.

For many years after the decision in *Caparo v Dickman* (1990), it was thought necessary to apply the three-stage test in every case to decide whether a duty existed. There were criticisms of this test because:
- The three-stage test overall was considered to lack clarity, making it difficult for lawyers to advise their clients whether to take a claim, and for judges deciding cases in court.
- The proximity test has never been fully established to show exactly who falls within a proximity of relationship. But, by not strictly defining such relationships, it does mean that new situations can always be developed and, as Lord Macmillan said in *Donoghue v Stevenson* (1932), 'the categories of negligence are never closed'.
- There is an overlap between the tests of reasonable foreseeability required for the existence of a duty of care and for remoteness of damage.
- The fair, just and reasonable test is vague, and it cannot be predicted when a judge will find it satisfied or not.

The decision in *Robinson v Chief Constable of West Yorkshire* (2018) does seem to have clarified when the *Caparo* three-stage test is required. According to this decision, it is not in every claim, only in a novel situation. Where it has been decided previously that a duty exists, then according to *Robinson*, the precedent can be applied directly.

27.1.2 Breach of duty

Many different factors determine whether a breach of duty was reasonable:
- Allowing the defendant's certain characteristics to be considered allows the law to be applied fairly to the particular defendant.
- Allowing individual characteristics of the claimant to be taken into account offers more vulnerable claimants greater protection. For example, in *Nettleship v Weston*, it would have been unfair to Mrs Weston to have treated her in the same way

as an experienced driver as she was on her third lesson. However, it could be said that there was a policy reason for the decision in this case. Every driver, whether a novice on their first lesson, or very experienced, has to have some form of insurance cover, and the experience or otherwise of the driver should not be a reason for an insurance company not to pay out.

● The same general principle applies to professionals. The standard of care is not reduced if a professional lacks experience so, for example, a junior doctor must exercise the same standard of care and skill as an experienced doctor.

On the other hand, in *Paris v Stepney Borough Council*, it was cheap and straightforward for the defendant Council to provide Mr Paris with goggles, or some other protective equipment: it was known that he was vulnerable and needed protection for the job he was expected to do.

Considering the size of the risk and the practicality of eliminating it means, in certain cases, that avoiding risk is not onerous for the defendant.

● In *Bolton v Stone* (1951), it was considered that the cricket club had done everything they could, in view of the small risk, to protect passers-by so that they should not be liable. Obviously, this was unfair on Miss Stone who was left without compensation for her injuries. Attitudes have changed since this decision – nowadays the club (through their insurers) would be liable as it would be considered that passers-by should receive greater protection than Miss Stone received.

● An early example of this view would be in *Haley v London Electricity Board* (1965), where greater protection should have been provided for blind pedestrians.

With greater emphasis on health and safety, working sites now have more barriers to protect all passers-by from injury. Courts will also consider whether all appropriate precautions have been taken by a defendant and balance this against the cost and effort of taking those precautions.

● So, in *Latimer v AEC* (1951), it was considered reasonable for the factory to spread sawdust over a previously flooded factory floor in order that production could restart. Again, with greater emphasis on health and safety, employers would now be required to take greater precautions to protect their workers in the workplace. This can be

Protective measures in the workplace to protect employees from Covid-19

seen with the requirements placed on employers to protect all employees in the Covid-19 pandemic.

It is fair that there should no liability if a risk has to be taken when the benefit to society is greater than the potential harm. For example:

● In both *Watt v Hertfordshire County Council* (1954) and *Day v High Performance Sports* (2003), it was essential for the defendants to act quickly.

● In emergency situations, it is possible that corners will be cut, and procedures overlooked as speed is of the essence. It would not be fair to penalise a defendant in this situation if the life of an accident victim is at stake.

It is fair that a defendant is judged against what is common practice and the knowledge of the time, especially in medical or scientific areas, where developments and changes in practice can take place in a short time. For example:

● In *Roe v Minister of Health* (1954), it would not be fair for the health authority to be liable for the contamination of a glass test tube if the reason for it was not known when the injection was administered. Of course, lessons would have been learned, as with any medical procedure, so that the same mistake should not have occurred in later years.

● Doctors treating Covid-19 patients in 2020, when the virus first came to light, should be treated legally according to the knowledge available at the time. Lessons were quickly learned during the first wave of infection in the spring, and procedures were developed for treating patients in the second wave during the autumn of that year.

On the other hand, what is reasonable is an objective question which could operate unfairly against

289

a defendant. The law does not take account of a defendant's actual experience, just the standard of skill that is expected at that level.

A claim may be defeated if a defendant's actions are considered reasonable even if others in the same profession have differing opinions about the actions taken.

- For many years 'Common Practice' as set out in *Bolam v Friern Barnet Hospital Management Committee* (1957) allowed professionals to set their own acceptable standards, and opinions within that profession could have differed, but were still acceptable. This approach meant that claims would be easier to defeat, and marginal or experimental practice could be deemed acceptable if some doctors approved of it.
- This test has been modified for the giving of consent by the decision in *Montgomery v Lanarkshire Health Board* (2015). As a result of this case, a doctor is under a duty to take reasonable care to ensure that a patient is aware of any material risks involved in any recommended treatment, and of any reasonable alternative or variant treatments.

27.1.3 Causation and remoteness

The third part of any negligence claim is for the claimant to prove that the injury or damage suffered was caused by a breach of the duty of care, and that the injury or damage was not too remote. There are two parts to this:

1 Factual causation using the 'but for' test.
2 Legal causation proving that the injury was reasonably foreseeable and not too remote from the defendant's negligence.

The principles of factual causation are generally fair, as the 'but for' test allows all claimants to be treated in the same way. However, this test is only appropriate where there is one defendant and one cause of damage. If there are many defendants and more than one cause of injury or damage, the claimant may not be able to prove which defendant was negligent. They might not receive compensation despite a duty of care having been breached, which is obviously unfair.

- In some cases, such as in *Barnett v Chelsea & Kensington Hospital Management Committee* (1969), the facts allow the factual causation test to apply in a straightforward manner. The victim of arsenic poisoning would have died, whether he had been treated at hospital or not.

- However, sometimes judges will ignore any problems applying the 'but for' test and find policy reasons in order to give a just result. This was the case in *Chester v Asfhar* (2004), where a consultant surgeon failed to warn a patient about the risk associated with an operation. She had the operation, which worsened her condition. Lord Hope in the House of Lords said:

> On policy grounds therefore I would hold that the test of causation is satisfied in this case. The injury was intimately involved with the duty to warn. The duty was owed by the doctor who performed the surgery that Miss Chester consented to. It was the product of the very risk that she should have been warned about when she gave her consent. So, I would hold that it can be regarded as having been caused, in the legal sense, by the breach of that duty.

Sometimes liability will not be imposed because the defendant's negligence does not cause the injury or damage, but instead sets the scene for something or someone else to inflict the loss. This is said to be the intervening act. The rules do not provide consistent outcomes as it must be decided whether the intervening cause is sufficiently significant to free the defendant from liability. For example:

- A natural event can amount to a *novus actus*. In *Carslogie Steamship Co. v Royal Norwegian Government* (1952), the defendant negligently caused damage to the claimant's ship. This caused the claimant to change the ship's schedule to send it for repairs when it would otherwise not have been at sea. It was further damaged in a severe storm. The defendant was only liable for the original damage, not the storm damage.
- In *Lamb v Camden Council* (1981), the claimant's house was flooded due to the defendant's negligence. The claimant vacated but squatters moved in and caused considerable damage. The Council was not liable for the damage caused by the squatters as the chain of causation had been broken.

If the claimant's actions are reasonable but they took a certain risk, then it must be considered whether the defendant should be liable for an injury associated with that risk.

- In *Spencer v Wincanton Holdings* (2009), the claimant had a leg amputated after an accident at work caused by the defendant employer's actions. The claimant fell and was injured while filling his car at a petrol station, while not using either crutches or a false leg. The defendant was held liable for the further injuries as the claimant's actions were considered reasonable and it was fair that he should be compensated for them. There was no *novus actus* present in this case.

The rules on remoteness of damage can be unfair to a claimant as they can operate in a way to limit the defendant's liability. The approach taken by the courts in determining what 'type' of damage may be foreseeable may not be fair. For example:

- In *Doughty v Turner Asbestos* (1964), the claimant did not succeed. The burn injuries received by him were not reasonably foreseeable, as knowledge at the time could not have predicted an explosion.

More recently the courts have developed tests as to whether a defendant made a 'material contribution' or 'material increase of risk of harm' to provide justice in specific instances – for example, with claimants suffering from mesothelioma.

- In *Fairchild v Glenhaven* (2002), the claimants had been exposed to asbestos by a number of different employers. They were unable to demonstrate, and medical science was unable to detect, which employer exposed each of them to the one fatal fibre. The House of Lords decided that if a claimant could show that one employer had materially increased the risk of contracting mesothelioma, they were entitled to claim full compensation from that one employer. This approach provided justice for the claimant in this particular case but could be unfair to a defendant employer who may not actually have been to blame.
- In *Barker v Corus* (2006), another asbestos case, the question was whether, if one of the employers that was responsible for increasing the risk of harm had gone out of business, should any existing employers be required to pay their portion? The House of Lords decided that an existing solvent employer should not. As a result, a successful claimant would only receive a proportion of the damages to which he or she was entitled.
- After this case, the Compensation Act 2006 was introduced to reverse the ruling in cases of mesothelioma and provide justice for claimants who will receive compensation in full. Whether the 'proportionate liability' idea will be applied to other claims remains to be seen.

Look online

There are arguments that we should have a no-fault system of tort liability. Read the following article and consider its content:

www.keepcalmtalklaw.co.uk/if-its-not-faulty-dont-fix-it-defending-fault-in-negligence/

27.2 Critical evaluation of occupiers' liability

The duty imposed on occupiers has been imposed by statute, whereas in negligence it is a common law duty.

The statutes imposing duties on occupiers were introduced at different times. The 1957 Act deals with liability to lawful visitors and the 1984 Act deals with liability to trespassers. There are some differences between the liability under the two Acts:

1. The 1957 Act allows for claims for personal injury and any damage to property suffered on another's property, whereas the 1984 Act allows more limited claims by trespassers to personal injury only. This can be justified because, as Lord Hoffman said in *Tomlinson v Congleton DC* (2003):

> Parliament recognised that it would often be unduly burdensome to require landowners to take steps to protect the safety of people who came upon their land without invitation or permission. They should not ordinarily be able to force duties upon unwilling hosts.

2. The two Acts set two different approaches to the imposition of a duty.
   - The 1957 Act requires an occupier to do everything that is reasonable to ensure the visitor will be reasonably safe – an objective test. This follows the standard approach to tort claims, where a defendant's acts or omissions are judged objectively.
   - However, for a duty to exist under the 1984 Act, the occupier has to be aware of the danger and has to know, or have reasonable grounds to believe, that the trespasser is in the vicinity of the danger. This is a subjective test so that if the occupier does not have the required knowledge of the existence of the danger or the trespasser, they will not owe a duty. This subjective test is inconsistent with most other torts.

This means that each claim under the 1984 Act will depend on its own facts. For example, in *Donoghue v Folkestone Properties* (2003), the occupier had no knowledge of the presence of the claimant trespasser and so owed no duty to him. This was because the accident happened at night in winter. A different result might have been achieved if the accident occurred in daytime or during summer months. It seems unusual that liability should depend on when the accident happened – the time of day or year.

3   For claims under both Acts, it is 'necessary to identify the particular danger before one can see to what (if anything) the occupier's duty is', per McCombe LJ in *Edwards v Sutton LBC* (2016). The 1984 Act requires the occupier to have actual knowledge of the danger, whereas this is not required by the 1957 Act. So, for a claim under the 1984 Act, if the occupier has no knowledge of the danger then they will not owe a duty. This was the case in *Rhind v Astby* (2004), where the occupier had no knowledge of a submerged container on which the claimant trespasser was injured, and was not liable. Also, under the 1984 Act, there is no obligation on the occupier to check for any danger on the premises.

4   Except for child visitors, the 1957 Act does not require the court to consider whether the premises are safe for the visitor who is injured. However, under the 1984 Act, a duty is owed if the occupier may reasonably be expected to offer the injured trespasser some protection. Whether the occupier is judged to have acted reasonably may depend on the injured trespasser – what is reasonable for that particular person?

5   The 1984 Act gives trespassers the right to make claims, but judges have found reasons not to allow this. This reflects public opinion, which does not agree that a person who should not be on premises can profit from their actions.

   ○   An example of this approach is where judges have introduced the concept of 'obvious dangers' into claims by trespassers. No duty is owed by an occupier when the trespasser is injured due to an obvious danger. For example, in *Ratcliff v McConnell* (1999), the claimant, as an adult, was not owed a duty due to the obvious danger in the swimming pool – he should have appreciated an obvious risk. Even though he was severely injured, he was not able to claim compensation.

   ○   Another example is the case of *Revill v Newbery* (1996). Eighty-two-year-old Ted Newbery injured a trespasser who burgled his allotment shed. There was a media-led outcry when Mark Revill, the trespasser, was granted legal aid to claim for his personal injuries against Newbery – the occupier. At the time of making the claim, Revill was serving a prison sentence for burgling Newbery's property. His claim for civil damages was based on the 1984 Act and trespass to the person. Revill was awarded damages in the civil court but the amount was reduced by two-thirds for his contributory negligence. The damages payable by Newbery were covered by public donations, and the judge received a considerable amount of hate mail for finding Newbery liable.

Lord Phillips, in *Donoghue v Folkestone Properties* (2003), summed up the judicial view of claims under the 1984 Act:

> There are, however, circumstances in which it may be foreseeable that a trespasser will appreciate that a dangerous feature of premises poses a risk of injury, but will nevertheless deliberately court the danger and risk the injury. It seems to me that, at least where the individual is an adult, it will be rare that those circumstances will be such that the occupier can reasonably be expected to offer some protection to the trespasser against the risk.

The concept of obvious dangers has also recently been introduced into claims under the 1957 Act. In *Edwards v Sutton LBC* (2016), the claimant was badly injured when he fell off a bridge over a stream in a public park. McCombe LJ said:

> The approach to the bridge was clear and unobstructed. The width of the bridge and the height of the parapets were also obvious to the eye. Any user of the bridge would appreciate the need to take care and any user limiting the width of the bridge's track, by pushing a bicycle to his side, would see the need to take extra care. It is not necessary to give a warning against obvious dangers ... Not every accident (even if it has serious consequences) has to have been the fault of another ... [and] an occupier is not an insurer against injuries sustained on his premises ... occupiers of land are not under a duty to protect, or even to warn, against obvious dangers.

On the one hand it is fair that a visitor should receive compensation if they are injured whilst on the premises of another when the occupier is at fault by not making their premises safe. However, over time this has developed into something of a compensation culture when claims are made at every opportunity, especially by lawful visitors. More recently, the courts seem to be sending a message that, despite the development of a compensation culture, visitors have to take personal responsibility for their safety and sometimes accidents do happen for which there is no remedy. Examples of this approach are *Laverton v Kiapasha Takeaway Supreme* (2002), which was reinforced in *The Dean and Chapter of Rochester Cathedral v Debell* (2016).

If these claims had been decided in favour of the claimants, other similar claims would follow, and the cost of liability insurance cover would rise for everyone.

Generally, it is fair that an occupier is responsible for the reasonable safety of their lawful visitors. This does not mean making premises completely safe but *reasonably* safe, and judges will support this approach. This strikes a fair balance between the rights and duties of occupiers to maintain the safety of their property and lawful visitors' personal responsibility for their safety, particularly in public areas or open spaces. If a lawful visitor is injured and can claim compensation, the aim of compensating a person injured by the tort of another is achieved. Often this will be via public liability insurance cover.

However, it seems to be different in the case of claims by trespassers. Public opinion supports the view that an occupier should not deliberately injure a trespasser. However, there is less support for allowing claims by trespassers who should not be on another's land without permission. This approach is achieved by judges ruling that, although statute allows claims, a trespasser cannot claim when injured by an obvious danger. The trespasser has to accept full personal responsibility for their actions as they should not be on land that does not belong to them. On the other hand, the aim of tort to compensate a person injured by the action of another has not been met. There does then seem to be an imbalance between the interests of the occupier and the trespasser.

Whatever the legal arguments for or against a claim, if the lawful visitor or trespasser is severely injured and is unsuccessful in claiming, the burden of caring for them for the rest of their life is likely to be passed to the state.

27.3 Critical evaluation of vicarious liability

Vicarious liability is justified because it gives a victim a just and practical remedy: in the event of a successful claim, the claimant is more likely to receive compensation than if they pursued just the employee. This is because an employer is more likely than an employee to have the financial means to pay any award.

- This justified the imposition of liability in *Limpus v London General* (1862) and *Rose v Plenty* (1976). These decisions operated harshly on the employers as they had prohibited the practices but were still found liable. The claimant is an innocent victim and the aim of tort law will be met by providing them with a remedy for their loss.

In addition, and more likely, the employer will have liability insurance cover which will pay any damages awarded. In practice:

- The employer will only be paying the premium for this cover, and any excess, so will not be paying the actual damages awarded.
- Insurers will spread the cost of paying damages among all their policy holders, which makes the burden of paying compensation manageable.
- If an employer has to make a claim, they are likely to find their future premiums will increase. This may act as a deterrent to having poor employment practices and encourage them to improve their recruitment, training and supervision of staff.
- The employer receives a benefit from the work being completed, so it is only fair that they should accept the liabilities.
- The employer can pass on the costs to their customers of complying with safe working practices as seen with some businesses, such as dentists, passing on the costs of using PPE equipment in their surgeries during the Covid-19 pandemic.
- Despite the burden of vicarious liability, it will only be enforced if the tortfeasor is an employee, the tort is committed in the course of employment and, in certain situations, there is a close connection between the tort and the employment.

On the other hand, the principle appears to contradict the concept of fault-based liability:

- The employer may have taken every step to choose, train and supervise its employees but will still be liable for their acts and omissions. This is fair when the employee commits the tortious act in the workplace, but is less fair where the act is committed outside the workplace, or while home working, when the employer has less control and supervision of the employee's actions.

- There have been some inconsistent and unfair decisions relating to road accidents and whether they were carried out in the course of employment.
  - If an employee is acting 'on a frolic', as in *Hilton v Thomas Burton (Rhodes)* (1961), the victim, or the victim's relatives, will be unsuccessful in claiming compensation. This is obviously unfair as Mrs Hilton clearly suffered loss, and her husband was killed in his work time and in the employer's van, but she was unsuccessful in proving vicarious liability. Unless she was successful in suing and recovering compensation from the negligent driver, she was not able to be compensated for her loss. Obviously, in a case such as this, the aim of tort law to compensate victims is not being met.
  - The decision in this case clearly contrasts with *Smith v Stages* (1989) where, on similar facts, the victim was able to claim vicarious liability. The difference in the decisions was merely related to the purpose of the employee's journey.
  - In *Beard v London General* (1900), the injured victim would not have been aware that the employee was not authorised to drive the bus, and, as a result, was not able to prove vicarious liability, which was obviously unfair on him.
  - Similarly, the decisions of *Rose v Plenty* (1976) and *Twine v Beans Express* (1946) showed that the courts were employing the principles inconsistently.

In contrast, where the employee commits a crime in the course of employment, or the employee has been dishonest, the courts are more prepared to make the employer vicariously liable. This can be seen with the development of the concept of 'close connection' with the employment, which has been developed to allow claims in cases such as *Lister v Hesley Hall* (2001), and *Mohamud v Morrisons* (2016). Further, the concept of 'akin' to employment has been used in cases such as *Cox v Minister of Justice* (2016) where there was no employment relationship at all.

It is obviously fair for the victims of the crimes that they should receive compensation for the injuries suffered, and they would be unlikely to obtain compensation from the person who inflicted those injuries as they are likely to be serving prison sentences. It could be argued, in favour of liability, that the employers in each of these cases should have supervised more closely the actions of their workers and those committing the offences. On the other hand, employers would not consider it fair that they should be liable for criminal actions where they were not committed directly in the course of employment but in situations 'akin' to employment.

As a result of the 'close connection' test, employers should take greater care when selecting their employees and on providing suitable training, and especially supervision, in the workplace.

- The decision in *Century Insurance v Northern Ireland Road Transport Board* (1942) is an example of this, as the employer should have made it totally clear to its employee that smoking while delivering petrol was dangerous.

It shows that employers have a social responsibility for their position and a business should see this responsibility as one of the underlying costs of being an employer. However:

- Modern methods of working from home, or more flexibly, mean that it is not always possible for employers to closely supervise their workforce, and it could be said to be unfair on them to accept liability for an employee's actions when they are working away from the employer's eyes.
- The tort will often have occurred before the employer realises that the employee has behaved negligently, criminally or against orders. If the employer takes disciplinary action against the employee as a result, this could be going against natural justice as any action should be taken at the time of and because of the tort, and not later.

For cases of dishonesty, the House of Lords decided in *Dubai Aluminium Company Limited v Salaam* (2002) that it is no longer possible to conclude that a firm will not be held to be vicariously liable for the acts of a partner simply because he or she has been dishonest. A firm, in this case a partnership, can be responsible for dishonest actions of fellow partners if the tortious acts are closely enough connected to the business of the firm.

An employer, or their insurer, can use the Civil Liability (Contribution) Act 1978 to recover from an employee any compensation paid out. If this message was given to employees, it could act as a deterrent to committing wrongs in the workplace. However, this right of recovery is unlikely to be effective in practice:

- The employee is unlikely to be earning sufficient to make it worth the employer (or their insurers) pursuing them for large amounts of money.
- The employee could leave the employment, or be dismissed, and the employer's rights of recovery will be difficult, or impossible, to enforce.
- This would certainly be the case if the employee has committed a crime during the employment and is serving a sentence of imprisonment. Rogue employees will know that there is little chance of them being sued or financially penalised by their employer, so there is little incentive to take care at work.

Summary

Negligence

- A duty of care establishes a legal relationship between the parties. It has been ruled that the three-stage *Caparo* test is not required to be satisfied in every case, just in novel situations.
- Breach of duty requires the court to consider various factors objectively, which may be unfair on certain defendants.
- The factual causation test may operate unfairly if there are multiple defendants. Remoteness of damage can also lead to some unfair results. In both cases judges have found policy reasons to overcome unfairness and reach just decisions.

Occupiers' liability

- The 1957 Act imposes an objective test for the occupier to do everything reasonable to ensure the visitor is reasonably safe whilst on the premises. This is consistent with the test used by other torts.

- The right to claim when injured on other person's property can be considered fair when the occupier has been at fault in some way. This right has led to a compensation culture that courts are trying to reign in to an extent.
- The 1984 Act uses a subjective test looking at every case on its facts, which is contrary to the approach of other torts.
- It is harder to claim under this Act, reflecting public opinion that wrong-doers should not profit from their actions.

Vicarious liability

- It is fair for victims of tort to receive compensation and it is unlikely they will receive any from a worker.
- Employers should take greater care to choose, train and supervise their employees.
- It contradicts the fault-based principle of liability.
- Courts have developed close connection and akin to employment tests to deal with 'new' situations.

Section 5

THE NATURE OF LAW

Chapter 28 Introduction to the nature of law

28.1 Law and rules: The difference between enforceable legal rules and principles and other rules and norms of behaviour

28.1.1 Laws

Laws are a set of rules, mostly created by law-makers acting on behalf of a state and which are imposed on all the citizens of the state. They will generally apply to the whole country – except for some forms of delegated legislation such as by-laws, which may only apply to a small area. In a criminal sense, laws will be enforced on the citizens by a system of courts which can impose sanctions for non-compliance. In a civil sense, laws regulate the conduct of citizens towards each other and can set rules requiring the payment of compensation, or some other order, for the benefit of an innocent party.

Judicial precedent allows judges to make decisions in court which have the effect of law. The principle of parliamentary sovereignty means that the will of Parliament, the Legislature, has greater authority over judicial precedent. This is because the Legislature is democratically elected and is carrying out the will of the people.

Laws will generally be written down and published. This is certainly the case when a law is made by the Legislature. Laws will apply to each and every citizen, whether they have lived in this country all their lives or whether they have just arrived. They will also apply whether the citizen knows of their existence or not and whether they have read and understood them or not. It can be seen that laws, whether criminal or civil in nature, are a form of social control and regulate the behaviour of citizens towards each other.

28.1.2 Rules

The term 'rule' has been defined by Twining and Miers as 'a general norm, mandating or guiding conduct' – in other words something that guides behaviour. A rule will often operate in a specific area such as a sport, or in a school or college. Each sport will have its own rules which set out how it should be played, who should officiate and any sanctions for unfair play. It will be appreciated that the rules will only apply to organised games and, in less official matches, it will be for the players to apply the rules to themselves. A school or college will have its own rules governing behaviour of all pupils and these may differ from institution to institution.

There may also be unwritten 'rules' that apply to a group or community. These may come from local custom or practice or they may be connected to religious beliefs. Breach of these types of rules can involve the disapproval of other members of the group or community, rather than any formal sanction. Each member may feel guilt if they break a rule and so will ensure that they keep to the rules. Members of the group or community are likely to accept the rules and abide by them in order to continue their membership of the group or community.

28.2 The connections between law, morality and justice

28.2.1 Law and morality

The moral values of communities lay down a framework for how people should behave. Concepts of morality differ from culture to culture, although most outlaw extreme behaviour such as murder.

The moral standards of a community have a profound influence on the development of law, but in complex societies, morality and law are never likely to be exactly the same. Major breaches of a moral code (such as murder and robbery) will be against the law, but in other matters there may not be consensus.

In England and Wales, there has been a move away from religious belief and the way that the law has developed reflects this:

- Abortion was legalised in 1967, yet many people still believe it is morally wrong.
- A limited form of euthanasia has been accepted as legal with the ruling in *Airedale NHS Trust v Bland* (1993), where it was ruled that medical staff could withdraw life-support systems from a patient who could breathe unaided, but who was in a persistent vegetative state. This ruling meant the feeding tubes of a patient could be withdrawn, despite the fact that this would inevitably cause the patient's death. Although causing this form of death by an omission is lawful, many would consider this is immoral as it denies the sanctity of human life.

The right to die is another area where law and morality can be in conflict. Doctors and nurses should act in the best interests of the patient, but this may be in conflict with the patient's wishes. Where a patient is mentally capable of deciding what treatment they wish to receive, then the medical staff must act in line with those wishes. A good example of this conflict is the case of *Re B (Adult: Refusal of Medical Treatment)* (2002).

There are also differences between law and morality in the way they develop and the sanctions imposed. For example:

1 Morality cannot be deliberately changed; it evolves slowly and changes according to the will of the people. Law can be altered deliberately by legislation: this means that behaviour which was against the law can be 'decriminalised' overnight. Equally, behaviour which was lawful can be declared unlawful.

Case study

Re B (Adult: Refusal of Medical Treatment) (2002)

Mrs B was a 43-year-old woman who was paralysed from the neck down. She needed a ventilator to help her breathe. There was no prospect of her ever recovering. She made numerous requests for her ventilator to be turned off, knowing that this would lead to her death. Her doctors refused her requests so she applied to the courts for a declaration that she had the necessary mental capacity to refuse treatment and for her ventilator to be turned off. It was decided that, as she was competent, she could decide on her treatment and it was unlawful to continue her treatment.

The judge stated that the fact that a patient's wishes go against the medical team's values and beliefs about what is in the patient's interests is not a valid justification for refusing the patient's request. If the team in charge of the patient is unwilling to act on the patient's request, they must find others who will.

2 Morality is voluntary with consequences, but generally carries no official sanction (though some religions may 'excommunicate' and reject members if they break the moral code). Morality relies for its effectiveness on the individual's sense of shame or guilt. Law makes certain behaviour obligatory, enforced by legal sanctions.

3 Breaches of morality are not usually subject to a formal process of adjudication. Breaches of law will be ruled on by a formal legal system.

Extension activity

In *Re A (conjoined twins)* (2000), the Court of Appeal had to decide whether an operation to separate conjoined twins should be allowed. The effect of the operation would be that one of the twins would die as she was incapable of independent existence.

1 Search for, and read a report of this case.
2 Discuss whether this sort of decision should be made by parents, doctors or judges.
3 Discuss whether it was right for the operation to go ahead, knowing that one life would be saved at the expense of the other.

28.2.2 Law and justice

It is often said that law provides justice, yet this is not always so. Justice is probably the ultimate goal towards which the law should strive, but it is unlikely that law will ever produce 'justice' in every case.

There is the problem of what is meant by 'justice'. The difficulty of defining justice was commented on by Lord Wright, a judge in the House of Lords in the mid-twentieth century, who said:

> the guiding principle of a judge in deciding cases is to do justice; that is justice according to the law, but still justice. I have not found any satisfactory definition of justice ... what is just in a particular case is what appears just to the just man, in the same way as what is reasonable appears to be reasonable to the reasonable man.

Different people's concept of what is justice may not be the same. Justice can be seen as applying the rules in the same way to all people, but even this may lead to perceived injustices – in fact, rigid application of rules may actually produce injustice:

- This can be seen in the statutory interpretation case of *London & North Eastern Railway Co. v Berriman* (1946), examined in Chapter 16. This case illustrates that following the exact wording of a law can lead to an injustice. It was correct that Mr Berriman was not 'relaying or repairing' the railway track, but most people would agree that he was doing his job, and applying the law strictly to deny his widow compensation in this way was not justice.
- In the law of tort, an example of justice not being seen to be done is the case of *Robinson v Chief Constable of West Yorkshire* (2018), detailed in Chapter 21. Mrs Robinson, an innocent elderly lady, was injured when police officers arrested a suspected drug dealer. The Supreme Court decided that she was not owed a duty of care in negligence and, despite being injured, was unable to claim compensation for her injuries.
- Similarly, in *Hilton v Thomas Burton (Rhodes) Ltd* (1961), the employers were not vicariously liable to compensate the widow of a man who was killed, during working hours, as the driver of the van in which he was travelling was said to be acting on a 'frolic' of his own. This case is detailed in Chapter 24.

On the other hand, it can be said that justice was done in the case of *Mohamud v Morrisons Supermarkets* (2016), also dealt with in Chapter 26. The employer was liable for the criminal assault carried out by one of their workers as it was said there was a 'close connection' between his assault and the work he was supposed to be doing.

28.2.3 Morality and justice

People's ideas of what justice is may be founded on their religious beliefs and the moral code they follow. In this way there is an overlap between morality and justice. However, many people with no religious views still have a sense of justice.

It is clear that the three concepts of law, morality and justice are quite distinct. There is, however, an overlap between law and morality, law and justice and also between morality and justice.

Activity ?

Write notes to compare and contrast the legal and moral issues in right to die cases.

28.3 The differences between civil and criminal law

In the English legal system, criminal and civil law are quite separate. The purpose of the law is different and cases are dealt with in different courts.

28.3.1 Civil law

Civil law is about private disputes between individuals and/or businesses. There are several different types of civil law, some of which are covered in this book. They include:

- the law of tort
- contract law
- human rights
- family law
- employment law
- company law.

28.3.2 Differences between civil and criminal law

Purpose of the law

- Civil law upholds the rights of individuals against other individuals or businesses. Compensation can be ordered to put the parties in the position they would have been in if there had not been any breach of the civil law.
- Criminal law is aimed at trying to maintain law and order in society. So, when a person is found guilty of an offence, that offender will be punished. There are also the aims of trying to protect society and trying to deter criminal behaviour, and these are the justifications for sending offenders to prison.

Person starting the case

- In civil cases:
  - The person starting the case is the individual or business which has suffered loss as a result of the breach of civil law.
  - They are called the claimant.
- Criminal cases are taken on behalf of the state:
  - The Crown Prosecution Service is responsible for conducting most cases.
  - They are referred to, in proceedings, as the prosecutor.

Courts

The cases take place in different courts.

Civil cases

- These are heard in the High Court (higher value cases) or the County Court (lower value cases). Family cases, however, take place in the Family Court.
- In both the High Court and the County Court, a judge will try the case, decide the liability and set the amount of compensation.

Criminal cases

- These are tried in either the Magistrates' Courts or the Crown Court. The Magistrates' Courts deal with less serious offences and the case is tried either by a panel of lay magistrates or by a single, legally qualified District Judge.
- Serious offences are tried in the Crown Court, where the case is tried by a judge sitting with a jury. The judge decides points of law and the jury decides the verdict of 'guilty' or 'not guilty'. The judge will impose a sentence.

Standard of proof

- Criminal cases must be proved 'beyond reasonable doubt'. This is a very high standard of proof, and is necessary since a conviction could result in the defendant serving a long prison sentence and a guilty verdict having a profound effect on their future.
- Civil cases have to be proved 'on the balance of probabilities'. This is a lower standard of proof, where the judge decides who is most likely to be right. This difference in the standard of proof means that it is possible for a defendant who has been acquitted in a criminal case to be found liable in a civil case based on the same facts. Such situations are rare, but do sometimes occur.

Outcome of case

Civil cases

- A defendant in a civil case is found 'liable' or 'not liable'.
- At the end of a civil case, the party found liable will be ordered to put right the matter as far as possible. This is usually done by an award of money in compensation, known as damages, though the court can make other orders such as an injunction.

Criminal cases

- A defendant in a criminal case is found 'guilty' or 'not guilty'. Another way of stating this in criminal cases is to say that the defendant is 'convicted' or 'acquitted'.
- At the end of a criminal case, a defendant found guilty of an offence will receive some form of punishment. There are a range of sentences available, depending on the seriousness of the offence.

	Civil cases	Criminal cases
Purpose of the law	To uphold the rights of individuals	To maintain law and order: to protect society
Person starting the case	The individual whose rights have been affected – known as the claimant	Usually the state through the Crown Prosecution Service – known as the prosecution
Courts hearing cases	County Court or High Court	Magistrates' Court or Crown Court
Standard of proof	The balance of probabilities	Beyond reasonable doubt
Person/s making the decision	Judge	Magistrates/District Judge in Magistrates' Court A judge and jury in Crown Court
Decision	Liable or not liable	Guilty (convicted) or not guilty (acquitted)
Powers of the court	Usually an award of damages (compensation) Other remedies are also possible, e.g. injunctions	Prison, community order, fine

Figure 28.1 Differences between criminal and civil cases

28.4 An overview of the development of English law

The law has developed through various sources of law including custom, common law, equity and statute law.

28.4.1 Custom

A custom is a rule of behaviour that develops in a community without being suddenly invented. Historically, customs are believed to have been very important as they were the basis of our common law (see the next section). It is thought that, following the Norman Conquest, judges were appointed by the king to travel around the land, making decisions in the king's name. The judges based at least some of their decisions on the common customs of the area and the country. This idea caused Lord Justice Coke in the seventeenth century to describe these customs as being 'one of the main triangles of the laws of England'.

Custom is a historical source of law and is unlikely to create new law today.

28.4.2 Common law

Clearly the legal system in England and Wales could not rely only on customs. After the Norman Conquest in 1066, a more organised system of courts was established, as the Norman kings realised that control of the country would be easier if they controlled, among other things, the legal system.

Judges were sent from London to major towns all around the country to decide important cases. In the time of Henry II (1154–89), these tours became more regular and Henry divided up the country into 'circuits', or areas, for the judges to visit.

Over a period of time the judges, on their return to London, would discuss the laws or customs they had used and the decisions they had made. Gradually, the judges selected the best customs, which were then used by all the judges throughout the country. The law became uniform or 'common' through the whole country, and it is from here that the phrase 'common law' seems to have developed.

Common law is the basis of our law today: it is unwritten law that developed from customs and judicial decisions. The phrase 'common law' is still used to distinguish laws that have been developed by judicial decisions (also known as judicial precedent), or created by statute or delegated legislation. For example, murder is a common law crime, while theft is a statutory crime. This means that murder has never been defined in any Act of Parliament, but theft is defined by the Theft Act 1968.

Judges can still create new law today in the form of judicial precedent, but they cannot make wide-ranging changes to the law – this can only be done by statute law.

> ## Key term 🔑
>
> Common law – this was largely unwritten law and relied on decisions of judges in court.

The King's Bench was founded in 1215

England and Wales use a common law system, as do many countries which were colonised by the British, such as the United States of America, Canada and Australia. A common law system does not use broad principles set out in a code. Instead, law is built up by individual case decisions on points raised in cases heard in court.

28.4.3 Statute law

An Act of Parliament is a law that has been passed by both Houses of Parliament and received Royal Assent. An Act of Parliament can change existing statute law or judicial precedent, or create new law. Statute law is useful to deal with new situations, such as terrorist activity or inventions such as computer technology. Parliament has created new offences such as those involving hacking of computers.

Because of the principle of Parliamentary sovereignty, law made by Parliament is the highest form of law. This is because the House of Commons is elected and, in theory, carries out the wishes of the electorate when making law. Acts of Parliament can overrule, amend or remove other forms of law such as delegated legislation or judicial precedent.

Statute law can:

- Consolidate (bring together) existing laws into a new single Act of Parliament. The Consumer Rights Act 2015 was an example of this.
- Codify existing law, both statutory and precedent, into one new Act. This was the case with the Theft Act 1978 when it was passed, though there have been many cases since interpreting the rules set out in the Act.

Both consolidation and codification make it easier for judges, lawyers and the general public to understand and apply the law.

However, judges still play an important role as they may have to interpret the meaning of words in a statute, if they are not clear, when deciding a court case.

Key term

Statute law – law that has been made by Parliament, which is the highest form of law.

28.5 The rule of law

28.5.1 Definition of the rule of law

The 'rule of law' is a symbolic idea. It can be defined in different ways. However, the main principles are:

- All people are subject to, and accountable to, law that is fairly applied and enforced.
- The process by which the laws of the country are enacted, administered and enforced must be fair.

Nobody can be above the law, so the rule of law must be sovereign. It is a safeguard against dictatorship, and supports democracy. This is because the government and its officials are accountable under the law. Also, authority is distributed in a manner that ensures that no single organ of government can exercise power in an unchecked way.

Many academics have written about the rule of law. The best known explanation of the 'rule of law' was given by Professor Dicey in the nineteenth century, but there have been other writers with different views on the topic.

Albert Venn Dicey

Dicey thought that the rule of law was an important feature that distinguished English law from law in other countries in Europe. He held that there were three elements that created the rule of law:

1 An absence of arbitrary power on the part of the state.
2 Equality before the law.
3 Supremacy of ordinary law.

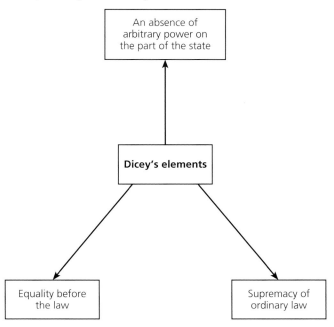

Figure 28.2 Dicey's elements in the rule of law

An absence of arbitrary power of the state

The state's power must be controlled by the law. The law must set limits on what the state can or cannot do. In the English legal system, government ministers' actions and decisions can be challenged in court by judicial review.

One of the main aims of the rule of law is to avoid the state having wide discretionary powers. Dicey recognised that discretion can be exercised in an arbitrary way, and this should be avoided to comply with the rule of law.

Everyone must be equal before the law

No person must be above the law. It does not matter how rich or powerful a person is, the law must deal with them in the same way as it would anyone else.

Those who carry out functions of state must be accountable under the law for their actions.

The law must be supreme

This was particularly true for the law of England and Wales in the time of Dicey, as many of the main developments up to that time were through judicial decisions rather than being created by Parliament. Today, most laws are made by legislation – Acts of

Parliament or delegated legislation – though judicial decisions do still create law.

Problems with Dicey's views

1   A major problem with Dicey's view of the rule of law is that it conflicts with another fundamental principle, that of Parliamentary Supremacy:
    ○ An Act of Parliament can overrule any other law.
    ○ No other body has the right to override or set aside an Act of Parliament.

So, under the rule of law there should be no arbitrary power on the part of the state, yet by Parliamentary Supremacy, Parliament has the right to make any law it wishes, and this can include granting arbitrary powers to the state.

Case study

The Case of Proclamations (1610)

This case considered whether the monarch could exercise arbitrary power by proclamation and change laws without Parliamentary consent. It was decided that the monarch did not have the power to create new offences without Parliament's consent. The justification for this was new laws required a lot of consideration and should be left to Parliament, not just one person.

Statutes passed by Parliament cannot be challenged through judicial review. This is different from some other countries where the legislative body is subject to the rule of law, so that laws passed by them can be challenged in the courts.

2   Another problem is that equality before the law in Dicey's theory refers to formal equality. It disregards the differences between people in terms of wealth, power and connections. Real equality can only be achieved if there are mechanisms in place to address these differences.

    For example, the cost of taking legal cases to court is very high. In order to allow the poorest in society to enforce their rights and so be equal under the law, it is necessary to have some form of state help in financing court cases.

3   Dicey's view of the rule of law is based on abstract ideas. This makes it difficult to apply in real-life situations.

Friedrich Von Hayek

Von Hayek was an academic economist, who also wrote on the inter-dependence of economics and institutions. He agreed with Dicey that the key component of the rule of law is the absence of any arbitrary power on the part of the state.

Joseph Raz

Joseph Raz, a professor of law in the late twentieth and early twenty-first centuries, recognised that the rule of law was a way of controlling discretion rather than preventing it completely. He saw the rule of law as of negative value, acting to minimise the danger of the use of discretionary power in an arbitrary way. He thought that the law must be capable of guiding the individual's behaviour.

Tony Honoré

This academic lawyer pointed out that the rule of law exists when a government's powers are limited by law and is bound to uphold this core of citizens' rights:

● No person shall be sanctioned except in accordance with the law: this is in both civil and criminal cases.
● There is equality before the law: there must be no discrimination on any grounds.
● There must be fairness and clarity of the law.

Within the English legal system there have been changes in the twenty-first century which support these principles. The Constitutional Reform Act 2005 recognised the rule of law and the importance of the independence of the Judiciary. Section 1 of that Act states:

> This Act does not adversely affect –
>
> **a** the existing constitutional principle of the rule of law; or
>
> **b** the Lord Chancellor's existing constitutional role in relation to that principle.

While s 3(1) states:

> The Lord Chancellor, other Ministers of the Crown and all with responsibility for matters relating to the Judiciary or otherwise to the administration of justice, must uphold the continued independence of the Judiciary.

These safeguards in the Constitutional Reform Act 2005 show the importance that is attached to the rule of law.

Dicey	Von Hayek	Raz
Absence of arbitrary power on the part of the state	Absence of arbitrary power on the part of the state	Clear rules and procedures for making laws
Equality before the law	Rule of law weakened by an increasingly interventionist state	Judicial independence must be guaranteed
Supremacy of ordinary law	Modern state is directly involved in regulating economic activity in conflict with the rule of law	Principles of natural justice should be observed. Courts should have the power to review the way in which the other principles are implemented

Figure 28.3 Key facts: comparing views of the rule of law

Lord Bingham

Lord Bingham, a former Lord Chief Justice and Senior Law Lord in the House of Lords, pointed out in 2006 that although the Constitutional Reform Act 2005 specifically states that it 'does not adversely affect the existing constitutional principle of the rule of law', the Act does not define the rule of law:

> all persons and authorities within the State, whether public or private, should be bound by and entitled to the benefit of laws.

He considered points which were essential in the rule of law:

- The law must be accessible and, so far as possible, intelligible, clear and predictable.
- Questions of legal right and liability should be resolved by the application of law.
- The laws of the land should apply equally to all, apart from when objective differences justify differentiation.
- The law must adequately protect fundamental human rights.
- The law must provide the means for resolving civil disputes which the parties are themselves unable to resolve, without excessive cost or delay.
- Ministers and public officers must exercise power conferred on them reasonably and in good faith and none of them is above the law. In Chapter 3, section 3.4.5, it was seen in *R (Miller) v The Prime Minister* (2019) that the Privy Council's advice to the Queen to prorogue Parliament was declared unlawful.
- Adjudicative procedures provided by the State should be fair.

28.5.2 The importance of the rule of law

The rule of law and law-making

The rule of law is very important when it comes to law-making. The process by which laws are made must be open and fair. Acts of Parliament have to be passed by both Houses of Parliament. In practice, the government of the day usually has a majority in the House of Commons. So most proposed new laws will be passed by the House of Commons, although there will be debate on all contentious issues, which can lead to changes being made.

The House of Lords exercises a check on the law-making process, as all proposed laws have also to be passed by them. One area where the House of Lords has consistently voted against change in the law has been in relation to allowing trial in the Crown Court without a jury.

The government can also make law by delegated legislation. Law made in this way does not always have to be considered by Parliament before it comes into force, so there are checks on this method of law-making:

1 Parliament must pass an Act granting a government minister power to make statutory instruments.
2 Parliament has power to scrutinise and check the statutory instruments.
3 Delegated legislation can be challenged in court through the process of judicial review to make sure that they have not gone beyond the power initially granted by Parliament.

The rule of law and the legal system

The way in which the legal system works is also covered by the rule of law. One of the most important points is that every defendant in a criminal case must have a fair trial. Trial by jury is seen as an important factor in maintaining fairness and protecting citizens' rights.

Another very important point is that no person can be imprisoned without a trial. In countries where the rule of law is disregarded, opponents of the government can be detained without a trial.

Civil justice system

The rule of law is also important in the civil justice system. Everyone should be able to resolve their disputes effectively through the civil justice system. This means that the system should be:

- free from discrimination
- free from corruption
- not improperly influenced by public officials.

The English legal system is trusted and recognised for being impartial.

The civil justice system should be accessible and affordable. This point is open to debate, as there have been major cuts to public funding of cases in the past twenty or so years, while the costs of taking a civil case to court have increased. However, there has been an increase in cheaper alternative ways of resolving civil disputes, such as arbitration and mediation.

The rule of law and substantive law

'Substantive' means the law in the different areas of law:

- The substantive law of criminal law sets out definitions of each offence.
- The substantive law of tort sets out what rights and responsibilities people owe to each other in everyday life.
- The substantive law of contract lays down the rules on issues such as when a contract is formed, what events may make that contract void or voidable, and what will amount to a breach of contract.
- The substantive law of human rights sets out the various rights that individuals are entitled to expect.

Whatever the area of substantive law, it is important that the rules recognise that people have key rights and that the laws are not oppressive.

Criminal law

- Many criminal laws, such as murder, manslaughter and non-fatal offences against the person, are aimed at protecting people.
- Other offences are aimed at protecting a person's property, such as theft, burglary or criminal damage.
- Other offences can be aimed at preventing disruptive behaviour and protecting public order.
- There are also regulatory offences, aimed at issues such as preventing pollution, ensuring that food sold in shops is fit for human consumption, and a wide range of driving offences aimed at safety on the roads.

For every offence the law has to be clear, and the prosecution has to prove that the defendant has committed the offence that has been charged. Unless they are charged with a strict liability offence, every person brought before a court can put forward a recognised defence.

All offences have a stated maximum penalty and the courts cannot impose a higher penalty. In fact, they usually impose a much lower sentence than the maximum allowed.

Law of tort

Many torts are aimed at protecting people and their property, and give the right to claim compensation for damage caused by breaches of the law. Unlike criminal law, where the prosecution is nearly always brought by the state, it is the person affected by the tort who claims. For example, if one person drives negligently and knocks down a pedestrian, that pedestrian has the right to claim compensation for their injuries.

One of the problems for a person seeking to use the law of tort is that public funding for making a claim is no longer available. This means that, although in theory everyone has the right to claim, so there appears to be equality before the law, in fact funding issues can make it difficult for many to bring a claim. 'No win, no fee' arrangements can be used to fund such cases, but there are still problems such as lawyers needing to be satisfied at the chance of success.

Contract law

Contract law recognises that, in most cases, people should be free to make what agreements they wish. However, it also recognises that a consumer may have little choice when making a contract with a business and that there is not really equality between the parties. In order to bring about greater equality, contract law provides rights for consumers. For example:

- The Sale of Goods Act 1979 created implied terms that goods must be of satisfactory quality and fit for their purpose. In this way, contract law supports real equality in the law.
- The Consumer Protection Act 1987 gives consumers rights when faulty goods cause injury or property damage. The Act allows any user of the goods to claim, not just the buyer. So, where an item is bought as a present for another person, that person can claim if there is a fault in the goods which causes them injury.

- The Consumer Rights Act 2015 has increased consumer protection when making a contract with a business. This now includes rights where the contract is for the supply of digital content. This is also an example of a law being created to keep up with changes in technology.

Human rights law

Human rights law supports the rule of law in many ways.

- All rights must be applied without discrimination. The European Convention on Human Rights sets out the right to liberty of the individual. This right should only be taken away where it is in accordance with the law, such as imprisoning someone who has been found guilty of a serious offence.
- The Convention also states that there is a right to a fair trial.

Criminal law	<ul><li>The defendant should only be charged with an offence known to law.</li><li>The defendant should only be charged with an offence which can be supported by evidence.</li><li>The defendant should have the opportunity to have access to legal advice and the chance to prepare a case to defend him/herself.</li><li>The state will not interfere with the evidence or the trial process.</li><li>In court, the prosecution and defence should be treated equally and be given the opportunity to present their case and call witnesses.</li><li>Neither the judge nor jury is under the control of the state.</li></ul>
Law of tort	<ul><li>A claimant should have the right to take action to protect him/herself and their property.</li><li>Both parties should be treated equally in pre-trial procedures and in the presentation of their case and call witnesses.</li><li>However, the availability of appropriate funding is an issue in being able to pursue legal rights.</li><li>Both parties should be given the opportunity to settle their case and for court to be available if settlement is not possible.</li><li>Liability should be decided by an independent judge according to principles of law.</li></ul>
Contract law	<ul><li>Both parties are at liberty to enter into a contract for whatever goods or services and on whatever terms they think fit.</li><li>The law will not interfere in the parties' rights to freely enter into a contract unless one of the parties is subject to a disability or undue pressure or influence is present.</li><li>The state will not interfere in the contractual arrangements of parties unless the subject of the contract is for illegal goods or services.</li><li>Both parties are at liberty to resolve any dispute out of court but a court should be available as a last resort.</li><li>Liability should be decided by an independent judge according to principles of law.</li></ul>
Human rights	<ul><li>The state should protect the human rights of each and every one of its citizens.</li><li>Every human right should be applied to every citizen without any form of discrimination.</li><li>Human rights should only be removed from an individual following fair process and in accordance with the law.</li><li>Human rights are indivisible so the state cannot pick and choose which rights it seeks to protect, or if it does not agree with the views or actions of certain individuals.</li><li>Public bodies should respect the rights of individuals.</li></ul>

Figure 28.4 Evaluation of the rule of law and substantive law

Tip

When discussing the importance of the rule of law, illustrate your answer with examples from different areas of law.

Quick questions

1 Explain the difference between laws and rules.
2 Explain the meaning of morality.
3 Compare and contrast the approach of English law to the way civil and criminal cases are conducted.
4 Compare and contrast the main features of common law and statutory law.

Summary

- Laws are created by a law-making body to regulate the conduct of citizens towards each other and for social control. They are generally written down and apply to everyone in the state. Breach of a law will generally lead to a sanction.
- Rules are norms guiding behaviour in certain areas. They may be written, forming a code of expected behaviour, or unwritten if they apply to a group or community, when observance is followed due to feelings of guilt.
- Morals are feelings of how people should behave. They can differ from society to society. Breach of a moral can lead to a person being excluded from the group or society but may be unlawful if a law is based on moral views.
- Achieving justice is the ultimate aim for any society or in an individual case. What is just will differ in every case and in the view of every individual. It is an aim but will not be achieved in every case.
- The purpose of civil law is to uphold the rights of individuals. The purpose of criminal law is to maintain law and order in society. There are different procedures, courts, ways of dealing with cases and outcomes in the two areas of law.
- English law originally developed by custom and by common law. Statute law is a more important source of law in today's society.
- The rule of law is symbolic in a democratic country. Everyone should be subject to the law, and no one is above the law, which should be applied fairly and equally.
- The making of law should have an open and fair procedure.
- Law should operate fairly and equally in every area of substantive law.

Chapter 29 Law and morality

Introduction

Behaviour which is considered immoral is often also illegal. Equally, illegal acts are often also considered immoral. The relationship between law and morality changes over time to reflect changes in law and in morality. For example, adultery is considered immoral but not illegal, whereas parking on yellow lines is illegal but not immoral. Murder is illegal and immoral.

29.1 The distinction between law and morals

29.1.1 What is law?

As we have seen, rules exist in many contexts. A rule is something that determines the way in which we behave, either because we submit ourselves to it voluntarily (moral rules) or because it is enforceable in some general way (laws).

Key term

Rule – 'a general norm mandating or guiding conduct' (Twining and Miers).

Some rules are not based on law or morality, but are often referred to as laws. These might be the laws of football or chess. They are generally observed in the context in which they operate. If these laws are broken, there are sanctions in the context of the sport. Many would view any form of cheating in a sport or game as wrong and possibly as immoral. Failure to follow these 'laws' is not illegal.

Some laws are laws relating to the operation of the universe, such as the three laws of thermodynamics. These laws are immutable – they are unchanging and cannot be broken. The rules we are concerned with are English law.

29.1.2 What is morality?

Morality is defined in the *Oxford English Dictionary* as: 'a particular system of values and principles of conduct, especially one held by a specified person or society'.

Morality can refer to a personal morality or a collective morality of society as a whole. Morality is 'normative' or prescriptive: it specifies what ought to be done and outlines acceptable and unacceptable behaviour.

In UK society and in many others, morality has been influenced to a large extent by religious beliefs. The Bible provides a moral code for Christian communities, both in the very basic and strict rules of the Ten Commandments, and in the more advanced, socially aware teachings of Jesus Christ. In Islam, the Koran provides a very extensive moral code for Muslims. The Torah does so for the Jewish faith.

Morality is the moral code that touches virtually every area of our lives: behaviour towards fellow human beings, money and property, and sexuality. There are 'core' moral beliefs such as issues surrounding birth, death and families.

Although morality is concerned with issues of 'right' and 'wrong', it is not at all black and white. Mary Warnock, an academic concerned with moral issues, said:

> I do not believe that there is a neat way of marking off moral issues from all others; some people, at some time, may regard things as matters of moral right and moral wrong, which at another time or in another place are thought to be matters of taste, or of no importance at all.

Moral attitudes change over time. This can be seen in attitudes to issues such as abortion, homosexuality, drugs and drink-driving. A common morality was easier to achieve when societies were insular, structured and not exposed to different beliefs and values. The customs of society formed the basis of a code of conduct that reflected that society, and members of the society accepted these customs in large measure. It was therefore part of the morality of that age. However, we now live in a multicultural society where there is a wide range of views.

Sociologist Emile Durkheim identified a range of factors as potentially contributing to the breakdown of a common morality. These included:

- the increasing specialisation of labour
- the growing ethnic diversity within society
- the fading influence of religious belief.

All of these factors are increasingly apparent in pluralist societies today. Under Durkheim's analysis, we should not be surprised to discover a parallel growth in the diversity of moral outlook and in norms of behaviour in modern Britain. There is, therefore, a more obvious difference between an individual's moral code and that of society as a whole:

- The essential core of society is based on a shared morality; without a shared morality, society disintegrates.
- Law aims to prevent the disintegration of society, and so will reflect morality.

29.1.3 Characteristics of legal and moral rules

In order to discover the characteristics of legal and moral rules, it is useful to compare them under a number of headings:

- their origins
- their date of commencement
- their enforcement
- their ease of change
- their certainty of content
- the way the rules are applied.

These characteristics help to identify the rules and distinguish legal and moral rules.

Their origins

It is generally possible to trace legal rules back to a source:

- In English law this was the common law. The law of tort and contract has been developed incrementally by judges.
- Today, statutes and delegated legislation have become an increasingly large source of law.
- European Union law has become a major source of law-making in the UK through treaties, directives, regulations and decisions.
- Conventions that the UK subscribes to such as the ECHR also play their part in the origin of law in the UK today.

Moral rules are more difficult to trace back to a precise origin. the Bible, Koran and Torah form the basis

for many individuals of their moral outlook. These codes inform attitudes towards issues such as pre-marital sex, theft and how one treats fellow humans.

For those who do not follow religious teaching, morality is based upon upbringing, education, peer views or the leanings of their own consciences. For most people, their morality is based on a combination of all these influences.

Their date of commencement

Legal rules generally have a start date. Acts of Parliament come into force at a specific time. Precedents operate from the date of the decision, although it can be argued they have retrospective effect, as with the decision in *R v R* (1991).

Moral rules are less straightforward. For example, Western attitudes towards pre-marital sex have undergone significant change in the last hundred years. It is not possible to attach a date to this change, as it is part of a wider change in social attitudes towards matters of sexual morality. Similarly, it is not possible to fix a date when a person's particular morality came into being – it evolves over time.

Their enforcement

Legal rules can be enforced by the courts following a set procedure and with appropriate sanctions such as criminal penalties or civil damages.

Sanctions may also be available for those who breach moral codes:

- Someone who uses offensive language may be excluded from a sports or social club.
- Moral rules are usually enforced through public disapproval through the media or privately through social ostracism rather than a formal sanction.
- Moral rules are less enforceable than legal rules, but it is often easier to hold different views about them.

Their ease of change

In theory, legal rules are relatively easy to change. Parliament has authority to pass a law whenever it wants. In practice, however, Parliament is often slow to respond to change. Courts also have the power to change legal rules but only when a case comes to court.

Moral rules tend to change gradually, perhaps over decades or centuries. It is often only in hindsight that we become aware of such change.

Sometimes the law leads morality, and sometimes the law follows the lead of morality.

Their certainty of content

It is normally possible to discover the precise content of legal rules through published statutes, delegated legislation and law reports.

The content of moral rules is less clear. Knowledge of the content of moral rules can often only be acquired informally, in the setting where they are applied such as the home.

Application of the rules

Legal rules generally apply to everyone in a situation covered by the law. The only difference is the ability of every individual to access the law.

Moral rules, on the other hand, range in application from enjoying almost universal adoption to having only marginal acceptance. Differing views are taken by different individuals and different sectors of society. This is particularly apparent in a pluralist society.

29.1.4 The main legal theories underpinning the law

There are two main theories relating to the nature of law:

1 Legal positivism
2 Natural law

Legal positivism

Legal positivists believe that laws are valid where they are made by the recognised legislative power in the state; they do not have to satisfy any higher moral authority.

Key term

Legal positivism – a theory of law: laws must be made by the state's highest legislative authority.

Each legal positivist has their own individual explanation of the theory. The nineteenth century philosophers are often referred to as classical legal positivists, such as Jeremy Bentham and John Austin.

Jeremy Bentham

Bentham was a utilitarian and law reformer. He made a distinction between what the law is, and commenting on its merits or otherwise. He believed that the philosophy of law should be concerned purely with what law is. He wrote:

> The existence of law is one thing, its merit or demerit is another. A law which exists is a law, though we happen to dislike it.

So, even though an individual or a group of individuals might find a law offensive, this does not affect its validity. In other words, morality is irrelevant to law.

Link

Utilitarianism is explored in more detail in Chapter 30.

John Austin

Austin developed the command theory of law. This has three main principles:

1 Laws are commands issued by the uncommanded commander – the sovereign.
2 Such commands are enforced by sanctions.
3 A sovereign is one who is obeyed by the majority.

Austin recognised a sovereign as one whom society obeys habitually. This sovereign might be a single person (the king, queen or dictator) or a collective sovereign such as a Parliament. The authority is given by Parliament, for example, to judges. Sanctions in criminal law are straightforward – disobey the law and suffer punishment (sanctions).

Modern legal positivists

Austin and his rather simplistic view have been criticised by modern legal positivists:

1 HLA Hart insists on the separation of law and morality. His model of law is more sophisticated than that of Austin. He argues that there are two categories of rules: primary and secondary. These combine to form the basis of a workable legal system:
   - Primary rules either impose legal obligations or grant powers. Obligations include behaviour that is subject to the criminal law – such as not to kill or steal – and powers enable an individual to, for example, make a will.
   - Secondary rules are concerned with the operation of primary legal rules.

   Hart identified three specific secondary rules:
   i The rule of recognition – this sets criteria for identifying primary rules.
   ii Rules of change – these identify how legal rules are formed, amended or repealed.
   iii Rules of adjudication – these enable the courts to settle disputes and interpret the law.
2 Hans Kelsen argues that morality is no part of law. It is neither good nor bad.

Legal philosopher	Basic premise
Jeremy Bentham	A utilitarian who wrote about what the law is and a commentary on its merits or otherwise. He believed that the philosophy of law should be concerned purely with what law is.
John Austin	He developed the command theory of law with its three main principles.
HLA Hart	A legal positivist who believed in the separation of law and morality. He argued that there are two categories of rules: primary and secondary. These combine to form the basis of a workable legal system.
Hans Kelsen	A legal positivist who argued that morality is no part of law.

Figure 29.1 Key facts: legal philosophers who are utilitarian and legal positivists

Natural law

Natural lawyers reject legal positivism. They believe that the validity of man-made laws depends upon the laws being compatible with a higher, moral authority. There are different views on natural law, reflected in the work of Saint Thomas Aquinas and Lon Fuller.

In ancient Athens, the philosopher Plato and his pupil Aristotle considered the question of how human beings should act. Both started by reflecting on the meaning of 'goodness'. For Aristotle, evil originates in naturally or morally failing to fulfil part or all of human nature and his definition of goodness. This is the basis for natural law.

Ethics involves defining human nature, and from that definition, deriving laws as principles of behaviour that either support or prevent human flourishing.

 Key term

Natural law – a moral theory of jurisprudence, which maintains that law should be based on morality and ethics.

Saint Thomas Aquinas

Aquinas combined the philosophy of Aristotle with Christian theology, including the Bible and the Ten Commandments, and Catholic Church tradition. He saw in Aristotle's philosophy a rational foundation for Christian doctrine. He sets out four kinds of law in his work, *Summa Theologica*:

1 Eternal law: all things have a natural tendency to pursue their own God-given goals because all things are created by God. Human beings can have some understanding of the eternal law. This would include the laws of gravity.
2 Natural law: the moral code in which human beings naturally incline towards good. Man-made law must conform to this as it comes from a higher authority.
3 Positive divine law comes from the commands of God – the Ten Commandments.
4 Positive human law must be in accordance with natural law.

Aquinas also stated that there are three natural ends or goals from which we can work out moral principles:
- Anything that exists has a natural tendency to go on existing. Natural law opposes death; therefore murder is wrong as it prevents human fulfilment.
- All animals have a natural tendency to mate and bring up their young. Therefore, the right to life is paramount, as is the protection of children.
- Humans have a rational nature which inclines us to live ordered lives in society. Natural law commands we should learn and live in harmony with others.

These goals help people work out our moral principles that should be reflected in man-made laws.

St Thomas Aquinas, philosopher and theologian

Lon Fuller

Fuller wrote *The Morality of Law* in 1964. He rejected legal positivism and also traditional religious forms of natural law theory. He argued that law serves a purpose:

> to achieve social order through subjecting people's conduct to the guidance of general rules by which they may themselves orient their behaviour.

If law is to achieve this purpose, it must satisfy the principles which make up an inner morality of law. This is described by Fuller as a procedural version of natural law. Under the principles, laws should be in existence; published and not retrospective; clear, concise and not contradictory; not be impossible to follow; not change rapidly; and be applied and administered fairly.

Hart criticises Fuller, not for the principles themselves, but for calling them a morality. This raises the question of what is morality.

Legal philosopher	Basic premise
Thomas Aquinas	Combined the philosophy of Aristotle with Christian theology, including the Bible and the Ten Commandments and Catholic church tradition. He sets out four kinds of law.
Lon Fuller	Argued that law provides general rules on which people can base their behaviour and achieve social order. If law is to achieve this purpose, it must satisfy the principles which make up an inner morality of law.

Figure 29.2 Key facts: legal philosophers who are natural lawyers

29.2 The diversity of moral views in a pluralist society

There is likely to be a variety of moral views in a pluralist society.

Key term

Pluralist society – a diverse society, where the people in it believe different things and tolerate each other's beliefs.

29.2.1 Pluralism in the UK

The UK has a multicultural society, with individuals having different or no religious beliefs. This leads to great variety in the moral values of the individuals in society. Often these individuals group together as a result of their moral views. An individual's views are protected under the ECHR, as is the right to express your views and assemble with others to express the collective views.

The country in which we live plays a significant role in shaping our lives. Other members of society and the laws of the country shape our views. The kinds of lives we can lead are constrained by the state, which has the right to punish individuals if they go beyond what the state deems to be appropriate behaviour.

One example is the conscientious objector who, when the country is at war, refuses to fight. The large majority of society accepts that they must be prepared to fight and may not fully accept the views of those who will not. Conscientious objectors believe it to be completely wrong in any circumstance, and accept that the state may punish them and society will shun them. Such a view is not necessarily a judgement about a government's policy but a moral judgement, drawn from personal beliefs. The difficulty arises when an individual changes his views.

The case of *R v Lyons* (2011) shows that refusal of a lawful order, even on the grounds of conscientious objection, is a punishable offence in the UK armed forces under the Armed Forces Act 2006.

Case study

R v Lyons (2011)

Lyons, aged 18, had joined the Royal Navy and became a Leading Medical Assistant in submarines. Five years later, he was told that he would be deployed to Afghanistan. He applied for discharge from the Royal Navy on the basis that he objected to the UK's role in Afghanistan. His application on grounds of conscientious objection was refused. Before his appeal against this refusal was decided, he was ordered to undertake a pre-deployment weapons training course, because of the risk he would face in Afghanistan. He refused to take the course and was convicted of insubordination.

Lyons argued that Article 9 ECHR (freedom of thought, conscience and religion) protected him from active service from the moment when he told his commanding officer of his objections, until his appeal on grounds of conscientious objection was finally determined.

The Court Martial Appeal Court ruled that moral objections to the UK's involvement in Afghanistan do not constitute a defence to an insubordination charge. The appellant was not entitled to disobey a lawful command on the ground of conscientious objection.

Similarly, there is the criminal who is prepared to steal but is not prepared to kill in order to steal. The majority of society and the state would agree with him that killing is wrong, but a small proportion would consider that stealing is not wrong.

29.2.2 Pluralism in Europe and the ECHR

The attempt to keep morality and religion out of politics and the law arises from the worry that, for example, religious fundamentalists will impose intolerant and coercive laws and practices on all of society. We have seen this in various countries with respect to attitudes towards abortion, stem-cell research on embryos and in-vitro fertilisation (IVF).

- In Ireland, while abortion was illegal, the case of *Open Door Counselling and Dublin Well Woman v Ireland* (1992) was heard by the European Court of Human Rights (ECtHR). The court found that the Ireland Supreme Court's injunction restraining counselling agencies from providing pregnant women with information concerning abortion facilities abroad violated Article 10 ECHR (right to freedom of expression).
- *Evans v United Kingdom* (2007) involved the refusal of one partner to the destruction of frozen embryos following the ending of their relationship. The ECtHR rejected the appeal, stated that for the right to respect for the decision to become a parent in the genetic sense under Article 8 (right to respect for private and family life) has to be a wide one.

Freedom of thought and expression is frequently restricted as being contrary to the moral views of the majority. The difficulty is deciding when the greater good of society as a whole should prevent the individual's unacceptable view, whether on the grounds of protection (anti-terrorism, online bullying), obscenity (likely to deprave or corrupt) or sexual matters (same-sex relationships, abortion, contraception).

29.3 The relationship between law and morality, and its importance

Law and morality often overlap, although there is often a period where one leads and the other follows. This relationship coincides for much of the time, and at other times, the one influences the other. This can be seen in the coincidence of legal and moral rules, and the influences of law and morality on each other. This is further developed later in this chapter in the sections on the legal enforcement of moral values in different areas of law.

29.3.1 The coincidence of legal and moral rules

Legal and moral rules, though distinctive, share certain characteristics:

- They are both concerned with setting standards, which are essential for governing the behaviour of individuals within society.
- They both dictate the way in which people are expected to behave.
- Legal and moral rules employ similar language: they distinguish between right and wrong, and they speak of duties, obligations and responsibilities.
- Legal rules are strengthened when they are the same as moral rules, and their enforcement can be justified more easily and accepted by society.

Sometimes legal rules possess no obvious moral content. Parking a car on a double yellow line in an empty town centre at four in the morning does not seem to infringe any moral code (other than the act itself of breaking the law). Most would think it was immoral to impose a parking fine in that situation and merely a money-raising exercise on behalf of a local council.

Activities

1 Think about three areas where law and morality coincide, and state the relevant law.
2 Then think about and state three areas where law and your personal morality do not coincide, and the reasons for that.

There are many moral rules that are not part of the law.

- Most people would agree that adultery is immoral and indeed may be the basis of a divorce, but it is not illegal in the UK, even though it is in some other countries of the world.
- Some acts that may be considered immoral are not criminal, but may be sufficient to support a claim in civil law. The line between them is blurred, as shown in some cases of gross negligence manslaughter.

29.3.2 The influences of law and morality on each other

Changing moral values can lead to developments in the law. This can be seen in the historical development of the law relating to rape within marriage. It was ruled in 1736 that 'a man cannot rape his wife', yet in *R v R* (1991), Owen J stated:

> I find it hard to believe that it ever was common law that a husband was in effect entitled to beat his wife into submission to sexual intercourse.

In this way, the law eventually caught up with perceived public morality.

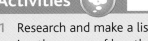

Activities

1. Research and make a list of key developments in other areas of law that have changed to reflect changing morality. You could use the examples of abortion or homosexuality.
2. Then perform the same research for areas of law where public morality has followed the lead of the law, such as discrimination on the grounds of gender or race.

Ideally, the law and morality change in harmony, with little lead or lag. For example, the Sexual Offences Act 1967 was passed following the *Wolfenden Report*. However, there were many more influences on the public's view at the time:

- There had been the famous case of *R v Penguin Books Ltd* (1961) which considered the novel *Lady Chatterley's Lover* by D.H. Lawrence not to be obscene under the Obscene Publications Act 1959.
- So-called underground magazines became available, such as *Oz* and *It*.
- Satirical magazines such as *Private Eye* developed a large circulation, reporting and commenting on current issues and scandals which many considered immoral and required action by the state and a change of the law.

29.4 The legal enforcement of moral values

As the UK is a multicultural society, it contains a diversity of moral views. This section explores the questions of whether and to what extent the law should seek to enforce any particular moral views. This is not just a subject of academic debate – judges are often forced to consider these questions before determining the law. There are two starting points for this debate:

1. The law, as the guardian of public morals, should intervene to ensure the continuation of the dominant morality within the state.
2. Individuals should be left free to decide their own morality.

These starting points appear to be diametrically opposite but, in practice, both these positions are modified.

29.4.1 The influence of John Stuart Mill

In his book *On Liberty*, John Stuart Mill, a nineteenth-century philosopher, explored the nature and limits of the power which can be legitimately exercised by society over the individual.

He stated that there is a limit to the legitimate interference of collective opinion with individual independence. Nevertheless, Mill accepted that rules governing an individual's conduct must be imposed upon them. The problem, though, is identifying where society should or should not be permitted to interfere with individual liberty. Therefore, Mill developed the harm principle as the appropriate test when considering this issue:

- Under this principle, an individual should be allowed to harm himself, and society can only intervene where his conduct harms others.

Mill limits the application of the harm principle in one significant way: it does not apply to those who are not in 'the maturity of their faculties' – children (over whom society enjoys absolute power) and presumably those suffering a severe mental disability. They must be protected against their own actions as well as against the actions of others.

Mill recognised that others might refuse to admit this distinction between that part of a person's life which concerns only himself and that which concerns others. The nineteenth-century judge, Sir James Stephen, opposed Mill's liberalism. Stephen argued that there is no distinction between acts that harm others and acts that harm oneself. He wrote:

> There are acts of wickedness so gross and outrageous that they must be punished at any cost to the offender.

Stephen argued that the prevention of wickedness and immorality is a proper end in itself and justifies state action: the law has a duty to proscribe behaviour condemned by society at large. Mill answered such objections by making a distinction between the harmful act itself and its particular consequences.

Mill argued that society should not impose morality on individuals. Individuals should be free to choose how they behave, provided that no harm is caused to other members of society. If harm is done, he argued, this should not outweigh the harm that denying individual liberty would do.

Problems with Mill's approach

Mill's approach raised questions, such as:

- What constitutes 'harm', physical or otherwise? Does it include, for example, pornography, drug-taking or sexual practices when carried out consensually or alone?
- Does an embryo or a foetus fall within the definition of other members of society?

A logical extension of Mill's approach is that crimes without victims should not really be crimes at all. Edwin Schur and Hugo Bedau in their book, *Victimless Crimes: Two Sides of a Controversy*, argue that a 'victimless crime' is a term used to refer to actions that have been made illegal but which do not directly violate or threaten the rights of any other individual. It often involves consensual acts, or solitary acts in which no other person is involved. Such acts would not lead to any person calling for help from the police. This would include recreational drug use.

They argue that some of these laws produce secondary crime and all create new criminals, many of whom are otherwise law-abiding citizens and people in authority. These victimless crimes that only do harm to the criminal should be decriminalised. They cite as examples drug use, homosexuality and abortion. If such activities are criminalised, demand will still be there and the activities will be pushed underground.

29.4.2 The Hart–Devlin debate

This debate between Lord Devlin and Professor HLA Hart was sparked by the publication of the *Wolfenden Report on Homosexual Offences and Prostitution*. The Report concluded that the law has a role in preserving public order and decency, but:

> It is not, in our view, the function of the law to intervene in the private life of citizens, or to seek to enforce any particular pattern of behaviour … [There] must remain a realm of private morality and immorality which is, in brief and crude terms, not the law's business.

In his book, *The Enforcement of Morals*, published in 1965, Lord Devlin wrote:

> Without shared ideas on politics, morals, and ethics, no society can exist.

Society, therefore, is constituted in part by its morality. He argued that the fabric of society depends on a shared or common morality. Where the bonds of that morality are loosened by private immoral conduct, the integrity of society will be lost and society will be liable to disintegrate. Society therefore has the right to defend itself against immorality. Even private wickedness and immorality may be punished because they are harmful to society. He stated:

> The suppression of vice is as much the law's business as the suppression of subversive activities.

Lord Devlin also recognised that there are limits to the right of society to interfere with private immoral conduct. He believed that individual freedom must be tolerated when it is consistent with the integrity of society. He accepted that personal preferences, or likes and dislikes, should not form the basis for decisions about what immoral conduct should be outlawed.

He therefore developed an apparently objective test, that of the reasonable or ordinary man, to help decide where the boundaries are to be drawn. Immoral conduct should only be prohibited by law when it is regarded by this ordinary man with 'intolerance, indignation or disgust'. This view can be seen in cases such as *R v Brown* (1993), when a group of homosexual men were convicted of assault after performing consensual acts of sado-masochism on each other (see Chapter 8, section 8.3.1 for case details).

Professor Hart proposed a more limited role for the law in the enforcement of morality. Whereas Lord Devlin started from the general principle that society has a duty to enforce its dominant morality, and then limited the application of this general principle to acts that the ordinary man regards with intolerance, Professor Hart started from the opposite end of the spectrum – that society should not interfere with private moral or immoral conduct.

However, Hart then limited the application of this general principle by sanctioning the enforcement of morality in certain situations:

- He accepted that enforcement is permitted when one of society's dominant moralities is being eroded by a true threat to the cohesion of society. Such a threat, though, has to be more than merely a challenge to society's code of conduct. There must be evidence that it creates a genuine public nuisance.

29.4.3 Legal enforcement of moral values in contract law

Judges and Parliament are often forced to confront complex moral issues. Parliament can choose whether to legislate, but judges have no choice. If a case comes to court they have to make a decision and, of course, if a case reaches the higher appeal courts, it becomes a precedent.

The principle that promises should be kept lies beneath the law of contract. Much of the law of equity was historically founded upon principles of conscience, with maxims such as 'equity will not allow a statute to be used as a cloak for fraud' and 'he who comes to equity must come with clean hands'.

Historically, certain contracts can be declared void because of their association with immorality. For example:

- *Pearce v Brooks* (1866): a cab owner failed to enforce a contract with a prostitute who used his cabs for trade because the courts were not prepared to allow contracts for immoral purposes.
- *Parkinson v College of Ambulance* (1925): the contract was void because its whole purpose was corruption in public life.

More recently, the courts have again stated their views on the relationship between law and morality:

- In *Otkritie International Investment Management Ltd v Urumov* (2013), the court specifically made the connection between morality and the law when it said:

> Public policy requires that the courts will not lend their aid to a man who founds his action upon an immoral or illegal act. The action will not be founded upon an immoral or illegal act, if it can be pleaded and proved without reliance upon such an act.

- In *Progress Bulk Carriers Ltd v Tube City* (2012), Lord Steyn stated:

> The aim of our commercial law ought to be to encourage fair dealing between parties. But it is a mistake for the law to set its sights too highly when the critical enquiry is not whether the conduct is lawful but whether it is morally or socially unacceptable. That is the enquiry in which we are engaged.

For there to be economic duress, the illegitimate pressure must be distinguished from the pressures of normal commercial bargaining.

Exclusion clauses can be seen as tough bargains. 'If you do not like the terms of a contract, do not enter it' is commonly stated as being a justification. However, when exclusion clauses are oppressive and there are no realistic alternatives, the law steps in by protecting consumers, either under the Consumer Rights Act 2015 or under the Unfair Contract Terms Act 1977. These, and related Acts of Parliament, have arguably swung the balance too far the other way.

The decisions in cases such as *L'Estrange v Graucob* (1934) and *Thompson v LMS Railway* (1930) are unlikely to be replicated if the cases were heard today (see Chapter 40 for these case details). However, it could be argued that these decisions are similar to claims against individuals at the hands of payday lenders, or businesses selling products to those who have no access to mainstream lines of credit. Even if the businesses might be acting in an immoral way, the consumer is unlikely to be willing or able to complain, even if they were aware that they could take legal action.

29.4.4 Legal enforcement of moral values in the law of tort

In the law of negligence, Lord Atkin's famously Biblical description of the duty of care as one owed to one's fellow man as a 'neighbour', in *Donoghue v Stevenson* (1932), reworked the parable of the Good Samaritan.

This can be applied in a way that perhaps does not reflect a moral view, as seen in *McFarlane v Tayside Health Board* (1999) (a case where, despite a vasectomy, Mr MacFarlane fathered a child, and he and his wife sought damages for the cost of care among other claims). The claim for damages in respect of the rearing of the child was dismissed. Lord Steyn stated:

> It may be objected that the House must act like a court of law and not like a court of morals. That would only be partly right. The court must apply positive law. But a judge's sense of the moral answer to a question, or the justice of the case, has been one of the great shaping forces of the common law. What may count in a situation of difficulty and uncertainty is not the subjective view of the judge but what he reasonably believes that the ordinary citizen would regard as right.

The situation is conflicted. Whether we talk of 'morals' or 'values', judges have to apply themselves to real cases with real facts and real people, and reflect the situation as they perceive it to be.

The duty of care to trespassers

Owing a duty of care to a trespasser was traditionally absent, as shown in *Addie v Dumbreck* (1929).

The change in the law in *British Railways Board v Herrington* (1972) brought in the concept of common humanity, and the subsequent Law Commission report led to the Occupiers' Liability Act 1984. The Act appears to have given trespassers a right to claim compensation when they have been injured while trespassing.

However, there have been a number of court decisions which have restricted when a duty is owed to trespassers and, if a duty is owed, whether the occupier is liable.

The idea of allowing a claim by a trespasser demonstrates the changing morality of society:

- Children, in particular, should be able to claim for injuries caused by hidden dangers as they are not expected to be aware of them, even if they are trespassing.
- This is not a huge move from the position where the child is in a public space but too young to read warning signs, as in *Glasgow Corporation v Taylor* (1922). The difficulty arises where the injured person is trespassing, even though trespassing in that place is common.

Section 1(3) sets out when there may be a legal duty. This reflected the morality of the time – over 35 years ago. The interpretation of the Act has been criticised for:

- allowing too much discretion to the Judiciary
- being too easy to refuse a claim on the grounds of public policy
- attempting to reduce the compensation culture that has been growing in recent years.

Activity

Write down the arguments for and against a *legal* duty of care owed to a pupil in a school building, and also whether there is a *moral* duty of care owed.

- Would the position be different if the pupil was a trespasser in the building?
- Does the age of the pupil matter?
- When is the pupil a trespasser and not a visitor – should that matter?

The rule in *Rylands v Fletcher*

This tort was developed to give a remedy where a person's property is damaged or destroyed by the escape of non-naturally stored material onto adjoining property. This rule of strict liability reflects a person's moral responsibility for the consequences of an escape of something brought onto land.

Originally this was almost always water. A reservoir was a valuable asset as it could drive a water wheel to power a mill. However, the water could seep out and flood an adjoining landowner's mine with disastrous consequences, including death of miners and financial ruin. Liability was made strict, otherwise the necessary proof for negligence or nuisance could be very difficult and the person with moral responsibility would be able to evade legal responsibility.

However, it could be argued that the modern interpretation of the rule shows a more legalistic rather than a moral viewpoint, in cases such as *Cambridge Water Co. v Eastern Counties Leather* (1994) and *Stannard (t/a Wyvern Tyres) v Gore* (2012).

The right of abatement allows someone who is suffering a nuisance to take action that would otherwise be illegal, such as cutting overhanging branches of a diseased tree to prevent possible injury or damage to property.

29.4.5 Legal enforcement of moral values in human rights law

Human rights are based on the principle of respect for the individual. Their fundamental assumption is that each person is a moral and rational being who deserves to be treated with dignity. We can therefore expect morality to be the dominant feature of human rights law.

The ECHR contains 14 Articles setting out different individual rights which are mainly civil and political in nature:

- Some, such as Articles 2 and 5, are absolute rights, where a state cannot justify interfering with them. These rights are based on morality.
- Others, such as Articles 8, 10 and 11, are qualified rights, so that if the state can justify limiting these rights, there will be no breach of the ECHR. These rights find a balance between law and morality.

The case of *Mengesha v Commissioner of Police of the Metropolis* (2013) shows the interrelationship of the articles, an absolute right and a qualified right.

Case study

Mengesha v Commissioner of Police of the Metropolis (2013)

On 30 November 2011, the claimant attended a public sector trades union march, acting with others as a legal observer. She was a law graduate and a member of the 'Bar in the Community' scheme at the Bar Pro Bono Unit. In the afternoon, the police authorised containment as they were entitled to do in the circumstances (also known as 'kettling'). About one hundred people were contained, including the claimant. The police had to review and assess the grounds of containment and bring it to an end once an imminent breach of the peace was no longer anticipated. This is lawful under Article 5 – justified deprivation of liberty for lawful arrest or detention – as it was a 'procedure prescribed by law'.

As the law then stood, the police could search those detained. The Chief Superintendent decided that those who were being released from the containment would be filmed and asked for their details. The claimant was held in a separate area, surrounded by police officers, and filmed. She was asked to give her name and address and date of birth. She attempted to ask what police power was relied upon, in authorising the police to film her and ask her details. Those questions were not answered and she was told she would not be released until she had been filmed and given her details. This is the potential breach of Article 8 – the right to respect for private and family life, home and correspondence.

The qualification to this right is that any restriction must be for one of the specified reasons, such as the prevention of disorder or crime. The court decided that the images and personal details were unlawfully obtained, so there was a breach of Article 8.

This case raises a number of issues with respect to morality:

- Article 5: clearly the unjustified deprivation of liberty is immoral. It does not matter whether this is temporary or permanent. However, in this case it was considered justified as it followed the commission of a number of offences by at least some of those kettled, and the kettling was done to prevent further offences being committed, which seemed likely. Therefore, there was no breach of Article 5 and the state acted in a moral manner to protect its citizens and their property against illegal and immoral activities.

- Article 8:
  1 Since the complainant was not suspected of any offence, it can be considered immoral to collect personal details and images without permission for police and security purposes.
  2 To make giving permission a condition of release is equally immoral, as it is effectively blackmail of an entirely innocent purpose.

29.5 Evaluation of the relationship of law and morality

Judges and Parliament are often forced to confront complex moral issues. In *Shaw v DPP* (1962), which concerned a magazine advertising the services of prostitutes, Shaw was convicted of 'conspiracy to corrupt public morals', a previously unknown offence. In that case, Viscount Simonds declared:

> there remains in the courts a residual power to enforce the supreme and fundamental purpose of the law, to conserve not only the safety and order, but also the moral welfare of the State.

In *R v Gibson* (1990), an artist was convicted under the common law offence of outraging public decency for exhibiting earrings made from freeze-dried human foetuses. Devlin would maintain that this is exactly the type of immoral conduct that would arouse the intolerance, indignation and disgust of the ordinary person, and so should be subjected to the full rigour of the criminal law. Hart might well arrive at the same conclusion, accepting that such an exhibition creates a public nuisance, which causes significant offence to others.

In *R v Brown and Others* (1993), all the activities were conducted in private, with no complaints from the victims and no medical attention ever sought. There were no permanent injuries. The activities only came to the attention of the police as a result of a video the men had made of the event. The judges decided the defence of consent was not available. This can be compared with the case of *R v Wilson* (1996) where, at his wife's request, he branded his initials on her buttocks, and was found not guilty of any offence.

These cases illustrate the tension that exists, and continues to exist, between the need to protect society at large against perceived immoral behaviour, and the right of individuals to conduct their private lives according to their own desires.

The question remains whether the state should interfere with the rights of an individual to live his or her life as he or she may choose, subject to ensuring a proper balance between the special interests of the individual and the general interests of the vast majority of the population.

Often the ECHR leaves it to individual nations to decide on these matters. In the UK this means the Judiciary and Parliament. Parliament's contribution is often minimal or belated. An example might be the Racial and Religious Hatred Act (2006). Enforcement can be inconsistent. For example, suggestions of racism within the police force continue, despite legislation.

The selection of material in this section is somewhat arbitrary. There are many entirely different issues such as stem-cell research, anti-smoking legislation, legalisation of all drugs or internet pornography that can be explored.

One case illustrates concern for the autonomy of the individual: *St George's NHS Healthcare Trust v S* (1998). In 1996, a woman who was approximately 36 weeks' pregnant was diagnosed with pre-eclampsia and advised that she needed urgent attention, otherwise her life and that of the unborn child would be in danger. When she rejected this advice, she was detained under Section 2 of the Mental Health Act 1983, and a court order was granted to carry out a Caesarean section operation without her consent. However, the Court of Appeal ruled that an adult of sound mind is entitled to refuse medical treatment, and this entitlement is not reduced because her decision might appear morally repugnant, bizarre or irrational.

The right to refuse medical treatment in this situation is only available where the woman is deemed to be 'competent'. In *Gillick v West Norfolk and Wisbech Area Health Authority and the DHSS* (1985), the mother of girls under the age of consent had sought a court declaration that their doctors would not be allowed to prescribe them contraceptive pills without her knowledge. The House of Lords declared that a 'competent child', who had sufficient understanding of the issues involved, could decide for herself without her parents being informed.

However, such autonomy is not absolute. Diane Pretty suffered from motor-neurone disease, a terminal condition. She wanted her husband to be allowed to help her to end her life peacefully and with dignity. In 2001, the House of Lords and the European Court of Human Rights rejected her application, ruling that a right to life does not include a right to die. Her application and many later cases conflicted with broader issues of public morality. Parliament must also confront issues of public morality such as in relation to human fertilisation and embryology, and assisted suicide.

Quick questions

1 Explain what is meant by legal positivism.
2 Explain what is meant by natural law.
3 Explain what is meant by a pluralist society.
4 Briefly explain the background to the Hart–Devlin debate.
5 Outline the legal enforcement of moral values in the law of tort.

Summary

- There are two main theories relating to the nature of law: legal positivism and natural law.
- Legal positivists believe that laws are valid where they are made by the recognised legislative power in the state; they do not have to satisfy any higher authority.
- Natural law is a moral theory of jurisprudence, which maintains that law should be based on morality and ethics.
- Morality is 'normative' or prescriptive: that is, it specifies what ought to be done and delineates acceptable and unacceptable behaviour.

- There are six characteristics which help to identify the rules and distinguish legal and moral rules.
- Legal and moral rules, though distinctive, share a number of characteristics.
- Changing moral values can lead to developments in the law and vice versa.
- Judges and Parliament are often forced to confront complex moral issues. Parliament can choose whether to legislate. Judges have no choice.

Chapter 30 Law and justice

Introduction

Justice is a concept that can be described simply as fairness, equality or even-handedness. We have a sense of justice from a very young age. In the world of law, the idea includes treating all cases in the same manner, showing impartiality and acting in good faith. However, the term 'justice' has occupied the minds of some of the greatest thinkers across the ages. As a result, there is a wide range of theories available to explain its meaning and application.

30.1 The meaning of justice

One of the earliest attempts to define justice was set out by the fourth-century BC Greek philosopher, Plato. He regarded justice as:

- Harmony between the different sectors or classes in society.
- An overarching virtue of both individuals and societies, so that almost every issue he would classify as ethical comes in under the notion of justice. For example, it is unjust for a person to steal from someone else, or not to give what they owe them; these concepts are reflected in both criminal and civil law today.

Plato's work was continued by his pupil, Aristotle, who stressed the need for proportionality and for achieving the middle way – a balance between extremes. This can be seen today in the law's efforts to balance competing interests, such as:

- freedom of contract and protection of consumers
- the individual's right to freedom of expression and protection of society from extreme views.

In the thirteenth century, Thomas Aquinas continued attempts to define justice in a similar language to Aristotle. Aquinas considered justice as:

- governing our relationships with other people
- the constant willingness to deal with other people as they deserve.

The end result of justice is the common good, for the individual and for the community (society).

From the eighteenth century onwards, legal philosophy developed quickly. Leading this was utilitarianism, a philosophy that developed from the writings of Jeremy Bentham and John Stuart Mill.

Jeremy Bentham was a social reformer who developed the theory known today as utilitarianism. This philosophy is centred around these concepts:

- The more an action increases overall happiness, the more valuable it is.
- The more it decreases happiness, the more reprehensible.

Utilitarians are only interested in the outcome of an act, regardless of what the act itself is. For a utilitarian, maximising happiness is the object of justice.

One of the criticisms of utilitarianism is that the interest of an individual may be sacrificed for greater community happiness. For example, if a drunk person announces that they are about to drive home to see their child who has suddenly fallen ill, would you be justified in stealing their car keys so that they could not set off?

- Not having the car keys may well cause distress and inconvenience.
- The greater happiness brought to the larger community by your action might outweigh the pain of the individual.
- Would it be different if the person was about to set off to take part in a demonstration or a terrorist attack?

When drafting the Investigatory Powers Act 2016, the government called on the utilitarian principle:

> ... an Act to make provision about the interception of communications, equipment interference and the acquisition and retention of communications data, bulk personal datasets and other information ... and for connected purposes. **"**

Another view of the Investigatory Powers Act 2016 can be seen from whistle-blower Edward Snowden's tweet:

> 66 The UK has just legalised the most extreme surveillance in the history of western democracy. It goes further than many autocracies. 99

John Stuart Mill

John Stuart Mill was a nineteenth-century liberal, whose pamphlet *Utilitarianism*, published in 1861, supported the basic principles of utilitarianism put forward by Bentham.

Mill wrote that actions are

> 66 [right] in proportion as they tend to promote happiness, wrong as they tend to produce the reverse of happiness. 99

However, he focused upon the quality of happiness rather than merely upon its quantity. He wrote:

> 66 Better to be a human being dissatisfied than a pig satisfied. 99

Mill also linked utilitarianism to justice. Justice, he explained, includes respect for people, property and rights, as well as the need for good faith and impartiality. All of these are consistent with the principle of utility, since their application brings the greatest happiness to the greatest number.

It could also be argued that punishing wrong-doers also brings happiness to the greatest number. However, Mill argued that punishment is in itself an evil as it involves inflicting harm or pain, and can only be justified where it brings a greater benefit, such as public order.

30.1.1 Act and rule utilitarianism

The theory of utilitarianism has developed since Bentham and Mill.
- Under *act* utilitarianism, the rightness of an act is judged in isolation to see whether it adds to or reduces the sum of human happiness. For example, when I drive my car at 130 mph on an empty motorway, I am increasing my own happiness and causing pain to nobody else: the sum of human happiness is increased. However, I am polluting the atmosphere and wasting natural resources, as well as creating work and risk to others if I crash the car.
- According to *rule* utilitarianism, the rightness of an act is judged according to whether the sum of human happiness would be increased if everyone acted in the same way. Developing the example, if all car owners tried to drive along the same stretch

of motorway at the same speed and at the same time, an accident might well occur, resulting in pain and misery: the sum of human happiness would decrease.

Legal philosopher	Basic premise
Jeremy Bentham	He developed the legal and moral principle of utility: what makes an action right or wrong is the usefulness, or value, of the consequence it brings. The more an action increases overall happiness, the more valuable it is; and the more it decreases happiness, the more reprehensible.
John Stuart Mill	Justice includes respect for people, property and rights, as well as the need for good faith and impartiality. All of these are consistent with the principle of utility, since their application brings the greatest happiness to the greatest number.

Figure 30.1 Key facts: legal philosophers concerned with utilitarianism

Tip

Make sure you can explain the meaning of each type of justice and can link relevant philosophers to each.

30.2 Theories of justice and the extent to which the law achieves justice

There are many ways of categorising justice including:
- Distributive justice concerning the fair allocation of resources, including anti-discrimination laws, minimum wage and redistribution of wealth through taxation and the welfare state.
- Social justice is concerned with equal justice, not just in the courts, but in all aspects of society.
- Formal or procedural justice, which considers legal institutions including policing, courts, judiciary, magistrates and juries, and the appeals system.
- Substantive justice including the legal rules, the concept of fault, rights and freedoms.
- Corrective justice involving sentencing in criminal law and remedies in civil law.

30.2.1 Distributive justice

Several philosophers have expounded the idea of distributive justice, including:

- Aristotle
- Thomas Aquinas
- Karl Marx
- Chaïm Perelman.

Aristotle

Aristotle was a pupil of Plato. He joined Plato's Academy in Athens in the fourth century BC. Like Plato, he described justice as referring to individuals in their dealings with each other, and to the state in making and enforcing laws. He often stressed the need for proportionality, and for achieving the middle way – a balance between extremes.

Aristotle identified particular examples of justice that apply to different situations. Among these is distributive justice. Aristotle argued that:

- A just state will distribute its wealth on the basis of merit, giving to each according to his 'virtue' and to his contribution to society.
- This is a proportionate system where the worthiest, rather than the neediest, receive the greatest share.

He argued that to allocate resources on the basis of people's needs would be unjust, as it would reward the lazy at least as much as the hard-working. We might consider how this would apply today to paying for care for the elderly or by providing social security benefits to all.

Saint Thomas Aquinas

Aquinas, the thirteenth-century theologian, described justice in language similar to that of Aristotle. He identified particular forms of justice that govern our dealings with others. For Aquinas:

- Distributive justice concerns the fair allocation of goods and responsibilities throughout the community.
- This is governed by the principle of due proportion.
- People receive what they are due in accordance with their merit, rank and need.
- Concerning merit, it would be wrong to pay workers an equal amount for unequal work, or an unequal amount for equal work.

Aquinas based his doctrine on natural law.

Karl Marx

Karl Marx, regarded as the nineteenth-century founder of communism, developed a radically different model of distributive justice. This model was embodied in his slogan: 'from each according to his ability, to each according to his need'.

This enshrines two principles of the ideal of communism:

- Each will maximise their contribution to the common wealth by making full use of their abilities.
- Each will receive according to their need, irrespective of the personal contribution they have made to the production process.

Aristotle would have regarded this model of distribution as unjust, as it has the potential for giving the greatest rewards to the least productive and therefore least deserving members of society.

The main criticism of Marx's views is that no country has so far been able to successfully put them into practice to bring about the just society envisaged by Marx. However, capitalist societies that follow principles of distributive justice, closer to those held by Aristotle and Aquinas, are also criticised for social injustice.

Chaïm Perelman

In 1944, Perelman produced a study of justice entitled *De la Justice*. He concluded that justice cannot be studied logically, as each attempt to define it is based upon a person's subjective values.

Chaïm Perelman, author of *De la Justice*

In his book, Perelman discusses different understandings of justice:

- 'To each according to his merits'.
- 'To each according to his needs'.
- 'To each according to his works'.
- 'To each equally'.

- 'To each according to his rank'.
- 'To each according to his legal entitlement'.

Activity

Research each of the philosophers that have been discussed.

- How much were their views influenced by the times in which they lived?

You can continue this process with other philosophers that will be studied later in the chapter.

Legal philosopher	Basic premise
Aristotle	An ancient Greek philosopher. He described justice as referring to individuals in their dealings with each other, and to the state in making and enforcing laws.
Thomas Aquinas	A thirteenth-century theologian. He stated that justice governs our relationships with other people. It is the constant willingness to deal with other people as they deserve. The end result of justice is the common good, for the individual and for the community.
Karl Marx	Widely regarded as the founder of communism, he developed a radically different model of distributive justice. This model was embodied in his slogan, 'from each according to his ability, to each according to his need'.
Chaïm Perelman	He produced a study of justice, entitled *De la Justice*. He concluded that justice cannot be studied logically, as each attempt to define it is based upon a person's subjective values. He saw six possible models of distributive justice.

Figure 30.2 Key facts: legal philosophers concerned with distributive justice

30.2.2 Social justice

Social justice refers to our ability to realise our potential in the society where we live. It is concerned with equal justice, not just in the courts but in all aspects of society. This concept demands that people have equal rights and opportunities: everyone, from the poorest person on the margins of society to the wealthiest, deserves an even playing field.

The Department for Work and Pensions published a paper on this topic in 2012. In the document, the key expression was: 'Social justice is about making society function better – providing the support and tools to help turn lives around'.

This is not a new idea, as it has been expounded by philosophers including John Rawls and Robert Nozick.

John Rawls

John Rawls published *A Theory of Justice* in 1971, which set out the concept of social justice.

Rawls described justice as fairness, and then presented a hypothetical society where each member would distribute its resources in a disinterested manner. To make this possible, nobody would know in advance what their position in that society would be, nor what stage of that society's development they would be born into – they would operate behind a 'veil of ignorance'. Rawls believed that, on this basis, benefits and burdens would be distributed justly and therefore fairly.

He argued that two basic principles of justice would be evident within this society:

1 Each person would have 'an equal right to the most extensive scheme of basic liberties compatible with a similar scheme of liberties for others'. This would include certain basic freedoms, such as the right to own property, freedom of speech, freedom of association, and freedom from arbitrary arrest – many of the freedoms under the ECHR.
2 Social and economic inequalities may exist, but only:
   ○ where they benefit the least advantaged members of society, and
   ○ all offices and positions are open to everyone.

For example:
- It is acceptable for a surgeon to earn several times the average wage, live in a large detached house and drive a luxury car, etc. because their work benefits disadvantaged members of society.
- Their work would encourage others to imitate their example, further benefiting the disadvantaged.
- It is only acceptable provided that everyone with skills and abilities comparable to those of the neurosurgeon has a reasonable opportunity to pursue a similar path.

In employing the fiction of the 'veil of ignorance' to develop a society based upon consent, Rawls was promoting a rights-based system. So, basic human rights such as freedom of speech and association are 'inalienable' – they can never be sacrificed for the common good.

The state must always respect the autonomy of the individual. Rawls wrote:

> Each person possesses an inviolability founded on justice that even the welfare of society as a whole cannot override. Therefore, in a just society the rights secured by justice are not subject to political bargaining or to the calculus of social interests.

This distinguishes Rawls from Bentham and the utilitarians, against whom the final comment is directed — utilitarians might allow individual freedoms to be sacrificed where this promotes wider benefits for the greater number.

Robert Nozick

Robert Nozick published *Anarchy, State and Utopia* in 1974, in which he developed an entitlement theory of justice, which consisted of three principles:

1 Justice in acquisition: how property is initially acquired.
2 Justice in transfer: how property can change hands.
3 Rectification of injustice: injustices arising from the acquisition or transfer of property under the two principles above. This third principle would not be required if the world was entirely just.

In practice, this means that when a person obtains property:

- Legally, in accordance with the principles of acquisition or transfer: they are entitled to keep that property.
- By fraud or theft or other unjust means: the third principle provides a remedy.

This is different from Rawls, who argued that inequalities may exist only where they benefit the most disadvantaged members of society.

Nozick places no limits upon private ownership. Property justly acquired may not be appropriated simply as a form of redistribution of wealth, to reduce inequalities. He wrote:

> No one has a right to something whose realisation requires certain uses of things and activities that other people have rights and entitlements over.

This is a free-market, libertarian form of justice. Nozick revives John Locke's theory of justice. He argues that state interference should be kept to a minimum to achieve a just society and that it should be restricted to the basic needs — protecting the individual against force, theft/fraud and enforcing contractual obligations. The emphasis is on protecting the individual's rights, particularly their property rights. Nozick does not believe that property can be owned by the state, but by individuals.

Nozick's theory may be criticised, but many of the recent political moves in our society show this theory in practice, such as:

- privatisation of state-owned facilities
- making the individual more responsible for their own welfare — tightening the welfare net in terms of social security and pension provision
- reducing the dependence of the individual on the state.

Legal philosopher	Basic premise
John Rawls	He described justice as fairness. He argued that two basic principles of justice would be evident within society.
Robert Nozick	He developed an entitlement theory of justice, which consisted of three principles. This contrasts with Rawls, who provided a philosophical basis for the welfare state and the redistribution of wealth to help the disadvantaged.

Figure 30.3 Key facts: legal philosophers concerned with social justice

30.2.3 Formal procedural justice

Procedural justice is concerned with making and implementing decisions according to fair processes.

Legal aid

This can be considered from the aspect of legal aid availability. Everyone has a right to access justice, receive a fair hearing, and understand their legal rights and obligations. An effective and unbiased police system needs to be in operation. A court structure has to instil confidence in its users that justice will be the outcome and that an appeals structure ensures that deficiencies can be rectified. Everyone involved in the system should be seen to be impartial, including police, magistrates, juries and judges.

Many people need help to access and use these rights. Legal aid should do this. In 2010, when introducing the government's legal aid reforms, the then Justice Secretary Ken Clarke said, 'I genuinely believe access to justice is the hallmark of a civilised society'.

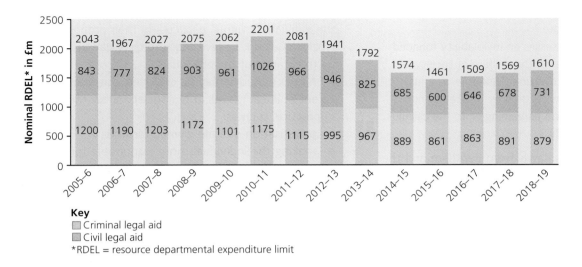

Figure 30.4 Criminal and civil legal aid in England and Wales from 2005–2006 to 2018–2019

Source: https://www.statista.com/statistics/1098628/legal-aid-spending-in-england-and-wales/

However, the effects of changes made by the Legal Aid Sentencing and Punishment of Offenders Act (LASPO) 2012 and subsequently have reduced the availability of legal aid. In April 2013, the government cut £350 million from the relatively small £2.2 billion budget, lopping off entire areas of law, including most of 'social welfare law':

- advice on welfare benefits
- employment
- housing (except homeless cases)
- immigration (except asylum)
- family (except in cases of domestic violence).

The decline since then can be seen in Figure 30.4.

Activities ❓

1 Research the latest legal aid figures.
2 Write down comments that have been made by the legal profession about this issue and its possible impact on justice.

Legal aid is important because if a person cannot afford legal representation, their right to a fair trial is being denied. This right is protected under Article 6 ECHR, enshrined in the Human Rights Act 1998. The right of access to a court must be meaningful and practical, not theoretical.

Chapter 4 discusses the process for gaining legal aid, and explores the issues that the cuts in funding have created. The consequences are:

- Legal aid 'deserts' have appeared – large areas where no legal aid is available, as firms can no longer afford to offer these services.

- Many firms have given up their criminal legal aid practices, raising serious concerns about increased risks of miscarriages of justice.

Legal aid lawyers are not 'fat cats' – in 2018, a social mobility report on young legal aid lawyers showed that half of its members earned less than £25,000 a year.

Justice requires access to the law, and those who are unable to act for themselves or pay for someone to act for them may be denied justice.

The criminal process

Trial by jury enables jury members to use their view of justice rather than adhere strictly to the rules of law and the evidence presented to them.

Case study

Ponting (1985)

A civil servant was charged under the Official Secrets Act for releasing secret information about the sinking of the Argentinian warship *General Belgrano* during the Falklands War. The judge told the jury that any public interest in the information did not provide a defence, but the jury acquitted him.

The rules of evidence adopted in criminal trials seek to balance the interests of the parties to the action. For this reason, evidence of previous convictions is not generally admissible unless the facts are strikingly similar to those in the current case.

On the other hand, even illegally obtained evidence may be admissible.

Case study

Jeffrey v Black (1978)

The police arrested a student for the theft of a sandwich, and then conducted an illegal search of his flat, where they discovered some drugs. The magistrates threw out the case after ruling the evidence inadmissible. However, the Divisional Court ruled that the illegality of the search did not justify excluding the evidence it had exposed.

This may at first seem to be unjust. Consider a situation where the police had discovered plans and materials to commit a terrorist attack. They would surely be justified in relying upon the material found in the 'illegal' search in court?

In general, justice is served by the criminal process, but individual cases sometimes expose a lack of justice that is not always remedied at a later date.

Appeals in criminal cases

In criminal cases heard in the Magistrates' Court, the defendant may appeal against conviction or sentence or on a point of law. Under the Criminal Justice Act 1998, the prosecution may appeal against 'unduly lenient' sentences. Convicted criminals appeal less frequently now that an appeal may result in a more severe sentence.

Under the Criminal Justice Act 1972, the Attorney-General may appeal on a point of law to the Court of Appeal where they wish to question the judge's direction that has led to an acquittal. For example, in *Attorney-General's Reference (No. 2 of 1992)*, the Court of Appeal considered the defence of automatism.

Appeals with respect to substantive law are always seen as achieving justice, but not necessarily for those who have been convicted under an 'old' law. In the interests of justice, today's sentencing guidelines are not applicable to offences committed before new guidelines come into force.

Miscarriages of justice in criminal cases

In spite of this system of appeals, injustices arise where people serve prison sentences for crimes they are not guilty of. Famous cases include the Birmingham Six and the Guildford Four. The publicity of these and other similar cases led to the establishment in 1997 of the Criminal Cases Review Commission (CCRC), whose role is to review the cases of those it feels have been wrongly convicted of criminal offences, or unfairly sentenced.

Look online

Look at cases that the CCRC have been involved with and their successes, at: www.ccrc.gov.uk/case-library/

The CCRC does not consider if a defendant is guilty or not guilty, but whether there is new evidence or argument that may cast doubt on the safety of the original decision. Derek Bentley and Sally Clark are among those who have had their convictions quashed by the Court of Appeal following reference from the CCRC.

The only comfort in terms of justice is the fact that systems exist to bring miscarriages of justice to the attention of the appeal courts, even if in some cases a long time can lapse before the miscarriage is put right, and in Bentley's case, many years after he had been hanged. Even then, compensation is unlikely to be paid unless it can be shown that their innocence was beyond all reasonable doubt as a result of fresh evidence.

Public funding for this area is limited. Procedural justice relies very heavily upon the integrity of those involved and the use of natural justice.

Rules of natural justice

Natural justice is often described as containing two basic principles:

1. The first is that the court must not only be impartial, but also seen to be so. Judges should have no personal interest in a case. When the *Pinochet* case (1998) was appealed in the House of Lords, Lord Hoffmann was not impartial because he was a director of one part of Amnesty International, who had been given permission to take part in the appeal. Clearly this infringed the principle of impartiality.

2. The second principle is that each party to the dispute must have a fair opportunity to present their own case and to answer the case of their opponent. In *Ridge v Baldwin* (1964), the House of Lords ruled that the decision by a police authority to dismiss its chief constable without a personal hearing contravened natural justice.

The rules of natural justice are designed to protect the interests of individuals against arbitrary decisions. In both the *Pinochet* case and *Ridge v Baldwin*, the original decision may have been correct. However, each was unreliable because of the breach of the rules of natural justice.

The application of justice must be fair, and must be seen to be fair.

30.2.4 Substantive justice

This is evaluated by considering different aspects of areas of law.

Substantive law – crime

The principle of proportionality generally governs the sentencing practice of judges and magistrates. This satisfies our expectations that the more serious the offence, the harsher the sanction that will be imposed.

Those convicted of murder are subject to a mandatory life sentence. The sentencing judge will then impose a tariff – the minimum term the murderer has to serve. Many agree that imposing a life sentence on a killer is just. Public opinion polls regularly show strong support for the return of the death penalty, to provide a degree of retributive justice.

Some murderers are viewed as worse than others: setting a tariff does not allow for proportionality, and so may lead to harsh decisions.

Case study

Cocker (1989)

The defendant suffocated his wife, at her insistence, with a pillow; she had been terminally ill and in much pain. The trial judge denied the defendant any partial defence that would reduce murder to manslaughter. Here, a life sentence may seem a disproportionate punishment.

However, the judge may provide a measure of justice by imposing a reduced tariff period.

Case study

R v Inglis (2010)

The trial judge imposed a nine-year tariff period, reduced on appeal to five years, when the defendant was found guilty of murdering her son. She killed him because she believed that she was acting in the best interests of her son and did not want him to suffer any further.

Lord Judge said:

> Mercy killing is murder. Until Parliament decides otherwise, the law recognises a distinction between the withdrawal of treatment supporting life, which may be lawful, and the active termination of life, which is unlawful.

Cases such as this show that, perhaps, justice is better served by allowing judges and magistrates to pass the sentence they feel to be most appropriate, rather than have a system of fixed sentences or a suggested tariff.

Not all premeditated killing is equally culpable. The partial defences of loss of control, diminished responsibility and for the survivor in a suicide pact were created to limit liability. The defences of self-defence and automatism excuse liability altogether.

One of the generally accepted characteristics of justice is that like cases are treated in like manner. However, the law gives more favourable treatment to those who kill while suffering diminished responsibility or with a loss of control than it does to those whose free will is overpowered by an external threat.

- The decision of the House of Lords in *Howe* (1987) clearly established that the defence of duress is not available on a charge of murder or attempted murder.
- Yet we feel much more sympathy for the defendant in *R v Gotts* (1991), a boy whose life was threatened by his own father, than we do for the defendant in *Byrne* (1960).

The Law Commission has proposed adding duress as a defence that would attract conviction for second degree murder. This would introduce parity of treatment under the law, and satisfy a basic requirement of justice that like cases are treated in like manner.

Substantive law – contract law

Link

See Section 7 on the law of contract for details of the cases mentioned in this section.

Formation of contract

In *Reveille Independent LLC v Anotech International (UK) Ltd* (2016), the court had to consider if a contract has come into existence between commercial parties when they were apparently still in negotiation. In examining the rules on offer and acceptance by conduct, the court wanted to preserve certainty and consider the reasonable expectations of honest, sensible business people. This was stressed in order to achieve justice in these business situations.

Exclusion clauses

Parties to a contract may try to limit their liability by relying upon exclusion clauses. The traditional rule of *caveat emptor* ('let the buyer beware') can work against the interests of the weaker bargaining party or where there is a pre-printed standard form of contract. The courts try to achieve a more just result.

- In *Olley v Marlborough Court Hotel* (1949), the exclusion clause was invalid as it had not been brought to Mrs Olley's attention when she booked in at reception.
- In *Spurling v Bradshaw* (1956), Lord Denning observed that some exclusion clauses were written in 'regrettably small print', and stated that the more harsh or unusual the term was, the more it needed to be brought to the attention of the person signing it, for example, by being 'printed in red ink, with a red hand pointing to it'.

> **Link**
>
> See Chapter 40 for case details for *Olley*.

The Unfair Contract Terms Act 1977 restricts the use of exclusion clauses. A person cannot exclude liability for death or personal injury resulting from their negligence, and other exclusion clauses are subjected to the test of reasonableness. This Act aims to prevent those with strong bargaining power from taking unfair advantage of weaker parties and provides a fairer balance between the bargaining parties.

Further protection is given to consumers by legislation such as the Consumer Rights Act 2015, which sets out both rights and remedies in consumer transactions. The question remains whether the pendulum has swung too far in favour of the consumer.

Penalty clauses

The justice of penalty clauses depends on the view of how far a person can force someone else to comply with what they have promised. European and international law allow a court to modify an excessive penalty in a contract term. Under UK law, the penalty clause is either invalid or not.

In *Cavendish Square Holding BV v Talal El Makdessi* (2015) and *ParkingEye Ltd v Beavis* (2015), the Supreme Court decision widened the previously applied tests regarding the enforceability of penalty clauses. Lord Hodge stated that:

> The correct test for a penalty is whether the sum or remedy stipulated as a consequence of a breach of contract is exorbitant or unconscionable when regard is had to the innocent party's interest in the performance of the contract.

This suggests an idea of justice being applied.

Third-party rights

Traditionally, a person could not sue unless they were a party to the contract. However, in *Jackson v Horizon Holidays* (1975), the claimant succeeded in seeking damages for himself and members of his family after a package holiday failed to match the advertised description, even though only he, and not his family members, had made the contract. This is not too surprising, given the law of agency.

- In 1999, Parliament passed the Contract (Rights of Third Parties) Act, allowing third parties to make a claim where the contract expressly provided for this, or where the contract gave them a benefit.
- These provisions were designed to avoid the obvious injustices caused in cases such as *Tweddle v Atkinson* (1861), and the subterfuges that were necessary to obtain a just result which occurred in *Beswick v Beswick* (1967).

> **Link**
>
> See Chapter 39 for case details for *Beswick*.

It does appear that the Contracts (Rights of Third Parties) Act 1999 would now allow the *Beswick* claim, even if she had not been an executor of the will. However, the parties did not intend the term to benefit a third party, the Act will not apply. The parties to the contract have therefore the right to exclude the Act from benefiting a third party. Most commercial contracts now include such a term, so the Act is not as useful as might be hoped.

Frustrated contracts

Parliament again was responsible for legislating to ensure that a just outcome can be reached where a contract is frustrated through no fault of either party:

- The Law Reform (Frustrated Contracts) Act 1943 enabled the courts to apportion the losses more fairly between the parties: the court may order 'a just sum' to be paid where either expenses have been incurred or a valuable benefit obtained.

However, the courts seem reluctant to find frustration of contract:

- *Armchair Answercall v People in Mind* (2016): the court made the inference that 'one or other party [had] assumed the risk of the occurrence of the event' and so there was no frustration of contract.
- *Canary Wharf v European Medicines Agency* (2019): the court decided that Brexit will not frustrate the EMA's lease of premises in London.

Substantive law – human rights law

As we have seen, corrective justice is involved when the law restores an imbalance between an individual and the state. Human rights law is concerned with this as a central theme.

Article 8 ECHR

Article 8 ECHR and its operation in the UK has again come under scrutiny with respect to the treatment of past convictions and other records of the individual with respect to job applications. Despite the progress made and the Law Commission proposals mentioned in Chapter 32, there are many problems, highlighted in the case of *R (on the application of P) v Secretary of State for Home Department* (2017).

> ### Case study
>
> #### *R (on the application of P) v Secretary of State for Home Department* (2017)
>
> This appeal consisted of four challenges. The three successful ones were as follows:
>
> 1   P committed two shoplifting offences in 1999 when suffering from undiagnosed schizophrenia. Fifteen years later, she wanted to be a care assistant. The Court of Appeal held that the multiple conviction rule was disproportionate in its current automatic form to the interference with P's life. It did not generate interests of public safety.
> 2   G, when aged 13, had had consensual anal intercourse with two boys aged 9 and 10 and was reprimanded in 2006 by the police. In 2011, he worked for an employment agency in a library of a local college. He was asked for an enhanced criminal record certificate ('ECRC') because his work involved contact with children. This challenge also succeeded: disclosure was not necessary, given G's age at the time of offending. If he sought an ECRC, it might be justifiable to include this as soft intelligence, but then he could potentially challenge it on the grounds of irrelevance.
> 3   W, when aged 16 in 1982, was convicted of actual bodily harm, for which he received a conditional discharge. At age 47, he wanted to teach English as a second language. Unsurprisingly, the court ruled it was disproportionate to have to disclose this conviction.

Clearly, the balance between state, society and the individual had swung too far in these instances, meaning that the retention and disclosures were unjust and a breach of Article 8.

Article 2 ECHR

Justice can also be seen in the courts' attitude to Article 2 ECHR – the right to life.

> ### Case study
>
> #### *Smith v Ministry of Defence* (2013)
>
> Several British soldiers had been killed, either as a result of 'friendly fire' (when soldiers on the same side accidentally kill one another) or the inability to check for hidden explosives, through poor training or inadequate equipment. The Supreme Court said they were protected by human rights law, even though they were acting abroad.

The positive obligations under Article 2 should apply where the individual should be given protection. This is, however, a matter of judgment, determined in light of the facts of each case and therefore requires justice.

30.2.5 Corrective justice

In criminal law, when judges or magistrates pass sentence on an offender, they take into consideration a number of factors:

- The aim of the sentence: to punish the offender for breaking the rules or to deter others from committing the same offence, balanced against the desire to rehabilitate the offender.
- Aggravating and mitigating factors relating to the offence and the offender.
- Sentencing guidelines.

In civil law, damages are awarded.

- In negligence, the aim of compensation is to restore the claimant to their pre-tort position, in so far as money can achieve this. To balance this, any contributory negligence on the part of the claimant will reduce their award. For example, in *Jebson v Ministry of Defence* (2000), 75 per cent of the claimant's award was deducted for his contributory negligence. This reduction is just because it is proportionate: it reflects that the claimant was largely responsible for his own harm.
- In contract law, the amount of damages is based on loss of bargain: the claimant is placed in the position they would have been in had the contract been performed. However, they can only recover reasonable losses. This can be seen in *Victoria Laundry v Newman* (1949), where exceptional losses were not recoverable.

The judgments in the two cases above reflect the 'concept of proportionality': damages are awarded according to the merits of the claim, and not automatically in relation to the harm suffered.

Under these tests, the awards of damages are just. However, it may not be seen as just where a claimant has a choice of claiming in contract or negligence, as the award of damages could be different.

Quick questions

1 Explain what is meant by utilitarianism.
2 Explain what is meant by distributive justice.
3 Explain what is meant by a social justice.
4 Briefly explain how the criminal justice system in England demonstrates justice.
5 Distinguish between substantive justice and procedural justice.

Summary

- Justice is a concept that can be described simply as fairness, equality or even-handedness.
- There are many theories and aspects of justice, including: justice as harmony; distributive justice; utilitarianism; social justice; procedural justice; corrective justice; substantive justice; natural justice.
- Justice is essential in the law. Achieving justice depends on different aspects of procedural and substantive law.
- Examples can be seen in both civil and criminal law.
- Judges are increasingly aware of the concept of justice, and use the law to achieve justice, even if this means overruling a previous case or distinguishing previous decisions on surprising grounds.

Chapter 31 Law and society

Introduction

Law plays a vital role in any society, maintaining public order and providing a vehicle for the settling of disputes. It can be used to bring about social change and acceptance of alternative approaches and beliefs.

31.1 The role law plays in society

31.1.1 What is society?

According to sociologists, a society is a group of people with common territory, interaction and culture. Law is just one aspect, but an important one, of social structure.

Members of a society must come in contact with one another. If a group of people within a country has no regular contact with another group, those groups cannot be considered part of the same society.

People of the same society share aspects of their culture, such as language or beliefs. Culture refers to the language, values, beliefs, behaviour and material objects that constitute a people's way of life. It is a defining element of society. Members of a society will not necessarily share every aspect of common culture.

There may be separate societies within a single geographical country. This is known as pluralism.

31.1.2 Pluralism

Pluralism has many definitions but in the context of this chapter, we can define it as a form of society in which the members of minority groups maintain their independent cultural traditions. A pluralist is, therefore, a person who believes that the existence of different types of people, beliefs and opinions within a society is a good thing. This requires tolerance from everyone concerned.

The United Kingdom is a society composed of many groups of people, some of whom originally belonged to other societies. There is a long history of invasion such as the Romans, the Vikings and the Norman Conquest, and relatively large immigrations such as the Huguenots who, in the seventeenth and eighteenth centuries, left France to escape persecution. The influence of the British Empire and Commonwealth enabled immigration from many parts of the world.

Successive governments have either encouraged or discouraged immigration from different countries and of different groups. For example:
- During the 1930s, there was a growth in the Jewish community due to Nazi policies in Germany.
- In the 1950s and 1960s, a large number of West Indians (the 'Windrush' generation) and, later, people from India and Pakistan, were encouraged to come to the UK for better work opportunities and a more prosperous life.

This helped to establish a pluralist society in the UK.

Members of a particular culture, religion or immigrant society tend to congregate together for comfort and also to preserve the cultural identity of their society.

Some practices that are common in other societies will inevitably offend or contradict the values and beliefs of the new society. Groups seeking to become part of a pluralistic society often have to give up many of their original traditions in order to fit in. This is known as assimilation, and can be seen in the gradual loss of immigrants' language as they assimilate society's use of English as the dominant language of society.

However, in pluralistic societies, groups do not have to give up all of their former beliefs and practices. Many groups within a pluralistic society retain their traditions, such as Chinese communities celebrating the Lunar New Year.

The UK contains people from different societies who blend together into a single population. This is referred to as multiculturalism, as even if a group has been in the UK for many generations, it can still retain some of its original heritage.

- The term 'multiculturalism' recognises that those who are originally from other societies do not necessarily have to lose their individual markers by becoming part of the mainstream.
- In a pluralistic society, no one group is officially considered more influential than another. However, powerful informal mechanisms, such as prejudice and discrimination, work to keep many groups out of the political process or out of certain neighbourhoods, or to prevent free expression of their values and beliefs.

31.1.3 The role of law in society

The rule of law cannot exist without a transparent legal system. This requires a clear set of laws that are freely and easily accessible to all, strong enforcement structures, and an independent judiciary to protect citizens against the arbitrary use of power by the state, individuals or any other organisation.

Lord Bingham set out the rule of law through eight principles that society, the state and the Judiciary must embrace.

Link

See Chapter 28 for Lord Bingham's list of principles.

Law plays four primary roles in society:
1 To protect people from harm – the criminal law system prohibits harm by other people or by dangerous things such as unsafe machinery or pollution.
2 To ensure a common good – by providing facilities for all such as education and health care.
3 To settle arguments and disputes regarding finite resources – this is the idea of a civil justice system.
4 To persuade people to do the right thing – by giving nudges through law such as encouraging giving to charity through gift aid.

The law strikes a balance between competing interests within society and the importance of fault. There is a two-way movement between law and society:
- The law can shape social norms and behaviour.
- Society can shape the law through protests, strikes and civil disobedience.

The difficulty is that the threats from small sectors of society are often exaggerated by the media, either because of their own views, or because the media outlet hopes to increase its influence and sales through sensationalism. Stanley Cohen in his book, *Folk Devils*

and Moral Panics (1972), points out that if someone is acting in a way that is not typical in society, then the media tends to overreact about it. The more the media covers this new behaviour, the more it becomes established. So rather than stopping it, which they were trying to do, they actually helped it to grow. Then government becomes enjoined to act. Examples of such media campaigns include knife crime, drug use and immigration.

31.2 The law as a social control mechanism

Social control may be either:
- Informal – it occurs through the family, a peer group, a local community or societal group.
- Formal – it occurs through specific social agencies which have the role of maintaining order in society:
  ○ the criminal justice system – including the police, the Judiciary, the probation and prison services
  ○ law-makers – Parliament, local authorities and the Judiciary
  ○ the civil justice system – settles disputes between individuals.

31.2.1 Social control through law

Rosco Pound's book, *Social Control Through Law*, was published in 1942. He suggested that the subject matter of law involves examining aspects of human nature which require social control to achieve individual expectations. Pound formulated a list of social-ethical principles to justify the making of laws:
1 They identify and explain human claims, demands or interests of a given social order.
2 They express what the majority of individuals in society want the law to do.
3 They guide the courts in applying the law.

He stated that individual interests, public interests and social interests overlap and that claims, demands and desires can be placed in all three categories. Rights, unlike interests, have many different meanings.

Today, law exerts greater control over the public and private lives of most members of society because our behaviour is less influenced by family and religious institutions. Law is now the dominant agency of social control.

Social control promotes rules of behaviour that should be followed by the members of a society. Some rules describe behaviour that is socially desirable (good manners) but not necessarily compulsory. Other rules of conduct are not optional and are enforced by laws.

Some laws, when introduced, were initially considered as being controversial, but in time have been accepted and are recognised as being beneficial. These include:

- A number of laws relating to driving that have been accepted as reducing the number of road accidents and deaths: the drink- and drug-driving limits, the compulsory wearing of seatbelts and using a phone while driving.
- The ban on smoking in enclosed areas, which has been recognised as having great health benefits.
- The legalising of homosexuality, which has led to much greater acceptance of LGBT issues.

Some areas of law are confusing because they are inconsistent or open to interpretation in different situations:

- Killing another individual is considered to be a serious crime, except in wartime. But there is a distinction between murder, manslaughter and other crimes where a death has occurred, such as causing death by dangerous or careless driving.
- Murder carries a mandatory life sentence. Other offences where the result is an unlawful killing do not, so there is a disparity in sentencing.

Social control is necessary to maintain social order, without chaos or continual disruption. It ensures that only the values and norms of society are acceptable. It provides predictability. When we cannot predict how others will act, peaceful and productive interaction between people becomes virtually impossible. Social control, therefore, makes a lawful society possible by policing the boundaries and dealing with deviant behaviours.

The consequences of a breakdown of social order are lawlessness and descent into anarchy. Although the aims of groups such as Extinction Rebellion are supported by many, the forms of their protests and the disruption caused do not receive popular support.

- Some members of society need legal protection such as children and vulnerable adults, particularly those with mental health issues. There are laws allowing social services to take action where there is the potential for harm, abuse or neglect.
- Assisted suicide is forbidden because of the potential for abuse.

Public safety is important regardless of the age and vulnerability of individual members of society. For this reason, there are laws to provide safety, for example, in the workplace, on the roads and in the consumption of certain drugs.

Social control fails where the law is weak, unclear or enforced without any degree of consistency. Eventually, rules may be changed when society's view on an issue changes, or the law is inconsistently enforced and falls into disrepute. It is arguable that this eventually happened to the law outlawing homosexuality.

Where an area of law affects a small number of people, it becomes of less public importance and the possibility of change is diminished. If there is illogicality and inconsistency, it is seen as just 'one of those things' and those not directly affected by it are not interested. This can be seen with the law on suicide:

- The law was aimed at reflecting traditional views of the sanctity of life and protecting the most vulnerable. Suicide is not a crime but aiding a suicide is, punishable by a maximum of 14 years in prison.
- This law has been brought into prominence in recent years by those choosing to end their lives in Switzerland, where assisted suicide is allowed. Whether family or friends who accompany them are prosecuted is a matter of prosecution policy.

Look online

1 Research the CPS policy for prosecuting those who accompany terminally ill people to suicide clinics abroad.
2 Research the case of Debbie Purdy.
  - Why did she take a case to court?
  - What was the final result of her case?
3 Research the case of Tony Nicklinson in 2014.
  - Why did he take a case to court?
  - What was the final result of his case?

Criminal and civil disputes are rarely simple matters in any society. Laws may be open to interpretation, and there may be different opinions of evidence.

- In criminal cases when guilt is established, there can be different views about an appropriate punishment.
- In civil cases there may be disagreement about the amount of damages or the wording of an injunction.

Because these issues are open to differing conclusions, society will leave the punishment or sanction to a legally qualified judge. Jurors do not choose the sentence in criminal cases as it is thought they would impose especially harsh sentences on those they find guilty. Juries do not now have a role in civil cases.

31.2.2 Social control through civil and criminal law

Criminal law

Self-defence

All members of society want to feel safe, especially in their own homes. In an unsafe situation, different people will react in different ways to protect themselves, members of their household and their property. Many argue that the balance between the interests of the householder and the burglar needs to be realigned, allowing the householder to decide on the appropriate degree of force when confronting a burglar in their own home.

This balance between the law and society was recognised by the revised statement issued in 2013 entitled 'Householders and the Use of Force Against Intruders', which was a Joint Public Statement from the CPS and the Association of Chief Police Officers. From the following statement it is clear that, in many cases, no prosecution will be taken in most cases where a householder uses reasonable self-defence against a personal attack in the home. It reads:

> The force you use must always be reasonable in the circumstances as you believe them to be. Where you are defending yourself or others from intruders in your home, it might still be reasonable in the circumstances for you to use a degree of force that is subsequently considered to be disproportionate, perhaps if you are acting in extreme circumstances in the heat of the moment and don't have a chance to think about exactly how much force would be necessary to repel the intruder: it might seem reasonable to you at the time but, with hindsight, your actions may seem disproportionate. The law will give you the benefit of the doubt in these circumstances.

> This only applies if you were acting in self-defence or to protect others in your home and the force you used was proportionate – disproportionate force to protect property is still unlawful.

Consent

Where the victim consents to an assault, the defendant may escape liability. Two cases illustrate how the courts balance the interests of the defendant against those of their victims: *R v Wilson* (1996) and *R v Brown and others* (1993).

The distinction in these two cases depended on the judges' views about the parties' relationships. On the one hand in *Wilson*, a heterosexual couple who subsequently married, were engaging in an extreme form of tattooing, where the pain was incidental to the desired outcome. On the other hand, a group of sado-masochistic homosexuals were engaged in forms of torture, where inflicting pain on each other was the purpose. In *Brown*, Lord Templeman spoke of the need for issues of policy and public interest to be weighed in the balance. Lord Mustill, however, spoke of the rights of an individual to live his or her life as he or she chooses, in *Wilson*.

Clearly, the judges had different views about which considerations should form part of the balancing exercise they were performing, and how society views activities that may revolt or disgust many people but are apparently consensual activities.

Activity

Prepare notes for a discussion on whether the law achieves social control in England through the use of criminal law.

Contract law

In contract law, courts are often confronted with the interests of two innocent parties, such as a business and a consumer, who believe they have a plausible legal argument. Consumer protection issues and the validity of standard terms in a contract are debated. Legislation such as the Consumer Rights Act 2015 can protect a consumer, though it has been criticised for protecting consumers at the expense of business.

The law of tort

Tort law is concerned with obligations or duties owed by one party to another. It seeks to provide a remedy, usually damages, for the harm that is caused by the wrongdoing of one person to another.

Often it is difficult to decide which party's interest should take precedence. Two cases involving cricket can be considered where the interests of a small sector of society, a cricket club, and individuals had to be resolved.

- In *Bolton v Stone* (1951) (see Chapter 21), the court decided in favour of the cricket club at the expense of the innocent victim. The court considered that the club had done everything possible in the circumstances to limit the risk to passers-by. If they were required to do more, it would make the game impossible to play.
- In *Miller v Jackson* (1977) (see Chapter 23), the court had to weigh up the claimant's private interest to peacefully enjoy their own home against the defendant's enjoyment of a valuable recreational activity. There was, in addition, the interest of the local community in enjoying the open space. Roscoe Pound had identified the balancing of a private interest with a social, or public, interest. He identified that the public interest would generally prevail, and that was the result of the case. In addition, the cricket club had acted reasonably in trying to limit the risk to the claimants.

When the state is an interested party, the situation appears to change. In *Dennis v Ministry of Defence* (2003), the private interest of Mr and Mrs Dennis had to be balanced with the public interest of the MOD and society as a whole. The claimants took action in Nuisance for the disturbance caused to them and their sheep by the regular flying of training jets over their property. Here it was decided that, although there was a public benefit to the continued training of fighter pilots, the Dennises should not be required to bear the cost of the public benefit. In contrast to *Miller v Jackson*, the private interest outweighed the public interest.

The balance between the individual in society and society as a whole (represented by the state) can be seen in the increased desire of individuals to claim compensation, whatever the overall effect on the state and society as a whole.

- Many local authorities complain about the compensation culture because defending claims is costly.
- In 2018–19, the NHS settled 44 per cent of the claims made against it without paying any compensation.
- The insurance industry, in general, takes a similar view.

All of society is affected by these claims in the form of higher council tax, insurance premiums and the NHS budget when money has to be set aside to cover the cost of litigation.

In March 2019, the NHS Litigation Authority released figures on medical negligence claims made in the previous year: 10,678 claims for clinical negligence were lodged and the total amount set aside for payment of all such claims amounted to £83.4 billion. There is a view that the number of claims, and the cost of meeting them, will continue to rise if the NHS is not fully funded.

- There are those that argue that barring all such claims would restore NHS funding at the expense of some unfortunate members of society.
- On the other hand, it is just that those injured as a result of medical negligence should receive some compensation.

31.3 The way in which law creates and deals with consensus and conflict

We have already seen in this chapter that judges clearly come to different opinions, deciding the cases on the facts presented to them and interpreting the law. Procedural law (Chapter 30) also creates and deals with conflict, but perhaps in a more negative way.

31.3.1 Theories of dealing with consensus and conflict

Both the criminal and civil processes have to balance the interests of those involved in a case and particularly in the trial. Achieving that balance can show how the interests of one sector of society dominate another's interests to provide social control.

There are three theories that need to be considered here:

1 the consensus theory
2 the conflict theory
3 the labelling theory.

The consensus theory

According to this theory, society generally works because most people are successfully socialised into shared values through the family and education. Socialisation produces agreement or consensus between people about appropriate behaviour and beliefs, without which no human could survive.

Consensus theorists believe that this process starts from a young age in the family and educational settings. These institutions enforce what are known as positive and negative sanctions, or rewarding good behaviour and punishing bad behaviour. Both of these institutions perform the function of social control, and this is a good thing for both the individual and society.

Consensus theory is a social theory that holds that a particular political or economic system is a fair system, and that social change should take place within the social institutions provided by it. This contrasts sharply with conflict theory, which holds that social change is only achieved through conflict. Consensus theory is concerned with the maintenance or continuation of social order in society.

Emile Durkheim's work is based upon the assumption that a consensus exists within society. A consensus provides people with an understanding of the acceptable and unacceptable forms of behaviour and conduct.

The conflict theory

Karl Marx's conflict theory claims that society is in a state of perpetual conflict due to competition for limited resources. It holds that social order is maintained by domination and power, rather than consensus and conformity.

According to the conflict theory, those with wealth and power try to hold on to it by any means possible, mainly by suppressing the poor and powerless.

The labelling theory

This theory suggests that most people commit deviant and criminal acts but only some are caught and punished for them. These individuals are stigmatised for their behaviour.

Most of us commit deviant and criminal acts at one time or another. However, we regard those who are categorised as 'criminal' as somehow different from the rest of us, and the only difference between the bulk of the population and criminals is that criminals are the ones who get caught. When sufficient people committing this behaviour are of similar age, race or appearance, they become stereotypes and society then expects those that conform to that stereotype to be deviant or criminal.

An example of this is the use of 'stop and search' powers by the police.

- Official figures from the Home Office in 2019 showed the number of stop and searches carried out by police officers in England and Wales increased by 32 per cent over the previous year.

- In the 12 months to March 2019, there were 370,454 stop and searches conducted, compared to 279,728 in the previous 12 months.

The rise follows a downward trend in the use of the powers between 2010 and 2018, although only 15 per cent, or 58,251, of people who were stopped and searched were arrested and 73 per cent resulted in no further action being taken.

- White people made up the largest ethnicity group searched under police powers, followed by black people. However, black, Asian and minority ethnic (BAME) people were still over four times more likely to be stopped than white people.

- For those who identified as black or black British, the disparity was even greater: they were 9.7 times more likely to be stopped and searched than a white person. Although the most common reason for carrying out a stop and search was on suspicion of drug possession (61 per cent of all instances), the number of people searched on suspicion of carrying knives or other weapons also rose. This may be an example of stereotyping, though the police are likely to dispute that they do target certain groups.

It can be seen that the stop and search figures target young BAME people more disproportionately. This may not have been the intention of the original law-makers but is certainly the act of the law enforcers.

31.3.2 Magistrates and stereotyping

The people who make decisions in legal cases are supposed to reflect society. The idea of trial by jury suggests that there will be a fair reflection, because those deciding if a defendant is guilty or not guilty are members of society, just like the accused. However, a House of Commons Select Committee reported in October 2016 on the role of magistrates, recommending changes so that they reflect society better.

- Greater diversity is needed: 12 per cent of magistrates are from a BAME background. Many benches have no or very few BAME lay magistrates. This means that in some areas of the UK, the magistrates' bench does not include a magistrate who is from the BAME community.

- The age profile of the magistracy needs rebalancing: in April 2019, 52 per cent of lay magistrates were aged 60 years or over, yet the age profile of most offenders in the Magistrates' Court is 18–25 years.

Only 12 per cent of magistrates are from a BAME background

Magistrates do not only deal with criminal cases – they also play a part in the Family Court. Here, age may be less of an issue but the racial background might raise concerns for those using the Family Court, even if magistrates have received diversity training.

The suggestion that offenders should be tried by their peers of exactly the same sector of society is unworkable. However, lay magistrates, like judges, need to be aware of the facts of life in different communities within society and be seen to act accordingly.

31.3.3 Access to justice and society

In theory, all citizens in a democratic society have a right to understand their legal rights and obligations, to access justice, and to receive a fair hearing in a court or tribunal. However, exercising the right is difficult for those who are not confident and articulate, and/or cannot afford to pay for a lawyer.

Campaign groups and professional bodies such as the Law Society and the Bar Council campaign on the need to improve access to justice for all, regardless of social background or wealth. Many people have found it more difficult to access justice because of cuts to legal aid, court closures and increased costs.

The fact that such campaigns are necessary indicates how society's relationship with the law is in danger of becoming even more lopsided and not reflecting the needs of the whole of society. This approach appears to be trying to recover consensus and avoid conflict.

31.4 The realist approach to law-making

Legal realism is the view that we should understand the law as it is practised in the courts, law offices and police stations, rather than as set out in statutes or books.

For legal realists such as Oliver Wendell Holmes, who wrote *The Common Law* in 1923, if the law were merely a system of rules, we would not need lawyers because judges could just apply the rules. However, judges have discretion on deciding a case, so in civil cases the outcome is not certain until the final judgment is given.

Legal realism is positivist – it first considers the law as it is. On the other hand, the law is the product of many factors, including social factors.

Legal realists are interested in the law rather than society. They do not give any importance to laws enacted by Parliament, as they regard only judge-made law as genuine law.

> **Key term**
>
> Legal realism – an understanding of the law as it is practised in reality (by judges), not the way it is presented in statutes or in academic theories.

A judge's understanding about law, society and psychology affects any judgment given by them. At the same time, in the same case, applying the same law, two judges could give different judgments. This is shown in dissenting judgments in the appeal courts. Realism rejects traditional legal rules and concepts, and concentrates more on what the courts actually do in reaching the final decision in the case. They define law as a generalised prediction of what the courts will do.

Realists believe that certainty of law is a myth:
- Law is intimately connected with society, and since society changes faster than the law, there can never be certainty about the law. This can be seen in the change (or lack of change) to the law on homosexuality and assisted suicide.
- A judge trying a criminal case has (subject to appeal) discretion in allowing the evidence that can be called and deciding any legal issues. The parties can never be entirely certain how their case can proceed.

31.4.1 Left realism

The left realists believe the main causes of crime are inequality, marginalisation, relative deprivation and subcultures. They believe that the main victims are going to be the working class and that work such as community-oriented programmes for controlling and reducing crime should be implemented, rather than focusing on white-collar crime.

It is believed that some commit crime because they feel relatively deprived. The media and the advertising of expensive products have raised expectations for material goods and there is pressure to keep up and have the latest products. But for many, they lack the opportunity to acquire those possessions, unless they resort to crime.

Marginalisation is where people lack the power or resources to fully participate in society. They lack both clear goals and organisations to represent their interests. Workers have clear goals (such as wanting better pay and conditions) and organisations to represent them (such as trades unions), and as such they have no need to resort to violence to achieve their goals. In contrast, unemployed youths are marginalised as they have no specific organisation to represent them and no clear sense of goals – which results in feelings of resentment and frustration. Having no access to legitimate political means to pursue their goals, frustration can become expressed through violence and crime.

Within society, there are likely to be sub-cultures which are prepared to resort to illegal means to acquire money and goods and thereby attain their desires. Theft, drug-dealing and robbery all become a way of life in communities which suffer from economic exclusion.

Left realism – controlling crime

Providing employment, paying living wages and affordable housing will all help to reduce deprivation and the need to commit crime.

Having a more accountable and democratic criminal justice system will reduce the marginalisation of groups. In other words, crime control should be a shared responsibility between several agencies, not just the police and law enforcement. Schools and social services also need to be involved.

By reducing marginalisation and relative deprivation, a criminal subculture will be less likely to develop. People will have more money to contribute to their local economy, which will help to create more jobs and allow a community to thrive.

31.4.2 Right realism

This theory believes that individuals make a rational choice to commit crime, and emphasises tough control measures to reduce crime – for example, zero-tolerance policing and more severe punishments.

It asks how governments can reduce crime here and now, and work within the constraints of the social system. It takes a victim-centred approach to crime, putting victims at the forefront.

It considers that the individual is responsible for crime – although it is accepted that high levels of 'social disorder' and low levels of 'social control' are associated with higher crime rates.

The rational choice theory considers that most criminals are rational actors. If there is a low risk of getting caught or that, if caught, there will be a light punishment, then there is a greater risk of committing crime, assuming the reward is high enough. In other words, the costs and benefits are weighed in order to assess whether a crime is worth committing.

On the other hand, if there was social control, such as parents or police, a lack of opportunity, and a risk of getting caught, there would be less crime. In run-down areas where there is disorder and less concern for others, there is the likelihood of more crime being committed. Without remedial action there can be a spiral of decline and the area becomes a magnet for crime and disorder.

Right realism – controlling crime

There are two main methods considered for preventing or reducing crime:
- Environmental crime prevention: focusses on making whole neighbourhoods more crime-resistant by, for example, putting more police or wardens on the streets, or adopting a 'zero tolerance' approach to minor crimes.
- Situational crime prevention (SCP): involves making buildings more secure and/or the use of CCTV, both of which are relatively cheap and simple to implement. It can be carried out by the police, local councils, institutions such as schools and colleges and private individuals.

Other sentencing policies associated with right realism include the use of ASBOs and the use of prison sentences for minor crimes, though this is unlikely by itself to reduce the level of crime in the long term, as offenders could lose their jobs, houses or families as a consequence and will resort to further crime as a form of survival.

Extension activity

Research an area of law where you think that a section of society is poorly protected by the law. Does your research alter your original view?

31.5 Evaluation of the law and society

- The UK is a pluralist and multi-cultural society with different values and beliefs that may be reflected in attitudes towards the law and issues such as the use of drugs, homosexuality and carrying of knives.
- The role of law in society is to have a fair and open legal system available to all for the protection of citizens from harm, the settling of disputes, maintaining the common good and persuading citizens to do the right thing. Access to the law is available to only a limited number. Many groups and communities feel marginalised and unable to access the law or legal advice.
- The media will often exaggerate threats to society and sensationalise issues, which may help in the growth of these issues rather than stopping their spread.
- Law is used as a form of social control often by the passing of more punitive laws and restricting freedoms. In today's society the law is a more likely use of control than families or religion.
- Law has influenced behaviour in positive ways, despite initial opposition such as in the introduction of many driving offences.
- Law, as a form of social control, is more effective if it is applied consistently to the whole country.

- The consensus theory where people are socialised by shared values, which leads to changes in behaviour, is likely to be more successful than the conflict theory, which tries to bring change by domination and power by the rich over the poor.
- Certain groups are subject to labelling – this is particularly seen in the use of stop and search by certain police forces.
- The left realist theory: relying on views of inequality, marginalisation, deprivation and the growth of sub-cultures, considers that change can be effected by improving all the causes of inequality. However, this approach is likely to be long term and expensive and needs the support of a community.
- The right realist theory: believing in tough measures to control crime is likely to be short term and require resources, but politically popular.

Quick questions

1. Briefly explain what is meant by 'society'.
2. Explain the meaning of the consensus theory.
3. Explain what is meant by legal realism.
4. Consider how law exercises social control in civil law.

Summary

Law plays the following roles in society:
- To protect citizens from harm.
- To ensure a common good.
- To settle arguments and disputes.
- To persuade citizens to do the right thing.
- Different areas of law reflect the balance between competing interests, which is often unequal, as considered by some communities and sectors of society.

- Legal realism is the view that we should understand the law as it is practised in court rather than as it is written.
- Right realism believes that individuals make a rational choice to commit crime. It argues for tough control measures to reduce crime.
- Left realism believes the main causes of crime are social issues and improving social conditions will help to reduce the level of crime.

Section 6

HUMAN RIGHTS LAW

Chapter 32 Rules and theory

Introduction

This chapter explains some of the underpinning principles which guide the operation of human rights law. It shows that there is a strong link between the constitutional mechanisms of the United Kingdom and human rights.

32.1 An outline of the rules of human rights law

32.1.1 What are human rights?

- Human rights belong to every individual, regardless of sex, race, nationality, socio-economic group, political opinion, sexual orientation or any other status.
- Human rights are owed by the state to the people. This means that public bodies must respect an individual's human rights, and the government must ensure that there are laws in place so that people respect each other's rights. For example, the right to life requires not only that the actions of those working on behalf of the state do not lead to a person's death, but that laws are also in place to protect an individual from the actions of others who might want to cause a person harm.

In addition to these basic rights, the UK government has, in recent years, tried to address what it refers to as social, economic and cultural rights granted to specific groups to improve the quality of their lives. These rights are sometimes referred to as 'second generation rights'. Examples of these rights are:
- equal pay at work
- the right not to be unfairly dismissed at work
- the right not to be discriminated against on the grounds of sex, race, or disability
- the rights given to consumers when buying goods or services.

Within the concept of human rights are ideas of natural justice, universality, the rule of law and due process.

Unlike many countries, the UK constitution is not written or contained in a single document or series of documents. Rights have been protected by:
- legislation made by Parliament, such as the Human Rights Act 1998
- judicial decisions
- documents such as Magna Carta and the Bill of Rights
- conventions such as the House of Lords passing legislation that appeared in the government's pre-election manifesto
- authoritative writings.

Magna Carta: a royal charter of rights

Concepts such as natural justice are also central to human rights. This is where the criminal trial or dispute-resolving process is fair and results in an objectively fair decision. It relies upon an independent court or tribunal where the judges have no interest in the case and both parties have the right to be heard in the process. Article 6 of the European Convention on Human Rights provides protection for these principles of natural justice.

It is important to note the difference between 'civil rights' and 'civil liberties'. The term 'civil rights' revolves around a basic right to be free from unequal treatment. 'Civil liberties' concern basic rights and freedoms that are guaranteed – either explicitly by a constitution, or interpreted as such by the Legislature and courts. Civil liberties include:

- freedom of speech
- the right to privacy
- the right to be free from unreasonable searches of your home
- the right to a fair trial in a court or tribunal
- the right to marry
- the right to vote.

Civil liberties are distinct from human rights:
- Human rights are universal rights and freedoms to which all people throughout the world are entitled.
- Civil liberties are those rights and freedoms recognised by a particular country.

People do not earn civil rights – citizenship automatically confers them. Civil liberties prevent governments from abusing their powers and restrict the level of interference in people's lives.

The UK does not have a written constitution setting out the civil liberties and rights of its citizens. It does, however, have a long history of recognising certain freedoms, and many written constitutions around the world are based on the rights long upheld by British courts. An example is 'habeas corpus' – which appears to have been in effect in the UK since at least the fourteenth century and may pre-date Magna Carta. Under this rule anyone who has been arrested, or deprived of their liberty, may request that they are presented before a judge so that the legality of their detention can be judicially decided.

One way to consider the difference between 'civil rights' and 'civil liberties' is to look at:
- what right is affected, and
- whose right is affected.

For example, as an employee, a worker does not have the legal right to be promoted, as obtaining promotion is not a guaranteed 'civil liberty'. But a female or disabled employee has the legal right to be free from discrimination in being considered for that promotion – an employee cannot legally be denied the promotion based on gender or disability. By choosing not to promote a female or disabled worker solely because of the employee's gender or disability, the employer has committed a civil rights violation and has engaged in unlawful employment discrimination based on gender or disability.

Figure 32.1 What are human rights?

Rights	Liberties
They are basic rights given to all citizens to be free from unequal treatment.	They are granted by a state.
They belong to everyone. They are universal in nature and international in scope.	They may be granted to certain sections or groups within a country.
They are inalienable and indivisible but can be limited.	Their extent is likely to be limited by the law granting them.

Figure 32.2 The differences between rights and liberties

For the OCR specification, you will need to know about the following specific rights:
- Article 5: the right to liberty and security of the person. This is a limited right, so there is an absolute prohibition on detentions which are outside the scope of Article 5(1).
- Article 6: the right to a fair trial. This again is a limited right, so there is a right to a fair hearing if a case falls within Article 6(1).
- Article 8: freedom of family life, private life, home and correspondence.
- Article 10: freedom of expression.
- Article 11: freedom of assembly and association.

Articles 8, 10 and 11 are all qualified rights, so that if the state can justify a limitation of these rights which is in accordance with law and meets a legitimate aim, there will be no breach of the EHCR.

32.1.2 Universality

Human rights are moral principles or standards of human behaviour that are protected by law. They are understood to be fundamental rights, 'to which a person is entitled simply because he or she is a human being'. They apply to all, regardless of their race, nationality, religion, ethnic origin or any other status. They apply everywhere and at all times and they apply in the same way to everyone. They should not be taken away except as a result of due process of law and of procedure.

Not everyone agrees with the concept of universality. Cultural relativists object to the idea that moral principles can be made to apply to all cultures. Their argument is that the principles contained in the Universal Declaration of Human Rights (1948), Magna Carta and the United States Bill of Rights (1791) are the product of western political history. They argue that universalism is a form of cultural imperialism and that the International Criminal Court illustrates that. Cultural relativists are generally supportive of 'traditional' or local approaches to justice, as they believe these will contribute more to post-conflict reconciliation. The counter-argument is that cultural relativism is often simply a mask for dictatorship and tyranny. What is culturally relative about the right not to be tortured?

32.1.3 Inalienable and indivisible rights

Which of your human rights would you sell? The right to life? The right to liberty and security? Surely no-one would seriously consider trading in their rights. The fact is that our rights are inalienable. They can't be taken away or sold. No-one can be lawfully sold into servitude or have their rights limited unless by the strict operation of law.

Similarly, it is problematic to think in terms of prioritising certain rights over another. The fact is that the rights are an indivisible package and are deeply interrelated. For example, it is hard to imagine the right to assemble and protest without the right to freedom of expression. Freedom from torture makes little sense without the right to life. The underpinning basis of our rights lies in the concept of the inherent dignity of human beings.

32.1.4 Dignity

Dignity is not easy to define in the way that we can define many legal topics. It is an aspect of our common humanity which recognises that there is a certain way that human beings ought to be treated. We know intuitively that this value should be respected whenever states and governments legislate for individuals. The origins of many human rights documents lie in situations where dignity has been abused or neglected. The ECHR was mainly a reaction to the industrial scale of abuse of dignity throughout the Second World War. Although we find it hard to define human dignity, we know instinctively when it is being abused. Dignity is based on the concepts of personal autonomy and democracy.

Autonomy is the right to live our lives according to our own values and not to be forced under the domination of others. For example, even when we enter into employment we do so voluntarily. One reason why zero-hours contracts are so troubling is that they offend against this notion of autonomy and dignity.

Democracy is the right to participate freely in the process of government and to be able to choose the direction of travel of the government to some extent. This also can be seen as providing an element of personal dignity.

Recognising dignity also includes the concept of difference. Our differences may include our religious or political beliefs, our sense of right and wrong, or our desires and interests. Our common humanity allows for such differences to prosper.

32.1.5 Pluralism

Pluralism is the idea that the constitution recognises not only the rights of the majority but the rights of all different groups, whether the differences arise from ethnicity, religious, social or political identity. It requires that the state does not impose a particular belief system or ideology on society as a whole. It means that people should be allowed to express their beliefs through associations and groups and to further their own different ways of life. This is so even when the views of the minority group may not be appealing to the majority.

Look online

Read the article at the link below.

https://eachother.org.uk/why-our-democracy-needs-more-black-political-journalists/

What aspects of human rights theory do you think this piece is reflecting?

32.2 An overview of the theory of human rights law

32.2.1 Rule of law

> " The rule of law is preferable to that of any man. "

The rule of law is seen as a fundamental principle of the legal system. It represents a guard against the exercise of arbitrary power. The European Convention on Human Rights describes the rule of law as part of the common heritage of Europe.

It has a part to play in human rights law too. The Universal Declaration of Human Rights along with many other international instruments link the rule of law with the protection of human rights; the ECtHR has made reference to 'the notion of the rule of law from which the Convention draws its inspiration', as stated in *Engel v Netherlands* (1976).

The rule of law has several elements:

- The law must be accessible, clear and predictable.
- Questions of legal right and liability should be resolved by application of law, not the use of discretion.
- The laws should apply equally to all.
- Ministers must exercise the power conferred on them fairly and without exceeding the limits of such powers.
- The law must give adequate protection to human rights.

32.2.2 Democracy

Democracy is a system of representative government which requires validation by the people through elections. It is built on the premise of involvement by the people in the business of the state. It also implies that a justice system should operate according to the rules of natural justice.

There is a strong link between Article 10, freedom of expression, and Article 11, freedom of association, and democracy as these rights are seen to underpin the functioning of a healthy democracy. The ECtHR has commented on the significance of democracy many times and has shown itself to be willing to act robustly in its defence, where needed.

> " Democracy appears to be the only political model contemplated by the Convention, and the only one compatible with it. "

Source: *Limited Communist Party of Turkey v Turkey* (1998)

Articles 8, 9, 10 and 11 of the Convention all specify that any interference with the exercise of the rights they contain must be only where it is seen to be 'necessary in a democratic society'.

32.2.3 Separation of powers

The separation of powers is an important constitutional theory. It explains how power should be divided and limited so that no single body is allowed to take too much power into their own hands. The idea has its origins in classical Greek and Roman times. Power should be divided between the three branches of state: the Executive, the Legislature and the Judiciary. The theory does not always work so well in practice, with the Executive in the UK being able to control the Legislature where there is a majority government and the absence of a free voting system. Judges are often accused of making law in their role as interpreters. The role of the Judiciary has been clarified in recent times by removing senior judges from sitting in Parliament under the Constitutional Reform Act 2005.

32.2.4 Approaches to interpretation

The ECtHR uses different approaches towards the interpretation of the Articles of the Convention than the rules of interpretation seen in the national courts. It has developed certain themes and approaches, which are set out below.

Balancing of rights

In a criminal case, the courts assess whether the defendant has created the necessary harm with the appropriate *mens rea* and has no relevant defence. In such cases, he or she will be found guilty. Similarly in contract and tort cases, if the relevant elements are present it is possible to predict the outcome with some certainty. In human rights cases, the situation is more nuanced. Judges are more often trying to balance competing rights. For example, it may be that the right to freedom of expression is balanced against the right to private life. Or the right to protest may be balanced against the threat of public order disturbances. The balance is most often between protecting the individual's right and that of the community in general.

In *Sporrong and Lonnroth v Sweden* (1983), the Court explained that the balance has to be struck:

> " between the demands of the general interests of the community and the requirements of the individual's fundamental rights ...the search for this balance is inherent in whole of the Convention. "

Proportionality

One of the key differences between the way human rights cases are decided, and other legal cases such as criminal or contract law, is the importance of the concept of proportionality.

The word 'proportionality' is not written anywhere in the Convention, rather it is a method of interpretation developed by the ECtHR when applying the Convention rights. A range of factors will be taken into account when deciding proportionality:

- Were there less restrictive alternative measures which could have been taken instead?
- Are the reasons appropriate? In *Stafford v UK* (2002), the reasons given did not justify the action taken.
- Were the safeguards inadequate?

Margin of appreciation

One of the underpinning mechanisms of the Convention has been the concept of the margin of appreciation. This is the idea that when the Convention is applied, a certain amount of leeway can be given to individual states to reflect their national priorities and cultural values. It is most often used in the interpretation of Articles 8–11 but can apply to other Articles too. The doctrine was developed in early cases such as *Handyside v United Kingdom* (1976).

The key points are:

- The duty to protect human rights lies primarily with the nation state.
- The ECtHR is subsidiary to the states.

- Member states are best placed to determine issues because they have greater local knowledge.
- The margin of appreciation varies from right to right. The ECtHR has determined that there is less room for margin of appreciation in relation to absolute rights, such as Article 3, compared to Articles 8–11.
- If the right at stake is seen as vital for the individual – such as matters concerning intimate rights such as sexuality or identity, then the margin will be less (see *Dudgeon v UK* (1982)).

An example of the margin of appreciation in action is the case of *Otto-Preminger Institute v Austria* (1994) in which a film made by the director Otto Preminger had been banned by the Austrian authorities for its offensive content. In particular, the content offended the religious sensibilities of the local Catholic community. Due to the importance of religion in the region, there was a narrow margin of appreciation. If the case had happened in a more secular society such as France, the margin would have been wider.

Quick questions

1. Name three of the ways in which human rights are protected in the UK.
2. Explain the meaning of 'inalienable rights'.
3. Explain the difference between rights and liberties.
4. Why is the concept of 'autonomy' significant in relation to human rights?
5. What does 'the doctrine of the margin of appreciation' mean?

Summary

- As the UK does not have a written constitution, individual rights have been protected in various ways including by legislation, judicial decisions, documents, conventions and authoritative writings.
- Civil liberties are granted by the Legislature or the courts.
- Civil liberties prevent governments from abusing their powers and restrict state interference in people's lives.
- Absolute rights are where a state cannot justify interfering with them.
- Limited rights are where rights are protected to a certain level.

- Qualified rights are where the state can justify their limitation, if the limitation is in accordance with law and meets a legitimate aim.
- Human rights belong to everyone.
- Human rights cannot be removed by the state but can be limited.
- Human rights are underpinned by long-standing constitutional ideas such as the rule of law, democracy and the separation of powers.
- The ECtHR has developed certain approaches to interpretation including the margin of appreciation and proportionality.
- Human rights are owed by the state to their people; they cannot be earned by individuals.

Chapter 33 Protection of the individual's human rights and freedoms in the UK

Introduction

This chapter deals with the key features of the European Convention on Human Rights and the European Court of Human Rights. It also sets out the key practical aspects of the Human Rights Act 1998 in relation to the Convention.

33.1 History of the European Convention on Human Rights and the European Court of Human Rights

33.1.1 The European Convention on Human Rights

In 1949, the Council of Europe was formed. Its main aim was to prevent any repetition of the events of the first half of the century which had seen Europe devastated twice by war. After the Second World War, the horrors of both war and the Holocaust had emphasised the need to enshrine in law a new respect for human dignity, and certain minimum standards of rights and freedoms that could be enjoyed by all citizens.

The Universal Declaration of Human Rights, adopted by the UN on 10 December 1948 under the stewardship of Eleanor Roosevelt, set the context of human rights against the recent historical backdrop:

> Disregard and contempt for human rights have resulted in barbarous acts which have outraged the conscience of mankind, and the advent of a world in which human beings shall enjoy freedom of speech and belief and freedom from fear and want has been proclaimed as the highest aspiration of the common people … All human beings are born free and equal in dignity and rights.

Echoing many of the aims of the United Nations and the Universal Declaration of Human Rights, the Council of Europe set out its own proposals in a document which created a system designed to promote and protect human rights.

The European Convention for the Protection of Human Rights and Fundamental Freedoms was drafted in 1950 by the Member States of the Council of Europe.

A common misconception which has been propagated in recent years is that the ECHR and its institutions were forced upon an unwilling UK as part of a wider European project. But the reality is that the UK was one of the architects of the Convention and the wider human rights agenda that followed the Second World War.

The Convention originally contained 14 articles but has been subsequently expanded by a series of Protocols including, amongst others, Protocol 1, Article 2 – the right not to be denied education, and Protocol 13 – the abolition of the death penalty in all circumstances.

The Convention also created the European Court of Human Rights to adjudicate matters relating to violations of the Convention rights.

The Council has since grown to 47 Member States and remains an active body.

33.1.2 History of the European Court of Human Rights

The European Court of Human Rights (ECtHR) is an international court established by the ECHR. When a Member State has allegedly breached the Convention, a case can be brought before the Court.

An application to the Court can be lodged by an individual after all domestic remedies have been tried and exhausted. The Court can issue both judgments and advisory opinions. It is based in Strasbourg, France.

The Court was established on 21 January 1959 on the basis of Article 19 ECHR. The jurisdiction of the Court is recognised by all 47 Member States of the Council of Europe.

The European Court of Human Rights, at Strasbourg

The accession of new states to the ECHR following the fall of the Berlin Wall in 1989 led to a sharp increase in applications filed in the Court. The efficiency of the Court was seriously threatened by the large number of applications it received:

- In 1999, 8400 applications were allocated to be heard.
- In 2003, 27,200 cases were filed and the number of pending applications was 65,000.
- In 2005, the Court opened 45,500 new case files.
- In 2009, 57,200 applications were allocated, with the number of pending applications rising to 119,300.

Look online

Explore the data relating to the numbers of violations by state from 1959–2019 using the following link:

www.echr.coe.int/Documents/Stats_violation_1959_2019_ENG.pdf

- Which countries are the worst offenders?
- Which articles are most often violated?
- How does the record of the United Kingdom compare with that of other countries?

Relationship with national courts

Most of the signatory states to the ECHR, including the UK, have incorporated the Convention into their own national legal systems, either through constitutional provision, statute or judicial decisions. In the UK, all courts are bound to give effect to decisions of the ECtHR.

An individual who argues that their human rights have been violated has to first take a case in their national courts. A claim can only be issued in ECtHR if all avenues and remedies have been exhausted in the national courts.

33.2 The impact of the Human Rights Act 1988

The UK ratified the European Convention on Human Rights in 1966.

The UK is a dualist system in respect of incorporating international law into the UK legal system. This means that Parliament must pass legislation to make international treaty provisions part of UK law and enforceable in a UK court. The opposite system is a monist system, when a treaty with another country or organisation automatically becomes part of the domestic law.

For the UK, this meant that before 2000, a person who alleged breach of their human rights could bring a case in the ECtHR, but could not argue any of their rights given by the Convention before a UK court. UK courts could use the Convention to help interpret ambiguous wording or clauses in legislation but could not decide a case based purely on a Convention right.

When Labour came to power in 1997, it put forward a Human Rights Bill to incorporate the ECHR into UK law. The Bill received Royal Assent in 1998 and came into effect in October 2000. This allowed time for judges, lawyers and public bodies to receive training on its effects and application.

Bringing a case: Sections 6 and 7

Section 7: Who is eligible to bring a case?

A person may bring a claim under the HRA in a court or other tribunal or rely on the Convention in other legal proceedings if:

> they are or would be a victim of the unlawful act.

A person must have 'standing' to be able to bring a case, meaning they must have been directly affected by the act of the public body.

Section 6: Who can the case be brought against?

The Act provides protection against violations by public bodies. This is known as a 'vertical' relationship between an individual and the state. Relations between individuals are seen as 'horizontal' and are not within the scope of HRA 1998.

Section 6 defines a public body as a body carrying out a public function, not private in nature.

There are two types of public body:

1. Core authorities, including government departments, local authorities and courts, but not Parliament. These only perform public duties.
2. Hybrid public authorities, which may be private in nature but they carry out public functions under a contract, such as residential care.

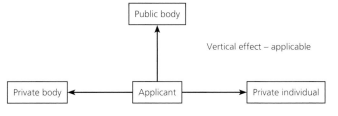

Figure 33.1 Vertical and horizontal effect

33.2.1 Judicial powers

Section 2: Case law from the ECtHR

Under s 2, a court or tribunal deciding a case under HRA 1998 must take into account all past judgments, decisions, declarations or opinions of the ECtHR.

If the court is faced with a conflicting domestic (UK) precedent and a decision of the ECtHR, it should follow the domestic precedent and refer the case to appeal.

Section 3: Interpretation and compatibility

Section 3 requires primary and subordinate legislation to be interpreted, and given effect to, in a way which is compatible with Convention rights 'so far as it is possible to do so'.

Case study

Bellringer v Bellringer (2003)

The Matrimonial Causes Act 1973 did not recognise as legitimate a marriage between a transgender woman and a man. A declaration of incompatibility was issued for the Act in relation to Articles 8 and 12. Parliament went on to pass the Gender Recognition Act 2004 to rectify this.

Section 4: Declarations of incompatibility

If, as in the *Bellringer* case, the court finds a piece of legislation is incompatible with a Convention right, it may make a declaration of incompatibility. This does not affect the original legislation so the parties in the case will still be bound by it. Parliamentary sovereignty remains as the court cannot declare a piece of legislation invalid.

When a declaration of incompatibility is issued, it is for Parliament to decide whether to repeal or amend the legislation, or to ignore the court judgment.

These cases are examples of section 4 in action:

Case studies

R (Anderson) v Secretary of State for the Home Department (2002)

Under the Crime (Sentences) Act 1997, the Home Secretary was given the power to fix a tariff period for a murderer subject to a life sentence. The House of Lords decided this power was incompatible with Article 6 ECHR. Parliament amended the law in the Criminal Justice Act 2003 and power to fix the tariff period passed to judges.

A v Secretary of State for the Home Department (2005)

The claimants were indefinitely detained under anti-terror legislation. When passing the legislation, Parliament had issued an order of derogation, as they were entitled to do under Article 15 ECHR in times of war or other public emergency. The claimants argued that there was no public emergency and powers allowing indefinite detention were disproportionate and unnecessary.

The House of Lords decided:

- that it was for the government to decide if there was an emergency situation, and
- the powers were disproportionate, discriminatory and incompatible with Articles 5 and 14 ECHR.

The government's response was to introduce legislation creating control orders – the Prevention of Terrorism Act 2005.

A government minister can, when promoting a bill through Parliament, certify that it is necessary to depart from the ECHR – perhaps because of terrorism issues. This power has mainly been used to derogate from Articles 5 and 6.

33.2.2 Section 8: Remedies

Under s 8, if the court finds that an act by a public authority is unlawful, it may grant damages or an injunction. Damages are usually only awarded if they are seen as necessary for just satisfaction. This was the case in *Commissioner of Police for the Metropolis v DSD, NBV* (2015), where a failure by the police to investigate rape was seen as breach of Article 3 and damages awarded accordingly. Normally, damages are seen as a last resort. Often the finding of a violation in itself will be considered as a victory.

33.2.3 Section 10: Remedial action

Under s 10, government ministers have the power to amend legislation that is subject to a declaration of incompatibility without having to go through the full parliamentary process, though it still has to be approved by a parliamentary resolution.

Although before HRA 1998 there was no right for an individual to bring an action for breach of ECHR rights in a domestic court, this did not mean that there was no protection of individual rights:

- Common law, through Magna Carta, protected the right to a fair trial and other fundamental rights and freedoms.
- Judicial review gave individuals the right to challenge decisions of government departments and other public bodies.
- Statutes created express rights, such as under the Police and Criminal Evidence Act 1984, for those arrested and detained by the police.

However, prior to HRA 1998, the UK's record in protecting ECHR rights was, in certain cases, inadequate. For example, in *Sunday Times v United Kingdom* (1979), the newspaper had an injunction placed on an article it had planned to publish. The article concerned the cause of birth defects in children whose mothers had used the drug thalidomide during pregnancy. The ECtHR held that such an injunction violated Article 10 ECHR because the interference did not correspond to public interests.

Even after HRA 1998 was passed, there have been cases heard by UK courts where a breach of human rights has not been accepted and the applicant has been forced to pursue a claim to the ECtHR.

The judgment in *Wainwright v United Kingdom* (2007) (see section 33.3.4 for case details) could be read as requiring the introduction into English law of a general tort of invasion of privacy. At the time of the visit (pre-2000), HRA 1998 was not in force. If it had occurred after HRA 1998, a remedy might have been available directly to the applicants.

33.3 The entrenched nature of the Human Rights Act 1988 and the devolution settlements

Entrenchment is a procedure which would make an Act of Parliament difficult to repeal or amend in the future. One way of doing this would be to include a provision that would require, for example, a 75 per cent majority of votes in the House of Commons before repeal or amendment could take place.

As is well known, under the principle of parliamentary sovereignty, Parliament is the supreme law-making body in the UK, and no one Parliament can bind its successors. This means that, in theory, a future Parliament could repeal or amend HRA 1998. The Human Rights Act contains no provision to stop or limit the powers of a successor Parliament from repealing or amending it. In practice, that is extremely unlikely because, in a political sense, it would suggest that the UK does not respect human rights.

In its 1997 White Paper, 'Rights Brought Home: The Human Rights Bill 1997', the government set out its view about entrenchment as follows:

> Although other legislatures had entrenched certain human rights protections into law, for example, the United States has added amendments to their constitution, it is considered that such an approach cannot be reconciled with our own constitutional traditions. Any attempt to entrench human rights provisions would be subject to the doctrine of parliamentary sovereignty, which would allow for repeal or amendment.

By three separate Acts, Parliament granted devolution, or law-making powers, to Scotland, Wales and Northern Ireland. None of these Acts contained entrenched provisions so again, in theory, these laws could be repealed by a future Westminster Parliament. However, politically, this would be extremely embarrassing and unlikely.

33.3.1 Scotland

Scotland was granted devolved powers by the Scotland Act 1998 and a Scottish Parliament was established. In constitutional terms, the Scotland Act makes provisions for the protection of human rights within Scotland. Specifically, s 57(2) states that:

> ... member of the Scottish Executive, or government, has no power to make any

subordinate, or delegated, legislation or to do any other act, so far as the legislation or act is incompatible with any of the ECHR rights.

Furthermore, Schedule 4(1) of the Act states that 'an Act of the Scottish Parliament cannot modify the Human Rights Act 1998'. Any Act which did so would be automatically rendered invalid. A decision on whether a decision of Scottish Ministers or an Act is invalidated by being noncompliant is ultimately for the UK Supreme Court, in considering any 'devolution issues' brought before it.

33.3.2 Wales

Wales was granted devolved powers by the Government of Wales Act 2006 which established the Welsh Assembly (now Welsh Parliament), with law-making powers. The Act provides, in s 108(6), that an Assembly Act (or Assembly Measure) which is incompatible with ECHR rights is outside the legislative competence of the National Assembly. This means that such a provision would be invalid and of no effect.

Also, by s 81 Welsh ministers have no power to make, confirm or approve any subordinate legislation, or to do any other act, so far as that legislation or act is incompatible with any ECHR rights. The Welsh ministers must not, therefore, in exercising any of their functions breach ECHR rights.

33.3.3 Northern Ireland

Northern Ireland was granted devolved powers by the Northern Ireland Act 1998, which established an Assembly with law-making powers. The Act provides in s 7, in a similar way to the other devolved countries, that HRA 1998 cannot be modified by an Act of the Assembly or by any subordinate legislation.

33.3.4 Recent developments

The Conservatives pledged in their manifesto for the 2015 General Election to repeal HRA 1998 and introduce a British Bill of Rights. This, the manifesto said, would break the formal link between the British courts and the ECtHR, making the Supreme Court the 'ultimate arbiter of human rights' in the UK.

Arguments for repeal were that the Act does little to protect the liberties or the safety of British people, and that it allows judges – who are not chosen by popular vote – to make substantive judgments about government policies. This has led, said the Conservatives, to 'perverse' rulings, such as allowing radical Islamist preacher Abu Qatada to remain in the UK, and the ban on prisoners being allowed to vote being declared unlawful.

There have been no attempts, at the time of writing, to introduce any attempt to repeal or amend the Act. It is thought that any such attempt would require the agreement of all three devolved legislatures, requiring them to pass what is known as a legislative consent motion. It is thought that this proposal would be vigorously opposed by all the governing parties in the devolved countries.

Activity

Using the infographic found at the link below, draft a simple timeline showing the development of the main human rights in the UK.

https://eachother.org.uk/everything-you-need-to-know-about-human-rights-2/

Issue	Before HRA 1998	After HRA 1998
An Act incompatible to ECHR	Courts could not set it aside or question its validity	Court can issue declaration of incompatibility or interpret Act in such a way to make it compatible. Section 4(2) HRA 1998
Duty of court in interpretation of Act	No duty to interpret in ECHR-friendly manner	A duty on court to interpret Act to comply with ECHR as far as possible. Section 3(1) HRA 1998
Use of ECtHR cases in domestic courts	Only used in a few limited situations	A duty is on courts to take ECtHR decisions into account
Claimants able to argue ECHR rights in domestic courts	No right to do so	Have directly enforceable right to do so
Remedy for breach of ECHR	Take case to ECHR after exhausting all domestic rights	Directly available in domestic courts. Section 8 HRA 1998
Effect of ECHR violation by public authority	Lawful – unless unlawful on other grounds	Unlawful

Figure 33.2 Comparison of the law before and after HRA 1998 came into effect

Wainwright v United Kingdom (2007)

On a prison visit to her stepson, a mother and her disabled son were strip-searched in a humiliating, discourteous and distressing manner. Although they had reluctantly consented to the search, the experience left them both badly affected, with the son suffering from PTSD as a result.

An original finding of battery and invasion of privacy was set aside by the Appeal Court, apart from the battery.

On appeal to the House of Lords, it was held by Lord Hoffmann that there was no tort of invasion of privacy as it was too uncertain in law. A claim under Articles 8 and 3 was also rejected.

The claimant appealed to ECtHR, which decided that there was no violation of Article 3, although there was a violation in respect of Article 8 which seeks to protect physical and moral integrity. The searches had been a disproportionate measure to the aim of preventing crime and disorder.

The applicants were awarded £3000 each in damages for the distress caused to them.

Case	Facts	Legal principle
Bellringer v Bellringer (2003)	A transgender woman 'married' a man. This was void as the parties were not of opposite sexes.	The House of Lords decided that the marriage was not valid: the law did not recognise a change of gender. A declaration of incompatibility was issued.
R (Anderson) v Secretary of State for the Home Department (2002)	The Home Secretary's power to fix a tariff period for a murderer subject to a life sentence was challenged.	The House of Lords decided this power was incompatible with Article 6. Parliament later removed this power from the Home Secretary in the Criminal Justice Act 2003.
A v Secretary of State for the Home Department (2005)	The claimants were indefinitely detained under anti-terror legislation. They argued there was no war or public emergency allowing derogation from the ECHR.	It was for the government to decide if there was an emergency situation; indefinite detention was disproportionate and discriminatory and incompatible with Articles 5 and 14.
Commissioner of Police for the Metropolis v DSD, NBV (2015)	The police failed to investigate offences of rape by a serial offender.	The police owe a duty to investigate acts of alleged ill-treatment by private individuals including serious, violent crime and there had been a breach of Article 3.
Malone v United Kingdom (1984)	The claimant was charged and acquitted of handling stolen goods. His telephone had been tapped and metered and letters intercepted.	The ECtHR decided there had been a violation of Article 8 – the right to respect for private life and correspondence.
Wainwright v United Kingdom (2007)	The claimant and his mother were required to undergo a strip-search before visiting a relative in prison. This caused the claimant to suffer from PTSD.	The ECtHR decided there was no breach of Article 3, but as the searches had not been proportionate to prevent crime and disorder, there was a violation of Article 8.

Figure 33.3 Key cases: human rights protection

Quick questions

1 Why was the European Convention of Human Rights drafted?
2 How are human rights enforced under the Convention?
3 What was the main reason that Parliament passed the Human Rights Act 1998?
4 What is a declaration of incompatibility? How does it affect a piece of legislation?
5 What are the remedies available under s 8 of the HRA?

Summary

- The European Convention of Human Rights (ECHR) sets out a number of protections given to individuals.
- The ECtHR hears applications by individuals who allege that their ECHR rights have been infringed by a state.
- The ECtHR is separate from the European Court of Justice and from national courts.
- Since 2000 when the Human Rights Act came into force, an individual in the UK can claim before a national court that there has been a breach of the Convention by a public body.
- The provisions of the Human Rights Act include guidance on judicial interpretation, compatibility and incompatibility, and remedies for breach.
- Parliament can pass legislation that derogates from the ECHR if a government minister issues a certificate of incompatibility.
- UK courts can issue a certificate of incompatibility if they find a law incompatible with the ECHR.

Chapter 34 Key provisions of the European Convention on Human Rights

Introduction

The European Convention on Human Rights (ECHR) was originally created in 1950 and sets out the core elements of human rights protection.

It is a document which has been added to on many occasions, with the addition of several protocols such as Protocol 13, Article 1, introduced in 2002, which abolished the death penalty.

Look online

The full text of the ECHR is available to download and read at:
www.echr.coe.int/Documents/Convention_ENG.pdf
- Identify the key Articles on the syllabus: Articles 5, 6, 8, 10 and 11.
- Write down the core rights within each Article.
- Find out how they might legally be limited, if at all.

34.1 Article 5: The right to liberty and security

34.1.1 Definitions of key terms

Meaning of 'liberty' and 'deprivation'

The idea of liberty here is used in the narrow, physical sense of not being under the direct physical control of another, not the wider, political sense.
- In *Engel v The Netherlands* (1976), the ECtHR said that liberty means: 'individual liberty in the classic sense, that is to say the physical liberty of the person It is not concerned with the broader ideas of liberty such as the sense of personal autonomy and the lack of psychological or social subordination'.
- In *Guzzardi v Italy* (1981), below, the ECtHR also explained that a deprivation of liberty was a question of the 'degree and intensity' of the restrictions placed on the individual.
- The 'acid test' for a deprivation of liberty was said in *Cheshire West and Chester Council v P* (2014) to be whether the individual was 'under continuous supervision and control and not free to leave'. As is made clear from Lady Hale's quotation here,

deprivation of liberty will not always be obvious by its appearance:

> What it means to be deprived of liberty must be the same for everyone, whether or not they have physical or mental disabilities ... the fact that my living arrangements are comfortable ... should make no difference. A gilded cage is still a cage.

- In *JJ v Secretary of State for the Home Department* (2007), a case about the use of control orders, it was said that deprivation consists of a combination of severe restrictions on ordinary life, as well as confinement.
- Further useful commentary on the meaning of deprivation could be found in *Austin v Commissioner of Police of the Metropolis* (2009), a case about the police tactic of 'kettling'.

Lord Hope explained it like this:
> A person can be deprived of his liberty even if his departure is not prevented by a locked door or other physical barrier and even though he may be allowed extensive social and other contact with the outside world.

Activity

Considering the definitions of deprivation above and, applying these tests, think about whether you have been deprived of your liberty at any time this week?

34.1.2 Article 5(1)

This Article guarantees the liberty and security of the person, with the aim of protecting an individual against arbitrary arrest and detention.

Article number	Exceptions to the general rule in Article 5(1)	Explanation and case law
5(1)(a)	Detention after due process includes detention after conviction for punishment.	*Stafford v UK* (2002): a convicted murderer was rejected for parole, as it was feared he would commit non-violent crimes. This was unlawful deprivation.
Article 5(1)(b)	Allows for the lawful arrest or detention of individuals who breach court orders or fail to fulfil an obligation prescribed by law.	For example, for non-payment of tax, contempt of court and breach of a bail condition.
Article 5(1)(c)	Allows for the lawful arrest or detention of a person suspected of having committed an offence.	*Fox, Campbell and Hartley v UK* (1990): an honest belief is not enough.
Article 5(1)(d)	Allows for the detention of a minor for educational supervision or bringing him before a competent legal authority such as a court.	
Article 5(1)(e)	Allows for the lawful detention of a person to prevent the spread of infectious diseases, and persons of unsound mind, alcoholics, drug addicts or vagrants. Also covers the provisions which allowed for the 2020 national lockdown during the COVID-19 pandemic.	In *HL v UK* (2004), the detention of a patient with autism was held to be unlawful. Powers were contained in s 45 Public Health (Control of Disease) Act 1984
Article 5(1)(f)	Allows for the lawful arrest or detention to stop a person unlawfully entering the country, or a person subject to deportation or extradition.	*Saadi v UK* (2008): UK policy of detaining asylum-seekers whilst dealing with applications compatible with Article 5 if a quick process

Figure 34.1 Exceptions to the general right in Article 5(1)

The Article requires that a deprivation of liberty must follow a prescribed procedure and it must be lawful.

'A prescribed procedure'

Any measure depriving a person of his liberty should only be carried out by someone or a body with the authority to do so and should not be arbitrary. A failure to allow a person to respond to the case against him may infringe Article 5(1).

'Lawful'

Any detention which is unlawful under English law will automatically be contrary to Article 5(1).

34.1.3 Exceptions to the general right in Article 5(1)

Article 5(1)(a)–(f) sets out the permitted exceptions to the general rule in 5(1). The list is exhaustive.

34.1.4 Article 5(2): Prompt reasons given

The provisions of this Article are mostly covered in PACE 1984: to allow a person to know why he or she has been arrested in a language he or she understands. It does not have to be given in full at the very moment of arrest but should be given promptly. In *Fox, Campbell, and Hartley v UK* (1990),

the ECtHR found that seven hours was an acceptable delay.

34.1.5 Article 5(3): Brought promptly before a judicial officer

This contains three separate parts:
1 Promptly: In *Brogan v UK* (1988), a period of four days and six hours between the arrest and being brought before a judge was too long.
2 Independent judicial officer: The officer must not be involved in the investigation.
3 Reasonable time and bail: There should be a presumption of bail which gets stronger as the detention continues. If denied, a court should give reasons why it is refused.

The purpose of the third provision is to ensure that no-one spends too long in detention before trial. There is a link here with Article 6(1). Time starts when the accused is first remanded into custody and ends when the court gives judgment. What is a reasonable time depends on the circumstances of each case, including the seriousness of the charge.

34.1.6 Article 5(4)

Everyone who is deprived of his liberty by arrest or detention can bring proceedings to have the lawfulness of his detention speedily decided by a court, and his release ordered if the detention is not lawful.

Where a person is in continued detention, it must be periodically reviewed (*Stafford v UK* (2002)).

Access to a court

Detained people must be able to challenge their detention in court. There is a positive duty on states to make this possible. Hearings of this kind, where liberty is involved, must not be delayed.

Lawfulness of detention

Lawfulness can be considered under both Convention rights and domestic law, by a court or a relevant tribunal such as a mental health review tribunal. For those of unsound mind, the detention should be reviewed regularly.

The court or tribunal must be impartial and independent. The Home Secretary used to set the minimum tariff to be served by an offender convicted of murder, until this was found to be in breach of Article 5. This function has now been transferred to the Judiciary, which is fair under the Article. The Parole Board decides on the suitability of prisoners for release once they have served the minimum term set by the court. As appointments to this body are made by the Home Secretary, there are questions as to whether the Parole Board is sufficiently independent to satisfy the requirements of the Article.

A judicial review of detention requires natural justice to be satisfied. This means that the offender is entitled to know the reasons for detention and to be able to put his case before the court, but there is no necessity for an oral hearing in every case.

Determinate and indeterminate sentences

A determinate sentence is a period fixed by the sentencing court. Once a sentence has been passed by a court, and any appeal process has finished, there is no right to have the lawfulness of the sentence reviewed by another court.

Indeterminate sentences are those where the offender is sentenced to a minimum term (the tariff) but will be released only when a body such as the Parole Board is satisfied that the offender is safe to be released and the public does not need further protection. Also covered are situations when an offender is returned to prison after early release or when licence conditions have been broken. These are considered executive actions which, under Article 5(4),

will need regular review by a court to ensure that continued detention does not breach the Article.

- In *James v UK* (2012), there were procedural delays in the process of deciding when a prisoner could be released. James could only be considered for release after attending rehabilitation courses, which he was unable to do as the prison authorities did not provide these courses. The claimant was unsuccessful under domestic law but took his case to the ECtHR. The court found that his rights under Articles 5(1), 5(4) and 13 had been violated.

The key principle is: a person cannot be detained forever without a proper chance of release.

It is important to note that imposing a whole-life tariff on prisoners in *Vintner and Others v UK* (2013) was not seen as a violation by the ECtHR as long as such sentences were subject to periodic review.

Speedy decision

Where liberty is at stake such hearings should not be delayed.

- In *R v Secretary of State for the Home Department ex parte Noorkoiv* (2002), it was decided that a Parole Board hearing three months after the expiry of a tariff period of a life sentence breached Article 5(4), even though this was a standard practice.
- In *R (KB) v Mental Health Review Tribunal* (2002), delays in hearing mental health cases were also in violation of Article 5.

34.1.7 Article 5(5)

This Article provides that everyone who has been the victim of unlawful arrest or detention shall have a right to compensation. This right is mandatory – if there has been a breach, compensation must be awarded. It is unlikely that compensation will be awarded for feelings of disappointment or frustration, though actual financial loss caused by the unlawful detention can be recovered.

34.1.8 Specific situations arising in relation to Article 5

Control orders and TPIMs

In the case of *A and Others v UK* (2004), it was held that the process of detaining nine foreign terror suspects in prison without charge or trial was unlawful. As a response, the government brought in the control orders scheme. Control orders enabled the Home Secretary to impose an almost unlimited range of restrictions on any person suspected of involvement in terrorism. This avoided the need to prosecute such individuals within the criminal justice system and was therefore seen as a controversial measure.

In January 2012, the government replaced control orders with terrorism prevention and investigation measures (TPIMs). TPIMs may be thought of as 'control order-lite'. These new measures are still outside of the criminal justice system and initiated by the Home Secretary. They also don't fall readily into any of the categories of permitted restrictions within Article 5(1) (a)–(f).

A TPIM:

- can include electronic tagging and an overnight residence requirement
- allows 'controlees' to use the internet, but they can be restricted on who they can meet and where they can go, including foreign travel bans
- they are limited to two years in length, but they are easily renewable if there is new evidence to do so.

Case studies

Guzzardi v Italy (1981)

A man suspected of being an active member of the Mafia was put under police supervision on the remote island of Asinara. He had a physical space of 2.5 square kilometers to move around in. He was required to:

- report to the authorities twice a day and as requested
- observe a curfew between 10 pm and 7 am
- not frequent bars or night-clubs
- lead an honest and law-abiding life.

The ECtHR decided that these restrictions amounted to a deprivation of his liberty.

Secretary of State for the Home Department v JJ (2007)

A deprivation of liberty took place, and subject to Article 5, when the controlees were subject to an 18-hour house curfew, visitors had to be authorised; during the six hours the controlees were permitted to leave their house there were severe limits on their movements. This was a deprivation.

Secretary of State for the Home Department v E (2007)

A person made subject to a control order was subject to a 12-hour curfew, in his own home where he lived with his wife and family. There were no geographical restrictions when he was allowed out of his house and no restriction on who he could meet. This did not amount to a deprivation of liberty subject to Article 5.

Care

There will normally be no deprivation of liberty if a person of sound mind is living with and cared for by his parents, friends or relatives in a family home, foster care or in sheltered accommodation. But what if the person has learning difficulties or other specific needs?

Online activity

Research the facts of *Cheshire West and Chester Council v P* (2014). Watch the Supreme Court video of Lady Hale explaining the judgment in *Cheshire West* and then attempt the questions.

www.youtube.com/watch?v=Nq1G9C7hKWk&list= UUdkf93h71xVAl28v 467Hk7w

What procedures have to be followed when a person is deprived of their liberty?

1   What does it mean that the arrangements must be periodically reviewed? Why is this done?
2   What was the main issue in this case according to Lady Hale?
3   What was the decision?
4   Which other case is she referring to when she says that the Strasbourg Court sees it as an issue of fact and degree?
5   The Court of Appeal felt that their rights were better determined by comparing them with people of similar disabilities and that there had been no deprivation. Which judgment do you prefer?

You can find the full report of this case online, at **www.supremecourt.uk/cases/docs/uksc-2012-0088-judgment.pdf.**

Activity

Now consider the case of *Hillingdon LBC v Neary* (2011).

A young man with autism and a severe learning disability was accepted into respite care with the local authority for a few days at the request of his father.

Do you think there was a deprivation of his liberty in any of the following situations?

- He was detained for a total of a year.
- The young man objected to being held in care.
- The father objected to him being kept in respite care.
- There was total control of his movements by carers at his every waking moment.

Now compare your thoughts with those of the judge. You can find the law report at **www.bailii.org/ew/cases/EWHC/COP/2011/1377.html.**

JE v DE, aka Re DE (2006)

DE suffered a stroke and was blind, with short-term memory impairment; he had dementia and lacked capacity to decide where he should live. DE and JE moved in together in 2004. DE then lived voluntarily at a care home but was then taken home by JE. A year later he was taken back to the care home and then to another care home. He had plenty of freedom within the homes, was taken for walks, had regular telephone contact with his wife and daughter, and received visits. However, his care notes indicated his wishes to leave and live with JE.

The ECtHR decided he was deprived of his liberty as, despite his freedoms, he was not 'free to leave' and the police would be contacted if he was missing. The Court also observed there is no requirement for a lock or physical barrier to be present for there to be a deprivation of liberty. For example, a Category C prisoner in an open prison is deprived of his liberty. Whether a patient is kept in locked or open conditions is not decisive.

Parents and children

Parental restrictions do not generally offend Article 5 but a two-year Secure Accommodation Order on a teenager imposed by a court was subject to the Article.

Public order and crowd control

'Kettling' is where a group of people are held by the police in an area as a means of controlling a demonstration. It is a relatively new tactic used by the police, which has no statutory authority. It does not expressly fall into any of the permitted restrictions under Article 5(1)(a–f).

Police 'kettling' students in London, 2010

Austin v Commissioner of Police of the Metropolis (2009)

The police stood in lines across the exits from Oxford Circus tube station in London during a demonstration. People were allowed to leave the 'kettle' only with permission but many were held for over seven hours. It was argued that this amounted to a deprivation of liberty under Article 5. The House of Lords held that if the kettling was done in good faith, proportionate, and for no longer than necessary, it would not violate Article 5. There was deemed no violation.

R (McClure and Moos) v Commissioner of Police of the Metropolis (2012)

The court ruled that the police had acted unlawfully in 'containing' (or kettling) G20 protestors. It made clear that police must anticipate an 'imminent breach of the peace' before taking 'preventative action'. Kettling should only be used as a 'last resort' to prevent violence. The police have no power to arbitrarily kettle protestors. The High Court confirmed its legality under these conditions.

Mengesha v Metropolitan Police Commissioner (2013)

The police authorised a 'kettle' of about one hundred people during a protest. No-one disputed that the containment was justified because serious damage and a breach of the peace had occurred.

As people were funnelled out of the containment area, they were filmed and only allowed to leave if they gave their name and address. A chief superintendent took the view this would help with any subsequent investigation. The claimant was held in a separate area and filmed. She was asked to give her name and address and date of birth. Police refused to answer her questions about the legal authority of the filming and request for details.

The court had to consider the legality of the police actions. No statutory powers enabled the police to take details and video before a person was allowed to leave a containment area. Powers existed under s 50 of the Police Reform Act 2002 relating to those arrested for anti-social behaviour; and s 64A of the Police and Criminal Evidence Act (PACE) 1984 relating to those under arrest. Neither law applied in this case and, as the giving of the video was not voluntary, the police requirement was unlawful.

Videoing a member of the public engaged Article 8 ECHR when the video was taken as the price of being required to leave a containment area. The retention of the video was not 'in accordance with the law' and the retention was therefore a breach of Article 8.

See section 34.3 for more information about Article 8.

Case	Facts	Legal principle
Guzzardi v Italy (1981)	A man suspected of being a member of the 'mafia' criminal organisation was put under supervision.	This amounted to a deprivation of liberty. Deprivation is a matter of 'degree and intensity'.
Cheshire West and Chester Council v P (2014)	P was incontinent, ate pieces of his pads, and so was put in an adult babygro.	The Supreme Court used the 'acid test': the individuals were being deprived of their liberty. Those with mental incapacity had the same right to liberty as everyone else.
P & Q by their litigation friend the Official Solicitor v Surrey CC (2011)	Two sisters with severe learning disabilities had to be continually supervised by their carers. They were not free to leave.	
JE v DE aka Re DE (2006)	DE suffered a stroke, was blind, had dementia and lived in care homes but wished to live with JE.	The ECtHR decided he was deprived of his liberty as he was not 'free to leave'.
Austin v Commissioner of Police of the Metropolis (2009)	Police 'kettled' demonstrators for over seven hours.	No breach of Article 5 as the measures were taken in good faith, were proportionate and enforced for no longer than necessary.
R (McClure and Moos) v Commissioner of Police of the Metropolis (2012)	G20 protestors were 'kettled'.	Kettling should only be used as a last resort when violence was imminent.
Mengesha v Metropolitan Police Commissioner (2013)	Police required demonstrators to be filmed as a condition of leaving a 'kettle'.	The police requirement was unlawful and breached Article 8.

Figure 34.2 Key cases: Article 5

34.2 Article 6: The right to a fair trial

34.2.1 Key elements of Article 6(1)

Article 6(1) covers both civil hearings and criminal trials. Articles 6(2) and 6(3) offer additional protection aimed solely at criminal proceedings.

The main aim of the Article is to protect citizens against the abuse of power by state and public authorities. The importance of this principle is seen by the fact that it permits no restriction; the only qualification is on the requirement of a public hearing. However, in certain situations the rights of the parties can be waived – for example, by the parties agreeing to settle a dispute by arbitration, rather than by a court hearing.

The key elements are:
- a determination of a civil right or obligation or a criminal charge
- an independent and impartial tribunal or court
- within a reasonable period of time
- in public
- fair.

Key element	Explanation	Examples
Civil rights and obligations	There must be a dispute in issue of a genuine and serious nature that directly affects civil rights and obligations. Covered by Article 6 if the right is a 'private' civil right. For example: ● Where financial interests are involved such as employment, personal injury, reputation and property. ● In child custody cases. Not covered if it is a public administrative right. For example: ● Cases challenging the allocation of a school, or a prisoner's claim to associate with other prisoners. ● Taxation and many immigration cases. ● Political areas like voting rights. ● Decisions to dismiss an employee.	Decision of a tribunal affecting the right to continue to practise – such as the Solicitors Disciplinary Tribunal. Child custody case: *Olsson v Sweden* (1992) Gender discrimination case: *Schuler-Zgraggen v Switzerland* (1993)
Criminal charge	Three criteria to decide whether a legal process should be regarded as a criminal charge: 1 The national classification of the action. 2 The nature of the offence. 3 Does it lead to a punishment? Making an anti-social behaviour order was classed as a civil, not criminal matter – *not for the purpose of punishment* but *for protection of the family*.	This was set out by the ECtHR in *Engel v Netherlands* (1976) *R (McCann) v Manchester Crown Court* [2002]
Independent and impartial tribunal	The ECtHR will consider several factors: ● How judges are appointed. ● For what period of time. ● Whether they are under pressure in their decision making. ● The overall 'appearance of independence'. The independence of the courts from any pressure by the Executive is a practical example of the principle of the separation of powers. The Criminal Justice Act 2003 allows for judge-only criminal trials where there is a serious risk of jury tampering or where tampering has taken place.	*Findlay v United Kingdom* [1997] *Scanfuture UK v Secretary of State for Trade and Industry* [2001] *R v Bow Street Magistrates ex parte Pinochet (No 2)* [2000] (see below) The first such case was *R v Twomey* (2011).
Delays	Justice delayed is justice denied. ● Those on remand are a clear priority. ● Excessive delay can be remedied by a lowering of sentence or even compensation. Delays also take into account any appeal procedure. *Konig v FRG* (1978) set out the factors to be considered in cases of delay: ● The complexity of the case. ● The applicant's conduct. ● The conduct of the state.	*Poiss v Austria* (1987) *Milasi v Italy* (1987): delay of 9 years and 7 months unreasonable in a case involving 35 defendants but no additional complexity. *Robins v UK* (1997): over four years to determine a simple dispute on costs was unreasonable. *Rinngeisen v Austria* (1972): delay of over five years not unreasonable in a complex fraud case where the defendant lodged requests and appeals and challenges against the judges in the case.

Key element	Explanation	Examples
Public hearing	The right to a public hearing is not an absolute right. There are many situations in which press and public can be excluded: ● The protection of morals, public order or national security. ● To protect children or the privacy of the parties. ● Where it is in the interests of justice to do so.	*B and P v United Kingdom* (2002): both applicants brought cases for residence orders under the Children Act 1989, claiming that holding these in private breached Article 6(1). The ECtHR decided that this provision did not breach Article 6.
Fairness	The ECtHR has identified features of fairness: ● Access to a court. ● Attendance and participation in proceedings. ● Equality of arms. ● Exclusion of unfair evidence.	*Golder v UKP* (1975): a prisoner was denied access to a solicitor. *T and V v UK* (2000): two boys were tried and convicted in an adult court for the murder of a two-year-old boy. Article 6 rights violated. Equality of arms means that both sides should have: ● equal access to the evidence ● equal participation in the proceedings ● equal treatment of witnesses ● the right to see and comment upon the evidence upon which the decision will be made. Evidence obtained by oppression or torture violates Article 6: *R v Mushtaq* [2005], *A v Secretary of State for the Home Department* [2005]

Figure 34.3 Explanation of key elements of Article 6(1)

Case study

R v Bow Street Magistrates ex parte Pinochet (No. 2) [2000]

Known as the *Pinochet* case, this came before the House of Lords on the question of whether the former Chilean dictator Augusto Pinochet could claim state immunity from torture allegations made by a Spanish court and therefore evade extradition to Spain. The original decision had to be set aside because one of the judges, Lord Hoffmann, failed to declare his links to Amnesty International before or during the hearing.

Look online

Read the online article about the case of *R v Twomey* (2011):

https://theoldbailey.wordpress.com/2010/03/31/found-guilty-with-no-juryr-vs-twomey-blake-hibberd-cameron/

● Why did the second trial not reach a conclusion?
● What happened during the third trial which led to the fourth trial being heard by a judge alone?
● Do you think that the four defendants eventually received a fair trial?

Reasons for a decision

The final judgment of the court must contain reasons that show that the main issues in the case have been taken into account and decided upon. There is no need to give reasons for every point on why one piece of evidence has been preferred to another. Once a final decision has been reached by a court, and any appeals exhausted, the case should be closed.

Case study

Brumarescu v Romania (1999)

Brumarescu's parents' house was nationalised by the state in 1950 without payment of compensation. In 1993, Brumarescu brought an action against the state, claiming that the nationalisation was unlawful. This claim was upheld, the time limit for an appeal passed and ownership was transferred to Brumarescu. The following year, the case was reopened before the Supreme Court who set aside the previous judgment and ruled that the house had passed into state ownership under a relevant law. Brumarescu complained to the ECtHR that there had been a violation of Article 6(1), and this was upheld on the grounds that there had been a final judgment in Brumarescu's favour which could not be reopened.

Equality of arms

In adversarial proceedings, both parties should have equal treatment and equal rights in the trial process. This is the idea of equality of arms.

Case study

Steel and Morris v United Kingdom (2005)

Fast-food chain McDonald's sued the claimants for libel when they issued leaflets outside one of their restaurants detailing the poor quality of the food and environmental impact of the company. The case lasted 313 days and is one of the longest running civil cases in English legal history. Steel and Morris were denied legal aid and had to pursue the case in their own time and using *pro bono* legal help. It was a clear case of David against Goliath.

Some of the claims they made were ultimately found to be accurate although some were also held to be false. The trial was a huge PR disaster for McDonald's. However, the defendants were ordered to pay £60,000 in damages to McDonald's.

At the ECtHR, the Court found against the UK in that the process had violated Article 6 and Article 10. They also found that the trial was biased due to the comparative lack of resources. It also found that the laws relating to libel were 'complex and oppressive'.

A full exploration of the legal case from the original libel trial to the case in the ECtHR is set out in the film *McLibel*.

McLibel – the film based on the Steel and Morris case

Disclosure is an important aspect of equality of arms

At the heart of many miscarriage of justice cases, such as the Guildford Four and the Bridgewater cases, has been the failure to properly disclose all the relevant evidence. The duty of full disclosure is not absolute and may be qualified.

This may be where it is necessary to protect a third party (for example, the life of a witness) or in the interests of national security or public interest immunity. It should only be limited where 'strictly necessary'.

In cases of national security, special advocates are appointed to represent the defendant in parts of the case that are closed to the defendant or his representatives. This would be where the defendant is unable to know secret material or evidence relevant to the case.

In the UK it is accepted that non-disclosure may be justified by public interest immunity. A procedure exists for such cases (both civil and criminal):

- The evidence is disclosed to a judge in chambers so that it can be decided if disclosure is necessary.
- The hearing may be without the defendant – *ex parte* – or even without them knowing at all.
- 'Special counsel' with security clearing may be used in this hearing to represent the defendant.
- Once special counsel has seen the sensitive material, they can no longer discuss the case or take any instruction from the defence.

Disclosure and national security

If a judge decides to authorise disclosure of the evidence, particularly where the trial has a national security aspect, then the government may try to hold the whole trial in secret to prevent the information coming to light.

Activity

Research the facts in the case of *Al Rawi v Security Services* [2011].

Was this a fair procedure?

Look online

Read the article 'Disclosure Is Essential To A Fair Trial. We Must Get It Right' by barrister Stefan Hyman and answer the questions.

https://eachother.org.uk/disclosure-is-essential-to-a-fair-trial-we-must-get-it-right/

1 Why did Liam Allen's trial collapse at the end of the first week?
2 What were the consequences of the collapse of the trial?
3 Explain how disclosure works in practice.
4 What are the difficulties involved in getting disclosure right? How could it be made easier in future?

Article 6(2) and 6(3)

Article 6(2) and 6(3) give extra protection in criminal trials.

At the heart of a fair trial is the concept of the presumption of innocence.

- If the state wishes to punish an individual they must take on the burden of proof to show guilt. It is not for the defendant to prove his innocence (see *DPP v Woolmington* (1935)).

However, not all crimes are always covered by this rule.

- In *Salabiaku v France* (1988), the ECtHR ruled that a strict liability drug-smuggling offence does not offend this Article as a defence was available to the charge.

34.2.3 Article 6(2): The right to silence

There are two elements to this right:

1 The accused should not be compelled to answer questions, on pain of punishment, if the answers are used to convict.
2 A court should not draw adverse inferences from an accused's refusal to answer questions, either during police interview or at trial.

Case study

Saunders v UK (1997)

The ECtHR found that there had been a violation when Saunders was required by government inspectors to answer questions during an investigation into a city takeover battle. A failure to answer them would have led to contempt of court proceedings. When Saunders was later prosecuted in a separate trial the earlier compelled transcripts were used as part of the evidence. This was a violation.

Adverse inferences and the right to silence

Since 1994 and the passage of the Criminal Justice and Public Order Act (CJPOA), there have been restrictions on the application of the right to silence. Sections 34–37 of CJPOA 1994 create situations where it is acceptable to draw adverse inferences from an accused's failure to answer certain questions.

In *Murray v UK* (1996), the ECtHR held that the right to silence is not absolute.

Case studies

Murray v UK (1996)

Murray was questioned by police after being arrested at a house used by the IRA to hold an informer captive. He remained silent and was convicted of aiding and abetting the false imprisonment. The judge had drawn adverse inferences from his silence. The ECtHR held there was no violation. The circumstances had to be taken into account, especially where there were facts which 'clearly called for an explanation'.

Condron v UK (2001)

The two defendants who were heroin addicts had remained silent during interviews on the advice of their solicitor. The judge allowed the jury to drawing an adverse inference from their silence. This was held to be a violation.

34.2.3 Article 6(3): The rights of the defence

Article 6(3) contains several specific rights which may also reflect aspects of the rights in Article 6(1).

These are the minimum rights for everyone charged with a criminal offence.

- 6(3)(a): The right to be informed of the accusation promptly, in a language the accused understands, and, in detail, the nature of the accusation.
- 6(3)(b): To have adequate time and facilities to prepare a defence. This may include access to a lawyer, especially if detained before trial, to obtain expert evidence and to call witnesses.
- 6(3)(c): The right to defend oneself in person or through legal assistance of his/her own choosing or, if he/she has not sufficient means to pay for legal assistance, to be given it free when the interests of justice so require. It is possible for the accused to waive his/her right to legal advice.

The right to attend the trial is seen as a part of 6(3)(c). The ECtHR has said that it would be senseless to talk about a fair trial without the right to attend – *Sejdovic v Italy* (2006). On the other hand, where a defendant refuses to attend, he or she may be tried *in absentia* without necessarily violating the right.

Representation

The right to legal representation applies to every stage of the investigation, including interviews at the police station. If the accused is denied representation, any evidence obtained may be excluded by s 78 PACE 1984. The right to representation is not absolute and in civil cases, the denial of legal aid may be reasonable. In criminal cases, especially where custody is a likely sentence, the denial of legal aid is likely to be a breach of the Article. In fact it is one of the grounds (the interests of justice) where it is likely to be granted.

In *Benham v UK* (1996), it was suggested that legal aid, as well as representation, was necessary where liberty was at stake. When Stephen Benham was imprisoned by magistrates for not paying the poll tax, the ECtHR held that his rights under Article 6 had been violated because he had not been able to get representation by a solicitor under the legal aid scheme.

Paying for legal representation

Normally, an accused will have complete freedom to have the lawyer of his choice to represent him in court. This right will cover the right to claim financial aid to pay for the representation in a criminal case if the alleged offender cannot afford to pay the legal fees.

However, in England this right is restricted by the requirement for the alleged offender to pass two tests to claim financial aid – the interests of justice test and the means test. Unless the alleged offender passes both tests, financial aid will not be available.

In addition, now the accused's right of choice will also be limited as those able to offer state-funded services have to be members of a panel who have entered into contracts with the Legal Aid Agency. In civil cases, state financial aid is much more restricted and is virtually non-existent.

Examination of witnesses

- Article 6(3)(d): The right to examine, and have examined, witnesses.

English law has always required witnesses to give their evidence in court in the presence of the accused, and no conviction should be based on the testimony of anonymous witnesses. A witness can give evidence by television link or video recording as long as the defence has the ability to question and challenge the witness at some stage.

Where the case is decided solely or decisively on evidence the defendant cannot test, this will amount to a violation.

Case study

R v Davis (2008)

Seven witnesses said they would be in fear for their lives if it was known that they gave evidence against the accused. Several methods were used to protect their identities including pseudonyms, withholding personal details, distorted voices and giving evidence from behind a screen. The House of Lords ruled that the combination of measures hampered the defence to the extent that it rendered the trial unfair, especially as it impaired the ability of defence lawyers to cross-examine the witnesses.

Activity

Read the *R v Davis* (2008) case study and answer these questions:

- Why were the prosecution arguments for a trial to be held in private?
- What parts of the trial did the Court of Appeal judges order could be reported?
- Do you think that the defendants could have received a fair trial?

Case study

R v Incedal (2014)

The Court of Appeal blocked attempts to hold a terror trial fully in secret.

Judges said that the 'core' of the terrorism trial could be partly heard in secret but parts must be in public. They said the media should also be allowed to name the two defendants as Erol Incedal and Mounir Rarmoul-Bouhadjar.

Look online

Read this article about why the Court of Appeal blocked the holding of this trial in secret, then answer the questions:

www.bbc.co.uk/news/uk-27806814/

- What were the prosecution arguments for a trial to be held in private?
- What parts of the trial did the Court of Appeal judges order could be reported?
- Do you think that the defendants could have received a fair trial?

Case	Facts	Legal principle
Brown v Stott (2001)	Defendant admitted she was drunk-driving and this admission was used in court. She argued this amounted to self-incrimination and a violation of Article 6.	The Privy Council decided Article 6 was complied with.
Osman v United Kingdom (2000)	The police were sued for failure to protect a family from harassment The police argued they had immunity from being sued for negligence.	ECtHR decided Article 6 had been violated by the blanket immunity as it was a disproportionate restriction on the claimant's right of access to a court.
R v Bow Street Magistrate, ex parte Pinochet Ugarte (2000)	One of the judges in the Pinochet case had not disclosed his links to Amnesty International.	Judges and panel members must disclose any links to anyone or any organisation with an interest in the case.
Steel and Morris v United Kingdom (2005)	Steel and Morris were sued for libel by McDonald's for publishing an alleged defamatory leaflet. Steel and Morris represented themselves in a long trial against experienced senior barristers.	The ECtHR decided that the complexity of the case and the different levels of legal support were so great to make the case unfair under Article 6.
T and V v United Kingdom (2000)	Two 11-year-old boys were tried for murder in a Crown Court room. They claimed an unfair trial in view of their age and trial in public in an adult court.	The ECtHR decided the boys were denied a fair hearing in breach of Article 6.
Secretary of State for the Home Department v AF (2009)	The applicants were subject to control orders but some of the evidence against them was based on 'closed' material.	The House of Lords decided that it was a breach of the right to a fair trial under Article 6 to hold someone under a control order without sufficient information about the allegations against him.
B and P v United Kingdom (2002)	The usual practice for hearing residence orders in family cases was to hold the hearings in private. It was claimed this breached Article 6.	The ECtHR ruled that there are certain cases, including this one, where the exclusion of the press and public may be justified. There was no breach of Article 6.

Case	Facts	Legal principle
Brumarescu v Romania (1999)	Brumarescu's parents' house was nationalised by the state in 1950. A later court ruled that the house had passed into state ownership under a relevant law. Brumarescu complained there had been a violation of Article 6(1).	ECtHR upheld Brumarescu's complaint as there had been a final judgment which could not be reopened.
Ibrahim v United Kingdom (2016)	Defendants were arrested in connection with the London bombings and were refused legal assistance to allow 'safety interviews' to be held.	The ECtHR ruled their rights had not been infringed and there was no breach of Article 6.
Murray v UK (1996)	Murray was questioned about his alleged connections with the IRA when he was arrested at a house being used to hold an informer captive. He refused to answer questions.	The ECtHR held there was no violation. The right is not absolute and there were facts which 'clearly called for an explanation'.
R v Davis (2008)	Several methods were used to protect the identities of witnesses against Davis as they feared for their lives if they were identified.	The House of Lords ruled that the combination of measures used to protect identities hampered the defence to render the trial unfair.
Othman (Abu Qatada) v United Kingdom (2012)	Othman was arrested and detained under terrorism laws; while he was subject to a control order he was served with a deportation notice.	The ECtHR ruled that, under Article 6, the UK could not lawfully deport the claimant to Jordan because of the risk of the use of evidence obtained by torture.

Figure 34.4 Key cases: Article 6

34.3 Article 8: The right to respect for family and private life

34.3.1 General aspects of qualified rights

Article 8 is a qualified right and, as such, the right to a private and family life and respect for the home and correspondence may be limited. Any limitation must have regard to the fair balance that has to be struck between the competing interests of the individual and of the community as a whole.

Article 8(2) states that any limitation must be:
- in accordance with law
- meet a legitimate aim; and
- necessary in a democratic society.

And for one or more of the following legitimate aims:
- the interests of national security
- the interests of public safety or the economic well-being of the country
- the prevention of disorder or crime
- the protection of health or morals, or
- the protection of the rights and freedoms of others.

If someone can show that there has been an interference with their rights, then the state has to show that this interference was justified. This can only be done if it is in accordance with the law, to meet a legitimate aim and necessary in a democratic society.

In looking at whether it is necessary, the ECtHR will have reference to the concept of proportionality. This simply means finding the balance between the individual right and the community. They will use the following criteria:

- Does the act meet the legitimate aim? Is the measure rationally connected with the objective in question?
- It is not arbitrary, unfair or irrational?
- Does it impact 'the very essence of the right'? Does it remove all of the protection of the right?
- Is it the minimum interference possible? Is it the least intrusive measure possible?
- Is there a fair balance between the competing interests of the individual and those of the community?

34.3.2 Key aspects of Article 8

There are four aspects to Article 8:
- private life
- family life
- home
- correspondence.

Article 8 is based on the concept of 'respect' for these aspects of our personal lives. It means that the state must take positive steps to protect these rights. This was considered by the ECtHR in *Sheffield and Horsham v United Kingdom* (1999).

Case study

Sheffield and Horsham v United Kingdom (1999)

The case concerned the UK's refusal to recognise for legal purposes the new sexual identities of the applicants who had undergone gender reassignment surgery. The ECtHR found that there was no violation in this case as it fell within the margin of appreciation granted to states. However, the ECtHR was critical of the UK's failing to keep this area of law under review.

English law has now been changed by the Gender Recognition Act 2004, which allows transgender individuals to apply for legal recognition for their new gender. The Marriage (Same Sex Couples) Act 2013 is also now in place, so fulfilling positive obligations.

Private life

Aspects of the right to private life include:
- the physical and psychological integrity of a person
- sex life and gender
- personal data
- reputation
- names.

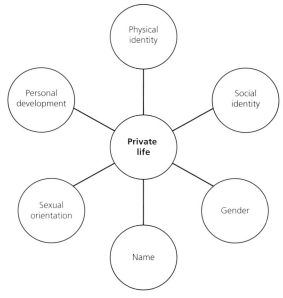

Figure 34.5 Aspects of the right to private life under Article 8

The meaning of 'private life' is very wide, and must not be confused with the idea of privacy. It has been given a very broad, inclusive meaning by the ECtHR and this meaning is still expanding over time.
- In *Peck v UK* (2003), it was said that it is not capable of 'exhaustive definition'.
- In *Pretty v UK* (2002), it set out the scope of Article 8 as including physical and social identity, gender identification, name, sexual orientation and personal development. The case emphasised the importance of personal autonomy and dignity as factors involved in decision making.
- In *Bensaid v UK* (2001), the ECtHR said that 'mental health must be regarded as a crucial part of private life'.

Surveillance is included, as shown in *Halford v United Kingdom* (1997).

Case study

Halford v United Kingdom (1997)

Alison Halford was an assistant chief constable. Her telephone calls were intercepted by senior police officers to obtain information regarding a sex discrimination claim she was pursuing in an employment tribunal. The interception of the telephone calls of an employee in a private exchange was a breach of the right of a private life under Article 8.

Sexual identity and gender

The right to a private life also includes sexual identity. We have seen this in terms of transgender men and women. Same-sex marriage need not, yet, be treated in the same way as heterosexual marriage although it is in the UK.

As the ECtHR is a dynamic institution, and the Convention is a 'living instrument', the landscape is fast changing. The growing view of marriage being made available to all regardless of their sexual orientation is not yet sufficiently firm that the court will find that a state has an obligation to provide identical rights.

However, where a state provides a civil partnership possibility, it should not do so in a discriminatory manner. This can be seen from the case of *Vallianatos v Greece* (2014).

Since 2019, the UK has allowed civil partnerships to be registered between persons of opposite sex. This was enacted under the Civil Partnership (Opposite-sex Couples) Regulations 2019. This demonstrates the ideas of equality and universality which are at the heart of human rights philosophy. If rights extend to one section of society, it is hard to see how they can justifiably be denied to another.

This shows how the ECtHR is extending the area of protection in relation to sexual identity to reflect the reality of relationships within society.

Laws which seek to regulate or restrict sexual orientation and sexual freedom engage Article 8.

- In *Dudgeon v UK* (1981), it was held that Section 11 of the Criminal Law Amendment Act 1885 which criminalised male homosexual acts violated the ECHR. Other cases in this area – *BB v UK* (2004) and *ADT v UK* (2000) – said that any laws which treated homosexuals less favourably than heterosexuals cannot be justified.
- In *Goodwin v UK* (2002), the ECtHR held that barriers imposed on a transgendered person violated their rights to private life.

Personal data

Personal information and data are also included. This means things such as DNA details and medical records.

- In *S and Marper v UK* (2009), a case about the retention of DNA samples by the police, it also said that included 'multiple aspects of a person's physical and social identity'.

- In *MS v Sweden* (1999), it was stated that 'respecting the confidentiality of health data is a vital principle in the legal systems of all contracting parties to the Convention'. These cases were about adults but the question arose as to whether they should also include children.
- This was the issue in *Axon v Secretary of State for Health* (2006). The case discussed the relationship of Gillick competence, Article 8 and the right to keep medical records private.
- In *Z v Finland* (1997), the release of medical records containing information about a person's HIV status was held to be disproportionate.

Case studies

Axon v Secretary of State for Health (2006)

Sue Axon sought a declaration that a doctor was under no obligation to keep confidential advice and treatment proposed to a young person, under the age of 16, in respect of contraception, sexually transmitted infections and abortion. She wanted a declaration from the court that a doctor must inform the parents unless that might prejudice the child's physical or mental health. At the time, medical professionals were bound by advice contained within professional guides. The claimant sought a declaration that this guidance was unlawful.

The court rejected the claimant's argument; provided the child is Gillick competent, the parental right to determine medical treatment is ended.

Roche v UK (2005)

The applicant was discharged from the army in 1968. Years later, from 1987, he suffered health problems which he claimed were a direct result of having participated in mustard gas and nerve gas tests in 1962 and 1963. There was no mention of these tests on his medical records. He was denied a service pension due to a lack of causation.

The UK was in breach of its obligation to allow him an effective procedure by having full access to his medical details. Article 8 had been violated.

Names

Names are seen as central to the idea of identity.

Case study

Johansson v Finland (2002)

Parents who wished to name their child 'Axl Mick' were denied this right by registrars in Finland. This was in breach of Article 8. Although the name 'Axl' was unusual in Finland, it was known in Denmark. The ECtHR held that the choice of a child's name was a private family matter. The name was not ridiculous or whimsical or likely to lead the child to suffer prejudice.

Private life or privacy in the UK?

In English law there has never been a right to privacy. While there was the possibility for a claim in the tort of breach of confidence, this was restricted to confidential information and confidential relationships. However, Article 8 is not available in private disputes. It can only be raised in cases involving a public authority. The court, however, must take into account ECHR as it must not make a decision that is incompatible with ECHR.

The Data Protection Act 1998 controls how personal information is used by organisations, businesses or the government. Everyone responsible for using data has to follow the strict rules – the 'data protection principles'. We have seen this in relation to medical records in the *Axon* case, but the law has developed in other ways to give some protection from what might be considered an invasion of privacy and thus a person's right to a private life.

The intrusion into private life has always been a feature of the tabloid press. The principle of freedom of expression under Article 10 is considered below, but the two articles do overlap. The difficulty is in establishing what is in the public interest and what is a mere invasion of privacy. The courts have had to balance individual rights to privacy and to freedom of expression.

The cases of *Wainwright v Home Office* (2003) and *Campbell v MGN Ltd* (2004) show a contrast in the development of the law in England.

Link

See Chapter 33 for more detail on *Wainwright v Home Office* (2003).

Case study

Campbell v MGN Ltd (2004)

Naomi Campbell was photographed coming out of a Narcotics Anonymous meeting in London. The newspaper published these photographs alongside the headline, 'Naomi: I'm a drug addict'.

As a model who had stated that she did not take drugs, this might be a legitimate matter to discuss under Article 10, freedom of expression. The question was whether this was a breach of her right to a private life and whether Article 8 takes precedence over Article 10.

The court stated that there is no question of priority of Article 10 over Article 8. The publication of photographs outside the clinic was a disproportionate interference with her right to privacy, even though the fact that she was receiving treatment was in the public domain.

Naomi Campbell succeeded even though the newspaper publisher was not a public authority.

The question of priority has been raised on a number of occasions, most recently in *PJS v News Group Newspapers Ltd* (2016). Here it was stated that case law establishes that neither Article 8 nor Article 10 has preference over the other. When the court is considering an injunction with respect to the right of an individual to a private life, it focuses on the comparative rights being claimed in the individual case.

Case study

PJS v News Group Newspapers Ltd (2016)

The claimant applied to the court for an injunction to prevent publication of the fact that, in 2011, he had a three-way sexual encounter. The Supreme Court decided that

- neither Article 8 nor Article 10 has preference over the other
- criticism of a person's conduct cannot be a pretext for invasion of privacy by disclosure of alleged sexual infidelity, which is of no real public interest in a legal sense. This rules out one defence to a claim for defamation.

Thus it seems that there is, as yet, no full privacy law in the UK, but Article 8, together with law on breach of confidence and defamation, give adequate, if confused, protection.

Case	Facts	Law
Niemietz v Germany (1992)	Police searched a lawyer's offices to try to identify a suspect.	The search was part of home and the lawyer's private life.
Halford v United Kingdom (1997)	Telephone calls were intercepted by senior police officers to obtain information.	Interception of the telephone calls of an employee in a private exchange was a breach of the right to a private life.
Axon v Secretary of State for Health (2006)	Mrs Axon queried whether a doctor was under an obligation to keep confidential advice and treatment to a young person under the age of 16.	Provided the child is Gillick competent, the parental right to determine medical treatment is ended or else there is a potential violation of Article 8.
Wainwright v Home Office (2003)	There was a strip-search by prison officers of Mrs Wainwright and her son during a visit to Armley Prison, Leeds.	Article 8 does include touching of the body as part of the right to a private life.
Campbell v MGN Ltd (2004)	Naomi Campbell was photographed coming out of a Narcotics Anonymous meeting in London.	Articles 8 and 10 are now part of a claim for breach of confidence.
PJS v News Group Newspapers Ltd (2016)	PJS applied to the court for an injunction to prevent publication of the fact that, in 2011, he had a three-way sexual encounter.	• Neither Article 8 nor Article 10 has preference over the other. • Criticism of a person's conduct cannot be a pretext for invasion of privacy.

Figure 34.6 Key cases: Article 8, the right to a private life

Family life

What is a family? Like many concepts under the ECHR, the answer develops over time to reflect social reality. In *Kroon v Netherlands* (1995), the ECtHR sought to define family in terms that do not allow legal forms to prevail over 'biological and social reality'.

Case study

Kroon v Netherlands (1995)

Kroon, who was married, started a new relationship outside of the marriage with A. It was a stable relationship – although they did not live together – and they had a child. Under Netherlands law, the child could not be registered as A's child. Only Kroon's husband could take legal steps to register a birth. This denied the legitimacy of Kroon's children. The court held that this was a violation of Article 8.

Some other ECtHR decisions about the scope of the family:
- Includes children and grandchildren – *Marckx v Belgium* (1979).
- Includes adoptive relationships – *Pini and Others v Romania* (2004).

- The concept of a family continues after divorce – *Berrehab v Netherlands* (1989).
- What constitutes a family depends on close family ties and is a matter of fact and degree – *Lebbink v Netherlands* (2004).
- Cohabiting heterosexual couples are included – *Kamal v UK* (2016).
- Foster relationships are also included – *X v Switzerland* (2017).
- Same-sex relationships are included and protected by Article 8(1) – *Schalk and Kopf v Austria* (2011).

Under Article 8, you have the right to enjoy family relationships without interference from the state. This includes the right to live with or have regular contact with your family.

There are many aspects of family life that can be affected by the state. For example:
- care proceedings and the possibility of a child being removed from the family home
- access to a child
- forced breakup of a relationship as a result of immigration rules.

Article 8 always extends to lawful and genuine marriages. A sham marriage to avoid immigration rules or to acquire nationality may not be protected.

A child born to parents who are married will therefore also always fall within Article 8. Unmarried couples who live together with their children fall within the Article, as the stable nature of the relationship makes it effectively the same as marriage.

Problems can arise when immigration rules cause a couple who are living together in England, with no suggestion of a sham marriage, find that one of them is not permitted to remain under immigration rules, while the other is a British citizen or otherwise has indefinite right to remain in the UK.

Agyarko and *Ikuga v Secretary of State for the Home Department* (2015) were precariousness cases involving people who had overstayed their permits to be in the UK.

Case study

Agyarko and *Ikuga v Secretary of State for the Home Department* (2015)

Mrs Agyarko and Mrs Ikuga had both been refused permission to remain or apply for judicial review proceedings of the Home Office's refusal to grant them leave to remain. Agyarko (a Ghanaian) and Ikuga (a Nigerian) had argued on the basis of their respective family lives. Their applications were refused because there were no insurmountable obstacles preventing them from continuing their relationships outside the UK, and no exceptional circumstances under Article 8 existed.

Extension activity

Research the problems highlighted by cases such as *Singh* and *Khalid v Secretary of State for the Home Department* (2015) and *MM (Lebanon) v Secretary of State for the Home Department* (2017).

The scope of the margin of appreciation differs according to the context of the case. It is particularly wide in child protection cases. An example of this can be seen in *Gaskin v United Kingdom* (1989).

Case study

Gaskin v United Kingdom (1989)

Graham Gaskin was placed in care when he was a baby. He complained of ill-treatment while he was in the care of a local authority and living with foster parents. He wanted access to his case records held by the local authority but his request was denied. He applied to the ECtHR.

The refusal to allow him access to his records breached his rights under Article 8. There was no independent mechanism to decide whether or not access should be permitted, if refused by those who made the decisions such as care workers. There must be specific justification for denying access to information pertaining to private and family life. The court stated that relationships between children and foster parents or carers fall within the definition of 'family' within the meaning of Article 8.

- In *Johannsen v Norway* (1996), the court had to consider a permanent placement of a child with a view to adoption in opposition to the natural parents' wishes. The question was, under Article 8, how the rights of the child and the parents should be balanced.
- In *Yousef v Netherlands* (2003), the court reiterated that in judicial decisions, where the rights under Article 8 of parents and those of a child are at stake, the child's rights must be the paramount consideration. This is entirely consistent with the principles in English family law.

These cases can be seen as the way in which different states' legal frameworks operate in a positive way to prevent harm to an individual who is part of a family.

Family and private life in the UK

The Human Rights Act 1998, along with Article 8, has influenced the development of the law in the UK. Some examples have been seen above. More recent examples often relate to immigration cases such as *Agyarko* and *Ikuga v Secretary of State for the Home Department* (2015).

In *Wood v Commissioner of Police for the Metropolis* (2009), the question again arose about the taking of photographs and their retention.

Case study

Wood v Commissioner of Police for the Metropolis (2009)

The taking and retention of photographs by the police of a person connected with a group opposed to the arms trade was an interference with that person's right to respect for his private life under Article 8, and the police failed to justify that interference as being proportionate.

The police action was a sufficient intrusion by the state into the individual's own space and integrity as to amount to a violation of Article 8.

Case study

AB v Secretary of State for Justice (2009)

The claimant asked for judicial review of a decision to keep her in a male prison and to not transfer her to a female prison. She suffered gender dysphoria and had been granted a certificate under the Gender Recognition Act 2004. The certificate provides that for all purposes the claimant is a female. The claimant wanted to have gender reassignment surgery but this could not be approved until she had lived as a woman for a period of time within a female prison. She was therefore unable to access the surgery.

The court said that the failure to transfer her violated her Article 8 rights. Justification for the infringement of her rights must be clear and weighty in order to be proportionate and there was no justification in this case.

In terms of sexuality and gender, the courts in England have been quite clear in their engagement of Article 8. In *AB v Secretary of State for Justice* (2009), it was decided that the continued detention of a pre-operative transgender woman in a male prison breached her right to privacy under Article 8.

Case	Facts	Law
Agyarko and *Ikuga v Secretary of State for the Home Department* (2015)	The applicants had overstayed their permits to be in the UK, and relied on their relationships with British citizens in order to obtain leave to remain.	The claims failed as there were no insurmountable obstacles preventing them from continuing their relationships outside the UK and no exceptional circumstances under Article 8 existed.
Gaskin v United Kingdom (1989)	The applicant wanted access to his case records held by the local authority to support claims of abuse, but his request was denied.	Refusal to allow him access to his records involved a breach of his rights under Article 8.
Johannsen v Norway (1996)	The natural parents of a child were opposed to the decision of the state with respect to adoption.	Particular weight should be attached to the best interests of the child, which may override those of the parent.
Wood v Commissioner of Police for the Metropolis (2009)	The police took and retained photographs of a person connected with a group opposed to the arms trade.	The photography had to be considered in context, and here it was an interference under Article 8.
AB v Secretary of State for Justice (2009)	The claimant, a pre-operative transgender woman who was in a male prison, asked for judicial review of a decision not to transfer her to a female prison.	The court said that the decision not to transfer her to a female prison was in violation of her Article 8 rights.

Figure 34.7 Key cases: Article 8, the right to family life

Home

Article 8 places a duty on a state to 'respect' a person's existing home. This means the state must allow a person to have access to their home and the right to live in it. It means they have to protect peaceful enjoyment of their property. It does not stretch to a general duty to house the homeless.

- It does not guarantee a right to a home: *Novoseletsky v Ukraine* (2005).
- Failure to provide alternative accommodation to an applicant with a severely disabled father fell under Article 8: *Marzari v Italy* (1999).

In *Khatun v United Kingdom* (1998), the ECtHR considered whether interference could be differentiated depending on whether the home was owned by the claimant or not. Whether or not somewhere was a home within the Article depends on the facts of each case.

Case study

Khatun v United Kingdom (1998)

The applicants suffered from pollution of the area of their home by dust caused by building works in London Docklands. A distinction had been made between those applicants with a proprietary interest in the land and those without such an interest, such as the applicants. The court stated that:

> Article 8(1) applies to all the applicants in the present case whether they are the owners of the property or merely occupiers living on the property, for example, the children of the owner of the property.

Usually the existence of sufficient and continuous links is enough to engage Article 8.

- In *Gillow v United Kingdom* (1986), the owners of a house in Guernsey were not given a licence to reside there by the authorities even though it was their home, so Article 8 was engaged.

Many of the cases brought against the UK with respect to 'home' relate to claims by travellers and others, such as travelling showmen, bringing caravans on to land.

- *Connors v UK* (2004) and *Price v Leeds City Council* (2005) explain that Article 8 is engaged where the dispute relates to eviction from a lawful site for traveller caravans but not where the occupation of the land is unauthorised, in the *Price* case on a playing field.

Article 8 operates only with respect to an individual's claim against a public body. Bizarrely, this would appear to include publicly owned housing rented to a tenant, but not where private landlords were concerned. This is seen in the case of *McDonald v McDonald* (2016).

Case studies

McDonald v McDonald (2016)

Fiona McDonald suffered with mental health issues. Her parents bought her a property to live in, subject to a mortgage. When the parents ran into financial difficulties, the mortgage company tried to evict her and sell the property. The Supreme Court decided that HRA 1998 and Article 8 do not require a court to consider whether it is proportionate to evict a residential occupier in a possession claim brought by a private residential landlord.

Niemietz v Germany (1992)

The police searched a lawyer's offices to try to identify a suspect. The search was part of 'home' and the lawyer's private life.

'Respect for private life must also comprise to a certain degree the right to establish and develop relationships with other human beings.' This includes being at work.

Correspondence

The interpretation is very wide, covering all forms of communication, including letters, telephone calls, faxes and emails. Interference must be justified under Article 8(2). This also covers those in prison, as was the case in *Golder v UK* (1975).

- In *Klass v Germany* (1978), the powers of secret surveillance of citizens were tolerable under the ECHR only in so far as strictly necessary for safeguarding the democratic institutions.

This means that, in some circumstances, a public authority may be able to interfere with your right to a private and family life in order to protect public safety or the freedoms of others. This has interesting but untested possibilities, including the operation of the Investigatory Powers Act 2016. This Act legalises a whole range of tools for snooping and hacking by the security services unmatched by any other country in Western Europe and the USA.

We have seen that the right of privacy extends to an office. With respect to private communications made while at work, the case of *Bărbulescu v Romania* (2016) indicates the current position. This decision reflects UK employment law good practice.

Case study

Bărbulescu v Romania (2016)

At his employer's request, Mr Bărbulescu set up a Yahoo Messenger account to deal with client enquiries. However, he also used the account to send personal messages, which was not allowed under the company rules. The company dismissed him for unauthorised use of the internet. The Grand Chamber held that Mr Bărbulescu's employers had breached Article 8 by not striking the right balance between its interests and his right to respect for his private life and correspondence.

The Grand Chamber said that although a right to private life could be reduced in the workplace, an employee could never lose all rights.

Restrictions permitted by the ECHR – interception of communications

Most UK employers allow or at least tolerate some personal internet and telephone use at work, so the situation is unlikely to be replicated in the UK.

The Investigatory Powers Act 2016 sets up a framework for protecting against the abuse of the wide powers granted to security services. This includes:

- combining the powers available to law enforcement, security and intelligence agencies to obtain communications data
- introducing a 'double-lock' for interception warrants so that, following Secretary of State authorisation, they cannot come into force until they have been approved by a judge
- creating an Investigatory Powers Commissioner to oversee how these powers are used
- ensuring the powers are fit for the digital age.

However this may not be seen as being compatible with EU law and the ECHR, as shown in the ruling from the CJEU in the joined cases of *Tele2 Sverige and Watson* (2016), where the court stated:

> That data taken as a whole is liable to allow very precise conclusions to be drawn concerning the private lives of the persons whose data has been retained, such as everyday habits, permanent or temporary places of residence, daily or other movements, the activities carried out, the social relationships of those persons and the social environments frequented by them ... In particular that data provides the means ... of establishing a profile of the individuals concerned, information that is no less sensitive, having regard to the right to privacy, than the actual content of communications.

Where national legislation provides for data retention, any retention must be strictly necessary for the purposes of investigating serious crime and linked to the investigation of serious crime.

Bulk interception of data

Thus the use of bulk interception of data has recently been challenged in the courts.

Case study

Big Brother Watch and Others v the United Kingdom (2018)

These applications were lodged after revelations by Edward Snowden (former contractor with the US National Security Agency) about the scale of surveillance and intelligence sharing between the USA and the United Kingdom. Journalists, individuals and rights organisations brought an action against the practices of:

1 the bulk interception of communications;
2 intelligence sharing with foreign governments; and
3 the obtaining of communications data from communications service providers.

The ECtHR held that the bulk interception regime violated Article 8.

Case	Facts	Law
McDonald v McDonald (2016)	The claimant's parents purchased a mortgaged property for her to live in, but ran into financial difficulties. The mortgage company wished to evict her.	Article 8 did not apply in this case so the court did not have to consider proportionality.
Bărbulescu v Romania (2016)	Mr Bărbulescu used a business Yahoo Messenger account to send personal messages. He was dismissed.	Article 8 rights had been engaged, but the interference had been proportionate within the state's margin of appreciation.
Tele2 Sverige and Watson (2016)	A Swedish electronic communications provider refused to retain electronic communications data following the finding in DRI that the Data Retention Directive was invalid was in question.	Where national legislation provides for data retention, any retention must be strictly necessary for the purposes of investigating serious crime and linked to the investigation of serious crime.
Big Brother Watch and Others v the United Kingdom (2018)	Journalists, individuals and rights organisations brought an action against the practices of bulk data interception, intelligence sharing and obtaining data from communications services providers.	The ECtHR held that the bulk interception regime violated Article 8.

Figure 34.8 Key cases: Article 8, the right to a home and correspondence

34.4 Article 10: The right to freedom of expression

Article 10(1) contains the meaning of expression and Article 10(2) sets out how the state can justify an interference with Article 10(1).

The concept of free speech has been with us for many years, and attempts to restrict it have been met with an outcry throughout history. Speakers' Corner is an area of Hyde Park, London, which is set aside for public speaking. The Parks Regulation Act 1872 passed that anyone can turn up here unannounced to speak on any subject, as long as the police consider their speeches lawful.

Before HRA 1998, freedom of expression was permitted as long as the law did not prevent it.

34.4.1 Key elements of Article 10(1)

This Article covers both the giving and receiving of information and ideas.
- Its scope is broader than just speech, including the right to express oneself through words, pictures, images and actions.
- It also covers public protest and demonstrations — showing a strong link with Article 11.

Crowds listen to a speaker in Hyde Park

Although we have a right to receive information, this does not create a duty on the state to actively provide information.
- In *Guerra v Italy* (1998), a case about toxic emissions, it was said that whilst a government could not prevent a person from receiving the information that others wish to give, nevertheless it had no positive obligation to collect and

disseminate information. Article 10 cannot be used to force a government to disclose information it chooses to keep secret.

- In *Leander v Sweden* (1987), the ECtHR found no violation when the government refused to allow the applicant access to the details of his security vetting.

There are three elements to freedom of expression:
1 Freedom to hold opinions.
2 Freedom to impart information and ideas.
3 Freedom to receive information and ideas.

Freedom to hold opinions

Freedom to hold opinions is an underpinning aspect of Article 10. The possible restrictions set out in Article 10(2) do not apply. Any restrictions to this right will be inconsistent with the nature of a democratic society.

States must not try to indoctrinate their citizens and should not be allowed to distinguish between individuals holding one opinion and another. The idea is to prevent prejudice against an individual because of his views by public authorities such as the police or a school.

This can be seen in the operation of the equality duty under the Equality Act 2010 where there is a potential conflict with Article 10. For example, a university must prevent unlawful discrimination and promote equality of opportunity, fostering good relationships between different groups, including those with 'protected characteristics', as designated in the Act.

Indoctrination could occur where the state failed to provide a balanced view.

An individual is free to hold opinions but is not forced to communicate them to others.

Freedom to impart information and ideas

The right to freedom of expression includes the right to 'offend, shock and disturb'. In *Handyside v United Kingdom* (1976), the ECtHR stated:

> The Court's supervisory functions oblige it to pay the utmost attention to the principles characterising a 'democratic society'. Freedom of expression constitutes one of the essential foundations of such a society, one of the basic conditions for its progress and for the development of every man.

Case study

Handyside v United Kingdom (1976)

Mr Handyside had published a 'Little Red Schoolbook'. The purpose of the book was to teach school children about sex, drugs and the use of pornography. He was convicted under the Obscene Publications Acts 1959 and 1964 as the book tended to deprave and corrupt its target audience – children.

The court found there was no breach of Article 10. The UK law was within the margin of appreciation of the member state, the 'wiggle room' or discretion granted to each state to fit the ECHR to its own laws.

Freedom of speech was not applicable only to inoffensive material, but also extends to protect activity which others may find shocking, disturbing or offensive.

The type of expression protected includes:
- political expression (including comment on matters of general public interest)
- artistic expression
- commercial expression, particularly when it raises matters of legitimate public debate.

High and low value expression

Political expression is given particular precedence and protection. This is an example of 'high value' expression, which means that there is less margin of appreciation. The ability of individuals to take part in political debate and free elections is considered to be 'the bedrock of any democratic system' (*Lingens v Austria* (1986)). Other high value forms of expression include religious expression and public interest expression. Lower value forms of expression include commercial expression. Here the margin of appreciation is wider. Whether artistic expression is high or low value may ultimately depend on the values of the state involved.

Freedom of the press

To ensure that free expression and debate are possible, there must be protection for elements of a free press, including protection of journalistic sources. The public and the media should be able to comment on political matters without hindrance. Journalists should not be forced to reveal their sources (*Goodwin v United Kingdom* (1996)).

Case study

Goodwin v United Kingdom (1996)

Mr Goodwin was a trainee journalist with *The Engineer* magazine. He received information about a company's financial information from an anonymous source. The company tried to force him to reveal the source using various court orders, including under s 10 of the Contempt of Court Act 1981, requiring him to name his source. He appealed unsuccessfully against this and continued to refuse to disclose his source. He was fined £5000 for contempt of court.

The ECtHR stated that as publication of the confidential information was already prohibited by injunction, the order for disclosure of the source was not necessary, and breached Article 10.

The case of *Axel Springer AG v Germany* (2012) set out criteria to be used in balancing Article 10 and Article 8. These criteria are:

- whether the information contributes to a debate of general interest
- the notoriety of the person concerned and the subject matter of the report
- the prior conduct of the person concerned
- the method of obtaining the information and its veracity
- the content, form and consequences of the publication
- the severity of the sanction imposed.

Case study

Axel Springer AG v Germany (2012)

A German newspaper published stories and photographs about the arrest and conviction for possession of drugs of an actor, who was well known for his portrayal of a police officer in a television series in Germany. On the facts, the court found that his right to privacy under Article 8 outweighed the newspaper's freedom of expression under Article 10. In coming to this conclusion, the court had applied the six criteria set out above.

Political and public expression

Political expression has a very broad meaning and can include political marches, demonstrations, and other forms of expression. In this wider sense it has very strong links with Article 11, freedom of association.

- In *Navalny v Russia* (2018), a political activist and opposition leader claimed that his arrest, detention and administrative conviction on seven occasions in 2012 and 2014 had breached his rights and had been politically motivated. The ECtHR found violations of both Article 5 and 10.

  They identified an ulterior purpose, which was to 'suppress that political pluralism which forms part of "effective political democracy"' governed by 'the rule of law'.
- In *Steel v UK* (1998), the ECtHR found that that Article 10 was engaged when demonstrators disrupted in one case a grouse shoot and in the second the construction of a motorway.
- A further example of this is the case of *Steel and Morris v United Kingdom* (2005), where the court found that there had been a violation of Article 10.

With respect to the overlap of Articles 8 and 10, where a court was considering whether to interfere with the freedom of the press, any interference has to be justified, even where there is no public interest in the material in question being published. This can be seen in the case of *A v B plc (Flitcroft v MGN Ltd)* (2002).

Case study

A v B plc (Flitcroft v MGN Ltd) (2002)

The newspaper appealed against an injunction preventing it naming a footballer who, it claimed, had been unfaithful to his wife. There remains a distinction between the right of privacy which attaches to sexual activities within and outside a marriage. An order restricting the freedom of the press requires positive and clear justification. The fact that there might be no proper public interest in the material to be published was not itself a sufficient reason.

Artistic expression

Different states place different values on artistic expression. Artistic expression is seen as a vital element in the development and fulfilment of the individual. There is generally a wide margin of appreciation to reflect different cultures and values in different states.

For example, in *Otto-Preminger-Institut v Austria* (1994) there was a conflict between freedom of expression and religion.

Case study

Otto-Preminger-Institut v Austria (1994)

The institute tried to show a film that was seen as offensive to Catholics, who formed a large part of the region of Tyrol, and in whose lives religion plays a very important role. The authorities had banned the showing of the film and confiscated it. The ECtHR found no violation.

Hate speech or incitement to hatred

Hate speech is dealt with by Article 17, which disallows actions which undermine the values of the Convention. However, incitement to racial hatred can also be seen in the context of Article 10 *Garaudy v France* (2003).

Case study

Garaudy v France (2003)

Garaudy's book, *The Founding Myths of Modern Israel*, challenged accepted views of the Holocaust and Hitler's 'Final Solution'. Garaudy was found guilty of disputing the existence of crimes against humanity, public defamation of a group of people (the Jewish community) and incitement to discrimination and racial hatred.

He argued that under Article 10, his right to freedom of expression had been unjustifiably infringed. He also argued that his book was a political work written with a view to combating Zionism and criticising Israeli policy, and had no racist or anti-Semitic content. He argued he should have unlimited freedom of expression.

The court found that there could be an interference with his right to freedom of expression. However unpalatable his views, his publication contained ideas, and as such should be protected under Article 10. Therefore there was no breach of Article 10.

Case	Facts	Law
Handyside v United Kingdom (1976)	Handyside was convicted under the Obscene Publications Acts 1959 and 1964.	There was no breach of Article 10 and the UK law fell within the margin of appreciation of the member state.
Goodwin v United Kingdom (1996)	Goodwin failed to disclose the source of company financial information and was fined.	The order for disclosure of the source was not necessary, and so was a breach of Article 10.
Axel Springer AG v Germany (2012)	A newspaper published stories about the arrest and conviction for possession of drugs of a well-known TV actor, together with photographs of him.	The actor's right to privacy under Article 8 outweighed the newspaper's freedom of expression under Article 10. The court had applied six criteria.
Steel and Morris v United Kingdom (2005)	Steel and Morris libelled McDonald's when they handed out leaflets criticising their products and policies. They were ordered to pay damages.	Given the lack of procedural fairness and the disproportionate award of damages, the court found that there was been a violation of Article 10.
A v B plc (Flitcroft v MGN Ltd) (2002)	The newspaper appealed against an injunction preventing it naming a footballer who, it claimed, had been unfaithful to his wife.	The fact that there might be no proper public interest in the material to be published was not itself a sufficient reason for an injunction.
Otto-Preminger-Institut v Austria (1994)	The Institute tried to show a film that offended the Catholic religion but the authorities banned it and confiscated the film.	The Institute claimed a violation of its freedom of speech under Article 10 of the Convention but failed in its attempt.
Garaudy v France (2003)	Garaudy was found guilty of disputing the existence of a number of crimes in relation to a book he had written.	Restriction was justifiable under Article 10(2) (so there had been no breach of Article 10).

Figure 34.9 Key cases: Article 10, freedom to impart information and ideas

Freedom to receive information and ideas

The freedom to receive information includes the right to gather information and to seek information through all possible lawful sources, including international television broadcasts and the internet. This freedom enables the media to impart such information and ideas to the public, who have a right to be adequately informed, in particular on matters of public interest. This relates to freedom of information.

This right does not put a general positive obligation to provide the information. This can be seen in *Guerra v Italy* (1998).

In the UK, the Freedom of Information Act 2000 gives everyone the right to access recorded information held by public sector organisations. Any request for information under the Act will be handled under different regulations, depending on the kind of information requested, and an organisation could refuse a request if the information is sensitive or the costs are too high.

The other side of freedom of information is the Investigatory Powers Act 2016. Whether this Act will have an effect on the interpretation of Articles 8 and 10 (as well as other Articles of the ECHR) remains to be seen.

Link

See Chapter 21, section 21.4.5, for more details of the Investigatory Powers Act 2016.

34.4.2 Limitations in Article 10

The limitations are set out in Article 10(2). There are three criteria. The interference must be:
- prescribed by law
- aimed at protecting a legitimate aim
- necessary in a democratic society.

Prescribed by law and protecting a legitimate aim

In *Sunday Times v United Kingdom* (1979), the court found that the British common law rules on contempt of court were sufficiently precise as to fall under the requirement 'provided by law'. They must also be for one of the legitimate aims shown in Figure 34.10.

Legitimate aim	Explanation	Case law
In the interests of national security	• Maintaining the secrecy of security services • Preserving order in the armed forces by suppressing unofficial magazines given to soldiers • Cases involving official secrecy	• *Observer and Guardian v UK* (1991) • *Vereinigung Demokratischer Soldaten Österreichs and Gubi v Austria* (1995) • *R v Shayler* (2002)
With respect to territorial integrity or public safety	Anti-terrorism laws have been used under this limb.	The armed struggle between the PKK and Turkey provides an example: *Surek v Turkey* (1991).
For the prevention of disorder or crime	The state could try to justify the interference by arguing that it would cause crime or disorder so the criminal offence is needed to protect against it. However, the question is whether the state's actions are proportionate. In the UK this can be seen through the mechanisms used by the government to ensure compliance of legislation with the various Articles in ECHR.	An example of this (and other limitations) can be seen in the case of *Surek v Turkey* (1999). The memorandum by the Home Office and Ministry of Justice with respect to the Serious Crime Bill (now the Serious Crime Act 2015) and the impact of ECHR states that: 'Serious Crime Prevention Orders may interfere with a person's rights under Articles 8, 10 and 11'.
For the protection of health or morals	Some forms of expression would not be allowed by any state, such as incitement to murder or the sale of pornography to or involving children. However, different states have a different view of morals and obscenity. The debate about abortion combines the issues of both health and morality. Article 10's application reflects the prevailing views at the time of any complaint brought before the court.	In *Müller v Switzerland* (1988), this was one of the main arguments. *Open Door and Dublin Well Woman v Ireland* (1992): the views prevailing then were in issue. **Cont.**

Legitimate aim	Explanation	Case law
For the protection of the reputation or rights of others	This includes the law of defamation (see Chapter 35). It covers the protection of intellectual property rights, through trademarks, copyright and patents.	*Twentieth Century Fox v British Telecommunications* [2011]: the claimants won an injunction against BT forcing them to block illegal downloads of their content.
For preventing the disclosure of information received in confidence	Secret documents cannot be published. Professional journalists must be aware of the confidential nature of information. Public interest in knowing about undue pressure and wrongdoing within public office outweighs the interest in maintaining public confidence in that office. There should be a fair balance between protecting the employer's reputation and rights, and the right to freedom of expression of the whistleblower. UK workers who disclose information about malpractice at their workplace are protected provided certain conditions are met.	*Bédat v Switzerland* (2016): the court stated that the journalist had not obtained the information by unlawful means. No violation of Article 10. *Guja v Moldova* (2008): ECtHR stressed that open discussion of topics of public concern was essential to democracy. *Heinisch v Germany* (2011): a whistleblower's rights had been violated under Article 10. This is enabled by the Public Interest Disclosure Act 1998.
For maintaining the authority and impartiality of the judiciary	Reporting trials in the media can be restricted in order to protect the rights of others such as children or the overall fairness of the trial under Article 6. Usually restrictions on recordings and photography in court, punishable as a criminal offence. Usually restrictions on the press disclosing details in advance of a trial so that the case can proceed fairly.	This was decided in *A v BBC* [2014]. The ECtHR considered 'maintaining the authority and impartiality of the Judiciary' in the case of *Pinto Coelho v Portugal (No. 2)* (2016). In *Sunday Times v United Kingdom* (1979), the government justified injunctions against publication of a newspaper article on the basis of this limitation.

Figure 34.10 Limitations in Article 10

Necessary in a democratic society

The ECtHR uses the principle of proportionality to assess this last point: 'Was the aim proportional with the means used to reach that legitimate aim?'

In *Observer and Guardian v United Kingdom* (1995), the ECtHR stated that 'necessary', within the meaning of Article 10(2), means the existence of a pressing social need.

Where the ECtHR finds that all three requirements are fulfilled, the interference will be considered legitimate. The burden of proof is on the state. If any of the three requirements fail then freedom of expression has been violated.

Case study

Observer and Guardian v United Kingdom (1995)

The newspapers challenged injunctions from the government preventing their publication of extracts from the *Spycatcher* memoir, authored by Peter Wright, a former member of the British Security Service, without obtaining the authorisation of the Security Service. He asserted that until the late 1970s, the Security Service had been engaged in various unlawful activities, such as bugging and burgling of friendly embassies.

In July 1986, the courts granted an interim injunction to prohibit publication, but by the time of the hearing for a permanent injunction, the book was published abroad including in the USA, and many copies had been imported into the UK.

The ECtHR stated that the temporary injunctions were justified prior to the publication in the United States. At that point, the information lost its confidential character and so the interference was no longer permissible.

Case	Facts	Law
Guerra v Italy (1998)	The applicants lived about 1 km from a chemical factory and demanded a right to receive information about the dangers to health from the factory.	The court held there is no positive obligation to collect and disseminate information.
Observer and Guardian v United Kingdom (1995)	The newspapers challenged injunctions preventing their publication of extracts of the *Spycatcher* book.	The ECtHR stated that the temporary injunctions were justified prior to the publication of the book but not thereafter.
R v Shayler (2002)	Shayler had been a member of the security services and disclosed documents to journalists that related to security and intelligence matters.	Shayler argued that the disclosures were in the public or national interest. This defence failed.
Surek v Turkey (1999)	The applicant was convicted of the offence of disseminating propaganda against the indivisibility of the state and provoking enmity and hatred among the people.	Surek argued that this was an interference by a public authority with his right to freedom of expression. No breach of Article 10 was found.
Müller v Switzerland (1988)	Müller was conviction of an offence of publishing obscene items, consisting of paintings.	Fining the exhibition organisers was not a violation of the right to freedom of expression.
Open Door and Dublin Well Woman v Ireland (1992)	The applicants were prohibited from providing any information to pregnant women about abortion clinics in Great Britain.	This prohibition was a breach of Article 10.
Bédat v Switzerland (2016)	In 2003 the applicant was fined for publishing an article questioning an accused motorist's state of mind and included a personal description, as well as photographs of letters sent by him to the investigating judge.	No violation of Article 10 and the Court found that the fine imposed on Mr Bédat was necessary in a democratic society.
Sunday Times v United Kingdom (1979)	The Attorney-General asked the Court to grant an injunction against the *Sunday Times* as the publication of the article on thalidomide victims would obstruct justice. The *Sunday Times* claimed a violation of Article 10.	This was a matter of public concern. The injunction was not granted.
Pinto Coelho v Portugal (No. 2) (2016)	The applicant was fined for broadcasting unauthorised audio recordings of a criminal trial.	The Court balanced the rights of the media to report on a matter of public interest with the interests of the participants. It found a breach of Article 10.

Figure 34.11 Key cases: Article 10

34.4.3 Article 10 and the internet

Technology has progressed significantly since the ECHR was conceived. The ECtHR has said that absence of proper legal frameworks allowing journalists to access materials on the internet without fear of sanction may hinder the freedom of the press (see *Editorial Board of Parvoye Delo and Shtekel v Ukraine* (2011)).

In *Yildirim v Turkey* (2012), the ECtHR unanimously held that the blanket blocking of access to sites.google.com breached the right to freedom of expression.

In *Delfi AS v Estonia* (2015), the Grand Chamber commented:

> While the Court acknowledges that important benefits can be derived from the internet in the exercise of freedom of expression, it is also mindful that liability for defamatory or other types of unlawful speech must, in principle, be retained and constitute an effective remedy for violations of personality rights.

Case	Facts	Law
Editorial Board of Parvoye Delo and Shtekel v Ukraine (2011)	*Pravoye Delo*, a Ukrainian newspaper, published an anonymous letter posted on an internet site that accused senior local officials of involvement in various criminal activities.	The Ukrainian ruling failed to meet the Article 10 requirement that any limitation of freedom of expression should be based on a clear, accessible and reasonably foreseeable law.
Yildirim v Turkey (2013)	The state had ordered blanket blocking of access to sites.google.com.	This breached the right to freedom of expression.
Magyar Jeti Zrt v Hungary (2018)	The applicant company had been found liable for having inserted a hyperlink to an interview on YouTube that was subsequently held to have defamatory content.	The court's decision amounted to a violation of the companies' Article 10 rights.

Figure 34.12 Key cases: Article 10 and the internet

To hyperlink or not to hyperlink?

In the case of *Magyar Jeti Zrt v Hungary* (2018), the applicant company had been found liable for having inserted a hyperlink to an interview on YouTube that was subsequently held to have defamatory content. The ECtHR expressed its strong view that there was a danger that freedom of the press could be supressed if it could not function properly.

To paraphrase the words of Tim Berners-Lee, hyperlinks are critical not merely to the digital revolution but to our continued prosperity – and even our liberty. Like democracy itself, they need defending.

34.5 Article 11: Freedom of assembly

There are three rights under Article 11(1):
1 Peaceful assembly
2 Association with others
3 Trade unions

These are qualified rights. The limitations are set out in Article 11(2):
- prescribed by law
- necessary in a democratic society
- for a legitimate aim:
  - in the interests of national security or public safety
  - for the prevention of disorder or crime
  - for the protection of health or morals
  - for the protection of the rights and freedoms of others.

The right must fulfil the criterion of proportionality. This involves looking at the following questions:
- Is the limitation effective?
- Is it the least intrusive measure possible?
- Does it deprive the very essence of the right?
- Is it balanced between the competing interests as a whole?

As with other Articles, the margin of appreciation will vary from case to case. However, the Council of Europe has expressed concerns about developments in some states during 2015, such as:
- Turkey: extending the powers of the police to use firearms in the Security Bill of March 2015.
- Spain: introducing heavy fines against organisers of spontaneous protests in a new law on citizens' security.
- The Russian Federation: with an amendment to the law on public gatherings, which permits the detention of any person participating in an unauthorised public assembly.

34.5.1 The rights under Article 11(1)

Article 11, as interpreted by the courts, has two closely related rights:
1 The right to meet and associate with others subject to the exceptions in Article 11(2).
2 A duty on the state to take positive measures to ensure effective protection of these rights.

Where individuals or businesses act in a way that undermines Article 11 rights, the state may be required to intervene to secure the protection of those rights.

Freedom of peaceful assembly

Freedom of peaceful assembly has a wide meaning include the organisation of, and participation in, marches or processions, static assemblies or sit-ins and both public and private events, whether formal or informal. The right must be exercised peacefully, without violence or the threat of violence, and in accordance with the law.

The right to freedom of assembly implies the right to choose the time, place and manner of conduct of the assembly, within the limits set by 2 of Article 11(2) (*Sáska v Hungary* (2012)). However, it does not grant any freedom of forum for the exercise of that right. It does not create any automatic rights of entry to private property, or even, necessarily, to all publicly owned property, such as government offices or university premises (*Appleby and Others v The United Kingdom* (2003)).

A totally peaceful assembly can still be disbanded without a violation of Article 11, as can be seen from the case of *Cisse v France* (2002).

Case study

Cisse v France (2002)

A group of two hundred illegal immigrants occupied a church and took part in a hunger strike as a protest about the difficulties they were having with their residency appeals. Despite the assembly being peaceful in nature, the Commissioner of Police ordered that they be evacuated from the church on the grounds of serious sanitary, health, peace, security and public order risks. His actions did not breach Article 11.

Assemblies may be peaceful even though they may lead to counter-demonstrations. The case of *Plattform 'Ärzte für das Leben' v Austria* (1988) shows that a peaceful demonstration may annoy or give offence to persons opposed to the ideas or claims that the demonstration is seeking to promote.

Case study

Plattform 'Ärzte für das Leben' v Austria (1988)

Plattform 'Ärzte für das Leben' was an association of doctors campaigning against abortion that organised a religious service and a march to the surgery of a doctor who carried out abortions. The ECtHR stated that a demonstration may annoy or give offence to persons opposed to the ideas or claims that it is seeking to promote. Participants must, however, be able to hold the demonstration without fear of physical violence by their opponents. While there is a right to counter-demonstrate, sometimes the state must interfere to protect its citizens and maintain order.

If the purpose of the assembly is to cause disorder, this is not protected under Article 11. *G v Federal Republic of Germany* (1989) concerned an illegal demonstration in front of US military barracks in support of nuclear disarmament. Here, demonstrators blocked the road for 12 minutes every hour, but the sit-in still fell within the accepted definition of a 'peaceful assembly'.

In the UK, the position can be seen in the case of *DPP v Jones (Margaret)* (1999).

Case study

DPP v Jones (Margaret) (1999)

There was a peaceful protest on the main road next to Stonehenge. The officer in charge concluded that it constituted a 'trespassory assembly' and told the protestors so. When asked to move off, some people were determined to remain and were convicted. The appeal was allowed. A peaceful assembly on the highway, which did not unreasonably interfere with or obstruct the highway, was not a trespassory assembly.

There is an increasing recognition that some tolerance of demonstrations that may shock, annoy or distress others is an integral part of ensuring that these rights are properly protected. This was the view taken in *Faber v Hungary* (2012), where restriction on the display of flags during a demonstration was a breach of Article 10.

Where the assembly takes place on private land, the owner of that land is able to prohibit the assembly, providing this does not prevent lawful protest taking place in a suitable alternative place or method. This can be seen in *Appleby v United Kingdom* (2003).

G20 protest march in London, 2009

Case	Facts	Law
Cisse v France (2002)	The applicant was a member of a group of people without residence permits who, in 1996, decided to take collective action to draw attention to the difficulties they were having in obtaining a review of their immigration status in France.	In the circumstances there was no violation of Article 11. The restrictions on the exercise of the applicant's right to assembly may have become necessary.
Plattform 'Ärzte für das Leben' v Austria (1988)	Plattform 'Ärzte für das Leben' held two demonstrations which were disrupted by counter-demonstrators, despite the presence of a large contingent of police.	A demonstration may annoy or give offence to persons opposed to the ideas or claims that it is seeking to promote, but sometimes the state must interfere.
DPP v Jones (Margaret) (1999)	On the road next to the perimeter fence at Stonehenge, 21 people protested peacefully. The officer in charge concluded that they constituted a 'trespassory assembly'.	A peaceful assembly on the highway, which did not unreasonably interfere with or obstruct the highway, was not a trespassory assembly.
Appleby v United Kingdom (2003)	The claimants wanted to demonstrate against a development in their home town of Washington.	Where the assembly takes place on private land, the owner of that land is able to prohibit the assembly, providing this does not prevent lawful protest taking place in a suitable alternative place or method.

Figure 34.13 Key cases: Article 11, freedom of assembly

Freedom of association with others

Freedom of association is the right to come together with others to form an association. This includes the right to form and join trade unions, and to join with others to pursue or advance common causes and interests (see *National Union of Belgian Police v Belgium* (1975)).

The converse is also part of the right, that is, the right not to belong to an association. This was stated in *Young, James and Webster v United Kingdom* (1981), where the ECtHR stated:

> Artical 11 guarantees not only freedom of association, including the right to form and to join trade unions, in the positive sense, but also, by implication, a 'negative right' not to be compelled to join an association or a union.

Association means something more than just socialising with others – *McFeeley v United Kingdom* (1981). A key element of the right is that the individuals taking part are doing so for a common purpose.

Case study

McFeeley v United Kingdom (1981)

The claimants had been convicted of terrorism offences in Northern Ireland and were prisoners in the Maze prison. A change of regime in 1976 resulted in them not being allowed to mix with the rest of the prison community. Article 11 did not apply to association in this sense.

Similarly, association does not include professional regulatory bodies set up by the state to regulate professions, as in *Le Compte, Van Leuven and De Meyere v Belgium* (1981), a case involving doctors and their regulatory body.

Political parties have been found to be an association, as in *Redfearn v United Kingdom* (2012).

Case study

Redfearn v United Kingdom (2012)

The appellant was a bus driver who worked in Bradford and most of his passengers were of Asian origin. He was summarily dismissed, after seven months, following his election to the local council of the British National Party. There were no specific allegations against him and he had been seen as a 'first class employee' by his line manager, who was of Asian origin.

In the ECtHR, he successfully argued that for an employee to lose his job for exercising his right to freedom of association 'struck at the "very substance" of that right', and that the government had a positive obligation under Article 11 to enact legislation that would protect that right even though he could not claim for unfair dismissal.

The right to form and to join trade unions for the protection of his interests

Trade unions are specifically recognised as associations, as is the right to form and join one. The state can restrict the right if the restriction can be justified. This might be the restriction on secondary picketing and the right of a trade union to expel members.

34.5.2 Restrictions set out in Article 11(2)

As this Article contains a qualified right, any interference depends on the conditions set out below.

'Prescribed by law'

This means there must be a clear, precise and predictable legal basis for the interference with Article 11. In the UK there are a number of restrictions. These restrictions come from both the common law and statute.

Link

These restrictions are outlined in more detail in Chapter 35.

'For a legitimate aim'

The legitimate aim must fall under one of the following categories:
- In the interests of national security or public safety
- For the prevention of disorder or crime
- For the protection of health or morals
- For the protection of the rights and freedoms of others

See Figure 34.15.

Case	Facts	Law
McFeeley v United Kingdom (1981)	The claimants had been convicted of terrorist offences, and they were not permitted to mix with the rest of the prison community.	The meaning of association is not defined, as is the case in many states. It does not mean the right to choose who to spend time with.
Redfearn v United Kingdom (2012)	The appellant was a bus driver and elected local councillor representing the British National Party. He was summarily dismissed after this election.	While association does not include professional regulatory bodies set up by the state to regulate professions, it does include political parties so there was a violation of Article 11.

Figure 34.14 Key cases: Article 11, freedom of association

Legitimate aim	Explanation	Case law
In the interests of national security or public safety	This includes counter-terrorism measures and counter-extremism measures. It overlaps with freedom of expression.	*R (Laporte) v Chief Constable of Gloucestershire* (2006) might be argued on the basis of public safety as well as the prevention of disorder or crime.
For the prevention of disorder or crime	The majority of references to ECtHR are dismissed as the Court takes the view that each state recognises the need to protect public safety.	States have a relatively wide margin of appreciation in this area, as we have seen in *Cisse v France* (2002).
For the protection of health or morals	States can be permitted to deny association registrations with the aim of protecting the health and morals of the country. Marches in favour of drug-taking can be banned.	*Larmela v Finland* (1997): the Finnish Minister of Justice refused to register the Cannabis Association of Finland, which aimed 'to influence intoxicant policy and legislation with a view to making the personal use of cannabis legal for Finnish citizens'.
For the protection of the rights and freedoms of others	Although the rights and freedoms of others are to be respected when considering such cases, this must be something more than the freedom to do as we please.	

Figure 34.15 Legitimate aims restrictions to Article 11

'Necessary in a democratic society'

'Necessary in a democratic society' implies two conditions:

1 There has to be a pressing social need for the interference.
2 The interference should be proportionate to the legitimate aims pursued.

National authorities need to decide whether or not there is a pressing social need in a particular case. There is a margin of appreciation, although the assessment of the national authorities is subject to supervision by the ECtHR. Furthermore, the Court's task is not to substitute its own view for that of the national authorities, but to review under Article 11 the decisions it delivered in the exercise of its discretion. This means that the Court must look at the interference complained of in the light of the case as a whole and determine whether it was 'proportionate to the legitimate aim pursued' and whether the reasons adduced by the national authorities to justify the interference are 'relevant and sufficient.'

The question of proportionality arose in the case of *R (Laporte) v Chief Constable of Gloucestershire* (2006).

Case study

R (Laporte) v Chief Constable of Gloucestershire (2006)

Police officers stopped three coaches from London carrying 120 anti-Iraq war protesters in March 2003. The protesters had been planning to join a large demonstration at RAF Fairford in Gloucestershire. Many of the protesters, including Laporte, had peaceful intentions, but some items which suggested a more violent intent were apparently discovered by the police on the coaches.

The coaches were sent back to London under police escort, the passengers unable to get off.

The Chief Constable had acted unlawfully as they were not prescribed by law and were disproportionate.

34.6 Restrictions permitted by the European Convention on Human Rights

The restrictions which are allowed by the ECHR are found within each specific article. These have been extensively discussed above.

The details are given in:
- Article 5(1)(a)–(f)
- Article 8(2)
- Article 10(2)
- Article 11(2).

Quick questions

1 Explain the meaning of 'deprivation of liberty'.
2 What is the 'acid test' for liberty in *Cheshire West and Chester Council v P*?
3 What are the implied elements of 'fairness' which form part of a fair trial?
4 Explain the meaning of the term 'private life' under Article 8 as it has been interpreted by
   the courts.
5 What are the three aspects of freedom of expression under Article 10?
6 Explain the meaning of 'high' and 'low value' expression. Why is this distinction important?
7 What is meant by 'freedom of association'?

Summary

- Article 5 of the ECHR describes the right to liberty and security.
  - A deprivation of liberty was said to be where the person was 'under continuous supervision and not free to leave'.
- Article 6 covers the right to a fair trial.
  - Elements of a fair trial include access to a court, participation in proceedings, equality of arms, and the exclusion of unfair evidence.
- Article 8 covers the right to respect for family and private life.
  - The concept of private life is very wide and is expanding over time. It includes physical and social identity, gender identification, name, sexual orientation and personal development.
  - The concept of family life reflects 'biological and social reality'.
  - Personal data is also protected under Article 8.
- Article 10 covers the right to freedom of expression. This means both the right to give and receive information.
  - The right to freedom of expression is seen as the fundamental basis of democracy. Political and religious expression are viewed as high value forms expression whereas commercial expression is seen as a low value form of expression.
- Article 11 covers the right to peaceful assembly and association.
  - Any restriction on Article 11 must be prescribed by law, for a legitimate aim, and necessary in a democratic society.

Chapter 35 Human rights and English law

Introduction

The rights contained within the ECHR have been imported into UK national law under the operation of s 1 HRA 1998. In addition to the HRA 1998, there are many pieces of domestic legislation and common law that place constraints on our ability to exercise our freedoms. These are the subject of this chapter.

35.1 Public order offences: restricting Articles 10 and 11

35.1.1 Breach of the peace

Breach of the peace is used to prevent unlawful violence against people or property. 'Peace' in this context refers to the Queen's peace.

The definition of breach of the peace can be found in *R v Howell* (1981):

> there is a breach of the peace whenever harm is actually done or is likely to be done to a person or in his presence to his property or a person is in fear of being so harmed through an assault, an affray, a riot, unlawful assembly or other disturbance.

The wide powers available to stop or prevent a breach mean that any use of the powers is closely examined by the courts to ensure that there has been no undue interference with respect for human rights. Examples of this can be seen with respect to kettling tactics by the police in:

- *R (McClure and Moos) v Commissioner of Police of the Metropolis* (2012)
- *Austin v Commissioner of Police of the Metropolis* (2012).

Link

See Chapter 34 for case details of *McClure and Moos* and *Austin*.

The Public Order Act 1986

The Public Order Act 1986 sets out various offences which can occur where there are demonstrations or protests. The Act replaces and largely replicates existing common law offences. Other offences include obstructing the highway under the Highways Act 1980 and aggravated trespass under the Criminal Justice and Public Order Act (CJPOA) 1994.

This means that when Articles 11 and 10 are considered, the state may have to show that the offence was committed and that the offence is a proportionate response to a legitimate aim.

35.1.2 Riot

Riot comes under s 1 of the Public Order Act 1986. Riot is defined as:

> Where 12 or more persons who are present together use or threaten unlawful violence for a common purpose and the conduct of them (taken together) is such as would cause a person of reasonable firmness present at the scene to fear for his personal safety, each of the persons using unlawful violence for the common purpose is guilty of riot.

35.1.3 Violent disorder

Under s 2 of the Public Order Act 1986, the offence of violent disorder is defined as:

> Where 3 or more persons who are present together use or threaten unlawful violence and the conduct of them (taken together) is such as would cause a person of reasonable firmness present at the scene to fear for his personal safety, each of the persons using or threatening unlawful violence is guilty of violent disorder.

This is therefore the same as riot but with fewer people involved.

35.1.4 Affray

Under s 3 of the Public Order Act 1986, affray is defined as follows:

> A person is guilty of affray if he uses or threatens unlawful violence towards another and his conduct is such as would cause a person of reasonable firmness present at the scene to fear for his personal safety.

Affray requires a specific threat to someone, not a general threat to the public at large.

Case study

I v DPP (2001)

Several youths carried petrol bombs with them in public. Although they did not actually threaten anyone specifically, they did anticipate a confrontation with another group. When they were dispersed by police, the bombs were put down.

The court held that carrying such equipment in public, even without overt threats or acts of violence, could constitute affray, but evidence was needed that one or more people actually present were or felt so threatened.

Causing fear or provocation of violence

Under s 4 of the Public Order Act 1986, the offence of causing fear or provocation of violence is defined as:

> ... if, with intent to cause a person harassment, alarm or distress, he (a) uses threatening, abusive or insulting words or behaviour, or (b) displays any writing, sign or other visible representation which is threatening, abusive or insulting, with intent to cause that person to believe that immediate unlawful violence will be used against him or another by any person, or to provoke the immediate use of unlawful violence by that person or another, or whereby that person is likely to believe that such violence will be used or it is likely that such violence will be provoked.

Causing intentional harassment, alarm or distress

Under s 4A of the Public Order Act 1986, the offence of causing intentional harassment, alarm or distress is defined as:

> A person is guilty of an offence if, with intent to cause a person harassment, alarm or distress, he–

> a uses threatening or abusive words or behaviour, or disorderly behaviour, or

> b displays any writing, sign or other visible representation which is threatening, abusive or insulting, thereby causing that or another person harassment, alarm or distress.

There is a defence if the accused can prove:
- that they were inside a dwelling and had no reason to believe that the words or behaviour used, or the writing, sign or other visible representation displayed, would be heard or seen by a person outside that or any other dwelling; or
- that their conduct was reasonable.

Harassment, alarm or distress

Under s 5 of the Public Order Act 1986, the offence of causing harassment, alarm or distress is defined as:

> A person is guilty of an offence if he–

> a uses threatening or abusive words or behaviour, or disorderly behaviour, or

> b displays any writing, sign or other visible representation which is threatening or abusive, within the hearing or sight of a person likely to be caused harassment, alarm or distress thereby.

There is a defence if the accused can prove:
- that they had no reason to believe that there was any person within hearing or sight who was likely to be caused harassment, alarm or distress;
- that they were inside a dwelling and had no reason to believe that the words or behaviour used, or the writing, sign or other visible representation displayed, would be heard or seen by a person outside that or any other dwelling; or
- that their conduct was reasonable.

This makes it clear that there are many options under UK law to control public order and also restrict the right to freedom of assembly.

35.1.5 Illegal forms of assembly

The police have an array of legal powers at their disposal to disperse and otherwise deal with other illegal forms of assembly, such as raves. These are mainly contained within the Public Order Act 1986 and the Criminal Justice and Public Order Act 1994.

Look online

Use the website at **www.legislation.gov.uk/** to research the details of the specific provisions below.

Statutory provision	Title
ss 11–13 Public Order Act 1986	Public processions – notice, conditions and prohibitions
s 14 Public Order Act 1986	Imposing orders on public assemblies
ss 63–66 CJPOA	Remove people attending a rave, powers of entry, search and seizure at a rave, attend or prepare for a rave, proceed to a rave
ss 68 and 69 CJPOA	Offence of aggravated trespass and powers to remove

Figure 35.1 Key provisions of the Public Order Act 1986 and the Criminal Justice and Public Order Act 1994

Following the case of *DPP v Chivers* (2010), the word 'land' includes a building.

Case study

DPP v Chivers (2010)

Daniel Chivers locked himself to a stair railing using a D-lock round his neck, Ian Fitzpatrick occupied a stairwell and Carl Von Tonda glued himself to the front door of the building.

The court decided that land includes a building so all three had been correctly charged with aggravated trespass.

The s 68 offence is capable of being committed by hunt saboteurs, climate change protesters, or motorway protesters or any protesters who are trespassing on land, but it is not formally limited to protest groups. It was used with respect to the UK Uncut protest at the Fortnum & Mason department store in Piccadilly, London.

Protestors at the UK Uncut demonstration at Fortnum & Mason department store

Raves

A rave is defined as a gathering on land in the open air of twenty or more persons, at which amplified music is played during the night and, by reason of its loudness and duration and the time at which it is played, is likely to cause serious distress to the inhabitants of the locality.

Section 63 CJPOA 1994 provides the police with powers to direct persons (other than exempt persons such as the occupier of the land and their family or assistants) gathering on land for a rave to leave. Failure to comply with a direction, or returning to the site within seven days, are offences.

35.2 Police powers: Articles 5 and 6

Police powers are most likely to become problematic in relation to:
- the deprivation of liberty under Article 5, and
- the right to a fair trial under Article 6.

35.2.1 Stop and search

There are two main powers to consider in relation to stop and search.

Sections 1 and 2 of Police and Criminal Evidence Act 1984:
- Contains the power to stop and search 'any person or vehicle'. It is an objective assessment requiring a constable to have 'reasonable grounds for suspecting that he or she will find stolen or prohibited articles'.
- Reasonable suspicion is not defined in PACE 1984. It 'can never be supported on the basis of personal factors. It must rely on intelligence or information about, or some specific behaviour by, the person concerned'.

This must be read in association with the guidance in Code A of the codes of practice.

Stop and search has the potential to interfere with several Convention rights, in particular the right to liberty and security under Article 5.

Look online

This webpage from the College of Policing website provides information on police powers for stop and search:

www.app.college.police.uk/app-content/stop-and-search/legal/

In particular, this must be exercised lawfully to be permitted under Article 5.1(c).

The second power in s 60 of the Criminal Justice and Public Order Act 1994 gives police the right to search people in a defined area during a specific time period when they believe, with good reason, that:

- serious violence will take place and it is necessary to use this power to prevent such violence
- a person is carrying a dangerous object or offensive weapon, or
- an incident involving serious violence has taken place and a dangerous instrument or offensive weapon used in the incident is being carried.

35.2.2 The power of arrest

This is contained in s 24 PACE 1984, as amended by the Serious Organised Crime and Police Act (2005).

Section 24 Arrest without warrant: constables

(1) A constable may arrest without a warrant:
   (a) anyone who is about to commit an offence;
   (b) anyone who is in the act of committing an offence;
   (c) anyone whom he or she has reasonable grounds for suspecting to be about to commit an offence;
   (d) anyone whom he or she has reasonable grounds for suspecting to be committing an offence.
(2) If a constable has reasonable grounds for suspecting that an offence has been committed, he or she may arrest without a warrant anyone whom he or she has reasonable grounds to suspect of being guilty of it.
(3) If an offence has been committed, a constable may arrest without a warrant:
   (a) anyone who is guilty of the offence;
   (b) anyone whom he or she has reasonable grounds for suspecting to be guilty of it.

What is reasonable suspicion?

> ### Case study
>
> #### Cumming and Others v Chief Constable of Northumbria Police (2003)
>
> All the CCTV controllers at a local authority had been arrested on suspicion of perverting the course of justice, as CCTV footage of a crime appeared to have been tampered with.
>
> They were all innocent and sought damages for wrongful arrest and false imprisonment.
>
> The claims failed but the Court of Appeal held that Article 5 should be taken into account in such situations.

> " The court must consider ... whether or not the decision to arrest was one which no police officer, applying his mind to the matter could reasonably take, bearing in mind the effect on the appellant's right to liberty. "

Section 28 PACE 1984 provides various requirements of a valid arrest:

- The person being arrested must be told of the fact of his or her arrest (s 28(1)) and of the grounds for his or her arrest (s 28(3)).
- The rule in s 28 PACE is a continuation of the decision in *Christie v Leachinsky* (1947).
- He or she should be cautioned according to CJPOA 1994, s 34.
- Under ss 34–37 CJPOA 1994, the suspect should be told of their right to remain silent and warned as to the inferences which might arise as a result of a silence.
- After arrest the person must be told of his rights including the right to consult privately with a solicitor (s 58 PACE 1984).
- If access to a solicitor is denied, this can lead to the case against the defendant being thrown out of court by the judge.

> ### Case studies
>
> #### R v Samuel (1988)
>
> A man was arrested and interviewed four times over two days. He was denied access to a solicitor on the grounds that it would lead to the alerting of other suspects. At his fourth interview, he confessed to two offences of burglary, and was charged with these. He continued to be denied access to his solicitor. He was then interviewed a fifth time and confessed to a robbery. The Court of Appeal quashed his subsequent conviction for robbery. It described the right to legal advice as 'one of the most important and fundamental rights of a citizen'. This fired a warning shot across the bows of the police, who had acted in breach of their duty in denying the suspect his legal right.
>
> #### R v Alladice (1988)
>
> The defendant had been denied access to a solicitor during a police interview. He appealed against his conviction, claiming he had given a confession under duress.
>
> There had been breaches of the Act and of the Codes of Practice, but they did not in this case render the admission of the confession unfair.

Exclusion of evidence

Unfairly obtained evidence may form the basis of a claim of a violation of Article 6 or, if this leads to an arrest or detention, Article 5.

Evidence may be excluded from the trial by the judge for two main reasons.

1 Under s 76 PACE 1984, where a confession was obtained:
    (a) by oppression of the person who made it; or
    (b) in consequence of anything said or done which was likely, in the circumstances existing at the time, to render unreliable any confession which might be made by him in consequence thereof, the court shall not allow the confession to be given in evidence against him.
2 Under s 78 PACE 1984, exclusion of unfair evidence.
    (a) In any proceedings the court may refuse to allow evidence on which the prosecution proposes to rely to be given if it appears to the court that, having regard to all the circumstances, including the circumstances in which the evidence was obtained, the admission of the evidence would have such an adverse effect on the fairness of the proceedings that the court ought not to admit it.

Detention

A person who has been arrested should be charged or released. Detention is possible in certain situations.

Under s 37 PACE 1984, a custody officer decides whether there is sufficient evidence to charge the arrested person. When charged, the person should be released or detained further under s 38 PACE 1984.

Pre-charge detention

A person may be detained for up to 24 hours under initial police detention.

This can be extended to 36 hours by a senior police officer in respect of indictable offences.

Further detention – beyond 36 hours – requires a magistrate's warrant.

A warrant can be renewed up to a maximum of 96 hours.

Detention and Article 5(3)

Any detention is permitted by Article 5(1)(c) but it must be done in accordance with the law – Article 5(3).

McKay v United Kingdom (2007) said there were two relevant periods of detention: the 'arrest period' and the 'pre-trial period'.

Arrest

A person must be brought 'promptly' before the courts. Although 'promptly' is not specifically defined, in the case of *Brogan v United Kingdom* (1989), it was said that a delay of more than four days was a violation.

The provisions in PACE would seem to meet the Article 5(3) benchmark.

Pre-trial or remand

Whilst on remand, Article 5(3) requires 'trial within a reasonable time or release pending trial'. Any detention must be compatible with Article 5(3), which creates a presumption in favour of release.

35.3 Interception of communications: restricting Article 8

35.3.1 The Regulation of Investigatory Powers Act 2000

This Act was passed with Article 8 in mind. It puts into place a complex structure of regulation over a number of forms of surveillance.

This includes:
- grounds for using the powers
- authority for granting the use of the powers
- available mechanisms of challenge to the use of the powers.

Section 32(2)(a) allows for authorisation of intrusive surveillance by the Secretary of State if it is considered necessary.

Section 32(3)

Subject to the following provisions of this section, an authorisation is necessary on grounds falling within this subsection if it is necessary:
(a) in the interests of national security;
(b) for the purpose of preventing or detecting serious crime; or
(c) in the interests of the economic well-being of the United Kingdom.

The power must be exercised proportionately.

Section 65(2)(a) contains a mechanism for challenge under s 7 HRA 1998.

This has to be through the Tribunal rather than the courts. The tribunal is the only effective mechanism set up for this process.

35.3.2 Investigatory Powers Act (2016)

The Investigatory Powers Act updated the regulatory framework of the security services.

- This creates a new framework to govern the use and oversight of investigatory powers by law enforcement, security and intelligence agencies.
- It gathers together all the powers relating to the agencies involved in obtaining communications data.
- It introduces a double-lock for interception warrants so that the authorisation of the Secretary of State must be approved by a judge.
- It allows for appeals against tribunal decisions.
- It also, controversially, allows for the hacking and accessing of mobile phone and computers of private individuals and access to the data thereon. The power to collect bulk data, which is used indiscriminately regardless of any reasonable suspicion of wrong-doing, is highly controversial.
- The Act also creates a mechanism for monitoring, including the creation of a commissioner who is tasked with overseeing that the powers are used correctly.

  Any interference must not be exercised arbitrarily.

Case study

Halford v United Kingdom (1997)

The interception of a claimant's private telephone calls by her employer was a breach of her Article 8 rights. She was pursuing a sex discrimination claim against her employer when she was put under surveillance. This was a serious breach of her rights.

Statutory provision	Title
s 23 IPA (2016)	Approval of warrants by judicial commissioners.
s 67 IPA (2016)	Appeals against Tribunal decisions are possible.
s 227 IPA (2016)	Creation of the office of Investigatory Powers Commissioner.
s 229 IPA (2016)	Main functions of Commissioner.

Figure 35.2 Framework of oversight created by the Investigatory Powers Act (2016)

Activity

Research the statutory provisions above to make sure you understand the content of the key provisions.

Case study

Official Secrets Act 1989

The Official Secrets Act 1989 replaced s 2 of the Official Secrets Act 1911. It set out the specific categories of public servants who are covered by a legal duty not to disclose sensitive information. Those working in security and intelligence (s 1), defence (s 2), international relations (s 3), crime and special investigations (s 4) will be unable to rely on the protection of Article 10 if disclosing such information.

35.4 Duty of confidentiality: rights under Articles 8 and 10

35.4.1 Breach of confidence

This covers situations where information is given in confidence with the expectation that it will remain private. The duty often engages both Article 8 and Article 10 in its scope.

What can be done about breach of confidence?

- If the breach has not yet occurred, it may be possible to obtain an injunction to prevent it.
- If the breach has already happened, action may be brought for the breach to recover compensation.

  A claimant must prove:
- The information was obtained in a way which gives rise to a duty of confidence (such as giving financial details to an accountant, or medical information to a doctor).
- It must have the 'quality of confidence'.
- It can arise within an employment contract.
- It must be used in an unauthorised way.
- The claimant must suffer a detriment from the use.

Defences to a claim of breach of confidence

- Information already in the public domain.
- Information was not confidential.
- Public interest in disclosure (the whistleblower's defence).

Case study

HRH Prince of Wales v Associated Newspapers (2006)

The newspaper published extracts obtained secretly from the Prince of Wales' handwritten diaries. He won a case for breach of confidence. On appeal it was held that:

> The judge was correct to hold that Prince Charles had an unanswerable claim for breach of privacy. When the breach of a confidential relationship is added to the balance, his case is overwhelming.

The duty covers private relationships such as between a husband and wife.

Case study

Duchess of Argyll v Duke of Argyll (1967)

An injunction was granted to prevent the publication of confidential information between the Duke and Duchess of Argyll. The newspaper to which the Duke had communicated these details was prevented from publishing.

It can apply to commercial agreements.

Case study

Douglas v Hello (2001)

Unauthorised pictures from the wedding of Michael Douglas and Catherine Zeta-Jones were published by *Hello!* magazine. The couple challenged the publication, claiming a violation of Article 8.

The court said that any right to private life had to be balanced against the right under Article 10, freedom of expression.

The court refused to make an injunction preventing *Hello!* from publishing the pictures. This refusal was mainly because Douglas and Zeta-Jones were prepared to have publicity of their wedding and had actually agreed that another magazine could publish pictures.

One factor in such cases is whether the individual claiming the breach is already in the public eye. Are they a role model? Do they have a high profile? These issues were considered in the cases of *A v B plc (Flitcroft v MGN Ltd)* (2002) and *Campbell v MGN* (2004). See Chapter 34 for more details.

Case studies

Mosley v News Group Newspapers (2008)

The newspaper published a story about the claimant's sexual activities with prostitutes. As he was the head of Formula One racing, the newspaper argued that the public had a right to know. The Court of Appeal held that there was no public interest in this story and his right to private life had been violated.

Von Hannover v Germany (2004)

Princess Caroline of Monaco was secretly photographed with her children whilst in a café and the photographs were published in a German magazine.

The ECtHR held that the photographs were highly intrusive and that there was no public interest to merit the publication.

A similar decision was reached in *Weller v Associated Newspapers* [2015], where the musician Paul Weller's children successfully challenged the publication of photographs of them taken in California.

35.5 Obscenity: restricting Article 10

Obscene publications are governed by the Obscene Publications Act 1959 and the Obscene Publications Act 1964.

35.5.1 Obscene Publications Act 1959

Section 1(1) of the Obscene Publications Act (OPA) 1959 sets out the legal test for obscenity. It describes an 'obscene' item as one that has the effect of tending to deprave and corrupt persons likely to read, see or hear it. This statutory definition is largely based on the common law test of obscenity, as laid down in the case of *R v Hicklin* (1868), namely:

> ... whether the tendency of the matter charged as obscenity is to deprave and corrupt those whose minds are open to such immoral influences, and into whose hands a publication of this sort may fall.

Famous cases in the UK include those of the novels *Lady Chatterley's Lover* by DH Lawrence and *Last Exit to Brooklyn* by Hubert Selby Jr. The courts have defined 'deprave' as meaning to make morally bad, to debase, to pervert or to corrupt morally, and 'corrupt' as meaning to render morally unsound or rotten, to destroy moral purity or chastity, to pervert or ruin a good quality, and to debase or defile.

The scope of obscenity

Under s 1(2) OPA 1959, obscenity applies to a wide range of media:

> 'article' means any description of article containing or embodying matter to be read or looked at or both, any sound record, and any film or other record of a picture or pictures.

The Theatres Act 1968 applies a similar definition of obscenity to plays and performances. This is also extended to live broadcasts under the Broadcasting Act 1990.

There is also a possible lesser offence of outraging public decency. Public decency requires a level of behaviour which is generally accepted in public and is not obscene, disgusting or shocking for the observers.

Galleries (and their staff, officers or directors) may be committing a criminal offence if, for example, they sell, show or distribute work that is considered to be obscene or which causes public outrage.

Defence to obscenity

Section 4 OPA 1959:

> ... a person shall not be convicted of an offence ... if it is proved that publication of the article in question is justified as being for the public good on the ground that it is in the interests of science, literature, art or learning, or of other objects of general concern.

35.5.2 Obscene Publications Act 1964

The second statute on obscenity includes some limited provisions to further restrict the law on obscenity. In particular, these tighten the rules on making a gain from obscene materials.

Look online

Film censorship and obscenity

Follow the link to the British Board of Film Classification website to find out what legislation exists to protect against harmful content in films.

www.bbfc.co.uk/education/students-guide/legislation/the-criminal-law

- Which 1996 film was accused of being obscene, despite no prosecution being brought?
- Do these restrictions seem sensible and appropriate?

Outraging public decency

The common law contains certain measures to protect against obscene materials or those likely to cause moral outrage. According to Viscount Simonds in the case of *Shaw v DPP*, the common law offence of outraging public decency could be used in situations where there was no obvious statutory provision to protect the public welfare.

Case studies

Shaw v DPP (1962)

The defendant had published a 'ladies directory' containing the contact details of prostitutes living in London. Conspiracy to corrupt public morals is a crime known to the law of England.

R v Gibson and Sylveire (1990)

Using freeze-dried human foetuses as earrings for a work of art was held to constitute the offence of outraging public decency.

35.6 Torts of defamation

35.6.1 Defamation: restricting Article 10

In the UK, the law of defamation sets out a position that is largely compatible with ECHR. Defamation comes in two forms: libel and slander.

- Libel is defamation in permanent form, including broadcasting.
- Slander is defamation in transient form – spoken, conduct or gestures.

In defamation, the words are taken to have their normal or natural meaning.

A claimant needs to show that the statement complained of:

- is defamatory, meaning that an ordinary person would think worse of the claimant as a result of the statement
- identifies or refers to him, and
- is published to a third party.

The Defamation Act 2013 requires claimants to show that the publication of the statement caused them, or is likely to cause them, serious harm. In the case of businesses, serious harm means serious financial loss.

A claim for slander also requires proof of special damage. This means financial loss. There are two exceptions to this requirement:

- A statement that the claimant has committed a criminal offence punishable by imprisonment, such as 'X is a thief'.

  Or:

- Where the words are calculated to disparage the claimant in any office, profession, calling, trade or business carried on by them at the time of publication, such as 'He [or she] is a doctor who is always amputating the wrong limb'.

Defences to a claim for defamation

There are a number of defences in English law with respect to defamation.

Defence	Explanation
Truth	s 2 of the Defamation Act 2013: ● Defendant must show that the imputation conveyed is substantially true.
Honest opinion	s 3 of the Defamation Act 2013: ● It provides a defence if the statement complained of was one of opinion which could have been held by an honest person on the basis of any fact which existed at the time the statement was published. ● If a claimant can show that the defendant did not hold the opinion, the defence will fail.
Publication on a matter of public interest	s 4 of the Defamation Act 2013: ● The defendant has to show that the statement complained of was, or formed part of, a statement on a matter of public interest. *And*: ● The defendant reasonably believed that publishing the statement complained of was in the public interest. Whether the defendant has a reasonable belief includes: ● attempts made to verify the truth of what is being published ● the nature of the sources of information ● the extent to which the claimant was given an opportunity to respond or comment. You will often see an article in a newspaper that 'X declined to comment'.
Internet defences	There are also a number of defences available to internet intermediaries, including: ● innocent dissemination ● a website operator's defence ● defences under the E-Commerce Regulations 2002.
Privilege	This comes in two forms: absolute and qualified. 1 Absolute privilege applies if there are clear public policy reasons limiting freedom of speech in this context. Such situations include: ● statements made in the course of judicial proceedings, parliamentary proceedings or papers ● contemporaneous reports of judicial proceedings. 2 Qualified privilege covers the publication of any fair and accurate report or statement on a matter of public interest. This defence can be defeated if there is evidence that the publication was made with malice. Examples of statutory qualified privilege include fair and accurate reports of: ● proceedings in public of Parliament or the courts ● courts or international organisations anywhere in the world ● a UK public company general meeting, or reporting. This has been extended to cover peer-reviewed statements published in scientific or academic journals.

Figure 35.3 Defences to a claim for defamation

Case study

Buckley v Dalziel [2007]

Statements made to the police were subject to absolute privilege. During a dispute between neighbours, statements were given to the police that the claimant said were defamatory. These were protected by absolute privilege – a decision based on public policy.

35.7 Trespass to land: Restricting Article 11

Those exercising a right under Article 11 have no enhanced rights in relation to others' land and cannot escape a claim of trespass simply by virtue of their protest or demonstration.

In *Appleby v UK* (2003), the ECtHR held that the property rights of the owners had to be taken into account.

Trespass is an unlawful and unjustifiable intrusion by a person onto the land of another. There is no need to show that any damage has been caused.

However, technically the slightest crossing of the claimant's boundary is sufficient to result in a trespass. In the case of *Ellis v Loftus Iron Co.* (1874), the court stated:

> ... if the defendant place[s] a part of his foot on the claimant's land unlawfully, it is in law as much a trespass as if he had walked half a mile on it.

This principle was used:

- to evict travellers parked on land belonging to others, typically the owners of woodland, as in the case of *Drury v Secretary of State for Environment, Food and Rural Affairs* (2004)
- in sit-ins such as that at Essex University in *University of Essex v Djemal* (1980).

These cases had mixed results for the landowners and so the criminal law was strengthened, as will be seen later in this chapter.

Examples of civil trespass include removing any part of the land in the possession of another, or any part of a building or other erection attached to the soil. It can also be a trespass to place something on, or in, land in the possession of another – such as dumping rubbish.

There are a number of legal justifications to trespass, including:

- licence to enter by law
- justification by right of way or easement (the use of someone else's property or land for a stated reason such as permitting the underground services of one property (such as drains) to pass beneath the land of a neighbouring property)
- justification by licence or necessity
- various powers of entry granted to officers of the law, such as the police.

Statutory restrictions

Removing trespassers from land

Section 61 of the Criminal Justice and Public Order Act (CJPOA) 1994 applies to trespassers who are on the land of another with the common purpose of remaining there. This section enables a police officer to direct trespassers on the land to leave the land where the occupier has already taken steps to ask them to do so, and either:

- they have damaged the land, or
- they have used threatening, abusive or insulting behaviour to the occupier, the occupier's family, employees or agents, or
- between them they have six or more vehicles on the land.

Failure to obey a direction to leave or returning to the land as a trespasser within three months is an offence. This deals with the problems occurring in *Drury v Secretary of State for Environment, Food and Rural Affairs* (2004) and *University of Essex v Djemal* (1980).

Section 62 provides a power for the police to seize vehicles of persons failing to comply with a direction under s 61.

Aggravated trespass under s 68 CJPOA 1994

See above at Section 35.1.5.

35.8 Harassment: Restricting Article 10

35.8.1 The Protection from Harassment Act 1997

The Protection from Harassment Act 1997 was originally introduced to deal with the problem of stalking. The Act covers stalking and harassment offences as well as remedies (sections 1–5).

There are two criminal offences:
- pursuing a course of conduct amounting to harassment
- a more serious offence where the conduct puts the victim in fear of violence.

Harassing a person includes alarming the person or causing the person distress.

A 'course of conduct', which can include speech, must normally involve conduct on at least two occasions, although there are exceptions to this.

In addition to the criminal offences, a civil court can impose civil injunctions in harassment cases, as well as awarding damages to the victim for the harassment. Breach of such an injunction is a criminal offence.

Case study

Majrowski v Guys and St Thomas' NHS Trust (2007)

The claimant employee sought damages from his employer for bullying which he said amounted to harassment under the Protection From Harassment Act 1997. The employer argued that the Act was designed solely to prosecute stalkers but this argument was rejected and they were found to be liable.

35.8.2 The Malicious Communications Act 1998

The Malicious Communications Act 1998 states that it is an offence to send another person a letter, electronic communication or article of any description that conveys:
- a message which is indecent or grossly offensive
- a threat
- information which is false and known or believed to be false by the sender.

Guilt requires the intention to cause distress or anxiety to the recipient or any other person. This is increasingly relevant with respect to cyberbullying.

Quick questions

1. What is the difference between riot and affray?
2. What are the elements of a valid arrest?
3. For what reasons may evidence be excluded from a trial?
4. What are the defences to a claim of breach of confidence?
5. What is the definition of obscenity?
6. What is unusual about the crime of outraging public decency?

Summary

- Articles 10 and 11 are subject to the limitations created by public order offences.
- Articles 5 and 6 may be subject to the range of police powers dealing with stop and search, arrest and detention. The gathering of evidence may also have an impact on the operation of these Articles.
- Article 8 may be limited by the statutory powers allowing for the gathering and retention of personal data contained in the Investigatory Powers Act 2016.
- A claim for breach of confidence may engage Article 8.
- Article 10 is limited by the scope of the laws relating to obscenity and defamation.
- The laws relating to trespass place limits on the availability of Article 11.
- Article 10 may be limited by the law of harassment.

Chapter 36 Enforcement of human rights law

Introduction

Since the passage of the Human Rights Act 1998, claims relating to human rights have been directly enforceable through the domestic courts. They may also form the basis of judicial review hearings. If a claimant has exhausted all the possible national hearings without success, they may take the case to the European Court of Human Rights in Strasbourg.

36.1 The role of domestic courts

36.1.1 The role before 2000

The UK has been subject to the ECHR since it came into force in 1953. But it was not until 1966 that the UK recognised the power of the ECHR to hear complaints from UK citizens and allowed an individual claiming breach of a Convention right to bring a case in the ECtHR.

There had been a debate over many years whether the ECHR should be incorporated into English law. The consequences of non-incorporation were that an individual had to take an action in the ECtHR rather than in English courts but only when all domestic remedies had been exhausted. This was unsatisfactory for individuals and the Judiciary. For the Judiciary, it was unsatisfactory as it had to make decisions in line with UK law, knowing there was a strong possibility of the decision being overturned on appeal to the ECtHR. It was also a concern that the jurisprudence of the ECtHR was being developed without any input from UK law. However, there were means of indirectly incorporating the effect of the ECHR by interpreting legislation using the purposive approach and in the spirit of decisions of the ECtHR.

In 1997 a White Paper, 'Rights Brought Home: The Human Rights Bill' said:

> It takes on average five years to get an action into the ECtHR once all domestic remedies have been exhausted; and costs an average of £30,000. Bringing these rights home will mean that the British people will be able to argue for their rights in the British courts – without this

inordinate delay and cost. It will also mean that the rights will be brought much more fully into the jurisprudence of the courts throughout the UK and their interpretation will thus be far more subtly and powerfully woven into our law.

This resulted in the Human Rights Act 1998, which came into force in October 2000, incorporating the ECHR into UK law and allowing an individual to assert his convention rights in English courts.

36.1.2 The role after 2000

For courts, s 2(1) of HRA 1998 says:

> A court or tribunal determining a question which has arisen in connection with a Convention right must take into account any –
>
> a judgment, decision, declaration or advisory opinion of the European Court of Human Rights.

The effect of this section is to require courts to take into account any previous decisions of the ECtHR. This affects judicial precedent as it allows the overruling of any previous English precedent that was in conflict with the ECHR.

This provision was commented on by Lord Slynn in *R (Holding & Barnes plc) v Secretary of State for the Environment, Transport and the Regions* (2001):

> Your Lordships have been referred to many decisions of the ECtHR on Article 6 of the Convention. Although the Human Rights Act 1998 does not provide that a national court is bound by these decisions, it is obliged to take account of them so far as they are relevant. In the absence of some special circumstances it seems clear to me that the court should follow

any clear and constant jurisprudence of the ECtHR. If it does not do so there is at least a possibility that the case will go to that court which is likely in the ordinary case, to follow its own jurisprudence. **"**

In relation to legislation, s 3 HRA 1998 says:

" 1 So far as it is possible to do so, primary legislation and subordinate legislation must be read and given effect in a way which is compatible with the Convention rights. **"**

This section has the potential to invalidate previously accepted (pre-2000) interpretations of Acts which were made without reference to the ECHR.

By s 4, if the court is satisfied that a provision of primary legislation is incompatible with a Convention right, it may make a declaration of that incompatibility. Note that the court cannot strike down the legislation, as can happen in some other countries; it can only make a declaration, which will have to be considered by Parliament. This power of a declaration is limited to the High Court, the Court of Appeal and the Supreme Court.

Section 8 allows for the granting of a relief or remedy which the court finds appropriate. This can include damages, although it must only do so where this is necessary to afford just satisfaction. Damages are therefore seen as a last resort. Case law has tended to emphasise the importance of ending the violation rather than awarding compensation.

Case study

Anufrijeva and others v Southwark LBC and others [2004]

Various claimants sought damages for breaches of their human rights involving maladministration under a statutory duty.

Damages were not assessed in the same way as for a breach of obligation in civil law but rather in the same way as the ombudsman. It means that damages are more likely to be seen as a measure of last resort. Costs in such cases were substantially higher than any likely damages awarded.

36.2 Judicial review

Judicial review is a hearing, usually in the Administrative Court, in which the judge reviews the lawfulness of a decision or action, or a failure to act, by a public body exercising a public function. It is only available where there is no other effective means of challenge. The Administrative Court is part of the Queen's Bench Division of the High Court.

Judicial review is concerned with whether the law has been correctly applied, and the right procedures have been followed. The court's decision must be followed, but its role is supervisory only and any remedies are discretionary.

The process of judicial review is quite separate from the normal appeal process.

In order to succeed, the claimant will need to show that:

- a public body is under a legal duty to act or make a decision in a certain way and is unlawfully refusing or failing to do so, or
- a decision or action has been taken by a public body that is beyond the powers it is given by law.

36.2.1 Whose decisions can be challenged by judicial review?

Decisions made by public bodies in a public law capacity may be challenged by judicial review. Examples of the bodies whose decisions can be challenged are:

- government ministries and departments
- local authorities
- health authorities
- chief constables
- prison governors
- some tribunals (but not if an appeal is available to a higher tribunal or court).

If a public body is not exercising a public function, for example, where it is an employer, or there is a claim of negligence against it, its actions are governed by private laws of employment and tort, not public law. These actions will not be subject to judicial review.

If public functions are contracted out to a private company, for example, a private company that is running a prison, it is carrying out a public function. Its actions in the running of the prison are governed by public law and are therefore subject to judicial review.

36.2.2 Who can bring a judicial review action?

The person bringing the action has to have an interest in the decision being challenged. This is called 'locus standi' or 'standing'. That means that the claimant has to have sufficient connection to the subject matter of the claim.

36.2.3 Alternatives to a judicial review

If there are other ways of challenging a decision or a delay, such as an appeal, those avenues have to be followed. If there are issues of maladministration, then a case should be made to the relevant ombudsman.

36.2.4 Time limits

A judicial review case must be brought before the court quickly and, in any event, within three months of the decision or action being challenged.

36.2.5 The grounds for judicial review

Illegality

Public bodies can only generally do what the law allows them to do. The law setting out their powers is usually contained in legislation. Public bodies may also have guidance and policy on the exercise of their legal powers. Guidance and policy do not have to be followed, but they should be followed unless there is good reason not to. Public bodies must correctly understand and apply the law that regulates their decision-making powers. If they do not follow the law correctly, then action or failure to act will be unlawful. This is known as being '*ultra vires*' and the decision will be void and of no effect.

An action or decision may be unlawful if:
- the decision-maker had no power to make it
- the decision-maker exceeded the powers given to him
- it misapplies the law
- the correct procedure was not followed.

An interesting and dramatic example of this kind of case was demonstrated in *R (on the application of Miller) v The Prime Minister* (2019).

Case study

R (on the application of Miller) v The Prime Minister (2019)

The Prime Minister, Boris Johnson, advised the Queen to suspend Parliament from sitting for a prolonged period of time – between 9 and 12 September until 14 October 2019. This process, known as 'prorogation', was challenged in the courts by judicial review, and the Prime Minister's advice was found to be unlawful.

Look online

Watch the judgment from the judicial review case below.

www.supremecourt.uk/watch/uksc-2019-0192/ judgment.html

1. What did the case decide about the existence and use of the prerogative power to suspend Parliament?
2. Which of the three grounds for review is relevant to this case?

Case studies

Attorney-General v Fulham Corporation (1921)

An Act gave the Corporation the power to set up a clothes-washing facility for the local population to use. The Corporation set up a commercial laundry where its employees washed the residents' clothes for payment. This was decided by the court to be *ultra vires* and illegal as the Act did not give any power to the Corporation to wash clothes for others.

Agricultural, Horticultural and Forestry Training Board v Aylesbury Mushrooms (1973)

The government minister failed to follow the correct procedures when introducing a new regulation. The procedure allowed for consultations with appropriate organisations but this procedure was not followed. In particular, the minister failed to consult the Mushroom Growers' Association, which represented the industry. Government proposals requiring the establishment of a training board were, as a result, *ultra vires* and void.

Fairness

A public body should never act so unfairly that it amounts to an abuse of power. If there are set procedures laid down by law that it must follow in order to reach a decision, then it must follow them. Claimants must be given a fair hearing which includes knowing the case against them, and having the opportunity to present their case. A public body must be impartial and not biased. The public body must consult people it has a duty to consult before a decision is made, or who have a legitimate expectation that they will be consulted, perhaps because they have been consulted in the past or they have an obvious interest in a matter.

A public body must keep its promises unless there is a good reason not to.

Irrationality and proportionality

The court may quash a decision when it is considered to be so demonstrably unreasonable as to be 'irrational' or 'perverse'. In practice, this is very difficult to show and it is usually argued alongside other grounds. The test was given by Lord Greene in *Associated Provincial Picture Houses Ltd v Wednesbury Corporation* (1948):

> If a decision on a competent matter is so unreasonable that no reasonable authority could ever had come to it, then the courts can interfere ... but to prove a case of that kind would require something overwhelming.

The test is a lower one, of proportionality, where human rights issues are involved. The concept of proportionality involves a balancing exercise between the legitimate aims of the state on one hand, and the protection of the individual's rights and interests on the other. The test is whether the means employed to achieve the aim correspond to the importance of the aim, and whether they are necessary to achieve the aim.

Case study

R (Rogers) v Swindon NHS Trust (2006)

A woman with early stage breast cancer was prescribed the drug Herceptin by her GP. The NHS Trust refused to supply the drug as it said it was non-approved and because – it said – her case was not exceptional. The Trust was not able to put forward in court any clear reasons for allowing some patients to have the drug treatment and not others, and it was ruled as irrational and unreasonable.

36.2.6 The approach of the Administrative Court

There are special procedures for handling judicial review claims:
- It proceeds as far as possible on the basis of agreed facts. The rules do not easily accommodate cases where the facts are in dispute.
- Both parties are expected to co-operate with the court and to take an open approach to the issue.
- The court will sometimes act proactively – bringing issues into play which have not been raised by either party.

- Depending on the nature of the decision being challenged, the court may show a degree of deference to the decision-maker, given their democratic mandate, or special expertise; the court may be reluctant to intervene in matters of public policy or in areas where a specialist expertise is needed.

The orders that the court can make

When a case is being brought for judicial review, a remedy will also be asked for. The Administrative Court can give these remedies:
- Quashing order – an order which overturns or undoes a decision already made.
- Prohibiting order – this stops a public body from taking an unlawful decision or action it has not yet taken.
- Injunction – a temporary order requiring a public body to do something or not to do something until a final decision has been made.
- Mandatory order – this makes a public body do something the law says it has to do.
- Declaration – the court can state what the law is or what the parties have a right to do.
- Damages – these may be awarded where a public body has breached the claimant's human rights.

The remedies outlined above are discretionary: even if the court finds that a public body has acted wrongly, it does not have to grant a remedy. It might decide not to do so if it thinks the claimant's own conduct has been wrong or unreasonable; for example, where the claimant has delayed unreasonably, has not acted in good faith, or where a remedy would impede a public body's ability to deliver fair administration.

There is a right of appeal from the Administrative Court to the Court of Appeal. The party that wants to appeal must first ask permission from the Administrative Court and, if that is refused, it can ask permission from the Court of Appeal directly. A further appeal may lie to the Supreme Court if the case is one of public importance.

36.3 The role of the ECtHR

The court can deal with complaints from one state against another state and from an individual against a state. The ECtHR has been successful in dealing with a large number of cases dealing with Convention rights. However, a problem of being accessible to every individual within the states in the Council of Europe is the sheer number of cases referred to it. Delay undermines the work of the Court and access to justice for people who may be suffering a violation of their rights. Another criticism is that only about 6 per cent of cases referred to it are admitted for hearings.

Protocol 14 was brought into force in 2010. The current structure of dealing with a case is shown in Figure 36.1.

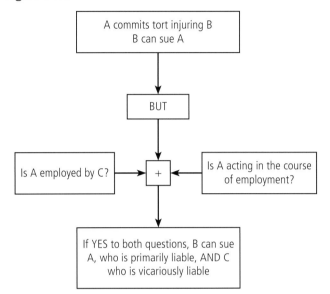

Figure 36.1 Claims procedure in the ECtHR

Some specific points about the court were introduced by Protocol 14:

- A judge will serve a single term of nine years.
- A single judge initially rules on the admissibility of the case – his (or her) decision is final.
- The three-judge committee can make a decision on the merits of the case if there is well-established case law on the issue.
- If the point has not previously been considered by the court, it must go before a chamber of seven judges.
- Infringement – if the Committee of Ministers (by 3–2 majority) finds a state refusing to abide by a judgment of the court, it can be referred back to the Grand Chamber for an infringement finding, which will then be referred back to the Committee to take action.
- An application is only admissible if the applicant has suffered a significant disadvantage.

Protocols 15 and 16 have been agreed in principle but are not yet in force. They were agreed after the Brighton Declaration on the future of the European Court of Human Rights 2012 in an attempt to reduce the number of cases referred. In 2014 there were 78,000 applications pending (down from 122,450 the year before). The focus of the protocols is subsidiarity – attempting to get referrals dealt with locally.

36.3.1 Criteria for admission

Under the ECHR, the admissibility criteria are as follows:

- The person referring the issue has to be a victim and directly affected by the act complained of (Article 34).
- Domestic remedies have to be exhausted (Article 35).
- An application has to be made within six months of the final decision of the domestic court – to be reduced to four months by Protocol 15.
- The complaint cannot be anonymous (Article 35).
- It cannot be substantially the same issue as a previously examined case (Article 35).
- It cannot be incompatible with the Convention, or ill-founded, or an abuse of process (Article 35).
- The individual must have suffered a significant disadvantage (Article 35).

36.3.2 The functions of the ECtHR

A living instrument

It is the role of the ECtHR to interpret the rights contained in the ECHR, and this interpretation should be followed in all Member States.

The court is not bound by previous precedent which allows it to develop human rights protections following changes in society; it can depart from previous approaches, which it has done in matters relating to the death penalty and prisoners' rights.

Effectiveness

The court has emphasised that it is important for individuals to be able to access Convention rights and that the court will enforce them.

Autonomy

The ECtHR can give an autonomous meaning to legal words that may be different from their meaning in Member States. This provides uniformity of meaning across all Member States and makes sure that states take their responsibilities seriously. This has been the case with the phrase 'criminal charge' in relation to Article 6.

Positive obligations

Convention rights are negative in the sense that they require the state not to act in a certain way that violates the right. However, the ECtHR interprets the Convention to require a state to take positive steps to prevent violations. This approach may place a burden on the state in terms of economic or social policy in order to meet its obligations, not so they are excessive.

The ECtHR has a vertical relationship between itself and the applicant who brings the case. Note that the applicant can only bring an action against a state and not another person. However, if a state is under a positive obligation, it may be required to control the behaviour of individuals within the state (such as in criminal law) or to take steps to protect a person from other individuals.

36.4 How well does the UK enforce ECHR rights?

A domestic court should take account of any previous decision of the ECtHR and this is supported by Lord Steyn's comments. Domestic courts can go further than the ECtHR but can also depart from ECtHR decisions. If a court is faced with a domestic decision that conflicts with a ECtHR decision, then it should follow the domestic decision and refer the case to appeal.

The procedures to enforce ECHR rights are in place but there are obstacles for an individual to enforce their rights before the ECtHR:
- Firstly, there is the necessity to exhaust all domestic remedies before bringing a claim to the ECtHR.

   Potentially, this can mean appealing all the way to the Supreme Court.
- There is also the issue of the cost of taking such action to the ECtHR when no state funding is available.
- Further, there will be the need to find a suitably specialised lawyer who is able and willing to pursue the claim.

It will have to be considered who a claim can be made against. Under s 6 HRA, the Act only applies to public bodies carrying out public functions. Increasingly, former public services such as residential care and social housing have been contracted out to private bodies, which are not covered by the Act.

Despite calls for legislation to define what a public authority is, it is often left to the courts to decide.

The provision can also operate to the detriment of an individual depending on who the claim is made against, even if the claim is based on similar grounds. This can be shown in *McDonald v McDonald* (2016) (see Chapter 34), where the vulnerable claimant was left without any remedy, whereas another claimant such as in *Connors v UK* (2004) was protected under the HRA.

Finally, even if a claim is accepted and reaches the ECtHR, the court may apply the margin of appreciation doctrine which considers the amount of discretion allowed to the state when considering alleged violations of qualified rights. For example:
- *Laskey, Jaggard and Brown v UK* (1997) (an appeal to the ECtHR from the case of *R v Brown* (1994): The court considered that outlawing homosexual sado-masochistic activity between consenting adults was acceptable for public health reasons.

   This doctrine can also be illustrated in the cases involving transgender men and women. In this area the court initially decided there was a lack of European consensus or standards, and it took over twenty years before a claim was accepted.

Case studies

Rees v United Kingdom (1987)

The applicant was a transgender man who wanted to change his name on his birth certificate. The ECtHR found there was a lack of common approach among Member States on this issue and found there was no violation of ECHR.

Cossey v United Kingdom (1991)

The claimant was a transgender woman who could not change her birth certificate sex to allow her to marry a man. The ECtHR found that there had been some developments in the approach of Member States since the decision in *Rees*, but not enough to rule that there had been a violation of Article 8.

Goodwin v United Kingdom (2002)

The applicant was transgender woman. In addition to the complaint of *Cossey*, she could not change her National Insurance details and was still regarded as male for pension purposes. She alleged this caused her to be discriminated against. The ECtHR recognised in this case that there had been scientific and social developments in the field since the previous decisions and that there had been a violation of Article 8.

Case name	Facts	Legal principle
R (on the application of Miller) (Appellant) v The Prime Minister (Respondent) (2019)	The Prime Minister advised the Queen to prorogue Parliament.	This was unlawful advice.
Attorney-General v Fulham Corporation (1921)	A council had power to set up a washing facility but instead set up a commercial laundry.	The council's decision was *ultra vires* and unlawful as it did not have the power to set up the laundry.
Agricultural, Horticultural and Forestry Training Board v Aylesbury Mushrooms (1973)	A minister did not consult the mushroom industry representatives before introducing new rules, as he was required to do.	The government proposals were *ultra vires* and void as required procedures had not been followed.
R (Rogers) v Swindon NHS Trust (2006)	An NHS trust refused to supply a cancer drug.	The decision was irrational and unreasonable as no reasons were put forward for the refusal. The decision was set aside.
Rees v United Kingdom (1981)	A transgender man wanted to change his name on his birth certificate.	Lack of common approach and no violation of ECHR.
Cossey v United Kingdom (1991)	A transgender woman could not change her birth certificate sex to marry a man.	Not enough development since *Rees* to rule a violation of Article 8.
Goodwin v United Kingdom (2002)	A transgender woman wanted to change her NI details for pension purposes.	There was a violation of Article 8 as there had been scientific and social developments.

Figure 3 6.2 Key cases: for the ECHR

Quick questions

1 Explain the advantages of enacting the Human Rights Act 1998.
2 What are the possible outcomes of a judicial review hearing?
3 What are 'positive obligations' arising from the ECHR?
4 Why is it important that the ECtHR can give an autonomous meaning to a word?
5 What is meant by the idea that the ECHR is a 'living instrument'? Can you give an example of this principle in action?

Summary

- The UK has been subject to the ECHR since 1953.
- Cases brought by a UK citizen alleging breach of a Convention right have only been heard by the ECtHR since 1966.
- Before 2000, a UK citizen had to exhaust all domestic court actions before bringing a claim before the ECtHR.
- Since 2000, a claim can be brought before a UK court alleging breach of a Convention right.
- The decision of a UK public body can be challenged by a judicial review action. The claimant has to have an interest in the action, which must be brought within three months of the decision being challenged.
- Actions can be brought on the grounds of illegality, unfairness or unreasonableness.
- If judicial review is granted, the Administrative Court can make various orders at its discretion.
- The ECtHR interprets the ECHR and is not bound by precedent.

Chapter 37 Evaluation of human rights protection and ideas for reform

Introduction

When considering the effectiveness of human rights protection in the UK, we have to look at both the broader issues concerning the relationship of the ECHR and the HRA below, and the effectiveness of individual Articles of the Convention.

37.1 An overview

Taking a human rights claim to the ECtHR can be a very time-consuming business.

A single case such as *Steel and Morris* concerned a libel action that started in 1997 but reached its conclusion in the ECHR in 2005. This is because the case first had to clear the domestic courts before being taken up to the ECtHR. There is also a huge caseload at the ECtHR which can delay the process even further.

Link

See Chapter 34, section 34.2.1, for more detail on *Steel and Morris v United Kingdom* (2005).

Look online

Have a look at the workload of the ECtHR via this link:

www.echr.coe.int/Documents/Stats_analysis_2019_ENG.pdf

Decisions of the ECtHR are not automatically incorporated into law in the UK. Where a decision has revealed an incompatible law, it is up to Parliament to decide whether to correct this or not. In *Hirst v United Kingdom (No. 2)* (2005), the ECtHR found that a blanket ban on prisoner voting was a violation of Article 3 of Protocol 1. A further five cases have all concluded the same but successive governments have refused to correct this anomaly, finding it politically difficult to do so.

This demonstrates that it ultimately down to Parliament to implement laws as it sees fit and that the decisions of the court are persuasive but not compulsory in nature. The English courts too may issue a declaration of incompatibility, but Parliament retains the discretion to act.

Look online

Read the factsheet issued by the press office of the ECtHR on prisoners' right to vote via this link:

www.echr.coe.int/Documents/FS_Prisoners_vote_ENG.pdf

Parliament can still pass law that is incompatible with the ECHR providing the government minister sponsoring the legislation signs a declaration of incompatibility. This has been done with anti-terrorism legislation introduced since 2001.

It is important to note that the European Court of Human Rights is completely separate from the European Court of Justice which hears cases relating to the European Union.

37.2 Evaluating Articles from the ECHR

37.2.1 Article 5

Article 5 contains fundamental values of liberty of the individual and the control of arbitrary state power. Any arrest or detention has to be for legal reasons, ensuring that a person only loses their freedom within strict rules that have the essential qualities of law and the rule of law.

These principles have been applied by the ECtHR, although it has been prepared to offer some flexibility to the state in cases such as the prevention of terrorism. This approach has been followed by domestic courts in relation to control orders that had to be replaced with the current system of Terrorism Prevention and Investigation Measures or TPIMs.

Both the ECtHR and domestic courts have insisted that minimum standards of the right of liberty and security of the person in Article 5 should not be abandoned. The UK government responded to the court's decisions in an attempt to ensure that legislation is compatible with Article 5, though this approach may alter if plans to repeal the HRA 1998 are pursued.

Violations of Article 5

Article 5 – the right to liberty and security – is second only to Article 6 – the right to a fair trial – in the number of violations registered at the European Court of Human Rights.

Between 1959 and 2019, there were 3,982 violations registered against states in respect of Article 5:

- The biggest transgressor was the Russian Federation with 1,121 violations, followed by Turkey with 771.
- The statistics reveal that protecting the right to freedom remains an urgent practical priority of the ECtHR.
- Over the same period, the UK registered a total of 70 violations.
- By comparison, Sweden and Denmark had only two registered violations each over the same period of time.

The fact that every state operates a criminal justice system which involves arresting and detaining large numbers of citizens means that the chances of breaching this article are high and emphasises the need to be vigilant.

Deprivations or restrictions?

Article 5 applies to deprivations of liberty. However there are many situations where the individual is not deprived of his liberty but only has it restricted. The difference between the two is one of degree (see *Guzzardi v Italy* (1981)).

Article 5 (1)(e) permits the detention of those with infectious diseases, persons of unsound mind, alcoholics, drug addicts and vagrants. The idea here is that such people may be dangerous to public safety or may need to be detained for their own benefit. However, it is clear that to detain a drug addict would require a high level of justification. The use of terms like 'vagrant' also shows that the language of the ECHR – now some 70 years old – can seem quite dated in places.

Article 5 and the vulnerable claimant

In relation to those of unsound mind, Article 5 creates a further dilemma. Should their rights be measured against other people with similar disabilities or should they have the same level of rights as everyone else? Lady Hale was unequivocal about this in *Cheshire West and Chester Council v P* (2014):

> The Supreme Court holds that people with mental disability have the same right to liberty as everyone else.

Her reasoning is that the vulnerability of such claimants means that courts should take a cautious approach when assessing any issue involving their rights. This shows, once again, the strength of the ECHR as a document which stands by the vulnerable, as well as everyone else.

This is the also the limb of Article 5(1) which allows for the kind of restrictions seen during the coronavirus pandemic. The use of extensive national lockdowns to control its spread has been the biggest collective restriction of liberty in the history of our country. Many people have been made much more aware of the need for any such restriction to be lawful and proportionate.

Special cases

TPIMs fall into a grey area. These orders, made by the Home Secretary, have the impact of placing quite stringent controls on the liberty of terror suspects. They are often subject to curfews and electronic tagging, as well as many other restrictions, despite not having been convicted of any offence. In some cases this has been seen to be a breach of Article 5. The deciding factor in such cases is the combination of confinement and severe restrictions on ordinary life.

Asylum seekers

Asylum seekers can be detained whilst their claim for asylum is being processed. This is seen as lawful as long as it is a proportionate measure and the claim is dealt with quickly. Many cases, however, do not pass this basic test.

37.2.2 Article 6

Article 6 provides for a fair trial in both criminal and civil cases.

As suggested above, the rights under Article 6 are the most violated under the Convention, with some 11,543 cases recorded by the ECtHR between 1959 and 2019. Statistics divide the rights into two main areas:

- the right to a fair trial, and
- the delay in proceedings.

Italy had 1,197 recorded violations for delaying proceedings and Turkey had 932 violations under the limb of right to a fair trial. By comparison, the UK clocked up 93 violations for breach of a fair trial and 30 further violations for delay.

All in all, there have been a total of 5,086 violations of the right to a fair trial and a further 5,884 violations registered under delay to proceedings (also Article 6), making this aspect of the Convention the most breached in practice.

Scope of Article 6

In evaluating the right it should be made clear that not all hearings are afforded the protection of Article 6. There are a number of notable civil exceptions that are not covered by the Convention. These include tax proceedings, immigration hearings and some school exclusions.

It is also not always clear as to the extent of the meaning of the term 'civil right'. This has been the subject of complex and lengthy legal argument.

Access to justice and Article 6

The concept of legal funding and the right to a fair trial have long been regarded as inextricably linked. A fair trial is only a theoretical right if the person relying on it cannot access the necessary funds to make it a practical reality.

The introduction of the reforms under the Legal Aid, Sentencing and Punishment of Offenders Act (LASPO) 2012 has had the effect of removing £279 million from civil legal aid, which resulted in 650,000 people losing funding for legal aid. This has led to widespread criticism of the Act. One effect in practical terms of the removal of such large sums of money was the creation of so-called 'legal aid deserts', areas of the country where firms of solicitors stopped offering legal aid altogether as it was no longer economically viable.

Open court and secret trials

One aspect of a fair trial is that it should be an open process. Increasingly, aspects of the trial are being held in secret – usually for reasons of national security. Such developments have the potential to undermine faith in the criminal justice system. In the case of *Incedal* (see Chapter 34 for more details), the Court of Appeal rejected the attempt to hold the entire trial in secret and insisted that parts of the trial were held in public and the two defendants were publicly named.

Evidence and equality of arms

Any analysis of the most serious miscarriage of justice cases, such as the Guildford Four and the Bridgewater case, shows that the most obvious cause of the miscarriage is often the failure to fully disclose evidence. This is partly due to an inherent imbalance in the framework for disclosure as set up in the Criminal Procedure and Investigations Act 1996.

These problems have become more acute in recent times due to the volume of available evidence in certain types of trial, which require huge amounts of police manpower to be processed properly, especially digital evidence existing in social media and on mobile phones. An example of this would the recent case of Liam Allen, in which a rape trial collapsed after key evidence came to light only when the trial was well underway.

Look online

Read this newspaper article to find out what happened in this case:

www.independent.co.uk/news/uk/crime/liam-allan-met-police-rape-accusation-false-evidence-disclosure-arrest-mistake-detectives-a8184916.html

37.2.3 Article 8

Article 8 is the most wide-ranging of the Articles of the Convention. It seeks to protect private life, family life, home and correspondence.

Many Article 8 decisions are an attempt to find a balance between the right and another Convention right. This will most often be Article 10. It is clear that in such situations there will be no obvious solution and the judges will be applying the doctrine of proportionality and margin of appreciation.

The scope of private life

This Article has been given a very wide, inclusive meaning by ECtHR, which it says in *Peck v UK* (2003) is not capable of exhaustive definition.

There is no general right to privacy in but Article 8 protects aspects of private life. It is developing on a case-by-case basis.

The case of *Pretty v UK* (2002) set out an explanation of the key areas covered by Article 8. It includes the following concepts:
- physical and social identity
- gender identification
- name
- sexual orientation.

It also covered a right to personal development and the right to establish and develop relationships with other human beings and the outside world. Personal autonomy was a very important underlying part of this principle. A further key issue was respect for human dignity and freedom.

Whilst the scope of this definition is clearly intended to open up Article 8 to the broadest possible range of situations, it has also been criticised for making the right too uncertain. In *R (Razgar) v Secretary of State for the Home Department* [2004], Lord Walker expressed his concerns that the words were unclear and that any rights developed from this could be seen as 'volatile and abstract'.

In other words, as the scope of Article 8 becomes wider, it becomes harder to define it accurately. This can lead to the possibility that the right may become harder to use in court to support a claim.

Celebrities and private life

It could be argued that those who have benefitted most are those able to bring high profile cases such as celebrities who aim to protect their private life. A string of cases including *Campbell v MGN* (2004), *Weller v Associated Newspapers* (2015) and more recently *Sir Cliff Richard v BBC* (2018) have strengthened the rights to privacy.

The print media would argue that this creates a danger of there being a 'chilling effect' around freedom of expression, which may make newspapers less willing to engage in investigative journalism. A gain under Article 8 can represent a loss under Article 10.

The issue of proportionality and balancing competing rights demonstrates that human rights law is an area where simple answers are not easy to find.

Sir Cliff Richard sued the BBC successfully over his right to privacy

The meaning of 'family life'

This has also been interpreted in a very broad sense by the ECtHR. The word 'family' has been interpreted in a flexible way, which has changed to stay in touch with societal change.
- The idea of a family is not simply based around the traditional arrangement of marriage but on 'biological and social responsibility' – *Kroon v Netherlands* (1995).
- The idea of a family includes grandparents, adoptive children, foster relationships, cohabiting couples and same-sex relationships.
- It has also been held to cover the ongoing ties which continue after a divorce – *Berrehab v Netherlands* (1989).
- The ECtHR has said that what constitutes a family depends on 'close family ties and is a matter of fact and degree' – *Lebbink v Netherlands* (2004). This is an example of the Court behaving in a pragmatic and inclusive manner.

These cases demonstrate the idea of the ECHR operating as a living instrument. A further example of this is seen in the approach of the ECtHR towards the environment.

Article 8 and the environment

The right to a healthy environment is not explicitly set out in the ECHR. In *Kryatakos v Greece* (2005), it was said that:

> neither Article 8 nor any of the other articles of the Convention are specifically designed to provide general protection of the environment as such.

Such rights are regarded as 'third generation rights'. However, in recent years there has been some movement by the ECtHR to cover such issues using the

Convention. Along with Articles 2, 3 and 6, there have been several attempts to use Article 8 in cases where an individual has suffered as a result of a degraded or dangerous environment. These cases have found infringements where the governments concerned have failed to properly regulate or enforce the law (see *Lopez Ostra v Spain* (1994)).

Such cases are not easy to prove. There has to be a causal link between the pollution and the effect on the individual and also a minimum level of severity before Article 8 would be engaged. The ECtHR has proved itself to be reluctant to develop this aspect of protection too far:

- In *Hatton v UK* (2003), a case about increasing light and noise pollution from Heathrow Airport, the Court was reluctant to attach any special status to environmental human rights.

Expanding the use of the Convention in this way shows how it can be used to reflect the changing landscape of human rights priorities. As climate change becomes a much more pressing issue, Article 8 may become more of a useful tool for protecting the right of the individual to have access to a healthy environment.

Technology and surveillance

One highly contentious area is the extent to which the police and other authorities are allowed to collect, store and retain biometric and other data.

Surveillance technology has become increasingly sophisticated in recent years and new forms of biometric data have been developed to assist with police investigations. This has led to challenges about the lawfulness of using, storing and retaining such data.

There are multiple examples of this in practice but two examples show how the courts view this data.

Facial recognition systems

The campaign group Liberty has long argued that automatic facial recognition (AFR) technology is 'an inherently oppressive and discriminatory surveillance tool'. In a recent case, *R (on the application of Edward Bridges) v The Chief Constable of South Wales Police* (2020), the Court of Appeal found that South Wales Police had failed to adequately take account of the discriminatory impact of facial recognition technology.

> **Look online**
>
> Read the case outline:
>
> www.libertyhumanrights.org.uk/issue/liberty-wins-ground-breaking-victory-against-facial-recognition-tech/

DNA retention

There is a delicate balance to be struck between the police being able to conduct their investigations thoroughly with sufficient evidence and the excessive retention of such evidence. *S and Marper v UK* (2008) said that the blanket retention of DNA was in breach of Article 8. This led to the government passing the Protection of Freedoms Act 2012, which set limits on this blanket retention. However, the campaign group Liberty has criticised the policy of retaining DNA, even where no charges are brought.

The issue is still a live issue as seen in the recent case of *Gaughran v the United Kingdom* (2020), where photographs, fingerprints and a DNA profile were retained after a conviction for a recordable offence of drink-driving.

The ECtHR observed that:

- The United Kingdom is one of the few Council of Europe jurisdictions to permit indefinite retention of DNA profiles, fingerprints and photographs of convicted persons.
- The applicant's biometric data and photographs were retained without reference to the seriousness of his offence and without regard to any continuing need to retain that data indefinitely.
- There is no provision allowing the applicant to apply to have the data concerning him deleted if conserving the data no longer appeared necessary
- The Court finds that the indiscriminate nature of the powers of retention of the DNA profile, fingerprints and photograph of the applicant as a person convicted of an offence, even if spent, without reference to the seriousness of the offence or the need for indefinite retention and in the absence of any real possibility of review, failed to strike a fair balance between the competing public and private interests.

Article 8 as an engine for change

Article 8 has been a positive engine for change in protecting the rights of both the vulnerable and minority groups, such as transgender rights. It encompasses mental as well as physical well-being, for example, *Bensaid v UK* (2001). It is the mark of a civilised society that it would seek to protect the rights of a vulnerable person such as one who is in the act of attempting suicide from having their image broadcast in public: *Peck v UK* (2003).

Article 8 has also been a useful vehicle for those campaigning for equality in relation to sexual orientation and gender rights. In other areas of protection, such as environmental human rights, the ECtHR has shown itself to be more cautious in its approach.

In addition, countries have a wide margin of appreciation in relation to this right and therefore will be able to avoid protecting rights in some situations. This could lead to the inconsistent interpretation of rights across the countries.

37.2.4 Article 10

This right has been called the 'cornerstone of a democratic society' and 'the bedrock of any democratic system' – *Lingens v Austria* (1986).

Importance of freedom of expression

This cannot be overstated. Freedom of expression is fundamental to the proper functioning of a democracy. This is because it allows individuals to participate fully in the process of debating and challenging ideas, which in turn helps to develop new ideas and approaches to politics.

When freedom of expression is restricted, this can have a chilling effect on levels of participation in democracy, which may, for example, make newspapers less willing to engage in investigative journalism. Rather than engaging with the process, individuals may become alienated from it and begin to see themselves as having no stake in the process. As freedom of expression is important in relation to other rights, such as the right to protest, when it is restricted then these other rights also are also impacted.

The Human Rights Act also recognises the significance of Article 10 rights. Section 12 singles this right out for particular consideration in any case which may result in the limitation of freedom of expression.

It is important to stress that freedom of expression has two main aspects:

- the right to give information, and
- the right to receive information.

When a person's right to give information is restricted, then the right of others to hear this is also limited. The right is a very broad right. It includes the right to say things which some may find shocking or offensive.

> The right to free expression would be meaningless if it only protected certain types of expression. So Article 10 protects both popular and unpopular expression – including speech that might shock others – subject to certain limitations.

Source: Liberty website

Where exactly the boundary lies between shocking forms of expression and unlawful ones is often difficult to assess exactly. A recent example would be when comedian Jo Brand made a joke which was felt by some to overstep this boundary.

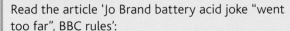

Activity

Read the article 'Jo Brand battery acid joke "went too far", BBC rules':

www.bbc.co.uk/news/entertainment-arts-49508231

- What is your view of Jo Brand's comment?
- Does this fall within Article 10 freedom of expression or should it be seen as unlawful?

States have a margin of appreciation in the way that Article 10 is applied and this allows them to take into account national and cultural priorities when deciding a case: *Handyside v UK* (1976).

One advantage of this is that the Convention is seen to be flexible to the needs of the state. It is also possible to argue that a wide margin of appreciation has the effect of undermining the Convention by giving too much discretionary power to the state to limit expression.

High and low value forms of expression

The margin of appreciation is slightly more complex in relation to Article 10 than other Articles. This is due to the fact that different forms of expression attract different levels of protection.

- Political, religious and public expression are seen as high value forms of expression and the margin of appreciation in such cases will be narrow. This allows the state much less wiggle room in applying the law.
- Where the expression is seen as low value, such as in artistic expression and commercial expression, then the margin of expression is wide and the state may more easily supress or limit expression.

In *Otto-Preminger-Institut v Austria* (1995), the state chose to prioritise Article 9, freedom of religion, over Article 10, artistic expression, in relation to a religiously offensive film. Such a solution might not be appropriate in other states. The ECtHR has said that artistic expression is also important within a democracy.

Hate speech and incitement to hatred

Article 10 and the internet

Access to the internet has been seen as an Article 10 right: *Yildirim v Turkey* (2013).

Denial of access to the internet or closure of social media accounts could be seen to be a form of digital 'no platforming'. This area is very controversial as social media platforms such as Facebook and Twitter are under pressure to remove harmful content, and content that could be seen as hate speech or incitement to hatred. The deletion of accounts can also be seen as quite a drastic limitation of freedom of speech and can lead to accusations of censorship.

> ### Extension activity
>
> Read the following article:
>
> **www.theguardian.com/us-news/2021/jan/11/opinion-divided-over-trump-being-banned-from-social-media**
>
> What are the arguments for and against denying people access to social media platforms?

> ### Activity
>
> David Icke, a former footballer and commentator, had his YouTube, Facebook and Twitter accounts suspended permanently for spreading multiple conspiracy theories, including the claim that 5G is a cause of Coronavirus, as well as many other unsubstantiated stories.
>
> Read the article on the BBC website and decide whether you think the deletion was justified.
>
> 'Twitter bans David Icke over Covid misinformation': **www.bbc.co.uk/news/technology-54804240**

> ### Look online
>
> Explore the importance of journalistic freedom of expression by reading online summaries of these cases:
> 1 *Goodwin v United Kingdom* (1996) – **https://eachother.org.uk/stories/protect-the-source/**
> 2 *Sunday Times v United Kingdom* (1979) – **https://eachother.org.uk/stories/free-to-report/**

37.2.5 Article 11

A qualified right

Unlike Articles 8 and 10, this qualified right to assembly and association is a collective right as it protects the rights of individuals to join together to take part in collective action.

As with other qualified rights, the court then has to decide whether the interference is justified by the state using the principles of proportionality and margin of appreciation. The limitations must be prescribed by law and necessary in a democratic society.

The assembly must be a peaceful one to have the positive obligation of protection of those assembling peacefully. This would include protection from violence or fear of violence from a counter-demonstration. Any counter-demonstration would also have to be protected, providing it is peaceful.

In the UK, two clashing demonstrations are usually kept apart by the police. This potentially affects an individual's freedom generally as they may be prevented from going where they wish to go or, indeed, be prevented from going anywhere. This can then lead to kettling, excessive force by the authorities or other interferences with human rights, as we have seen.

- The case of *Plattform 'Ärzte für das Leben' v Austria* (1988) shows that the protection is not an absolute guarantee, but does raise the question whether the protection given is sufficient and is given even-handedly to opposing views.
- In *Fáber v Hungary* (2012), a case based on Article 10, the court ruled that Hungary was wrong to arrest and fine Fáber, who had waved a flag with Fascist connotations less than 100 metres away from an anti-racism demonstration. It could be argued that this was sufficient protection for the anti-racist demonstration but could be said to be excessive force being used against Fáber with respect to his demonstration.

Police powers and the right to demonstrate

Restrictions on the right to demonstrate are always controversial and the courts have to rule on the balance between protecting the workers at the site, the right to protest, the need to protect public order and the rights of others.

The anti-fracking protests in North Yorkshire in 2017 are an obvious example of the different interests involved:
- the protestors who believe fracking is bad for the environment
- people who wish to travel past the protest site
- those living in the locality whose lives are disrupted
- those who have to pay for the police presence
- the disruption and cost to the fracking business
- those supplying materials to the fracking site.

Depending on your point of view, there is always an argument that the state through the police did or did not do enough.

The state is obliged to deal with these conflicting interests using the principle of proportionality. Proportionality is the balance between the individual right and the community. The criteria used for this include the effectiveness of the measures taken, the balance achieved, whether the actions of the state operate in the least intrusive manner possible and whether the effect is to deprive the individual of the right under Article 11.

Variation in the margin of appreciation between different states

We have seen that the Council of Europe has commented unfavourably on the variation in the margin of appreciation in different states, with particular reference to Spain, Turkey and Russia. It is interesting to note that in all these countries there has been, arguably, a further erosion of human rights, particularly under Article 11.

People turn to Article 11 when the state attempts to stop a demonstration going ahead, takes steps in advance to disrupt a demonstration or stores personal information on those taking part.

Where there has been a violation of Article 11, the state may then have to change its law to ensure no further breach of the convention. This is often a lengthy process in the UK and it can be argued that remedying the law is not seen as a serious and urgent matter by the UK government. It would be interesting to speculate about the changes to police powers that have occurred since the *Laporte* decision in 2006.

37.3 The Human Rights Act 1998

The biggest single advantage of the HRA 1998 was that it allowed individuals to pursue human rights claims directly in the domestic courts for the first time since the ECHR was passed in 1950.

Element	Changes introduced by HRA 1998
Ministers	<ul><li>Section 19 requires ministers to consider whether any legislation they are proposing is compatible with human rights and to make a statement of compatibility.</li><li>The statement has no legal effect but is a clear signal that human rights issues should be considered from an early stage.</li></ul>
Judges	<ul><li>Section 2 requires courts to 'take into account' decisions of the ECtHR when deciding cases that are connected with human rights. The Strasbourg decisions therefore are not automatically part of our domestic precedent but are persuasive in nature.</li><li>In fact, where there is a clash between the principles laid down by the ECtHR and domestic law, then the domestic principles should be followed. The effect of the HRA is, therefore, to encourage consideration of human rights issues at all stages of the legal process but not to tie the hands of the domestic courts or Parliament.</li></ul>
Universalism	<ul><li>The Human Rights Act 1998 has, since its inception in 2000, provided a new dynamism in areas of the law where protections were otherwise slow to emerge.</li><li>This can be seen in cases protecting the vulnerable or disempowered such as care home residents, the mentally ill, or in the development of LGBTQ rights.</li><li>Other areas have been seen to be more controversial, such as protection for the rights of asylum seekers, prisoner voting rights or the rights of suspected terrorists.</li><li>Universal rights means not only protecting those within society who are seen as merit-worthy, but also those who are seen as morally unworthy or unpopular.</li><li>Attempts to filter out rights from one group ultimately only succeed in diminishing the power of human rights for all. This is the difficulty that critics of the HRA struggle to come to terms with.</li></ul>
Difficult cases	<ul><li>Cases such as *Othman (Abu Qatada) v UK* (2012) (where the claimant, a terror suspect, was said to have abused the system by using repeated legal challenges under the HRA in an attempt to resist extradition on terrorism charges) have been used to argue that the whole framework of human rights is somehow at fault.</li><li>This case, and *R (on the application of Begum) (Respondent) v Secretary of State for the Home Department (Appellant)* (2020), are rare. They have to be set against the numerous cases where human rights have been protected and extended, such as *Cheshire West and Chester Council* (2014), upholding the rights of those with mental incapacity.</li></ul>

Figure 37.1 Changes introduced by HRA 1998

- Research the case of *R (on the application of Begum) (Respondent) v Secretary of State for the Home Department (Appellant)* (2020) – undecided at the time of publication.
- How many cases can you find which show that human rights have developed in a positive way to protect vulnerable, disempowered or minority groups within society?

37.3.1 Ideas for reform: a UK Bill of Rights?

Despite the obvious advantages of having domestic human rights legislation, many argue that the HRA should be scrapped in favour of a new British Bill of Rights.

Consider the following:
- Which aspects of the HRA 1998 would you consider scrapping or reforming?
- How would you adapt the Act?
- What would you replace it with?

A commission on a Bill of Rights 2012 was set up by the Conservative government in 2012, following an election manifesto promise. It reported in 2014 but failed to reach consensus, leading to a split report. Two Conservative Members, Lord Faulks QC and Jonathan Fisher QC, argued for withdrawing from the ECHR, and said (in their minority view):

> There are strong arguments that the cause of human rights, both in the UK and internationally, would be better served by withdrawal from the Convention ...

Seven members suggested there should be a new bill in principle, but could not agree precisely what form it might take. The chairman of the commission, Sir Leigh Lewis went with the majority view.

He said:

> Our current human rights structures do not enjoy great public support and ownership and are seen very much as someone else's creation [from abroad]. We were struck by the fact that [within Europe] we are unique in neither having our own constitution nor our own Bill of Rights decided by our own parliament.

However, the idea that the ECHR is somehow the creation of foreign lawyers is a relatively new idea that would have seemed strange at the time of drafting. This is due to the fact that the Convention was largely drafted with the full assistance of British lawyers and, according to Francesca Klug (see below), 'is as British as custard'.

In a minority view, two of the commission members, Philippe Sands QC, a Liberal Democrat adviser, and the Labour peer Baroness Kennedy QC, opposed the introduction of a UK Bill of Rights for fear it would be used to lever the UK out of the ECHR. Their view was: 'We believe that such a path would be catastrophic for the UK, for Europe and for the protection of human rights around the world.'

Francesca Klug, a professor and expert in human rights laws, said:

> There is no political appetite to [change the Human Rights Act] which is only 12 years old, maintains parliamentary sovereignty and is compatible with remaining within the ECHR. That is the gist of over 80 per cent of the responses to the commission's consultation, most of which maintain that the HRA is a UK Bill of Rights in all but name.

Ben Emmerson QC, said:

> The Human Rights Act has been interpreted and applied by British judges in a balanced and intelligent way that reflects British legal traditions, and the judgments of our supreme court now exert a powerful influence over the court in Strasbourg precisely because they are interpreting the same set of rights, but with a distinctively British character.

His view was that, 'to embark on an ill-thought-through process of altering the language and content of our human rights legislation at this time is irresponsible madness'.

Stephen Bowen, director of the British Institute of Human Rights, said:

> The commission asked for the public's views about whether we need a Bill of Rights, and the message from the majority was clear: the Human Rights Act is our Bill of Rights, and should remain part of our law.

The end result was a recommendation that nothing should be altered until after the outcome of the Scottish referendum on independence in 2014, when a constitutional convention should be held. However, after this vote came the 2015 General Election and in 2016 the vote on the UK's continued membership of the EU. This vote, in favour of withdrawing from the EU, appears to have put the issue of reform of the HRA to one side and no further action is proposed at this time.

A British Bill of Rights

If a British Bill of Rights were to be implemented, it would see that the UK would continue to respect the rights within ECHR. There would be specific limitations in respect of deportation and immigration cases, which might involve a redefining of the meaning of terms such as 'private life' or 'degrading treatment'. Whether this is a path the government wishes to tread remains to be seen.

Devolution and reform

Any reform of the HRA would have a significant impact on the devolution arrangements in Scotland, Wales and Northern Ireland, as respect for the Human Rights Act was effectively embedded into the devolution arrangements.

Of more concern would be the effect on the Good Friday Agreement, which brought peace to Northern Ireland, as repealing the Act would undermine this settlement too.

Quick questions

1. What are the arguments for and against prisoners having the vote?
2. Discuss whether TPIMs represent an unacceptable invasion of the right to liberty or a practical system designed to prevent acts of terror.
3. Article 6 is the most violated of all of the Convention rights. Can you explain why this is?
4. It has been said that the term 'private life' is not capable of exhaustive definition. Does this present a problem for the protection of rights under Article 8?
5. Discuss the arguments for and against the use of the concept of the margin of appreciation in deciding human rights cases.

Summary

- There are areas not expressly catered for by Article 5 such as TPIMs and Kettling which means the protection in these cases is less certain.
  - The right to liberty is not dependent on a person's status. A mentally incapacitated person has the same right to liberty as everyone else.
- Article 6 rights are the most violated of all the Convention rights, particularly relating to a delay of proceedings.
  - A number of hearings are not covered by the right to a fair trial. These include tax and immigration hearings.
  - The financial limitations imposed by the LASPO have resulted in a dramatic fall in the availability of legal aid and led to the creation of 'legal aid deserts', restricting access to justice.
  - A recent increase in the use of secret trials and anonymous witnesses has raised concerns about fairness.
- Article 8: the term 'private life' is very broadly defined under the Convention which can be seen as both positive in scope but also negative in the sense of being 'volatile and abstract'.
  - The greater the protection afforded under Article 8 the more of a 'chilling effect' this can have on the freedom of journalists under Article 10. There is a clear trade-off between these two rights.

- Article 8 provides ample evidence of the concept of the 'living instrument' doctrine of the ECtHR as it very frequently evolves to meet social change.
- Article 10 rights of freedom of expression are inextricably linked with the rights needed in a democratic society.
  - Access to the internet has been seen as a human right under Article 10. Denying people access to social media platforms by banning them is a controversial limitation of freedom of expression.
- Article 11 rights are inextricably linked with the rights under Article 10 and must be considered together.
  - Some states have been accused of using the margin of appreciation to limit the availability of rights under article 11.
  - Police powers to limit the right to peaceful assembly should only be used where it is necessary and proportionate to do so. This is often a controversial area of law.

Section 7

THE LAW OF CONTRACT

Chapter 38 Contract law rules and theory

Introduction

A contract can be defined as an agreement that the law will enforce. Contract law is largely derived from the common law (case law).

38.1 An outline of the rules of the law of contract

The rules for contract law have been developed over many years – we will consider *Pinnel*'s case (1602) later. Originally, judges travelled the land making judgments to settle disputes. Cases involving the buying and selling of goods were often decided according to local rules or customs. These rules were gradually extended over wider areas, eventually becoming the common law of the land. These were developed and refined into the modern law of contract.

> **Key term**
>
> Contract – a contract is an agreement the law will enforce.

The general rule of contract law is that only a party to a contract can take legal action to enforce it.

Contract law follows the rules for other civil cases: if a party to the contract takes legal action, the burden of proof is on the claimant, who must prove their case against the defendant on the balance of probabilities.

Some statutes deal with problems that have arisen in the common law:

- The Sale of Goods Act 1979 is a modern incarnation of the Sale of Goods Act 1893. This first Act was created by Parliament to reflect Victorian case law on the sale of goods, to codify commercial law so that it could easily be used throughout the world.
- European law has influenced today's contract law by making regulations that are often designed to help consumers. The Unfair Terms in Consumer Contracts Regulations 1999 are one example. These regulations are now subsumed in the Consumer Rights Act 2015, which also provides a range of different remedies.

Equity provides some ways of overcoming aspects of inherent unfairness in the common law. We can see this, for example, with equitable, discretionary, remedies available for breach of contract used where the main remedy of damages is inappropriate.

Below is a summary of the rules for the different aspects of contract law required for the OCR specification. You will need to apply and evaluate the first two areas.

- **Formation** – this is about making an agreement to do something, for example, buy a car. Formation is governed by the principle of privity of contract. An agreement requires an offer and acceptance, an intention to create legal relations and the consideration needed for a valid contract.
- **The terms of the contract** – these are the obligations and rights of each party to the contract. The terms for buying a car would be for one party to pay the agreed price for the car and for the other party to hand over legal ownership of the car. However, some terms are specifically agreed by the parties, while others are implied; that is, they are part of the contract whether or not the parties have thought about it.
- **The validity of that agreement** – this area covers factors that may make a contract invalid (called 'vitiating factors'). Here we are considering the law of misrepresentation and economic duress. Misrepresentation might be where the seller of the car stated its mileage was 20,000 when in fact it was 80,000.

- **Discharge of contract** – this involves examining exactly what amounts to performance of a contract, when the contract is breached (broken) through non- or part-performance, and what happens when performance of the contract is prevented by events outside the control of either party.
- **Remedies** – what a party to the contract is entitled to when the contract has been breached or affected by a vitiating factor.

Look online

XYcoms Ltd have failed to deliver you a new phone and have failed to return your payment of £600.

Look at **www.gov.uk/make-court-claim-for-money** and set out what information you need to start a court claim against them.

How easy do you think this is?

38.2 The theory of the law of contract

38.2.1 Freedom of contract theory and inequality of bargaining power

The usual or classical principle of the common law is freedom of contract and the sanctity of contracts.

Under this theory, contract law is based on making promises. An agreement requires the making of a promise in return for a promise (or for performance), and if an agreement is recognised as a contract in law, the law recognises a contracting party as legally obliged to perform their promise.

Promises relate to things to be done or refrained from, either now or in the future. This is the basis of formation of contract and the concept of consideration.

One argument against allowing past consideration (see later) as a valid form of consideration, is to prevent opening the floodgates to dubious cases. This would seem a poor argument, as few minor cases would ever go to court given the cost of litigation. The consequences of breach may be agreed in the contract itself, or negotiated after breach and even during litigation.

The theory of freedom of contract can lead to injustice where there is inequality of bargaining power. An individual cannot negotiate terms with large organisations. Few people read the terms and conditions of trading when making an online contract – think of Amazon or eBay. There is some protection through legislation such as the Consumer Rights Act 2015 and the Unfair Contract terms Act 1977.

38.2.2 Reliance theory

Reliance theories see contractual obligations as being imposed by the law to ensure that those induced to rely upon other parties are not made worse off as a consequence. Under the reliance theory, an agreement specifies the performance of a contracting party. The contract is not based on promising but on what is described as the assumption of responsibility. Each party assumes responsibility for reliance incurred by the other party on the assumption that the specified performance will be provided.

The classical theory can be seen as, 'I promise to do this, and you promise to do that'. Reliance theory can be seen as: 'We will proceed on the assumption that I am to do this and you are to do that. I do not promise that I will do this but I accept responsibility for your reliance on the assumption that I will do it. Similarly, you will accept responsibility for my reliance in the same way.'

The appropriate measure of damages to protect the interest of a promisee under the classical theory is that the promisee must be entitled to the value of the performance, less the saving of the cost of his own performance. The appropriate measure of damages to satisfy the reliance interest should not exceed the expectation measure. A party will not make a contract unless he or she considers at the time of the contract that the value to of the contract to him or her will be at least equal to whatever he or she gives up.

In contract law, specific performance is not available as a matter of course, but only where damages are inadequate. However, if the defendant is under a legal obligation to perform why should they not, as a rule, be ordered to carry it out? If the claimant is entitled to performance, they should be able to at least decide whether to claim damages or to insist on specific performance. Under the reliance theory, each party is liable to satisfy the reliance interest of the other party rather than a duty to perform the contract. This means there would be no general right to specific performance from the nature of the agreement. The decision whether damages are adequate to protect the reliance interest, or whether only specific performance can do so has to be taken by the court.

38.2.3 Certainty of terms and consumer protection

Whichever of the above theories is considered, the agreed terms must be certain. This is a principle in contract law.

An offer must be certain before it can be accepted, so in the case of *Guthing v Lynn* (1831), the offer to pay £5 more for a horse if it was 'lucky' was too vague and not an offer.

This leads to problems where two businesses try to deal with each other, but both businesses have their own conditions of trading. It may not be clear which set of contract terms apply.

If there is no certainty, there would appear to be no contract, but in many cases the parties have gone on with the deal without formally agreeing whose terms are the contract terms. This can be seen in *Butler Machine Tool Co. Ltd v Ex-Cell-O Corporation* (1979), where Lord Denning suggested that the *subjective* view of the contract terms that the parties to the contract have is replaced by an *objective* view that the parties must have agreed, as is the case with implied terms in a contract. *Reveille Independent LLC v Anotech International (UK) Ltd* (2016) is another example of the courts working out the actual terms of a contract from the dealings between the parties.

Implied terms are also placed in a contract that neither party may have agreed. This is apparent in the way in which the law protects consumers. The Consumer Rights Act 2015 is a major example of this, but the common law approach can be seen in cases such as *Olley v Marlborough Court Hotel* (1949).

This is moving away from the idea that a contract is a freely negotiated deal under the freedom of contract theory, although the courts are very careful when departing from the common law principle of freedom of contract. They will therefore be reluctant to imply terms into a contract, especially in cases where this would set a general implication of a term into all similar contracts.

It could be argued that the courts try to avoid this because of the criticism of judge-made law, and the argument that only Parliament should make changes to the law. However, when Parliament changes the law, we tend to get a confusing situation where there is clarity and extension of rights in one situation, for example, the Consumer Rights Act 2015, but not in other situations. For example, this legislation does not protect the purchaser of goods in a private sale, and does not state whether an online purchase (such as on eBay) is a private sale.

38.2.4 Good faith

The ideas of reliance and responsibility are also present in English contract law.

For contracts and commerce to work, both parties are expected to do what they said they will do. If they do not do so, then the law will settle the dispute. Criminal sanctions are reserved for the worst cases (fraud).

Contract law applies corrective justice. Damages are assessed on the loss of bargain: the claimant is placed in the position they would have been in had the contract been performed. In other words, both parties entered the contract relying on each other to perform their obligations, and responsibility for the losses is taken by the person at fault.

However, parties can only recover reasonable losses, as can be seen in *Victoria Laundry v Newman* (1949).

Link

See Chapter 43 for this case and remedies for damage.

In *Wellesley Partners LLP v Withers LLP* (2015), the basic rule in contract was summarised:

A contract breaker is liable for damage resulting from his breach if, at the time of making the contract, a reasonable person in his shoes would have had damage of that kind in mind as not unlikely to result from a breach.

This is another objective test that may not, therefore, reflect the freedom of contract principle. It seems to indicate that contracts are expected to be made between the parties in good faith.

Good faith is incorporated as an underlying principle in contracts of insurance, where all material facts must be disclosed if there is not to be a misrepresentation.

However, imposing a duty of good faith in all contracts would run contrary to the general principle of contract law. Businesses enter into contracts, and their aim is to make as much profit as possible within a competitive market, subject to the law as it stands at the time. However, contract parties are involved in a competitive situation and cannot be expected to disclose every aspect of their business deal.

What the law does is to attempt to balance the interests of the parties to a contract by legislation, interpretation of the contract and the common law with a smattering of equity. The results of this lack certainty.

Article 7 of the United Nations Convention on Contracts for the International Sale of Goods (1980) states:

> In the interpretation of this Convention, regard is to be had to its international character and to the need to promote uniformity in its application and the observance of good faith in international trade.

Most international commercial contracts state as a term of the contract that English law will apply, and disputes will be settled in accordance with English law in London.

For contracts to work, both parties are expected to do what they said they will do

38.2.5 Balancing interests and justice

Judges often have to balance competing interests in their judgments. This can lead to unusual results.

Parliament also sets out to balance rights between contracting parties, which seems to go against the theory of freedom of contract. Parties to a contract may try to limit their liability by relying upon exclusion clauses. The traditional rule of *caveat emptor* ('let the buyer beware') could operate harshly against the interests of the weaker bargaining party.

There are apparently conflicting decisions such as:
- *Olley v Marlborough Court Hotel* (1949) – the exclusion clause was invalid as it had not been brought to Mrs Olley's attention when she made the contract.
- *Thompson v LMS Railway* (1930) – an exclusion clause was incorporated even though she could not read the printed terms which referred to another document she would have had to locate.

Link

See Chapter 40 for case details for *Olley* and *Thompson*.

If we are aware of a risk and take it, why should death and personal injury not be excluded from a voluntary contract? This cannot be excluded under the Unfair Contract Terms Act 1977.

As only a party to a contract can take legal action on it, this can lead to injustice, despite the legal position of an agent.

Key term

Agent – a person who is authorised to act for another (the principal) in the making of a contract with third parties. The resulting contract is made between the principal and the third party, and not with the agent.

- In *Jackson v Horizon Holidays* (1975), the claimant succeeded in seeking damages for himself and for members of his family after a package holiday failed to match the advertised description, even though only he, and not his family members, had signed the contract. This case, amongst others, led to the Contract (Rights of Third Parties) Act 1999. This Act modified the law by allowing third parties to make a claim where the contract expressly provided for it, or where the contract purported to confer a benefit on them.
- This Act remedied obvious injustices such as *Tweddle v Atkinson* (1861), but the provisions of the Act are frequently excluded in standard form contracts and so the benefit of the Act is largely negated for consumers.

Link

See Chapter 39 for case details for *Jackson* and *Tweddle*.

The law regarding frustration of contract has also been modified by Parliament. The Law Reform (Frustrated Contracts) Act 1943 enabled the courts to distribute the losses more fairly between the parties: the court may order 'a just sum' to be paid, where either expenses have been incurred or a valuable benefit obtained.

38.2.6 The principle of fault

The principle of fault has two distinct elements:
1 the degree of responsibility for actions
2 the liability under the law.

A misrepresentation is an untrue statement of fact made by one party to the contract, which encourages the other party to enter into the contract. It is a vitiating factor in a contract and different remedies are available, depending on the perceived amount of fault and the type of misrepresentation – either innocent, negligent or fraudulent.

Sometimes statements are recognised as no more than advertising slogans and so do not create liability. If the statement is considered one of fact rather than opinion, it can give rise to liability. This happened in *Smith v Land and House Property* (1884).

Case study

Smith v Land and House Property (1884)

A tenant was described by his landlord, the defendant, as 'most desirable'. In fact, the tenant was completely unreliable, and the defendant knew he was likely to be made bankrupt in the near future. As the other party relied upon this misrepresentation, the maker of the statement could be sued; he was at fault for the statement and therefore for the loss it caused.

Generally, silence will not amount to misrepresentation. After all, there is freedom of contract, and if you do not ask about something, there is no obligation to be told about it unless it is a contract where good faith is required, such as a contract of insurance.

Look online

Look at this guide to insurance and consider how this reinforces the existing law: **www.simplybusiness.co.uk/legal/insurance-act-2015/**

- *With v O'Flanagan* (1936) (see Chapter 41 for details): If there is a deliberate attempt to conceal an important fact, there will be liability.
- *Poussard v Spiers and Pond* (1876) and *Bettini v Gye* (1876) (see Chapter 40 for details): Breach of contract depends on the level of fault to work out the injured party's rights. Whether there is a breach of a condition or a breach of warranty will determine whether a person can end the contract or must continue it, but can claim some compensation.

In 1995, the Law Commission considered the situation where there could be punitive damages.

Key term

Punitive damages – damages greater than mere compensation. The aim is to punish the defendant for their wrongful conduct and to deter them and others from acting similarly in the future.

The recommendation was that punitive damages must not be awarded for breach of contract. They were never available for breach of contract, no matter how deliberate the breach. This was seen in the case of *Addis v Gramophone Co. Ltd* (1909). However, the law on penalty clauses in contract seems to allow what might appear to be punitive damages, subject to the judge's view as to what is commercially justifiable.

- In *Parking Eye v Beavis* (2015), a penalty charge of £85 for parking was upheld by the court. Lords Sumption and Neuberger emphasised the context in which the contract was made in reaching their decision:

> The penalty rule is an interference with freedom of contract. In a negotiated contract between properly advised parties of comparable bargaining power, the strong initial presumption must be that the parties themselves are the best judges of what is legitimate in a provision dealing with the consequences of breach.

Link

See Chapter 43 for details of *Addis* and *Parking Eye*.

38.2.7 Morality and the law of contract

We have explored the relationship between morality and the law in Chapter 29. Morality is most obviously intertwined with criminal law, but aspects of contract law are also affected by morality.

Contracts can be declared void because of their association with immorality. In *Pearce v Brooks* (1866), a cab owner's contract with a prostitute to use his cabs for her trade was void because it was a contract for immoral purposes.

Other examples of contracts being void because of illegality include:

- *Parkinson v The College of Ambulance* (1925): the whole purpose of the contract was to buy an honour (knighthood, OBE, etc.) – that is, corruption in public life.

- *Dann v Curzon* (1910): the courts were not prepared to enforce a contract to commit a tort or a crime.
- *Napier v National Business Agency* (1951): the courts will not allow parties to take advantage of contracts that set out to defraud.

Today, there are frequent press reports about contracts obtained as a result of bribery. Should these be illegal and unenforceable in the courts? Contracts made to hide the true tax situation may be viewed as immoral, but are only illegal if involving tax evasion rather than tax avoidance. The same is true for methods to avoid contractual obligations with respect to wages and minimum wage regulation. Economic duress may be considered immoral (as would physical duress, as in *Welch v Cheeseman* (1974) where property was sold at an undervalue as a result of threats by the owner's violent partner).

Equitable remedies are a reflection of morality and justice in contract law. The area of fraudulent misrepresentation developed in *Derry v Peek* (1889) is based on the tort of deceit but still reflects the view in contract law that it would be wrong to allow a contract to be obtained by fraud.

Freedom of contract allows any contract to be made, subject to illegality. Some contracts are so outrageous that they are immoral, but they are rarely illegal. Under the Victorian Moneylenders Acts, the courts could not enforce a contract to lend money with a rate of interest above 50 per cent. Today we allow much higher rates of interest to be used and enforced, despite most religions taking a strong view about charging interest to lend money. Is this a changing view of morality in business?

Quick questions

1. State the main sources of English contract law.
2. What is meant by certainty of terms in contract law?
3. What is meant by freedom of contract?
4. Explain the principle of fault in contract law.
5. Give an example of the law attempting to balance the interests of the parties to a contract?

Summary

- Contracts have a number of elements that can be considered as a whole or individually.
- Contract law is largely based on common law, so most of the law comes from decided cases.
- The elements that come from Acts of Parliament are mostly to do with consumer protection.
- The main theory of contract law is freedom of contract. This means that a person can make any contract they like, even if it is disadvantageous to them. There is, however, some statutory protection.

- The principle of good faith is an underlying principle; a person assumes that the other party will fulfil their promise and that the law will help when they do not.
- The law tries to balance interests between parties, particularly where exclusion clauses are concerned.
- The concept of fault applies, particularly to the law on misrepresentation in contracts.
- Morality is present in contract law, particularly with illegal contracts, economic duress, terms imposed in contracts and equitable remedies.

Chapter 39 Formation of contract

Introduction

This chapter deals with the formation of a contract, which requires an offer and acceptance, an intention to create legal relations, and the consideration needed for a valid contract. The rules of privity of contract are examined, and the topic is evaluated in Chapter 44.

39.1 Offer and acceptance

This section deals with the idea of agreement in formation of a contract. This requires an offer and acceptance, so that there is agreement between the parties to create a contract.

39.1.1 Offer

An offer is the starting point for a contract. Contract law sets out what amounts to an offer, when the offer comes into existence and when it comes to an end. Once an offer is communicated to the offeree by the offeror, the offeree can choose whether to accept that offer or not until the offer ends.

Key terms

Offer – a proposal (or promise) showing a willingness to contract on firm and definite terms.

Offeror – the person who makes the offer.

Offeree – the person to whom an offer is made

Invitation to treat – an indication that one person is willing to negotiate a contract with another, but that they are not yet willing to make a legal offer.

The offer must be definite in its terms. The difficulty is in deciding whether a statement amounts to an offer or whether it is just a statement preparatory to an offer, which is known as an invitation to treat. Words such as 'might be prepared to' or 'may be able to' indicate uncertainty. This can be seen in the case of *Gibson v Manchester City Council* (1979) (see next section).

An acceptance of the offer forms the basis of a valid contract.

An offer or an invitation to treat?

The law distinguishes between an offer and an invitation to treat. An invitation to treat is not an offer and therefore it cannot be accepted to make a contract, as shown in *Gibson v Manchester City Council* (1979).

Case study

Gibson v Manchester City Council (1979)

Mr Gibson was a council tenant. The council wrote to him stating:

> The Corporation may be prepared to sell the house to you ... If you would like to make formal application to buy your Council house, please complete the enclosed application form.

He completed the application but the council refused to accept his application. It was decided that the council's letter was not an offer. The reason was that it was not a firm and definite proposal, as it stated that the council 'may be prepared to sell the house', but not that it definitely would. His formal application was the offer that the council could accept or reject.

There are a number of examples of invitations to treat.

Advertisements

Generally, an advertisement cannot be an offer, and is thus only an invitation to treat. This can be seen in the case of *Partridge v Crittenden* (1968).

Case study

Partridge v Crittenden (1968)

Crittenden placed an advertisement stating 'Bramblefinch cocks, bramblefinch hens, 25s [£1.25] each'. He was prosecuted for 'offering for sale' a wild bird under the Protection of Birds Act 1954. He was not guilty as the advertisement was not an offer but an invitation to treat. Any offer leading to a contract would be made by the person responding to the advertisement.

Exceptionally, if an advertisement contains a clear indication that there is an 'offer' because it is expected to be taken seriously, then the court may well decide it is an offer. This usually occurs in a unilateral rather than a bilateral contract.

- In a unilateral contract, the offeror makes a promise in exchange for an act by another party. For example, a reward offered for someone finding and returning a missing pet. There is no obligation to look for the missing pet, but there is an offer to pay the reward to the finder. A unilateral contract arises only when the offeree completely performs the required act.
- In a bilateral contract, there is an exchange of mutual promises. An example is a contract to buy a loaf of bread for £1. Both parties have an obligation – to provide the bread on one party, to pay £1 on the other party.

Key terms

Bilateral contract – this type of contract requires both offeror and offeree to do something. Both parties have obligations.

Unilateral contract – in a unilateral contract there is an agreement to pay in exchange for performance, if the potential performer chooses to act. There is no obligation to perform the act.

A unilateral contract can be seen in the case of *Carlill v Carbolic Smokeball Co.* (1893).

Case study

Carlill v Carbolic Smoke Ball Co. (1893)

The company advertised a patent medicine, the smoke ball. The advertisement stated that if someone used it correctly and still got flu, then the company would pay them £100. Mrs Carlill did get flu after using the smoke ball as instructed. The court awarded her the £100. The promise was an offer that could be accepted by anyone who used the smoke ball correctly and still contracted the flu, because the advertisement was a unilateral offer.

Advertisement from 1894

Goods in a shop window or on a shop shelf

The goods on the shelf or in the customer's basket are an invitation to treat. This is consistent with *R v Morris* (1983), discussed in Chapter 9, section 9.1.1.

The contents of the basket become an offer when the customer presents them to the checkout operator (or self-service scanner). The shop then accepts or declines the customer's offer through their checkout operator or assistant at the self-service scanner.

The goods in a shop window are similar to those on the shelves, in that the shop has no obligation to sell the items to a potential customer. This can be seen in the case of *Fisher v Bell* (1961).

Case study

Fisher v Bell (1961)

A shopkeeper displayed a flick-knife with a price tag in his shop window for sale. He was charged with 'offering the knife for sale', an offence under the Offensive Weapons Act 1959. The display of the knife in the window was an invitation to treat so the knife had not been offered for sale. He was therefore not guilty of the offence.

In *Pharmaceutical Society of Great Britain v Boots Cash Chemists* (1953), Boots were charged with selling controlled pharmaceutical products other than under the supervision of a pharmacist.

Case study

Pharmaceutical Society of Great Britain v Boots Cash Chemists (1953)

Some items that had to be sold by a pharmacist were on a shelf for customers to select. Boots were found not guilty, as the offer was made by the customer at the till where there *was* a pharmacist present to approve the acceptance of the offer.

This principle makes good sense. A seller of goods is not obliged to sell the goods to you. The goods might be a display item (that is, the actual item itself is not for sale), even with a price ticket on the item. There may be none left to sell, or there are legal restrictions on the sale of some goods such as fireworks, alcoholic drinks and knives.

Lots at an auction

At an auction, the bidder makes the offer that the auctioneer then accepts by banging his hammer. This means that the lots available at an auction are an invitation to treat. This can be seen in the case of *British Car Auctions v Wright* (1972).

Case study

British Car Auctions v Wright (1972)

The auctioneers were prosecuted for offering to sell an unfit vehicle at an auction. However, the prosecution failed because there was no offer, only an invitation to treat.

A request for information

A request for information and a reply to such a request is not an offer. This might be just a general enquiry such as when an item displayed for sale does not have a price in it. An example of this is where a person enquires about the price of an item – 'How much is the red dress?' An example of this is *Harvey v Facey* (1893).

Case study

Harvey v Facey (1893)

Harvey wanted to buy Facey's farm and sent a message: 'Will you sell me Bumper Hall Pen [the farm]? State lowest price.'

Facey replied: 'Lowest price acceptable £900.'

Harvey tried to buy the farm for £900 but could not as the reply was merely a reply to the request for information, not an offer.

Offer or invitation to treat?	Brief legal rule	Case example
An advertisement	An advertisement is usually an invitation to treat, not an offer	*Partridge v Crittenden* (1968)
An advertisement containing an offer	Where there is a unilateral contract, the advertisement may be an offer rather than invitation to treat	*Carlill v Carbolic Smokeball Co.* (1893)
Goods in a shop window	An invitation to treat	*Fisher v Bell* (1961)
Goods on a supermarket shelf	An invitation to treat	*Pharmaceutical Society of Great Britain v Boots Cash Chemists* (1953)
Goods at an auction	Each lot is an invitation to treat; offer made by the bidder	*British Car Auctions v Wright* (1972)
Request for information and reply to the request	An invitation to treat	*Harvey v Facey* (1893)

Figure 39.1 Key facts: invitation to treat

Who can make an offer?

An offer can be made by anyone. This can be by an individual, a partnership, limited company or other organisation. An offer made other than by an individual is made by an employee of the business or an agent. It can also be made through a notice or a machine, as in *Thornton v Shoe Lane Parking* (1971).

Thornton v Shoe Lane Parking (1971)

Mr Thornton put money into a machine and was given a ticket at the entrance to a car park. The offer was made by the machine on behalf of the company owning the car park. The acceptance was made by putting the money into the machine. This was where the contract was made, which dictated what terms were in the contract – the terms displayed by the machine.

To whom can an offer be made?

An offer can be made to:
- a named individual, as in *Gibson v Manchester City Council* (1979)
- a group of people
- the world at large, as in *Carlill v Carbolic Smokeball Co.* (1893).

An offer can be targeted at particular individuals and may be conditional on another contract being made. An example of this which had disastrous consequences was the Hoover free flights fiasco. Here was an offer to give a free flight if you bought a Hoover product costing more than £100. Inevitably, the offer was taken up by many people who realised that this was effectively a flight to the US for £100, with a free hoover product thrown in! Hoover nearly went bankrupt as a result – it sold £30 million worth of its products but had to pay £50 million for the flights!

Hoover's offer of free flights nearly bankrupted the company

Communicating the offer

An offer comes into existence when it is communicated to the offeree. Communication requires the offeree to know of the existence of the offer, as in the case of *Taylor v Laird* (1856).

Taylor v Laird (1856)

Taylor gave up the captaincy of a ship overseas. He worked as an ordinary crew member on the ship in order to get back to England, but received no wages. The ship owner had not received any communication of his offer to work as an ordinary crew member. Therefore, there was no contract for the payment of wages on this voyage.

Exact timing can be critical – this can be seen in the case of *Stevenson v McLean* (1880).

Stevenson v McLean (1880)

On Saturday, the offeror offered to sell iron to the offeree. The offer was stated to be open until Monday. On Monday at 10 a.m., the offeree sent a telegram asking if he could have credit terms, but got no reply. At 1.34 p.m. the offeree sent a telegram accepting the offer, but at 1.25 p.m. the offeror had sent a telegram, 'Sold iron to third party', arriving at 1.46 p.m. The offeree sued for the breach of contract but the offeror argued that the query about credit ended the offer so there could be no acceptance.

It was decided that the query about credit did not end the offer, so a binding contract was made at 1.34 p.m.

How an offer can end

An offer can come to an end in the following ways:
- revocation
- rejection
- lapse of time
- death
- acceptance.

Revocation

An offer can be revoked (withdrawn) at any time before acceptance. The offeror must communicate the revocation to the offeree before the revocation can take effect, as in *Routledge v Grant* (1828). This can have implications where there is an offer to the whole world – the *Carlill v Carbolic Smokeball* type of offer. In these circumstances, the offer can end in three ways:

1 Set a time limit in the offer, such as by stating the 'reward' will only be available to be paid until a particular date.
2 The expiry of a reasonable time.
3 Publish revocation of the offer in the same way as the original offer was made.

Case study

Routledge v Grant (1828)

Grant had offered his house for sale, stating that the offer would remain open for six weeks. When he told Routledge that he no longer wished to sell the house, this was effective revocation of the offer, even though it was within the six-week period. Routledge could no longer accept the offer as it had ended.

Tip

Note that an offer is revoked as soon as the revocation is communicated to the offeree. This is shown in *Stevenson v McLean* (1880) as well as *Routledge v Grant* (1828).

An offeree can make a separate contract with the offeror to keep the offer open, or only to sell to them. This is known as a collateral contract, and can be enforced if the offeror refuses to sell within the agreed period or sells the item to someone else.

The revocation must be communicated by a reliable person, not necessarily the offeror:

- In *Routledge v Grant* (1828), the offeror communicated the revocation of the offer to the offeree.
- In *Dickinson v Dodds* (1876), the offeree heard about the revocation of the offer from a reliable source. This was effective communication of revocation.

Case study

Dickinson v Dodds (1876)

Dodds had offered to sell houses to Dickinson. When a reliable person known to both of them told Dickinson that Dodds had withdrawn the offer, this was effective revocation.

In cases where conduct indicates acceptance, the offer cannot be revoked when the expected conduct continues. This can be seen in *Errington v Errington and Woods* (1952).

Case study

Errington v Errington and Woods (1952)

A father bought and paid a deposit for a house for his son and daughter-in-law to live in. The offer was that the son and his wife would pay the mortgage instalments and then the house would be transferred to them. The instalments continued to be paid as expected until the father's death. The offer could not then be revoked, because of the continuing conduct.
    Unclear – need more detail?

Rejection

- Once an offer is rejected, this ends the offer.
- If the offer is made to more than one person, rejection by one person does not mean the other offerees can no longer accept the offer.
- The rejection must be communicated to the offeror before it takes effect as in revocation.

An offer can be rejected in two ways:

1 Specifically responding to the offer by saying 'No'.
2 Making a counter offer: this could be, for example, a different price or delivery date. An example of rejection through a counter offer occurs in *Hyde v Wrench* (1840).

Key term

Counter offer – a response to an offer that makes a firm proposal that materially alters the terms of the offer.

Case study

Hyde v Wrench (1840)

Wrench offered to sell his farm for £1000 to Hyde. Hyde replied with a counter offer of £950. Wrench rejected this counter offer. Hyde then replied that he accepted Wrench's earlier offer to sell for £1000. However, as the counter offer ended Wrench's original offer, Hyde could not accept it. Wrench could have accepted Hyde's offer of £1000 but did not do so.

Sometimes there are enquiries during negotiations. As has been seen in *Stevenson v McLean*, these are generally treated as requests for information and not counter offers. Although a counter offer operates as a rejection of the offer, a request for information does not. Thus, the offeree can accept the offer following the request for information.

Tip

It is not always easy to decide whether there has been a request for information or a counter offer. This confusion can be seen from the status of an enquiry about credit in *Stevenson v McLean*. A request for information is usually drafted as a question, whereas a counter offer is not.

Lapse of time

An offer can end by lapse of time. If a fixed period for the duration of the offer is stated, then as soon as that expires, there is no offer to accept.

The problem arises when no time is set. In this situation, the time is a reasonable time, which will obviously vary, depending on the nature of the offer. You would expect a longer time for the duration of an offer to buy a metal tank than an offer to buy a cake from a cake stall in a market.

An example is *Ramsgate Victoria Hotel v Montefiore* (1866).

Case study

Ramsgate Victoria Hotel v Montefiore (1866)

On 8 June, Montefiore offered to buy shares at a fixed price in the hotel. On 23 November, his offer was accepted but he no longer wanted them as the share price had fallen; he refused to pay. It was held that the long delay between the offer and the acceptance meant the offer had lapsed and could no longer be accepted, so he did not have to pay for the shares.

Death

The effect of the death of either the offeror or the offeree depends on which party died and the type of contract involved.

- If the offeree dies, then the offer ends, and those dealing with his estate cannot accept on his behalf. The executors or administrators of his estate can make a new offer, as can the offeror.
- When an offeror dies, acceptance can still take place until the offeree learns of the offeror's death.

However, this is obviously not the case where the offer is to perform some personal service, such as to provide personal tuition.

	Brief legal rule	Case example
Offer not communicated to offeree	No offer exists	*Taylor v Laird* (1856)
Offer must exist to be open for existence	The exact timing of the duration of the offer is critical	*Stevenson v McLean* (1880)
Revocation of offer	Can be made at any time	*Routledge v Grant* (1828)
Communication of revocation of offer	Must be effectively communicated, not necessarily by the offeror	*Dickinson v Dodds* (1876)
Offer rejected	Once rejected, the offer ends and cannot be accepted	*Hyde v Wrench* (1840)
Offer lapsed	Lapses after end of fixed time, or if no time, after a reasonable time	*Ramsgate Victoria Hotel v Montefiore* (1866)
Death of one party	Ends the offer when known or if the offer is for personal services by the deceased	No case

Figure 39.2 Key facts: duration of an offer

Acceptance

- Acceptance must be positive and unqualified.
- It must be acceptance of the whole offer and all the terms in it.
- There is no acceptance if the response to the offer is 'Yes, if ...' or Yes, but ...'. This would be a counter offer unless it is just a request for information.

Key term

Acceptance – the final and unconditional agreement to all the terms of the offer.

39.1.2 Acceptance

Acceptance of all the terms in a contract can be seen when you tap on 'I agree' to accept the contract on your phone or computer. This then incorporates all the terms and conditions that you have indicated you have read, whatever they might be.

How do you accept an offer?

Acceptance can be in any form, provided it is definite and communicated to the offeror. It does not have to be in the same format, so an email can be responded to by a text, letter, telephone call, etc.

However, acceptance cannot be by silence; there must be some positive act for acceptance. This can be seen in the case of *Felthouse v Bindley* (1863).

Case study

Felthouse v Bindley (1863)

There were discussions about the purchase of a horse. The final letter from the offeror stated: 'If I hear no more, I consider the horse mine.' There was no further response, but the court decided there was no contract as an offer could not be accepted by silence or inactivity on the part of the offeree.

Although there can be any form of acceptance, providing it is effectively communicated, the offeror can require a specific method for acceptance. For example, the acceptance must be made personally.

If the offer requires a particular manner of acceptance, it must usually be complied with for a valid acceptance. There can sometimes be a waiver of the requirement stated. This can be seen in the case of *Yates v Pulleyn* (1975).

Case study

Yates v Pulleyn (1975)

An option to purchase land was required to be agreed in writing 'sent by registered or recorded delivery post'. When a letter was sent by ordinary post, it was argued that there was no acceptance.

This argument was rejected as it was a convenience for the offeree, sent by registered post to be certain that the acceptance had arrived. Lord Denning made the distinction between the requirement being mandatory and being directory:

- A mandatory instruction would have to be followed exactly (acceptance must be registered post).
- A directory instruction only requires completion within the time frame set – so any form of post would do.

The requirement of a signature can cause problems where negotiations are conducted electronically.

Case study

Neocleous v Rees (2019)

It was held that the autogeneration by a computer on emails can be the same as a signature. This is reflected in the Law Commission's 2019 report on Electronic Execution of documents, which stated the law:

> An electronic signature is capable in law of being used to execute a document (including a deed) provided that (i) the person signing the document intends to authenticate the document and (ii) any formalities relating to execution of that document are satisfied.

The report has been accepted by the government and further action to clarify the law will no doubt follow in due course.

There are similar problems with contracts made by telephone, in particular the problem of evidence of what was actually stated.

Case study

Wells v Devani (2019)

An estate agent brought proceedings against his client for not paying commission. Following a telephone call between them, the parties had agreed that the agent's commission rate but the trigger event for payment had not been discussed.

The court implied terms that gave business efficacy to the contract in the absence of written terms.

The case is an example of the circumstances in which the court implied a term into a contract to give it business efficacy where there appears to be an offer and an acceptance.

When does acceptance take place?

As we have seen in *Stevenson v McLean*, the actual time of revocation of an offer is critical. This is equally important with acceptance.

The general rule is that acceptance takes place when the acceptance is communicated to the offeror.

There are three ways of accepting an offer that need special attention:

1 acceptance by conduct
2 acceptance by use of the post – the postal rules
3 electronic methods of communication

Acceptance by conduct

This has been seen in *Carlill v Carbolic Smokeball Co*. The case of *Reveille Independent LLC v Anotech International (UK) Ltd* (2016) reflects what occurs quite often in business contracts – the job begins before the formal contract is agreed in all its detail, with numerous offers and counter offers.

Case study

Reveille Independent LLC v Anotech International (UK) Ltd (2016)

In common with many potential contracts, there was a written offer document which stated that it was not binding until signed by both parties. The offeree made some alterations and signed the document, but the alterations amounted to a counter offer and the document remained unsigned by the offeror. However, there was performance: products were integrated and promoted in episodes of the US version of the *Masterchef* TV series, even though the document remained unsigned.

The counter offer had been accepted by conduct, because the prescribed mode of acceptance was said to have been waived by the original offeror. Acceptance was by conduct.

The court confirmed the principle that the reasonable expectations of honest, sensible business persons must be protected.

Acceptance by use of the post – the postal rules

The postal rules were developed in the nineteenth century to deal with the problem of when a contract came into existence and where the loss should fall if a letter is not delivered correctly. The rule also adapted the idea that once you have posted a letter, you cannot get it back.

The postal rules only apply to letters of acceptance, not to offers or counter offers, and are as follows:

1 The rules only apply if post is the usual or expected means of communication.

2 The letter must be properly addressed and stamped.
3 The offeree must be able to prove the letter was posted.

If the rules apply, acceptance takes place at the moment the letter is properly posted.

The rules were set out in the case of *Adams v Lindsell* (1818).

Case study

Adams v Lindsell (1818)

Lindsell wrote to Adams, offering to sell them some wool and asking for a reply 'in the course of post'. The letter was delayed in the post. On receiving the letter, Adams posted a letter of acceptance the same day. However, because of the delay Lindsell assumed Adams did not want the wool and sold it to someone else. There was a valid contract because acceptance took place as soon as the letter was placed in the post box, and there had been no communication about revoking the offer.

Electronic methods of communication

The law has struggled to deal with the issues arising from modern methods of communication. The principle is that acceptance, apart from the postal rules, occurs when the offeror is aware of the acceptance. This can be seen in the statement of Lord Denning in *Entores v Miles Far East* (1955):

> If a man shouts an offer to a man across a river but the reply is not heard because of a plane flying overhead, there is no contract. The offeree must wait and then shout back his acceptance so that the offeror can hear it.

The situation of electronic signatures applies here.

The case of *Brinkibon Ltd v Stahag Stahl* (1983) dealt with the problem of out-of-hours messages – the court held that these are only effective once the office is reopened.

Fax, text and email are more modern forms of communication, and the same problems and principles very often apply. An offer is accepted provided that

1 the person signing the document intends to authenticate the document, and

2 any formalities relating to executing that document are satisfied such as clicking on an icon in a website accepting terms and conditions.

The question remains as to whether actually reading of the email/fax/text is required before acceptance.

The Consumer Protection (Distance Selling) Regulations 2000 give consumers a number of rights, which were added to the Consumer Rights Act 2015. If key information to the consumer is omitted, no contract is formed. The Regulations apply to telephone, fax, internet shopping, mail order, email and television shopping.

Article 11 of the Electronic Commerce (EC Directive) Regulations 2002 states that where a buyer is required to give his consent through technological means (such as clicking on an icon), the contract is made when the buyer has received from the service provider electronically an acknowledgement of receipt of the acceptance. Thus many online businesses state, 'Your order has been received and is now being processed' or words to that effect, rather than 'Your order has been accepted'. This ensures that online sellers are not required to accept the order at this point.

Silence and acceptance

The law on formation of contracts will consider what the parties intended to do. This is a subjective approach. In practice, an objective test is often applied, disguised as a subjective judgment. In *Felthouse v Bindley* (1863), both parties wanted there to be a contract. The court said that from an objective viewpoint there was no evidence of an acceptance from the seller. In fact the seller had contacted the auctioneer holding the horse to remove it from the auction, which might contradict that view.

However, for the court to decide there is a valid contract there should be clear and identifiable evidence. The offer has to be communicated and so, logically, must the acceptance.

The Unsolicited Goods and Services Act 1971 states that, for example, where goods are received without request there can be no contract unless the acceptance is communicated to the sender. So the individual may benefit and the business may lose out and be prosecuted, but is it moral to keep the goods?

Of course, the need to communicate an acceptance might have been waived, as in *Carlill* and *Reveille*.

 Tip

When considering offer and acceptance cases, you need to adopt a logical and precise approach. Consider the facts to establish the order of events and the legal effect of each event. Use appropriate authority – usually decided cases.

Let's consider the facts of *Adams v Lindsell* (1818). Assume that A found out (from L or a reliable source) that L had sold the wool on 9 September:

2 Sept	L wrote to A offering to sell wool
5 Sept	A received the letter
5 Sept	A sent a letter of acceptance
8 Sept	L sold the goods to X
9 Sept	L received the letter of acceptance

The offer opened when A received the letter. The offer ended when A learned the wool had been sold (9 September). The acceptance took place when the letter of acceptance was posted. The contract was therefore made on 5 September between A and L.

A slightly more complicated case is *Byrne v Van Tienhoven* (1880):

1 Oct	V T posted a letter offering goods for sale
7 Oct	Letter of 1 Oct arrived with B
8 Oct	V T revoked the offer in a letter
11 Oct	B accepted the offer by telegram
15 Oct	B posted a letter confirming acceptance
20 Oct	Letter of revocation arrived with B

Here, the revocation was not effective until it was received on 20 October. This was too late, as the contract was made on 15 October when the letter of acceptance was posted or when the telegram arrived, whichever is earlier.

 Activity

Look at the case of *Stevenson v McLean* (1880) and follow the same techniques as shown above to decide when the contract was made.

	Brief legal rule	Case example
Acceptance by conduct	Valid Particularly in unilateral contracts	*Carlill v Carbolic Smokeball Co.* (1893)
Prescribed method of acceptance may be waived	Acceptance by a different method to that in the offer may be permitted	*Reveille Independent LLC v Anotech International (UK) Ltd* (2016)
Postal rules	If they apply, acceptance takes place at the moment of posting the letter	*Adams v Lindsell* (1818)
Electronic methods of communication	Acceptance occurs when the offeror is aware of the acceptance	Electronic Commerce (EC Directive) Regulations 2002), Article 11
Email autosignatures	Autogeneration by a computer on emails can be the same as a signature	*Neocleous v Rees* (2019)

Figure 39.3 Key facts: acceptance of an offer

Case	Judgment
Gibson v Manchester City Council (1979)	An offer must have definite terms, not vague such as 'may be prepared to'
Partridge v Crittenden (1968)	An advertisement is usually an invitation to treat and not an offer
Carlill v Carbolic Smoke Ball Co. (1893)	Here the advertisement contained promises that were intended to be taken seriously so it was an offer leading to a unilateral contract
Fisher v Bell (1961)	Goods in a shop window are an invitation to treat
Pharmaceutical Society of Great Britain v Boots Cash Chemists (1953)	Goods in a self-service shop are an invitation to treat
British Car Auctions v Wright (1972)	The bidder makes the offer at an auction; the auctioneer accepts it
Harvey v Facey (1893)	A request for information and the response to the request are not an offer
Thornton v Shoe Lane Parking (1971)	In a vending machine or ticket machine the offer is made by the person inserting the coin
Taylor v Laird (1856)	An offer only comes into existence when it is communicated to the offeree
Stevenson v McLean (1880)	Exact timing of the offer and acceptance are critical in deciding when a contract comes into existence
Routledge v Grant (1828)	An offer can be revoked at any time, providing revocation is communicated to the offeree
Dickinson v Dodds (1876)	Revocation can be via a reliable source rather than directly communicated
Hyde v Wrench (1840)	Once an offer is rejected it cannot be accepted
Ramsgate Victoria Hotel v Montefiore (1866)	An offer ends through lapse of time when a reasonable time has elapsed
Felthouse v Bindley (1863)	Acceptance cannot be made through silence
Yates v Pulleyn (1975)	A mandatory method of acceptance by a particular method must be complied with
Neocleous v Rees (2019)	Autogeneration by a computer on emails can be the same as a signature
Wells v Devani (2019)	Telephone records can imply a term into a contract to give it business efficacy where there appears to be an offer and an acceptance
Reveille Independent LLC v Anotech International (UK) Ltd (2016)	A directory method of acceptance by a particular method does not have to be complied with
Adams v Lindsell (1818)	If the posting rules apply, acceptance takes place at the moment of posting
Entores v Miles Far East (1955)	With non-postal acceptance, acceptance takes place when the offeror is aware of the acceptance
Brinkibon Ltd v Stahag Stahl (1983)	Acceptance takes place when a message is opened
Byrne v Van Tienhoven (1880)	An example of the working of offer and acceptance issues in negotiations

Figure 39.4 Key cases: offer and acceptance in contract law

39.2 Intention to create legal relations

Once offer and acceptance have taken place and an agreement is formed, it would appear that there is a contract. However, as a contract requires an agreement that the law will recognise, there must be an intention to create legal relations and make the contract legally binding.

This is presumed in a business agreement, and is presumed not to exist where the agreement is purely of a social and domestic nature.

This means that where an agreement is made between a business and someone else (whether another business or a consumer), the law **presumes** that the agreement is intended to be legally binding and a contract. There can, however, be evidence that the agreement is not intended to be legally binding and then it will not be a contract. This is when the presumption is **rebutted** (evidence is shown that the there was no presumption), as seen in *Jones v Vernons Pools* (1938) (see section 39.2.2).

Similarly, where the agreement is merely a social agreement, the presumption is that it is not legally binding, although, as we shall see, this presumption may also be rebutted.

Key term 🔑

Intention to create legal relations – the parties to a contract expressly or impliedly agree that the contract is legally binding and therefore enforceable in court.

39.2.1 Social and domestic arrangements

These are presumed not to be legally binding, but the presumption can be rebutted. The distinction can be seen in *Balfour v Balfour* (1919) and *Merritt v Merritt* (1970).

Case study

Balfour v Balfour (1919)

Mr Balfour worked abroad. His wife stayed in England. He promised her an income of £30 per month. Later the marriage failed and she petitioned for divorce and claimed her £30 per month. As the agreement had been made at an amicable point in their relationship, not in contemplation of divorce, it was a purely domestic arrangement and not legally enforceable.

However, where husband and wife are already separated, an agreement between them may be taken as intended to be legally binding.

Case study

Merritt v Merritt (1970)

Mr Merritt had left his wife. An agreement to pay the wife an income if she paid the outstanding mortgage was held to be intended to create legally binding obligations, and was enforced by the court.

Sometimes families make arrangements that appear to be business arrangements because of the nature of what they are doing. In such cases, the court must examine the real purpose of the arrangement – was it purely a social matter or something with much more legal intent? An example is *Jones v Padavatton* (1969).

Case study

Jones v Padavatton (1969)

A woman was persuaded by her mother to come to England to study for the Bar, promising to allow her to stay in her house. Several years later, the daughter had still not passed any Bar examinations. They fell out and the mother wanted to evict her. The daughter said that there had been a contract for her to stay there.

At the time when the first arrangement was made, the mother and daughter were very close, so the court was satisfied that neither party at that time intended to enter into a legally binding contract.

If money has changed hands, then even if the arrangement is made socially, it is more likely to be a business arrangement and therefore legally binding, as in *Simpkins v Pays* (1955).

Case study

Simpkins v Pays (1955)

A lodger and two members of the household entered competitions. The lodger filled in the form in the landlady's name. One of the entries won. The claim was made by the lodger on the basis there was understanding that they would share any winnings. Their action succeeded as this was more than just a social arrangement.

This is usually the case with arrangements such as lottery ticket syndicates. It is, of course, wise to make some record of the agreement, as it is difficult to decide whether an agreement has been made or is merely social chatter with insufficient evidence of a binding agreement, as in *Wilson v Burnett* (2007) where a similar situation was tested objectively.

Case study

Wilson v Burnett (2007)

Three young women worked together. They attended a bingo session, where one of them won a local prize of £153 and then a national prize of over £100,000.

The question was whether there was a contract between them to share any winnings over £10. The suggestion of a prior agreement was undermined by the fact that when one of them won the local prize of £153 and they were waiting to hear the national result, others repeatedly asked if she was 'going to share'. This suggested that an intention to create a legal relationship did *not* exist at that time, so the claim for a share failed.

However, if parties put their financial security at risk for an agreement, then it must have been intended that the agreement should be legally binding, as in *Parker v Clarke* (1960).

Case study

Parker v Clarke (1960)

A young couple were persuaded by an older couple to sell their house to move in with them, with the promise also that they would inherit the property on their death. Later, the couples fell out and the young couple was asked to leave.

The young couple successfully argued that they had a legally binding agreement. Giving up their security indicated that the arrangement was intended to be legally binding.

39.2.2 Commercial agreements

Commercial agreements are presumed to be legally binding. This is quite logical but does not take into account the fact that the presumption can be rebutted by showing the opposite is the case. This can be seen in a so-called gentlemen's agreement which is usually discovered by a term that states the contract is binding in honour only, as in the case of *Jones v Vernons Pools* (1938).

Case study

Jones v Vernons Pools (1938)

Mr Jones claimed that he had a winning football pool coupon. The coupon, which he signed, stated that the transaction was 'binding in honour only'. As the agreement was based on the honour of the parties and not legally binding, there was no intent to create legal relations and no legal contract.

A football pools coupon

The burden of proof in a business situation is on the person seeking to establish there is *no* legal intention – that the presumption has been rebutted. An example of this is seen in *Edwards v Skyways Ltd* (1969).

Case study

Edwards v Skyways Ltd (1969)

Negotiations had taken place about rights and payments to redundant airline pilots. Skyways tried to avoid making the agreed *ex gratia* (this means – without admitting the payment was a legal requirement) payment in Edwards' redundancy. This failed because, while *ex gratia* suggests a voluntary payment with no liability to make it, the agreement here was seen as a business agreement. There was therefore a presumption that the agreement was intended to be legally binding, which the claimant had failed to rebut.

In *Edmunds v Lawson* (2000), a case about a pupillage contract with a barrister and minimum wage regulations, the court stated:

> " Whether the parties intended to enter into legally binding relations ... is an issue to be determined objectively. "

Each case will be decided on its own facts.

The offer of a free gift also creates problems. Where this is to promote a business, it can still be held to be legally binding, as in *Esso Petroleum Co. Ltd v Commissioners of Customs and Excise* (1976).

Case study

Esso Petroleum Co. Ltd v Commissioners of Customs and Excise (1976)

Esso gave a World Cup coin with every four gallons of petrol purchased. Should this free gift attract tax? As Esso was clearly trying to gain more business from the promotion, there was held to be intention to be bound by the arrangement, as a contract to supply but not sell the coins. As there was no sale of the coins, no purchase tax was payable.

Another situation is where prizes are offered in competitions. Just as the free gift is designed to promote the company offering it, the same occurs where a company offers a competition prize, as in *McGowan v Radio Buxton* (2001).

Case study

McGowan v Radio Buxton (2001)

The claimant entered a radio competition. The prize was stated to be a Renault Clio car. The winner was given a four-inch scale model of a Renault Clio. Radio Buxton argued that there was no intention to create legal relations. The court decided that there *was* legal intention, in line with previous cases.

The same problem arises with a letter of comfort, which is not usually intended to be legally binding. This occurs where the parent company wishes to give some assurance to the lender regarding the subsidiary's ability to repay a loan, but has no obligation to pay on its behalf.

Key term 🔑

Letter of comfort – a written assurance, usually provided by a parent company in respect of its subsidiary's financial obligations to a bank.

This can be seen in *Kleinwort Benson Ltd v Malaysian Mining Corporation* (1989), where the courts found that there was no legal contractual obligation, only a moral obligation.

Case study

Kleinwort Benson Ltd v Malaysian Mining Corporation (1989)

Kleinwort lent £10 million to Metals Ltd, a subsidiary of the Malaysian Mining Corporation (MMC). MMC would not guarantee this loan but issued a comfort letter stating its intention to ensure Metals had sufficient funds for repayment. When Metals went out of business without repaying Kleinwort, a claim based on the comfort letter failed as there was no legal intention. If Kleinwort had required a guarantee, it should have insisted on one.

The Court of Appeal decided that MMC had not made a promise to do anything, but represented a fact that it was their present intention to ensure that Metals Ltd would be able to meet its liabilities. As a result, intention to create legal relations was irrelevant.

	Brief legal rule	Case example
The presumption with social and domestic arrangements	Social and domestic arrangements are presumed not to be legally binding	*Balfour v Balfour* (1919)
Rebutting the presumption in social and domestic arrangements	The presumption can be rebutted by showing the opposite is the case	*Merritt v Merritt* (1971)
The presumption with business contracts	Business agreements are presumed to be legally binding	*Edwards v Skyways Ltd* (1969)
Rebutting the presumption in business contracts	The presumption can be rebutted by showing the opposite is the case	*Jones v Vernons Pools* (1938)
The position of letters of comfort	A letter of comfort is not usually intended to be a legally binding document but, confusingly, it may give rise to a legally binding obligation depending on the wording	*Kleinwort Benson Ltd v Malaysian Mining Corporation* (1989)
Social arrangements can be like business arrangements	If money has changed hands, then even if the arrangement is made socially, it is more likely to be a commercial arrangement and therefore legally binding	*Simpkins v Pays* (1955)

Figure 39.5 Key facts: intention to create legal relations

Case	Judgment
Edwards v Skyways Ltd (1969)	The agreement to actually pay a redundancy package is binding even though it is described as *ex gratia*
Jones v Vernons Pools (1938)	The football pool coupon, which he signed, stated that the transaction was 'binding in honour only' This rebutted the presumption in the business contract
Esso Petroleum Co. Ltd v Commissioners of Customs and Excise (1976)	As Esso were clearly trying to gain more business from the promotion, there was held to be legal intention in the arrangement
McGowan v Radio Buxton (2001)	A prize in a competition is part of a legally binding contract
Kleinwort Benson Ltd v Malaysian Mining Corporation (1989)	The claim based on the comfort letter failed as there was no legal intention If Kleinwort had required a legally binding guarantee it should have insisted on one
Balfour v Balfour (1919)	The agreement was not binding as it was a domestic arrangement between an amicable married couple
Merritt v Merritt (1971)	The agreement was binding as it was an arrangement between a separated married couple about future maintenance payments
Jones v Padavatton (1969)	There is a presumption that cohabitants would not intend to create enforceable contractual obligations between themselves
Simpkins v Pays (1955)	If money has changed hands, then even if the arrangement is made socially, it is more likely to be a commercial arrangement and therefore legally binding
Parker v Clarke (1960)	If parties put their financial security at risk for an agreement, then it must have been intended that the agreement should be legally binding

Figure 39.6 Key cases: intention to create legal relations

Activity

Here are two short scenarios. In each case, write down the arguments for and against there being a valid contract on the basis of intention to create legal relations. Discuss your arguments in a group and justify your conclusions.

1   Three students share a flat. They take it in turns to buy milk for the fridge. As people often forget to do this, they have instituted a fine system of 50p each time someone forgets their turn. All money collected to go towards an end-of-term meal out. One member of the flat refuses to pay the 50p 'fine'.

2   Anna's Uncle Paul said he would let her have his car if she got into a degree course at a top university. She has now achieved this but he refuses to give her his car as he has just spent most of his savings on a brand new Ferrari.

39.3 Consideration

Consideration is essential for every valid contract because contract law requires a bargain and not a gift. This means that both parties to a contract will give something to the other by way of exchange.

Consideration is defined in *Currie v Misa* (1875) as:

> some right, interest, profit or benefit accruing to one party or some forbearance, detriment, loss or responsibility given, suffered or undertaken by the other.

The definition given by Sir Frederick Pollock and approved by Lord Dunedin in *Dunlop v Selfridge Ltd* (1915) is:

> An act or forbearance of one party, or the promise thereof, is the price for which the promise of the other is bought, and the promise thus given for value is enforceable.

In our everyday contracts this might be paying money for a cup of coffee.
- When the consideration has been performed it is said to be executed.
- If it is yet to be performed, it is said to be executory.

Key terms

Executed consideration – an act in return for a promise.
Executory consideration – a promise for a promise.

Over time, a number of rules have been developed that are applied to the principle of consideration:

1 Consideration need not be adequate but must be sufficient.
2 Past consideration is not good consideration.
3 Consideration must move from the promisee.
4 Performing an existing duty cannot be the consideration for a new contract.
5 A promise to accept part payment of a pre-existing debt in place of the whole debt is not consideration.

39.3.1 Adequacy of consideration

The law is concerned with bargains and not gifts. This can be seen in cases such as *Chappell v Nestlé Co. Ltd* (1960) and *Esso Petroleum Co. Ltd v Commissioners of Customs and Excise* (1976) (already considered above).

The idea of adequacy is that the parties to the contract themselves agree that the value of things being exchanged is acceptable. This can be seen in the cases of *Thomas v Thomas* (1842) and *Chappell v Nestlé Co. Ltd* (1960).

Case studies

Thomas v Thomas (1842)

Before he died, a man expressed the wish that his wife should be allowed to remain in the house after he died. This wish was not stated in his will. The executors carried out this wish and charged the widow a nominal rent of £1 per year. When they later tried to evict her, they failed because consideration was provided by the £1 per year rent.

Chappell v Nestlé Co. Ltd (1960)

Nestlé's customers were able to claim a recording of a song at a fraction of the normal cost if they sent in some Nestlé chocolate bar wrappers.

The total consideration was the payment and the chocolate bar wrappers. The House of Lords stressed that even if the contract had been to supply the record merely for the wrappers alone, without any money, the wrappers would have constituted consideration, even though they were of only nominal value.

Paying a sum of money to abandon a claim is valid consideration, even though the claim had little chance of success (but was not fraudulent). This makes an agreement to settle a claim, for example, for alleged defective goods, enforceable as a contract, whether or not the original claim would have succeeded.

39.3.2 Sufficiency of consideration

Sufficiency means the consideration must be real, and have some value.

- Real means the consideration must exist.
- Consideration must be definite, and having some value means it has at least a nominal amount of value (as in *Chappell v Nestlé Co. Ltd*).

However, there is little consistency in approach – *White v Bluett* (1853) and *Ward v Byham* (1956) show conflicting decisions.

Case studies

White v Bluett (1853)

A son owed his father money and had given him a promissory note (a written promise to pay a sum of money) to cover the debt. The father died with the promissory note unpaid. The father's executors sued for the money. The son claimed that his father had promised to write off the debt if he stopped complaining about the way his father was handing out his assets, which he had done. There was no consideration, as he had no legal right to complain, and natural love and affection were not consideration, so he still had to pay the debt.

Ward v Byham (1956)

The parties were the parents of an illegitimate daughter. The child lived with the father at first, but the mother asked for the child to live with her. The father agreed subject to a letter saying:

> Mildred, I am prepared to let you have Carol and pay you up to £1 per week allowance for her providing you can prove that she will be well looked after and happy and also that she is allowed to decide for herself whether or not she wishes to come and live with you.

The father eventually stopped making the payments. As there was no legal obligation to keep the child happy, the court considered this to be consideration.

39.3.3 Past consideration is no consideration

This means that consideration has no value where it has already been done at the time the agreement is made. It is clearly not the price for which the promise is bought, as it had been completed before the agreement was made. This can be seen in *Re McArdle* (1951).

Case study

Re McArdle (1951)

Mrs McArdle had carried out work on the bungalow in which she lived with her husband and his mother. The bungalow was part of the estate of her husband's father. After the work had been carried out, those inheriting the bungalow signed a document stating 'in consideration of you carrying out the repairs we agree that the executors pay you £488 from the estate'.

As the promise to make payment came after the work had been done, it was past consideration. There was, therefore, no contract to pay her the £488.

There is an exception to this rule – when the promisor makes an express or implied request for a particular task, and there must be an implied understanding that the task should be paid for. This is often the case in commercial agreements such as *Re Casey's Patent* (1892), and occasionally can be seen in other 'important' matters such as in the case of *Lampleigh v Braithwait* (1615).

Key terms

Promisor – in contract law, a person who makes a promise to another.
Promisee – in contract law, the person who is promised something.

Case studies

Re Casey's Patent (1892)

The claimant worked on patents for a company. The company later promised him a one-third share in the patents. The company then refused to hand over the share of the patents on the basis that there was no contract as the consideration was past consideration.

The court decided the claimant was entitled to the share as it was implied that when he worked on the patents he would receive some payment.

Lampleigh v Braithwait (1615)

Braithwait had been convicted of murder and was to be hanged. Lampleigh agreed to do what he could to obtain a royal pardon (the only way to avoid being executed). Lampleigh negotiated the pardon, and Braithwait then promised to pay him £100, but did not do so. Braithwait's argument was that the gaining of the pardon was past consideration so there was no obligation to pay the £100.

The court decided that although the consideration had preceded the promise, the actions taken were at the defendant's request and were so important that a fee must have been implied.

There must be all of the following for these exceptions to apply:
- an express or implied request by the promisor to the promisee to perform a task
- an implied promise inherent in the request that the promisor will pay the promisee a reasonable sum for performing the task
- the performance of the task, and
- the payment of money by the promisor to the promisee for that performance.

While it is sometimes said that this is an exception to 'past consideration is no consideration', it is not – the performance of the task occurs after the implied promise to pay by the promisor.

39.3.4 Consideration must move from the promisee

Consideration moving from the promisee means that a person cannot sue or be sued under a contract unless they have provided consideration for it.

In a bilateral contract, each person is a promisor and a promisee, but in a unilateral contract, one party makes the promise and the other does the act rather than make a promise. An example can be seen in *Tweddle v Atkinson* (1861).

Tweddle v Atkinson (1861)

Both fathers of a young couple who intended to marry agreed in writing to each give a sum of money to the couple. The woman's father died before giving over the money and the husband then sued the executors of the estate when they refused to pay the money. Even though the husband was named in the agreement, his claim failed because he had given no consideration and was not a party to the agreement himself.

39.3.5 Performing a pre-existing duty owed to the promisor cannot be the consideration for a new contract

A pre-existing duty is something that you are already legally required to do. This can occur in three ways:

1 A duty imposed under a public duty to act, such as the police doing what they are required to do under their public duty.
2 A duty imposed under an existing contract with the promisor such as, in a contract of employment, merely doing one's job.
3 A promise to make payment of an already existing debt, such as repaying a loan.

Examples include a public duty, as in the case of *Collins v Godefroy* (1831), or an obligation under an existing contract, as in *Stilk v Myrick* (1809).

Case studies

Collins v Godefroy (1831)

A policeman was under a court order to attend and give evidence at a trial. It was important to the defendant that the policeman attended, so the defendant promised to pay the policeman some money to make sure he did. There was no consideration as the policeman was already under a duty to be in court.

Stilk v Myrick (1809)

Stilk agreed to sail as crew with Myrick for £5 per month. Part way through the voyage, two of the crew deserted and the captain asked the remaining crew to do the extra work, sharing the wages saved. The claim for the additional wages failed because there was no consideration – crew agree to do everything possible in the event of emergencies.

However, if there is an extra element required for the new payment, there is consideration. This was demonstrated in *Glasbrook Bros v Glamorgan County Council* (1925) and in *Hartley v Ponsonby* (1857).

Case studies

Glasbrook Bros v Glamorgan County Council (1925)

During a strike, a pit-owner asked for extra protection from the police by having police officers live on site. For this there would be a payment. When the strike was over, the pit-owner refused to pay, arguing that the police were in any case bound to protect his pit. As the police had provided more men and in a different way than they would normally have done, there was consideration for the promise.

Hartley v Ponsonby (1857)

This case involved similar facts to *Stilk v Myrick* (1809). However, after desertion only 19 members of a crew of 36 remained. A similar promise to pay more money to the remaining crew was enforceable because the reduction in numbers made the voyage much more dangerous, so there was an extra element amounting to good consideration.

Case study

Williams v Roffey Bros and Nicholls (Contractors) Ltd (1990)

Roffey subcontracted the carpentry on a number of flats it was refurbishing to Williams for £20,000. Williams had underquoted for the work and ran into financial difficulties. There was a clause in Roffey's building contract that it would have to pay its client if the flats were not finished on time. Therefore, Roffey agreed to pay Williams another £10,300 if he would complete the carpentry on time.

Williams completed the work on time but Roffey failed to pay the extra £10,300. Even though Williams was only doing what he was already contractually bound to do, Roffey was gaining the extra benefit of not having to pay the money for delay to its client. Williams was thus providing consideration for Roffey's promise to pay him more for the work merely by completing his existing obligations on time. The reason why Roffey refused to pay Williams the additional sum was that, in completing the work on time, Williams was merely performing his pre-existing contractual duty.

The court decided that the promise for extra pay was enforceable.

More modern examples can be seen in which the courts regard contracts that might appear to have no consideration as enforceable. The current situation can be seen in *Williams v Roffey Bros and Nicholls (Contractors) Ltd* (1990).

39.3.6 A promise to accept part payment of an existing debt in place of the whole debt is not consideration

This rule arises from *Pinnel*'s case (1602), where the judge said that the payment of a lesser sum on the day a debt is due cannot be in satisfaction of the greater debt. This means that a creditor is able to claim the reminder of a debt, even if they have agreed with the debtor that a part payment will clear the debt, unless there is early repayment or something additional is given.

This rule was confirmed in the case of *Foakes v Beer* (1884), where an agreement to pay a debt by instalments was no consideration for not claiming the whole debt at once.

Case study

Foakes v Beer (1884)

Dr Foakes owed Mrs Beer £2090 after a court gave judgment in favour of Mrs Beer. The two reached an agreement for Foakes to pay in instalments, with Mrs Beer agreeing that no further action would be taken if the debt was paid off by an agreed date. Later Mrs Beer demanded the interest to which she was entitled under a judgment debt, and sued when Foakes refused to pay. She was successful following the rule in *Pinnel*'s case.

The rule in *Pinnel*'s case is harsh.

One exception is the principle of accord and satisfaction, where there is agreement (accord) to end a contract and satisfaction (consideration) that has been acted upon voluntarily. For example, accepting something other than money for the whole debt is good consideration, even if it is not of equal value to the debt. This must be done at the request of the creditor, not the debtor. An example of this is if A owed B £1000 and A suggested that B gives him £200 and B's car (even if the car was not worth £800), and B agrees to that arrangement.

	Brief legal rule	Case example
Consideration must be sufficient	Sufficiency means the consideration must be real, and have some value	*Chappell v Nestlé Co. Ltd* (1960) *White v Bluett* (1853)
Past consideration is no consideration	Consideration has no value where it has already been done at the time the agreement is made	*Re McArdle* (1951)
Consideration must move from the promisee	A person cannot sue or be sued under a contract unless he or she has provided consideration for it	*Tweddle v Atkinson* (1861)
Performing an existing duty is not consideration	Performing an existing duty cannot be the consideration for a new contract	*Stilk v Myrick* (1809)
Where there is acceptance of part payment of a debt	Payment of a lesser sum on the day a debt is due cannot be in satisfaction of the greater debt	*Foakes v Beer* (1884)

Figure 39.7 Key facts: consideration

Case	Judgment
Thomas v Thomas (1842)	Payment of the very small rent was consideration, not the moral obligation to carry out the dead man's wishes
Chappell v Nestlé Co. Ltd (1960)	The chocolate bar wrappers amounted to consideration for the record
White v Bluett (1853)	An intangible benefit is not consideration
Ward v Byham (1956)	Going beyond one's existing legal duty can amount to consideration
Re McArdle (1951)	The promise to make payment came after the work had been done, so it was past consideration and of no value
Re Casey's Patent (1892)	The court can find an implied term as to make some payment to circumvent the past consideration rule
Lampleigh v Braithwait (1615)	The matter was so important that some payment could be implied as intended by the parties

Case	Judgment
Tweddle v Atkinson (1861)	The claim failed because he had given no consideration and was not a party to the agreement himself
Collins v Godefroy (1831)	There was no consideration for it as the policeman was already under a duty to be in court
Stilk v Myrick (1809)	A pre-existing contractual obligation was not sufficient consideration to create a contract
Glasbrook Bros v Glamorgan County Council (1925)	The police had provided more men and in a different way than they would normally have done, so there was consideration for the promise
Hartley v Ponsonby (1857)	A great change in circumstances and workload amounted to consideration
Williams v Roffey Bros and Nicholls (Contractors) Ltd (1990)	The extra benefit of not having to pay a sum for delay to a client is consideration
Pinnel's case (1602)	Payment of a lesser sum on the day a debt is due cannot be in satisfaction of the greater debt
Foakes v Beer (1884)	*Pinnel's* case was applied

Figure 39.8 Key cases: consideration

39.4 Privity of contract

39.4.1 The general principle of privity of contract

The principle of privity of contract is: a contract cannot confer rights nor impose obligations on someone who is not a party to the contract. A contract between A and B cannot result in C claiming rights (or having obligations imposed) under the contract.

> **Key term**
>
> Privity of contract – only those who are parties to a contract are bound by it and can benefit from it.

The rule of privity can be seen in *Dunlop Pneumatic Tyre Co. Ltd v Selfridge* (1915).

> **Case study**
>
> ### *Dunlop Pneumatic Tyre Co. Ltd v Selfridge* (1915)
>
> Dunlop manufactured tyres and sold some to Dew, who agreed not to resell them below a certain price. Dew resold to Selfridge on the basis of the same term, not to resell below a certain price. Selfridge then resold below this price. As Dew refused to sue Selfridge, Dunlop sued them. Because Dunlop was not a party to the contract between Dew and Selfridge, it could not sue Selfridge for selling below the agreed price.

39.4.2 The relationship between privity and consideration

The rule of privity is based on the rule that consideration must move from the promisee, as in *Tweddle v Atkinson* (1861). The privity rule is seen as causing injustice, and the courts have tried to find ways of avoiding the rule. There are special cases, where a contracting party may sue on behalf of another who was intended to benefit from the contract. In *Jackson v Horizon Holidays Ltd* (1975), it was decided that the rule does not apply to contracts where one person would be expected to make contracts on behalf of themselves and others, such as holidays and restaurants.

> **Case study**
>
> ### *Jackson v Horizon Holidays Ltd* (1975)
>
> Mr Jackson booked a holiday for himself and his family. The holiday was very disappointing. He sued for damages for himself and his family. The court decided that it would be unfair to limit the award of damages to Mr Jackson. Damages awarded reflected the loss suffered by all the members of the holiday party.

> **Look online**
>
> Research and look for legal justifications in other cases such as those discussed in this article about *Jackson v Horizon Holidays*: www.lawgazette.co.uk/law/claiming-damages-for-a-ruined-holiday/55929.article

39.4.3 Common law exceptions

There are some exceptions when the rule of privity does not apply.

Agency

An agency arises when one person, the agent, is authorised to make a contract on behalf of another person, the principal. The principal and the agent are treated as being the same person, so the principal is a party to the contract.

This occurs, for example, when an employee makes a contract on behalf of a company.

The doctrine of privity usually prevents a third party from relying on the terms of a contract. This means that an exclusion clause in a contract may not offer protection to anyone other than the parties to the contract. This can be seen in *Scruttons Ltd v Midland Silicones Ltd* (1961).

Case study

Scruttons Ltd v Midland Silicones Ltd (1961)

The claimant was the owner of goods which were shipped for it by a carrier. The contract limited the liability of the carrier for damage caused to the goods to $500. The carrier contracted with the defendant to unload the goods. When doing so, the defendant negligently damaged them.

The defendant was not party to the contract between the owner and the carrier, and so the doctrine of privity of contract prevented the defendant from being awarded the $500.

Collateral contracts

The court may be able to avoid the strict rule of privity by finding a second contract alongside the main agreement, as in the case of *Shanklin Pier Ltd v Detel Products Ltd* (1951).

Case study

Shanklin Pier Ltd v Detel Products Ltd (1951)

Contractors employed to paint the pier were told by the pier company to use paint manufactured by Detel. The paint was bought by the contractors from Detel. Detel made a representation to the pier company that the paint would last for seven years. The paint only lasted three months.

There was no privity of contract between the pier company and the defendant paint manufacturer, but the court found that there was a collateral contract between them to the effect that the paint would last for seven years. The consideration was the instruction given by the pier company to its contractors to order the paint from the defendant.

Restrictive covenants

In English land law, if a purchaser of land promises the seller in a contract for the purchase of land that they will not do something on the land, then this is a restrictive covenant. An example might be not to keep a caravan on the land.

This becomes part of the title to land that an owner has. That promise will 'run with the land', which means that all subsequent purchasers of that land are legally bound by that promise even though they are not parties to that initial contract. This can be seen in the case of *Tulk v Moxhay* (1848).

Case study

Tulk v Moxhay (1848)

Tulk sold a house and the centre gardens in Leicester Square to Elms. The contract included a restrictive covenant that the gardens were not to be built on. Elms sold the gardens to Moxhay who intended to build on them. Because the covenant ran with the land, Tulk could enforce it against Moxhay even though they had no direct contract.

39.4.4 Statutory exceptions

Contracts (Rights of Third Parties) Act 1999

Section 1 of the Contracts (Rights of Third Parties) Act 1999 states:

> (1) Subject to the provisions of this Act, a person who is not a party to a contract (a 'third party') may in his own right enforce a term of the contract if—
>
> (a) the contract expressly provides that he may, or
>
> (b) subject to subsection (2), the term purports to confer a benefit on him.
>
> (2) Subsection (1)(b) does not apply if on a proper construction of the contract it appears that the parties did not intend the term to be enforceable by the third party.
>
> (3) The third party must be expressly identified in the contract by name, as a member of a class or as answering a particular description but need not be in existence when the contract is entered into.

Thus, someone who is not a party to a contract (a 'third party') may enforce the contract against either or both of the actual parties to the contract if:

- the third party is expressly identified by name, or as a member of a class or as answering a particular description, and
- the contract expressly provides that the third party may enforce the contract, or
- the contract term is an attempt to confer the benefit of the term on the third party.

This seems to get round the difficulty that occurred in *Beswick v Beswick* (1967).

Case study

Beswick v Beswick (1967)

Mr Beswick made a contract with his nephew to sell his coal merchant's business, in exchange for weekly payments to the uncle for life and, after his death, to his wife, the nephew's aunt. After the death of the uncle, the nephew refused to pay the weekly payments to his aunt.

The court decided that the aunt was not a party to the contract and so there was no privity of contract.

The reason why the aunt would now be able to claim under the Contracts (Rights of Third Parties) Act 1999 is that she was named in the contract, and the contract intended to confer a benefit on her.

Nisshin Shipping Company Limited v Cleaves & Co Limited & Others [2003] makes it clear that if parties to a contract wish to ensure that a benefit is not conferred upon third parties, the parties should use an express term in their contract to rebut any presumption that might be made under s 1(1)(b) of the 1999 Act.

The parties to the contract have the right to exclude the Act from benefiting a third party.

Where the Act applies, under s 3 if the contract is being enforced by a third party, the person who made the contract can rely on any defence or valid exclusion clause that was available to the original contracting party: if A books a holiday with B and the list given to A of those going on that holiday includes another, C, C will be able to claim rights under the contract.

A will, however, be able to rely on any defence they might have, including relying on any valid term of the contract limiting their liability for any breach of that contract.

One success among many attempts to evade the consequences of the privity rule in this context is found in *New Zealand Shipping Co. v Satterthwaite* (1974).

Other statutory exceptions

There are a number of statutory exceptions:

- These include giving rights to third parties under insurance contracts, both marine and motor.
- For motor insurance, this would include named drivers on a policy, and someone driving another car in an emergency under 'driver of other cars' terms in the insurance policy.
- Some aspects of life assurance also fall within these exceptions.

Case study

New Zealand Shipping Co. v Satterthwaite (1974)

The facts were very similar to those in *Scruttons Ltd v Midland Silicones Ltd*, but the exclusion clause between the owner and the carrier was expressly stated to cover *anyone* engaged by the carrier to assist in dealing with the goods, even though not party to the contract between owner and carrier.

The court got round the privity of contract difficulty by holding that, when the owner entered into the contract with the carrier, the owner was in effect also making an offer (promise) to anyone who would assist the carrier that the exclusion clause would extend to that person. The act of assisting the carrier, performed by the defendant in unloading the goods, was both the acceptance of the owner's offer and the consideration for the owner's promise.

So, the exclusion clause created a separate unilateral contract between the owner and the defendant and is an example also of consideration being the performance of an existing duty owed to a third person, as the defendant was already bound by contract with the carrier to unload the goods.

	Brief legal rule	Case example
The rule of privity of contract	Only those who are parties to a contract are bound by it and can benefit from it	*Dunlop Pneumatic Tyre Co. Ltd v Selfridge* (1915)
Relationship with consideration	In certain circumstances the courts try to avoid the strict rule of privity by allowing for damages for distress	*Jackson v Horizon Holidays Ltd* (1975)
Agency provides an exception to privity	An agent is authorised to make a contract on behalf of another person, the principal	
Collateral contracts can provide an exception to privity	The court may be able to avoid the strict rule of privity by finding a second contract alongside the main agreement	*Shanklin Pier Ltd v Detel Products Ltd* (1951)
Contracts (Rights of Third Parties) Act 1999	The Act allows someone who is not a party to a contract (a 'third party'), in some circumstances, to enforce the contract against either or both of the actual parties to the contract	*Beswick v Beswick* (1967)

Figure 39.9 Key facts: privity of contract

Case	Judgment
Dunlop Pneumatic Tyre Co. Ltd v Selfridge (1915)	As Dunlop was not a party to the contract between Dew and Selfridge, it could not sue Selfridge for selling below the agreed price
Jackson v Horizon Holidays Ltd (1975)	The claims of Jackson's family were allowed even though, strictly, they were not parties to the holiday contract
Shanklin Pier Ltd v Detel Products Ltd (1951)	There was found to be a collateral contract between them to the effect that the paint would last for seven years
Beswick v Beswick (1967)	The aunt was not a party to the contract, so there was no privity of contract

Figure 39.10 Key cases: privity of contract

Extension activity

You can explore further issues, cases and principles for this area of the law:

- Common law exceptions – *Linden Gardens Trust Ltd v Lenesta Sludge Disposals Ltd; St Martins Property Corporation Ltd v Sir Robert McAlpine* (1993).
- Interpretation of contracts (Rights of Third Parties) Act 1999 s 1 (1) (b) in arbitration law – *Nisshin Shipping Co. Ltd v Cleaves & Co. Ltd* (2003).

Quick questions

1. State the ways in which an offer can be rejected.
2. State the rules with respect to acceptance by post
3. State the presumptions with respect to the law on the intention to create legal relations. Give examples of rebuttal of these presumptions.
4. What is meant by 'sufficiency of consideration'?
5. Explain the general principle of privity of contract.

Summary

- Agreement in the formation of contract requires an offer to be accepted while it is open.
- An offer is a statement of the terms upon which a person is prepared to be bound by a contract.
- An offer differs from an invitation to treat, as only an offer can form the basis of a contract.
- An advertisement is an invitation to treat. It can only be an offer when there is a unilateral contract.
- Other invitations to treat include goods in a shop window or on a shop shelf, lots at an auction and requests for information.
- It is essential to know when an offer has been communicated so that it is open and when it ends.
- An offer can end through revocation, rejection, lapse of time, death and when accepted.
- Acceptance must be communicated to be effective; there are special rules in some circumstances where there is acceptance using the post.
- There must be an intention to create legal relations for there to be a valid contract.
- There is a distinction between business or commercial contracts and those that are of a social and domestic nature.
- Consideration involves each party to a contract giving something of value to the other.
- There are five rules with respect to what amounts to consideration.
- Privity of contract means that only a party to the contract can take legal action on it.
- There are exceptions to the doctrine of privity, both from case law and statute.

Chapter 40 Terms

Introduction

The terms of a contract are what the parties to the contract have agreed. These terms can either be specifically agreed between the parties, known as express terms, or implied in the contract. For example, if I buy a cup of coffee for £1:
- The express terms are coffee and £1 – this is the consideration in the contract.
- Other terms may be implied, for example, that the coffee will be hot.

There are different types of express and implied terms – conditions, warranties, innominate terms – which have different consequences if not complied with.

40.1 Is a statement a representation or a term of the contract?

When negotiations are taking place, many things are discussed so that the terms of the contract are agreed. The difficulty is deciding whether what is said is a term or remains a representation.

The courts will take into account the following factors:
1 The importance attached to the representation.
2 Special knowledge or skill of the person making the statement.
3 Any time lag between making the statement and making the contract.
4 Whether there is a written contract.

The distinction between a term and a representation is important in relation to remedies:
- If a term is not observed, there can be a claim for breach of contract.
- If a representation is untrue, the remedy is for misrepresentation.

The importance attached to the representation

Where the statement is obviously important to the contract, it will be seen as a term of the contract. This was demonstrated in *Couchman v Hill* (1947).

Case study

Couchman v Hill (1947)

An auction catalogue stated that a heifer was unserved (not pregnant). The auctioneer and the farmer selling the animal confirmed this. In fact the heifer was pregnant and died while calving. The statement was clearly important to the purchaser of the animal and so was taken as a contract term rather than a representation.

Special knowledge or skill of the person making the statement

There are two contrasting cases that show the importance of the skill expected of a person making a statement. In these examples, the private seller of a car is not expected to have the same level of understanding about cars as a car dealer.
- *Oscar Chess v Williams* (1957): the private seller of a car believed it to be a 1948 model but it was actually much older. This statement was not a term of the contract.
- *Dick Bentley v Harold Smith Motors* (1965): the car dealer stated the car had done 20,000 miles when in fact it had done 100,000 miles. Even though that statement was not written in the contract, it was taken to be a term of the contract rather than a mere representation.

This distinction is important as the purchaser of the car could take action for breach of contract rather than for misrepresentation. In the *Dick Bentley* case, it is crucial because the purchaser of the car would have lost his rights under the misrepresentation law at that time.

The time lag between making the statement and making the contract

Where a contract is made some time after negotiations and does not refer to the statement that has been made during negotiations, it is likely that the statement will not become a term of the contract. This can be seen in *Routledge v McKay* (1954).

Case study

Routledge v McKay (1954)

Both parties were private individuals and relied on the registration documents of a motorbike. The contract was made seven days after the date of the vehicle's manufacture was mentioned, and did not refer to the date of the vehicle. The actual date of manufacture was misstated by 12 years.

Because of the time gap between negotiations and the written contract, the statement was a mere representation and not a term of the contract.

Whether there is a written contract

As we have seen in *Routledge v McKay*, the court tends to presume that everything the parties wanted to include as a term of the contract is put in the written contract.

	Brief legal rule	Case example
The importance attached to the representation	Where the statement is obviously important to the contract it will be seen as a term of the contract	*Couchman v Hill* (1947)
Special knowledge or skill of the person making the statement	Where there is special knowledge or skill, the statement is more likely to be a term of the contract	*Oscar Chess v Williams* (1957) *Dick Bentley v Harold Smith Motors* (1965)
The time lag between making the statement and making the contract	Where a contract is made later and does not refer to the statement, it is likely that the statement does not become a term of the contract	*Routledge v Mackay* (1954)
Whether there is a written contract	The court tends to presume that everything the parties wanted to include as a term of the contract is put in the written contract	*Routledge v Mackay* (1954)

Figure 40.1 Key facts: term or representation in a contract

Case	Judgment
Couchman v Hill (1947)	The statement was clearly important to the purchaser of the animal and so was taken as a contract term rather than a representation
Oscar Chess v Williams (1957)	A private seller of a car believed it to be a 1948 model but was actually much older This statement was not a term of the contract, just a representation
Dick Bentley v Harold Smith Motors (1965)	The misleading mileage of a car was a term of the contract rather than a mere statement
Routledge v Mackay (1954)	It was presumed that the actual date of manufacture of the vehicle was not seen as important as it was not in the written contract

Figure 40.2 Key cases: term or representation in a contract

40.2 Express terms

Express terms are words agreed by the parties to be incorporated in their contract. They are terms which are written in a contract or stated verbally at the time the contract is made. There can be a combination of written and oral express terms. Where terms are expressly agreed there may be problems with incorporation or interpretation. Incorporation involves deciding what terms are in the contract, and interpretation (sometimes called construction) is concerned with what the incorporated terms mean.

Express terms deal with matters such as price and what must be provided for the price. They may specify how the contract is to be performed and the obligations of the parties under the contract. There may be exclusion clauses that will limit or extinguish one party's rights under the contract. We have seen that in the previous chapter with respect to exclusion of the provisions of the Contract (Rights of Third Parties) Act 1999. Exclusion clauses are dealt with in more detail below where cases involving signed documents, notices and tickets are dealt with.

Some terms can be considered particularly harsh. The law struggles to deal with very harsh terms.

Extension activity

An example of a very harsh term can be seen in *Interfoto v Stiletto Visual* (1987). Find the case on the internet and list terms that you consider harsh and those you consider reasonable.

40.3 Implied terms

Terms can be implied into the contract by the common law or by statute. Statutory implied terms are contained in different Acts such as the Consumer Rights Act 2015.

40.3.1 Terms implied by common law

Terms can be implied by common law in two ways:
1 Through business efficacy and the officious bystander test.
2 By custom or prior dealings between the parties.

Business efficacy and the officious bystander test

The courts will imply a term into a contract if the term is necessary to make sure that the contract works on a business-like basis. There is a two-part test for this:
1 Is the term necessary to make the contract effective?
2 If the parties to the contract had thought about it, would they have agreed that the suggested term was obviously going to be in the contract?

An example of business efficacy can be seen in the case of *The Moorcock* (1889).

Case study

The Moorcock (1889)

The defendants owned a wharf with a jetty on the River Thames. They agreed to dock a ship and unload cargoes at the wharf. Both parties were aware at the time of contracting that this could involve the vessel being there at low tide, and that then the ship would rest on the bottom. When the ship grounded it broke up on a ridge of rock.

The defendants stated there was no term covering this. The court implied a term that the ship would be at a safe mooring and that the ship would not be damaged when it settled at low tide.

The officious bystander test can be seen in *Shirlaw v Southern Foundries Ltd* (1939), where it was stated:

> *Prima facie* that which in any contract is left to be implied and need not be expressed is something so obvious that it goes without saying; so that if, while the parties were making their bargain, an officious bystander were to suggest some express provision for it in their agreement, they would testily suppress him with a common 'Oh, of course!'

In *Hollier v Rambler Motors* (1972), the court accepted that a failure to sign a document on one occasion did not prevent the terms in that document being present in the contract, if it was merely an oversight in not signing the document on that particular occasion.

Terms will not be implied if the parties would never have agreed to it had they thought about it. This was shown in *Shell UK Ltd v Lostock Garage Ltd* (1977).

Shell UK Ltd v Lostock Garage Ltd (1977)

In the contract, Shell supplied petrol and oil to Lostock who, in return, agreed to buy these products only from Shell. Shell later supplied petrol to other garages at lower prices as part of a price war. This forced Lostock to sell at a loss. Lostock argued there was a term in the contract that Shell would not abnormally discriminate against it. This argument failed as Shell would never have agreed to such a term.

Genuinely implied terms are what a reasonable person would have understood to be the intention of both parties in the context of the contract. *Egan v Static Control Components (Europe) Ltd* (2004) is a good example.

Case study

Egan v Static Control Components (Europe) Ltd (2004)

Static Control Components supplied Egan's company with components. Before 1999, Egan had signed three guarantees, making him personally liable for the company's debts up to £75,000. In 1999, with the debt rising, Egan was asked to repay in six weekly instalments and to sign a new guarantee for up to £150,000 in the same form as the previous guarantees. When the company went into liquidation, Egan tried to argue that the 1999 guarantee only applied to goods supplied after it was signed.

The court decided that a reasonable person would assume that the guarantee applied to both existing and future debts.

In *Marks and Spencer plc v BNP Paribas Securities Services Trust Company (Jersey) Ltd* (2015), the Supreme Court clarified the law relating to implied terms in contracts:

- Reasonableness is to be judged objectively, according to what the 'notional reasonable' person would agree to.
- Fairness and acceptability to the parties are not enough to imply a term.
- The requirement for reasonableness and equitableness will usually add nothing to the other tests – 'if a term satisfies the other requirements, it is hard to think that it would not be reasonable and equitable'.

- Only one test needs to be satisfied – the business efficacy or officious bystander test. However 'it would be a rare case where only one of those two requirements would be met'.
- The officious bystander test may not be straightforward – it is important to take 'the utmost care' in forming the question to be posed by the officious bystander.
- The test of necessity for business efficacy involves a value judgement – it is not a test of absolute necessity, because the necessity is judged by reference to business efficacy. Lord Sumption suggested that it may be more helpful to say that 'a term can only be implied if, without the term, the contract would lack commercial or practical coherence'.

Terms implied by custom

Much of English law is founded on the law of custom. Some local customs survive, such as the one in the case of *Hutton v Warren* (1836) where local custom meant that at the end of an agricultural lease, a tenant farmer was entitled to an allowance for seed and labour on the land. The court decided that the terms of the lease must be viewed in the light of the custom.

Terms implied by prior dealings between the parties

The prior conduct of the parties may indicate terms to be implied, as shown in *Hillas v Arcos* (1932).

Case study

Hillas v Arcos (1932)

A contract drawn up in 1930 between the two parties included an option clause, allowing the claimants to buy a further 100,000 lengths of timber during 1931. The agreement for 1931 was otherwise quite vague as to the type of timber, etc. The 1930 timber contract was fulfilled.

In 1931, the claimants then wanted the further 100,000 lengths of timber but the defendants refused to deliver them. Their argument was that since the 1931 agreement was vague in many major aspects, it was therefore no more than a basis for further negotiations.

The court decided that, while the option clause lacked specific detail, it was implied that it would be on the same terms as the previous contract.

	Brief legal rule	Case example
Business efficacy and the officious bystander test	Is the term necessary to make the contract effective?	*The Moorcock* (1889)
Terms can be implied by custom	The terms of the lease must be viewed in the light of the custom	*Hutton v Warren* (1836)
Terms can be implied by a course of dealing between the parties	The court may imply a term that reflects the previous dealings between the parties	*Hillas v Arcos* (1932)
Terms will not be implied if the parties would never have agreed to them had they thought about them	Terms will not be implied if the parties would never have agreed to them had they thought about them	*Shell UK Ltd v Lostock Garage Ltd* (1977)
The implied terms reflect the clear intention of the parties	Genuinely implied terms are what a reasonable person would have understood to be the intention of both parties in the context of the contract	*Egan v Static Control Components (Europe) Ltd* (2004)
Reasonableness is to be judged objectively	It is not strictly concerned with the hypothetical answer of the actual parties, but with that of notional reasonable people in the position of the parties at the time at which they were contracting	*Marks and Spencer plc v BNP Paribas Securities Services Trust Company (Jersey) Ltd* (2015)

Figure 40.3 Key facts: implied terms in a contract

Case	Judgment
The Moorcock (1889)	There was an implied undertaking that the ship would be at a safe mooring that would not damage the ship
Hutton v Warren *(1836)*	Local custom meant that at the end of an agricultural lease, a tenant farmer was entitled to an allowance for seed and labour on the land
Hillas v Arcos (1932)	While the option clause lacked specific detail, nevertheless it was in the same terms as the contract of sale that had been completed if the option were to be taken up
Hollier v Rambler Motors (1972)	A failure to sign a document on one occasion did not prevent the terms in that document being present in the contract if it was merely an oversight in not signing the document on that particular occasion
Shell UK Ltd v Lostock Garage Ltd (1977)	Lostock argued there was a term in the contract that Shell would not abnormally discriminate against it This argument failed as Shell would never have agreed to such a term
Egan v Static Control Components (Europe) Ltd (2004)	The court decided that a reasonable person would assume that the guarantee applied to both existing and future debts
Marks and Spencer plc v BNP Paribas Securities Services Trust Company (Jersey) Ltd (2015)	The court set out the current position with respect to when terms may be implied in a contract

Figure 40.4 Key cases: implied terms in a contract

40.3.2 Terms implied by statute: the Consumer Rights Act 2015

The Consumer Rights Act 2015 brings together rights and remedies available to consumers when making a contract with a business. These contracts are defined as being between consumer and trader in the Act, with both 'consumer' and 'trader' being defined. With these contracts, terms are implied in the contract and 'rights' are given to the consumer and impose a duty on the trader.

The Act also
- reforms and consolidates the law relating to unfair terms in consumer contracts
- sets out specific remedies available to consumers in contracts to which the Act applies.

The Act defines a consumer as: 'an individual acting for purposes that are wholly or mainly outside that individual's trade, business, craft or profession'.

A company cannot therefore be a 'consumer', as it is not an 'individual'.

This definition is wider than existing definitions, as it includes individuals who enter into contracts for a mixture of business and personal reasons, so long as the contracts are mainly for personal reasons. This means that if an author of a textbook, who is otherwise retired from work, buys computer software for his home computer and then uses the software to write part of the book, he or she will still be classified as a consumer. It is the trader who has to prove that an individual is not a consumer in the circumstances.

A trader is described in the Consumer Rights Act 2015 as:

> a person acting for purposes relating to that person's trade, business, craft or profession, whether acting personally or through another person acting in the trader's name or on the trader's behalf.

So a trader can be a sole trader, a company, business partnership or any other form of business organisation.

This definition expressly provides that traders remain liable when dealing through a third party, as, for example, when dealing through an agent.

The Consumer Rights Act 2015 applies to contracts of sale, hire, hire-purchase and other contracts for the transfer of goods.

We will now look at the implied terms, called rights (of the consumer) in the Act.

For the supply of goods:
- s 9 – the right of satisfactory quality
- s 10 – the right of fitness for particular purpose
- s 11 – the right relating to description.

For the supply of services:
- s 49 – reasonable care and skill
- s 52 – performance within a reasonable time.

Section 9 – the right of satisfactory quality

Section 9 of the Consumer Rights Act 2015 states:

> Every contract to supply goods is to be treated as including a term that the quality of the goods is satisfactory.

Satisfactory quality is defined as being where the goods meet the standard that a reasonable person would consider satisfactory, taking account of:
- any description of the goods
- the price or other consideration for the goods (if relevant)
- all the other relevant circumstances.

The Act goes on to explain that the quality of goods includes their state and condition and takes into account:
- the fitness for all the purposes for which goods of that kind are usually supplied and their durability
- appearance and finish of the goods
- freedom from minor defects of the goods
- the safety of the goods.

However, this will not apply:
- with respect to defects specifically drawn to the consumer's attention before the contract is made
- where the consumer examines the goods before the contract is made in relation to any defect that the examination would have revealed, or
- where the goods have been sold after inspection of a sample and the defect would have been apparent on a reasonable examination of the sample.

Whether the goods are of satisfactory quality is an objective test based on the views of a 'reasonable person' rather than those of the trader/supplier or of the consumer.

In *Rogers v Parish (Scarborough) Ltd* (1987), a case involving the sale of a new Range Rover car, Lord Mustill stated:

> To identify the relevant expectation one must look at the factors listed in the subsection. The first is the description applied to the goods. In the present case the vehicle was sold as new. Deficiencies which might be acceptable in a second-hand vehicle were not to be expected in one purchased as new. Next, the description 'Range Rover' would conjure up a particular set of expectations, not the same as those relating to an ordinary saloon car, as to the balance between performance, handling, comfort and resilience. The factor of price was also significant.

This is very similar to the law under the Sale of Goods Act 1979, and we can assume that the case law under that Act will continue to apply.

Section 10 – the right of fitness for particular purpose

This section applies to a contract to supply goods if, before the contract is made, the consumer lets the trader know the particular purpose for which they are contracting for the goods. The consumer can make the purpose known either expressly or impliedly.

In these circumstances, where the buyer is relying on the skill and judgement of the seller, there is an implied term that the goods are reasonably fit for that purpose, whether or not goods of that kind are usually supplied for that purpose. This term is again similar to the provision in the Sale of Goods Act 1979.

There is no need to state a purpose where the goods are being bought for their normal use, as in *Grant v Australian Knitting Mills Ltd* (1936) which involved underwear. There was no need to state that the underpants were to be worn by a human for the section to apply.

Where, however, the purchaser has a particular sensitivity that is not known to the seller, then so long as the goods are fit for the normal purpose to most people, there will be no breach of the requirement. This can be seen in the case of *Griffiths v Peter Conway Ltd* (1939), where the claimant had abnormally sensitive skin and suffered dermatitis from a new coat made especially for her. Since she had not made the seller aware of this, the seller was not in breach of the implied term as to fitness for purpose.

These cases show:
- There must be fitness for the purpose such goods are normally used.
- Where a purchaser has a specialist need, that need must be made known to the trader before the contract is made. This could include a particular food allergy to a food trader, sensitivity to a hair-colouring dye to a hairdresser or a particular strength of a fixing to a builder's merchant.

Section 11 – the right relating to description

Section 11 of the Consumer Rights Act 2015 states:

> Every contract to supply goods by description is to be treated as including a term that the goods will match the description.

This is again much the same as the equivalent in the Sale of Goods Act 1979.

The description can be an implied description, for example, when the goods are on a display. The description also includes relevant information that must be included in any statutory information relating to goods as set out in the Consumer Contracts (Information, Cancellation and Additional Charges) Regulations 2013.

Under these Regulations, information which the trader must provide for distance selling includes:
- a description of the goods, service or digital content provided
- the duration of any agreement
- the total price of the contract
- additional delivery charges and other costs
- information about the seller.

There is also a provision that where goods are supplied after being seen or examined by the consumer, the goods must match the model.

This could include the way in which goods are logoed, as in *Beale v Taylor* (1967).

Case study

Beale v Taylor (1967)

The purchaser bought a car advertised as a 1961 Triumph Herald convertible. The two halves had been welded together: the rear half of the car was part of a 1961 Herald convertible car, but the front half was part of an earlier model. The rear of the car had a badge on it – '1200', which was first applied to the 1961 model. The front half had a smaller engine in it, not a 1200. The badge amounted to the description.

Remedies for breach of terms to supply goods

A three-tier remedy structure will usually apply when a trader breaches the standards contained in the Act. The customer's rights are cumulative, and are in addition to the usual contract remedies such as damages. The rights are:
- The short-term right to reject – s 20 of the Consumer Rights Act 2015.
- The right to repair or replacement – s 23 of the Consumer Rights Act 2015.
- The right to a price reduction or the final right to reject – s 24 of the Consumer Rights Act 2015.

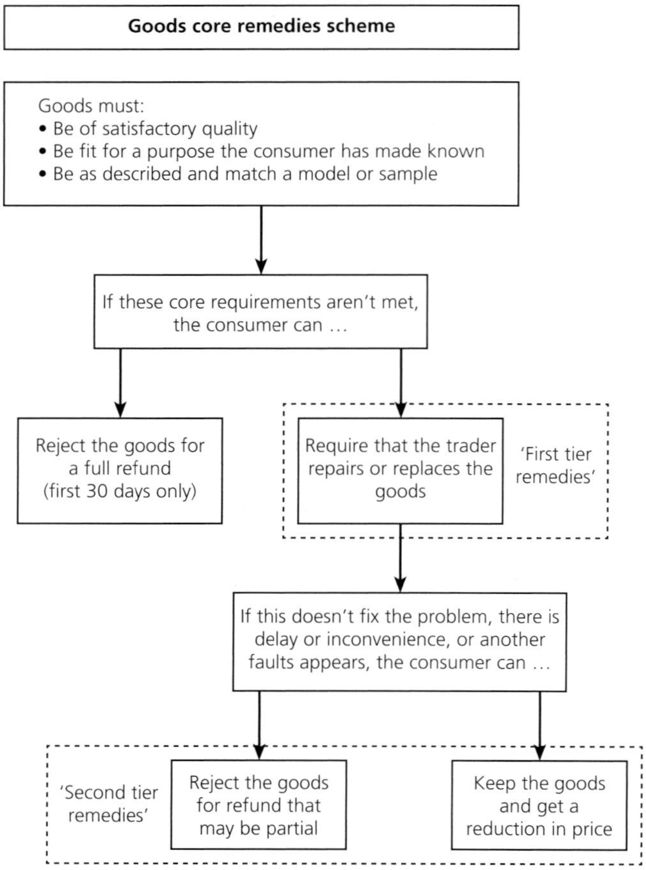

Figure 40.5 A flowchart showing the goods core remedies scheme

Source: Department for Business Innovation and Skills, *Consumer Rights Act: Goods – Guidance for Business* (September 2015). Crown copyright 2015.

Section 20 – the short-term right to reject

The short-term right to reject under s 20 must be exercised within 30 days of the delivery of the goods. The period will be shorter where the goods are perishable.

- The consumer must clearly indicate to the trader that they are rejecting the goods and ending the contract.
- As long as the consumer makes the goods available to the trader, they are entitled to a full refund.
- The trader must pay for reasonable costs of returning the goods (although this doesn't include the consumer's costs in returning the goods in person). This is usually done with a prepaid label, and is particularly important with respect to distance selling.
- A refund must be given within 14 days, beginning with the day on which the trader agrees that the consumer is entitled to a refund.

- The refund must be given using the same means of payment as the consumer used, unless the consumer expressly agrees otherwise.
- The trader must not impose any fee on the consumer for making the refund. More bulky items such as a bike may incur costs to the consumer, but these are then repayable by the trader.

Section 23 – the right to repair or replacement

If the s 20 right is not exercised by the consumer, they will have the right to repair or replacement under s 23. The trader must:

- Repair or replace the item in reasonable time, taking into account the nature of the goods and the purpose for which they were acquired.
- Do this without significant inconvenience to the consumer.
- Bear any necessary costs incurred in doing so. This includes the cost of any labour, materials or carriage relating to the exercise of this right.

The fault complained of must have been present at the time of the original delivery.

The consumer cannot require the trader to repair or replace the goods if it would be impossible, or disproportionate compared to other remedies. It would be impossible, for example, to replace faulty goods if they were unique. A replacement would also have to be identical, so that if the same make and model was no longer available, replacement would be impossible.

A major factor determining whether either repair or replacement is disproportionate is if it would impose an unreasonable cost on the trader compared with an alternative remedy.

If the consumer requests a repair or replacement within the first thirty days of the goods being supplied, then the short term right to reject is paused. Once the goods are repaired or replaced goods, the consumer has either the remainder of the thirty-day period or seven days, whichever is the longer, in which to reject the goods if they still do not conform to the contract.

- For example, a phone develops a fault on day 26 and is returned to the phone shop for repair; the phone is returned on day 29 supposedly repaired. If it has not been repaired satisfactorily, the consumer has until day 36 to reject the phone.

The consumer only has to accept one repair or replacement. If the goods still do not meet the consumer's rights, whether because the original issue persists or a new one has arisen, the consumer can exercise their right to a price reduction or final right to reject.

Section 24 – the right to a price reduction or the final right to reject

If s 23 does not bring satisfaction, the consumer has the right to a price reduction or a final right to reject the goods and claim a refund under s 24. The trader can have only one attempt at repair or replacement for the consumer to have this right. Any refund is subject to a deduction for use. During the first six months, any deduction for use is, at present, limited to motor vehicles.

Consumer remedies under the Consumer Rights Act 2015 for the implied terms are sometimes said to be sequential and tiered:

1 a short-term right to reject and claim a refund within 30 days, which if not exercised leads to
2 the right to repair or replacement, and if this is unsatisfactory, then
3 the right to a price reduction or a final right to reject (and claim a refund) with a possible reduction for use of the item.

Look online

To help you with this area, look at the flowchart showing core statutory goods remedies on page 38 of the Guidance for Business at: www. businesscompanion.info/sites/default/files/CRA-Goods-Guidance-for-Business-Sep-2015.pdf

Who has to show the non-conformity at time of supply for a breach of ss 9–11 (apart from short-term right to reject)?

Under ss 19(14) and (15) of the Consumer Rights Act 2015, if a breach of the statutory rights, for example, a fault in the goods supplied, arises in the first six months from delivery, it is presumed to have been present at the time of delivery. Therefore, if a fault is discovered within the first six months after buying the product, it is presumed to have been there since the time of purchase – unless the trader can prove otherwise. This applies where the consumer exercises his or her right to a repair or replacement or his or her right to a price reduction or the final right to reject. This does not apply where the consumer exercises the short-term right to reject.

If a fault develops after the first six months, the burden is on the consumer to prove that the product was faulty at the time of delivery.

Section 49 – reasonable care and skill

A contract to supply a service implies that the trader must perform the service with reasonable care and skill.

A contract to supply a service might be a contract to carry out building work, or to service a car. Such contracts often include both goods and services. The service element would include deciding what was needed and the fitting of the parts to the car. The parts themselves are a supply of goods. This is equivalent to the relevant section of the Supply of Goods and Services Act 1982, which the Consumer Rights Act 2015 replaced.

Here the standard of care is equivalent to the standard of care expected in a claim in the tort of negligence. This is decided on a case-by-case basis, and can be seen in the cases of *Thake v Maurice* (1986) and *Wilson v Best Travel* (1993).

Case studies

Thake v Maurice (1986)

Mr and Mrs Thake already had five children so they decided that the husband should have a vasectomy. However, after the operation Mrs Thake became pregnant again and sued for breach of contract. There was an implied term that the surgeon would perform the operation to the standard of care and skill of a competent surgeon.

The evidence was that he had reached that level of care and skill so the claim was unsuccessful.

Wilson v Best Travel (1993)

While on holiday in Greece, the claimant fell through a glass door and suffered injuries. The glass conformed to Greek but not British safety requirements. The court stated that, as the tour company had checked the premises to ensure the local safety regulations had been complied with and the danger posed by the glass would not cause 'reasonable holidaymakers' to decline to stay there, they had not breached the implied term.

Section 52 – performance within a reasonable time

This term applies where the contract does not include a specific time and the service has not been completed or has taken longer than expected. What is a reasonable time is a question of fact, which will depend on the circumstances.

The rights under ss 49 and 52, and the right of the trader to be paid a reasonable sum where no price is agreed, are sometimes included in pre-contract statements incorporated into the contract. These are likely to be quite detailed, particularly where the contract is for building work.

Remedies for breach of terms to supply services

If the service does not conform to the contract, the consumer's rights are:
- the right to require repeat performance (s 55)
- the right to a price reduction (s 56).

Section 55 – the right to require repeat performance

This right requires the trader to perform the service again, to complete its performance in accordance with the contract.

If the right is demanded, and assuming that performance is not impossible, the trader must provide it within a reasonable time and without significant inconvenience to the consumer. The trader must also bear any necessary costs incurred in doing so such as the cost of any labour or materials.

Section 56 – the right to a price reduction

This right is to reduce the price to the consumer by an appropriate amount for the trader's failure to perform the contract. This may result in the trader giving a refund, up to the full contract price.

This remedy is available only in two situations:
- where completion by repeat performance is impossible, or
- if the consumer has asked for repeat performance but the trader breaches the requirement to do it within a reasonable time and without significant interference to the consumer.

40.4 Types of term

There are two approaches to classification of terms – term based and breach based. Term based means using the traditional method of categorising a term as either a condition or warranty, The more modern breach-based approach recognises that the effect of breach of a term will vary depending on the seriousness of the breach, hence the term being considered intermediate or innominate. The innominate approach is less certain. It can be difficult to decide if the effect of the breach is

sufficiently serious to justify termination of the contract as if it were a condition.

40.4.1 Condition

A condition is a term in a contract so important that a failure to perform the obligation would destroy the main purpose of the contract.
- For example, if I make a contract to buy a sim card to fit an iPhone, it is central to the contract that the sim card will fit an iPhone. There would be either an express term in the contract (for example, 'suitable for iPhone') or an implied term to that effect. The term would be a condition. This is important because if a condition is broken, the person suffering the failure to perform is entitled to end the contract.

A condition is said to go to the root of a contract. This can be seen in the case of *Poussard v Spiers and Pond* (1876).

Case study

Poussard v Spiers and Pond (1876)

An actress agreed to perform the lead role in a production. She failed to attend the first few performances. Her role was given to an understudy. When she did attend, she was not allowed to take up the role. She had broken her contract by not turning up for the performances. As the lead, her presence was central. It was therefore a condition in the contract so the contract could be repudiated.

40.4.2 Warranty

A warranty is a minor term of the contract. Only damages can be claimed for a breach of warranty – the contract is not ended and the main purpose of the contract can continue to be performed despite the breach.
- For example, for a phone, it is not central to the contract if the phone will only store 99 contacts rather than the 100 stated in the contract. It still performs the main purpose of making phone calls. One fewer contact available in the memory is not central to the contract.

Key terms

Condition – a term in a contract that is central to the contract. Breach of this term may allow the contract to be repudiated.

Warranty – a minor term in a contract. Breach of this term does not end the contract but allows a claim for damages only.

An example of a breach of warranty can be seen in *Bettini v Gye* (1876).

Bettini v Gye (1876)

A singer was contracted to perform at a series of concerts and six days of rehearsal. He failed to attend the first three days of rehearsals. He was replaced as the singer for his failure to turn up to these rehearsals. When he did turn up, he was not permitted to continue the contract.

This was a breach of warranty, so the concert organiser could not end his contract, which continued. The singer was, therefore, awarded damages for loss of earnings for the breach of his contract.

40.4.3 Innominate term

An innominate term is a term in a contract that is not clearly a condition or a warranty. They are 'intermediate or indeterminate terms'.

The consequences of the breach of an innominate term can be the same as for a condition or a warranty, depending on the seriousness of the breach. The parties wait until the effect of the breach when it is treated as a condition or warranty.

Key term

Innominate term – a term in a contract that is not defined as a condition or a warranty.

An example of an innominate term can be seen in *Hong Kong Fir Shipping Co. Ltd v Kawasaki Kisen Kaisha Ltd* (1962).

Case study

Hong Kong Fir Shipping Co. Ltd v Kawasaki Kisen Kaisha Ltd (1962)

The defendants chartered a cargo ship from the claimants for two years. A term in the contract required that the ship should be 'in every way fitted for ordinary cargo service'. In fact there were problems with the ship's engine and the ship was not fully seaworthy. Eighteen weeks' use of the ship was lost while the ship was being repaired. The defendants repudiated the contract. Was the term a condition or a warranty?

The court said that not all contract terms could be simply divided into conditions and warranties; many contracts are more complex and:

> some breaches will, and others will not, give rise to an event which will deprive the party not in default of substantially the whole benefit which it was intended that he should obtain from the contract.

The court decided this was to be treated as a breach of warranty so only damages could be awarded.

Unless expressly stated in the contract, classifying a term as a condition or a warranty depends on the consequences of the breach. A term may also be classified as a condition as a result of a precedent.

This is a straightforward solution to the problem where general terms can have a variety of breaches. The proper remedy is only discovered after the consequences of the breach have been identified.

However, there is an element of uncertainty to the innominate term. The outcome of a particular breach is uncertain until the term has been construed as either a condition or a warranty, taking into account the severity of the breach that has occurred.

	Brief legal rule	Case example
Condition in a contract	A term in a contract that is central to the contract, breach of which may allow the contract to be repudiated	*Poussard v Spiers and Pond* (1876)
Warranty in a contract	A minor term in a contract, breach of which does not end the contract but allows a claim for damages only	*Bettini v Gye* (1876)
Innominate term in a contract	A term in a contract that is not defined as a condition or a warranty. Whether it is treated as a condition or a warranty depends on the consequences of any breach of the term	*Hong Kong Fir Shipping Co. Ltd v Kawasaki Kisen Kaisha Ltd* (1962)

Figure 40.6 Key facts: terms in a contract

Case	Judgment
Poussard v Spiers and Pond (1876)	Her presence was central to the production; it was a condition entitling the producers to repudiate her contract for her non-attendance
Bettini v Gye (1876)	The rehearsals were not central to the contract to sing, so the concert organiser could not repudiate his contract He had not broken a condition in the contract
Hong Kong Fir Shipping Co. Ltd v Kawasaki Kisen Kaisha Ltd (1962)	Not all contracts could be simply divided into terms that are conditions and terms that are warranties Many contracts are more complex

Figure 40.7 Key cases: terms in a contract

40.5 Exclusion and limitation clauses

Exclusion clauses are terms in a contract that exclude or limit liability if the contract is breached. They may also attempt to exclude liability in other areas of law, for example, under the tort of negligence.

Exclusion clauses are often found in standard form contracts and on notices.

There are many ways that a term of the contract tries to limit or exclude liability:

- A term may restrict the value of any claim to the purchase price of the goods.
- It may try to exclude a claim for a defect after 14 days from the date of the contract.

We have already seen that many contracts attempt to exclude the operation of the Contract (Rights of Third Parties) Act 1999 in Chapter 39, section 39.4.3.

Key term

Exclusion clause – a term in a contract that prevents one party being liable for a breach of contract.

40.5.1 The nature of exclusion and limitation clauses

Courts generally accept that the parties to a contract can agree any terms they like under the principle of freedom of contract.

However, this view is balanced by the idea that often during negotiations, one party is in a much stronger position than another. For example, as an individual or even as a business, you have little opportunity to negotiate the terms of a contract for a rail ticket or a mobile phone contract.

The courts and Parliament have tried to find ways of limiting the effectiveness of an exclusion clause.

Tips

- When considering exclusion clauses, first look at the common law approach through case law and see the result.
- If the clause is effective to exclude or limit liability, then look at the statutory provisions and see whether they reduce its effectiveness.

40.5.2 Rules relating to construction and interpretation of contracts

Many disputes are about the meaning of contracts and the terms that are in the contracts.

The assumption is that each party to the contract understands that the terms agreed accurately record the contract. A dispute arises when one party argues that a term of the contract has one particular meaning and the other party disagrees.

This is particularly important for exclusion clauses as they are usually put in a contract by someone in a stronger bargaining position. You can see this when you look at the terms and conditions of everyday contracts, such as a mobile phone contract or a streaming contract. Most people agree to the terms without reading them or enquiring about the meaning of the terms. It is only when there is a problem that the contract and the meaning of the terms are considered. This is known as interpretation of the contract.

Contract interpretation is not an exact science. The rules of contract interpretation have developed over many years and there is no strictly defined approach. The cases suggest only guidelines, which does not help certainty. As with statutory interpretation, in recent years the general trend has been to move away from a literal approach to a purposive approach.

Link

See Chapter 16 for a reminder of the literal and purposive approaches.

The starting point for analysis is the use of language in the contract.

- In *Pink Floyd Music Ltd v EMI Records Ltd* (2010), it was stated that ordinary English words will mean what they say. If the words of the contract are clear and unambiguous, then it is assumed that is what the parties intended.

If the words are not clear and unambiguous, an objective test should be applied.

- *Investors Compensation Scheme Ltd v West Bromwich Building Society* (1998) set out an objective test – what would a reasonable man interpret to be the meaning of the contract?

This is wider than just the words in the contract and can include relevant background information and contextual information. The key issue is what the parties' understanding and intention were at the time the contract was made.

- In *M T Højgaard v E.ON Climate and Renewables UK Robin Rigg East Ltd* (2014), the court said that post-contract conduct is not usually a guide to interpretation.

It is possible to add a commercial, common sense angle to contract interpretation. This is obviously very wide but does allow common sense when the actual meaning of the words is unclear and ambiguous.

Common law controls

A clause in a contract that seeks either to limit or exclude liability for contract breach is subject to all of the normal rules regarding terms, particularly those concerning incorporation of the term. Such terms will seriously limit a party's rights under the contract. The first question to be considered by the court is whether the term is part of the contract. There are three matters to consider:

1 Is the agreement signed?
2 Is any notice with the term in it incorporated in the contract?
3 Is the term incorporated as a result of the previous dealings of the parties?

Is the agreement signed?

Where a party has signed a written agreement, they are bound by that agreement, as in *L'Estrange v Graucob* (1934).

Case study

L'Estrange v Graucob (1934)

Mrs L'Estrange bought a cigarette-vending machine from the defendant for use in her café. She signed a contract including a clause which excluded all implied conditions and warranties. The machine did not work properly and Mrs L'Estrange relied on the implied term that it was fit for purpose. However, she was bound by the exclusion clause in the contract as she had signed it, even though she had not read the contract.

However, if a party relying on an exclusion clause in a written document asks the other to sign it and, in response to a query from the other, misrepresents the effect of the clause, the clause will be interpreted in accordance with the misrepresentation and not with the written document. This is so even if the document is signed by the other. This was shown in *Curtis v Chemical Cleaning and Dyeing Co. Ltd* (1951).

Case study

Curtis v Chemical Cleaning and Dyeing Co. Ltd (1951)

Mrs Curtis took her wedding dress to be cleaned and was asked to sign a document that exempted the cleaners from liability for any damage 'howsoever arising'. Before signing the document, she asked what she was signing. She was told that it only referred to the fact that the cleaners would not accept liability for beads or sequins attached to the dress.

When the dress was returned, it had a large stain on it. The cleaners could not rely on the exclusion clause because of the verbal assurances made to Mrs Curtis that they were only excluding liability for damage to beads and sequins.

Is any notice with the term in it incorporated in the contract?

Incorporation can only happen if, at the time the contract was made, the unsigned document was brought to the attention of the person suffering the exclusion clause.

Any attempt to introduce new terms to the contract after acceptance will fail, unless there is a new contract changing the original one or the original contract allows for terms to change. An example of price change can be seen in most mobile phone contracts.

The problem of incorporation arises when the terms are not made clear when the contract is made. This can be seen in *Olley v Marlborough Court Hotel* (1949).

Case study

Olley v Marlborough Court Hotel (1949)

The claimants booked into the hotel at its reception desk. At this point a contract was formed. They later went out, leaving the key at reception as required. In their absence, someone took the key, entered their room and stole some of their belongings. The hotel claimed that they were not liable because of an exclusion clause. However, the clause was not incorporated in the contract, since it was on a notice inside the Olleys' bedroom in the hotel and could not have been known about when they made the contract. This was the case even though the claimants had the opportunity to read the notice before they left their belongings in the room and handed the key to reception as they went out.

The key point is whether it was brought to the attention of the other party before the contract was made. In *Olley v Marlborough Court*, it had not. The combination of notices, tickets and other documents may make it difficult for someone trying to rely on an exclusion clause to prove it was brought to the attention of the other party.

Activity

Compare the three ticket cases below and decide whether the exclusion clause in each case has been incorporated. You will need to justify your decision.

Case studies

Chapelton v Barry Urban District Council (1940)

Mr Chapelton hired two deckchairs on the beach at Barry Island, and received two tickets from the council's beach attendant when he paid the hire charge. Next to the deckchairs was a sign that gave the price and time limit, but did not refer to any exclusion clauses. However, on the back of the tickets it stated, 'The council will not be liable for any accident or damage arising from the hire of the chair'.

Mr Chapelton did not read the ticket as he thought it was merely a receipt so he would not be asked to pay again during the day. The canvas on one chair was defective and the chair collapsed, injuring him. The council tried to rely on their exclusion clause as a defence to a claim for his injuries.

Thompson v LMS Railway (1930)

Mrs Thompson was illiterate and could not read. She went on a railway excursion, and was given a ticket with the words, 'Excursion: for conditions see back'. On the back of the ticket was a notice referring customers to the conditions printed in the company's timetables. These conditions excluded liability for any injury. She was injured on the journey and claimed for damages.

Thornton v Shoe Lane Parking Ltd (1971)

The claimant was injured in a car park owned by the defendants. There was a notice by the ticket machine that gave the charges and stated that parking was at the owner's risk. On the ticket was printed the words, 'This ticket is issued subject to the conditions of issue as displayed on the premises'. Notices inside the car park then listed the conditions of the contract, including an exclusion clause covering both damage and personal injury.

On this basis, an exclusion clause will only be incorporated into a contract when it is contained in a document that has contractual significance.

In summary, for reasonable notice:

1. There must be a contractual document, with reference to the distinction between such a document and a receipt: *Chapelton v Barry*.
2. There must be reasonable steps to draw the exclusion clause to the other party's attention: *Thompson v LMS Railway*.

3 The reasonable notice must be given before conclusion of a contract by acceptance of an offer: *Olley*, *Thornton*.

Is the term incorporated as a result of the previous dealings of the parties?

If the parties have dealt on the same terms in the past, it is possible to imply knowledge of the clause from these past dealings.

Case study

Hollier v Rambler Motors (1972)

Hollier had used this garage about three or four times over five years, and he had usually signed an invoice that said, 'The company is not responsible for damage caused by fire to customers' cars on the premises'.

Mr Hollier telephoned Rambler and spoke to the manager. He told him that he wanted some repair work done to the car. The manager said that the defendants could not do anything about it for the moment, but if the claimant had the car towed or sent in they would attend to the defects. Mr Hollier agreed. Those were the only terms of the agreement, expressed over the telephone. If he had taken the car to the garage, he would probably have signed the document with the exclusion clause in it.

A fire broke out at the garage, causing substantial damage to the car. The court decided that it was possible that the terms would be implied, but the contract wasn't made frequently enough to justify that conclusion in this case.

However, the courts are reluctant to find an exclusion clause present, for example, in *McCutcheon v David MacBrayne Ltd* (1964).

The effect of exclusion clauses on third parties to the contract

The doctrine of privity usually prevents a third party from relying on the terms of a contract. So an exclusion clause in a contract may not offer protection to parties other than the parties to the contract. This has already been seen in seen in *Scruttons Ltd v Midland Silicones Ltd* (1961) (see section 39.4.3 in Chapter 39).

The court set out four conditions to be fulfilled before it can be said that contract was made as agent for a third party so that the third party can take a benefit:

1 Was the third party intended to benefit from the contractual term?
2 Was it clear that the contracting party was also contracting as agent for the third party?
3 Had they authority so to do?
4 Was any difficulty with consideration overcome?

The *contra proferentem* rule

The *contra proferentem* 'rule' is a principle designed to help with contract interpretation. The rule is: if the meaning or scope of a term is uncertain, the term should be interpreted least favourably against the person who introduced it, and who seeks to rely on it. For consumer contracts, this is stated in the Consumer Rights Act 2015 s 69.

Key term

Contra proferentem – if the meaning of a term is unclear, the words will be construed against the person who put them in the contract.

Cases such as *Transocean Drilling UK Ltd v Providence Resources plc* (2016) and *Persimmon Homes Ltd v Ove Arup and Partners Ltd* (2017) show that the *contra proferentem* rule does not apply to commercial contracts where the parties bargain on equal and clear terms.

Case study

McCutcheon v David MacBrayne Ltd (1964)

The claimant had often used the defendants' ferries. Sometimes, but not always, he was asked to sign a document (a risk note) including an exclusion clause. On this occasion, one of his relatives took the car to the ferry. The relative received a receipt which referred to notices containing conditions displayed on the ferry company premises. He did not read the receipt and was not asked to sign it. The ferry sank and the car was destroyed.

The court decided there was no consistent course of action to assume that the claimant knew that the exclusion clause was always present, so it was not incorporated in the contract.

461

In *Oliver Nobahar-Cookson v The Hut Group* (2016), the court stated that exclusion clauses should be narrowly construed.

The Consumer Rights Act 2015 and exclusion clauses

Other aspects of exclusion clauses are dealt with later in this chapter.

The Consumer Rights Act 2015 sets out restrictions on exclusion clauses in contracts between traders and consumers. These are:
- a 'fairness test' for enforceability of terms and of consumer notices
- a 'grey list' of potentially unfair clauses in consumer contracts
- the test of fairness doesn't apply to the main subject matter of the contract or terms that set the price if they are 'transparent and prominent'.

Bars on exclusion clauses

There are three main sections of the Act which set out the bars on exclusion clauses – ss 31, 57 and 65.

Section 31 prohibits a term excluding or limiting liability, including for the following sections of the Act with respect to sale of goods:
- s 9 (goods to be of satisfactory quality)
- s 10 (goods to be fit for particular purpose)
- s 11 (goods to be as described)
- s 14 (goods to match a model seen or examined)
- s 15 (installation as part of conformity of the goods with the contract).

Section 57 prohibits a term excluding or limiting liability, for the supply of services under the following sections of the Act:
- s 49 (service to be performed with reasonable care and skill)
- s 50 (information about trader or service to be binding)
- s 51 (reasonable price)
- s 52 (reasonable time).

Section 65 prohibits exclusion or restriction of liability for death or personal injury resulting from negligence.

General fairness of terms

Under s 62, all consumer contract terms and notices must be fair. The Act defines 'unfair' terms as those which put the consumer at a disadvantage, by limiting the consumer's rights or disproportionately increasing their obligations as compared to the trader's rights and obligations.

However, a court should take into account the specific circumstances existing when the term was agreed, other terms in the contract and the nature of the subject matter of the contract.

This fairness test is supplemented by a so-called 'grey list' of terms. This is a non-exhaustive list of terms that may be unfair. A term can be fair even if it is included on the grey list, and can be unfair even if it is not.

Terms on the grey list include those which:
- allow disproportionate charges
- require the consumer to pay for services which have not been supplied when the consumer ends the contract
- allow the trader to change the price after the consumer is bound.

Look online

The 'grey list' of terms is defined on page 64 of the Government's 'Unfair Contract Terms Guidance' document. Find this online at: www.gov.uk/government/uploads/system/uploads/attachment_data/file/450440/Unfair_Terms_Main_Guidance.pdf

Terms about the main subject matter of the contract or that set the price must be:
- transparent – in plain and intelligible language and, if in writing, legible
- prominent – brought to the consumer's attention in such a way that the average consumer would be aware of the term.

Written terms in consumer notices must also be transparent. This could be in any communication or announcement, as long as it would be seen or heard by a consumer.

With respect to the *contra proferentem* rule discussed later in this chapter, in a consumer contract, s 69 of the Consumer Rights Act 2015 states that if a term or consumer notice could have different meanings, the meaning that is most favourable to the consumer should prevail.

Activity ?

Read this scenario:

You have just bought a cup of coffee at a café. You have a loyalty card with the café, and as you have enough points on the card, you get given a free toy.

The coffee makes you ill.

You give the toy to your niece but when she opens the box, the toy is broken.

1 List the express and implied terms or rights in each part of the scenario.
2 What rights do you have, and what rights does your niece have?

You later discover that the café limits liability for its food and drink to the price paid for the food and drink. Additionally, the loyalty card specifically excludes the Contracts (Rights of Third Parties) Act 1999. How would this change your answers to that scenario?

	Brief legal rule	Case example
Exclusion clause definition	Exclusion clauses are terms in a contract that exclude or limit liability for a breach of the contract	
Is the term incorporated in the contract? (1)	Where a party has signed a written agreement, he or she is bound by that agreement	*L'Estrange v Graucob* (1934)
Is the term incorporated in the contract? (2)	Whether exclusion clauses are only incorporated into a contract requires the party subject to the clause to know of the clause at the time the contract was made	*Olley v Marlborough Court Hotel* (1949)
Is the term incorporated in the contract? – the ticket cases	The combination of notices, tickets and other documents may make it difficult for someone trying to rely on an exclusion clause to prove it was brought to the attention of the other party	*Chapelton v Barry Urban District Council* (1940) *Thompson v LMS Railway* (1930) *Thornton v Shoe Lane Parking Ltd* (1971)
Is the term incorporated in the contract? (3)	Is the term incorporated as a result of the previous dealings of the parties?	*McCutcheon v David MacBrayne Ltd* (1964)
The *contra proferentem* rule	The *contra proferentem* principle is an approach to be used only where the term is both one-sided and ambiguous	*Transocean Drilling UK Ltd v Providence Resources plc* (2016) *Persimmon Homes Ltd v Ove Arup and Partners Ltd* (2017) *Oliver Nobahar-Cookson v The Hut Group* (2016)

Figure 40.8 Key facts: exclusion clauses

Case	Judgment
L'Estrange v Graucob (1934)	Mrs L'Estrange was bound by the exclusion clause in the contract for the cigarette-vending machine, regardless of the fact that she had not read it
Curtis v Chemical Cleaning and Dyeing Co. Ltd (1951)	The cleaners could not rely on the exclusion clause because of the verbal explanation made to Mrs Curtis that they were only excluding liability for damage to beads and sequins
Olley v Marlborough Court Hotel (1949)	The clause was not incorporated in the contract since it was on a notice on a wall inside the Olleys' bedroom in the hotel and could not have been known about when they made the contract
Chapelton v Barry Urban District Council (1940)	It was unreasonable to assume that Mr Chapelton would automatically understand that the ticket was a contractual document, and the council was liable for his injuries
Thompson v LMS Railway (1930)	It was common knowledge that railway journeys were contracts and that there were terms of carriage involved The fact that Mrs Thompson was illiterate and could not read the ticket did not alter the legal position
Thornton v Shoe Lane Parking Ltd (1971)	The customer is bound by the terms of the contract as he or she can assume that all the terms are set out in the first notice as in *Chapelton v Barry Urban District Council* (1940)
McCutcheon v David MacBrayne Ltd (1964)	Previous dealings are only relevant if they prove knowledge of the terms and actual, not constructive, assent to them
Transocean Drilling UK Ltd v Providence Resources plc (2016)	If the exclusion clause is clear, *contra proferentem* has no application
Persimmon Homes Ltd v Ove Arup and Partners Ltd (2017)	Where the meaning of the clauses are clear and unambiguous they should be given effect, so the *contra proferentem* rule was not relevant
Oliver Nobahar-Cookson v The Hut Group (2016)	If necessary to resolve ambiguity, exclusion clauses should be narrowly construed

Figure 40.9 Key cases: exclusion clauses

40.5.3 The Unfair Contract Terms Act 1977 and the Consumer Rights Act 2015

Where an exclusion clause is incorporated as part of a contract, statutory provisions might make the clause invalid and of no effect.

Statutory controls exist to deal with an imbalance between the parties to a contract. As we have seen, exclusion clauses are put in a contract by the party with the stronger bargaining position. In most consumer contracts, there is no opportunity to negotiate most of the terms of the contract.

However, there are two principal provisions provided by Parliament:

1 The Unfair Contract Terms Act 1977 – applies to exclusions for liability in tort as well as contractual breaches.

2 The Consumer Rights Act 2015 – applies to contracts between traders and consumers which was discussed in section 40.3.2.

The Unfair Contract Terms Act 1977 provides the main protection against exclusion clauses in non-consumer contracts. It contains a test of reasonableness to be applied to exclusion clauses.

Exclusions and limitations made void by the Act

Certain types of exclusion clauses are invalidated by the Act and will therefore be unenforceable:

- Under s 2(1), a person cannot exclude liability for death or personal injury caused by negligence.
- Under s 6(1), the implied condition as to title (transferring a person's rights over the goods) (the Sale of Goods Act 1979 and s 7 of the Supply of Goods and Services Act 1982) cannot be excluded.

Exclusions depending for their validity on a test of reasonableness

Section 3 imposes a reasonableness test to contracts where one party is subject to the other's standard written terms of business. Guidelines on what is reasonable are contained in both s 11 and s 2 of the Act. This can be seen in the case of *Smith v Eric S Bush* (1990).

Case study

Smith v Eric S Bush (1990)

Surveyors negligently carried out a paid-for valuation on a building, and missed a defect which later resulted in loss to the purchaser. The surveyors and the mortgage application contained clauses excluding liability for the accuracy of the valuation report. Including the exclusion clause was not reasonable.

As these are only guidelines, the test depends on all the circumstances of the case, and ultimately is for judges to interpret.

Section 11(5) requires the party who inserts the clause in the contract, and who seeks to rely on it, to show that it is reasonable in all the circumstances.

The tests of reasonableness include Section 11(1) which concerns exclusion clauses in general. The test is whether the insertion of the term in the contract is reasonable in the light of what was known to the parties when the contract was made. This is sometimes called the knowledge test.

The two cases (*Warren v Turprint Ltd; Smith v Eric S. Bush*) were both consumer cases. However, Section 11(2) covers exclusion clauses involving breaches of the implied conditions in the Sale of Goods Act 1979 and Supply of Goods and Service, Act 1982 in business-to-business dealings. The criteria are set out in schedule 2 of the Unfair Contract Terms Act 1977:

- the strength of the bargaining position of the parties
- whether the customer received an inducement to agree to the term
- whether the customer knew of the existence and extent of the term
- where the term excludes or restricts any relevant liability if some condition is not complied with, whether it was reasonable to expect such compliance
- whether the goods were manufactured, processed or adapted to the special order of the customer.

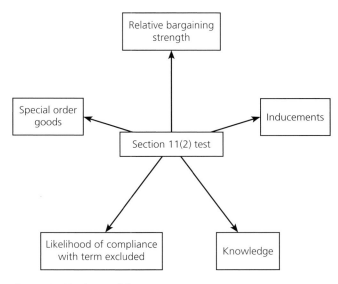

Figure 40.10 The s 11(2) test

An example of an exclusion clause being found to be reasonable can be seen in *Watford Electronics Ltd v Sanderson CFL Ltd* (2001).

Case study

Watford Electronics Ltd v Sanderson CFL Ltd (2001)

The claimant bought software from the defendant. The system failed to perform. In the defendant's standard terms there was a clause limiting any liability to the price of the goods supplied.

The court said that it was a reasonable term since the parties were of equal bargaining power and the limitation clause was subject to negotiation when the contract was made.

Section 11(4) specifically relates to limitation clauses. There are two criteria:

1 The resources that the defendant could expect to be available for meeting their liability.
2 How far it was open to the defendant to cover themselves by insurance against any successful claim.

Key term

Limitation clause – a term in a contract that sets an upper limit on liability for breach of contract.

An example is *George Mitchell Ltd v Finney Lock Seeds Ltd* (1983).

George Mitchell Ltd v Finney Lock Seeds Ltd (1983)

The claimant ordered winter cabbage seed from the defendant at a cost of £201.60. The seed did not match the description and produced plants that were unfit for resale. The entire crop was lost, at a cost of £61,000.

The contract limited liability to replacement of the goods or a refund in price. The court stated the clause was not reasonable because:

● the breach arose from the seller's negligence
● the seller could have insured against crop failure at a modest cost
● in the past, the seller had settled claims which exceeded the limitation sum – this showed that the seller himself did not always consider the clause fair and reasonable.

Contractual relationship	Description of term(s)	Method of incorporation	Exclusion/limitation of liability for breach
Trader/Consumer	Title, description, satisfactory quality, fitness for purpose	Consumer Rights Act 2015	Prohibited by Consumer Rights Act 2015
	Reasonable care and skill Reasonable time for performance	Consumer Rights Act 2015	Prohibited by Consumer Rights Act 2015
	Other	Express or implied	Permitted if 'fair'
Business/Business	Title, description	Sale of Goods Act 1979 Supply of Goods and Services Act 1982	Prohibited by Unfair Contract Terms Act 1977
	Satisfactory quality, fitness for purpose	Sale of Goods Act 1979 Supply of Goods and Services Act 1982	Permitted by Unfair Contract Terms Act 1977 subject to 'reasonableness'
	Reasonable care and skill Reasonable time for performance	Supply of Goods and Services Act 1982	Permitted, but if one party deals on the other's written standard terms of business, it must satisfy 'reasonableness'
	Other	Express or implied	Permitted, but if one party deals on the other's written standard terms of business, it must satisfy 'reasonableness'
Private	Title, description	Sale of Goods Act 1979 Supply of Goods and Services Act 1982	Prohibited by Unfair Contract Terms Act 1977
	Other	Express or implied	Permitted

Figure 40.11 Summary of availability of exclusion clauses

Case	Judgment
Warren v Truprint Ltd (1986)	Section 11(5) of the Unfair Contract Terms Act 1977 requires the party who inserts the clause in the contract, and who seeks to rely on it, to show that it is reasonable in all the circumstances
Smith v Eric S Bush (1990)	The test is whether the insertion of the term in the contract is reasonable in the light of what was known to the parties at the time when the contract was made This is sometimes called the knowledge test
Watford Electronics Ltd v Sanderson CFL Ltd (2001)	The exclusion clause was a reasonable term since the parties were of equal bargaining power and the limitation clause was subject to negotiation when the contract was made
George Mitchell Ltd v Finney Lock Seeds Ltd (1983)	Section 11(4) of the Unfair Contract Terms Act 1977 specifically relates to limitation clauses and not exclusion clauses, as in this case

Figure 40.12 Key cases: statutory controls of exclusion clauses

Quick questions

1 Explain what is meant by an innominate term in a contract.
2 State case examples of incorporation of terms in a contract.
3 Explain the *contra proferentem* rule.
4 State the main Acts of Parliament that relate to exclusion clauses.
5 Explain the short-term right to reject under s 20 of the Consumer Rights Act 2015.

Summary

- The courts have to decide whether a statement is a representation or a term.
- Terms can be implied in a contract by the common law and/or by statute.
- Breach of a term gives rise to different possible remedies.
- The Consumer Rights Act 2015 uses the nomenclature of terms which provide 'rights' of consumers and duties of traders.
- The Consumer Rights Act 2015 applies to contracts and notices between a 'consumer' and a 'trader'.
- The Consumer Rights Act 2015 applies to contracts of sale, hire, hire-purchase and other contracts for the transfer of goods.
- Terms implied into a contract to supply goods under the Consumer Rights Act 2015 are with respect to satisfactory quality, fitness for particular purpose and description.
- Rights under the Consumer Rights Act 2015 include:
  - the short-term right to reject
  - the right to repair or replacement
  - the right to a price reduction
  - the final right to reject.

Terms are of three types:
- conditions
- warranties
- innominate terms.

- Terms implied into a contract to supply services under the Consumer Rights Act 2015 are to provide the service with reasonable care and skill and for performance within a reasonable time.
- Remedies for the breach of a term implied into a contract to supply services under the Consumer Rights Act 2015 are a right to repeat performance and a right to a price reduction.
- Exclusion clauses are sometimes excluded from a contract by the operation of the common law.
- Judges have done their best to make the exclusion clauses ineffective.
- Statutory protection is more geared to consumers than to businesses.
- Different statutes cover different types of contract, which can lead to confusion.
- The Consumer Rights Act 2015 may need to be interpreted by reference to cases on legislation such as the Sale of Goods Act 1979.
- The combined effect of terms and restrictions on their use is beneficial to consumers, but goes against the principle of freedom of contract.

Chapter 41 Vitiating factors

41.1 Misrepresentation

In Chapter 40 we considered whether a statement is a mere representation or a term of the contract. Representations are statements that influence a decision on whether or not to make a contract, and are misrepresentations if they are false.

A misrepresentation only occurs during the formation of a contract.

The effect of misrepresentation is to make the contract voidable. This means that the contract is valid unless the party who has suffered the misrepresentation takes action to end the contract. This is known as rescission of the contract.

Rescission for misrepresentation applies in cases where a party relied on a statement by the other party to enter the contract, and the statement was not true. Rescission treats the contract as if it had never existed: it becomes a void contract. This means the parties would be put back in the positions they were in before the contract was made. This is known as *restitutio in integrum*.

Key terms

Misrepresentation – a false statement of material fact made by a party to the contract that induces the other party to enter the contract.

Voidable contract – a contract which could be made void if there has been misrepresentation.

Void contract – a contract that is declared to be null: it never had legal effect.

Rescission – when the innocent party ends the contract because of a misrepresentation. Rescission makes the contract a nullity.

The elements of the definition of misrepresentation are:

- a false statement
- of material fact
- made by a party to the contract
- that induces the other party to enter the contract.

41.1.1 False statement

A statement is usually written or verbal, but doesn't have to be. It could be anything that would influence the other's decision, such as hiding a fault as in *Gordon v Selico Ltd* (1986), where painting over dry rot immediately before selling a property was a fraudulent misrepresentation. *Spice Girls Ltd v Aprilia World Service BV* (2000) is an example of false statement.

Case study

Spice Girls Ltd v Aprilia World Service BV (2000)

The Spice Girls had signed a sponsorship agreement with Aprilia. While the agreement was being negotiated, unknown to Aprilia, a member of the group, Geri Halliwell, had given notice to leave the group. Filming of promotional material took place with all the girls together, but when one left it made the films worthless for promotional purposes. The court decided that by all of them attending, the group represented that none of them intended to leave the group and none of them was aware that one member intended to. This was a misrepresentation.

The Spice Girls

To be a misrepresentation, the statement made must be false – untrue or inaccurate. Whether or not the defendant knew that the statement was false defines the type of misrepresentation it might be.

Because there must be a statement to be a misrepresentation, silence cannot be a misrepresentation. There is no obligation on a person wishing to enter a contract to make any statement about what is being offered – but anything said in that respect must be true, as in *Fletcher v Krell* (1873).

Case study

Fletcher v Krell (1873)

A woman applied for a job of governess. She was not asked and she did not state that she was divorced. In Victorian times this would mean she would not be offered the job. The court decided that there was no misrepresentation as she was under no duty to disclose her marital status and she had not been asked about it.

There are, however, factors which affect this principle:
- change of circumstances
- the making of a half-truth
- confidential relationships.

Change of circumstance

Even if a statement is true when it is made, it can become a misrepresentation if it becomes false before the contract is made. This was shown in *With v O'Flanagan* (1936).

Case study

With v O'Flanagan (1936)

A doctor accurately stated the profits of his medical practice with a view to inducing purchasers to buy the practice. However, between the statement and the contract being made, the doctor fell ill and many of the patients left the practice. This made the original statement inaccurate.

The court decided he had to tell the purchaser of the changed situation.

Therefore, a person must correct information where the situation has changed between making the representation and the acceptance of the offer.

Half-truth

Silence can be a misrepresentation where a statement made is a half-truth. What is not said is a non-disclosure, and may be a misrepresentation as the maker of the statement has a duty to reveal the whole truth of the situation. This can be seen in the case of *Dimmock v Hallett* (1866).

Case study

Dimmock v Hallett (1866)

A seller of land told the purchaser truthfully that there were tenants on the land. This was exactly what the purchaser wanted. However, he did not complete the statement by telling the purchaser that all the tenants were leaving. The court decided that this part-truth was a misrepresentation.

Confidential relationships

Where the relationship between the parties is based on trust then silence may be a misrepresentation. This was shown in *Tate v Williamson* (1866).

Case study

Tate v Williamson (1866)

A financial adviser advised his client to sell some land for less than half its value so that his client could clear his debts. The adviser then purchased the land himself but did not tell his client that he had done so.

The court decided that this was a breach of trust and was therefore a misrepresentation.

Where a contract is a contract of 'utmost good faith' (*uberrimae fidei*) then all material facts must be disclosed, whether asked about or not. This is usually seen in contracts of insurance, for example, in *Lambert v Co-operative Insurance Society* (1975).

Case study

Lambert v Co-operative Insurance Society (1975)

A woman renewed her jewellery insurance policy. She did not tell the insurance company that her husband had recently been convicted of conspiracy to steal. This was an important fact that would have affected the insurance society's decision whether to renew the insurance and, if so, at what premium.

Her silence about the conviction was a misrepresentation. The company was entitled to make the policy void and refuse to pay her claim.

The Consumer Insurance (Disclose and Representations) Act 2012 replaces the consumer's duty to volunteer information with a duty to answer the insurer's questions honestly and reasonably. The questions must be clear and specific. The consumer must take reasonable care not to make a misrepresentation which could induce the insurer to enter the contract. This modifies the consumer's duty of utmost good faith by removing the obligation to disclose all material facts. He or she must reply honestly and with reasonable care to questions asked only.

41.1.2 Material fact

The misrepresentation must be of a material fact. This means that it must have led a person to make the contract.

It must be a statement of fact rather than a statement of opinion. A statement of future intention can be seen as a 'fact' if the person intended to do this when they made the statement. If they did not really intend to do something, they misrepresented their state of mind, which is a fact.

Statements of opinion

In general, if a person honestly believes in their statement of opinion and it proves to be false, it will not be a misrepresentation. This is illustrated by *Bisset v Wilkinson* (1927) and *Edgington v Fitzmaurice* (1885).

Case studies

Bisset v Wilkinson (1927)

The seller of farmland that had never had sheep on it was asked by the buyer how many sheep it could take. Although he was not a sheep farmer, he stated that he thought it would support about two thousand. This turned out to be false. However, as he genuinely believed his opinion to be accurate, it was not a misrepresentation.

Edgington v Fitzmaurice (1885)

The claimant invested in a company. The directors of the company falsely stated that the investment was to be used to complete alterations to the buildings of the company and other developments. In fact, it was used to pay off existing debts.

The representation was seen as a statement of fact rather than just future intention, as the directors did not have the intention to make alterations, etc. This was a misrepresentation.

But if the person does not honestly believe their own opinion, it is regarded as a statement of fact rather than one of opinion, as in *Smith v Land and House Property Corporation* (1884).

Case study

Smith v Land and House Property Corporation (1884)

The seller of an investment property described it as being let to a most desirable tenant. The purchaser refused to complete the purchase when he discovered that the tenant (Fleck) owed rent to the owner.

The statement that Fleck was a 'most desirable tenant' was not one of opinion but of fact – because the seller knew that this was false, he had misrepresented the fact that he held that opinion.

Statements of intention

A statement of intention – a promise to do something in the future – is generally not a statement of fact, because a fact relates to a past event or something in existence. However, a statement of intention becomes a statement of fact if the maker of the statement has no intention of carrying it out – because they are misrepresenting the fact that they possess the intention.

41.1.3 Made by a party to the contract

A person is not liable for statements made by others unless it is by their agent. This means, for example, that a newspaper review of an item cannot be a misrepresentation in contract law.

41.1.4 Induces the other party to enter the contract

The statement must be a critical part of leading the other party to make the contract. In *BV Nederlandse Industrie Van Eiprodukten v Rembrandt Enterprises Inc* (2018), the court held that the relevant test is whether the claimant would not have entered into the contract without the representation. The claimant can establish that a misrepresentation was a factor in their decision to enter the contract, but it does not have to be the only or the deciding factor.

However, they must have relied on the statement made rather than their own judgement or information they obtained elsewhere, for there to be a misrepresentation. This was shown in *Attwood v Small* (1838).

Case study

Attwood v Small (1838)

The seller made a false statement to the purchaser about the earnings from his mine. The buyer instructed a surveyor to confirm this statement, which he did (incorrectly). The purchaser bought the mine and then discovered the statement to be untrue. There was no misrepresentation as the purchaser relied on the survey report and not the seller's statement.

It does not matter if the victim could have discovered the truth by taking reasonable steps or it was unreasonable to rely on the untrue statement. The fact that the untrue statement was relied upon is enough to make it a misrepresentation, as in *Redgrave v Hurd* (1881).

Case study

Redgrave v Hurd (1881)

The purchaser of a solicitor's practice was given a set of accounts to look at. The seller verbally misled the purchaser as to the true earnings. The purchaser relied on the statement and did not look at the accounts. If he had done so, he would have seen that the seller's statement was false. He was entitled to rely on the seller's statement, and because this was untrue, it was a misrepresentation.

In *Museprime Properties Ltd v Adhill Properties Ltd* (1990), it was decided that what the reasonable person would or would not have done is irrelevant.

Case study

Museprime Properties Ltd v Adhill Properties Ltd (1990)

The purchaser of property relied on inaccurate statements about rents made in auction particulars. The defendant argued that no 'reasonable' purchaser would have relied on these statements and would have made other enquiries. However, as the purchaser had relied on the statements, there was reliance, and this could be a misrepresentation.

41.1.5 Omissions in a consumer context

Section 12 of the Consumer Rights Act 2015 covers pre-contract information for a contract to supply goods. The trader has to provide certain information to the consumer before the contract becomes binding. If any of that information changes before entering into the contract or later, it is not effective unless expressly agreed between the consumer and the trader.

All consumer information must be displayed clearly. Under the Consumer Protection (Amendment) Regulations 2014, a misleading omission is where a trader deliberately misses out key information that the consumer might need to make an informed decision about buying the goods or services. For example, it is misleading if a trader:

- omits material information that the average consumer needs, according to the context, to make an informed transactional decision
- hides or provides material information in an unclear, unintelligible, ambiguous or untimely manner

- fails to identify the commercial intent of the commercial practice if this is not already clear from the context.

The obscure presentation of consumer information will be treated as a misleading omission. The Consumer Protection from Unfair Trading Regulations 2008 ban misleading omissions and aggressive sales tactics.

	Brief legal rule	Case example
Misrepresentation definition	Misrepresentation is a false statement of material fact made by a party to the contract that induces the other party to enter the contract	
There must be a false statement	If nothing is said or asked, it cannot be a statement and, if false, misrepresentation	*Fletcher v Krell* (1873)
Silence is not usually a misrepresentation unless there are changed facts	A statement which is true when made but becomes false before the contract is made must be corrected	*With v O'Flanagan* (1936)
The statement does not have to be written or verbal	The statement can be made pictorially or by appearance	*Spice Girls Ltd v Aprilia World Service BV* (2000)
The misrepresentation must be of a material fact	It must be a statement of fact rather than a statement of opinion.	*Bisset v Wilkinson* (1927)
It must induce the other party to enter the contract	The statement must be important to the person making the contract and they must have relied on the statement made rather than their own judgement	*Redgrave v Hurd* (1881)
Consumer must be given clear information	Failure to do so is a misleading omission	S 12 Consumer Rights Act 2015

Figure 41.1 Key facts: misrepresentation

Case	Judgment
Fletcher v Krell (1873)	There was no misrepresentation as she was under no duty to disclose her marital status and she had not been asked about it
With v O'Flanagan (1936)	There was a continuing representation; he had to tell any prospective purchaser of changes to the situation
Dimmock v Hallett (1866)	A part-truth was a misrepresentation
Tate v Williamson (1866)	The adviser's failure to disclose that he was intending to buy the land personally was a breach of trust and was therefore a misrepresentation
Lambert v Co-operative Insurance Society (1975)	Where a contract is a contract of 'utmost good faith', then all material facts must be disclosed. This is now subject to the Consumer Insurance (Disclose and Representations) Act 2012 An example is a contract of insurance
Spice Girls Ltd v Aprilia World Service BV (2000)	By attending a photoshoot, the group represented that none of them intended to leave the group
Bisset v Wilkinson (1927)	An expression of the seller's honestly held opinions was not a misrepresentation
Edgington v Fitzmaurice (1885)	A statement of future intention can be seen as a statement of fact if it was proved that the maker had no such intention and therefore it is a misrepresentation
Attwood v Small (1838)	A person must have relied on the statement for there to be a misrepresentation
Redgrave v Hurd (1881)	Relying on an untrue statement can amount to a misrepresentation
Museprime Properties Ltd v Adhill Properties Ltd (1990)	What the reasonable person would or would not have done is irrelevant; there can be misrepresentation if a false statement is relied on

Figure 41.2 Key cases: misrepresentation

41.1.6 Types of misrepresentation: the Misrepresentation Act 1967

There are three possible types of misrepresentation, and each has different possible remedies:

1 Fraudulent
2 Negligent, including under the Misrepresentation Act 1967
3 Innocent.

Fraudulent misrepresentation

Fraudulent misrepresentation occurs when a person induces the contract by making a statement that they know is untrue, or is reckless as to whether or not it is true.

This can include hiding defects, as we have seen in *Gordon v Selico Ltd* (1986). To avoid being found to have made a fraudulent misrepresentation, the person who made the statement must believe it is true.

A fraudulent misrepresentation includes not only an out-and-out incorrect answer to an inquiry, but can also be an overly optimistic view of the position. This was seen in *Greenridge Luton One Ltd v Kempton Investments Ltd* (2016).

Case study

Greenridge Luton One Ltd v Kempton Investments Ltd (2016)

The High Court held that a buyer of a commercial property was entitled to have its deposit returned because of an untrue representation made recklessly or fraudulently by the seller, that there were no service charge arrears, when in fact there were such arrears. There was fraudulent misrepresentation and the buyer was also entitled to damages for deceit of £395,948.

As shown in this case, the remedy for fraudulent misrepresentation can be rescission *and* damages.

Negligent misrepresentation

Negligent misrepresentation is a false statement made by a person who believed the statement was true, but had no reasonable grounds for believing it to be true.

The Misrepresentation Act 1967 s 2(1) created a statutory liability for negligent misrepresentation. All that is needed is for there to be a misrepresentation which results in a contract and the victim suffers loss. This is much broader than any of the previous possible claims. It is particularly useful where the claimant is unable to prove fraud.

Under the Act, once the victim has proved there was a misrepresentation, the burden of proof is on the person making the statement that there were reasonable grounds to believe the statement was true. This reverses the usual burden of proof in civil cases when it is for the victim to prove the case. An example can be seen in the case of *Howard Marine v Ogden and Sons* (1978).

Case study

Howard Marine v Ogden and Sons (1978)

Ogden hired two dredgers from Howard Marine for £1800 per week to carry out works for Northumbrian Water Authority. In order to complete a tender for the work, Ogden asked Howard for the capacity of the dredger. Howard checked Lloyds' Register of Shipping, which stated the capacity was 850 cubic metres. In fact, the entry was incorrect and the capacity was much lower. Therefore, the work carried out by Ogden took much longer and cost much more to perform.

Howard argued that they had reasonable grounds for believing the statement to be true as they had checked Lloyds' Register. However, as they had the registration document of the dredger, which stated the correct capacity, this argument failed.

If the misrepresentation is negligently made, the claimant has the choice of suing under the Misrepresentation Act 1967 or under the law of tort following the principles set out in *Hedley Byrne v Heller*. If the Act is chosen, then the relationship required for a claim using *Hedley Byrne v Heller* does not need to be established.

The remedy for negligent misrepresentation can be rescission *and* damages.

Innocent misrepresentation

The Misrepresentation Act 1967 provides the definition of innocent misrepresentation as: a representation which is genuinely held on reasonable grounds. This is a false statement made honestly – the person making the statement always believed it to be true and there is no element of negligence in that belief. There is still a misrepresentation, albeit an innocent misrepresentation.

The remedy is either rescission *or* damages instead of rescission. This is under the courts' discretion, as stated in the Misrepresentation Act 1967.

Type	Level of truth	Remedy	Example
Innocent misrepresentation	The maker of the statement always believed it to be true and had good grounds for doing so	Rescission or damages under Misrepresentation Act 1967, s 2(2)	*Leaf v International Galleries* (1950)
Negligent misrepresentation	The maker of the statement believed the statement to be true, but had no reasonable grounds for believing it to be true	Rescission and/or damages Misrepresentation Act 1967, ss 2(1) and (2)	*Howard Marine v Ogden and Sons* (1978)
Fraudulent misrepresentation	The maker of the statement knew that the statement was false	Rescission and damages in the tort of deceit	*Greenridge Luton One Ltd v Kempton Investments Ltd* (2016)

Figure 41.3 Key facts: types of misrepresentation

41.1.7 Remedies for misrepresentation

- Rescission, setting aside the contract, is possible in all cases of misrepresentation. The aim of rescission is to put the parties back in their original position, as though the contract had not been made.
- Damages can also be awarded, as stated in the Misrepresentation Act 1967.

Innocent misrepresentation: rescission

The usual remedy for misrepresentation is rescission, as stated in *Salt v Stratstone Specialist Ltd (t/a Stratstone Cadillac Newcastle)* (2015), where a car which was described as brand new was not in fact brand new.

Rescission is an equitable remedy. All equitable remedies are discretionary, which means that the court will only award them if it is fair to do so in all the circumstances.

However, the remedy of rescission will not be available in the following situations:
- restitution to the original pre-contract position is impossible
- the contract is affirmed
- delay
- a third party has gained rights over the property.

Restitution to the original pre-contract position is impossible

This was shown in *Clarke v Dickson* (1858), where the claimant was misled into becoming a partner in a business. The business changed to become a limited company before the claimant wanted to rescind the contract. Rescission was not available – he could not return the partnership as the firm had become a limited company.

The contract is affirmed

Affirmation is where the innocent party decides to carry on with the contract despite being aware of the misrepresentation. The right to seek to rescind the contract is then lost, as in *Long v Lloyd* (1958).

Case study

Long v Lloyd (1958)

The claimant was told by the seller that a lorry was in excellent condition, but shortly after the sale it broke down. The claimant noticed faults with the lorry and contacted the defendant, who offered to pay half the repairs, which he agreed to. The lorry broke down again shortly afterwards and the claimant wanted to rescind the contract. The court refused to grant rescission because by persevering with the lorry after the first breakdown and agreeing to share the cost of repairs, he had indicated his willingness to continue with the contract and so affirmed the contract.

Delay

One maxim of equity is that delay defeats equity. The idea behind this is that once a contract has been completed, any complaints are likely to arise within a short time and after that you can assume there are no major problems. This can be seen in *Leaf v International Galleries* (1950).

Case study

Leaf v International Galleries (1950)

In 1944, the claimant had purchased a picture of Salisbury Cathedral from the defendant. He was told that it was by Constable but only found out it was not by him when he tried to sell it five years later. Rescission was not allowed because of the delay in bringing his claim.

A third party has gained rights over the property

Where someone else has gained an interest in the subject matter of the contract, then rescission will not be granted as this would be unfair on the innocent third party. An example is *Lewis v Averay* (1972).

Case study

Lewis v Averay (1972)

Lewis sold his car and let the buyer take it away in exchange for a cheque. The cheque was worthless. The buyer had accepted it as he was persuaded by the fraudster that he was the well-known actor Richard Greene who had played Robin Hood on television. In fact, the rogue posed as Richard Greene but signed the cheque 'R A Green'. The buyer then sold the car to the defendant, an innocent third party.

The original seller's only effective remedy was to claim rescission and to ask for the car to be returned to him by the innocent third party. The claim for rescission failed as, between the two innocent parties, it would be more unfair to deprive the third party of the car purchased in good faith.

Innocent misrepresentation: damages

The court has discretion to award damages instead of rescission under s 2(2) of the Misrepresentation Act 1967. This section describes the circumstances in which a court might regard rescission as inequitable and award damages instead:

> if of opinion that it would be equitable to do so, having regard to the nature of the misrepresentation and the loss that would be caused by it if the contract were upheld, as well as to the loss that rescission would cause to the other party.

This means that if there is no longer a right to rescind the contract, for example, because of delay, there is no possibility of damages under this section.

Case study

Sindall v Cambridgeshire County Council (1993)

The claimant paid £5 million to Cambridgeshire County Council for building land, not knowing that it contained a buried sewer pipe that would obstruct its building plans. By the time the claimant found out, the property market had collapsed and the land was worth a much smaller amount, so the claimant wanted to rescind and get back the full purchase price, plus interest. It was held that there was no misrepresentation but, if there had been, it would have been innocent. Then rescission would be denied because the only loss to the claimant was the £18,000 which would have been required to relocate the pipe. This could easily have been recompensed in damages, whereas rescission would cost the council a huge amount in restoring the purchase price plus interest, and this was inequitable.

The measure of damages under s 2(2) must be recompense for loss related specifically to the misrepresentation. In *Sindall v Cambridgeshire County Council*, that would have been the £18,000 necessary to preserve the value of the land as it was agreed in the contract. There would have been no compensation for the loss in market value of the land, which had nothing to do with the misrepresentation.

Negligent misrepresentation

The remedies for negligent misrepresentation are rescission and/or damages. The remedy of rescission has been discussed above.

- If the claim is under the Misrepresentation Act 1967, s 2(1), damages are calculated as in fraud.
- As discussed above, s 2(2) also gives the court discretion to make an award of damages instead of rescission for a negligent or innocent misrepresentation. For negligent misrepresentation, this could be in addition to damages under s 2(1) but would have to take account of such damages.

Case study

East v Maurer (1991)

The claimant had bought a hairdressing salon from the defendant, who continued to trade from another he owned, despite telling the purchaser that he did not intend to continue to work at his other salon. As a result, the purchaser lost business to the defendant.

The claimant had established that he had suffered a loss due to the defendant's misrepresentation which arose from the misrepresentation.

Fraudulent misrepresentation

The remedies are rescission and damages in the tort of deceit. Both of these have been discussed above.

An example of damages in the tort of deceit can be seen in the case of *Smith New Court v Scrimgeour Vickers* (1996), where the court awarded the victim damages based on the difference between the amount paid for shares and the final sale price – more than the usual award of damages in a contract.

Damages based on fraudulent misrepresentation aim to put the victim in the position they were in before the misrepresentation occurred. However, the court seems willing to take the view that damages in the tort of deceit may be appropriate in certain circumstances. In *East v Maurer* (1991), the Court of Appeal stated that it was possible in principle to recover damages for loss of profit following a fraudulent misrepresentation.

	Brief legal rule	Case example
Rescission definition	It is an equitable remedy: the parties are returned to the positions they were in before the contract was made	
Rescission is not allowed (1) – cannot restore the pre-contract situation	Rescission is not allowed if the parties cannot be restored to their pre-contractual position	*Clarke v Dickson* (1858)
Rescission is not allowed (2) – affirmation	Affirmation is where the innocent party decides to carry on with the contract despite being aware of the misrepresentation	*Long v Lloyd* (1958)
Rescission is not allowed (3) – delay	Delay defeats equity: rescission is not available as a remedy if there is a delay in coming to court	*Leaf v International Galleries* (1950)
Rescission is not allowed (4) – a third party has gained rights over the property	Rescission will not be granted if this would be unfair on an innocent third party	*Lewis v Averay* (1972)

Figure 41.4 Key facts: remedies for misrepresentation

Case	Judgment
Clarke v Dickson (1858)	Rescission was not available as the victim could not return to the original position
Long v Lloyd (1958)	By persevering with the lorry after the first breakdown, he had indicated his willingness to continue with the contract and so affirmed the contract
Leaf v International Galleries (1950)	Even though he had no means of finding out the truth until he came to sell the painting, rescission was not allowed because of the delay in bringing his claim
Lewis v Averay (1972)	The claim for rescission failed as in the circumstances it would be unfair to deprive the third party of the car purchased in good faith
Howard Marine v Ogden and Sons (1978)	They had not discharged the burden of proof by demonstrating they had reasonable grounds for believing it to be true; they had the registration document of the dredger which stated the correct capacity, so it could not be innocent misrepresentation
East v Maurer (1991)	It is possible to recover damages for loss of profit following a fraudulent misrepresentation

Figure 41.5 Key cases: remedies for misrepresentation

Read this scenario and answer the questions that follow:

Dodd.G Motors have sold several cars this week, but not all the customers are happy.

- Alphonso knew nothing about cars so just asked for an Italian car. He was sold a car made for an Italian company in Poland.
- Beryl wanted a car with low mileage. She was sold a car with the odometer showing 17,000 miles. Dodd.G Motors knew that it had done 70,000 miles.
- Cal asked for a particular make and model of car with the more powerful engine option. The car he was sold had the less powerful engine. Dodd.G Motors could have checked this from the car's identity but did not bother to do so.
- Desi bought a car that was described as 'one owner'. The car's document showed one registered keeper, but did not show that it had been specially imported to the UK from Japan, where it had had two previous owners. Dodd.G Motors had no reason to believe the car was an import.

1 Decide what type of misrepresentation is present (if any) in each scenario.
2 Explain what remedies might be available in each possible claim against Dodd.G Motors.

41.2 Economic duress

Any contract made where one party is forced into it is void. This could be as result of undue influence, duress or economic duress.

- **Undue influence** occurs where one party is pressured into entering the contract, where there is a trusting relationship and one party will benefit at the expense of another.
- A contract signed under **duress** might involve threats, such as blackmail, or even violence to persuade one party to sign the contract.
- Economic duress – the threat to damage a business or a person financially – is a common form of duress, and the court will consider each case according to its individual circumstances. The threats must be 'improperly coercive', though not necessarily unlawful. The difficulty is to decide when the line is crossed between, say, tough business bargaining, exploiting weaknesses to advantage, and the use of improper pressure.

Key term

Economic duress – when someone enters into a contract as a result of financial threats.

Economic duress occurs when someone is effectively saying, 'make a contract with me on these terms or else there will be no contract and you will be ruined'. This can easily be seen where there is a shortage of an item and the supplier of that item can effectively name their price. The court has to distinguish between legitimate commercial pressure and economic duress.

41.2.1 The nature of the threat

In the case of *The Siboen and The Sibotre* (1976), the court said that serious threats to property should be considered as duress. Where someone is coerced so much that they cannot properly consent, the contract can be put aside. However, commercial pressure is not enough.

This idea was developed in *Atlas Express v Kafco* (1989).

Case study

Atlas Express v Kafco (1989)

Kafco signed a contract with Atlas Express to deliver the goods to Woolworth stores. The parties agreed a delivery charge per small box. There was no agreement about the number of boxes per load, but it was estimated that there would be a minimum of 400 boxes per load. Atlas then discovered that each delivery was going to be in smaller quantities as the first delivery only contained 200 boxes.

Atlas demanded more money per load or it would not deliver the consignments. Kafco had no other option but to agree to pay extra money to Atlas – Kafco was a small company which had just secured a big order from a major company and it was essential that it delivered on time. Kafco agreed to pay the extra money, but then refused to pay it as this agreement was made under economic duress. The court decided in favour of Kafco.

41.2.2 The consequences of the threat

For economic duress, there must be pressure that:

- takes away the victim's choice
- is illegitimate
- is a significant cause for inducing the victim to enter into the contract.

This can be seen in *Universe Tankships Inc. of Monrovia v International Transport Workers Federation (The Universe Sentinel)* (1983).

Case study

Universe Tankships Inc. of Monrovia v International Transport Workers Federation (The Universe Sentinel) (1983)

The vessel, *The Universe Sentinel*, was threatened by the International Transport Workers Federation (ITWF) as it was a vessel sailing under what ITWF regarded as a flag of convenience. The threat was that unless the owners of the vessel comply with ITWF's demands to the rates of pay and other terms of employment of the crew, and also to paying money into a workers' welfare fund, they would not tug the ship so it could not leave the port. The ship owners agreed so the ship could leave port.

The court decided that the money had been extracted as a result of economic duress and must be repaid.

41.2.3 Additional criteria to help identify economic duress

The question is: what makes the pressure illegitimate and not just commercial hard bargaining? The court in *Pao on v Lau yiu Long* (1979) identified the following factors to help decide whether economic duress was present:

- Did the person claiming to be coerced protest about the pressure?
- Did that person have any other available course of action that was reasonable?
- Was he or she independently advised before taking the action?
- After entering into the contract, did he or she take steps to make the contract void?

Case study

Pao on v Lau yiu Long (1979)

This was a dispute about the terms of the purchase of a business and a guarantee given to the seller protecting against a fall in share price. The court set out factors to help decide whether economic duress was present.

In *CTN Cash and Carry v Gallagher* (1994), it was decided that duress was not available when the action threatened was lawful.

Case study

CTN Cash and Carry v Gallagher (1994)

Gallagher sent a consignment of cigarettes to the wrong address and the cigarettes were stolen. Gallagher believed that the cigarettes were at CTN's risk and sent them an invoice for the cigarettes. Gallagher then threatened to withdraw the claimant's credit facility unless the invoice was paid. CTN needed the credit facilities and so paid the invoice. Was this economic duress?

Gallagher genuinely believed the money to be owed to them, so that they were not trying to exploit a weakness to gain an unfair advantage, but were simply trying to get back what they were entitled to.

The court accepted that 'illegitimate' is not synonymous with 'unlawful'.

In *Progress Bulk Carriers Ltd v Tube City* (2012), it was decided that pressure could be illegitimate even when lawful.

Case study

Progress Bulk Carriers Ltd v Tube City (2012)

Ship owners contracted to hire their ship to charterers to transport a cargo. The charterers had a buyer for the cargo. The ship owners broke the contract by failing to provide the ship, but agreed with the charterers to provide a substitute ship and to compensate them for any losses. The delays led to a reduction in the price of the cargo, so the charterers requested a reduction in the cost of the hire of the ship. By this time, the charterers were under great pressure to deliver the cargo, and the ship owners now refused to supply the ship at a discount unless the charterers agreed that no compensation should be paid by the ship owners for the earlier breach of contract.

This 'take it or leave it offer' was reluctantly accepted by the charterers, who then sued for losses, arguing that their agreement was forced on them by economic duress.

The court upheld their claim. The conduct of the ship owners had to be viewed in the light of their initial breach of contract, and their willingness to take advantage of the consequences of that breach. This was 'illegitimate' pressure, even if not unlawful in itself.

The question of when lawful pressure amounts to duress was considered in *Times Travel (UK) Limited v Pakistan International Airlines Corporation* (2019).

Case study

Times Travel (UK) Limited v Pakistan International Airlines Corporation (2019)

Times Travel was a small family business which sold tickets for Pakistan Airlines' flights. At the time, the airline was the only operator of direct flights between the UK and Pakistan, and Times Travel's business was almost exclusively tied to that route.

The two parties were in dispute about commission. Pakistan Airlines gave notice to terminate the contract. As a condition of entry into a new contract, Pakistan Airlines required a waiver of any prior claims by Times Travel, including those in the dispute about commission.

Where only lawful acts have been committed, economic duress will not be available as a defence unless bad faith can be proved, which was not the case here.

Tip

In circumstances where there is a character who is facing financial difficulties, consider whether economic duress might be present.

41.2.4 Remedies for economic duress

A claim based on economic duress does not result in an award of damages. The courts can:
- make an order for the restitution of property or money extracted under such duress
- declare the contract void.

Restitution is an equitable remedy that restores a person to the position they would have been in without the other party's improper action. Because it is an equitable remedy, it is discretionary, as we have seen for rescission.

	Brief legal rule	Case example
Economic duress definition	The threat to damage a business or person financially	
Economic duress does not normally cover a threat towards property	Economic duress does not normally cover a threat towards property except in severe circumstances	*Atlas Express v Kafco* (1989)
Economic duress involves: 1 Compulsion or a lack of practical choice for the victim	A practical effect must be that there is compulsion on, or a lack of practical choice for, the victim	*Universe Tankships Inc. of Monrovia v International Transport Workers Federation (The Universe Sentinel)* (1983)
2 Illegitimate pressure	Commercial pressure is not enough to amount to economic duress. There are a number of factors to consider	*Pao on v Lau yiu Long* (1979)
3 Actions that are not lawful	Illegitimate is not synonymous with unlawful	*CTN Cash and Carry v Gallagher* (1994)
4 Pressure could be illegitimate even when lawful	'Illegitimate pressure' can be constituted by conduct which is not in itself unlawful, although it will be an unusual case where that is so	*Progress Bulk Carriers Ltd v Tube City* (2012)

Figure 41.6 Key facts: economic duress

Case	Judgment
Atlas Express v Kafco (1989)	Economic duress was established as the agreement was induced by illegitimate pressure of great magnitude
Universe Tankships Inc. of Monrovia v International Transport Workers Federation (The Universe Sentinel) (1983)	Several demands were made in relation to pay and conditions – this amounted to compulsion
Pao on v Lau yiu Long (1979)	The court identified four factors to be considered if there was to be economic duress
CTN Cash and Carry v Gallagher (1994)	The threat to withdraw the credit facility was a lawful threat as Gallagher genuinely believed they were entitled to the money
Progress Bulk Carriers Ltd v Tube City (2012)	The charterers faced 'catastrophic' losses if they delayed any longer The agreement to waive all claims against them was obtained by economic duress
Times Travel (UK) Limited v Pakistan International Airlines Corporation (2019)	Where only lawful acts have been committed, economic duress will not be available as a defence unless bad faith can be proved, which was not the case here

Figure 41.7 Key cases: economic duress

Quick questions

1 Distinguish between the different types of misrepresentation.
2 Explain whether silence can be a misrepresentation.
3 Explain what is meant by 'rescission'.
4 When can a court award damages for innocent misrepresentation?
5 Explain the remedies for economic duress.

Summary

- Vitiating factors include misrepresentation and economic duress.
- Misrepresentation occurs where a person is induced to enter a contract as a result of statements made that are false.
- There are three types of misrepresentation: innocent, negligent and fraudulent, each with its own remedies.
- Economic duress arises where there is the threat to damage a business or a person financially. The court will consider each case involving economic duress according to its individual circumstances.

Chapter 42 Discharge of contract

Introduction

Discharge of contract merely means the end of the contract. The usual method of discharge of a contract is through performance, when both parties have done what they agreed in the contract.

A contract may be discharged by frustration, where unforeseen events make performance impossible, or by breach, if it has not been performed as agreed.

42.1 Discharge by performance

The strict rule of discharge by performance is that performance must be complete and exact.

Activity

Jen arranged a minicab home from a club late one night for £20. She had given the driver her precise address. The driver was in a hurry to pick up his next, very lucrative, fare so told Jen to get out at the end of her street, about 100 metres from her house, as it was a one-way street and would require him to take a long and time-consuming detour.

- Do you think she should pay the driver £20, a little less than £20 or nothing?
- If you think she should pay nothing, how close do you think the driver should get to her house to be paid?
- Write down the arguments for Jen and for the minicab driver.

An early case showing the rule is *Cutter v Powell* (1795).

Case study

Cutter v Powell (1795)

Cutter agreed to work as second mate on a voyage for a fixed fee. He died at sea near the end of the voyage, and his widow sued for a proportion of his fee. However, she was entitled to nothing as he had agreed to work the entire voyage and had not done so.

Another example is *Re Moore and Co. Ltd and Landauer and Co.'s Arbitration* (1921), where even though the total number of the tins was correct, the number of tins in each carton was incorrect and so the goods did not correspond with the description in the contract.

The harshness of the rule has been lessened in these circumstances:

- tender of performance
- severable contracts
  substantial performance
  acceptance of partial performance
- delayed performance

42.1.1 Tender of performance

If one party prevents the other from carrying out his contract, then the innocent party can claim to be paid on a *quantum meruit* basis. This can be seen in *Planche v Colburn* (1831).

Case study

Planche v Colburn (1831)

A publisher hired an author to write one of a series of books. When the publisher decided to abandon the whole series, the author was prevented from completing the work through no fault of his own. He was entitled to recover a fee for his wasted work.

Key term

Quantum meruit – as much as it is worth.

42.1.2 Severable contracts

Where a contract can be seen as being separate parts, non-completion of one part is not a breach of the whole contract. So, if Mr Cutter's contract in *Cutter v Powell* had been described as, for example, £1 per day, then the contract for the voyage would have been divisible. This can be seen in *Ritchie v Atkinson* (1808).

Case study

Ritchie v Atkinson (1808)

A ship owner agreed to carry a cargo at an agreed rate per ton, but he carried only a part of the cargo. He was entitled to be paid for the part of the cargo he had carried at the agreed price per ton, but was liable in damages for breach of contract for not carrying the whole cargo.

42.1.3 Substantial performance

If a party has done almost everything that was required under the contract, the doctrine of substantial performance may apply. Where it does apply, there must be payment of the amount for what has been done.

This does not apply where the contract is considered to be an entire contract, and all of the obligations in the contract are seen as a single transaction that cannot be broken down, as in *Cutter v Powell*.

Substantial performance often occurs in large contracts where little things are not performed exactly, as in *Dakin and Co. v Lee* (1916).

Case study

Dakin and Co. v Lee (1916)

Builders agreed to repair the defendant's premises for £1500. They performed the contract completely but there were three relatively poorly performed aspects. These cost £80 to put right.

The court decided that the contract had been substantially, if not precisely, performed. The fact that the work was done badly did not mean it had not been performed at all. The builder was entitled to be paid the price, with a deduction for the defective work.

The difficulty is in establishing what amounts to substantial performance. There are no percentages to indicate when the work has been substantially completed, and it is decided on the circumstances of each case. Two contrasting examples are *Hoenig v Isaacs* (1952) and *Bolton v Mahadeva* (1972).

Case studies

Hoenig v Isaacs (1952)

A decorator was contracted to decorate and furnish a room for £750. Some of the furniture was defective but could be repaired for £55. The court decided that the contract was substantially completed on a financial basis. The decorator was entitled to be paid for what he had done on a *quantum meruit* basis.

Bolton v Mahadeva (1972)

A builder agreed to install a central heating system for £560. However, the installation was defective, as the system gave off fumes and did not work properly. Repairs cost £170. The court decided that the builder was entitled to nothing, as there had not been substantial performance of the contract.

The court used their discretion to reach a just and fair decision through *quantum meruit* in *Young v Thames Properties Ltd* (1999).

Case study

Young v Thames Properties Ltd (1999)

A contract was made for resurfacing a car park, but the contractor did not resurface to the exact specifications with respect to the depth of some of the materials. The court decided that the defects made little difference to the quality of the car park, so the contractor was entitled to the contract price minus the savings to the contractor of not completing the contract with the correct depth of materials.

42.1.4 Acceptance of part-performance

If one party has agreed the other party need not complete the entire contract, the contract must be paid for on a *quantum meruit* basis. However, the consent must acknowledge that the defaulting party is entitled to be paid for what they have completed so far, and the agreement was made without undue pressure.

If the innocent party has no option but to accept the work partially done, this is not considered consent to part-performance. This was shown in *Sumpter v Hedges* (1898).

Case study

Sumpter v Hedges (1898)

A builder agreed to build two houses. He completed just over half of the work and then ran out of money. The customer completed the outstanding work. The builder argued that in completing the work himself, the defendant accepted part-performance.

The court said the defendant had no choice but to accept part-performance as he was left with half a completed house on his land. Therefore, the builder was not entitled to be paid for the work he had done so far. There was insufficient work done for substantial performance.

However, as some of the materials left behind by the builder were used in completing the work, the builder was awarded a sum for the use of those materials.

42.1.5 Delayed performance and the effect of time for performance of a contract

In many contracts it is useful to insert a term stipulating time. This is particularly important when an item is needed at a particular time, for example, a wedding dress.

There are often terms in contracts about the time for performance of the contract. The question here is: how exactly must terms as to time be performed? If it is exact, can the injured party reject the contract for breach of this term?

The court regards time as a condition if:
- the parties have expressly stated in the contract that time of performance of the contract is a critical part of performance (time is of the essence)
- in the circumstances, time for completion of the contract is critical, or
- one party has failed to perform on time and the other has insisted on a new date for completion of the contract (making time of the essence of the contract).

The effect of delay to performance is to be treated as a breach of condition if any of these points are present. If none of these points are present, the default position is for the delay to be treated as breach of an innominate term, so the effect of the breach is examined.

This can be seen in cases such as *Charles Rickards Ltd v Oppenheim* (1950) and *Union Eagle Ltd v Golden Achievement Ltd* (1997).

Case study

Charles Rickards Ltd v Oppenheim (1950)

A buyer of a Rolls-Royce car chassis agreed for a body to be built upon it by a fixed date. The body was not completed by that date. The buyer kept pushing for delivery, and eventually gave notice that unless delivery of the car with a completed body was ready within four weeks, he would cancel the contract. The car was not delivered within the period of four weeks. When the car was completed, he rejected it.

The claimant was entitled to cancel the contract as time had been made of the essence and that term had not been complied with.

The result can be harsh.

Case study

Union Eagle Ltd v Golden Achievement Ltd (1997)

In a contract for the sale of a flat, the time for completion of the contract had been specified as 5.00 p.m. and time was expressly stated to be 'of the essence'. The purchaser delivered the purchase price at 5.10 p.m. and the seller repudiated the contract. The court decided that the seller was entitled to repudiate the contract as the time for completion had been made a condition of the contract.

Most contracts for the sale of land including houses include terms about time for performance of the contract. It is essential that once time being of the essence has been waived, it is then reinstated as a term by giving notice, if such a term is to be relied on. This is apparent from the case of *Hakimzay Ltd v Swailes* (2015), a case involving the sale of a residential property.

	Brief legal rule	Case example
Discharge by performance – general rule	Performance must be complete and exact	*Cutter v Powell* (1795)
Some contracts can be seen as divisible contracts	If a contract can be seen as being separate parts, then non-completion of one part is not a breach of the whole contract	*Ritchie v Atkinson* (1808)
The doctrine of substantial performance	If a party has done substantially what was required under the contract, then the doctrine of substantial performance can apply	*Dakin and Co. v Lee* (1916)
Full performance prevented by actions of the other party	If one party prevents the other from carrying out his or her contract, the innocent party can claim to be paid on a *quantum meruit* basis	*Planche v Colburn* (1831)
One party accepts part-performance	If one party has agreed the other party need not complete the entire contract, the strict rule will not apply	*Sumpter v Hedges* (1898)
The effect of a term as to time for performance of a contract	A term as to time is treated as a condition if it falls within one of three categories If not it is treated as a warranty	*Union Eagle Ltd v Golden Achievement Ltd* (1997)
Time can be made of the essence of a contract	This also means the right to treat it as a condition can be waived	*Charles Rickards Ltd v Oppenheim* (1950)

Figure 42.1 Key facts: discharge by performance

Case	Judgment
Cutter v Powell (1795)	As the contract was for the whole voyage, he had not performed his contract
Ritchie v Atkinson (1808)	The ship owner was entitled to be paid for the part of the cargo he had carried as the contract was divisible
Dakin and Co. v Lee (1916)	Substantial performance applied as there were relatively minor defects in the work
Hoenig v Isaacs (1952)	*Quantum meruit* was used to establish payment to be made
Bolton v Mahadeva (1972)	The defects were too great to amount to substantial performance
Young v Thames Properties Ltd (1999)	The court used its discretion to reach a just and fair decision
Planche v Colburn (1831)	An author was prevented from carrying out his contract so was paid on a *quantum meruit* basis
Sumpter v Hedges (1898)	The builder was not entitled to be paid for the work he had done so far as the customer had no alternative and had not consented to the builder's part performance
Charles Rickards Ltd v Oppenheim (1950)	He was entitled to cancel the contract as time had been made of the essence and that term had not been complied with
Union Eagle Ltd v Golden Achievement Ltd (1997)	Time was expressly stated to be 'of the essence' – the purchase price was delivered 10 minutes late and the seller was entitled to repudiate the contract

Figure 42.2 Key cases: discharge by performance

42.2 Discharge by frustration

Historically the law held that a party was bound to perform their obligations under the contract, whatever happened. In *Paradine v Jane* (1647), the defendant was still liable to pay rent on land even though he had been forced off the land by an invading army during the English Civil War!

The injustice of this strict rule led to the development of a new doctrine in the nineteenth century. If a party to a contract was prevented from keeping the promise because of an unforeseeable, intervening event, they would not be liable for a breach of contract.

For a successful claim of frustration, the following must be shown:

- The frustrating event occurred after the contract was made.
- The event is so fundamental that it goes to the root of the contract and goes beyond what was contemplated by the parties when they made the contract.
  The event makes performance of the contract impossible or, at least, radically different.
- The event is entirely beyond the parties' control.

The frustrating event must be as a result of:

- Destruction of the subject matter including unavailability of a party in a contract for personal services such as through death or serious illness of the performer.
- Subsequent illegality, for example, by fulfilling a contract for goods that are subsequently banned from being imported.
- Destruction/frustration of the common venture – this is the situation where there is no physical destruction but the essential commercial purpose of the contract cannot be achieved.

42.2.1 Grounds for claiming frustration

These can be seen under the following headings:

- impossibility
- illegality
  radical change in circumstances
  frustration in specific situations
  ○ leases
  ○ employment contracts

Impossibility

This was shown in *Taylor v Caldwell* (1863).

Case study

Taylor v Caldwell (1863)

The owner contracted to rent out his music hall. Through no one's fault, and before the rental could take place, the music hall burned down. The hirer had spent money advertising the events for which he would not be paid until after the events. As it was now impossible to complete the contract, it was frustrated. This ended the contract and there was no recompense for the wasted expenses.

Frustration also applies where the subject matter becomes unavailable through no fault of the contracting parties. An example is *Jackson v Union Marine Insurance Co. Ltd* (1874).

Case study

Jackson v Union Marine Insurance Co. Ltd (1874)

A ship was chartered to sail from Liverpool to Newport and from there, load a cargo for San Francisco. It ran aground and could not be loaded for a long time. This was seen as 'the perils of the sea'.

The court agreed there was an implied term that the ship should be available for loading in a reasonable time, so the long delay frustrated the contract.

Illegality

A contract may be frustrated as the result of a change in the law that makes the contract illegal to perform, for example, as a result of war.

Case studies

Denny, Mott and Dickson Ltd v James B Fraser and Co. Ltd (1944)

The court said that a contract to import certain goods would be frustrated if importing goods of that kind became illegal after the contract was made.

Re Shipton Anderson and Co. and Harrison Bros and Co. (1915)

A cargo of grain was sold, but before it could be delivered, war broke out. The government requisitioned the cargo so the contract was frustrated.

Radical change in circumstances

There is a radical change of circumstances as the essential commercial purpose of the contract cannot be achieved.

If the main purpose of the contract is based on a particular event and the event will not take place, the contract may be frustrated. The contrasting cases of *Krell v Henry* (1903) and *Herne Bay Steamboat Co. v Hutton* (1903) illustrate this.

Case studies

Krell v Henry (1903)

A man hired a hotel room in order to view Edward VII's coronation procession. The Prince became ill so the coronation and procession were postponed. The court said that the event was the main purpose of the contract; as it would not occur, the contract was frustrated even though the room could still have been used.

Herne Bay Steamboat Co. v Hutton (1903)

Hutton hired a boat in order to see the fleet when the King reviewed it as part of his coronation celebrations. Hutton claimed he did not have to pay as the King was ill and did not attend. However, the court said the contract was not frustrated as one main reason for the contract still remained, to view the fleet. All that was missing was the King's presence. This was not enough to frustrate the contract.

- In *Krell*, the commercial purpose of the contract was to watch the procession. The contract was frustrated because the outside event beyond the control of the parties (the King's illness) destroyed the commercial purpose.
- In *Hutton*, the commercial purpose was not destroyed as he could still go and see the fleet of ships that assembled, so the contract was not frustrated.

Frustration in specific situations

Leases

In *National Carriers Ltd v Panalpina (Northern) Ltd* (1980), the tenant's access to the premises was closed by the local authority because it passed by a derelict and dangerous building. The tenant argued that its tenancy was frustrated. However, the lease was not frustrated as the lease had a term of ten years, and the interruption was temporary.

In *Canary Wharf v European Medicines Agency* (2019), the court decided that Brexit will not frustrate the EMA's lease of premises in London, as the premises could still be used or sub-let.

Employment contracts

In a contract for services, the frustrating event may be the unavailability of the party who is to perform the service because of illness, as in *Robinson v Davidson* (1871), or failure to perform on medical advice, as in *Condor v The Baron Knights* (1966).

Case studies

Robinson v Davidson (1871)

A pianist made a contract to perform. Shortly before the performance was due, she became ill and informed the claimant that she would be unable to attend. The court decided that the contract was conditional on the woman being well enough to perform and her illness was a frustrating event.

Condor v The Baron Knights (1966)

A contract entered into by a band required all members of the band to be available to perform for seven evenings a week if necessary. The drummer became ill and was advised to work no more than four nights per week. On occasion, he ignored this advice, but the court still held that the contract was frustrated since it was necessary to have a stand-in musician in case he fell ill.

42.2.2 Limits to frustration – when frustration cannot apply

These events are sometimes categorised as:
- self-induced frustration
- the contract becoming less profitable
- the event being a foreseeable risk or the event was mentioned in the contract.

Self-induced frustration

Frustration will not apply when the frustrating event is within the control of one party.

Case study

Maritime National Fish Ltd v Ocean Trawlers Ltd (1935)

A fishing company owned two trawlers and had a contract to hire a third. The company needed a licence for each vessel but was only allocated two licences, which it allocated to its own boats. The company then claimed frustration of the hire contract as it could not use the hire boat.

The court held that frustration did not apply and the contract was still valid. The 'frustrating' event was within the company's control as it could have allocated a licence to the hired boat rather than another of its boats, which it had chosen to do.

This can be contrasted with *Gamerco SA v ICM Fair Warning (Agency) Ltd and Missouri Storm Inc.* (1995). Here the lack of a licence was a frustrating event as the issue of the licence was not under the control of either party and the contract was to perform at the particular location at a particular time.

Case study

Gamerco SA v ICM Fair Warning (Agency) Ltd and Missouri Storm Inc. (1995)

A Spanish concert promoter and the defendant rock group, Guns N' Roses (their corporate persona is Missouri Storm Inc.) agreed to put on a concert at Atletico Madrid's stadium. Shortly before it was due to take place, the stadium was deemed unfit and its licence withdrawn by the Spanish authorities. No other stadium was available.

The contract had been frustrated: the promoter could not erect the stage and the band could not perform.

For this reason, many contracts contain a *force majeure* clause.

Key term

Force majeure clause – a clause often found in commercial contracts. It excludes liability for the parties for delay in performance or the non-performance if there are extraordinary events.

If the contract does not contain a force majeure clause, it may still be possible to rely on frustration to avoid being in breach of contract. However, what may constitute a frustrating event depends on the circumstances of each case.

Guns N' Roses concert, Los Angeles, 2016

The contract has become less profitable

A contract becoming less profitable or more difficult to complete is not a reason for frustration of that contract.

Case studies

Davis Contractors Ltd v Fareham Urban District Council (1956)

Builders were contracted to build houses for the urban district council for £94,000 but then discovered it would cost £115,000 to complete the contract due to labour shortages. The builders claimed frustration of the contract.

The court rejected this as the contract was not radically different to what the parties had originally intended, just less profitable.

Tsakiroglou and Co. Ltd v Noblee Thorl GmbH (1962)

The defendants agreed to ship peanuts from Sudan during November or December 1956 to Hamburg. Both parties anticipated that the ship would sail through the Suez Canal but the actual route was not specified in the contract. However, the Suez crisis of 1956 meant that on 2 November, the Suez Canal was closed to shipping. The defendant could still have transported the peanuts within the contractually agreed time but this would mean going via the Cape of Good Hope, which would have taken much longer and cost much more.

The court held that the contract was not frustrated.

The event being a foreseeable risk was mentioned in the contract

Case study

Amalgamated Investment and Property Co. Ltd v John Walker and Sons Ltd (1977)

This involved a contract to sell a building to the investment company who wanted it for redevelopment. After the contract was made, the Department of the Environment made the building a listed building, meaning that it could not be used for development. This resulted in a huge drop in the value of the building.

The court rejected a claim of frustration, as listing was a risk associated with all old buildings, and pre-contract enquiries showed the developers were aware of this possibility.

In general, the courts are reluctant to find that there has been frustration of contract. This can be seen in the case of *Armchair Answercall v People in Mind* (2016).

Case study

Armchair Answercall v People in Mind (2016)

People in Mind's role was to support Armchair Answercall in moving the business to a new management model for existing franchisees and potential new customers. The contract for services was commercially undermined when third-party franchisees refused to vary the way the business was carried out.

For an event to be frustrating, it had to be a 'supervening outside event which the parties could not reasonably be thought to have foreseen as a real possibility'. This was not the case here, as the franchisees' departure was promoted by the acts of Armchair Answercall.

42.2.3 The financial consequences of frustration

The Law Reform (Frustrated Contracts) Act 1943 sets out the remedies available. The Act does not affect the law on the situations when frustration may occur, and only sets out how frustrated contracts should be settled.

The key sections of the Act are ss 1(2)–1(4).

Section 1(2) provides that:
- Money paid before the frustrating event occurs is recoverable – this includes paying in advance for goods and then having the order cancelled because new legislation has prohibited those goods.
- When the contract is frustrated, there is no longer an obligation to pay the price agreed for goods or services.
- The court may award the injured party expenses incurred before the contract is discharged, to a maximum of the sum of money paid or payable before the frustrating event.

In *Gamerco SA v ICM Fair Warning (Agency) Ltd and Missouri Storm Inc.* (1995), mentioned above, the judge ordered the repayment of the whole sum paid in advance of $412,500 and, as both parties had incurred some expenditure in advance of the proposed performance, justice was done by both parties bearing the loss of their own expenses.

Section 1(3) provides that:
- If one party has obtained a valuable benefit from the contract before the frustrating event, the court may order them to pay a just sum, depending on the circumstances of the case.

The purpose of judicial discretion on this is to fairly compensate the claimant from the date the loss is suffered. This can be seen in the case of *BP Exploration v Hunt (No. 2)* (1979).

Case study

BP Exploration v Hunt (No. 2) (1979)

Hunt had a concession to explore for oil in Libya. BP financed him, in return for a half share of the concession. Its expenses were set out by a formula in the contract. Oil came on stream in 1967 but in 1971 the Libyan government seized BP's interest.

BP had not received all its initial expenditure from Hunt's share, and claimed a just sum at the discretion of the judge.

Section 1(4) provides that in estimating the expenses incurred by any party to the contract, the court should consider:
- overhead expenses
- any work or services performed personally by a party to the contract.

This explains the nature of expenses mentioned in s 1(2).

The rules under the Act are summarised as follows:
- Money already paid (e.g. a deposit) is recoverable.
- Money already due under the contract is not payable.
- The court can use its discretion to order compensation to be paid for work done and expenses incurred under the contract before the

frustrating event. The principle of *quantum meruit* is applied to work out the just amount.
- The court may order compensation to be paid for any valuable benefit one party may acquire under the frustrated contract.

	Brief legal rule	Case example
Discharge by frustration – general rule	Where a party to a contract was prevented from keeping the promise because of an unforeseeable, intervening event, they are not liable for a breach of contract	*Taylor v Caldwell* (1863)
For there to be frustration the contract must be impossible to perform	The court must decide whether performance is impossible in fact	*Jackson v Union Marine Insurance Co. Ltd* (1874)
Subsequent illegality can amount to frustration of contract	A contract becoming illegal to perform after it is made frustrates the contract	*Denny, Mott and Dickson Ltd v James B Fraser and Co. Ltd* (1944)
A radical change of the main purpose of the contract can amount to frustration of contract	The main purpose of the contract must be affected by the change, not just some aspect of it	*Krell v Henry* (1903) *Herne Bay Steamboat Co. v Hutton* (1903)
Self-induced frustration is breach not frustration	Frustration will not apply when the frustrating event is within the control of one party	*Maritime National Fish Ltd v Ocean Trawlers Ltd* (1935)
A contract becoming less profitable is not frustration	Merely because a contract becomes less profitable or more difficult to complete is not a reason for frustration of that contract	*Davis Contractors Ltd v Fareham UDC* (1956)
Remedies for frustration of contract	These are dealt with in the Law Reform (Frustrated Contracts) Act 1943	

Figure 42.4 Key facts: discharge by frustration

Case	Judgment
Taylor v Caldwell (1863)	As the destruction of the music hall was not the fault of either party, so the contract was frustrated
Jackson v Union Marine Insurance Co. Ltd (1874)	The long delay in loading caused by it running aground amounted to frustration of the contract
Robinson v Davidson (1871)	Illness of a person who is to perform personally can amount to frustration
Condor v The Baron Knights (1966)	Acting on medical advice can be sufficient for frustration of contract
Denny, Mott and Dickson Ltd v James B Fraser and Co. Ltd (1944)	The law was changed so that importing those goods became illegal after the contract was made. This frustrated the contract
Re Shipton Anderson and Co. and Harrison Bros and Co. (1915)	The government requisitioned the cargo so the contract was frustrated
Krell v Henry (1903)	The event, which was the main purpose of the contract, would not occur therefore the contract was frustrated

Case	Judgment
Herne Bay Steamboat Co. v Hutton (1903)	The contract was not frustrated as one main reason for the contract still remained
Maritime National Fish Ltd v Ocean Trawlers Ltd (1935)	The choice of which boat to allocate a licence to amounted to self-induced frustration
Gamerco SA v ICM Fair Warning (Agency) Ltd and Missouri Storm Inc. (1995)	The licence was withdrawn by a third party so the contract was frustrated
Armchair Answercall v People in Mind (2016)	In general, the courts are reluctant to find there has been frustration of contract

Figure 42.5 Key cases: discharge by frustration

42.3 Discharge by breach

Breach of contract can occur by:
- actual breach – there has been a failure to perform the contract
- anticipatory breach – one party indicates that they will not be performing the contract.

42.3.1 Actual breach

When a party fails to perform their obligations under a contract, that party may be sued for breach of contract. The differences between conditions, warranties and innominate terms have been considered in Chapter 40.

If a repudiatory breach is established, the other party who is not in breach may terminate the contract and claim damages or continue the contract and claim damages. Repudiatory breach can occur in three ways:
- a breach of condition
- a refusal to perform the contract
- a serious breach of an innominate term that would be considered a breach of condition.

Key term 🔑

Repudiatory breach of contract – this occurs when a party commits a breach of contract so serious that it entitles the innocent party to treat the contract as terminated,

Either or both parties to the contract may be in breach of contract. The victim will always be entitled to claim for damages, but ending the contract depends on the type of term that has been breached:
- Breaching any term of a contract gives the right to claim damages, but only a breach of condition gives the right to repudiate and end the contract, and/or sue for damages.
- Breach of a condition includes breach of an innominate term where the term is treated as a condition.

Breach can be a total failure to perform, for example, non-delivery or non-payment, or failure to perform in accordance with the terms of the contract (and could be seen as part-performance).

The three sets of circumstances giving rise to a breach of contract are:
1 Renunciation by a party of their liabilities under it – such as not paying a bill on the due date.
2 Impossibility created by own action – such as closing a hairdresser's business for holidays with appointments during that time.
3 Total or partial failure of performance – such as delivering defective goods.

Sometimes contracts contain express termination provisions, which means that the contract can be terminated in the event of any of the circumstances set out in the contract (such as non-payment of a stage payment or suspension of work on a project). This was illustrated in *Stocznia Gdynia SA v Gearbulk Holdings* (2009). These rights are in addition to any right to terminate set out by the common law.

Case study

Stocznia Gdynia SA v Gearbulk Holdings (2009)

Orders were placed for the construction of ships which were not delivered. The buyer, Gearbulk, cancelled the orders. The contract provided a right to terminate the contract corresponding to that right under contract law of a breach that goes to the root of the contract. In such cases, the injured party simply has to make clear that he is treating the contract as discharged.

42.3.2 Anticipatory breach

An anticipatory breach occurs when a party to a contract gives advance notice to the other party that they will not be performing or completing the contract. The innocent party in this situation has a choice:

- To sue immediately for breach of a condition, or
- To wait for the time agreed for performance of the contract and to sue if performance does not take place then.

The injured party can treat the contract as repudiated immediately and/or claim damages. An example is *Hochster v de la Tour* (1853).

Case study

Hochster v de la Tour (1853)

Hochester agreed to work as a courier on a tour due to start in June. However, the company told him in May that it no longer required his services. In that situation he was entitled to sue immediately and did not have to wait until the actual breach of contract, which would have occurred in June.

This is a good right to have – if the injured party had to wait to see if performance would take place, the other party could run out of money or other events could occur that result in discharge by frustration.

If one of the parties to a contract, either expressly or by conduct, leads the other party to reasonably conclude that they do not mean to carry out the contract, this amounts to a repudiation. The other party can treat the contract as at an end.

In *Geden Operations Ltd v Drybulk Handy Holdings Inc. (Bulk Uruguay)* (2014), the principle was summarised as conduct. The inevitability of non-performance entitled the innocent party to treat the contract as at an end prior to the time for performance. However, unlikelihood or uncertainty in future performance is not enough to prove anticipatory breach.

42.3.3 Remedies for breach

- If the victim claims an anticipatory breach, they may claim damages immediately, to put them in the same position they would have been in had the contract been completed. However, they must mitigate their losses within reason.
- The victim may choose not to accept the anticipatory breach but to see if the defendant commits an actual breach. The damages are assessed at the time when performance should occur, and the loss might increase due to a change in market factors. Alternatively, an event may occur which discharges the contract, such as frustration of contract for which there are different remedies.
- The victim may also repudiate the contract under anticipatory breach. They would no longer be bound to perform any obligations under the contract.
- For a breach of condition, the victim can claim for damages and/or repudiation.
- For a breach of warranty, the claim is limited to damages.

	Brief legal rule	Case example
Discharge by breach – general rule	When a party fails to perform his or her obligations under a contract, that party may be sued for breach of contract	*Poussard v Spiers and Pond* (1876) (see Chapter 40)
Types of breach	Breach can be actual breach or anticipatory breach	*Hochster v de la Tour* (1853)
When can it be taken as anticipatory breech?	This can be by renunciation or self-induced impossibility. Unlikelihood or uncertainty in future performance is not enough	*Geden Operations Ltd v Drybulk Handy Holdings Inc. (Bulk Uruguay)* (2014)
Effect of breach	This depends on the type of term broken	

Figure 42.6 Key facts: discharge by breach

Case	Judgment
Hochster v de la Tour (1853)	An anticipatory breach occurs when a party to a contract gives notice in advance to the other party that they will not be performing the contract
Geden Operations Ltd v Drybulk Handy Holdings Inc. (Bulk Uruguay) (2014)	Sets out when a breach can be treated as an anticipatory breach.

Figure 42.7 Key cases: discharge by breach

Tip

Consider whether the event preventing the performance of the contract comes from outside the contracting parties. If it does not, breach is a more likely reason for discharge of contract.

Quick questions

1 Explain the meaning of 'discharge by performance'.
2 Explain the meaning of 'severable contract'.
3 What must be proved for a successful claim of frustration?
4 Explain three situations when frustration cannot apply.
5 Distinguish between actual breach and anticipatory breach.

Summary

- A contract can be discharged by performance (the usual method), frustration or breach (failure to perform in whole or in part).
- Performance must be complete and exact but there are exceptions such as where part-performance is accepted.
- If the contract is not discharged by frustration, there will be a breach of contract.
- Breach and frustration have different remedies.
- Breach can be of a condition, a warranty or an innominate term.
- Breach can be actual or anticipatory.

Chapter 43 Remedies

Introduction

Remedies in contract law are divided into:

- Legal remedies – available against a person in breach of contract as of right. These can be damages, which is financial compensation, or remedies against the goods.
- Equitable remedies – these are discretionary: you do not have a right to an equitable remedy.
- Remedies under a specific statute – we will examine remedies under the Consumer Rights Act 2015.

43.1 Damages

The purpose of damages is to put the victim in the position they would have been in if the contract had been properly completed and performed by the defendant. The court is therefore looking at what should have happened and the consequences of non- or part-performance.

Damages are normally awarded for expectation loss (loss of a bargain) or reliance loss (wasted expenditure).

43.1.1 Basis for a claim in damages

The problem for the courts is to establish how much the loss will be. As damages are compensatory, they will not include losses that are too remote to be awarded. Compensatory damages are the main type of damages. We need to consider:

- loss of a bargain
- reliance loss
- restitution.

Loss of a bargain (expectation loss)

The idea here is to place the claimant in the same financial position as if the contract had been properly performed. This can be seen in a number of ways:

- The difference in value between the goods or services required in the contract and those actually provided. An example of this is *Bence Graphics International Ltd v Fasson UK Ltd* (1996).

Case study

Bence Graphics International Ltd v Fasson UK Ltd (1996)

The defendant supplied vinyl film on which the claimant printed identifying markers (decals) to put on bulk containers. There was an implied term that the decals would survive in a readable form for five years, but they lasted only two years. The court awarded damages amounting to the actual loss incurred by having to replace the decals.

- Where there is a market, damages will be the difference between the contract price and the price in the market. If the claimant's profit remains, there is no loss. This can be seen in the case of *Charter v Sullivan* (1957). However, if there is no available market then the claimant can recover the full loss, as in *WL Thompson Ltd v Robinson Gunmakers Ltd* (1955).

Case studies

Charter v Sullivan (1957)

The defendant contracted to buy a Hillman Minx car then refused to take delivery. Because demand for this particular car easily outstripped supply, the seller could easily sell the car and make his profit. Therefore, only nominal damages were awarded.

WL Thompson Ltd v Robinson Gunmakers Ltd (1955)

The defendant agreed to buy a Standard Vanguard car but later refused to accept and pay for it. Supply of Standard Vanguard cars exceeded the demand. Had the garage found another customer and sold to him or her as well as the defendant, then there would have been two sales and two profits. Therefore, damages were awarded for the loss of profit on one sale.

- Loss of profit not just for goods, but also in other contracts – as in *Victoria Laundry Ltd v Newman Industries Ltd* (1949), where the claimant recovered the profit that he would have been able to make but for the breach of contract.
- Loss of a chance – generally a speculative loss is not recoverable in contract, and most cases are based in negligence rather than contract. There was an exception in *Chaplin v Hicks* (1911), where the actress lost the chance of being selected for the part. The court stated that the mere fact that damages were difficult to calculate should not prevent them being awarded.

Reliance loss

This is the expense incurred by a claimant who relied on a contract being performed. A claimant may also recover expenses he or she has had to spend in advance of a contract that has been breached. An example of this can be seen in *Anglia Television Ltd v Reed* (1972).

Case study

Anglia Television Ltd v Reed (1972)

Anglia TV spent a lot of money preparing for a film, including fees paid to the director, designer and stage manager. Robert Reed, an American actor, agreed to be the main actor but then pulled out. A suitable replacement could not be found so the film was not made. As Anglia TV could not predict what its profit on the film would have been, the court awarded damages based on reliance loss. Robert Reed must have known that such expenditure was likely and was liable for the expenses incurred by Anglia TV, both before and after the contract was made, up to breach.

It is also possible sometimes to recover damages for the loss of an amenity, as in *Farley v Skinner* (2001).

Case study

Farley v Skinner (2001)

The claimant asked the defendant surveyor whether the house he was to buy was subject to aircraft noise. The surveyor incorrectly reassured him that it was not. The court said that an innocent party was entitled to be placed in the position that he would have been in had the party in breach exercised due care.

Damages were recoverable for distress and inconvenience where the matter was important to the claimant, that had been made clear to the defendant, and the required action had been incorporated into the contract. The court viewed as appropriate an award of £10,000 for the discomfort of suffering aircraft noise.

The distinction between expectation loss and reliance loss

Expectation loss

This is the normal measure of damages for breach of contract. It refers to the innocent party's loss of bargain. This includes the profits that it would have expected to receive had the contract been performed, taking into account the costs it would have incurred to earn that profit. The aim of expectation loss damages is to put the innocent party in the same position as if the contract had been performed.

Reliance loss

This is wasted expenditure. It refers to the expenses incurred by the claimant in reliance of the contract being performed. The aim of damages for reliance loss is to put the claimant in the position he or she would have been in had the contract never been made; here the claimant has incurred expense in preparation for the contract that is expected to be performed, but it has not been performed.

Expectation loss and reliance loss are mutually exclusive to prevent double recovery of damages.

Restitution

Restitution is a repayment of any money or other benefits passed to the defendant in advance of the contract that is breached.

43.1.2 Special situations

There are some situations that do not fit the normal pattern.

Nominal damages

If no loss is actually suffered but there is breach, the court may award 'nominal damages'. In *Staniforth v Lyall* (1830), the award of nominal damages was made as the claimant had made no loss. In fact, the main purpose of bringing the case was to have proof that the contract was at an end.

Experience Hendrix LLC v PPX Enterprises Inc. (2003) involved Jimi Hendrix master recordings

Case study

Staniforth v Lyall (1830)

Lyall was under a duty to load his cargo onto the claimant's boat by a certain date. He failed and the boat owner sued for breach of contract. The claimant hired his boat out to another party immediately following the breach for a greater profit than he would have made from the defendant.

He succeeded in having the contract declared terminated but having suffered no loss, was awarded a nominal sum only. Then there was no risk of being in breach of contract or of being unable to rehire the boat to someone else without being in breach of contract, as the contract had been terminated by the breach.

In some cases, substantial damages have been awarded where nominal damages might have been considered more appropriate. One example is *Experience Hendrix LLC v PPX Enterprises Inc.* (2003).

Case study

Experience Hendrix LLC v PPX Enterprises Inc. (2003)

After the death of Jimi Hendrix, the defendant had been granting licences to exploit master recordings containing works featuring Hendrix, in breach of a 1973 agreement settling earlier litigation. There was no evidence to show or quantify any financial losses suffered as a result of the breaches.

The court stated that the defendant should make a reasonable payment for its uses of master recordings in breach of the settlement agreement – that is, more than just nominal damages.

This is sometimes called a '*Wrotham Park*' award, following the case of *Wrotham Park Estate Co. Ltd v Parkside Homes Ltd* (1974), but is now known as negotiating damages.

Case study

Wrotham Park Estate Co. Ltd v Parkside Homes Ltd (1974)

The claimant sold land which was subject to a restrictive covenant preventing building on it. However, the defendant built and sold houses on the land. The claimant asked the court for an injunction order that the houses be demolished. The court would not grant an order for the demolition of the houses, on the basis that to do so would be unfair to the inhabitants of the houses. Instead, the court decided to award damages to represent the amount that the claimant might have accepted in exchange for the release of the restrictive covenant (even though the claimant would never have agreed to this at any price).

Instead of working out how much the innocent party has lost, or how much the wrong-doer has gained, *Wrotham Park* damages try to quantify the sum which might reasonably have been negotiated between the parties for giving permission to the wrong-doer to act as they did.

The difficulty with *Wrotham Park* damages is that it is not clear when they should be awarded. In *Morris-Garner v OneStep (Support) Ltd* (2018), it was stated that *Wrotham Park* damages:

- should be awarded when the claimant would have very real problems in establishing financial loss
- is a 'just' response to a breach of contract
- should not be restricted to exceptional circumstances.

495

This type of damages is now known as negotiating damages. They can be awarded for breach of contract where the loss suffered by the claimant is measured for its econ-omic value. The defendant has taken something for nothing, for which the claimant is entitled to require payment. Typically this may occur in cases involving breach of confidentiality, breach of restrictive covenants over land or breach of an intellectual property agreement.

Speculative damages

The courts have been careful to avoid granting speculative damages.

Case study

Addis v The Gramophone Company (1909)

The court refused a claim for damages in contract for injury to reputation and mental distress caused by the humiliating manner of Mr Addis's dismissal from his job, as this was a matter for the law of tort. He was awarded damages only for the loss of salary and commission owed.

However, in *Chaplin v Hicks* (1911), the claimant succeeded.

Case study

Chaplin v Hicks (1911)

A contract was breached when the claimant was not notified of her selection in time to go to a beauty contest and acting audition. She was awarded damages on the basis that she had been deprived of a 24 per cent chance of being engaged as an actor – 12 of the other 50 contestants were subsequently engaged.

There are cases allowing damages of a highly speculative nature for mental distress, while also recognising the problems with respect to privity of contract, such as *Jackson v Horizon Holidays Ltd* (1975) (details given in Chapter 39).

Damages for loss of amenity have been allowed where the sole purpose of the contract was to provide the pleasurable amenity. *Ruxley Electronics and Construction Ltd v Forsyth* (1996) is an example.

Case study

Ruxley Electronics and Construction Ltd v Forsyth (1996)

The contract for a swimming pool stated the depth but the builder completed the pool with a depth about 10 per cent less. There was nothing wrong with the pool apart from the depth – it was still worth its cost, it did not affect the value of the property as a whole and it could still be used as originally intended. The cost to correct the pool was £21,650, which was equivalent to the original cost of building the pool.

The court stated that in building contracts there are two bases for quantification of damages – the cost of reinstatement or the difference in value. The cost of reinstatement was totally unreasonable in this case. As there was no real difference in value of the pool, technically, Mr Forsyth was entitled to nothing. However, as he had not received that which he had contracted for, the court awarded him £2500 for loss of amenity.

43.1.3 Causation and remoteness of damage

Compensatory damages are relevant once it has been established which losses are to be compensated.

- Causation: losses may have been foreseeable at the time of making the contract, but they will only be recoverable if those losses were caused by the breach of contract. Therefore, the claimant must prove that the breach caused the loss, not just provided the opportunity for loss. This is the 'but for' test – but for the breach of contract, would the claimant have suffered the loss claimed? If the loss would have happened in any event, then the breach could not be said to have caused the loss.
- Remoteness of damage: this does not establish how much compensation will be payable (damages), but merely which losses can be the subject of compensation (damage).

Tip

To remember the difference between damage and damages, think of damages as being money – damage$. The measure of damages is the term used to describe the quantum (amount) of damages awarded.

The test of remoteness was set out in *Hadley v Baxendale* (1854).

Case study

Hadley v Baxendale (1854)

A mill owner made a contract with a carrier to deliver a crankshaft for his mill. The mill was unable to operate as the existing crankshaft was broken. The carrier did not know this. The carrier was late with delivery. The mill owner sued unsuccessfully because the carrier was unaware of the importance of prompt delivery.

The remoteness test is in two parts:

1   The objective test: what loss is a natural consequence of the breach? In this case, the loss was late delivery.

2   The subjective test: this is based on specific knowledge of potential losses in the minds of both parties when the contract is formed. Did the carrier know that the mill could not operate without the crankshaft?

The test has been developed in subsequent decisions, as in *Victoria Laundry Ltd v Newman Industries Ltd* (1949).

Case study

Victoria Laundry Ltd v Newman Industries Ltd (1949)

There was a contract to deliver a boiler to the laundry company but it was not delivered until five months after the contract date. The laundry successfully sued for loss of its usual profits from the date of the breach. This was a natural consequence loss.

The laundry also sued in respect of additional lost profits from a special, one-off contract that it had been unable to take up without the boiler. This claim failed as the defendant did not know about the special contract at the time the contract was made.

The remoteness test is:

●   Recoverable loss should be measured against a test of reasonable foreseeability.

●   Foreseeability of loss depends on knowledge at the time the contract was made.

●   There are two types of knowledge: common knowledge and actual knowledge of the defendant, as in *Hadley v Baxendale* (1854).

Knowledge can be implied on the basis of what a reasonable man may have contemplated in the circumstances. This is shown in *Czarnikow Ltd v Koufos (The Heron II)* (1969).

Case study

Czarnikow Ltd v Koufos (The Heron II) (1969)

A contract for the carriage of a cargo of sugar arrived late. The buyers of the cargo had intended to sell the cargo of sugar promptly upon arrival. They claimed for the loss of profit resulting from the fall in the market price of the sugar during the period of delay.

The ship owners did not know what the buyers intended to do with the sugar. But they did know that there was a market in sugar and, if they had thought about it, must have realised that it was 'not unlikely' that the sugar would be sold in the market at its market price on arrival. Since the defendant must have known that market prices fluctuate, he must have contemplated the loss (or equally a profit) as a possible result of the breach.

This principle was considered in *H Parsons (Livestock) Ltd v Uttley Ingham* (1978).

Case study

H Parsons (Livestock) Ltd v Uttley Ingham (1978)

The defendants had installed a pig nut hopper. The ventilation hatch was sealed during transit. The installers then forgot to open it. Lack of ventilation caused the nuts that were added by the customer to go mouldy. Many pigs died from eating the mouldy nuts.

The court decided that the death of the pigs would have been within the contemplation of the parties when they made their contract and damages were not too remote.

In *Wellesley Partners LLP v Withers LLP* (2015), the position was clarified where a claim is made in both contract and negligence, by stating that the contract interpretation of the law as set out here should prevail.

Once the tests of causation and remoteness have established that there is liability for the loss claimed, the court then has to determine how much the claimant can recover.

Case	Judgment
Hadley v Baxendale (1854)	Sets out the two-part test for remoteness of damage
Victoria Laundry Ltd v Newman Industries Ltd (1949)	Modifies the test set out in *Hadley v Baxendale* (1854)
Czarnikow Ltd v Koufos (The Heron II) (1969)	The court decided that under the subjective part of the test in *Hadley v Baxendale* it was only necessary to show that the losses were in the reasonable contemplation of the parties as a possible result of the breach
H Parsons (Livestock) Ltd v Uttley Ingham (1978)	The court must determine what was in the contemplation of the parties at the time that the contract was made
Wellesley Partners LLP v Withers LLP (2015)	Summarises the position on damage

Figure 43.1 Key cases: remoteness of damage

	Brief legal rule	Case example
Damages – purpose	The purpose of damages is to put the victim in the position he or she would have been in if the contract had been properly completed and performed by the defendant	
Nominal damages	If no loss is actually suffered but the breach has been established then the court may award 'nominal damages'	*Staniforth v Lyall* (1830)
Wrotham Park damages	Awarded where the claimant would have very real problems in establishing financial loss and it is a 'just' response to a breach of contract	*Wrotham Park Estate Co. Ltd v Parkside Homes Ltd* (1974)
Damages for loss of a bargain	The idea here is to place the claimant in the same financial position as if the contract had been properly performed In other words, the claimant is put in the same financial position as if the main purpose of the contract had been achieved by proper performance	*Bence Graphics International Ltd v Fasson UK Ltd* (1996)
Damages where there is a market	Where there is a market, damages will be the difference between the contract price and the price obtained or required to be paid in the market	*Charter v Sullivan* (1957)
Damages for future contracts	There can be a claim for the profit that he or she would have been able to complete but for the breach of contract	*Victoria Laundry Ltd v Newman Industries Ltd* (1949)
Damages for loss of a chance	In rare circumstances the courts have allowed claimants to recover a loss that is entirely speculative; such claims are normally based on negligence	*Chaplin v Hicks* (1911)
Reliance loss	This refers to the expenses incurred by a claimant who relied on a contract being performed, but it was not performed	*Anglia Television Ltd v Reed* (1972)
Restitution	A repayment of any money or other benefits passed to the defendant in advance of the contract that is breached	
Speculative damages	Contract law has developed cases allowing damages of a highly speculative nature for mental distress while also recognising the problems with respect to privity of contract	*Ruxley Electronics and Construction Ltd v Forsyth* (1996)

Figure 43.2 Key facts: damages

Case	Judgment
Staniforth v Lyall (1830)	Upon breach, the claimant hired the boat to someone else for a greater profit than he would have made under the original contract As he had suffered no loss, he was awarded a nominal sum as damages
Wrotham Park Estate Co. Ltd v Parkside Homes Ltd (1974)	The claimant had suffered no loss but damages were awarded on the basis of the hypothetical sum the claimant could have charged to release the covenants
Experience Hendrix LLC v PPX Enterprises Inc. (2003)	The court decided that the publisher should pay a reasonable sum to Hendrix's estate, even though the estate had suffered no actual loss
Bence Graphics International Ltd v Fasson UK Ltd (1996)	Damages are assessed according to the difference in cost of shorter lifespan
Charter v Sullivan (1957)	Where demand exceeds supply, the claimant can still make his or her profit so there is no loss to be compensated
W L Thompson Ltd v Robinson Gunmakers Ltd (1955)	Supply exceeded demand; had the claimant found another customer and sold to him or her as well as the defendant, then there would have been two sales and two profits So loss of profit is the measure of damages
Victoria Laundry Ltd v Newman Industries Ltd (1949)	The claimant may recover for the profit that he or she would have been able to make from contracts but for the breach of contract
Chaplin v Hicks (1911)	The mere fact that damages were difficult to calculate should not prevent them being awarded
Anglia Television Ltd v Reed (1972)	The main actor pulled out and a suitable replacement could not be made so a film was not made The question of damages was decided that, as Anglia TV could not predict what its profit on the film would have been, the court awarded damages based on reliance loss
Farley v Skinner (2001)	It is possible to recover damages for the loss of an amenity under reliance loss
Ruxley Electronics and Construction Ltd v Forsyth (1996)	As he had not received the exact swimming pool that he had contracted for, the court awarded him £2500 for loss of amenity

Figure 43.3 Key cases: damages

43.1.4 Mitigation of loss

The injured party must take reasonable steps to minimise the effects of the breach. This is known as mitigation of loss. How this works can be seen in *British Westinghouse Electric v Underground Electric Railways* (1912).

Case study

British Westinghouse Electric v Underground Electric Railways (1912)

The goods delivered were defective. The railway company purchased replacements, which turned out to be more efficient than the original ones. They obtained benefits over and above what they would have got from the original contract.

The court said that additional benefits obtained as a result of taking reasonable steps to mitigate loss were to be accounted for when calculating damages. The court will balance loss against gain when calculating the amount of damages.

Key term

Mitigation of loss – the injured party must take reasonable steps to minimise the effects of the breach.

However, a claimant is not bound to go to extraordinary lengths to mitigate the loss, only to do what is reasonable in the circumstances. In an anticipatory breach, they are not bound to sue immediately they know of the possibility of the breach, but may continue until the breach is an actual breach. This can be seen in *White and Carter (Councils) Ltd v McGregor* (1962).

Case study

White and Carter (Councils) Ltd v McGregor (1962)

The claimant made a contract to display advertisements of McGregor's garage company for three years on litter bins. The day the contract started, McGregor said they no longer wished their advertisements to be on bins. The claimants refused cancellation and continued to display the advertisements, and brought an action for the contract price.

The argument that the claimants might have mitigated the loss by not continuing to fit the advertisements on bins failed as the contract was essentially a claim for a debt – payment of the price – so mitigation of loss did not apply.

The case of *Thai Airways v KI Holdings* (2015) shows the principle of mitigation when calculating damages.

Case study

Thai Airways v KI Holdings (2015)

The defendant company had contracted to supply the claimant with seats for its aircraft, but the seats were not delivered on time, and some not delivered at all. The airline leased substitute planes to mitigate its loss. The leased substitute aircraft were more fuel-efficient and this had to be taken into account.

This resulted in damages being reduced by the amount of fuel saved, so that the overall effect was that there was no loss and no profit to the claimant.

43.1.5 Liquidated damages

Liquidated damages are where the amount of damages has been fixed by a term in the contract. However, the courts will only accept this sum as the award of damages if the sum identified in the contract represents an accurate and proper assessment of loss. If it is not, it is seen as a penalty and will be unenforceable. The courts developed rules for determining the difference between genuine liquidated damages and a penalty in *Dunlop Pneumatic Tyre Co. v New Garage and Motor Co.* (1914):
- An extravagant sum will always be a penalty.
- Payment of a large sum for failure to settle a small debt is probably a penalty.
- A single sum operating in respect of a variety of different breaches is likely to be a penalty.

- The wording used by the parties is not necessarily conclusive.
- It does not matter that actual assessment of the loss was impossible before the contract.

Key term

Liquidated damages – where the amount of damages has been fixed by a term in the contract.

The rule on penalties has been updated in the case of *Cavendish Square Holding BV v Talal El Makdessi* (2015) and *ParkingEye Ltd v Beavis* (2015).

Case studies

Cavendish Square Holding BV v Talal El Makdessi (2015)

This involved the sale of a Middle Eastern media business. The contract stated that if the seller did not comply with the terms of the contract preventing him from competing with the buyer, then he would lose his right to future payments and he would have to sell his remaining shares to the buyer at a greatly reduced price.

The court held that the provisions contained in the agreements were there to protect the legitimate interests of the buyer.

ParkingEye Ltd v Beavis (2015)

An £85 parking fine was given for overstaying the two-hour parking limit at a privately owned car park. Mr Beavis tried to argue that the fine was a penalty and therefore unenforceable.

It was not a penalty. The correct test for a penalty is whether the sum or remedy stipulated as a consequence of a breach of contract is exorbitant or unconscionable (too much or unreasonable) considering the innocent party's interest in the performance of the contract.

Under the new test, the party relying on a term in a contract which sets out the damages to be paid must be able to show that the clause is to protect a legitimate interest and that the amount is not exorbitant or unconscionable (excessive). The following principles will apply:
- The amount no longer has to be a genuine pre-estimate of loss.
- This rule applies to commercial and consumer cases.
- The party seeking to rely on the term does not have to have suffered loss.

- The purpose of the term can be to act as a deterrent against a specific breach of contract.
- The recompense under the term does not have to be financial.
- The term can only apply to a breach of a primary obligation, not a secondary one, such as not paying a contractual penalty.
- The traditional tests in the *Dunlop* case are useful for cases concerning standard damages clauses but are of little use in more complex cases. The tests are not fixed rules of general application to all situations and were never intended to be this.
- In more complex cases, a broader approach is more suitable, which focuses on the nature and extent of the innocent party's interest in performance.
- A term with respect to damages may be justified apart from the desire to recover compensation for a breach. This is the commercial justification approach.
- The old penalty rule is an interference with freedom of contract. In a negotiated contract between parties of similar bargaining power, the strong initial presumption must be that the parties themselves are the best judges of what is legitimate in a provision dealing with the consequences of breach.

This makes it easier to enforce penalty clauses. The court must consider the wider commercial context of the agreement. If it can be shown that there is a legitimate reason why breach of contract damages would not be sufficient in the case in question, then even if the amount stated in the term seems to have no correlation to the actual loss suffered, it may be enforceable.

43.1.6 *Quantum meruit*

We have seen the operation of *quantum meruit* in relation to part-performance.

There are three common circumstances in which such an award is made:

1   In a contract for services where no price is stated, as in *Upton Rural District Council v Powell* (1942), where a retained fireman provided services with no fixed agreement as to wages; the court awarded a reasonable amount.
2   Where the circumstances of the case show that a fresh agreement can be implied in place of the original one, as in *Steven v Bromley* (1919). Here Steven had agreed to carry a cargo of steel at a specified rate. When the steel was delivered, there were also additional items. Steven was able to claim extra for the additional items.
3   Where a party considers the contract discharged by the other's breach, or where a party has been prevented from performing by the other party. In either case, they might claim for work they have already done, as in *De Barnady v Harding* (1853): a principal wrongly revoked his agent's authority to act on his behalf. The agent was then entitled to claim for the work he had already done and for expenses incurred.

	Brief legal rule	Case example
The duty to mitigate the loss	The party injured by a breach of contract must take reasonable steps to minimise the effects of the breach	*British Westinghouse Electric v Underground Electric Railways* (1912)
Liquidated damages	Liquidated damages are where the amount of damages has been fixed by a term in the contract	*Dunlop Pneumatic Tyre Co. v New Garage and Motor Co.* (1914)
Quantum meruit	Recovery of an unqualified sum for services already rendered	*Upton Rural District Council v Powell* (1942)

Figure 43.4 Key facts: mitigation of loss and terms attempting to quantify damages

Case	Judgment
British Westinghouse Electric v Underground Electric Railways (1912)	It was necessary to balance loss against gain when the amount of the damages was being calculated
Thai Airways v KI Holdings (2015)	The lease of substitute aircraft which were more fuel efficient had to be taken into account
Dunlop Pneumatic Tyre Co. v New Garage and Motor Co. (1914)	The case sets out the traditional rules as to when the term is a liquidated damages clause or a penalty
Cavendish Square Holding BV v Talal El Makdessi ParkingEye Ltd v Beavis (2015)	Sets out new tests for being able to rely on a penalty clause
Upton Rural District Council v Powell (1942)	Where a contract for services is silent on the issue of remuneration, *quantum meruit applies*
Steven v Bromley (1919)	Where the circumstances of the case show that a fresh agreement can be implied in place of the original one, *quantum meruit applies*
De Barnady v Harding (1853)	Where a party has elected to consider the contract discharged by the other's breach or where a party has been prevented from performing by the other party, *quantum meruit applies*

Figure 43.5 Key cases: mitigation of loss and terms attempting to quantify damages

43.1.7 The difference between damages in contract and in tort

In contract, the aim of a damages award is to put the innocent party in the position he or she would have been in had the contract been performed. In tort, the claimant is not complaining of failure to implement a promise. Damages in tort aim to restore the claimant to his or her pre-incident position. In tort, it is not a question of loss of bargain.

For example: D is selling his classic car. He tells C that it was once owned by John Lennon. D genuinely believes this but has no reasonable grounds for doing so. In fact, it is untrue. If true, the car is worth £80,000. If false, it is worth £50,000. C buys the car from D for £60,000. Assume that the representation becomes a term of the contract. If he had got what he bargained for, the car would be worth £80,000 but it is actually worth only £50,000. In contract, the damages for breach of the term are £30,000 (expected value minus actual value).

If the statement remained a mere representation, the tort measure for negligent (s 2(1)) misrepresentation would be £10,000. He has an asset worth £50,000 but he paid £60,000 for it. To restore him to his position prior to entering the contract, he needs £10,000 (value of purchase minus actual value).

In simple practical terms, if the representee would have made a good bargain had everything been as it was stated to be, he should try to sue in contract. If he would have made a bad bargain, he should try to sue for fraudulent or negligent misrepresentation.

Activity

NH Hospitals placed an order with BigPharm for one million doses of a new vaccine to be delivered by 20 December at a cost of £10 million. A vaccination programme was set up by NH to take place between Christmas and New Year, costing NH £5million to deliver.

Explain what remedies are available to and against each of the parties in the following circumstances:

- BigPharm knew about the vaccination programme, but the delivery is delayed until after the New Year, costing a further £3 million.
- BigPharm did not know about the vaccination programme, but the delivery is delayed until after the New Year, costing a further £3 million.
- The government withdrew approval of the vaccine and forbade its import.

43.2 Equitable remedies

Equitable remedies are awarded where the remedy of damages is inadequate and justice would not be served merely by damages.

Equitable remedies are not a right as they are at the discretion of the court. Unlike damages, equitable remedies are not constrained by remoteness of damage or causation. We will consider injunctions and specific performance.

43.2.1 Injunction

An injunction in contract law is a court order instructing someone not to breach a term of their contract.

- The idea is that the prohibition will prevent someone interfering with the rights of another. This is the most usual type of injunction and is known as a prohibitory injunction.
- Occasionally an injunction will order a party to do something. This is known as a mandatory injunction.

Key terms

Prohibitory injunction – a court order instructing someone not to do something.
Mandatory injunction – a court order requiring a party to do something.

An injunction will not be awarded for a party to complete a personal service, as the court is unable to supervise such an order. This was shown in *Page One Records Ltd v Britton* (1967).

Case studies

Page One Records Ltd v Britton (1967)

The band, The Troggs, agreed that Page One Records would be their manager and sole agent for five years. The Troggs agreed not to appoint anyone else as a manager during the contract. The relationship broke down.

Page One wanted an injunction to prevent The Troggs from appointing a new manager. The injunction was refused and Page One could only claim damages. This was because the contract involved obligations of trust and confidence. An injunction would amount to forcing the band to remain idle, or to continue to employ a manager and agent in whom it had lost confidence. Forcing them to work together with the manager could not be supervised by the court.

An injunction can be permanent or temporary, for example, until a full trial of the issues in a dispute. A temporary injunction is called an interim injunction.

Injunctions are often applied for with respect to:

- intellectual property rights
- employment contracts, to prevent an employee competing when leaving employment or when a business owner is selling the business.

43.2.2 Specific performance

This equitable remedy is the opposite of an injunction. When the court orders specific performance, it is ordering one party to perform their contractual obligation, rather like a mandatory injunction.

There are clear examples of where the judge exercises his discretion, such as *Airport Industrial GP Ltd v Heathrow Airport Ltd* (2015). Here the judge was concerned that making an order for specific performance would inevitably force a company into liquidation, so he did not make an order for specific performance of the construction of a car park.

In general, equitable remedies such as specific performance will not be available in the following circumstances:

- Where damages would be an adequate remedy, for example, where substitute goods are available.
- Contracts involving personal service and contracts of employment, as we have seen in the case of *Page One Records Ltd v Britton* (1967).
- Where the court cannot supervise the enforcement of the contract – this would clearly be the case with a contract of personal service such as in *Page One Records*, but would not be the case where a unique item such as a work of art was the subject matter of the contract. The court could easily enforce delivery of a painting.
- Impossibility – where a defendant cannot perform their obligations under the contract, or could only do so illegally, the court will not grant specific performance, for example, the export of a famous painting without the required export licence.
- Where the claimant cannot (or is not sure whether they can) perform their part of contract.
- Laches – if a claimant is aware of the defendant's breach of contract, they must quickly apply to the court for an order of specific performance, otherwise it suggests that they are content with the contract. An example of laches was seen in the case of *Leaf v International Galleries* (1950).
- The conduct of the claimant – one of the maxims of equity is 'He or she who seeks equity must do equity', and the court will not grant a claimant specific performance if they have in some way behaved dishonestly.

Key term

Laches – an equitable defence that the claimant has delayed asserting its rights and is no longer entitled to bring an equitable claim.

Case	Judgment
Page One Records Ltd v Britton (1967)	An injunction will not be awarded for a party to complete a personal service as the court is unable to supervise such an order
Airport Industrial GP Ltd v Heathrow Airport Ltd (2015)	Specific performance was not ordered as it would force a company into liquidation, which would be unjust in the circumstances

Figure 43.6 Key cases chart: equitable remedies

43.3 Consumer remedies under the Consumer Rights Act 2015

Link

See Chapter 40 for information on this topic.

Quick questions

1 State the test for remoteness of damage.
2 Explain the meaning of speculative damages.
3 Explain the legal principle with respect to mitigation of loss.
4 Distinguish between liquidated damages and a penalty.
5 Explain the legal principles behind an order for specific performance of a contract.

Summary

- Remedies for breach of contract can be either legal or equitable remedies.
- Damages are the most common form of remedy and are compensation for losses suffered.
- In specific circumstances, more than the actual loss suffered will be awarded.
- Contracts sometimes try to establish what damages will be payable if there is a breach. These are valid terms if considered liquidated damages, but not if they are considered a penalty.
- Equitable remedies are discretionary.
- Specific performance requires delivery of goods but is not available for contracts of service.

Chapter 44 Contract law evaluation

Introduction

In this chapter we will concentrate on the evaluation of two topics from this part of the specification: formation and contract terms. Both sections will be broken down to the topics studied in Chapters 39 and 40, and ideas for reform will be incorporated in the sections.

Contract law has changed little over the years and has therefore developed piecemeal to reflect changes in society and technology. This may be seen as firefighting, or as an acknowledgement that the law is satisfactory and just needs a little tinkering around the edges to polish it.

44.1 Formation of contract

44.1.1 Offer

The distinction between an offer and an invitation to treat

The distinction between an offer and an invitation to treat is confusing to both parties to a contract, as the differences are often very slight.

- In *Fisher v Bell* (1961), the justification for the decision is based on the traditional view of freedom of contract. If the shop window display was an offer, this would remove the shop owner's right to decide whether to contract with that particular customer or not. The customer could enter the shop, accept the offer and create a legally binding contract. The shop owner may then be liable for selling prohibited goods to a person who is under a particular age, for example, a knife, or have insufficient stock to satisfy a customer.

- In a self-service shop, people generally believe the goods can be bought there and then, or at least when brought from a store room. If the goods are not in stock, the customer believes the seller will be able to provide them at a later date but recognises that both sides have the option to decline the contract. It has been suggested that all invitations to treat should be treated as offers, so that the law would mirror the public's belief in the situation. However, this would again cause problems with respect to age-restricted goods. At present, that is avoided by having sales staff authorising a purchase at the checkout.

- If the item on the shelf had the status of an offer, then once the item is placed in the customer's basket a contract would be made, and the customer would have to pay for the item or possibly be charged with theft. This would also prevent a customer changing their mind without being in breach of contract. If there was a pricing error, neither party could rectify the situation – subject to the possible criminal offence where there has been label switching.

- Similar difficulties arise with online shopping which has, to some extent, been solved by legislation as we have seen.

It appears that the word 'offer' is generally used to encompass invitations to treat. This is not just in the general public's mind, but can be seen in most guidance given to retailers by local authorities. It would seem that the term 'invitation to treat' is redundant, except to lawyers.

Advertisements and unilateral contracts

There is much legislation about misleading advertisements, which suggests that these advertisements only have legal significance if they lead to a contract:

- While the legislation leads to criminal sanctions, the individual affected by the advertisement is usually only left with a claim for misrepresentation, unless some part of the advertisement has become a term of the contract or there is protection under the Consumer Rights Act 2015.

Duration of offer, information or counter offer?

The law can be confusing as to what exactly forms the offer and how long it remains open. There are many ways an offer can come to an end.

- A counter offer ends the original offer. This seems a fair rule, as an attempt to go back to the original offer is rarely refused during negotiations – the price rarely goes up during negotiations.
- However, it is not always clear when there is a counter offer and when there is just a request for information. This confusion can be seen from the status of an enquiry about credit in *Stevenson v McLean* (1880).
- If you state the length of time the offer will be open, you can still change your mind, as in *Routledge v Grant* (1828), so long as you communicate to the other party that you revoke the offer. If you do not state the length of time it will be open, and do not revoke the offer, then it is open for a reasonable time as in *Ramsgate Victoria Hotel v Montefiore* (1866).
- But how long is a reasonable time? It all depends on the circumstances. This leads to confusion. The balance is between doing what is morally right and losing money, or arguing the point and losing goodwill. This seems to be a poor choice for a business.

44.1.2 Acceptance

Whatever method of acceptance is used, the way in which the rules work is open to criticism.

Silence

The courts claim the law on formation of contracts will consider what the parties intended to do. This is a subjective approach. In practice, an objective test is often applied, disguised as a subjective judgment.

- In *Felthouse v Bindley* (1863), both parties wanted there to be a contract. The court said that from an objective viewpoint there was no evidence of an acceptance from the nephew. In fact the nephew had asked the auctioneer holding the horse to remove it from the auction, which might contradict that view. However, for the court to decide there is a valid contract there should be clear and identifiable evidence. The offer has to be communicated and so, logically, must the acceptance.
- Silence as a form of acceptance creates many problems, so the Unsolicited Goods and Services

Act 1971 states that, for example, where goods are received without request, there can be no contract unless the acceptance is communicated to the sender. So the individual may benefit and the business may lose out and be prosecuted, but is it morally right to keep the goods?

Sometimes the need to communicate an acceptance may be said to have been waived, as in *Carlill* and *Reveille*.

The postal rules

The postal rule appears to be unfair on an offeror who may never receive the letter of acceptance or it is delivered late. The rule was established when the post was the usual method of communication.

- The offeror is a party to a legally binding contract without realising so. The offeror may have contracted with another party in the meantime, so the courts have to make a decision that is only satisfactory to one of the offerees.
- A further problem with the postal rule is whether it applies to any other method of communication. The *Entores* and *Brinkibon* cases indicate the courts' unwillingness to expand the rule to more modern methods of communication. This unwillingness may be due to the courts' belief that an offeree should take reasonable steps to ensure the acceptance is received, and that the postal rule should be restricted because it is out of date.

Modern communication methods

If key information for the consumer is omitted, then no contract is formed. However, the seller may still have received payment, and it may be difficult to regain the payment made under a non-existent contract.

Article 11 of the Electronic Commerce (EC Directive) Regulations 2002 sets out when acceptance takes place.

- Thus many online businesses state, 'Your order has been received and is now being processed' or words to that effect, rather than 'Your order has been accepted'.
- This ensures that online sellers are not required to accept the order at that point, but merely acknowledge receipt of the offer to buy the goods or service.
- The question remains as to when they:
  - have accepted the customer's offer
  - can take the money from the buyer's bank.

The requirement of a signature can cause problems where negotiations are conducted electronically.

In *Neocleous v Rees* (2019), it was held that the autogeneration by a computer on emails can be the same as a signature. This is reflected in the Law Commission's 2019 report on Electronic Execution of Documents.

In *Bernuth Lines Ltd v High Seas Shipping Ltd* (2006), it was stated that clicking on the 'send' icon still raised questions of effective acceptance. For example:

- The email must be sent to the email address of the intended recipient.
- It must not be rejected by the system or otherwise delayed.
- If the sender does not require confirmation of receipt, they may not be able to show that receipt has occurred.
- There may be circumstances where, for instance, there are several email addresses for a recipient, or different devices will only receive emails to particular addresses.
- Even if it is received, is the device being used by the intended recipient, a colleague or merely a family member?

The law is failing to address problems raised by modern communications methods. The case of *Thomas and Gander v BPE Solicitors* (2010) demonstrates this. Here the question was whether an email acceptance is effective when it arrives, or at the time when the offeror could reasonably be expected to have read it, which was not straightforward.

Problems can be raised by modern communications methods such as email

Case study

Thomas and Gander v BPE Solicitors (2010)

An email of acceptance was received at or close to 6 p.m. on 24 August 2007, a Friday night before a Bank Holiday. The email was available to be read at that time but was not in fact read until the Tuesday morning. The question is whether the defendants were correct that acceptance was not effective from the moment the email was received, because it was sent after working hours.

The court stated that it must be resolved 'by reference to the intentions of the parties, by sound business practice and in some cases by a judgment where the risks should lie', as had been stated in the case in *Brinkibon*.

In the context in which the 6 p.m. email was sent – this was a transaction that could have been completed that evening, and the court did not consider that 6 p.m. was outside working hours. The email was available to be read on a portable device within working hours, despite the fact that the recipient had in fact gone home. So there was a valid acceptance.

The effect of *Thomas and Gander* is that each case is decided on its particular facts. As mobile phones with email capabilities are a normal part of business communications today, and the use of automated messages indicate that an email or text has been read, the courts will look at each case on the basis of its particular facts and the business practices that have been in use in the negotiations. Thus the result might be different for booking a restaurant table, buying a car or selling a business.

Look online

Consider the points made by the Law Commission in their 2019 report. How effective do you consider the proposals are?

www.lawcom.gov.uk/project/electronic-execution-of-documents/

44.1.3 Intention to create legal relations

There are a few issues to resolve here:

- Do the parties intend to form a contract at all? In *Kleinwort Benson Ltd v Malaysian Mining Corporation* (1989), the courts had to decide whether or not the document was in fact intended to be legally binding. Courts can view individual letters of comfort as a contract or not, depending on all the evidence in the case.

- Is the contract commercial or social? *Sadler v Reynolds* (2005) suggested that some situations fall into a sort of 'halfway house' between domestic and commercial. If that is the case, the presumption will vary, depending on which side the decision is made.

The two presumptions created by the courts help to decide whether or not an agreement has legal validity. However, the court will always consider all the circumstances surrounding the case and, particularly in respect of social and domestic arrangements, the final decision will not always be obvious:

- The case of *Jones v Padavatton* (1968) divided the Court of Appeal as to the existence of legal intent.
- In *Ellis v Chief Adjudication Officer* (1997), there was not a legally binding contract as the court found that the parties did not intend that to be the case.
- However, in *Hardwick v Johnson* (1978), the agreement had legal intent on similar facts.

The presumption against legal intent for social and domestic arrangements is understandable but, by considering the surrounding circumstances, the courts reach inconsistent decisions.

This is also the case in business situations:

- In *Esso Petroleum Co. Ltd v Commissioners of Customs and Excise* (1976), the court considered that the offer of the free coin was enough to allow the presumption for legal intent to remain, as it was inextricably linked to the purchase of fuel.

It can also be argued that there should be no need to prove legal intent. Offer, acceptance and consideration are the foundations on which a contract is made. If these elements are all present and there is no clear statement that the agreement is not to be legally binding, then it should be a valid contract. Indeed, it has been argued that this should be the case even where there is no consideration. A straightforward objective test might be a satisfactory solution to the issue.

44.1.4 Commercial or domestic agreement?

It has been suggested in *Sadler v Reynolds* (2005) that there may be situations which fall into a sort of 'halfway house' between domestic and commercial, and that in this case the burden of overturning the presumption may be affected.

Case study

Sadler v Reynolds (2005)

The alleged contract was between a journalist and a businessman who were friends. The journalist wanted to ghost-write the autobiography of the businessman. The judge suggested that the agreement fell 'somewhere between an obviously commercial transaction and a social exchange'.

The burden was on the journalist to prove that there was an intention to create legal relations, that it was a business agreement and not a social one.

There is unlikely to be legal intention where business people meet in social setting and any agreement was intended to be taken seriously, as in *Blue v Ashley* (2017).

Case study

Blue v Ashley (2017)

While drinking in a pub, Mr Ashley said that he would pay Mr Blue £15 million if he could get the Sports Direct share price to £8 per share. The key issue was whether this would have been understood as a serious offer, creating a legally binding contract. The evidence suggested that no one in the group in the pub thought this was a serious legal offer.

The amount of court time and legal fees expended can be considerable as, for example, in *Blue v Ashley* (2017).

Look online

Read the briefing note written by a pupil barrister about *Blue v Ashley* (2017) at **https://cornwallstreet. co.uk/back-basics-contract-law-blue-v-ashley-2017-ewhc-1928-comm/**

Make notes on the points raised about formation of contract.

44.1.5 Consideration

The general principles and reform

Consideration confirms that the law is concerned with bargains and not gifts. So a 'free gift' attached to a contract appears not to form part of the consideration as the recipient gives no additional value for it. Despite this, we would expect the 'free gift' to be safe and to be provided, as the contract is for the main item plus the 'free gift' in exchange for the other party's consideration, usually money. This can be seen in cases such as *Chappell v Nestlé Co. Ltd* (1960) and *Esso Petroleum Co. Ltd v Commissioners of Customs and Excise* (1976).

There have been no proposals for reform of the law on consideration since a 1937 Law Commission report, which effectively led to no change. Any reform has been in the area of third party rights and legislation referred to below.

- The most radical proposal for reform is to abandon the concept of consideration and thus allow gifts to be legally actionable. This is unlikely to be adopted as there is a fear of spurious claims.
- If the law were reformed to redefine consideration by looking at factual benefits rather than legal benefits, recent legislation would be easier to apply and would have less focus on consumers only. This could also be a mechanism for preventing general use of an exclusion clause with respect to the 1999 Act.

The development of the law on economic duress effectively avoids a person relying on a consideration that is not freely given.

Sufficiency

The rule of consideration that it must be sufficient, as in the *Nestlé* case, may be viewed by a member of the public as ridiculous, as the chocolate wrapper has no value in the real world. The justification for this rule is often said to be the courts' willingness to validate an agreement.

- If a party wishes to give something to another party and this is to form the basis of the agreement, then the court will always attempt to allow the agreement to exist and be enforceable.
- This means that anyone who understands the courts' attitude need not use a deed of gift, but can merely agree to sell something at a gross undervalue to achieve the objective. This was the case in *Thomas v Thomas* (1842).

- This may then conflict with the criminal law of fraud, or be evidence of coercion on the part of the beneficiary that may be more difficult to prove where there is a deed.

Past consideration

Re McArdle (1951) explains past consideration. However, it seems that the court can sometimes find an implied promise to pay, as in *Lampleigh v Braithwait* (1615).

The argument against allowing past consideration as a valid form of consideration is made to prevent opening the floodgates to dubious cases. This would seem a poor argument, as few minor cases would ever go to court given the cost of litigation. Bigger cases tend to be resolved on the basis of commercial reality and a reasonable sum on the basis of *quantum meruit*, which might well be agreed after the event.

Performing an existing duty cannot be the consideration for a new contract

This rule concerns variation of contract, interpretation of terms in a contract or replacement by a new contract to be decided.

In *Stilk v Myrick* (1809), the crew members did not receive the extra payment as they were only carrying out an existing duty – an interpretation of the terms. The same applied in *Hartley v Ponsonby* (1857), except for the greater number of crew members who had deserted, so there was a variation of the terms of the contract or possibly a new contract.

- In *Stilk*, there was a hint of pressure from the crew on the captain for the extra payment or they would all desert.
- In *Hartley*, the remaining crew had to get the ship to its destination under the possible threat of desertion if they did not.
- In *Williams v Roffey Bros and Nicholls (Contractors) Ltd* (1990), there was no pressure as it was the defendant builder who offered the extra payment to the claimant roofer.

Today's courts take the view that there is a commercial reality in applying the strict rules of consideration.

A promise to accept part payment of the existing debt in place of the whole debt is not consideration

It has always been a commercial reality that some customers will be unable to pay their debts as they fall due. The idea of bankruptcy and company insolvency rules recognise this and provide a means of distributing assets in the event of insolvency. The development of rules to combat agreements made near to the date of insolvency, such as those on fraudulent preference, reflect this. Many businesses accept a part payment in settlement of a debt as they will have to wait longer and possibly receive less if there is an insolvency.

The strict legal position would appear to be modified only by the very special circumstances in the doctrine of promissory estoppel, which only applies when it is inequitable for the creditor to insist on his full rights. Practical considerations mean that, subject to the principle of fraud and duress, the reality reflects the principle of freedom of contract. There is a conflict between the morality of breaking a promise and the strict rule of law that consideration is required for a valid contract.

44.1.6 Privity of contract

- The decision in *Tweddle v Atkinson* (1861) does not give effect to the arrangement made by the families. It would appear to be more than just a social arrangement yet is not enforced because the young couple were not a party to the agreement.
- A similar result was the outcome in *Beswick v Beswick* (1967). In that case, the aunt did succeed as she could carry out her late husband's contracts as the executor of his estate.

The Law Commission's 1996 report which led to the Contracts (Rights of Third Parties) Act 1999 (although not adopting all the proposals) identified a number of difficulties with privity of contract. These included:

- The intentions of the original contracting parties are thwarted where the original intention of the parties to the contract were to allow third party rights.
- The injustice to the third party, where a valid contract has raised reasonable hope of having the legal right to enforce the contract, particularly where the third party has relied on that contract.
- The person who has suffered the loss cannot sue, while the person who has suffered no loss can sue (as was the case in *Beswick v Beswick*).
- Even if the promisee can obtain a satisfactory remedy for the third party, they may not be able to sue, because it is too expensive or too time-consuming.
- The development of exceptions, both in statute and common law.
- The different rules in the law of tort that may allow some claims and not others on the basis of

negligence. For example, in *Ross v Caunters* (1980), an improperly executed will deprived a beneficiary of an intended benefit, which they recovered in tort against the negligent solicitor. This effectively enforced a contract benefitting a third party.

- The existence of the rule, together with the exceptions to it, has given rise to a complex body of law and to elaborate strategies to give third parties enforceable rights.
- Uncertainty is commercially inconvenient, and the law on privity of contract is out of line with many trading partner countries' law in the EU and jurisdictions further afield. It is illogical to have wildly different rights, depending on which law applies to a contract or even by buying goods for someone else in a different country.
- The rule causes difficulties in commercial life, particularly in construction contracts and insurance contracts.

The 1999 Act would apply in the situations in *Tweddle v Atkinson* and *Beswick v Beswick*. However, the parties to the contract may specifically exclude the Act's application, so that a carefully drafted contract will not allow a third party to obtain the benefit of the contract. Many commercial contracts contain this exclusion. Are these exclusions unfair contract terms under the Unfair Contract Terms Act 1977 for business-to-business contracts or under the Consumer Rights Act 2015 for consumers?

Much of the difficulty encountered in such cases is eliminated by s 1(6) of the Contracts (Rights of Third Parties) Act 1999, which permits the third party to enforce any terms which would exclude or limit liability.

- In *New Zealand Shipping Co. v Satterthwaite*, for instance, the contract between the owner and the carrier 'expressly identified the defendant ... as a member of a class or as answering a particular description' (s 1(3)) and expressly provided that the defendant 'may in his own right enforce a term of the contract' (s 1(2)) by extending the cover provided by the exclusion clause to the defendant.

In consumer contracts, there are often rights where goods are bought for someone else, such as when a gift receipt is obtained. However, the parties to the contract have the right to exclude the Act from benefitting a third party. Most commercial contracts now include such a term, so the Act is not as useful as might be hoped.

Whilst the Act made the law clearer and received more publicity than changes brought about through case law, there is still potential for uncertainty in identifying when a contract purports to give an enforceable right to a third party.

General rights given under the Act are well structured and easier to understand than a series of common law exceptions. The Act means that original parties' intentions are now respected – if they want the third party to have rights, they can put them in the contract. This requires the original parties to be clear about exactly what, if any, rights the third party can have and assumes that there is agreement between the parties on this point.

44.2 Contract terms

44.2.1 The distinction between different types of term

Until the development of the idea of innominate terms, the distinction between types of term was straightforward. Today the important question is how the court will interpret the terms of a contract. Judges use the following principles:

- Where terms are implied by law, judges apply the classification given to them in the statute.
- Where terms are implied by fact, the judges will interpret them according to the presumed intention of the parties.
- Where the parties have identified how the express terms are to be classified or what remedies attach to them, the judges will usually try to accommodate the wishes of the parties.
- Where the terms are express but the parties have not identified what type they are or what is the appropriate remedy in a breach, judges will interpret those terms according to what they believe is the true intention of the parties.

In doing this, the court might ignore the literal interpretation of the words used and look at context and background, if it feels that there is some error in expression of the intention of the parties in the formal agreement.

An example of how these rules can be bypassed by a stronger party to the contract is seen where all terms in a contract are stated to be conditions:

- Judges may feel that it is impossible to follow the express classification of the terms.
- In this way, a term stated as being a condition may be construed in fact as a warranty.

- This can lead to different approaches, depending on whether the court thinks the term is clear or is open to different interpretations. This was demonstrated in *Arnold v Britton* (2015) and *Rainy Sky v Kookmin Bank* (2011).

Lord Clarke said:

> the ultimate aim of interpreting a provision in a contract, especially a commercial contract, is to determine what the parties meant by the language used, which involves ascertaining what a reasonable person would have understood the parties to have meant.

If there are two possible constructions, the court is entitled to prefer the construction which is consistent with business common sense, and to reject the other.

44.2.2 The use of the officious bystander test

The officious bystander test is still used, and is an adequate way of showing that the court is giving effect to the presumed intention of the parties. However, it imposes a very strict standard and possibly an unrealistic one:

- While one party will usually be very willing to accept that the implied term at issue was what they actually intended to be part of the contract, the other party almost inevitably will be arguing the exact reverse, or there would be no dispute.

As a result, there are circumstances when the 'officious bystander rule' cannot apply. One example is where one party is totally unaware of the term which the other suggests should be implied into the agreement. In this case, it could never have been their intention to include it, so the test fails.

44.2.3 Non-incorporation of previous terms

In *Hollier v Rambler Motors* (1972), it could be argued that the court was trying to avoid an exclusion clause in a standard form contract. If he had gone to the garage in person, he probably would have signed the document with the exclusion clause in it.

44.2.4 Departure from the principle of freedom of contract

The courts will be very careful when departing from the common law principle of freedom of contract. They will therefore be reluctant to imply terms into a contract, especially where this would set a general implication of a term into all similar contracts.

The courts might be trying to avoid this because of the long-debated criticism of judge-made law, and the argument that Parliament should make changes to the law. However, when Parliament changes the law, we tend to get a confusing situation where the clarity and extension of rights in one situation, for example, the Consumer Rights Act 2015, is balanced by areas which lack clarity. For example, what protection is afforded by the law, if any, for the purchaser of goods in a private sale? Is a sale on eBay a private sale?

44.2.5 Lack of certainty in implied terms

The traditional use of conditions and warranties promotes certainty. If a condition is breached and the contract has not been fully performed, then it may be terminated. But if it is a warranty, there is no right to terminate. This approach is inflexible and can lead to unfair results, as it does not consider the consequences of a breach.

A minor breach of a condition gives the right to terminate the contract. This is always the case, except when there is a contract for the sale of goods and then s 15A of the Sale of Goods Act 1979 applies. This is where the buyer has the right to reject the goods because the seller breached one of the implied terms in ss 13–15 of the Act, but the breach is so slight that it would be unreasonable to reject them. In this case, the breach is not to be treated as a breach of condition, but may be treated as a breach of warranty.

There is, however, an exception to this exception. This section applies unless a contrary intention appears in, or is to be implied from, the contract. Presumably this means that a term of a contract stating that all terms, express or implied, are to be treated as conditions would then nullify this section of the Sale of Goods Act 1979. That term may, however, be an unfair and ineffective contract term.

- A similar effect is produced as a result of s 5A of the Supply of Goods and Services Act 1982. However, if an innocent party suffers a major breach of a warranty, no termination is possible.
- The innominate terms approach is less certain. It can be difficult to decide if the effect of the breach is serious enough to justify termination. This is important in relation to remedies available and may mean that if a party terminates when they are not entitled to do so, they will be in breach of the contract.

Despite the problems that could be caused, it is possible to see that the innominate terms approach of considering the effect of the breach is more flexible. This is particularly true as many contract terms protect the party with the stronger bargaining power. There would be one less hurdle for the weaker party if all terms were innominate terms.

44.2.6 Implied terms are default terms

In contracts for the sale of goods and the supply of services, both for businesses and consumers, there are a number of implied terms and terms that are implied not to exist. Examples include:

- goods corresponding with description
- care and skill in carrying out a service
- the inability to exclude liability for death or personal injury.

We can make sense of the emphasis that the House of Lords placed in *Liverpool City Council v Irwin* (1977) on the courts only implying a term by law into a contract when it is necessary to do so. However, 'necessary' here is not the same as 'necessary to give business efficacy' to the contract.

Case study

Liverpool City Council v Irwin (1977)
The court considered the nature and extent of the obligations of landlords of a building in multiple occupation to repair essential means of access. It was an implied term of a tenancy agreement that the lessor was to be responsible for repairing, and lighting the common parts of the building was a necessary term.

44.2.7 The Supreme Court

The Supreme Court has apparently clarified the law on when the court can imply a term in a contract. They have endorsed the traditional approach that the term either must be so obvious as to go without saying, or must be necessary to give business efficacy to the contract. But which test is favoured?

- In *Marks and Spencer plc v BNP Paribas Securities Services Trust Company (Jersey) Ltd* (2015), the court considered the Privy Council's decision in *Attorney General of Belize v Belize Telecom* (2009), which had generally been accepted as the leading modern case on the implication of terms.
- In *Belize*, Lord Hoffmann suggested that in the process of implying terms, the only question was whether a reasonable reader of the contract, with the

relevant background knowledge, would understand the term to be implied. That decision led to a great deal of academic debate as to whether it had changed the law, so that reasonableness could now be seen as a sufficient ground for implying a term.

In the *Marks and Spencer* case, the Supreme Court is unanimous in emphasising that *Belize* should not be interpreted as having watered down the traditional, highly restrictive approach to the implication of terms. Reasonableness in itself is not sufficient; the tests of obviousness or business efficacy must be met.

44.2.8 Approaches to the purpose of exclusion clauses

There are two different approaches:
1   Use the whole of the contract, including any exclusion clauses, to define the obligations set out in it.
2   Define the obligations set out in the contract without reference to the exclusion clauses. The exclusion clauses would then be used as a defence when necessary.

Cheshire, Fifoot and Furmston's *Law of Contract* suggests that the approach usually depends upon the wording of the exclusion clause being considered. However, exclusion clauses are more commonly viewed as a defence.

The common law first looks to see whether the clause has been incorporated in the contract:
- If it is not incorporated in the contract, it will not be effective.
- If it is incorporated in the contract, legislation will decide whether it is effective or not.

This two-stage test leads to uncertainty. This helps the stronger party to a contract that has more resources to undertake litigation. There are more perceived obstacles to an individual taking legal action, whether in their capacity as an individual or a business. Taking on big corporations such as telecoms providers, banks and airlines is often too daunting a prospect for the individual. Such businesses know this and design their help lines and compensation offers to minimise their costs and liability and discourage claims being pursued.

44.2.9 The *contra proferentem* rule

Cases such as *Transocean Drilling UK Ltd v Providence Resources plc* (2016), *Persimmon Homes Ltd v Ove Arup and Partners Ltd* (2017) show that the *contra proferentem* rule now has little application to commercial contracts where the parties bargain on equal terms, allocating potential losses between each other, and doing so in clear and unambiguous words. This is in direct contrast to the law under the Consumer Rights Act 2015.

> ### Quick questions
>
> 1   What is meant by the officious bystander test?
> 2   Explain how the law can be confusing as to what exactly forms the offer and how long it remains open.
> 3   Explain the ways in which silence can be a problem with respect to formation of contract.
> 4   *Chappell v Nestlé Co. Ltd* (1960) and *Esso Petroleum Co. Ltd v Commissioners of Customs and Excise* (1976) both involved what could be considered something for nothing. How does the law justify these decisions?
> 5   It has been suggested in *Sadler v Reynolds* (2005) that there may be situations which fall into a sort of 'halfway house' between domestic and commercial contracts. Is this further distinction needed?

Summary

Formation of contract

- The distinction between an offer and an invitation to treat is confusing to both parties to a contract.
- The law can be confusing as to what exactly forms the offer and how long it remains open.
- Silence as a form of acceptance creates many problems.
- The posting rules do not match up with modern methods of communication.
- The distinction between a commercial contract and a domestic agreement is unclear.
- The law on consideration is difficult to reconcile with the law on economic duress.
- The law on privity of contract is too easily avoided.

Contract terms

- The difference between condition and warranty is difficult to apply to innominate terms with certainty.
- There is a lack of certainty in implied terms.
- There are different approaches to the application of exclusion clauses.
- The balance between consumers and traders has shifted too.

Study skills

What you will gain from studying OCR A Level Law

This course has been designed to inspire you as well as foster your interest and enjoyment in law. It also aims to develop your knowledge and skills for the further study of law or progressing into the workplace. You will gain an understanding of the law in England and Wales as well as its role in a European and global context. You will learn how the legal system and law work, understand the changing nature of law and the interaction between law, morals, justice and society.

There are several key aspects to studying law:

- You will develop your knowledge and understanding of the English legal system and areas of both private and public law within the law of England and Wales.
- You will develop an understanding of legal method and reasoning as used by lawyers and the judiciary.
- You will learn to apply the techniques of legal method and reasoning to analyse and offer answers to problems, based on legal principles, legislation and case law.
- You will develop the ability to construct conclusions and communicate persuasive legal arguments by reference to appropriate legal authorities.
- You will be able to demonstrate critical awareness of the influence and operation of the law in society.

Thinking and planning ahead: some useful tips for studying OCR A Level Law

- Be positive – believe that the road to success starts right at the beginning of your course and remember that in each lesson and for each piece of work you complete.
- Decide what you want to achieve and make a plan to get you there.

- Be organised from the outset – work out a realistic timetable for when you are going to do your work and do your best to stick to it. Also decide how you are going to store your notes and completed work; check where you are weekly so you keep on top of your work.
- If you are given a scheme of work that shows the order in which topics will be studied, use this to help your organisation; keep all the material you are given and the work you do for each topic together so it is easy to find when you need it.
- Do whatever work you are set as well as you can; get feedback on that work and make use of it in the next piece of work you do – learning how to improve is a key element of a successful revision strategy.
- Revise thoroughly for all tests – building an embedded base of knowledge as you go along takes the pressure off you when it comes to exam revision.
- Work steadily – prepare as you go along by making revision notes or mind maps when you complete a topic; you can improve and refine these when you come to exam revision, but you will already have something to work from.
- Focus on mastering skills just as much as on learning information – what you know is important in an exam, but showing that knowledge in the appropriate way is equally crucial.
- Don't struggle alone – if you have questions or haven't understood something, ask your teacher.

Revision study skills: useful tips

- Be methodical: make a list of topics to be revised like the one in the table below and tick the boxes as you go.
  - ○ **Revised** means you have made revision notes or a mind map – whatever system works for you.

Topic	Revised	Factual test	Peer test	Past paper test	Consolidate	Exam ready
Civil courts						
ADR						

- ○ **Factual test** means you have checked what you know – it's a good idea to revise a topic in the morning and check what you can remember later that day or the next day.
- ○ **Peer test** means having a revision buddy – it might be a friend in your class but it can be anyone else. They ask you some questions about what you have revised and you explain your answers to them; this helps you to clarify your thinking and articulate your thoughts.
- ○ **Past paper test** means writing an answer to a previous exam question in the appropriate amount of time for the exam and getting some feedback on what you have written.
- ○ **Consolidate** means reflecting on the previous steps and then refining further the information you need and the skills you have to demonstrate.
- ○ **Exam ready** – this means what it says, you are confident with this topic.
- Factual knowledge is important so you need to make sure that your notes are made in a way that is useful for you; you will need factual information in each type of question on an exam paper.
- Learning key terms and ideas: makes sure what you learn is accurate and that you can explain what you have learned clearly.
- Learning Acts of Parliament: names and dates are crucial; section numbers and subsection numbers might be necessary too, depending on the area of law. Aim to be precise and learn key definitions. For those that are very long, learn a form of words that makes it clear what the law means.
- Learning cases: this can be difficult as there are a lot. You need some kind of system based on each different unit or topic area so take the time to find a system that works for you – it might be notes or index cards, for example. Whatever method you use the key things you need are:
  - ○ **Name and date** – the name is key and even if you can't remember the actual date of the case having a sense of chronology is important;
  - ○ **Key facts** – this means just enough to highlight the issues in the case and to show your use of the case is accurate;
  - ○ **Decision and court** – this means what the court decided and it may be important to know

which court, for example whether it was the Supreme Court or the Court of Appeal;
  - ○ **Importance of the case** – this means the reason why you have learned about this case and how you would use it. Don't learn too many cases – a long list is a great memory feat but it doesn't help you get more marks. Have a smaller number of cases and use them to make points in essays or to help you apply the law in case-study questions.
- Analysis and evaluation (AO3): work out these points as you go along – they are essential components in some answers in order to reach the higher mark bands. Factual information is not enough on its own. Rather than simply making a long list of points, work on creating a smaller number of points which you can develop and extend; also think about how you can express what you want to say clearly in your own words so you don't have to learn your evaluation word for word.
- Active revision works best. Just reading a book or your notes is less efficient than doing something that keeps you focused. Make sure you make notes, key cards or mind maps when revising.
- Be honest and realistic in your revision schedule and strategies: if you don't feel you know what works for you spend some time trying different things in the early stages of your revision to give yourself confidence – you can measure what works by test results. Once you have done that, make a plan you can stick to. Think about times of day when you work best and build your plan around them. If you know you can't sit still for more than an hour, don't plan to sit at your desk for a three-hour stretch. Build in breaks but stick to them. Have time to do things you enjoy to give your brain a break.
- If you are able to, have somewhere suitable to revise – at a table or desk if you can and put distractions, such as your phone, somewhere you can't see or hear them while you are working or use one of the focus apps available to stop you being distracted. Be honest as to whether you need silence to work; if you do, earplugs can be helpful. If you listen to music, make sure it isn't going to distract you.

- Your revision needs to be user friendly – pages and pages of notes can become unwieldy so think about using ever briefer notes or key cards you can carry around and look at from time to time. Make your notes memorable – layout, colours and images can all help reinforce information and trigger your memory in an exam situation. Your mobile phone can help you here as you can use apps to generate study aids such as notes, key cards and mind maps.
- Practise working to time limits: look at the information on exam question papers to be sure you have this right.
- Use sample exam questions, mark schemes and other information provided by OCR to build strong answers.
- Look after yourself: you need to be at your best when you sit your exams so eat and sleep well, get exercise and don't give up all the things that are important to you. You may need to put some things on hold for a while, but don't stop having some fun or you might end up resenting your revision and that makes it hard to do your best.

Know your exam

There are three different exams for OCR A Level Law:
- H418/01 The legal system and criminal law
- H418/02 Law making and the law of tort
- H418/03 The nature of law and human rights OR H418/04 The nature of law and the law of contract

Make sure you know which paper you are sitting on a particular day.

H418/01 The legal system and criminal law

This paper consists of two sections:
- Section A: The legal system
- Section B: Criminal law

Written paper: 2 hours
33.3% of total A Level – 80 marks
Section A is worth 20 marks. There will be a choice of medium tariff questions.
Section B is worth 60 marks. There will be legal scenario and extended response questions.

Section A

- Questions 1–2 focus on knowledge and understanding of the English legal system (AO1). One question from two should be answered; each question is worth 8 marks.

- Questions 3–4 will focus on analysis and evaluation legal concepts (AO3). One question from two should be answered; each question is worth 12 marks and there is no need to include a conclusion.

Section B

All Section B questions are worth 20 marks. You have a choice between Part 1 and Part 2, each comprising of two scenario questions and one essay question.
- Questions 5 and 6 (Part 1), and 8 and 9 (Part 2) focus on knowledge and understanding (AO1) and the application of legal rules and principles to scenarios (AO2). The assessment material will make it clear whether or not the scenarios are related.
- Questions 7 and 10 will be identical. They will focus on knowledge and understanding (AO1) and analysis and evaluation (AO3). This question is separate from the scenarios and should be treated as an essay requiring a conclusion.

H418/02 Law making and the law of tort

This paper consists of two sections:
- Section A: Law making
- Section B: The law of tort

Written paper: 2 hours
33.3% of total A Level – 80 marks
Section A is worth 20 marks. There will be a choice of medium tariff questions.
Section B is worth 60 marks. There will be legal scenario and extended response questions.
The structure of this paper and the breakdown between the questions is the same as for H418/01.

H418/03 The nature of law and human rights

This paper consists of two sections:
- Section A: The nature of law
- Section B: Human rights law

OR

H418/04 The nature of law and the law of contract

This paper consists of two sections:
- Section A: The nature of law
- Section B: The law of contract

Written paper: 2 hours

33.3% of total A Level – 80 marks

Section A is worth 20 marks. There will be a choice of extended response questions.

Section B is worth 60 marks. There will be legal scenario and extended response questions.

Section A

Both questions are worth 20 marks and are identical across the human rights and contract options. One question from two should be answered.

- Questions 1–2 focus on knowledge and understanding (AO1) and analysis and evaluation (AO3). It is important to draw together knowledge and understanding from across the full course of study in the form of an essay requiring a conclusion.

Section B

The breakdown between the questions is the same as for Section B in H418/01 and H418/02.

Note that all the components include synoptic assessment. This means you can bring in material from the full range of your studies of the English legal system and areas of substantive law. In addition, all papers apply the two-year rule – this means that while you are encouraged to be aware of the changing nature of law, you are not required to be familiar with innovations coming into effect in the two years immediately preceding the examination.

The OCR website has a large array of resources to help with understanding the assessment and preparing for your exam. Make sure you look at the following material from **https://www.ocr.org.uk/qualifications/ as-and-a-level/law-h018-h418-from-2020/assessment/**

- Question papers, mark schemes and reports.
- Sample assessment materials (sample question papers and mark schemes).
- Candidate exemplars (candidate style answers with examiner commentary).
- Assessment guide.

Using your time in the exam

As each paper is two hours in length it is important to make the best use of your time.

- Start by reading all the instructions on the answer book and the question paper carefully to check what you have to do.

- Use the first 5 minutes to calmly read all the questions carefully.
- Select the ones you are going to answer where that is appropriate and make some brief notes of things that come into your head as you are reading.
- Then make a plan for each question before you begin your answer – resist the urge to start writing straight away as a plan will help you construct an answer which fits what you have been asked to do.
- Use your time wisely – resist the temptation to spend too long on any one question.
- Try to leave time at the end of the exam to read through your script again so you can amend any points and correct any errors. Read carefully so that you can pick up changes that need to be made.
- If you do find yourself short of time use bullet points in the last few minutes of the exam.

Understanding command words

It is important to answer the question which has been set and understanding the command word in a question can help you with that.

If a question uses the command words '**Explain**' or '**Describe**' the focus will be on demonstrating your knowledge and understanding (AO1). You will only see these words in questions 1-2 of Section A questions on H418/01 and H418/02.

If a question uses the command word '**Advise**' the focus will be on demonstrating your knowledge and understanding of legal rules and principles (AO1), as well as applying legal rules and principles to scenario questions (AO2). You will only see this word in questions 3-4 or 6-7 of Section B on H418/01, H418/02, H418/03 and H418/04.

If a question uses the command word '**Discuss**' the focus is on analysis and evaluation (AO3) but there is no need to reach a conclusion. You will only see this word in questions 3-4 of Section A on H418/01 and H418/02.

If a question uses the command phrase '**Discuss the extent to which**' the focus is on knowledge and understanding (AO1) as well as analysis and evaluation (AO3) in an essay which reaches a conclusion. You are most likely to see this phrase in questions 7 or 10 on H418/01 and H418/02 as well as in questions 5 or 8 on H418/03 and H418/04.

Exam preparation

- Practise writing questions to the appropriate time limit so you know how much you can do and what the time limit feels like so it isn't a nasty shock on exam day.
- If there have been several previous examinations for this course by the time you take your exam, use past paper questions to see the sort of things that have been asked in the past. However, don't assume they will come up in an identical way again! Instead use them to refine your answering technique and to think through analytical and evaluative points.
- Unpack questions so you know what to do – use a highlighter to indicate key words or important pieces of information in a case study.
- Understand the command words in the question as these will help you select key information, use it appropriately and approach the task you have been set in the best way to maximise your potential marks.
- Understand how your paper is going to be marked – look at OCR published mark schemes that go with exam papers and the published sample assessment material. These show how marks are awarded; the mark scheme is the document an examiner has by their side when they are marking your paper. Think about the assessment objectives, the levels for the different questions and how you can move through them.
- Check the mark allocations in relation to the levels for each of your exam papers in the specification and in the mark schemes to help you balance your time and write answers of an appropriate length.
- Read the reports on past papers as they become available. These are written by the lead marker once marking is completed and they contain information about how the paper performed, as well as good advice for future candidates. The most up to date ones are on an OCR site used by teachers so ask them about the most recent reports.

Make the best of what you have in any exam

- Make sure you answer the correct number and combination of questions.
- Read all the questions carefully and take the time to decide which optional questions are best for you.

- Write down a few key points for each question before you start writing any answers so you have some triggers for each question as you come back to it.
- Highlight key terms and commands about what to do in the question.
- Plan your answer – this will keep you focused and help you stay calm.
- Demonstrate a wide, accurate and detailed base of knowledge that is relevant to the context of the question; for example, if you are using cases, focus on the law rather than a lengthy retelling of the facts.
- Practise linking cases and statute law to legal principles and analysis of the law.
- Have a range of evaluative points at your disposal so you can select the most appropriate ones based on the question.
- Answer the question you have been asked – don't rely on pre-planned answers to previous questions.
- Answer questions in the order that suits you best – you might prefer to answer case study or application questions first while you are mentally fresh and have time to think.
- Remember that your script is marked by its quality rather than its length. Writing pages and pages for an answer won't necessarily get you a good mark.
- Take care with your presentation. Make your script easy to navigate with clear and accurate numbering of questions and don't rush – use your best handwriting so that it is easy to read everything you have written.
- Try to avoid lots of crossings out and arrows to different parts of your script. If you need to do this, perhaps because you have missed something out, help the examiner with clear directions so they can find what they need.

Wider things you can do

- Studying law requires effort and the mastery of good skills but it is rooted in an understanding of wider societal values and issues.
- Use high quality and objective news websites to develop your understanding of topical legal issues and wider matters that can impact on the law.
- Read the blogs of people writing about the law. For example, search for articles by the BBC legal affairs correspondent.
- Search for programmes like *Law in Action* to find out about wider topical legal issues – you can listen

to all programmes as podcasts. BBC Sounds allows you to search for other law related podcasts, as will other podcast providers. You can learn a lot about other legal systems this way too to build up your wider awareness

- Read a good quality newspaper – you can access a lot of material free online; titles such as *The Guardian* and *The Independent* have pages devoted to law.
- Watch videos – you can search for law-related videos but make sure you select ones that deal with the English legal system; this is particularly important if you use websites such as TED. Also be selective in the quality of what you watch – look at videos posted by reputable universities which you can find through links on their department website pages; some have their own YouTube channels too; universities such as Oxford, Cambridge, LSE, UCL and King's College London are good ones to start with. Most universities also provide material on how you will be taught and what you will learn if you join their department which is useful if you are thinking of applying for a law degree.
- Follow law-related issues on social media but take the time to investigate their objectivity.

Glossary

A broad approach of the rule – if a clear meaning of the words would lead to a repugnant result, the judge will modify the meaning of the words. An example is Sigsworth (1935).

A narrow approach of the rule – the court chooses a possible meaning of words but if there is only one meaning, that must be given. Examples are Adler v George (1964) and R v Allen (1872).

Acceptance – the final and unconditional agreement to all the terms of the offer.

Acquittal – the defendant is found not guilty.

Actus reus – the physical element of the crime.

Agent – a person who is authorised to act for another (the principal) in the making of a contract with third parties. The resulting contract is made between the principal and the third party, and not with the agent.

Allurement – something on the premises that may be attractive to children and which may cause them injury.

Automatism – a defence to a criminal offence: an act done by the muscles without any control by the mind or by a person who is not conscious of what they are doing.

Bilateral contract – this type of contract requires both offeror and offeree to do something. Both parties have obligations.

Burden of proof – the prosecution must prove that the defendant is guilty.

Causation – a link between the defendant's act or omission and the injury, loss or damage suffered by the claimant.

Claim – an action taken in a civil court, either the County Court or the High Court, when a person or business believes that their rights have been infringed and they are due compensation or some other remedy.

Claimant – an injured victim of a wrongdoing. The claimant brings an action to recover compensation for their loss or damage.

Common law – this was largely unwritten law and relied on decisions of judges in court.

Compensation – the amount of money claimed to make good the loss or damage to the claimant. This will also be known in tort and contract claims as damages.

Condition – a term in a contract that is central to the contract. Breach of this term may allow the contract to be repudiated.

Contempt of court – failure to comply with an order of a civil court. The court can order punishment in the form of a fine or even imprisonment for failure to comply with an injunction.

Contra proferentem – if the meaning of a term is unclear, the words will be construed against the person who put them in the contract.

Contract – a contract is an agreement the law will enforce.

Counter offer – a response to an offer that makes a firm proposal that materially alters the terms of the offer.

Crime – conduct which is forbidden by the state and for which there is a punishment.

Crime of strict liability – a crime that can be committed by proof of *actus reus* alone.

Damage – the legal test that a claimant's loss was caused by a breach of a duty of care.

Damages – the payment of money as compensation for the loss or damage suffered.

Defendant – the person or body responsible for the loss or damage and who, generally, has been at fault.

Delegated legislation – laws or rules written outside Parliament when a person or body has been given the authority, by Parliament, to make those laws or rules.

Diminished responsibility – a partial defence to a charge of murder which reduces the offence to one of voluntary manslaughter.

Direct effect – an EU law that an individual can rely on as authority for their case. This applies to laws in Treaties and Regulations.

Due diligence – where the defendant has done all that was within his power not to commit an offence.

Duress by threats – a defence in criminal law: the defendant has been effectively forced to commit the crime by threats made to him.

Economic duress – when someone enters into a contract as a result of financial threats.

Enabling Act – a law passed by Parliament which gives a person or body the authority to make laws.

EU Directives – laws issued by the Council of Ministers requiring Member States to bring in their own law so that harmony of law is achieved throughout the EU.

EU Regulations – laws issued by the Council of Ministers which are binding on Member States, automatically apply and have direct effect, allowing an individual to rely on that law.

Exclusion clause – a term in a contract that prevents one party being liable for a breach of contract.

Executed consideration – an act in return for a promise.

Executory consideration – a promise for a promise.

Force majeure **clause** – a clause often found in commercial contracts. It excludes liability for the parties for delay in performance or the non-performance if there are extraordinary events.

Gross negligence manslaughter – a form of involuntary manslaughter where the defendant is grossly negligent in breach of a duty of care towards the victim, and this results in the victim's death.

Inchoate offence – an offence relating to a criminal act which has not, or not yet, been committed.

Independent contractor – also known as a self-employed person who is responsible for their own actions and can be sued by a victim of a tort committed by an independent contractor. No third party will be vicariously liable for the wrongdoings of an independent contractor.

Injunction – a court order addressed to the defendant to stop doing something.

Innominate term – a term in a contract that is not defined as a condition or a warranty.

Intention to create legal relations – the parties to a contract expressly or impliedly agree that the contract is legally binding and therefore enforceable in court.

Invitation to treat – an indication that one person is willing to negotiate a contract with another, but that they are not yet willing to make a legal offer.

Laches – an equitable defence that the claimant has delayed asserting its rights and is no longer entitled to bring an equitable claim.

Legal positivism – a theory of law: laws must be made by the state's highest legislative authority.

Legal realism – an understanding of the law as it is practised in reality (by judges), not the way it is presented in statutes or in academic theories.

Letter of comfort – a written assurance, usually provided by a parent company in respect of its subsidiary's financial obligations to a bank.

Limitation clause – a term in a contract that sets an upper limit on liability for breach of contract.

Liquidated damages – where the amount of damages has been fixed by a term in the contract.

Loss of control – a partial defence to a charge of murder which reduces the offence to one of manslaughter under s 54(1) of the Coroners and Justice Act 2009.

Mandatory injunction – a court order requiring a party to do something.

Mediator – a trained person who acts as a go-between in an attempt to help people in a dispute come to an agreement.

Mens rea – the mental element of the crime.

Misrepresentation – a false statement of material fact made by a party to the contract that induces the other party to enter the contract.

Mitigation of loss – the injured party must take reasonable steps to minimise the effects of the breach.

Natural law – a moral theory of jurisprudence, which maintains that law should be based on morality and ethics.

Negligence – an act or a failure to act which causes injury to another person or damage to their property.

Offer – a proposal (or promise) showing a willingness to contract on firm and definite terms.

Offeree – the person to whom an offer is made.

Offeror – the person who makes the offer.

Pluralist society – a diverse society, where the people in it believe different things and tolerate each other's beliefs.

Primary legislation – laws passed by Parliament.

Privity of contract – only those who are parties to a contract are bound by it and can benefit from it.

Prohibitory injunction – a court order instructing someone not to do something.

Promisee – in contract law, the person who is promised something.

Promisor – in contract law, a person who makes a promise to another.

Punitive damages – damages greater than mere compensation. The aim is to punish the defendant for their wrongful conduct and to deter them and others from acting similarly in the future.

Quantum meruit – as much as it is worth.

Reasonable person – the ordinary person on the street or someone doing the same task as the defendant.

Reasonably foreseeable – loss, damage or injury which a reasonable person should predict or expect from his negligent act or omission.

Recklessness – where the defendant realised the risk, but decided to take it.

Remedy – an order made by a court to enforce or satisfy a tort claim. It is usually damages or an injunction.

Repudiatory breach of contract – this occurs when a party commits a breach of contract so serious that it entitles the innocent party to treat the contract as terminated.

Rescission – when the innocent party ends the contract because of a misrepresentation. Rescission makes the contract a nullity.

Reverse onus – shifting the burden of proof to the defendant.

Rights of audience – the right to present a case in court, as an advocate.

Rule – 'a general norm mandating or guiding conduct' (Twining and Miers).

Standard of proof – the extent to which the burden of proof must be made.

Statute law – law that has been made by Parliament, which is the highest form of law.

Statutory Instrument – a piece of delegated legislation created by a government minister under the authority of an enabling Act. It will often be used to complete the detail of the enabling Act.

The golden rule – a judge can choose the best interpretation of ambiguous words OR avoid an absurd or repugnant result.

The literal rule – words in an Act are given their ordinary, natural, dictionary meaning.

The Lord Chancellor – due to the Constitutional Reform Act 2005, the role of the Lord Chancellor was changed. Rather than being the head of the Judiciary, the role is now managing the Judiciary system and the courts. The Lord Chancellor is an MP, so a member of the Legislature, and a member of the Cabinet, so part of the Executive.

The mischief rule – the judge looks at the gap in the law before the Act was passed and interprets the words to cover the gap and deal with the mischief.

The neighbour principle – the person who is owed a duty of care by the defendant. It is not the person living next door: it is anyone you ought to bear in mind, who could be injured by your act or omission.

Three-part test – an update of the neighbour principle to show who is owed a duty of care in negligence.

Tort – a civil wrong. The word comes from the French for 'wrong'. The aim of the law of tort is to compensate an injured victim for the wrong done to them.

Unilateral contract – in a unilateral contract there is an agreement to pay in exchange for performance, if the potential performer chooses to act. There is no obligation to perform the act.

Void contract – a contract that is declared to be null: it never had legal effect.

Voidable contract – a contract which could be made void if there has been misrepresentation.

Voluntary manslaughter – the verdict when the defendant has a partial defence to murder, where the killing was carried out when the defendant was suffering from loss of control or diminished responsibility.

Warranty – a minor term in a contract. Breach of this term does not end the contract but allows a claim for damages only.

Index